16th SIGMORPHON Workshop on Computational Research in Phonetics, Phonology, and Morphology (SIGMORPHON 2019)

Florence, Italy
2 August 2019

ISBN: 978-1-5108-9102-9

SIGMORPHON 2019

The 16th SIGMORPHON Workshop on Computational Research in Phonetics Phonology, and Morphology

Proceedings of the Workshop

August 2, 2019
Florence, Italy

Preface

Welcome to the 16th SIGMORPHON Workshop on Computational Research in Phonetics, Phonology, and Morphology, to be held on August 2, 2019 in Florence, Italy. The workshop aims to bring together researchers interested in applying computational techniques to problems in morphology, phonology, and phonetics. Our program this year highlights the ongoing and important interaction between work in computational linguistics and work in theoretical linguistics. This year, work in both theoretical phonology and computational morphology were strongly represented in the workshop submissions. We received 20 submissions, and after a competitive reviewing process, we accepted 12. The workshop is privileged to present four invited talks this year, all from very respected members of the SIGMORPHON community.

This year also marks the fourth iteration of the SIGMORPHON Shared Task in Morphological Inflection, previously co-located with CoNLL. This year's task encouraged submissions in two important inflectional sub-tasks: cross-lingual inflection generation, and contextual morphological tagging.

23 teams participated in the task, with 14 teams submitting system papers describing their work, one of which is non-archival.

We are grateful to the program committee for their careful and thoughtful reviews of the papers submitted this year. Likewise, we are thankful to the shared task organizers for their hard work in preparing the shared task. We are looking forward to a workshop covering a wide range of topics, and we hope for lively discussions.

Garrett Nicolai
Ryan Cotterell

Organizers:

Garrett Nicolai, Johns Hopkins University
Ryan Cotterell, University of Cambridge

Program Committee:

Noor Abo Mokh, Indiana University
Jane Chandlee, Haverford College
Çağrı Çöltekin, University of Tübingen
Daniel Dakota, Indiana University
Ewan Dunbar, Université Paris Diderot
Jason Eisner, Johns Hopkins University
Micha Elsner, The Ohio State University
Kyle Gorman, CUNY / Google AI
Nizar Habash, NYU Abu Dhabi
Mans Hulden, University of Colorado
Adam Jardine, Rutgers University
Gaja Jarosz, University of Massachusetts Amherst
Christo Kirov, Google AI
Greg Kobele, Universität Leipzig
Greg Kondrak, University of Alberta
Sandra Kübler, Indiana University
Andrew Lamont, University of Massachusetts Amherst
Karen Livescu, TTI Chicago
Arya D. McCarthy, Johns Hopkins University
Kevin McMullin, University of Ottawa
Kemal Oflazer, CMU Qatar
Jeff Parker, Brigham Young University
Gerald Penn, University of Toronto
Jelena Prokic, Ludwig-Maximilians-University Munich
Mohamad Salameh, Diffbot
Miikka Silfverberg, University of Colorado
Kairit Sirts, University of Tartu
Kenneth Steimel, Indiana University
Francis Tyers, Indiana University
Anssi Yli-Jyrä, University of Helsinki
Kristine Yu, University of Massachusetts Amherst

Shared Task Organizers:

Arya D. McCarthy, Johns Hopkins University
Ekaterina Vylomova, University of Melbourne
Shijie Wu, Johns Hopkins University
Chaitanya Malaviya, Allen Institute for Artificial Intelligence
Lawrence Wolf-Sonkin, Google AI
Garrett Nicolai, Johns Hopkins University
Christo Kirov, Google AI
Miikka Silfverberg, University of Helsinki
Sebastian J. Mielke, Johns Hopkins University
Svetlana Toldova, National Research University Higher School of Economics
Olga Lyashevskaya, National Research University Higher School of Economics
Karina Mishchenkova
Elena Klyachko
Jeffrey Heinz, Stony Brook University
Ryan Cotterell, University of Cambridge
Mans Hulden , University of Colorado

Invited Speakers:

Sharon Goldwater, University of Edinburgh
Janet Pierrehumbert, Oxford University
Adina Williams, Facebook AI
Géraldine Walther, University of Zurich
Benoît Sagot, Inria

Table of Contents

Conference Program

August 2, 2019

8:30–10:30   **Morning Session**

8:30–9:30   *Invited Speaker*: Adina Williams

9:30–10:30   *Invited Speaker*: Janet Pierrehumbert

10:30–11:00   **Break**

11:00–12:30   **Shared Task**

11:00–11:30   *Shared Task Wrapup*
TBA

11:30–12:30   *Shared Task Poster Session*
Multiple

AX Semantics' Submission to the SIGMORPHON 2019 Shared Task
Andreas Madsack and Robert Weißgraeber

Cognate Projection for Low-Resource Inflection Generation
Bradley Hauer, Amir Ahmad Habibi, Yixing Luan, Rashed Rubby Riyadh and Grzegorz Kondrak

Cross-Lingual Lemmatization and Morphology Tagging with Two-Stage Multilingual BERT Fine-Tuning
Dan Kondratyuk

CBNU System for SIGMORPHON 2019 Shared Task 2: a Pipeline Model
Uygun Shadikhodjaev and Jae Sung Lee

Morpheus: A Neural Network for Jointly Learning Contextual Lemmatization and Morphological Tagging
Eray Yildiz and A. Cüneyd Tantuğ

AX Semantics' Submission to the SIGMORPHON 2019 Shared Task

Andreas Madsack and **Robert Weißgraeber**
AX Semantics, Stuttgart, Germany
{firstname.lastname}@ax-semantics.com

Abstract

This paper describes the AX Semantics' submission to the SIGMORPHON 2019 shared task on morphological reinflection. We implemented two systems, both tackling the task for all languages in one codebase, without any underlying language specific features. The first one is an encoder-decoder model using AllenNLP; the second system uses the same model modified by a custom trainer that trains only with the target language resources after a specific threshold. We especially focused on building an implementation using AllenNLP with out-of-the-box methods to facilitate easy operation and reuse.

1 Introduction

This paper describes our implementation and results for Task 1 of the 2019 Shared Task (McCarthy et al., 2019). The task is to generate inflected word forms given the lemma and a morphological feature specification (Kirov et al., 2018). See Figure 1 for an example in German, where a verb lemma is inflected according to the specified number, mood, tense and person.

sehen (V;IND;PST;3;PL) → sahen

Figure 1: Task 1 Example, German: putting the verb "sehen" into 3rd person past tense indicative plural.

In contrast to last year, where the training data was only in the respective target language, this year the given data consists of up to 10000 exemplars of one high resource language combined with up to 100 exemplars of a low resource language. The target language is the low resource language. The task is to use the high resource data to improve the inflection of the low resource language. Including the surprise language pairs the task consists of 99 language pairs.

2 Motivation

After participating last year (Madsack et al., 2018) we started to rebuild everything we needed for our production system using AllenNLP (Gardner et al., 2017). Our main goal here is reproducibility and full logging of everything as default. In our experience AllenNLP brings best practices that, while sometimes opinionated, are way better than building everything from scratch, and which we wanted to apply to this problem.

Our two systems represent our learning curve in the attempt to solve the given shared task. The first system is a solution entirely based on given AllenNLP components. The second system has a custom trainer that, only at the start, trains with all given training data for a pair and then continues only with the (low-resource) target language.

The source code of our submission can be found at: https://301.ax/github-sigmorphon2019

3 System 1 - softmax baseline in AllenNLP

Our first system is the soft-attention baseline rebuilt in AllenNLP. It basically serves as a starting point for our second system.

The model is an encoder-decoder (Cho et al., 2014) and is using the readily implemented version in AllenNLP (named SimpleSeq2Seq). We modified the model code to add accuracy and edit-distance metrics. The attention used is dot-product attention (Luong et al., 2015). All other hyperparameters are inspired by Wu et al. (2018) and shown in Table 1.

We trained two kinds of System 1. One with only low data as baseline and another with high and low data concatenated. All systems used here are character based and the input sequence is first the lemma followed by a next marker (we

Proceedings of the 16th Workshop on Computational Research in Phonetics, Phonology, and Morphology, pages 1–5
Florence, Italy. August 2, 2019 ©2019 Association for Computational Linguistics

used a tabulator) followed by the morphological features as a string. One example input of the encoder looks like the following: `zmrzlina N;DAT;SG`. Besides, AllenNLP wraps inputs and target outputs with start and end markers.

parameter	value	
	System 1	System 2
embedding dimension	200	100
beam size	10	10
hidden size	400	200
number of hidden encoder layers	2	1
encoder dropout	0.4	0.3
optimizer	adam	adam

Table 1: hyper parameters for System 1 and System 2

4   System 2 - transfer learning

The second system uses the same encoder-decoder-model as System 1. The major modification is a trainer that first learns on all training data (high and low resource data) and after a threshold is reached continues learning only with the target language. This threshold marks the transfer learning point: The cross-lingual model is reused as a basis for training with the monolingual data.

The first 10 epochs are always trained with all training data. The switch to only training with low resource data happens after 5 epochs without training improvement. As metric for this improvement a lower loss on validation data is used. Most hyper parameters (Table 1) for System 2 were halved after some experimental evaluation. We did not do an exhaustive search of these parameters, so minor improvements with the help of hyperparameter optimization (e.g. using cross-validated grid search) are possible here.

Figure 3 shows a loss curve where training with only the target language Khakas (and without the high-resource language Bashkir) started at epoch 17. For comparison the loss curve of System 1 for the same language pair is shown in Figure 2. In this example System 2 gains a smaller loss than System 1 on the validation data - System 2 reaches with about 0.2 half as much loss as System 1 with about 0.4.

5   Results

The results for System 1 and System 2 shown in Table 2 and Table 3 together with the soft-attention

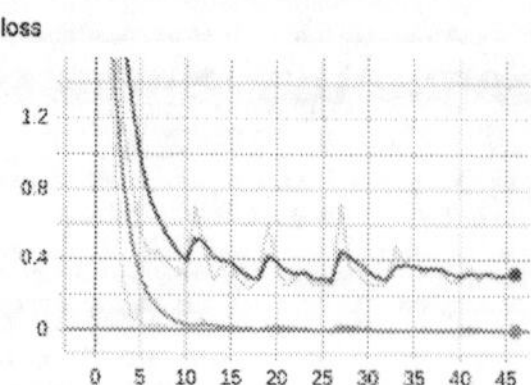

Figure 2: Loss for train (orange) and validation (blue) for **System 1** language pair "bashkir–khakas"

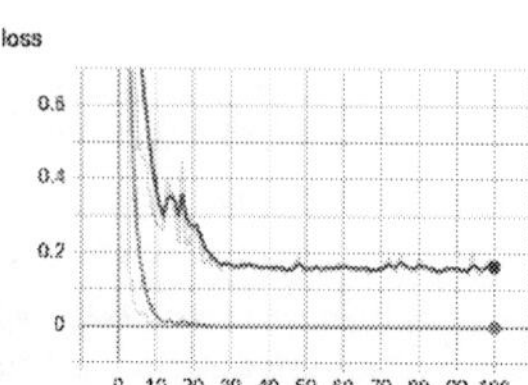

Figure 3: Loss for train (orange) and validation (blue) for **System 2** language pair "bashkir–khakas"

baseline from the organizers (Wu and Cotterell, 2019) are the unmodified results from the submission to the task. We found minor tooling mistakes on the surprise languages after the submission deadline which we didn't correct in the table.

In the trained models we can observe big differences in the accuracy for different language pairs. To better understand the results we trained a new version of System 1 with only the low data given and ignored the high-resource language data completely. As expected this version of System 1 performed worst in comparison to the other systems due to the lack of a sufficient amount of training data.

In general, the very low results on some pairs seem to be based on very different character sets and/or feature sets between the concerning language pairs. For example a language pair with a lot of different characters and different features is "bengali–greek". The amount of Greek data alone is not enough to train an encoder-decoder-model (see System 1 low results) and the data for Bengali doesn't help either way (see System 1, System 2 and baseline results).

Thus, the results indicate that a difference in features and/or character sets has a big impact on the usefulness of the high resource training data. For the character set a phonological mapping to a phonetic alphabet could improve on that issue.

language pair	characters in low	features not in high	System 1 (low)	System 1	System 2	Baseline (tune) (0-soft)
adyghe–kabardian	0	0	2	85	91	**93**
albanian–breton	2	7	0	10	11	**21**
arabic–classical-syriac	22	11	0	33	27	**52**
arabic–maltese	29	2	0	0	2	**16**
arabic–turkmen	30	3	6	8	12	**32**
armenian–kabardian	32	4	2	5	39	**68**
asturian–occitan	6	0	0	6	14	**47**
bashkir–azeri	32	10	0	19	11	**34**
bashkir–crimean-tatar	33	7	0	30	0	**51**
bashkir–kazakh	3	1	14	64	72	**76**
bashkir–khakas	3	3	2	*62*	*74*	*74*
bashkir–tatar	35	6	0	35	8	**37**
bashkir–turkmen	30	0	0	**52**	42	50
basque–kashubian	14	10	6	2	8	**20**
belarusian–old-irish	25	18	0	**4**	**4**	**4**
bengali–greek	82	16	0	0	0	**3.6**
bulgarian–old-church-slavonic	31	5	0	24	17	**40**
czech–kashubian	8	0	6	10	**52**	40
czech–latin	9	6	0	4.4	**6.7**	3.9
danish–middle-high-german	5	6	14	34	**70**	68
danish–middle-low-german	12	13	10	24	14	**36**
danish–north-frisian	3	10	0	7	20	**23**
danish–west-frisian	4	6	0	37	26	**48**
danish–yiddish	35	16	0	0	42	**44**
dutch–middle-high-german	2	5	10	50	**60**	54
dutch–middle-low-german	9	10	4	18	**38**	**38**
dutch–north-frisian	3	7	0	12	14	**21**
dutch–west-frisian	3	2	3	16	38	**43**
dutch–yiddish	35	13	0	-	-	**43**
english–murrinhpatha	0	7	0	12	**22**	12
english–north-frisian	4	12	0	2	19	**23**
english–west-frisian	5	8	0	19	33	**41**
estonian–ingrian	1	2	0	14	6	**30**
estonian–karelian	3	4	0	0	**46**	**46**
estonian–livonian	16	12	0	2	19	**25**
estonian–votic	3	1	3	14	17	**25**
finnish–ingrian	1	1	0	**36**	34	26
finnish–karelian	2	2	0	0	**52**	32
finnish–livonian	17	11	1	18	2	**25**
finnish–votic	4	2	2	27	**32**	22
french–occitan	3	1	0	24	**37**	33
german–middle-high-german	3	0	12	38	**72**	66
german–middle-low-german	10	7	8	2	20	**46**
german–yiddish	35	14	0	0	20	**46**
greek–bengali	*45*	*12*	1	*0*	7	*31*
hebrew–classical-syriac	22	10	0	48	32	**61**
hebrew–maltese	30	4	0	7	6	**16**
hindi–bengali	45	12	0	3	6	**35**
hungarian–ingrian	2	4	0	**24**	18	10
hungarian–karelian	3	8	2	0	**36**	30
hungarian–livonian	19	18	0	2	11	**19**
hungarian–votic	5	4	1	**17**	15	16
irish–breton	3	5	0	3	3	**19**
irish–cornish	3	8	0	2	**8**	**8**
irish–old-irish	1	12	0	2	**4**	0
irish–scottish-gaelic	5	2	0	42	26	**60**
italian–friulian	7	1	0	27	27	**33**
italian–ladin	2	3	1	13	23	**47**
italian–maltese	5	5	0	11	**16**	9
italian–neapolitan	2	2	6	**60**	48	41
kannada–telugu	23	1	20	44	**68**	60
kurmanji–sorani	9	12	0	2	0.8	**8.1**
latin–czech	17	8	0	0	9.1	**13.5**

Table 2: Left: Feature/character differences between language pairs. (in low, not in high language)
Right: Results (accuracy) for test data compared to baseline (Part 1)

language pair	characters in low not in high	features	System 1 (low)	System 1	System 2	Baseline (tune) (0-soft)
latvian–lithuanian	29	6	0	0.7	7.7	**10.9**
latvian–scottish-gaelic	11	0	0	30	**48**	48
persian–azeri	32	13	0	0	1	**23**
persian–pashto	15	9	0	0	1	**14**
polish–kashubian	6	0	6	48	**68**	66
polish–old-church-slavonic	57	1	0	10	0	**30**
portuguese–russian	36	15	0	0	0	**11.9**
romanian–latin	13	9	0	0	0.1	**4.5**
russian–old-church-slavonic	31	2	0	22	24	**32**
russian–portuguese	35	8	0	0.3	0.5	**32.3**
sanskrit–bengali	46	19	0	11	1	**21**
sanskrit–pashto	38	12	0	2	3	**7**
slovak–kashubian	9	1	2	22	40	**52**
slovene–old-saxon	7	6	0	4	6.7	**7.8**
sorani–irish	26	18	0	0.3	**3.3**	2.6
spanish–friulian	8	1	0	28	37	**38**
spanish–occitan	5	1	0	26	39	**50**
swahili–quechua	5	34	0	0	0.2	**3**
turkish–azeri	3	1	0	60	64	**66**
turkish–crimean-tatar	2	3	0	69	**74**	65
turkish–kazakh	31	1	18	54	68	**74**
turkish–khakas	25	3	2	68	54	**78**
turkish–tatar	4	2	0	**79**	68	69
turkish–turkmen	4	0	0	56	**86**	80
urdu–bengali	45	9	0	3	5	**30**
urdu–old-english	38	6	0.2	0.3	0.1	**8**
uzbek–azeri	12	6	0	5	4	**27**
uzbek–crimean-tatar	13	8	0	0	0	**13**
uzbek–kazakh	31	1	22	12	46	**56**
uzbek–khakas	25	3	0	10	28	**76**
uzbek–tatar	16	7	0	1	2	**21**
uzbek–turkmen	11	0	0	8	16	**36**
welsh–breton	6	8	0	17	20	**34**
welsh–cornish	4	11	2	0	12	**26**
welsh–old-irish	8	18	2	2	4	**8**
welsh–scottish-gaelic	12	11	0	20	16	**28**
zulu–swahili	0	19	0	0	19	**36**

Table 3: Left: Feature/character differences between language pairs. (in low, not in high language) Right: Results (accuracy) for test data compared to baseline (Part 2)

6 Conclusion

Our continual goal is to improve our morphology system component in our Natural Language Generation SaaS (Weißgraeber and Madsack, 2017).

In our production setup the System 1 described above competes against a handcrafted morphology and a reasonable lexicon (which were not used for the Shared Task). This handcrafted morphology together with the lexicon is always better on very regular part of speech (POS) types (i.e. German adjectives). Therefore not for every language POS combination a system shown here is used in our production NLG inflection system. For every language and POS type we evaluate which solution fits best.

AllenNLP successfully helped us to reproduce the same results even with newer versions of libraries (i.e. PyTorch, CUDA, Python), which is an important quality for our NLG system.

References

Kyunghyun Cho, Bart van Merrienboer, Caglar Gulcehre, Dzmitry Bahdanau, Fethi Bougares, Holger Schwenk, and Yoshua Bengio. 2014. Learning phrase representations using RNN encoder–decoder for statistical machine translation. In *Proceedings of the 2014 Conference on Empirical Methods in Natural Language Processing (EMNLP)*, pages 1724–1734, Doha, Qatar. Association for Computational Linguistics.

Matt Gardner, Joel Grus, Mark Neumann, Oyvind Tafjord, Pradeep Dasigi, Nelson F. Liu, Matthew Peters, Michael Schmitz, and Luke S. Zettlemoyer. 2017. Allennlp: A deep semantic natural language processing platform.

Christo Kirov, Ryan Cotterell, John Sylak-Glassman, Géraldine Walther, Ekaterina Vylomova, Patrick

Xia, Manaal Faruqui, Sebastian J. Mielke, Arya Mc-Carthy, Sandra Kübler, David Yarowsky, Jason Eisner, and Mans Hulden. 2018. UniMorph 2.0: Universal Morphology. In *Proceedings of the 11th Language Resources and Evaluation Conference*, Miyazaki, Japan. European Language Resource Association.

Thang Luong, Hieu Pham, and Christopher D. Manning. 2015. Effective approaches to attention-based neural machine translation. In *Proceedings of the 2015 Conference on Empirical Methods in Natural Language Processing*, pages 1412–1421, Lisbon, Portugal. Association for Computational Linguistics.

Andreas Madsack, Alessia Cavallo, Johanna Heininger, and Robert Weißgraeber. 2018. AX semantics' submission to the CoNLL–SIGMORPHON 2018 shared task. In *Proceedings of the CoNLL–SIGMORPHON 2018 Shared Task: Universal Morphological Reinflection*, pages 43–47, Brussels. Association for Computational Linguistics.

Arya D. McCarthy, Ekaterina Vylomova, Shijie Wu, Chaitanya Malaviya, Lawrence Wolf-Sonkin, Garrett Nicolai, Christo Kirov, Miikka Silfverberg, Sebastian Mielke, Jeffrey Heinz, Ryan Cotterell, and Mans Hulden. 2019. The SIGMORPHON 2019 shared task: Crosslinguality and context in morphology. In *Proceedings of the 16th SIGMORPHON Workshop on Computational Research in Phonetics, Phonology, and Morphology*, Florence, Italy. Association for Computational Linguistics.

Robert Weißgraeber and Andreas Madsack. 2017. A working, non-trivial, topically indifferent nlg system for 17 languages. In *Proceedings of the 10th International Conference on Natural Language Generation*, pages 156–157. Association for Computational Linguistics.

Shijie Wu and Ryan Cotterell. 2019. Exact hard monotonic attention for character-level transduction. *arXiv preprint arXiv:1905.06319*.

Shijie Wu, Pamela Shapiro, and Ryan Cotterell. 2018. Hard non-monotonic attention for character-level transduction. In *Proceedings of the 2018 Conference on Empirical Methods in Natural Language Processing*, pages 4425–4438, Brussels, Belgium. Association for Computational Linguistics.

Cognate Projection for Low-Resource Inflection Generation

Bradley Hauer, Amir A. Habibi, Yixing Luan, Rashed Rubby Riyadh, Grzegorz Kondrak
Department of Computing Science
University of Alberta, Edmonton, Canada
`{bmhauer,amirahmad,yixing1,riyadh,gkondrak}@ualberta.ca`

Abstract

We propose cognate projection as a method of crosslingual transfer for inflection generation in the context of the SIGMORPHON 2019 Shared Task. The results on four language pairs show the method is effective when no low-resource training data is available.

1 Introduction

In this description of the University of Alberta systems, we discuss our approach to Crosslingual Transfer for Inflection Generation (Task 1) in the SIGMORPHON 2019 Shared Task on Crosslinguality and Context in Morphology (McCarthy et al., 2019). The task of inflection generation is to produce an inflected word-form given a lemma and a sequence of abstract morphological tags. For example, the Latin citation form *fucō* with the tag V;IND;FUT;3;SG should yield the form *fucābit*.[1] The goal is to examine how best to do this in a cross-lingual setting.

We focus on depth over breadth, performing experiments on only four language pairs which represent a range of diachronic relationships. Kashubian is so closely related to Polish that it is sometimes viewed as a dialect. Occitan and Spanish are less closely related, but share many morphological features. Romanian evolved from Latin over the course of 1500 years. Hindi and Bengali are also related, but written in distinct scripts.

In order to alleviate the training data sparsity in the low-resource setting, we attempt to leverage external text corpora, from which we extract target language word lists for both inflection generation and cognate projection. The results show that this strategy improves the overall results for some of the tested language pairs.

2 Prior Work

Our methods build upon the prior work of the University of Alberta teams for three previous SIGMORPHON shared tasks on type-level morphological generation (Cotterell et al., 2016, 2017, 2018). We view inflection as a string transduction task. Our discriminative transduction models stem from the DIRECTL+ transducer of Jiampojamarn et al. (2008), which was originally designed for grapheme-to-phoneme conversion.

Nicolai et al. (2016) apply discriminative string transduction to morphological reinflection. They show that the approach of Nicolai et al. (2015) performs well on typologically diverse languages. They also discuss language-specific heuristics and errors.

Nicolai et al. (2017) combine a discriminative transduction system with neural models. The results on five languages show that the approach works well in the low-resource setting. Additionally, they propose adaptations designed to handle small training sets, such as tag re-ordering and particle processing.

Najafi et al. (2018a) make further progress on the combination of neural and non-neural models for low-resource reinflection. Their best system obtains the highest accuracy on 34 out of 103 languages. They achieve additional improvements in accuracy by leveraging unannotated text corpora using the non-standard approaches of Nicolai et al. (2018) and Najafi et al. (2019).

---

[1] For an unknown reason, only the inflected Latin forms in the data include vowel length diacritics.

Proceedings of the 16th Workshop on Computational Research in Phonetics, Phonology, and Morphology, pages 6–11
Florence, Italy. August 2, 2019 ©2019 Association for Computational Linguistics

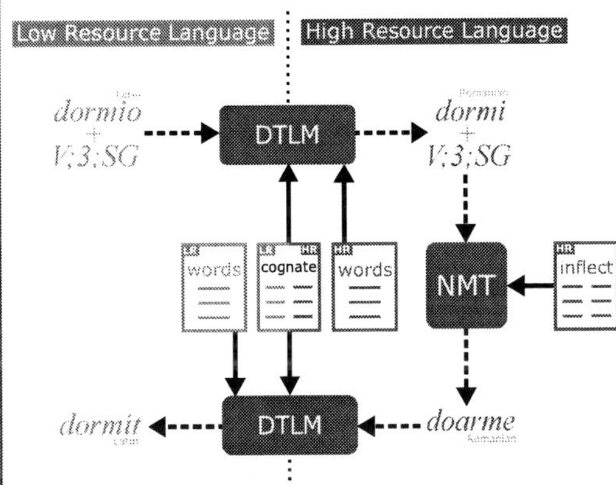

Figure 1: Two approaches to applying cognate projection to inflection generation. DTLM and NMT denote projection and inflection models, respectively. Dashed arrows show transduction. Solid arrows indicate training data. The LR and HR components are shown in orange and blue.

3 Tools

In this section, we describe our two principal tools: DTLM for cognate projection and low-resource inflection generation, and OpenNMT for high-resource inflection generation.

3.1 DTLM

DTLM (Nicolai et al., 2018) combines discriminative transduction with character and word language models derived from large unannotated corpora, with the language-model features integrated into the transducer. DTLM employs a many-to-many alignment method, which is referred to as precision alignment.

Nicolai et al. (2018) demonstrate that DTLM achieves superior results in low-data scenarios on several transduction tasks, including inflection generation, transliteration, phoneme-to-grapheme conversion, and cognate projection. In the CoNLL–SIGMORPHON 2018 Shared Task on Universal Morphological Reinflection (Cotterell et al., 2018), DTLM was our best performing individual system. It was also successfully used in the NEWS 2018 shared task on transliteration (Najafi et al., 2018b).

3.2 OpenNMT

OpenNMT (Klein et al., 2017) is an open-source neural machine translation tool based on sequence to sequence model with attention mechanism. Klein et al. (2017) demonstrates that Open-NMT generally performs better quality of machine translation than other existing open-source machine translation systems and is fairly efficient in terms of training and test speed.

Machine translation models have been successfully applied to other transduction tasks (Kann and Schütze, 2016). We employ OpenNMT as a vanilla HR morphological inflection tool, by simply concatenating the lemma and the tags to form the input sequence. Each individual tag is encoded as a single input token. No target wordlists are used.

4 Cognate Projection Methods

Each dataset in this shared task pairs a low-resource (LR) language with a related high-resource (HR) language. Genetically related languages share *cognates*, words with a common linguistic origin (St Arnaud et al., 2017). For example, the Latin word *oculus* 'eye' is cognate with the Romanian word *ochi*. Cognate pairs exhibit phonetic and semantic similarity (Kondrak, 2013). The correspondences between substrings in cognates tend to follow regular patterns (Kondrak, 2009).

Cognate projection, also referred to as cognate production (Beinborn et al., 2013; Ciobanu, 2016), is the task of predicting the spelling of a hypothetical cognate in another language. For example, the projection of *oculus* from Latin to Romanian should generate *ochi*. Even if a cognate

Language	Source	UniMorph	Words
Kashubian	Wikipedia	509	60286
Occitan	Wikipedia	8316	318706
Latin	UniMorph	509182	357951
Bengali	UniMorph	4443	2752

Table 1: The size of the UniMorph datasets and our target word lists.

Pair	k	t	Train	Dev	Test
pol↔csb	7500	0.4	6500	500	500
spa↔oci	5300	0.4	4500	500	300
ron↔lat	4612	0.4	4000	300	312
hin↔ben	1816	0.5	1456	180	180

Table 2: Our cognate projection datasets.

word does not exist, cognate projection should produce a target form that incorporates the inter-lingual sound correspondences and the phonotactic constraints of the target language. We hypothesize that the projected forms exhibit some of the morpho-phonetic properties of the actual words. For example, the projection of the Spanish verbal form *tomaré* ('I will take') into a (non-existent) Latin word *tomābō* could provide useful information for inflecting actual Latin verbs.

We propose two projection-based approaches for inflection generation which are based on the above hypothesis (Figure 1). We refer to those approaches as *Data Projection* and *Instance Projection* respectively. Both approaches aim at taking advantage of the HR inflection training data to perform LR inflection. Morphological tags are left unchanged. For cognate projection, we train transduction models (Section 3.1) on lists of cognate pairs extracted from small bitexts. The projection models are strengthened by target wordlists extracted from freely-available monolingual corpora.

The *Data Projection* approach simply projects the entire HR training data, which consists of lemmas and the corresponding inflected forms, into the LR language. For example, the Romanian training pair *"dormi+V;3;SG = doarme"* projects into Latin *"dormio+V;3;SG = dormit"*. This produces a relatively large, synthetic LR training set from which an LR inflection model can be derived (Section 3.2). The underlying idea is that the HR inflection patterns may be reflected in the corresponding LR inflection patterns, especially if the languages are closely related.

The *Instance Projection* approach is more complex, consisting of three transduction steps: (1) project an individual LR test instance into the HR language; (2) inflect the resulting form using a model trained on the HR training data, and (3) project the result back into the LR language. For example, Latin *"dormio+V;3;SG"* would first be

projected into Romanian *"dormi+V;3;SG"*, then inflected using the Romanian model into *doarme*, and finally projected back into Latin as *dormit*. Unlike in Data Projection, inflection is performed entirely in the HR language. We aim to determine whether the higher HR inflection accuracy can offset the errors introduced at either of the projection steps.

5 Development

In this section, we describe our external resources and development results.

5.1 External Resources

For low-resource tasks, in both inflection generation and cognate projection, it makes obvious sense to leverage additional resources, which are freely available for many under-resourced languages. We extract the target word lists for DTLM from UniMorph[2] (Kirov et al., 2018). and Wikipedia[3], as summarized in Table 1.[4]

For cognate projection, we need training sets composed of cognate pairs, Finding good parallel bitexts for low-resource languages is quite challenging. Small bitexts exist in special domains, such as technical documentation or Bible translations. For Polish-Kashubian and Spanish-Occitan, we use software documentation from OPUS[5] (Tiedemann, 2012). For Hindi-Bengali, we use the OpenSubtitles (v2018) data, also from OPUS. For Romanian-Latin, we use a parallel corpus which contains a verse-by-verse alignment of the Bible translations in 100 languages (Christodouloupoulos and Steedman, 2015).

---

[2]`https://unimorph.github.io`
[3]`https://dumps.wikimedia.org`
[4]We are aware that the test data for the shared task may come from UniMorph. We use UniMorph solely for deriving the target word language model, without taking advantage of the morphological annotations. All our submissions that use external data are declared as non-standard.
[5]`http://opus.nlpl.eu/`

Data	System	ID	Word Accuracy				Levenshtein Distance			
			csb	oci	lat	ben	csb	oci	lat	ben
None	Copy Baseline	5	12.0	1.0	2.4	1.0	1.90	3.01	3.83	3.56
LR only	DTLM (standard)	1	60.0	**64.0**	14.3	55.0	0.58	**0.93**	2.56	0.86
	DTLM + wordlists	2	58.0	63.0	**34.0**	**64.0**	**0.56**	0.97	**1.85**	**0.72**
HR only	No Projection	-	16.0	7.0	0.3	n/a	1.72	2.91	5.13	n/a
	Instance Projection	4	28.0	5.0	0.0	0.0	2.02	2.99	6.58	6.51
	Data Projection	3	30.0	3.0	0.8	0.0	1.54	3.20	4.85	6.63
LR + HR	Data Projection	6	**66.0**	23.0	1.4	17.0	0.78	2.22	4.25	3.33
	1-MONO	-	62.0	60.0	5.1	31.0	0.60	1.11	3.34	1.91

Table 3: Inflection results on test sets of the shared task.

5.2 Inflection Generation

We perform inflection generation with DTLM in the low-resource setting, and OpenNMT in the high-resource setting. For DTLM, we apply the tag splitting and particle handling techniques described in Nicolai et al. (2017). In particular, we split tag sequences into component tags, and append them at both the beginning and end of the lemma, treating each of them as an atomic symbol. We tune the hyper-parameters of both the aligner and transducer using grid search for each language. For OpenNMT, we split tag sequences, and append them to the lemma. All parameters are set to default values.

The task of leveraging HR training data for LR inflection generation is complicated by two types of inconsistencies. First, there are unavoidable typological differences, especially between less similar languages. For example, Latin nominal inflection paradigms include six cases, most of which do not exist in Romanian, which instead distinguishes between definite and indefinite forms. Second, the order of the tags in the data may differ. For example, the person tag follows the tense tag in the Spanish data, while the order is reversed in the Occitan data. We do not perform any tag re-ordering in the current shared task, but see Nicolai et al. (2017) for a principled solution to this problem.

5.3 Cognate Projection

We train our cognate models on lists of HR-LR word pairs acquired from the bitexts. The bitexts are aligned with FAST_ALIGN (Dyer et al., 2013). We extract all aligned word pairs, and sort them by the alignment frequency. For Hindi and Bengali, which are written in different scripts, we compute the inter-lingual orthographic similarity after romanizing all words using *uroman* (Herm-

jakob et al., 2018). We discard all pairs with orthographic similarity below a threshold t, which is manually tuned for each language pair. The similarity is computed as $1 - D/L$, where D is the Levenshtein distance, and L is the length of the longer of the two strings. Furthermore, we discard pairs which involve any words that are English, are shorter than 4 characters, or include digits. We take the top k HR-LR pairs, and randomly divide them into training, development, and test sets, as summarized in Table 2.

For each language pair, we train a DTLM model in each direction on the training set, using the development set to prevent over-fitting, as well as a target-language word list (Section 5.1). The results of the intrinsic evaluation of the projection models on the in-domain test sets are shown in Table 4. The accuracy of the Romanian-Latin is relatively low, which may be due to the Bible domain.

6 Results and Discussion

We test several systems, as listed in Table 3. (Submission IDs are given here in parentheses.) A naive copy baseline (5) simply outputs the unchanged input lemmas. DTLM models with and without target wordlists (2 and 1) make no use of HR data (the latter is our only standard submission, which uses no external resources). The next three systems make use of only the HR training sets provided as part of the shared task. This emulates a scenario[6] where no LR inflection data is available. *Data Projection* (3) and *Instance Projection* (4) implement the two methods illustrated in Figure 1, while *No Projection* simply applies an inflection model trained on HR data to LR in-

---

[6]We note the similarity to the setup in the shared task on Cross-lingual Morphological Analysis of VarDial 2019 (Zampieri et al., 2019).

Pair	WA (LD)	Pair	WA (LD)
pol→csb	28.6 (1.97)	csb→pol	49.8 (1.32)
spa→oci	47.3 (1.76)	oci→spa	46.7 (2.15)
ron→lat	5.5 (2.88)	lat→ron	17.9 (2.26)
hin→ben	22.2 (2.92)	ben→hin	29.8 (2.62)

Table 4: Intrinsic evaluation of cognate projection.

stances. The last system (6) combines the projected HR inflection data with LR data, which probably comes closest to the spirit of this shared task. 1-MONO is the first-order monotonic hard attention system of Wu and Cotterell (2019).

The test results are shown in Table 3. The best result on each language is shown in bold. When only LR data is used, the results confirm the finding of (Nicolai et al., 2018) that leveraging target wordlists from monolingual corpora can improve inflection accuracy for less-closely related languages. With the exception of Polish-Kashubian, the standard DTLM model is better than the competitive baselines. However, the Polish-Kashubian results demonstrate that cognate projection can outperform the *Copy* and *No Projection* baselines when only HR data is used. Finally, augmenting the LR training data with the projected HR data does not improve the inflection accuracy in most cases.

7 Conclusion

We described the details of the systems that we tested on four language pairs in the SIGMORPHON 2019 Shared Task. In particular, we successfully experimented with leveraging cognate projection for inflection generation. We view our Polish-Kashubian results as a proof of concept that should motivate further research on this new idea.

Acknowledgments

We thank Garrett Nicolai for the assistance with DTLM. We thank the shared task organizers for their effort.

This research was supported by the Natural Sciences and Engineering Research Council of Canada.

References

Lisa Beinborn, Torsten Zesch, and Iryna Gurevych. 2013. Cognate production using character-based machine translation. In *Proceedings of the Sixth International Joint Conference on Natural Language Processing*, pages 883–891, Nagoya, Japan. Asian Federation of Natural Language Processing.

Christos Christodouloupoulos and Mark Steedman. 2015. A massively parallel corpus: the Bible in 100 languages. *Language Resources and Evaluation*, 49(2):375–395.

Alina Maria Ciobanu. 2016. Sequence labeling for cognate production. In *Knowledge-Based and Intelligent Information and Engineering Systems: Proceedings of the 20th International Conference KES-2016*, pages 1391–1399. Elsevier.

Ryan Cotterell, Christo Kirov, John Sylak-Glassman, Géraldine Walther, Ekaterina Vylomova, Arya D. McCarthy, Katharina Kann, Sebastian Mielke, Garrett Nicolai, Miikka Silfverberg, David Yarowsky, Jason Eisner, and Mans Hulden. 2018. The CoNLL–SIGMORPHON 2018 shared task: Universal morphological reinflection. In *Proceedings of the CoNLL–SIGMORPHON 2018 Shared Task: Universal Morphological Reinflection*, pages 1–27, Brussels. Association for Computational Linguistics.

Ryan Cotterell, Christo Kirov, John Sylak-Glassman, Géraldine Walther, Ekaterina Vylomova, Patrick Xia, Manaal Faruqui, Sandra Kübler, David Yarowsky, Jason Eisner, and Mans Hulden. 2017. The CoNLL-SIGMORPHON 2017 shared task: Universal morphological reinflection in 52 languages. In *Proceedings of the CoNLL-SIGMORPHON 2017 Shared Task: Universal Morphological Reinflection*, Vancouver, Canada. Association for Computational Linguistics.

Ryan Cotterell, Christo Kirov, John Sylak-Glassman, David Yarowsky, Jason Eisner, and Mans Hulden. 2016. The SIGMORPHON 2016 shared task—morphological reinflection. In *Proceedings of the 2016 Meeting of SIGMORPHON*, Berlin, Germany. Association for Computational Linguistics.

Chris Dyer, Victor Chahuneau, and Noah A. Smith. 2013. A simple, fast, and effective reparameterization of IBM model 2. In *Proceedings of the 2013 Conference of the North American Chapter of the Association for Computational Linguistics: Human Language Technologies*, pages 644–648, Atlanta, Georgia. Association for Computational Linguistics.

Ulf Hermjakob, Jonathan May, and Kevin Knight. 2018. Out-of-the-box universal Romanization tool uroman. In *Proceedings of ACL 2018, System Demonstrations*, pages 13–18, Melbourne, Australia. Association for Computational Linguistics.

Sittichai Jiampojamarn, Colin Cherry, and Grzegorz Kondrak. 2008. Joint processing and discriminative training for letter-to-phoneme conversion. In *Proceedings of ACL-08: HLT*, pages 905–913, Columbus, Ohio. Association for Computational Linguistics.

Katharina Kann and Hinrich Schütze. 2016. MED: The LMU system for the SIGMORPHON 2016 shared task on morphological reinflection. In *Proceedings of the 14th SIGMORPHON Workshop on Computational Research in Phonetics, Phonology, and Morphology*, pages 62–70, Berlin, Germany. Association for Computational Linguistics.

Christo Kirov, Ryan Cotterell, John Sylak-Glassman, Géraldine Walther, Ekaterina Vylomova, Patrick Xia, Manaal Faruqui, Sebastian J Mielke, Arya McCarthy, Sandra Kübler, et al. 2018. Unimorph 2.0: Universal morphology. In *Proceedings of the Eleventh International Conference on Language Resources and Evaluation (LREC-2018)*.

Guillaume Klein, Yoon Kim, Yuntian Deng, Jean Senellart, and Alexander M. Rush. 2017. OpenNMT: Open-source toolkit for neural machine translation. In *Proceedings of the 55th Annual Meeting of the Association for Computational Linguistics - System Demonstrations*, pages 67–72. Association for Computational Linguistics.

Grzegorz Kondrak. 2009. Identification of cognates and recurrent sound correspondences in word lists. *Traitement automatique des langues et langues anciennes (TAL)*, 50(2):201–235.

Grzegorz Kondrak. 2013. Word similarity, cognation, and translational equivalence. In Lars Borin and Anju Saxena, editors, *Approaches to Measuring Linguistic Differences*, volume 265 of *Trends in Linguistics*, pages 375–386. De Gruyter Mouton.

Arya D. McCarthy, Ekaterina Vylomova, Shijie Wu, Chaitanya Malaviya, Lawrence Wolf-Sonkin, Garrett Nicolai, Christo Kirov, Miikka Silfverberg, Sebastian Mielke, Jeffrey Heinz, Ryan Cotterell, and Mans Hulden. 2019. The SIGMORPHON 2019 shared task: Crosslinguality and context in morphology. In *Proceedings of the 16th SIGMORPHON Workshop on Computational Research in Phonetics, Phonology, and Morphology*, Florence, Italy. Association for Computational Linguistics.

Saeed Najafi, Colin Cherry, and Grzegorz Kondrak. 2019. Efficient sequence labeling with actor-critic training. In *Canadian Conference on Artificial Intelligence*, pages 466–471. Springer.

Saeed Najafi, Bradley Hauer, Rashed Rubby Riyadh, Leyuan Yu, and Grzegorz Kondrak. 2018a. Combining neural and non-neural methods for low-resource morphological reinflection. In *Proceedings of the CoNLL–SIGMORPHON 2018 Shared Task: Universal Morphological Reinflection*, pages 116–120, Brussels. Association for Computational Linguistics.

Saeed Najafi, Bradley Hauer, Rashed Rubby Riyadh, Leyuan Yu, and Grzegorz Kondrak. 2018b. Comparison of assorted models for transliteration. In *Proceedings of the Seventh Named Entities Workshop*, pages 84–88, Melbourne, Australia. Association for Computational Linguistics.

Garrett Nicolai, Colin Cherry, and Grzegorz Kondrak. 2015. Inflection generation as discriminative string transduction. In *Proceedings of the 2015 Conference of the North American Chapter of the Association for Computational Linguistics: Human Language Technologies*, pages 922–931. Association for Computational Linguistics.

Garrett Nicolai, Bradley Hauer, Mohammad Motallebi, Saeed Najafi, and Grzegorz Kondrak. 2017. If you can't beat them, join them: the University of Alberta system description. *Proceedings of the CoNLL SIGMORPHON 2017 Shared Task: Universal Morphological Reinflection*, pages 79–84.

Garrett Nicolai, Bradley Hauer, Adam St Arnaud, and Grzegorz Kondrak. 2016. Morphological reinflection via discriminative string transduction. In *Proceedings of the 14th SIGMORPHON Workshop on Computational Research in Phonetics, Phonology, and Morphology*, pages 31–35, Berlin, Germany. Association for Computational Linguistics.

Garrett Nicolai, Saeed Najafi, and Grzegorz Kondrak. 2018. String transduction with target language models and insertion handling. In *Proceedings of the Fifteenth Workshop on Computational Research in Phonetics, Phonology, and Morphology*, pages 43–53.

Adam St Arnaud, David Beck, and Grzegorz Kondrak. 2017. Identifying cognate sets across dictionaries of related languages. In *Proceedings of the 2017 Conference on Empirical Methods in Natural Language Processing*, pages 2519–2528.

Jrg Tiedemann. 2012. Parallel data, tools and interfaces in opus. In *Proceedings of the Eight International Conference on Language Resources and Evaluation (LREC'12)*, Istanbul, Turkey. European Language Resources Association (ELRA).

Shijie Wu and Ryan Cotterell. 2019. Exact hard monotonic attention for character-level transduction. *arXiv preprint arXiv:1905.06319*.

Marcos Zampieri, Shervin Malmasi, Yves Scherrer, Tanja Samardžić, Francis Tyers, Miikka Silfverberg, Natalia Klyueva, Tung-Le Pan, Chu-Ren Huang, Radu Tudor Ionescu, Andrei M. Butnaru, and Tommi Jauhiainen. 2019. A report on the third VarDial evaluation campaign. In *Proceedings of the Sixth Workshop on NLP for Similar Languages, Varieties and Dialects*, pages 1–16. Association for Computational Linguistics.

Cross-Lingual Lemmatization and Morphology Tagging with Two-Stage Multilingual BERT Fine-Tuning

Daniel Kondratyuk

Charles University

Institute of Formal and Applied Linguistics

Saarland University

Department of Computational Linguistics

dankondratyuk@gmail.com

Abstract

We present our CHARLES-SAARLAND system for the SIGMORPHON 2019 Shared Task on Crosslinguality and Context in Morphology, in task 2, Morphological Analysis and Lemmatization in Context. We leverage the multilingual BERT model and apply several fine-tuning strategies introduced by UDify demonstrating exceptional evaluation performance on morpho-syntactic tasks. Our results show that fine-tuning multilingual BERT on the concatenation of all available treebanks allows the model to learn cross-lingual information that is able to boost lemmatization and morphology tagging accuracy over fine-tuning it purely monolingually. Unlike UDify, however, we show that when paired with additional character-level and word-level LSTM layers, a second stage of fine-tuning on each treebank individually can improve evaluation even further. Out of all submissions for this shared task, our system achieves the highest average accuracy and f1 score in morphology tagging and places second in average lemmatization accuracy.

1 Introduction

We focus on track 2 of the SIGMORPHON 2019 Shared Task (McCarthy et al., 2019), which requires systems to predict lemmas and morphosyntactic descriptions (MSDs) of words given sentences of pre-tokenized words. The data relies on treebanks provided by the Universal Dependencies (UD) project (Nivre et al., 2018), where MSDs are converted from UD format to the UniMorph schema (McCarthy et al., 2018; Kirov et al., 2018). Systems must predict from sentences given test data provided in 107 separate treebanks each representing one of 66 different languages.

Recent advances in contextual word representations show that pretraining language models on a large corpus of unsupervised text can be used to

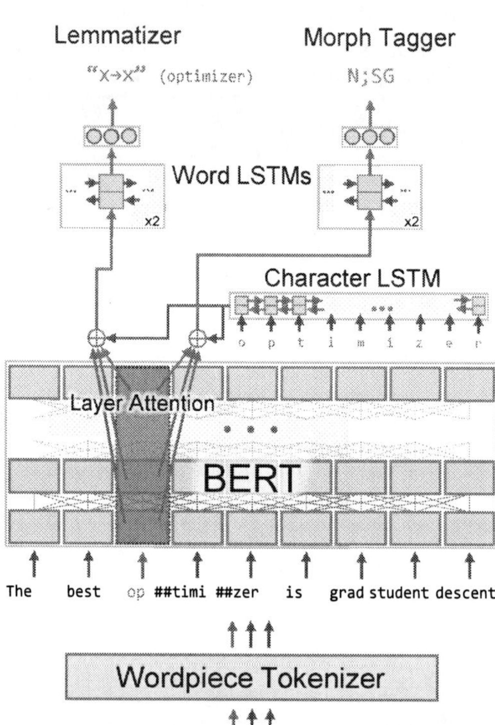

Figure 1: An illustration of our model architecture with task-specific layer attention, inputting word tokens and predicting lemma edit scripts and morphology tags for each token.

transfer their internal knowledge representations to other NLP tasks to boost evaluation scores significantly (Howard and Ruder, 2018; Peters et al., 2018; Devlin et al., 2018). We utilize the BERT base multilingual cased model pretrained on raw sentences found in the top 104 most-resourced languages of Wikipedia (Devlin et al., 2018) for all of our experiments. In addition, we use methods introduced by UDify (Kondratyuk, 2019) to

Proceedings of the 16th Workshop on Computational Research in Phonetics, Phonology, and Morphology, pages 12–18

Florence, Italy. August 2, 2019 ©2019 Association for Computational Linguistics

further fine-tune and regularize BERT, which has been shown to be especially helpful in predicting morpho-syntactic tasks.

Our system defines a simple multi-task multilingual neural architecture for predicting lemmas and MSDs jointly. Our contributions to achieve high lemmatization and morphology tagging performance are as follows:

1. We leverage the pretrained multilingual BERT cased model to encode input sentences and apply additional word-level and character-level LSTM layers before jointly decoding lemmas and morphology tags using simple sequence tagging layers.

2. Instead of only training models for each treebank separately, we use a two-stage training process to incorporate cross-linguistic information present in other treebanks, training multilingually over all treebanks in the first stage and then monolingually using saved multilingual weights in the second stage.

Our results show that applying an intermediate multilingual fine-tuning stage on BERT is superior to just fine-tuning monolingually in nearly all cases. Code for our model is released along with UDify at `https://github.com/hyperparticle/udify`.

2 Model Architecture

We describe the architecture of our system as follows. See Figure 1 for an illustration of this description. Our network consists of a shared BERT encoder followed by joint lemma and morphology tag decoders.

Given an input sentence consisting of a sequence of word tokens, we apply BERT's multilingual cased tokenizer to each word, potentially splitting it into multiple subword tokens. We encode this token sequence with the pretrained multilingual cased BERT base model consisting of 12 layers with 12 attention heads per layer and hidden output dimensions of 768. Following this, we take the subset of wordpieces corresponding to the first wordpiece of each word to align the BERT encoding with the sequence of input words[1].

Once BERT encoding is complete, we apply two separate instances of layer attention defined

---

[1] Kondratyuk (2019) and Kitaev and Klein (2018) found that first, last, or average of the wordpieces did not make a noticeable difference.

in UDify which is similar to ELMo (Peters et al., 2018), i.e., a trainable weighted sum of all 12 layers of BERT, which has been shown to improve evaluation performance over just computing representations on the last layer. The layer attention instances generate embeddings specific to each task, one for lemmatization and the other for morphology tagging.

But before decoding, we also apply character-level embeddings (Santos and Zadrozny, 2014; Ling et al., 2015; Kim et al., 2016) to produce an enhanced morphological representation by encoding the sequence of character tokens for each word through a bidirectional LSTM with a residual connection (Schuster and Paliwal, 1997; Kim et al., 2017), keeping the hidden layers fixed to dimensions of 384. We concatenate the final hidden states of both LSTM directions, and then sum these character-level word representations with each of the two encoded representations produced by the task-specific layer attention.

Similar to Kondratyuk et al. (2018) and Straka (2018), both the lemmatizer and morphological tagger employ two successive layers of word-level bidirectional residual LSTMs computed over the entire task layer attention sequence with hidden dimensions of 768, summing both directions together along each output state.

For lemmatization, we precompute edit scripts representing a minimal sequence of character operations to transduce a word form to its lemma counterpart, as seen in Chrupała (2006); Straka (2018). As is typical for neural sequence tagging, we apply a feedforward layer to the final layer of the lemmatizer LSTM, representing the activations of classes of all edit scripts found in the training data.

Similarly for morphology tagging, we apply a feedforward layer whose units correspond to the vocabulary over all unfactored MSD strings. We apply the method of Inoue et al. (2017) to jointly predict the classes of unfactored and factored morphology tags, i.e., we also predict each dimension of the morphology tag whose subcategories are defined by the UniMorph schema (e.g., case, mood, person, tense, etc.). We only use the factored tags to improve training, and for prediction we use the full unfactored tags.

Hyperparameter	Value
Character-level embedding dimension	256
Character-level LSTM hidden dimension	384
Word-level LSTM hidden dimension	768
Final feedforward learning rate	$4e^{-3}$
LSTM, layer attention learning rate	$1e^{-3}$
BERT learning rate (layers 7-12)	$5e^{-5}$
BERT learning rate (layers 1-6)	$1e^{-5}$
LSTM embedding dropout	0.5
BERT internal dropout	0.25
Mask probability	0.25
Layer dropout	0.2
Batch size	32
Epochs	50

Table 1: A summary of hyperparameters applicable to each model configuration.

3 Experiments

We train our system on the provided treebank training data with three separate configurations.

3.1 Configurations

Mono We train the network (as seen in Figure 1) monolingually by simply fine-tuning it on each treebank separately.

Multi We fine-tune the network as in Mono, except on a dataset consisting of all treebank training data concatenated together, as seen in UDify. All word, character, and tag vocabularies of each language are combined together.

Multi+Mono We train the network monolingually as in Mono, but using the BERT weights saved from the model fine-tuned according to Multi. This effectively defines a two-stage training process: the first stage involves multilingual fine-tuning of BERT, and the second stage re-trains the layer attention, LSTMs and feedforward taggers from scratch on each treebank with a reduced monolingual vocabulary (keeping fine-tuned BERT intact).

For all Mono and the second stage of Multi+Mono, we ensure that we do not combine multiple treebanks of the same language but always fine-tune on just the training data from each provided treebank.

3.2 Hyperparameters

A summary of specific values for each of the hyperparameters discussed can be seen in Table 1.

We train each configuration using a batch size of 32 over 50 epochs. We employ the Adam optimizer, computing the loss as the softmax cross entropy between the predicted tags and the

Model	Lemma		Morph	
	Acc	Dist	Acc	F1
Baseline	93.13	0.13	73.16	87.92
Mono	92.80	0.17	90.26	93.44
Multi	90.39	0.27	85.18	90.18
Multi+Mono	**95.00**	**0.12**	**93.23**	**96.02**

Table 2: A summary of the average results of each model configuration with a comparison to the baseline (Malaviya et al., 2019).

gold labels. We apply discriminative fine-tuning (Howard and Ruder, 2018) by defining four separate parameter groups each with their own base learning rate, decreasing as the layers get closer to the input: the first 6 layers of BERT, the last 6 layers of BERT, the layer attention and LSTM layers, and the final feedforward layers.

We apply regularization as defined by UDify, with a few extra modifications. We raise the layer dropout, BERT dropout, input mask probability slightly to prevent overfitting, especially for the Mono and Multi+Mono configurations. We also apply dropout to all intermediate word-embedding representations between each of the word-level LSTM layers.

4 Results

We display comparisons between each of the three configurations. We compute lemma accuracy, lemma Levenstein distance, morphology tag accuracy, and morphology f1 scores for each of the 107 treebanks. A summary of the averages of all scores for each configuration can be found in Table 2. The full results are shown in Tables 3, 4, 5, and 6.

5 Discussion

Our results show that not only does fine-tuning BERT provide excellent lemmatization and morphology tagging performance, two-stage Multi+Mono training can provide significant improvements for practically every treebank when compared to Mono. While some of these improvements can be attributed to learning from monolingual data from multiple treebanks of the same language, we can see improvements even for languages possessing just one treebank. This provides evidence that the Multi and Multi+Mono models regularize well to multilingual training. This could be explained by a combination of: multilingual learning providing

Treebank	Model	Lemma Acc	Lemma Dist	Morph Acc	Morph F1
Afrikaans AfriBooms	Mono	98.66	0.03	98.4	98.63
	Multi	97.19	0.05	98.06	98.58
	Multi+Mono	**98.95**	**0.02**	**99.23**	**99.36**
Akkadian PISANDUB	Mono	49.78	2.14	86.22	86.41
	Multi	23.56	3.63	60.44	60.89
	Multi+Mono	**65.35**	**0.97**	**89.11**	**89.06**
Amharic ATT	Mono	**100.0**	**0.00**	86.8	90.74
	Multi	**100.0**	**0.00**	81.0	86.14
	Multi+Mono	**100.0**	**0.00**	**87.43**	**91.34**
Ancient Greek PROIEL	Mono	92.15	0.22	90.85	96.95
	Multi	85.75	0.43	88.99	96.2
	Multi+Mono	**92.34**	**0.20**	**92.37**	**97.68**
Ancient Greek Perseus	Mono	88.88	0.32	88.9	94.74
	Multi	80.98	0.56	86.38	93.4
	Multi+Mono	**89.69**	**0.29**	**90.88**	**96.26**
Arabic PADT	Mono	94.24	0.17	94.09	96.91
	Multi	75.54	0.85	93.66	96.88
	Multi+Mono	**94.45**	**0.16**	**95.66**	**97.65**
Arabic PUD	Mono	71.0	1.50	84.03	93.78
	Multi	36.65	5.03	65.25	85.59
	Multi+Mono	**81.92**	**0.48**	**84.53**	**94.09**
Armenian ArmTDP	Mono	94.5	0.10	91.05	95.48
	Multi	91.48	0.17	82.49	89.92
	Multi+Mono	**95.58**	**0.08**	**92.77**	**96.66**
Bambara CRB	Mono	**90.08**	**0.18**	92.7	94.02
	Multi	72.25	0.58	77.09	81.81
	Multi+Mono	88.76	0.21	**93.32**	**95.34**
Basque BDT	Mono	96.3	0.08	90.03	94.72
	Multi	93.72	0.14	85.54	92.76
	Multi+Mono	**96.5**	**0.07**	**92.07**	**96.3**
Belarusian HSE	Mono	87.76	0.21	78.62	89.47
	Multi	87.62	0.22	73.56	81.76
	Multi+Mono	**92.51**	**0.12**	**89.93**	**95.68**
Breton KEB	Mono	91.19	**0.20**	90.88	92.93
	Multi	80.24	0.55	76.49	79.07
	Multi+Mono	87.66	0.32	90.35	91.77
Bulgarian BTB	Mono	96.72	0.10	96.61	98.3
	Multi	95.06	0.16	95.64	98.02
	Multi+Mono	**98.05**	**0.07**	**98.01**	**99.18**
Buryat BDT	Mono	85.48	0.33	80.29	82.5
	Multi	73.48	0.57	64.25	67.12
	Multi+Mono	**86.35**	**0.30**	**85.67**	**88.42**
Cantonese HK	Mono	99.49	0.01	92.11	90.19
	Multi	98.63	0.02	87.31	84.65
	Multi+Mono	**100.0**	**0.00**	**94.29**	92.83
Catalan AnCora	Mono	99.2	**0.01**	98.36	99.19
	Multi	98.87	0.02	98.58	99.37
	Multi+Mono	**99.38**	**0.01**	**98.82**	**99.45**
Chinese CFL	Mono	**100.0**	**0.00**	92.52	91.46
	Multi	**100.0**	**0.00**	84.9	85.56
	Multi+Mono	99.65	**0.00**	**92.55**	91.5
Chinese GSD	Mono	99.94	**0.00**	94.56	94.44
	Multi	**100.0**	**0.00**	97.03	96.96
	Multi+Mono	99.97	**0.00**	**97.13**	**97.04**
Coptic Scriptorium	Mono	92.52	0.17	89.93	92.28
	Multi	84.75	0.33	78.69	82.32
	Multi+Mono	**96.13**	**0.08**	**93.3**	**94.81**
Croatian SET	Mono	96.73	0.06	92.07	96.86
	Multi	96.54	0.06	91.01	96.74
	Multi+Mono	**97.51**	**0.05**	**94.11**	**97.82**
Czech CAC	Mono	99.03	0.02	96.43	98.67
	Multi	99.04	0.02	97.09	99.07
	Multi+Mono	**99.45**	**0.01**	**98.48**	**99.48**
Czech CLTT	Mono	98.09	0.03	92.35	96.63
	Multi	99.29	**0.01**	92.99	97.49
	Multi+Mono	**99.3**	**0.01**	**95.31**	**98.2**
Czech FicTree	Mono	98.11	0.03	93.39	97.14
	Multi	98.62	0.03	92.06	97.39
	Multi+Mono	**99.01**	**0.02**	**97.13**	**98.9**
Czech PDT	Mono	99.14	**0.01**	97.01	98.84
	Multi	99.12	0.02	97.48	99.12
	Multi+Mono	**99.42**	**0.01**	**98.54**	**99.47**
Czech PUD	Mono	92.71	0.12	80.71	92.13
	Multi	**97.91**	**0.03**	**92.71**	**97.64**
	Multi+Mono	96.74	0.06	92.38	97.43
Danish DDT	Mono	96.48	0.06	95.72	97.15
	Multi	96.47	0.07	96.25	97.73
	Multi+Mono	**98.15**	**0.03**	**97.98**	**98.68**
Dutch Alpino	Mono	97.63	0.04	96.64	97.43
	Multi	96.71	0.07	97.51	98.24
	Multi+Mono	**98.62**	**0.03**	**98.12**	**98.62**
Dutch LassySmall	Mono	96.77	0.06	96.11	97.0
	Multi	97.41	0.06	98.04	98.6
	Multi+Mono	**98.08**	**0.03**	**98.5**	**98.83**

Table 3: Main results (part 1 of 4).

Treebank	Model	Lemma Acc	Lemma Dist	Morph Acc	Morph F1
English EWT	Mono	98.56	0.02	96.44	97.38
	Multi	98.49	0.03	96.98	97.99
	Multi+Mono	**99.19**	**0.01**	**97.85**	**98.52**
English GUM	Mono	97.75	0.04	96.17	97.11
	Multi	94.97	0.09	93.6	96.15
	Multi+Mono	**98.45**	**0.02**	**97.52**	**98.11**
English LinES	Mono	98.31	0.03	96.76	97.51
	Multi	96.6	0.07	93.06	95.48
	Multi+Mono	**98.62**	**0.02**	**97.77**	**98.3**
English PUD	Mono	95.98	0.06	95.89	97.0
	Multi	94.05	0.13	92.65	95.76
	Multi+Mono	**97.89**	**0.03**	**96.67**	**97.58**
English ParTUT	Mono	97.87	0.03	96.02	96.55
	Multi	97.8	0.04	92.72	94.98
	Multi+Mono	**98.51**	**0.02**	**96.65**	**97.35**
Estonian EDT	Mono	**93.21**	**0.15**	95.3	97.56
	Multi	89.13	0.23	96.13	98.18
	Multi+Mono	88.16	0.22	**97.23**	**98.69**
Faroese OFT	Mono	**89.14**	0.22	**86.97**	92.27
	Multi	79.94	0.40	75.8	83.55
	Multi+Mono	88.95	**0.20**	86.74	**93.47**
Finnish FTB	Mono	93.74	0.13	93.61	96.3
	Multi	93.25	0.12	92.67	96.75
	Multi+Mono	**95.45**	**0.08**	**96.85**	**98.38**
Finnish PUD	Mono	75.7	0.54	89.28	94.22
	Multi	**85.71**	**0.21**	94.76	97.69
	Multi+Mono	85.48	0.28	**95.62**	**97.98**
Finnish TDT	Mono	93.89	0.12	95.05	97.05
	Multi	92.76	0.13	93.41	97.1
	Multi+Mono	**95.73**	**0.08**	**97.1**	**98.54**
French GSD	Mono	98.51	0.03	97.51	98.57
	Multi	98.44	0.03	97.64	98.85
	Multi+Mono	**99.01**	**0.02**	**98.31**	**99.07**
French ParTUT	Mono	94.88	0.10	94.35	97.2
	Multi	94.1	0.13	91.56	96.74
	Multi+Mono	**96.66**	**0.06**	**95.46**	**97.95**
French Sequoia	Mono	97.86	0.04	96.57	98.2
	Multi	98.36	0.03	92.56	97.45
	Multi+Mono	**98.81**	**0.02**	**97.75**	**98.99**
French Spoken	Mono	97.67	0.04	98.07	98.09
	Multi	98.42	0.03	97.17	97.2
	Multi+Mono	**98.85**	**0.02**	**98.6**	**98.65**
Galician CTG	Mono	98.58	**0.02**	98.23	98.07
	Multi	98.19	0.03	96.94	96.47
	Multi+Mono	**98.96**	**0.02**	**98.44**	**98.29**
Galician TreeGal	Mono	95.32	0.07	92.14	95.32
	Multi	96.24	0.05	84.58	92.1
	Multi+Mono	**98.46**	**0.03**	**96.21**	**97.88**
German GSD	Mono	97.18	0.06	88.01	94.75
	Multi	95.89	0.10	89.33	95.46
	Multi+Mono	**97.62**	**0.05**	**90.43**	**95.9**
Gothic PROIEL	Mono	93.25	0.14	85.95	93.72
	Multi	86.86	0.29	86.06	94.16
	Multi+Mono	**94.54**	**0.13**	**91.02**	**96.64**
Greek GDT	Mono	**94.64**	**0.13**	92.74	97.21
	Multi	90.99	0.25	92.36	97.12
	Multi+Mono	82.95	0.42	**95.61**	**98.23**
Hebrew HTB	Mono	96.55	0.07	95.99	97.2
	Multi	95.25	0.09	95.45	97.3
	Multi+Mono	**97.85**	**0.04**	**97.67**	**98.47**
Hindi HDTB	Mono	98.7	0.02	91.95	97.16
	Multi	98.63	0.02	92.16	97.4
	Multi+Mono	**98.84**	**0.01**	**93.65**	**98.04**
Hungarian Szeged	Mono	93.68	0.12	84.9	94.42
	Multi	92.82	0.12	79.01	92.69
	Multi+Mono	**96.99**	**0.06**	**91.5**	**97.51**
Indonesian GSD	Mono	99.4	**0.01**	90.62	93.84
	Multi	98.92	0.02	90.84	94.01
	Multi+Mono	**99.51**	**0.01**	**92.48**	**95.16**
Irish IDT	Mono	**89.07**	**0.26**	80.44	86.01
	Multi	85.9	0.33	75.72	84.6
	Multi+Mono	88.09	0.27	**84.4**	**90.04**
Italian ISDT	Mono	98.33	0.03	97.88	98.77
	Multi	98.34	0.03	98.31	99.17
	Multi+Mono	**98.88**	**0.02**	**98.49**	**99.19**
Italian PUD	Mono	94.82	0.10	95.1	97.67
	Multi	96.19	0.09	59.07	84.9
	Multi+Mono	**97.69**	**0.04**	**96.37**	**98.42**
Italian ParTUT	Mono	97.32	0.05	97.32	98.24
	Multi	98.24	0.04	97.92	98.8
	Multi+Mono	**98.87**	**0.02**	**98.4**	**99.2**
Italian PoSTWITA	Mono	96.15	0.08	95.87	96.82
	Multi	95.24	0.12	96.56	97.58
	Multi+Mono	**97.24**	**0.06**	**96.88**	**97.9**

Table 4: Main results (part 2 of 4).

Treebank	Model	Lemma		Morph	
		Acc	Dist	Acc	F1
Japanese GSD	Mono	99.36	0.01	97.36	97.04
	Multi	99.49	0.01	98.07	97.83
	Multi+Mono	**99.65**	**0.00**	**98.41**	**98.21**
Japanese Modern	Mono	96.17	0.05	96.1	96.17
	Multi	94.57	0.08	90.05	90.16
	Multi+Mono	**98.67**	**0.01**	**97.47**	**97.5**
Japanese PUD	Mono	98.89	0.02	96.78	96.45
	Multi	**99.5**	**0.01**	97.9	97.7
	Multi+Mono	99.36	**0.01**	**98.56**	**98.39**
Komi Zyrian IKDP	Mono	56.63	0.88	45.78	49.74
	Multi	63.86	0.83	38.55	37.04
	Multi+Mono	**78.91**	**0.38**	**67.97**	**75.05**
Komi Zyrian Lattice	Mono	63.74	0.82	44.51	52.06
	Multi	60.44	1.05	39.56	45.87
	Multi+Mono	**80.77**	**0.36**	**67.58**	**78.01**
Korean GSD	Mono	87.47	0.26	96.18	95.66
	Multi	83.82	0.35	94.06	93.22
	Multi+Mono	**91.95**	**0.16**	**96.77**	**96.27**
Korean Kaist	Mono	92.62	0.14	96.97	96.59
	Multi	89.3	0.23	97.54	97.24
	Multi+Mono	**93.18**	**0.12**	**97.85**	**97.58**
Korean PUD	Mono	98.56	0.03	92.36	95.51
	Multi	68.19	0.99	64.7	70.71
	Multi+Mono	**99.57**	**0.01**	**94.67**	**96.76**
Kurmanji MG	Mono	87.54	0.24	80.69	86.67
	Multi	78.91	0.45	65.04	72.29
	Multi+Mono	**93.73**	**0.12**	**84.23**	**90.26**
Latin ITTB	Mono	98.68	0.03	95.17	97.65
	Multi	98.53	0.04	96.38	98.44
	Multi+Mono	**99.2**	**0.02**	**97.64**	**98.96**
Latin PROIEL	Mono	95.75	0.09	88.81	95.43
	Multi	94.67	0.12	91.15	96.78
	Multi+Mono	**97.36**	**0.05**	**93.68**	**97.87**
Latin Perseus	Mono	79.04	0.43	72.1	83.21
	Multi	86.43	0.27	80.53	90.8
	Multi+Mono	**89.68**	**0.19**	**85.94**	**93.79**
Latvian LVTB	Mono	95.15	0.08	92.59	95.85
	Multi	94.73	0.09	91.88	95.75
	Multi+Mono	**97.14**	**0.05**	**95.78**	**98.04**
Lithuanian HSE	Mono	74.46	0.53	67.6	75.01
	Multi	73.61	0.48	66.09	78.74
	Multi+Mono	**85.57**	**0.25**	**79.46**	**87.97**
Marathi UFAL	Mono	73.65	0.67	59.53	74.76
	Multi	75.53	0.65	55.53	75.05
	Multi+Mono	**76.69**	**0.61**	**67.75**	**80.19**
Naija NSC	Mono	99.84	0.01	95.64	94.16
	Multi	99.43	0.01	92.33	89.49
	Multi+Mono	**100.0**	**0.00**	**96.5**	**95.31**
North Sami Giella	Mono	85.74	0.30	84.66	90.44
	Multi	79.06	0.42	83.28	90.03
	Multi+Mono	**90.17**	**0.21**	**92.46**	**95.33**
Norwegian Bokmaal	Mono	98.76	0.02	97.13	98.32
	Multi	98.62	0.02	97.73	98.83
	Multi+Mono	**99.18**	**0.01**	**98.25**	**99.02**
Norwegian Nynorsk	Mono	98.45	0.02	96.89	98.17
	Multi	98.34	0.03	97.62	98.77
	Multi+Mono	**99.0**	**0.01**	**98.11**	**98.97**
Norwegian NynorskLIA	Mono	96.24	0.07	93.37	94.96
	Multi	97.28	0.05	93.96	96.29
	Multi+Mono	**98.08**	**0.04**	**96.8**	**97.39**
Old Church Slavonic PROIEL	Mono	91.09	0.19	86.24	93.22
	Multi	82.79	0.39	80.18	89.63
	Multi+Mono	**93.7**	**0.15**	**91.71**	**96.45**
Persian Seraji	Mono	95.34	0.23	97.17	97.69
	Multi	92.17	0.41	96.85	97.73
	Multi+Mono	**96.63**	**0.17**	**98.31**	**98.67**
Polish LFG	Mono	96.25	0.07	92.44	96.74
	Multi	96.01	0.09	89.63	96.47
	Multi+Mono	**97.94**	**0.04**	**97.13**	**98.86**
Polish SZ	Mono	96.54	0.07	88.15	94.79
	Multi	96.22	0.08	69.63	91.35
	Multi+Mono	**97.43**	**0.05**	**95.11**	**98.11**
Portuguese Bosque	Mono	98.26	0.03	95.1	97.57
	Multi	97.48	0.05	94.45	97.34
	Multi+Mono	**98.65**	**0.02**	**96.22**	**98.26**
Portuguese GSD	Mono	98.64	0.07	98.63	98.74
	Multi	97.73	0.11	98.05	98.03
	Multi+Mono	**99.09**	**0.05**	**99.03**	**99.1**
Romanian Nonstandard	Mono	95.66	0.08	93.15	96.26
	Multi	92.88	0.13	93.8	96.99
	Multi+Mono	**96.52**	**0.06**	**95.01**	**97.65**
Romanian RRT	Mono	97.98	0.03	97.34	98.19
	Multi	97.14	0.05	97.15	98.36
	Multi+Mono	**98.58**	**0.02**	**98.19**	**98.89**
Russian GSD	Mono	96.41	0.06	90.73	95.92
	Multi	97.34	**0.04**	90.6	96.58
	Multi+Mono	**97.74**	**0.04**	**94.92**	**97.95**

Table 5: Main results (part 3 of 4).

Treebank	Model	Lemma		Morph	
		Acc	Dist	Acc	F1
Russian PUD	Mono	89.44	0.19	86.15	93.84
	Multi	94.38	0.10	64.26	89.43
	Multi+Mono	**95.49**	**0.08**	**91.15**	**96.27**
Russian SynTagRus	Mono	98.6	0.03	97.22	98.61
	Multi	98.28	0.04	97.76	98.97
	Multi+Mono	**99.01**	**0.02**	**98.38**	**99.23**
Russian Taiga	Mono	88.91	0.20	82.64	88.88
	Multi	**94.13**	**0.13**	88.61	**94.89**
	Multi+Mono	93.49	**0.13**	**90.15**	94.88
Sanskrit UFAL	Mono	57.22	1.12	43.81	58.11
	Multi	49.48	1.24	33.51	43.14
	Multi+Mono	**63.32**	**0.89**	**47.74**	**69.52**
Serbian SET	Mono	96.74	0.06	93.86	97.02
	Multi	97.36	0.05	93.22	97.18
	Multi+Mono	**98.08**	**0.03**	**97.02**	**98.64**
Slovak SNK	Mono	96.31	0.06	89.24	95.15
	Multi	95.73	0.07	90.61	96.23
	Multi+Mono	**97.57**	**0.04**	**95.41**	**98.24**
Slovenian SSJ	Mono	97.22	0.04	92.56	96.37
	Multi	97.6	0.04	92.97	97.2
	Multi+Mono	**98.87**	**0.02**	**97.01**	**98.8**
Slovenian SST	Mono	93.46	0.10	83.46	90.38
	Multi	**97.24**	**0.05**	87.76	94.06
	Multi+Mono	97.2	**0.05**	**92.76**	**96.2**
Spanish AnCora	Mono	99.07	0.02	98.15	99.04
	Multi	98.87	0.02	98.36	99.19
	Multi+Mono	**99.4**	**0.01**	**98.79**	**99.4**
Spanish GSD	Mono	99.0	**0.01**	95.93	98.05
	Multi	98.35	0.02	95.63	97.96
	Multi+Mono	**99.16**	**0.01**	95.88	**98.08**
Swedish LinES	Mono	96.24	0.07	93.49	96.42
	Multi	94.94	0.09	92.43	96.6
	Multi+Mono	**97.83**	**0.04**	**94.75**	**97.67**
Swedish PUD	Mono	91.83	0.12	93.26	95.64
	Multi	90.81	0.14	93.46	96.37
	Multi+Mono	**95.85**	**0.07**	**95.62**	**97.25**
Swedish Talbanken	Mono	97.54	0.04	96.46	97.92
	Multi	97.17	0.05	96.65	98.52
	Multi+Mono	**98.62**	**0.02**	**98.09**	**99.05**
Tagalog TRG	Mono	76.0	0.48	72.0	79.17
	Multi	72.0	0.60	28.0	38.2
	Multi+Mono	**91.89**	**0.19**	**91.89**	**95.04**
Tamil TTB	Mono	88.96	0.27	84.78	92.41
	Multi	90.58	0.22	80.21	88.04
	Multi+Mono	**91.52**	**0.20**	**91.07**	**95.64**
Turkish IMST	Mono	93.43	**0.11**	85.51	91.71
	Multi	91.77	0.12	76.86	87.72
	Multi+Mono	**94.77**	**0.11**	**90.55**	**95.38**
Turkish PUD	Mono	83.11	0.37	84.34	92.13
	Multi	84.92	0.36	49.33	76.78
	Multi+Mono	**86.52**	**0.32**	**87.47**	**94.43**
Ukrainian IU	Mono	96.14	0.06	90.68	95.59
	Multi	96.31	0.06	91.42	96.32
	Multi+Mono	**97.84**	**0.03**	**95.78**	**98.1**
Upper Sorbian UFAL	Mono	85.25	0.25	74.19	81.49
	Multi	83.19	0.31	71.96	81.55
	Multi+Mono	**93.74**	**0.10**	**86.37**	**92.54**
Urdu UDTB	Mono	96.34	0.07	78.57	92.0
	Multi	96.08	0.07	79.26	92.44
	Multi+Mono	**96.92**	**0.06**	**80.67**	**93.45**
Vietnamese VTB	Mono	**99.81**	**0.00**	93.5	92.99
	Multi	99.35	0.01	93.96	93.47
	Multi+Mono	99.75	**0.00**	**94.54**	**94.02**
Yoruba YTB	Mono	97.6	**0.02**	88.0	85.33
	Multi	96.4	0.04	75.6	70.99
	Multi+Mono	**98.45**	**0.02**	**93.02**	**93.15**

Table 6: Main results (part 4 of 4).

language-invariant generalizations, out-of-domain data providing noise to reduce overfitting, or warm restarts aiding in improved convergence of model parameters. More experimentation is necessary to quantify these possible contributors.

Unlike the results shown by UDify, we see that the MULTI configuration provides overall inferior predictions on almost every treebank when compared to both MONO and MULTI+MONO.

This is likely due to the added LSTM layers and character-level embeddings, which provide additional information that improves monolingual training representations far more than it improves multilingual. Our intuition is that the LSTM layers pose an information bottleneck for massively multilingual data, unlike the BERT encoder, whose large capacity has been shown to be able to scale to more than 100 languages. Predictions using a smaller vocabulary subset could provide a much stronger signal to the LSTM layers to incorporate character-level morphology more accurately. But we do see that learning MULTI still learns useful cross-lingual information, just that it requires the LSTMs and character embeddings to be reconfigured to the specific treebank at hand to gain the benefits of both types of training.

Note that we specifically do not perform any extensive hyperparameter search or use ensembling. As such, we predict that our evaluation results could still be raised much higher.

6 Conclusion

We have demonstrated our system consisting of fine-tuning a multi-task enhanced BERT model for lemmatization and morphology tagging using a two-stage multilingual training scheme. We show that while pretrained BERT does provide word representations capable of surpassing the baseline, we are able to improve this significantly by also incorporating multilingual pretraining on all available treebanks, allowing the model to regularize and likely incorporate cross-lingual information useful for morphological parsing. We leave a more detailed analysis as to what extent multilingual fine-tuning and BERT pretraining contribute to model performance for future work.

7 Acknowledgements

Daniel Kondratyuk has been supported by the Erasmus Mundus program in Language & Communication Technologies (LCT).

References

Grzegorz Chrupała. 2006. Simple data-driven context-sensitive lemmatization. *Procesamiento del Lenguaje Natural*, 37.

Jacob Devlin, Ming-Wei Chang, Kenton Lee, and Kristina Toutanova. 2018. Bert: Pre-training of deep bidirectional transformers for language understanding. *arXiv preprint arXiv:1810.04805*.

Jeremy Howard and Sebastian Ruder. 2018. Universal language model fine-tuning for text classification. In *Proceedings of the 56th Annual Meeting of the Association for Computational Linguistics (Volume 1: Long Papers)*, volume 1, pages 328–339.

Go Inoue, Hiroyuki Shindo, and Yuji Matsumoto. 2017. Joint prediction of morphosyntactic categories for fine-grained arabic part-of-speech tagging exploiting tag dictionary information. In *Proceedings of the 21st Conference on Computational Natural Language Learning (CoNLL 2017)*, pages 421–431.

Jaeyoung Kim, Mostafa El-Khamy, and Jungwon Lee. 2017. Residual lstm: Design of a deep recurrent architecture for distant speech recognition. *Proc. Interspeech 2017*, pages 1591–1595.

Yoon Kim, Yacine Jernite, David Sontag, and Alexander M Rush. 2016. Character-aware neural language models. In *Thirtieth AAAI Conference on Artificial Intelligence*.

Christo Kirov, Ryan Cotterell, John Sylak-Glassman, Géraldine Walther, Ekaterina Vylomova, Patrick Xia, Manaal Faruqui, Sebastian J. Mielke, Arya McCarthy, Sandra Kübler, David Yarowsky, Jason Eisner, and Mans Hulden. 2018. UniMorph 2.0: Universal Morphology. In *Proceedings of the 11th Language Resources and Evaluation Conference*, Miyazaki, Japan. European Language Resource Association.

Nikita Kitaev and Dan Klein. 2018. Constituency parsing with a self-attentive encoder. *arXiv preprint arXiv:1805.01052*.

Daniel Kondratyuk. 2019. 75 languages, 1 model: Parsing universal dependencies universally. *arXiv preprint arXiv:1904.02099*.

Daniel Kondratyuk, Tomáš Gavenčiak, Milan Straka, and Jan Hajič. 2018. Lemmatag: Jointly tagging and lemmatizing for morphologically rich languages with brnns. In *Proceedings of the 2018 Conference on Empirical Methods in Natural Language Processing*, pages 4921–4928.

Wang Ling, Chris Dyer, Alan W Black, Isabel Trancoso, Ramon Fermandez, Silvio Amir, Luis Marujo, and Tiago Luis. 2015. Finding function in form: Compositional character models for open vocabulary word representation. In *Proceedings of the 2015 Conference on Empirical Methods in Natural Language Processing*, pages 1520–1530.

Chaitanya Malaviya, Shijie Wu, and Ryan Cotterell. 2019. A simple joint model for improved contextual neural lemmatization. *arXiv preprint arXiv:1904.02306v2*.

Arya D. McCarthy, Miikka Silfverberg, Ryan Cotterell, Mans Hulden, and David Yarowsky. 2018. Marrying Universal Dependencies and Universal Morphology. In *Proceedings of the Second Workshop on Universal Dependencies (UDW 2018)*, pages 91–101, Brussels, Belgium. Association for Computational Linguistics.

Arya D. McCarthy, Ekaterina Vylomova, Shijie Wu, Chaitanya Malaviya, Lawrence Wolf-Sonkin, Garrett Nicolai, Christo Kirov, Miikka Silfverberg, Sebastian Mielke, Jeffrey Heinz, Ryan Cotterell, and Mans Hulden. 2019. The SIGMORPHON 2019 shared task: Crosslinguality and context in morphology. In *Proceedings of the 16th SIGMORPHON Workshop on Computational Research in Phonetics, Phonology, and Morphology*, Florence, Italy. Association for Computational Linguistics.

Joakim Nivre, Mitchell Abrams, Željko Agić, and Ahrenberg. 2018. Universal dependencies 2.3. LINDAT/CLARIN digital library at the Institute of Formal and Applied Linguistics (ÚFAL), Faculty of Mathematics and Physics, Charles University.

Matthew E. Peters, Mark Neumann, Mohit Iyyer, Matt Gardner, Christopher Clark, Kenton Lee, and Luke Zettlemoyer. 2018. Deep contextualized word representations. In *Proc. of NAACL*.

Cicero D Santos and Bianca Zadrozny. 2014. Learning character-level representations for part-of-speech tagging. In *Proceedings of the 31st International Conference on Machine Learning (ICML-14)*, pages 1818–1826.

Mike Schuster and Kuldip K Paliwal. 1997. Bidirectional recurrent neural networks. *IEEE TRANSACTIONS ON SIGNAL PROCESSING*, 45(11):2673.

Milan Straka. 2018. UDPipe 2.0 prototype at CoNLL 2018 UD shared task. In *Proceedings of the CoNLL 2018 Shared Task: Multilingual Parsing from Raw Text to Universal Dependencies*, pages 197–207, Brussels, Belgium. Association for Computational Linguistics.

CBNU System for SIGMORPHON 2019 Shared Task 2:
a Pipeline Model

Uygun Shadikhodjaev and Jae Sung Lee
Department of Computer Science
Chungbuk National University
Cheongju City, Chungbuk Province, South Korea
ushadikhodjaev@gmail.com, jasonlee@cbnu.ac.kr

Abstract

In this paper we describe our system for morphological analysis and lemmatization in context, using a transformer-based sequence to sequence model and a biaffine attention based BiLSTM model. First, a lemma is produced for a given word, and then both the lemma and the given word are used for morphological analysis. We also make use of character level word encodings and trainable encodings to improve accuracy. Overall, our system ranked fifth in lemmatization and sixth in morphological accuracy among twelve systems, and demonstrated considerable improvements over the baseline in morphological analysis.

1 Introduction

In this paper we present our neural network architecture that we have used for the SIGMORPHON 2019 shared task 2 (McCarthy et al., 2019). We use two models by pipelining them in the sequence of operations. Our approach is based on the idea that lemmatization is an *m-to-n* mapping task where given a word of m characters we need to produce its lemma consisting of n characters. Unlike lemmatization, morphological analysis calls for a different approach where given a sentence consisting of m words, we need to choose one label from a fixed set of labels for each word. Hence, morphological analysis/tagging is a classification task for an input sequence.

	Word	Lemma	MSD
1	these	these	PL;DET
2	guys	guy	N;PL
3	were	be	PST;IND;V;FIN
4	fantastic	fantastic	ADJ
5	!	!	_

Table 1: Sample data of SIGMORPHON 2019 Shared Task 2

2 Task and Dataset

There are two tasks in SIGMORPHON 2019 and we chose task 2. The idea of the task is simple: the input is a sentence made of words and the output is a lemma and morphosyntactic description (MSD) for each word. Table 1 shows sample data for task 2: the first column is the input, the second is the lemma, and the last is the MSD for each word. There may be a difference in the result if a lemma is used as an additional input for MSD tagging. Our experiments showed improved performance when a lemma was incorporated.

The dataset consists of initial 98 datasets of more than 60 distinct languages, and additional nine surprise languages/datasets that were added later. Some of the datasets consist of languages that are not widespread in terms of their usage and amount of available training data. For example, Akkadian has only 80 sentences in training data, and other low-resource languages similarly have small numbers of sentences: Amharic has 859, Bambara 820, Buryat 741, Cantonese 520, etc. On the other hand, Russian SynTagRus and Czech PDT respectively have 49,511 and 70,330 sentences in their training data. In addition to

Proceedings of the 16th Workshop on Computational Research in Phonetics, Phonology, and Morphology, pages 19–24
Florence, Italy. August 2, 2019 ©2019 Association for Computational Linguistics

having less training data, some of the low-resource languages also do not have pre-trained word vectors. In such cases, we use other related languages' word vectors as a substitute, as will be discussed later.

3   Model

The baseline model (Malaviya et al., 2019) provided by the task organizers approaches task 2 by first finding a MSD tag for a given word and incorporating that information in lemmatization. Given a sequence of words w, a sequence of morphological tags m, and a sequence of lemmas l, they define their model as:

$$p(l, m \mid w) = p\,(l|m, w)p(m|w) \qquad (1)$$

This illustrates the importance of MSD tags in the lemmatization process. However, lemmatization can be done effectively even without consideration of morphological tags. Therefore, our approach flips the order of operations: we first find the lemma for a given word and input the original sentence with the generated lemma to the MSD tagger. Equation 2 summarizes this idea:

$$p(m, l \mid w) = p\,(m|l, w)p(l|w) \qquad (2)$$

Overall, given the nature of the required tasks, an *m-to-n* sequence to sequence model for lemmatization and a label classifier model for morphological analysis are used. The two models are trained separately and pipelined as shown in Figure 1. As an example, when given an initial sentence "these guys are fantastic!", we lemmatize each input word as "these guy be fantastic!" We then input the derived lemmas and the original input to the MSD tagger. At the end, we obtain MSD tag for each input word.

3.1   Lemmatizer

Our lemmatizer is a sequence to sequence model and is based on an encoder-decoder architecture using Google's transformer (Vaswani et al., 2017). Lemmatization is a similar task to translation, where an input sequence is mapped to an output sequence of a different length. Therefore, our approach is justified by the model's robust performance in neural machine

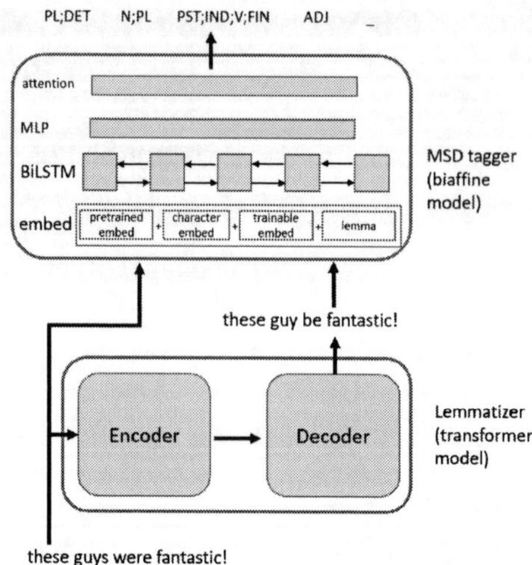

Figure 1: Pipeline Model

translation, particularly for WMT 2014 English-to-German and WMT 2014 EN-FR datasets. An informal leaderboard at http://nlpprogress.com demonstrates that the best performing teams use a transformer architecture for their encoder-decoder architecture (cf. Edunov et al., 2018, Wu et al., 2019).

A more formal leaderboard for the GLUE benchmark (Wang et al. 2018) consists of tasks that mainly use the encoder part of the encoder-decoder architecture. Therefore, the tasks of the GLUE benchmark are not directly comparable with lemmatization, but even in this case, at least the top 10 performers use BERT (Devlin et al., 2018), which uses a transformer encoder architecture (cf. Liu et al., 2019, Keskar et al., 2019).

The specific code for lemmatization is taken from the tensor2tensor library [1] version 1.13.4 with some modification added for our task. We chose the built-in hyperparameter configuration of *transformer_tiny*. The input and the output is a sequence of characters and no pre-trained embedding is used. One word is input at a time, and thus no consideration is taken of context words. For instance, in the mentioned example, the encoder input is "t h e s e" as a sequence of characters and the decoder output is "t h e s e". Likewise, "g u y s" and "g u y", "w e r e" and "b e", etc. are input and output one by one. Overall, the number of attention layers or heads is 4 as opposed to 8 in the original paper and hence it

---

[1] https://github.com/tensorflow/tensor2tensor

requires less computational power without substantial loss in the accuracy. The model performs quite well and with this basic setup was ranked fifth among 12 participating systems.

3.2 MSD tagger

The task of morphological analysis uses the output of lemmatization after pipelining it. Furthermore, MSD tagging is very similar to another well researched NLP task: head-dependent relation labelling in dependency parsing. Like head-dependent relation labelling, an MSD tag of a word is dependent on the word itself and its position within the sentence. As an example, let's consider two sentences: "I live in an apartment" and "I like live music". Even though "live" occurs in both sentences, the label we attach is dependent on the context. In other words, context words and the word itself determine its MSD tag. Therefore, we use the modified dependency parser reported by Dozat et al. (2017), which is based on Kiperwasser et al. (2016). The original model won in the CoNLL 2017 shared task (Nivre et al. 2017a, Nivre et al. 2017b) and its subsequent modifications won in the CoNLL 2018 shared task (Zeman et al., 2018, Che et al., 2018). Unlike dependency parsing, for the morphological analysis it is not necessary to find the head of a word. Therefore, we amend the dependency parser by Dozat et al. (2017) and use only the model's head-dependent relation labeling functionality for the MSD tagging.

The model's input is an elementwise addition of four embeddings for an input word. We then pass the vector representation for each input word through BiLSTM layers with subsequent multilayer perceptron (MLP) and biaffine attention layers. The MSD tagging assigns a tag to each word while the dependency parsing assigns a tag to a relation between a pair of words. In the latter case, even though we need to tag a relation between a pair of words, each word needs a label. Furthermore, information from two words only is not enough and the parser has to attend actually to the whole context to assign the correct label. Therefore, we need attention over all input words in the dependency parsing and we leave this feature for the MSD tagger too.

The optimization is done by the Adam optimizer (Knigma and Ba 2014). We trained the model until there were no improvements after 5000 steps. The number of BiLSTM layers was

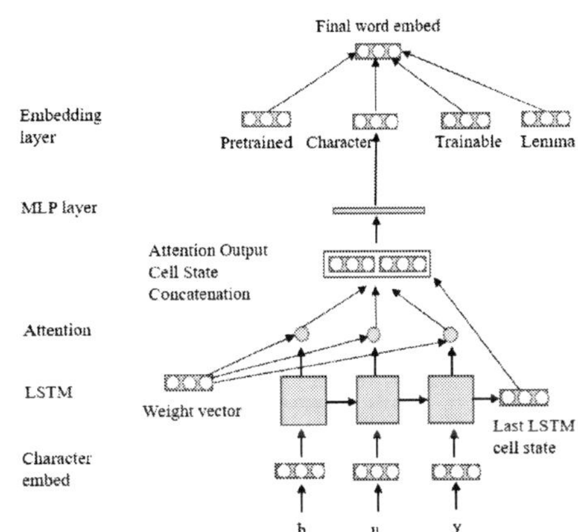

Figure 2: Character level embedding

three and the dimension of each LSTM cell as well as the word vector was 100 (300 when fastText[2] is used). We mainly used pre-trained embeddings of words from the CoNLL 2017 shared task (Nivre et al. 2017a, Nivre et al. 2017b) trained on word2vec (Mikolov et al., 2013). For Akkadian, Amharic, and Japanese we used fastText (Bojanowski et al., 2017). Interestingly, using the pre-trained word vector of Dutch from the CoNLL 2017 shared task demonstrates better performance than the Afrikaans pre-trained word vector of fastText for Afrikaans-AfriBooms treebank. Similar results were observed for some other datasets and therefore we used fastText only for the mentioned languages. At the same time, using the word vector for a related language is also in the spirit of cross-lingual learning transfer from a resource-rich to a resource-lean language (Ruder et al., 2017).

For each word, there are four embeddings, which are summed elementwise: pre-trained, trainable, character level, and lemma. Trainable embeddings are vectors that are initialized randomly and then trained as the training proceeds. Likewise, lemma vectors are also initialized randomly. The process of character level embedding generation is more involved and is based on the character level word representation by Cao and Rei (2016). Character level embeddings are a sequence of characters that pass through unidirectional LSTM cells (Hochreiter and Schmidhuber, 1997) and are then

---

[2] https://fasttext.cc/

21

summed after the conventional attention layer (Bahdanau et al., 2015). Figure 2 summarizes this process.

4 Results

After experiments with different hyperparameter settings, we were able to choose optimal settings, as was described earlier. Table 2 summarizes the results of lemmatization and MSD tagging by the sequence to sequence transformer model and the biaffine attention based BiLSTM model.

Our choice of lemmatization followed by an MSD tagging was an important step for increasing MSD tag accuracy. Although, a full-scale ablation

Treebanks	lemma acc.	lemma Leven.	morph acc.	morph F1
Afri. AfriBooms	98.49	0.03	98.45	98.66
Akk.PISANDUB	67.82	0.89	82.18	81.77
Amharic-ATT	99.91	0.00	88.19	92.41
A. Greek-Perseus	94.48	0.14	81.75	91.58
A. Greek-PROIEL	96.75	0.08	83.82	93.86
Arabic-PADT	94.16	0.16	93.22	96.32
Arabic-PUD	85.29	0.42	79.16	91.27
Armenian-ArmTDP	94.34	0.11	76.80	84.91
Bambara-CRB	83.90	0.30	92.79	94.74
Basque-BDT	95.75	0.10	87.63	92.80
Belarusian-HSE	89.81	0.19	58.67	65.26
Breton-KEB	92.54	0.19	87.36	90.13
Bulgarian-BTB	96.56	0.09	96.02	98.00
Buryat-BDT	89.23	0.26	80.48	82.93
Cantonese-HK	100	0.00	90.00	87.40
Catalan-AnCora	97.20	0.05	96.19	97.71
Chinese-CFL	99.76	0.00	91.49	90.37
Chinese-GSD	99.98	0.00	94.60	94.42
Coptic-Scriptorium	89.95	0.21	94.81	95.93
Croatian-SET	95.14	0.09	88.64	94.64
Czech-CAC	98.22	0.05	91.76	96.86
Czech-CLTT	98.41	0.03	90.01	94.98
Czech-FicTree	97.89	0.04	91.49	95.6
Czech-PDT	98.08	0.03	89.88	95.84
Czech-PUD	93.06	0.12	76.17	89.38
Danish-DDT	94.86	0.08	95.52	96.96
Dutch-Alpino	97.37	0.05	96.45	97.18
Dutch-LassySmall	96.45	0.07	96.38	97.00
English-EWT	97.31	0.08	95.82	97.01
English-GUM	97.09	0.05	95.46	96.54
English-LinES	97.87	0.04	96.34	97.16
English-ParTUT	97.30	0.05	94.75	95.56
English-PUD	94.90	0.07	93.43	94.95
Estonian-EDT	95.76	0.09	93.08	96.45
Faroese-OFT	88.28	0.22	81.08	88.28
Finnish-FTB	95.87	0.09	92.55	95.59
Finnish-PUD	89.09	0.23	88.52	93.32
Finnish-TDT	95.68	0.10	93.62	96.22
French-GSD	97.56	0.04	96.76	97.98
French-ParTUT	95.81	0.07	93.10	96.54
French-Sequoia	97.32	0.05	96.27	98.13
French-Spoken	97.17	0.06	97.25	97.31
Galician-CTG	97.00	0.04	97.94	97.73
Galician-TreeGal	94.05	0.08	92.74	95.58
German-GSD	97.11	0.06	86.05	93.73
Gothic-PROIEL	96.62	0.09	82.33	91.77
Greek-GDT	95.98	0.08	93.24	97.26
Hebrew-HTB	96.83	0.06	95.84	97.22
Hindi-HDTB	96.40	0.04	91.05	96.65
Hungarian-Szeged	95.19	0.09	88.11	94.63
Indonesian-GSD	99.50	0.01	90.17	93.15
Irish-IDT	91.24	0.20	82.40	88.35
Italian-ISDT	96.82	0.07	96.81	98.05
Italian-ParTUT	96.34	0.09	96.08	97.59
Italian-PoSTWITA	95.26	0.11	95.12	96.33

Treebanks	lemma acc.	lemma Leven.	morph acc.	morph F1
Italian-PUD	94.14	0.13	93.32	96.40
Japanese-GSD	98.13	0.02	97.74	97.46
Japanese-Modern	96.94	0.04	96.74	96.74
Japanese-PUD	97.46	0.03	97.88	97.65
Komi_Zyrian-IKDP	80.47	0.30	53.12	42.98
Komi_Zyrian-Lattice	84.07	0.38	57.14	65.07
Korean-GSD	93.19	0.12	95.87	95.25
Korean-Kaist	95.57	0.07	96.71	96.30
Korean-PUD	97.96	0.04	91.02	93.99
Kurmanji-MG	91.40	0.17	79.48	87.13
Latin-ITTB	97.44	0.06	93.32	96.62
Latin-Perseus	91.16	0.19	78.68	88.54
Latin-PROIEL	96.51	0.08	87.99	95.16
Latvian-LVTB	95.77	0.07	91.60	95.10
Lithuanian-HSE	86.42	0.30	56.03	57.49
Marathi-UFAL	74.25	0.65	47.43	59.40
Naija-NSC	99.93	0.00	94.94	93.17
North_Sami-Giella	91.96	0.16	87.04	91.90
Norwegian-Bokmaal	97.83	0.03	95.81	97.40
Norwegian-Nynorsk	97.74	0.04	94.87	96.60
N.NynorskLIA	97.51	0.04	93.03	94.29
OCS-PROIEL	96.51	0.08	83.44	91.82
Persian-Seraji	96.27	0.17	97.06	97.70
Polish-LFG	95.66	0.08	92.19	96.23
Polish-SZ	94.99	0.09	89.17	94.58
Portuguese-Bosque	95.13	0.08	93.39	96.48
Portuguese-GSD	87.82	0.25	96.91	97.14
Rom.-Nonstandard	93.40	0.14	91.91	95.60
Romanian-RRT	95.53	0.09	96.85	97.99
Russian-GSD	95.89	0.07	88.91	94.20
Russian-PUD	90.72	0.16	79.88	90.15
Russian-SynTagRus	96.97	0.06	93.28	96.46
Russian-Taiga	89.86	0.22	76.53	84.11
Sanskrit-UFAL	61.81	0.92	33.17	46.19
Serbian-SET	96.42	0.07	91.76	95.34
Slovak-SNK	96.24	0.07	89.24	94.68
Slovenian-SSJ	96.38	0.06	91.56	95.27
Slovenian-SST	93.79	0.13	83.44	90.24
Spanish-AnCora	97.69	0.04	96.64	97.98
Spanish-GSD	98.31	0.03	93.97	96.78
Swedish-LinES	95.37	0.08	92.57	96.24
Swedish-PUD	91.65	0.12	92.66	95.43
Swedish-Talbanken	96.56	0.05	96.66	98.16
Tagalog-TRG	83.78	0.54	72.97	79.70
Tamil-TTB	91.52	0.23	79.13	88.48
Turkish-IMST	96.34	0.07	87.37	91.37
Turkish-PUD	85.13	0.37	81.89	89.47
Ukrainian-IU	95.42	0.09	88.70	94.23
Upper_Sorbian-UFAL	90.66	0.14	66.95	76.85
Urdu-UDTB	94.25	0.08	79.06	92.21
Vietnamese-VTB	99.93	0.00	91.79	90.69
Yoruba-YTB	98.84	0.01	91.47	92.05
Mean	**94.07**	**0.12**	**88.09**	**91.84**
Median	**95.87**	**0.08**	**91.76**	**95.16**
Mean – baseline by the task organizers	**94.17**	**0.13**	**72.18**	**86.25**
Median – baseline by the task organizers	**95.92**	**0.08**	**76.40**	**89.45**

Table 2: Test set scores

study was not performed due to time constraints, an experiment for MSD tagging without lemma on English-PUD and Korean-Kaist treebanks were performed. On both datasets, a decrease in accuracy was observed. For English-PUD's morph accuracy and F1 scores decreased by 1.18 and 0.43 percentage points, while Korean-Kaist's respective scores decreased by 7.50 and 8.41 percentage points. We conjecture that the larger decrease in Korean is due to its higher morphological complexity than English; a lemma itself is more important to find MSD tags for morphological rich languages.

In general, as more training data were available, higher scores were obtained in absolute terms. As an example, for Russian, among four available datasets (Russian-GSD, Russian-PUD, Russian-SynTagRus, and Russian-Taiga) Russian-SynTagRus was the largest, and its accuracy was best by all four metrics used.

Some languages have more MSD tags than others and therefore present another dimension for the task complexity. For instance, Czech-PDT treebank has 2895 unique MSD tags while English-EWT has only 179, i.e. 16 times less. This, therefore, partly affects the accuracy of the MSD tagger, where Czech-PDT treebank's morphological accuracy is 89.88% while English-EWT's is 95.82%.

While there is a lot of variance in the number of MSD tags among languages, most of the languages have around twenty to sixty characters in their alphabet. Hence, the number of characters in the alphabet does not seem to affect lemmatization. At the same time, Chinese uses distinct characters for each word and does not have word inflections. Despite having 3536 unique characters, Chinese-GSD treebank's lemma accuracy is 99.98%. It also has only 40 MSD tags due to the absence of inflections.

Overall, lemmatization appears to be a slightly easier task than MSD tagging, and in our case, incorporating lemma information in MSD tagging yielded more accurate results for the latter.

5   Conclusion

Our pipeline model has shown favorable results in SIGMORPHON Shared Task 2 and scored fifth and sixth place, respectively, for lemmatization and MSD tagging. For future work, it would be interesting to assess how incorporating the output of MSD tagging into lemmatization would affect lemma accuracy.

Acknowledgments

This research was supported by the Basic Science Research Program through the National Research Foundation of Korea (NRF) funded by the Ministry of Education (grant number: 2017R1D1A3B03035676).

References

Dzmitry Bahdanau, Kyunghyun Cho, and Yoshua Bengio. 2015. Neural machine translation by jointly learning to align and translate. In *3rd International Conference on Learning Representations, ICLR 2015*, San Diego, CA, USA.

Piotr Bojanowski, Edouard Grave, Armand Joulin, and Tomas Mikolov. 2017. Enriching word vectors with subword information. *Transactions of the Association for Computational Linguistics*, 5:135–146

Kris Cao and Marek Rei. A joint model for word embedding and word morphology. 2016. In *Proceedings of the 1st Workshop on Representation Learning for NLP*, pages 18–26, Berlin, Germany. Association for Computational Linguistics.

Wanxiang Che, Yijia Liu, Yuxuan Wang, Bo Zheng, and Ting Liu. Towards better UD parsing: Deep contextualized word embeddings, ensemble, and treebank concatenation. 2018. In *Proceedings of the CoNLL 2018 Shared Task: Multilingual Parsing from Raw Text to Universal Dependencies*, pages 55–64, Brussels, Belgium. Association for Computational Linguistics.

Jacob Devlin, Ming-Wei Chang, Kenton Lee, and Kristina Toutanova. 2018. BERT: pre-training of deep bidirectional transformers for language understanding. CoRR, abs/1810.04805.

Timothy Dozat, Peng Qi, and Christopher D. Manning. Stanford's graph-based neural dependency parser at the CoNLL 2017 shared task. 2017. In *Proceedings of the CoNLL 2017 Shared Task: Multilingual Parsing from Raw Text to Universal Dependencies*, pages 20–30, Vancouver, Canada. Association for Computational Linguistics.

Sergey Edunov, Myle Ott, Michael Auli, and David Grangier. 2018. Understanding back-translation at scale. In *Proceedings of the 2018 Conference on Empirical Methods in Natural Language*

Processing, pages 489–500, Brussels, Belgium. Association for Computational Linguistics.

Sepp Hochreiter and Jurgen Schmidhuber. 1997. Long short-term memory. Neural Comput.,9(8):1735–1780.

Nivre Joakim, Agić Željko, Ahrenberg Lars, et al., 2017a, Universal Dependencies 2.0, LINDAT/CLARIN digital library at the Institute of Formal and Applied Linguistics (ÚFAL), Faculty of Mathematics and Physics, Charles University, http://hdl.handle.net/11234/1-1983.

Nivre Joakim, Agić Željko, Ahrenberg Lars, et al., 2017b, Universal Dependencies 2.0 – CoNLL 2017 Shared Task Development and Test Data, LINDAT/CLARIN digital library at the Institute of Formal and Applied Linguistics (ÚFAL), Faculty of Mathematics and Physics, Charles University, http://hdl.handle.net/11234/1-2184.

Eliyahu Kiperwasser and Yoav Goldberg. 2016. Simple and accurate dependency parsing using bidirectional LSTM feature representations. *Transactions of the Association for Computational Linguistics*, 4:313–327.

Xiaodong Liu, Pengcheng He, Weizhu Chen, and Jianfeng Gao. 2019. Multi-task deep neural networks for natural language understanding. *CoRR*, abs/1901.11504.

Chaitanya Malaviya, Shijie Wu, and Ryan Cotterell. 2019. A simple joint model for improved contextual neural lemmatization. arXiv preprint arXiv:1904.02306v2.

Arya D. McCarthy, Ekaterina Vylomova, Shijie Wu, Chaitanya Malaviya, Lawrence Wolf-Sonkin, Garrett Nicolai, Christo Kirov, Miikka Silfverberg, Sebastian Mielke, Jeffrey Heinz, Ryan Cotterell, and Mans Hulden. 2019. The SIGMORPHON 2019 shared task: Crosslinguality and context in morphology. In *Proceedings of the 16th SIGMORPHON Workshop on Computational Research in Phonetics, Phonology, and Morphology*, Florence, Italy. Association for Computational Linguistics.

Tomas Mikolov, Kai Chen, Greg Corrado, and Jeffrey Dean. 2013. Efficient estimation of word representations in vector space. *CoRR*, abs/1301.3781.

Diederik P. Kingma and Jimmy Ba. 2015. Adam: A method for stochastic optimization. In *3rd International Conference on Learning Representations, ICLR 2015*, San Diego, CA, USA.

Sebastian Ruder, Ivan Vulic, and Anders Sogaard. 2017. A survey of cross-lingual word embedding models. cite arxiv:1706.04902.

Nitish Shirish Keskar, Bryan McCann, Caiming Xiong, and Richard Socher. 2019. Unifying question answering and text classification via span extraction. *CoRR*, abs/1904.09286.

Ashish Vaswani, Noam Shazeer, Niki Parmar, Jakob Uszkoreit, Llion Jones, Aidan N Gomez, Lukasz Kaiser, and Illia Polosukhin. 2017. Attention is all you need. In *Advances in Neural Information Processing Systems* 30, pages 5998–6008. Curran Associates, Inc.

Alex Wang, Amanpreet Singh, Julian Michael, Felix Hill, Omer Levy, and Samuel Bowman. GLUE: A multi-task benchmark and analysis platform for natural language understanding. 2018. In *Proceedings of the 2018 EMNLP Workshop Blackbox NLP: Analyzing and Interpreting Neural Networks for NLP*, pages 353–355, Brussels, Belgium. Association for Computational Linguistics.

Felix Wu, Angela Fan, Alexei Baevski, Yann Dauphin, and Michael Auli. 2019. Pay less attention with lightweight and dynamic convolutions. In *International Conference on Learning Representations*.

Daniel Zeman, Jan Hajic, Martin Popel, Martin Potthast, Milan Straka, Filip Ginter, Joakim Nivre, and Slav Petrov. 2018. CoNLL 2018 shared task: Multilingual parsing from raw text to universal dependencies. In *Proceedings of the CoNLL 2018 Shared Task: Multilingual Parsing from Raw Text to Universal Dependencies*, pages 1–21, Brussels, Belgium, Association for Computational Linguistics.

Morpheus: A Neural Network for Jointly Learning Contextual Lemmatization and Morphological Tagging

Eray Yildiz
Faculty of Computer and
Informatics Engineering
Istanbul Technical University
yildiz17@itu.edu.tr

A. Cuneyd Tantug
Faculty of Computer and
Informatics Engineering
Istanbul Technical University
tantug@itu.edu.tr

Abstract

In this study, we present *Morpheus*, a joint contextual lemmatizer and morphological tagger. *Morpheus* is based on a neural sequential architecture where inputs are the characters of the surface words in a sentence and the outputs are the minimum edit operations between surface words and their lemmata as well as the morphological tags assigned to the words. The experiments on the datasets in nearly 100 languages provided by SigMorphon 2019 Shared Task 2 organizers show that the performance of *Morpheus* is comparable to the state-of-the-art system in terms of lemmatization. In morphological tagging, on the other hand, *Morpheus* significantly outperforms the SigMorphon baseline. In our experiments, we also show that the neural encoder-decoder architecture trained to predict the minimum edit operations can produce considerably better results than the architecture trained to predict the characters in lemmata directly as in previous studies. According to the SigMorphon 2019 Shared Task 2 results, *Morpheus* has placed 3rd in lemmatization and reached the 9th place in morphological tagging among all participant teams.

1 Introduction

Lemmatization is the process of reducing an inflected word into its dictionary form known as the lemma. Morphological tagging, on the other hand, is the process of marking up words with their morphological information and part of speech (POS) tags. Lemmatization and morphological tagging are essential tasks in natural language processing since they usually represent initial steps of subsequent tasks such as dependency parsing (Chen and Manning, 2014; McDonald and Pereira, 2006) and semantic role labeling (Haghighi et al., 2005). Morphological information of words is utilized in various tasks including statistical machine trans-lation (Huck et al., 2017), neural machine translation (Conforti et al., 2018) and named entity recognition (Güngör et al., 2019) to improve the performance. Morphological tagging and lemmatization is crucial especially in morphologically rich languages such as Turkish and Finnish since inflected and derived words carry a substantial amount of information such as number, person, case, tense and aspect. Moreover, lexical ambiguities can occur in highly inflectional and derivational languages such as Turkish. The correct lemma and morphological tags may differ according to the context in which words appear. As shown in table 1, the Turkish word *"dolar"* may have different lemma and morphological properties according to the context it is used.

To achieve lemmatization and morphological tagging in highly inflectional languages, traditional approaches employ finite state machines which are constructed to model grammatical rules of a language (Oflazer, 1993; Karttunen et al., 1992). Building a state machine for morphological analysis is not a trivial task and requires considerable effort necessitating linguistic knowledge. Furthermore, morphological analyzers frequently produce multiple analyzes for each word which introduces morphological ambiguities. Morphological disambiguation which is the process of selecting correct analyzes of words according to the context (Yildiz et al., 2016; Shen et al., 2016) is mostly needed after morphological analysis step. Morphological disambiguation is also a difficult problem due to the fact that it requires the classification of both lemmata and the corresponding labels. Therefore, researchers have studied language-agnostic data-driven solutions for both lemmatization and morphological tagging. In most of the studies, applying machine learning or statistical methods over morphologically an-

Proceedings of the 16th Workshop on Computational Research in Phonetics, Phonology, and Morphology, pages 25–34
Florence, Italy. August 2, 2019 ©2019 Association for Computational Linguistics

Table 1: Different lemmata and morphological properties of Turkish word "dolar" according to the context

Turkish Sentence	English Translation	Lemma of the word "dolar"	Morhoplogical Properties of the word "dolar"
atkıyı boynuna **dolar**	She/he **wraps** the scarf around his/her neck	dola *(Eng. wrap)*	Verb, Third Person Singular, Present Tense
su kovaya **dolar**	The water **fills** the bucket	dol *(Eng. fill)*	Verb, Third Person Singular, Present Tense
dolar yine yükseldi	The **dollar** increased again	dolar *(Eng. dollar)*	Noun, Nominative, Singular

notated corpora (mostly on *UniMorph* dataset[1] (Kirov et al., 2018)) have been proposed to perform joint morphological tagging and lemmatization. One of the early studies, *Morfette* (Chrupała et al., 2008) utilized a Maximum Entropy Classifier to find lemmata and morphological tags of each word in a sentence. Two separate classifiers are employed in their architecture: one for assigning morphological tags to the words and one for predicting the shortest edit script between the surface word and its lemma. Shortest edit script is the shortest sequence of instructions (insertions, deletions, and replacements) which transforms a string into another one. In this way, the system is able to apply lemmatization to out of vocabulary words by predicting the transformation which should be applied to the surface word to obtain the lemma of the word. More recent work, namely *Lemming* (Müller et al., 2015) has out-performed *Morfette* by using a Conditional Random Field classifier to classify each candidate sequences of lemmata and morphological tags jointly. The feature space of *Lemming* differs from *Morfette* as *Lemming* also uses external lexical features such as the occurrences of a candidate lemma in a dictionary. As deep neural networks gain popularity and lead state-of-the-art results in various natural language processing tasks, sequential neural networks have been successfully employed for lemmatization and morphological tagging in recent studies (Bergmanis and Goldwater, 2018; Malaviya et al., 2019; Dayanık et al., 2018; Chakrabarty et al., 2017). Promising results are obtained through standard encoder-decoder neural architectures where inputs are the character sequences of the words and outputs are the character sequences of lemmata and morphological tags (Bergmanis and Goldwater, 2018; Dayanık et al., 2018). Neural architectures which are designed to predict the edit operations between surface words and lemmata are also proposed in recent works (Chakrabarty et al., 2017). The current state of the art is held by Malaviya et al. (2019) using a neural hard attention mechanism to align the characters of surface words and

lemmata. Morphological tagging and lemmatization are jointly modeled in their architecture and a dynamic programming approach is used to maximize both morphological tagging and lemmatization scores.

In SigMorphon 2019 workshop, a shared task about morphological tagging and contextual lemmatization in nearly 100 distinct languages is organized (McCarthy et al., 2019). In this study, we propose a neural network architecture, namely *Morpheus* for SigMorphon 2019 Shared Task 2. Our architecture is inspired by *MorphNet* (Dayanık et al., 2018), which has produced promising results in Turkish using an encoder-decoder neural architecture. In *MorphNet*, all characters are represented with a vector, and word vectors are generated by using long short term memories (LSTM) over character vectors. Another bidirectional LSTM is applied over word vectors to obtain context-aware representations of each word in a sentence. An LSTM based decoder inputs context-aware word representations and produces lemmata and morphological tags, respectively. Our architecture differs from *MorphNet* as we use two separate decoders for generating lemmata and morphological tags. Another difference of our architecture is that we follow the minimum edit script prediction approach considering the promising performance outputs of prior work (Chrupała et al., 2008; Müller et al., 2015; Chakrabarty et al., 2017). The lemma decoder of our network is optimized to predict the minimum edit operations between surface words and lemmata instead of predicting the character sequences of the lemmata as in *MorphNet* and *Lematus*.

Our experiments show that predicting the minimum edit operations instead of characters improves the performance significantly on *UniMorph* dataset, which is provided in SigMorphon 2019 Shared Task 2. The performance of the proposed architecture is comparable to the current state-of-the-art system (Malaviya et al., 2019), which is provided as a strong baseline by SigMorphon 2019 organizers. All of the experiments in this paper are reproducible using the codes we

---

[1] https://unimorph.github.io/

make publicly available[2].

2 Method

The input of our neural network based model is a sentence containing surface form words and the outputs are edit operations between surface words and their lemmata and morphological tags assigned to the words. The problem can be defined as we are searching a function whose inputs are surface words of a sentence $f([w_o, .., w_n])$ and whose output is the set of (o_i, m_i) tuples $[(o_0, m_0), .., (o_n, m_n)]$ where o_i is the set of edit operations to generate the lemma of the surface form w_i and m_i is the set of morphological tags assigned to the surface form w_i. The overall architecture of the system is illustrated in Figure 1. The system comprises 3 neural components that are running sequentially:

- The first component generates word vectors using LSTMs over the vector representations of its characters.

- The second component generates context-aware word vectors applying bidirectional LSTMs over word vectors

- Two separate LSTM decoders accept the same context-aware word vectors. The first decoder generates edit operations between surface words and lemmata while the second decoder generates morphological tags

In the final step, lemmata are generated by applying predicted edit operations to the surface words.

2.1 Generating minimum edit operations

The proposed model is designed to predict minimum edit operations to obtain the lemma from a surface word. The fundamental edit operations are *Same*, *Delete*, *Replace*, and *Insert* operations. To find minimum edit operations between surface word and its lemma, we use a dynamic programming approach[3] which is based on *Levenshtein* distance. Some sample edit operations between surface words and lemmata are given in Figure 2 for several languages. As seen in Figure 2, *Same* and *Delete* operations have only one version whereas *Replace* and *Insert* operations have multiple versions combined with the character to be

replaced or inserted. So the actual number of elements in the edit operations set are determined for each language separately by processing the training data.

Generally, the length of a lemma is shorter than or equals to the length of the corresponding surface form and consequently, the number of edit operations are usually the same as the length of the surface form. However, for some languages, lemmata longer than the corresponding surface forms are observed. Since our minimum edit prediction decoder predicts an edit operation label for each character in the surface (see Section 2.4.1 for details), it fails in generating lemmata longer than the surface forms. Thus we make some modifications over the base operations generated by standard *Levenshtein* distance based algorithm. To ensure the length of the operation labels is the same as the length of the surface words, we merge consecutive *Insert* labels in the same position into one *Insert* label with multiple characters. We also combine the *Replace* labels and the following consequent *Insert* labels in the same position into one *Replace* label with multiple characters. For example, the minimum edit operations for the Russian surface-lemma pair "видна"-"видный" have four *Same* operation labels and one Replace_ый label, respectively. Note that the last character in the surface word "а" is replaced with the character "ы" and then the character й is inserted into the end. The base labels Replace_ы and Insert_й are merged into one label Replace_ый to ensure that edit operations and surface words have the same length (Figure 2).

2.2 Word representations

The first component of our network inputs character sequences of each word in a sentence and generates vector representations of the words using an LSTM network. Let w_i represents the ith word with L_i characters in a sentence and w_{ij} is j^{th} character in w_i. In our model, each character w_{ij} is represented by a vector $a_{ij} \in \mathbb{R}^{d_a}$ and we calculate the vector representation of ith word $\mathbf{e}_i \in \mathbb{R}^{d_e}$ by applying an LSTM over the vector representations of its constituent characters from left to right as shown in eq. (1). The last hidden state vector of the LSTM $h_{L_i} \in \mathbb{R}^{d_e}$ is considered as the vector representation of the word w_i.

$$\mathbf{e}_i = h_{L_i} = LSTM(a_{L_i}, h_{L_{i-1}}) \qquad (1)$$

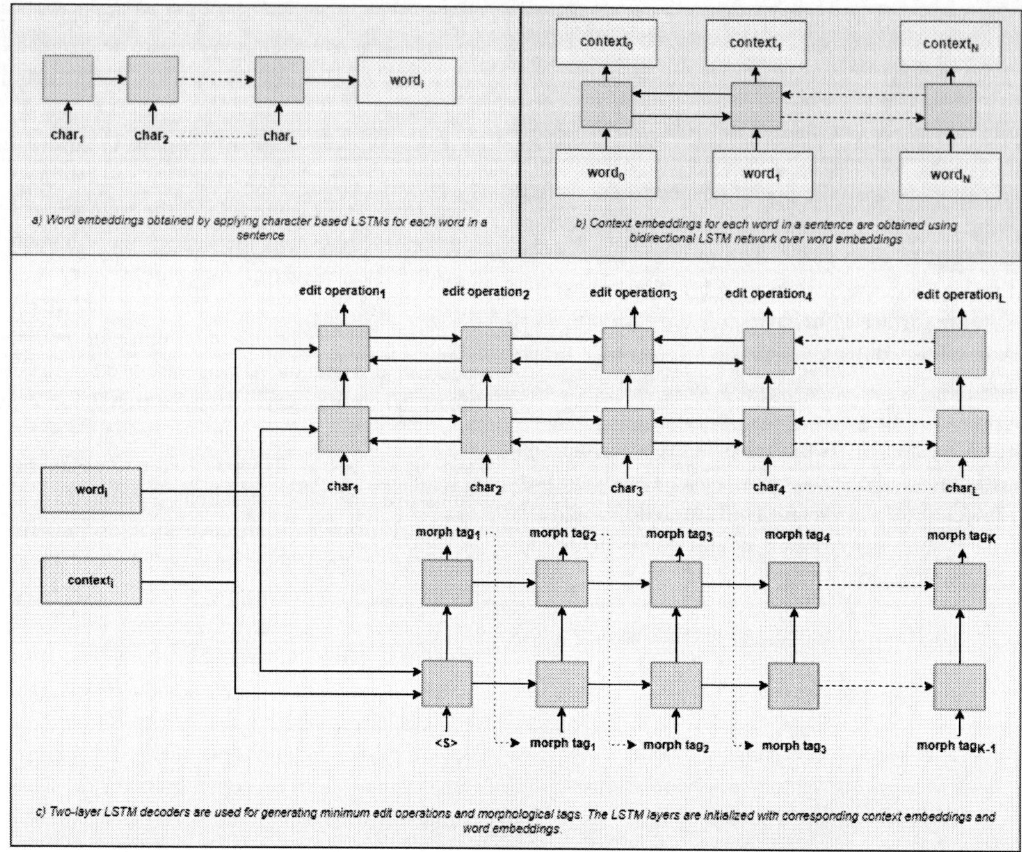

Figure 1: The illustration of the proposed neural network architecture which consists of 3 components: (a) word vector generator (b) context vector generator (c) decoders to generate minimum edit operations for lemmatization and morphological tags. (N indicates the number of words in the sentence. L indicates both the number of characters in the word and the number of edit operations between the word and the lemma. K represents the number of morphological tags assigned to the word)

2.3 Context-aware word representations

The context of the words have a substantial impact on morphological tagging and lemmatization in most languages (Shen et al., 2016; Malaviya et al., 2019). In order to take into account the context of the words we employ another LSTM which is bidirectional and inputs vector representations e_i and outputs context-aware representations $c_i \in \mathbb{R}^{d_c}$ for each surface word in the context as shown in eqs. (2) to (4)

$$\overrightarrow{c_i} = LSTM(e_i, \overrightarrow{c_{i-1}}) \qquad (2)$$

$$\overleftarrow{c_i} = LSTM(e_i, \overleftarrow{c_{i+1}}) \qquad (3)$$

$$\mathbf{c}_i = [\overrightarrow{c_i}, \overleftarrow{c_i}] \qquad (4)$$

The final output is context-aware vector representation $\mathbf{c}_i$ for each word w_i in the sentence.

2.4 Decoding Components

One of the important differences of the proposed network from previous studies (Bergmanis and Goldwater, 2018; Dayanık et al., 2018) is that it has two separate decoders for lemmatization and morphological tagging. The parameters of the decoders are not shared. However, they are both fed with the same word vectors e_i and context-aware word vectors $\mathbf{c}_i$ that are generated in the encoding step.

2.4.1 Minimum edit prediction decoder

The minimum edit prediction decoder component consists of a two layer bidirectional LSTM network and an embedding layer which maps each character w_{ij} in surface word to a one dimensional

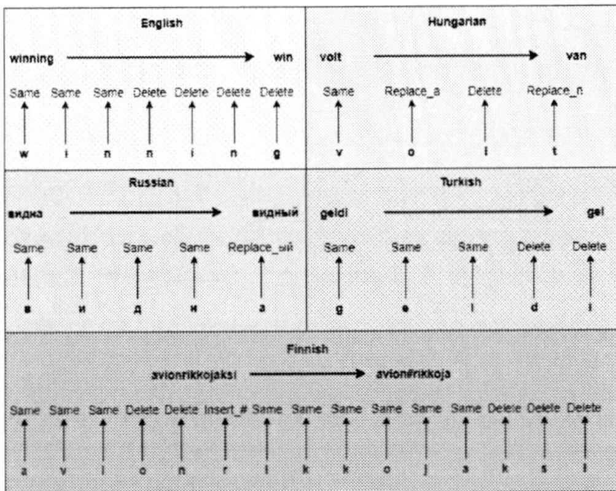

Figure 2: Minimum edit operations between surface words and their lemmata

vector $u_{ij} \in \mathbb{R}^{d_u}$. Forward LSTM network inputs previous hidden states $g_{j-1}^{\rightarrow 1}, g_{j-1}^{\rightarrow 2} \in \mathbb{R}^{d_g}$ and outputs current hidden states $g_j^{\rightarrow 1}, g_j^{\rightarrow 2}$ and an output vector $y_j^{\rightarrow} \in \mathbb{R}^{d_y}$. Backward LSTM network, on the other hand, applies the same operations in opposite direction and outputs $g_j^{\leftarrow 1}, g_j^{\leftarrow 2} \in \mathbb{R}^{d_g}$ and $y_j^{\leftarrow}$. *Softmax* function is then applied to the multiplication of trainable matrix $\mathbf{W}_o \in \mathbb{R}^{d_y \times |o|}$ with the concatenation vector of output vectors $y_j^{\rightarrow}$ and $y_j^{\leftarrow}$ where $|o|$ represents the number of distinct edit operations observed in the dataset. The output of *softmax* operation is the probabilities of each minimum edit operation $p(o_{ij})$ corresponding to the character w_{ij} as shown in eqs. (5) to (7).

$$y_j^{\rightarrow}, g_j^{\rightarrow 1}, g_j^{\rightarrow 2} = LSTM(u_{ij}, g_{j-1}^{\rightarrow 1}, g_{j-1}^{\rightarrow 2}) \quad (5)$$

$$y_j^{\leftarrow}, g_j^{\leftarrow 1}, g_j^{\leftarrow 2} = LSTM(u_{ij}, g_{j+1}^{\leftarrow 1}, g_{j+1}^{\leftarrow 2}) \quad (6)$$

$$p(o_{ij}) = softmax(\mathbf{W}_o \times [y_j^{\rightarrow}, y_j^{\leftarrow}]) \quad (7)$$

The first hidden states of both forward and backward LSTMs are initialized with the word vector $\mathbf{e}_i$ (see section 2.2) and a linear transformation of the context-aware word vector: $\mathbf{W}_c \times \mathbf{c}_i$ where $\mathbf{W}_c$ is a matrix in $\mathbb{R}^{d_c \times d_e}$ (see section 2.3), respectively (see eq. (11)).

$$g_0^{\rightarrow 1} = \mathbf{e}_i \quad (8)$$

$$g_0^{\rightarrow 2} = \mathbf{W}_c \times \mathbf{c}_i \quad (9)$$

$$g_{L_i}^{\leftarrow 1} = \mathbf{e}_i \quad (10)$$

$$g_{L_i}^{\leftarrow 1} = \mathbf{W}_c \times \mathbf{c}_i \quad (11)$$

2.4.2 Morphological tagging decoder

The morphological tagging decoder component is another LSTM decoder which is able to generate morphological tags without length restriction. Each word w_i has K_i morphological tags and each morphological tag m_{il} is represented by a one dimensional vector $v_{il} \in \mathbb{R}^{d_v}$. A two layer LSTM network which is unidirectional is initialized same as in minimum edit prediction component. An LSTM cell inputs the vector representation $v_{i(l-1)}$ of previously predicted tag m_{il}' and previous hidden states $q_{l-1}^1, q_{l-1}^2 \in \mathbb{R}^{d_q}$ in each step. The outputs of the LSTM cell are current hidden states q_l^1, q_l^2 and an output vector $z_{ij} \in \mathbb{R}^{d_z}$. *Softmax* function is then applied to multiplication of the output vector z_{ij} and trainable matrix $\mathbf{W}_m \in \mathbb{R}^{d_z \times |m|}$ where m equals to the number of distinct morphological tags in the dataset. The first input to the decoder is the vector representation of a special start symbol $v_{start} \in \mathbb{R}^{d_v}$. In this way the probabilities of each morphological tags $p(m_{il})$ in given position i, l are calculated as shown in eqs. (5), (12) and (13).

$$z_1, q_1^1, q_1^2 = LSTM(v_{start}, \mathbf{e}_i, \mathbf{W}_c \times \mathbf{c}_i) \quad (12)$$

$$z_l, q_l^1, q_l^2 = LSTM(v_{i(l-1)}, q_{l-1}^1, q_{l-1}^2) \quad (13)$$

$$p(m_{il}) = softmax(\mathbf{W}_m \times z_l) \quad (14)$$

2.5 Character prediction decoder

The character prediction decoder component which sequentially predicts the characters occur in lemmata is not employed in the proposed architecture. However, we build an alternative model in which the character prediction decoder component is used instead of a minimum edit prediction decoder. In this way, we aim to evaluate the impact of predicting minimum edit operations instead of characters in lemmata. The character prediction decoder used in the experiments has the same architecture and parameter set with the morphological tagging decoder.

2.6 Training objective

All the parameters in whole architecture including all LSTM parameters and the trainable matrices $\mathbf{W}_c, \mathbf{W}_o, \mathbf{W}_m$ are optimized jointly in training

Method	Lemmatization Accuracy (%)	Morphological Tagging F1 Score (%)
Turku NLP (Kanerva et al., 2018)	92.18	86.7
UPPSALA Uni. (Moor, 2018)	58.5	88.32
SigMorphon 2019 Baseline (Malaviya et al., 2019)	93.95	68.72
Morpheus (Character Prediction)	88.03	88.94
Morpheus (Edit Operation Prediction)	**94.15**	**90.52**

Table 2: Average lemmatization and morphological tagging performances of the systems on *UniMorph* dataset

phase by minimizing the sum of two cross entropy losses as follow:

$$\mathcal{L}_{lemma} = -\frac{1}{N} \sum_{i}^{N} \frac{1}{L_i} \sum_{j}^{L_i} \log p(o_{ij}) \qquad (15)$$

$$\mathcal{L}_{morph} = -\frac{1}{N} \sum_{i}^{N} \frac{1}{K_i} \sum_{j}^{K_i} \log p(m_{ij}) \qquad (16)$$

$$\mathcal{L}_{total} = \mathcal{L}_{lemma} + \mathcal{L}_{morph} \qquad (17)$$

The loss for lemmatization is calculated by taking cross entropy over predicted minimum edit operations $p(o_{ij})$ as in eq. (15) where N stands for the number of words in the sentence and L_i stands for the number of characters in the word w_i. The loss for morphological tagging is cross entropy over predicted tag probabilities $p(m_{il})$ as in eq. (16) where K_i stands for the number of morphological tags assigned to the word w_i. The total loss to minimize is the sum of the lemmatization loss and morphological tagging loss (see eq. (17)).

3 Experiments

In our experiments, we train and evaluate the proposed architecture on *UniMorph* dataset collection (Kirov et al., 2018) for each language. Same architecture with the same hyper-parameters is used for all the languages. To investigate the impact of the minimum edit prediction component on the performance, we also train the network in which the character prediction decoder component is used instead of a minimum edit prediction component. The results of the experiments are provided in section 3.3 and table 2

3.1 Dataset

UniMorph dataset collection, which includes a various number of sentences consist of surface words with annotated lemmata and morphological

tags in 97 different languages are provided in SigMorphon 2019 shared task 2. The dataset for each language is split into train and validation sets, and the size of the dataset differs in each language. In our experiments, we train our architecture on train sets and evaluate the performances on validation sets. The experimental results presented in section 3.3 are obtained on the validation sets. Note that final results which are presented in SigMorphon paper (McCarthy et al., 2019) are calculated over the test sets which were not available to the systems before the final submission stage.

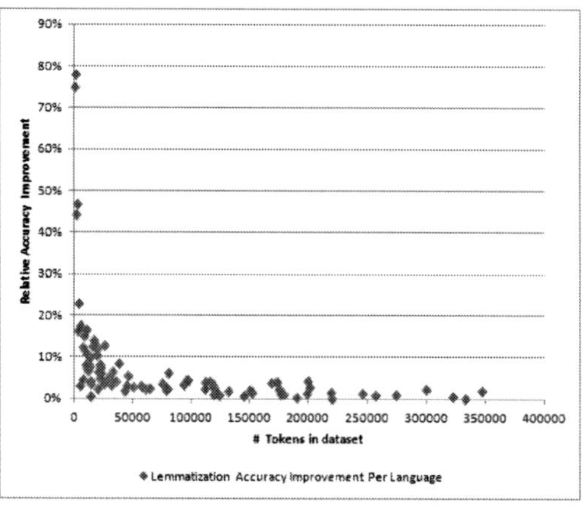

Figure 3: Relative lemmatization accuracy improvement vs dataset size per language

3.2 Experimental Setup

The same settings are used in the training of the architecture for each language. The input character embedding length d_a is set to 128 while the length of the word vectors d_e is set to 1024 and the length of the context-aware word vectors d_c is set to 2048. The length of character vectors in the minimum edit prediction component d_u and the length of the morphological tag vectors d_v are set to 256 while the hidden unit sizes in decoder LSTMs d_g and d_q are set to 1024. We use *Adam* optimization algorithm (Kingma and Ba, 2014) with learning rate $3e - 4$ for minimizing the loss

Language	Dataset Size	Lemmatization Accuracy (%)		Morph. Tagging F1 (%)	
		Character Pred.	Edit Pred.	Character Pred.	Edit Pred.
North-Sami-Giella	29K	87.53	**91.90**	88.89	**92.83**
French-GSD	360K	97.06	**98.47**	97.58	**97.99**
Japanese-Modern	14K	85.39	**93.88**	**93.06**	92.44
Swedish-PUD	18K	82.79	**93.05**	89.23	**92.09**
Arabic-PADT	256K	94.39	**95.18**	95.01	**95.40**
Basque-BDT	119K	95.42	**96.49**	93.06	**94.47**
Urdu-UDTB	123K	95.20	**96.02**	90.79	**91.20**
Irish-IDT	21K	85.07	**89.23**	**80.60**	71.52
Bambara-CRB	14K	88.24	**88.85**	93.47	**93.56**
Dutch-Alpino	200K	94.97	**97.81**	95.63	**96.45**
Czech-FicTree	175K	97.39	**98.49**	94.15	**96.39**
Danish-DDT	94K	93.16	**97.26**	94.17	**95.62**
Latin-ITTB	332K	98.65	**98.75**	96.84	**97.34**
French-Sequoia	64K	95.54	**98.17**	95.96	**96.82**
Italian-PoSTWITA	115K	92.71	**96.61**	94.43	**95.62**
Polish-SZ	93K	93.59	**96.86**	90.23	**93.26**
Czech-CLTT	32K	92.11	**98.03**	89.03	**93.82**
Cantonese-HK	7K	90.05	**94.17**	85.41	**86.14**
Galician-TreeGal	23K	89.68	**95.19**	89.78	**90.72**
Slovenian-SSJ	131K	95.25	**96.94**	93.47	**95.79**
French-ParTUT	25K	92.67	**96.10**	93.09	**94.55**
Lithuanian-HSE	5K	70.60	**83.05**	43.37	**70.70**
French-Spoken	35K	94.47	**98.48**	95.46	**96.66**
Russian-Taiga	22K	83.59	**90.57**	76.62	**83.80**
Latvian-LVTB	150K	94.29	**96.22**	93.51	**95.87**
Czech-PDT	1515K	84.86	**98.41**	87.65	**95.27**
Japanese-GSD	168K	95.21	**98.91**	95.35	**95.61**
Indonesian-GSD	111K	97.06	**99.49**	92.69	**93.11**
Gothic-PROIEL	62K	**96.60**	96.58	93.04	**95.12**
Latin-PROIEL	219K	96.31	**96.37**	93.75	**95.05**
Czech-PUD	19K	83.55	**93.57**	81.30	**86.70**
Dutch-LassySmall	96K	93.44	**97.58**	94.51	**95.47**
Romanian-RRT	198K	96.54	**97.88**	96.81	**97.44**
Korean-Kaist	346K	93.31	**95.07**	95.70	**95.46**
Amharic-ATT	11K	93.80	**100.00**	91.02	**91.39**
English-GUM	79K	95.58	**97.85**	93.92	**95.48**
Estonian-EDT	421K	93.10	**96.27**	95.64	**96.70**
Chinese-GSD	111K	95.22	**99.15**	89.25	**90.78**
Korean-GSD	80K	87.55	**92.89**	93.43	**94.16**
Marathi-UFAL	4K	74.59	**76.94**	68.26	**69.26**
Akkadian	2K	42.22	**60.89**	**78.13**	66.52
Faroese-OFT	13K	83.56	**89.97**	88.08	**89.49**
English-EWT	246K	96.78	**98.11**	95.61	**95.95**
Sanskrit-UFAL	3K	53.61	**65.98**	52.59	**55.36**
Turkish-IMST	60K	94.13	**96.43**	91.67	**93.72**
English-PUD	20K	89.40	**95.22**	88.88	**89.89**
Korean-PUD	18K	87.19	**98.86**	91.42	**92.75**
Finnish-PUD	16K	77.72	**87.55**	85.49	**92.05**
Russian-SynTag	1036K	95.31	**97.76**	94.99	**95.13**
Croatian-SET	179K	94.91	**96.01**	94.31	**95.47**
Tagalog-TRG	406	48.00	**84.00**	**74.23**	71.74
Slovenian-SST	31K	91.83	**94.97**	85.34	**89.23**
Finnish-FTB	172K	90.70	**94.46**	94.13	**95.85**
Polish-LFG	174K	93.85	**96.09**	92.93	**95.35**
Portuguese-Bosque	218K	96.43	**97.86**	96.07	**96.59**
Coptic-Scriptorium	20K	93.47	**95.68**	95.17	**94.76**
Chinese-CFL	7K	82.55	**92.66**	81.51	**83.76**
Spanish-AnCora	497K	98.32	**98.92**	98.29	**98.46**
Greek-GDT	57K	93.73	**96.65**	94.71	**96.12**
Serbian-SET	78K	94.82	**97.06**	94.36	**96.06**
Naija-NSC	14K	95.80	**99.84**	91.15	**92.02**
Vietnamese-VTB	42K	98.17	**99.95**	89.45	**89.71**
Yoruba-YTB	2K	83.60	**97.20**	**80.49**	70.67
Italian-PUD	22K	89.51	**96.11**	92.63	**94.22**
Finnish-TDT	198K	91.37	**95.38**	95.67	**96.76**
English-ParTUT	44K	94.87	**97.85**	92.32	**93.46**
Upper-Sorbian-U.	11K	77.79	**90.74**	69.47	**77.46**
Norwegian-Ny.	14K	93.89	**97.42**	90.45	**92.20**
Galician-CTG	121K	97.18	**98.69**	97.29	**97.30**
Old-Church-Slv.	66K	96.48	**95.66**	93.33	**94.91**
Russian-GSD	92K	**92.90**	91.51	91.98	**93.91**
Kurmanji-MG	10K	85.66	**92.69**	**85.99**	85.22
Norwegian-Bk.	299K	96.65	**98.94**	96.75	**97.41**
Italian-ISDT	273K	96.90	**97.90**	97.34	**97.89**
Komi-Zyrian-IKDP	1K	38.55	**68.67**	**45.50**	36.89
Hebrew-HTB	144K	96.49	**97.35**	95.35	**95.70**
Tamil-TTB	10K	86.77	**96.10**	83.07	**88.50**
Buryat-BDT	10K	83.33	**89.61**	78.24	**82.30**
Breton-KEB	12K	85.61	**92.81**	88.65	**90.12**
Latin-Perseus	29K	**87.30**	86.26	79.21	**82.88**
Romanian-Nonstd	189K	96.10	**96.37**	95.52	**96.36**
Italian-ParTUT	50K	94.65	**97.44**	94.83	**96.30**
Catalan-AnCora	481K	98.17	**98.92**	98.42	**98.65**
Arabic-PUD	22K	**81.31**	80.90	87.23	**88.00**
Komi-Zyrian-L.	2K	52.75	**77.47**	55.79	**57.02**
Japanese-PUD	25K	86.30	**97.32**	93.46	**94.02**
Slovak-SNK	119K	94.52	**96.95**	91.88	**94.55**
Ukrainian-IU	118K	93.63	**96.80**	91.24	**93.68**
Turkish-PUD	17K	78.20	**89.19**	86.71	**91.28**
Bulgarian-BTB	152K	95.98	**97.58**	97.16	**97.83**
Russian-PUD	19K	83.78	**92.54**	81.73	**87.79**
Belarusian-HSE	8K	78.06	**89.87**	69.39	**71.95**
Hindi-HDTB	322K	98.15	**98.82**	96.12	**96.60**
Czech-CAC	474K	98.01	**98.86**	96.52	**97.54**
Hungarian-Szeged	38K	87.89	**95.26**	89.63	**91.65**
Swedish-LinES	74K	93.52	**96.82**	93.25	**94.88**
Afrikaans-Af.B.	45K	93.75	**98.74**	95.08	**95.96**
English-LinES	77K	96.19	**98.27**	94.57	**95.43**

Table 3: Lemmatization and Morphological Tagging performances of minimum edit prediction model and character prediction model on development sets

function. *Dropout* rate 0.4 is applied to all connections during model training for regularization. All the weights are initialized with *Xavier* initialization method (Glorot and Bengio, 2010). We use an early stop mechanism which stops the training after four consecutive epochs without improvement on validation set.

3.3 Results

Table 2 presents the lemmatization and morphological performances of the proposed method on UniMorph dataset collection. The lemmatization accuracy on a dataset is the proportion of the number of correctly found lemmata over the total lemmata count. The lemmatization accuracy given in table 2 is the average of the accuracies obtained over the validation sets of all languages. The performance of morphological tagging is measured by the F1 score calculated over the predicted and actual individual morphological tags. In addition to the performance of the proposed architecture with minimum edit prediction decoder, the performance of the architecture with character prediction decoder is also given. The performances of SigMorphon 2019 neural baseline, *Turku NLP* system (Kanerva et al., 2018) which is the best lemmatization performer in CONLL 2018 Shared Task (Zeman and Hajič, 2018) and *UPPSALA Uni* system which is the best morphological tagging performer in CONLL 2018 are also given. Although the dataset provided in CONLL 2018 share the same basis with the dataset provided in SigMorphon, important differences exist between them. Hence the performances of *Turku NLP* and *UPPSALA Uni* are not directly comparable to our systems and SigMorphon baselines. However, we present the performances of those systems averaged on the same languages in SigMorphon dataset to provide an idea of how much improvement is achieved over a year.

According to the results, the proposed architecture, *Morpheus* performs slightly better than the SigMorphon neural baseline in terms of the average lemmatization accuracy. Similarly, for the morphological tagging task, *Morpheus* with a minimum edit prediction decoder significantly outperforms the baseline and *Morpheus* with character prediction decoder The experiments show that the performance is improved considerably when the minimum edit prediction decoder is used instead of the character prediction decoder. An impressive result is that the performance of morphological tagging is also enhanced by employing the minimum edit prediction decoder.

Table 3 shows the lemmatization and morphological performances of both character prediction and minimum edit prediction models for each language. The performance of the minimum edit prediction model is better than the character prediction model in almost all languages. Figure 3 shows that there is a correlation between the size of the training data and the improvement on the performance when the minimum edit prediction decoder is employed. For instance, the relative lemmatization improvement is extreme in languages with relatively small dataset such as Tagalog-TRG (400 tokens/0.75 relative improvements), Komi-Zyrian (1.1K tokens/0.78 relative improvement) and Akkadian (1.7 tokens/0.44 relative improvement). On the other hand, in languages with large size dataset such as Spanish-AnCora (496K tokens), Catalan-AnCora (480K tokens) and French-GSD (359K tokens), the improvement is relatively low (0.006, 0.007 and 0.01, respectively). Although improvement magnitude is highly correlated with the training dataset size, there must be other factors specific to the properties of the language. For instance, the dataset size of the language Marathi-UFAL is small (4.1K tokens). However, the improvement degree is also small (0.03 relative improvement).

Language	Surface word	Edit pred. based model output	Char. pred. based model output
English	Thurlow Cosmic sorrows Vietnam	Thurlow Cosmic sorrow Vietnam	Throughlough Comsic sorw Vietman
Turkish	YPK kokainle Islık	Ypk kokain ıslık	YYk koki sılık

Table 4: Some examples of the errors made by character prediction model and corrected by the edit prediction based model

To investigate in which cases the edit prediction model performs better, we explore the outputs of the models for English and Turkish languages. A significant portion of the errors in the character prediction model is observed in unseen words and proper nouns. Some of the errors made by the character prediction based model and corrected by the edit prediction based model are shown in Table 4. A possible reason is that the lemmatization of

a singular nominative noun which is rarely seen in the training data is easier to edit prediction model since all of the edit operations are *Same* and the model should only produce a sequence of *Same* labels. Character prediction based model, on the other hand, have to learn to reproduce the word from scratch. Additionally, we observe a significant amount of samples in which the edit prediction model produced morphological tags and lemmata more appropriate to the context than the outputs of the character prediction model. As a result, further research is needed to understand in which cases the edit prediction decoder helps to better learning of morphological properties of a language.

4 Conclusion

In this study, we propose a neural architecture, namely *Morpheus*, which is based on sequential neural encoder-decoders. The input words are encoded in context-aware vector representations using two-level LSTM network and the decoders initialized with context-aware word vectors generates both morphological tags assigned to the words and minimum edit operations between surface words and their lemmata. We perform experiments to evaluate the performance of *Morpheus* on *UniMorph* dataset collection (Kirov et al., 2018), which comprised nearly 100 language datasets. The experiments show that the lemmatization performance of the *Morpheus* is comparable to the SigMorphon neural baseline system (Malaviya et al., 2019), which has obtained current state-of-the-art results on *UniMorph* dataset collection. Regarding morphological tagging performance, *Morpheus* outperforms SigMorphon morphological tagger baseline significantly (0.3 relative improvement). In lemmatization, *Morpheus* has placed 3rd in the SigMorphon 2019 Shared Task 2, and it has reached the 9th place in morphological tagging. In our experiments, we also show that predicting the minimum edit operations between surface words and their lemmata instead of directly predicting the characters improves the performances of the system significantly especially when the dataset is small.

Acknowledgments

We would like to thank the SigMorphon 2019 organizers for the great effort and the reviewers for the insightful comments.

References

Toms Bergmanis and Sharon Goldwater. 2018. Context sensitive neural lemmatization with lematus. In *Proceedings of the 2018 Conference of the North American Chapter of the Association for Computational Linguistics: Human Language Technologies, Volume 1 (Long Papers)*, pages 1391–1400.

Abhisek Chakrabarty, Onkar Arun Pandit, and Utpal Garain. 2017. Context sensitive lemmatization using two successive bidirectional gated recurrent networks. In *Proceedings of the 55th Annual Meeting of the Association for Computational Linguistics (Volume 1: Long Papers)*, pages 1481–1491.

Danqi Chen and Christopher Manning. 2014. A fast and accurate dependency parser using neural networks. In *Proceedings of the 2014 conference on empirical methods in natural language processing (EMNLP)*, pages 740–750.

Grzegorz Chrupała, Georgiana Dinu, and Josef Van Genabith. 2008. Learning morphology with morfette.

Costanza Conforti, Matthias Huck, and Alexander Fraser. 2018. Neural morphological tagging of lemma sequences for machine translation. In *Proceedings of the 13th Conference of the Association for Machine Translation in the Americas (Volume 1: Research Papers)*, volume 1, pages 39–53.

Erenay Dayanık, Ekin Akyürek, and Deniz Yuret. 2018. Morphnet: A sequence-to-sequence model that combines morphological analysis and disambiguation. *arXiv preprint arXiv:1805.07946*.

Xavier Glorot and Yoshua Bengio. 2010. Understanding the difficulty of training deep feedforward neural networks. In *Proceedings of the thirteenth international conference on artificial intelligence and statistics*, pages 249–256.

Onur Güngör, Tunga Güngör, and Suzan Üsküdarli. 2019. The effect of morphology in named entity recognition with sequence tagging. *Natural Language Engineering*, 25(1):147–169.

Aria Haghighi, Kristina Toutanova, and Christopher D Manning. 2005. A joint model for semantic role labeling. In *Proceedings of the Ninth Conference on Computational Natural Language Learning*, pages 173–176. Association for Computational Linguistics.

Matthias Huck, Aleš Tamchyna, Ondřej Bojar, and Alexander Fraser. 2017. Producing unseen morphological variants in statistical machine translation. In *Proceedings of the 15th Conference of the European Chapter of the Association for Computational Linguistics: Volume 2, Short Papers*, pages 369–375.

Jenna Kanerva, Filip Ginter, Niko Miekka, Akseli Leino, and Tapio Salakoski. 2018. Turku neural parser pipeline: An end-to-end system for the conll 2018 shared task. In *Proceedings of the CoNLL 2018 Shared Task: Multilingual Parsing from Raw Text to Universal Dependencies*, pages 133–142.

Lauri Karttunen, Ronald M Kaplan, and Annie Zaenen. 1992. Two-level morphology with composition. In *COLING 1992 Volume 1: The 15th International Conference on Computational Linguistics*, volume 1.

Diederik P Kingma and Jimmy Ba. 2014. Adam: A method for stochastic optimization. *arXiv preprint arXiv:1412.6980*.

Christo Kirov, Ryan Cotterell, John Sylak-Glassman, Géraldine Walther, Ekaterina Vylomova, Patrick Xia, Manaal Faruqui, Sebastian J. Mielke, Arya McCarthy, Sandra Kübler, David Yarowsky, Jason Eisner, and Mans Hulden. 2018. UniMorph 2.0: Universal Morphology. In *Proceedings of the 11th Language Resources and Evaluation Conference*, Miyazaki, Japan. European Language Resource Association.

Chaitanya Malaviya, Shijie Wu, and Ryan Cotterell. 2019. A simple joint model for improved contextual neural lemmatization. *arXiv preprint arXiv:1904.02306*.

Arya D. McCarthy, Ekaterina Vylomova, Shijie Wu, Chaitanya Malaviya, Lawrence Wolf-Sonkin, Garrett Nicolai, Christo Kirov, Miikka Silfverberg, Sebastian Mielke, Jeffrey Heinz, Ryan Cotterell, and Mans Hulden. 2019. The SIGMORPHON 2019 shared task: Crosslinguality and context in morphology. In *Proceedings of the 16th SIGMORPHON Workshop on Computational Research in Phonetics, Phonology, and Morphology*, Florence, Italy. Association for Computational Linguistics.

Ryan T McDonald and Fernando CN Pereira. 2006. Online learning of approximate dependency parsing algorithms. In *EACL*, pages 81–88.

Christophe Moor. 2018. *Multilingual Dependency Parsing from Raw Text to Universal Dependencies: The CLCL entry*. Ph.D. thesis, University of Geneva.

Thomas Müller, Ryan Cotterell, Alexander Fraser, and Hinrich Schütze. 2015. Joint lemmatization and morphological tagging with lemming. In *Proceedings of the 2015 Conference on Empirical Methods in Natural Language Processing*, pages 2268–2274.

Kemal Oflazer. 1993. Two-level description of turkish morphology. In *Proceedings of the Sixth Conference on European Chapter of the Association for Computational Linguistics*, EACL '93, pages 472–472, Stroudsburg, PA, USA. Association for Computational Linguistics.

Qinlan Shen, Daniel Clothiaux, Emily Tagtow, Patrick Littell, and Chris Dyer. 2016. The role of context in neural morphological disambiguation. In *COLING*, pages 181–191.

Eray Yildiz, Caglar Tirkaz, Bahadir Sahin, Mustafa Tolga Eren, and Ozan Sonmez. 2016. A morphology-aware network for morphological disambiguation.

Daniel Zeman and Jan Hajič, editors. 2018. *Proceedings of the CoNLL 2018 Shared Task: Multilingual Parsing from Raw Text to Universal Dependencies*. Association for Computational Linguistics, Brussels, Belgium.

Multi-Team: A Multi-attention, Multi-decoder Approach to Morphological Analysis.

Ahmet Üstün   Rob van der Goot   Gosse Bouma   Gertjan van Noord

University of Groningen

{a.ustun, r.van.der.goot, g.bouma, g.j.m.van.noord}@rug.nl

Abstract

This paper describes our submission to SIG-MORPHON 2019 Task 2: Morphological analysis and lemmatization in context. Our model is a multi-task sequence to sequence neural network, which jointly learns morphological tagging and lemmatization. On the encoding side, we exploit character-level as well as contextual information. We introduce a multi-attention decoder to selectively focus on different parts of character and word sequences. To further improve the model, we train on multiple datasets simultaneously and use external embeddings for initialization. Our final model reaches an average morphological tagging F1 score of 94.54 and a lemma accuracy of 93.91 on the test data, ranking respectively 3rd and 6th out of 13 teams in the SIG-MORPHON 2019 shared task.

1 Introduction

This paper presents our model for the SIGMOR-PHON 2019 Task 2 on morphological analysis and lemmatization in context (McCarthy et al., 2019). The task is to generate a lemma and a sequence of morphological tags, which are called morphosyntactic descriptions (MSD), for each word in a given sentence. This task is important because it can be used to improve several downstream NLP applications such as grammatical error correction (Ng et al., 2014), machine translation (Conforti et al., 2018) and multilingual parsing (Zeman et al., 2018). Table 1 shows the lemma and morphological tags of: *Johnny likes cats*.

The first sub-task, Lemmatization, is to transform an inflected word form to its lemma which is its base-form (or dictionary form), as in the example of *likes* to *like*. The second sub-task, morphological tagging, is to predict morphological properties of words as a sequence of tags, including a part of speech tag. These morphological tags specify the inflections encoded in word-forms. In the

Orig	Johnny	likes	cats	.
Lemma	Johnny	like	cat	.
MSD	PROPN;SG	V;SG;3;IND;PRS	N;PL	_

Table 1: Example sentence, annotated with lemmas and morphological tags.

example sentence, the word *likes* is annotated with a morphological tag set of {*V,SG,3,IND,PRS*}. Both tasks are dependent on context. For example, while *walking* is annotated with the lemma *walk* and tag set {*N,SG*} in the sentence: *The beach is within walking distance*; it is annotated with *walking* and {*V.PTCP;PRS;V*} in: *I was walking*.

These two tasks have a clear relation; in most languages the categories found in the morphological tags indicate how the lemma of the word was inflected to the word-form. In other words, syntactic inflections have a strong correlation with the morphological properties of the words.

Our approach to solve both of these tasks consists of an encoder and two separate decoders within a multi-task architecture based on a sequence-to-sequence network. The shared encoder reads words and sentences to learn character-level and word-level representations. The decoders then separately generate lemmas and morphological tags using these representations by using multiple attention mechanisms. Our contributions are threefold:

- We introduce the use of multiple attention mechanisms that selectively focus character and word sequences in the sentence context.

- We evaluate the effect of a variety of types of external embeddings for lemmatization and morphological tagging.

- We evaluate the effect of combining annotated datasets from related languages for both tasks

Proceedings of the 16th Workshop on Computational Research in Phonetics, Phonology, and Morphology, pages 35–49
Florence, Italy. August 2, 2019 ©2019 Association for Computational Linguistics

using dataset embeddings.

2 Related work

Our system is based on three main approaches which are heavily studied in existing literature. These are sequence-to-sequence learning, multi-task learning and multi-lingual learning.

Recent work on computational morphology showed that neural sequence-to-sequence (seq2seq) models (Sutskever et al., 2014; Bahdanau et al., 2014) have yielded new state-of-the-art performance on various tasks including morphological reinflection and lemmatization (Cotterell et al., 2016, 2017, 2018). Building on this, Dayanık et al. (2018) utilize different levels of representations such as character-level, word-level and sentence-level in the encoder of their seq2seq architecture based on previous work (Heigold et al., 2017).

Multi-task learning approaches for jointly learning related tasks have been successfully employed on syntactic and semantic tasks (Søgaard and Goldberg, 2016; Plank et al., 2016). In the context of morphological analysis, this has been used by Kementchedjhieva et al. (2018), who jointly learn morphosyntactic tags and inflections for a word in a given context, and use a shared encoder within a multi-task architecture consisting of multiple decoder similar to our model.

Multi-lingual learning approaches which benefit from joint learning for multiple languages is also studied on various tasks with different architectures. Ammar et al. (2016) uses a language embedding that contains information considering the language, word-order properties and typological properties for dependency parsing. In multilingual neural machine translation, Johnson et al. (2017) use a special token to indicate the target language. In this work, our model uses the approach of Smith et al. (2018) who introduce the treebank embedding approach to combine several treebanks for a single language or closely related languages.

Most similar to our model, Kondratyuk et al. (2018) use a joint decoder approach for morphological tagging and lemmatization. However, our model differs from theirs in substantial ways. Our model employs an encoder-decoder architecture which utilizes different levels of attention components with a multi-lingual/multi-dataset signal. Moreover, our model solves the tagging problem as a sequential prediction task instead of multi-layer classification so that we can use the same architecture for both lemmatization and tagging which are described in Section 3.2 and 3.3.

3 System Description

Our model is inspired by the architecture of Dayanık et al. (2018). We employ an encoder-decoder model over the character and word sequences. Following Dayanık et al. (2018), the encoder in our model consists of two parts. First, a word encoder which runs on the character level, is used to generate embeddings for each word (Section 3.1.1). Second, a context encoder is initialized with these word embeddings, and runs on the sentence level (Section 3.1.4). We also experiment with two methods to complement the word-level embeddings (Section 3.1.2 and 3.1.3).

The representations at the different levels which are generated by the encoder are then passed into the decoders. Unlike Dayanık et al. (2018) which uses one decoder for both the lemmas and the morphological tags, we use two different decoders in a multi-task architecture. The tag decoder produces a set of morphological tags by using word representations and joint attention mechanism that one attention focuses on words and other focuses on characters (Section 3.2). The lemma decoder produces a lemma by using the same information complemented with output embeddings of the tag decoder (Section 3.3).

Multi-task Learning The decoders work jointly in a multi-task fashion and they share all internal representations of the encoder. The whole network is trained by backpropagating the sum of the losses of the decoders without any weighting:

$$\mathbf{L}(\theta) \;=\; L_{tag} + L_{lemma} \tag{1}$$

where the morphological tag loss L_{tag} and the lemma loss L_{lemma} are separately computed as the negative log likelihood loss over their softmax outputs.

Notation Given a sentence $S = w_1, ..., w_n$ and $w_i = c_1, ..., c_m$ where w denotes words and c denotes characters, our model processes S and w in encoders and jointly produces a set of morphological tags $t_i = t_{i,1}, ..., t_{i,\gamma}$ and a lemma $l_i = l_{i,1}, ..., l_{i,\phi}$ which is a sequence of characters.

3.1 Encoder

In the following subsections, we explain the different parts of the encoder. An overview of the encoder architecture is shown in Figure 1.

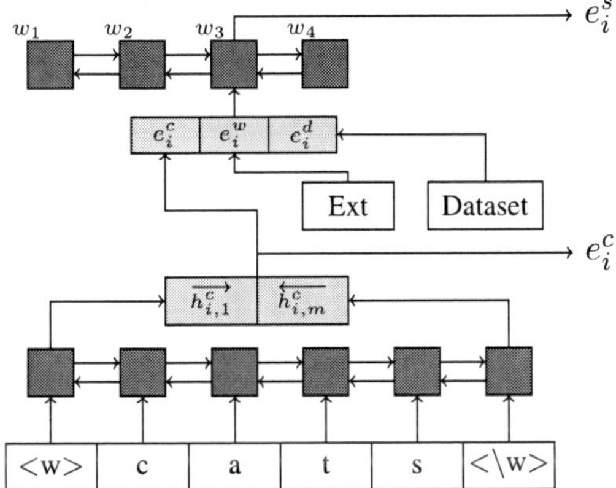

Figure 1: Overview of the encoder when processing the third word of the sentence: "Johnny likes cats .". Red:word level embeddings. Green: Character level embeddings.

3.1.1 Word Encoder

We use a bidirectional GRU layer (Cho et al., 2014) to encode character sequences in the word encoder. We first pass each character of a word w_i to an embedding layer to map them into the fixed dimensional character embeddings. The bi-GRUs process character embeddings in both directions and produce the hidden states $h_{i,1}^c, ..., h_{i,m}^c$. The resulting word embedding e_i^c is computed by concatenating the final states of forward and backward GRUs for the given word:

$$h_{i,1:m}^c = \text{bi-GRU}(c_{i,1:m}) \quad (2)$$

$$e_i^c = [\overrightarrow{h_{i,m}^c}; \overleftarrow{h_{i,1}^c}] \quad (3)$$

3.1.2 Word-Surface Embeddings

In addition to the character-level word embeddings, we use surface-level word embeddings which are either learned in a standalone embedding layer or taken from the pre-trained external embeddings. Word-surface embeddings are denoted by e_i^w. For the unknown words, we used a *word droupout* to overcome the sparsity issue. Following Kiperwasser and Goldberg (2016), we replace unknown tokens with a probability that is inversely proportional to the frequency of the word so that the word representation for an unknown token is learned based on infrequent words and their context.

3.1.3 Dataset Embeddings

In order to train our model on multiple datasets at once, we use dataset embedding e_a^d for each

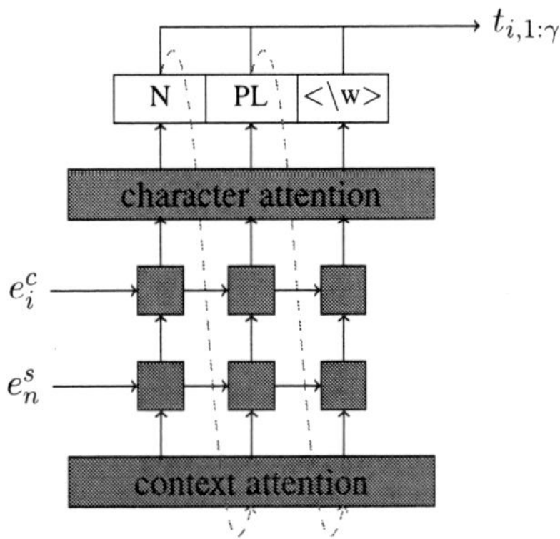

Figure 2: An overview of the morphological tag decoder.

dataset a which is mapped into a fixed dimensional vector in an embedding layer. The idea of dataset embeddings is introduced by Smith et al. (2018). These embeddings enable us to combine multiple datasets without losing their monolingual and heterogeneous characters. The strategy that we use to pick and combine datasets is described in Section 4.2

3.1.4 Context Encoder

In order to encode sentence level contextual information, we use another bidirectional GRU layer. For a given sentence, we first concatenate the output of the word encoder e_i^c, the word-surface embedding e_i^w and the dataset embedding e_a^d, for each word in the sentence. The resulting embedding sequence $e_1^{in}, ..., e_n^{in}$ is then passed into the bi-GRU. The output of the bi-GRU is a sequence of embeddings $e_1^s, ..., e_n^s$ each representing a word in the sentence:

$$e_i^{in} = [e_i^c; e_i^w; e_a^d] \quad (4)$$

$$e_{1:n}^s = \text{bi-GRU}(e_{1:n}^{in}) \quad (5)$$

3.2 Tag Decoder

As the tag decoder shows in Figure 2, we use a 2 layer stacked bidirectional GRU as the tag decoder to generate morphological tags $t_i = t_{i,1}, ..., t_{i,\gamma}$ for the target word w_i in a given sentence. In order to utilize both character-level representations and contextual representations during decoding, we initialize the first layer of the decoder with the context-level word embedding e_i^s and the second layer of the decoder with the character-level word embedding e_i^c after passing them through a *relu* layer. The decoder outputs the morphological tags over a softmax layer based on the final hidden states $\widetilde{h}_t$, which are computed in a joint attention mechanism described in the following section.

$$\widetilde{h}_t = \text{decoder}(h_t, c_t^c, c_t^s) \quad (6)$$
$$p(t_{i,t}|\widetilde{h}_t) = \text{softmax}(\widetilde{h}_t) \quad (7)$$

3.2.1 Joint Context and Character Attention

We employ two different attention mechanisms to allow the decoder to focus on multiple parts of the sentence and the target word at the same time. We use the attention mechanism introduced by Bahdanau et al. (2014) for the context attention layer. In the context attention, the alignment vector a_t^s, which consists of weights for each word in the sentence, is computed based on the previous hidden state h_{t-1} at the top layer of the stacked bi-GRU and context-level embeddings e^s of words by using the *concat* function described in Luong et al. (2015). The sentence-level context vector c_t^s which is calculated as a weighted average over word embeddings, is then passed into a simple concatenation layer W_c^s to produce the new hidden state h_t through the stacked bi-GRU:

$$a_t^s(i) = \text{align}^s(h_{t-1}, e_i^s) \quad (8)$$
$$c_t^s = \sum_i a_t^s e_i^s \quad (9)$$
$$h_t = \text{bi-GRU}(W_c^s[c_t^s; h_{t-1}], h_{t-1}) \quad (10)$$

Together with the context attention, we also employ a character-level attention model to take into account the entire output of the word encoder. We use the global attention mechanism with the *general* score function for alignment vectors (Luong et al., 2015), for the character attention. The source-side character-level attention vector c_t^c is computed as a weighted average of the outputs of the word encoder, each denoted by $h_{i,j}^c$. The resulting output state $\widetilde{h}_t$ of the tag decoder is then generated by concatenating the current hidden state at the top of the stacked bi-GRU h_t and the context vector c_t^c in a concatenation layer which has a *tanh* activation:

$$a_t^c(j) = \text{align}^c(h_t, h_{i,j}^c) \quad (11)$$
$$c_t^c = \sum_j a_t^c h_{i,j}^c \quad (12)$$
$$\widetilde{h}_t = \tanh(W_c^c[c_t^c; h_t]) \quad (13)$$

3.3 Lemma Decoder

The lemma decoder (Figure 3) produces one character at a time to sequentially form a lemma $l_i =$

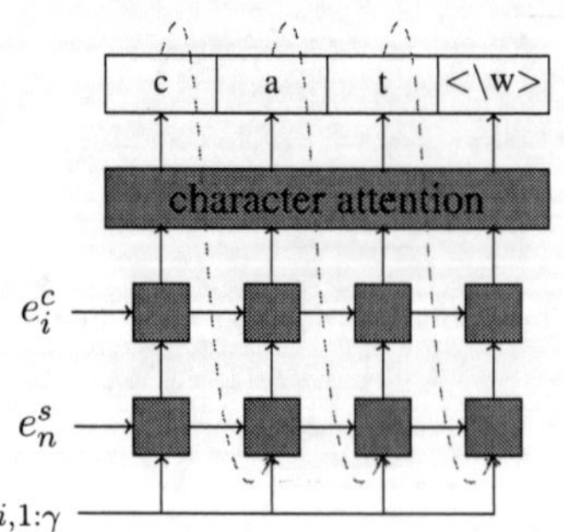

Figure 3: An overview of the lemma decoder.

$l_{i,1}, ..., l_{i,\phi}$ for a target word w_i. Similar to the tag encoder, we use a 2 layer stacked bi-GRU as lemma decoder. The initial states of the decoder layers are taken from the word encoder output e_i^c and the context encoder output e_i^s through a *relu* layer similarly as in the tag decoder. The output of the lemma decoder $l_{i,t}$ is conditioned on the current state of the decoder h_t, the character attention c_t^c and the morphological tags $t_{i,1:\gamma}$ of the target word. The probability of the output lemma characters are then predicted through a softmax layer.

$$\widetilde{h}_t = \text{decoder}(h_t, c_t^c, t_{i,1:\gamma}) \quad (14)$$
$$p(l_{i,t}|\widetilde{h}_t) = \text{softmax}(\widetilde{h}_t) \quad (15)$$

In order to exploit morphological features during lemmatization, we give the morphological tags $t_{i:\gamma}$ which are predicted by the tag decoder, as part of input to the lemma decoder. Independent of their order, the entire set of the tags are encoded by a simple *feed-forward* layer as described in the baseline model (Malaviya et al., 2019) and the resulting vector is concatenated with the input embeddings for each target word.

The last part of the lemma decoder is the attention network which is the same character-level attention model as in the tag decoder. The character attention mechanism allows the lemma decoder to compute an attention vector c_t^c based on the output states of the word encoder. The attention vector is then passed into a concatenation layer to generate the output state $\widetilde{h}_t$ of the decoder for each lemma character $l_{i,t}$.

$$a_t^c(j) = \text{align}^c(h_t, h_{i,j}^c) \quad (16)$$
$$c_t^c = \sum_j a_t^c h_{i,j}^c \quad (17)$$
$$\widetilde{h}_t = \tanh(W_c^c[c_t^c; h_t]) \quad (18)$$

Parameter	Val.	Parameter	Val.
teacher forcing ratio	0.5	dataset embbedding size (e_a^d)	32
dropout	0.25	word enc. hidden size (h_i^c)	1,024
patience	4	context enc. hidden size (h_i^s)	1,024
word enc. input size	128	dec. input size	128
word embedding size (e_i^w)	256	dec. hidden size (h_t)	1,024

Table 2: Default hyperparameter settings. Encoder and decoder are denoted by *enc* and *dec* respectively.

4 Setup

In this section we will give the details regarding our experimental setup. The hyperparameters we used in our experiments are shown in Table 2. These hyperparameters have been tuned on the datasets described in Section 5.1. For the training, we used ADAM (Kingma and Ba, 2014) and we applied an early stopping strategy with a minimum number of 100 epochs. We stop training if there is no improvement in the development set for 4 consecutive epochs (patience).

4.1 External Embeddings

Because of time-constraints and the large number of languages in the dataset, we used out-of-the-box embeddings. We compared the performance of three well-known pre-trained embedding repositories for different training methods. We use two word-based embeddings: Polyglot embeddings (Al-Rfou et al., 2013), and FastText embeddings (Grave et al., 2018). For FastText, two sets of pre-trained embeddings are available: one is trained only on Wikipedia (Bojanowski et al., 2017), whereas the newer versions are also trained on CommonCrawl (Grave et al., 2018). Whenever available, we pick the newer embeddings, but for many low-resource languages we fall back to the older, smaller version. We also experiment with context-based embeddings, namely ELMo embeddings (Peters et al., 2018), we use the pre-trained models from Che et al. (2018).

All of these embeddings have been trained using the default settings for the embedding type, hence their dimensions are substantially different (Polyglot; 64, FastText:300, ELMo:1,024) . We decided not to transform these, as their default dimensions are tuned towards their training algorithm and we want to provide a fair comparison for all out-of-the-box settings.

4.2 Dataset Embeddings

For the dataset embeddings, we only consider combining pairs of two for efficiency reasons. To ensure that we match datasets which are informative, we use word overlap (excluding numberals and punctuation). As this method is expected to be most benficial for small datasets, we searched for datasets which are closest (ie. have a large word overlap) to the 50 smallest datasets. The final pairs of datasets can be found in Appendix A.

5 Experiments

In this section, we will describe the data used in our experiments as well as evaluate the effectiveness of our external embeddings setup and the dataset embeddings with in a variety of settings. In all experiments we use +E and -E to indicate the model with and without external embeddings, and +D and -D for dataset embeddings.

5.1 Data

The test data of SIGMORPHON 2019 task 2 consists of a collection of datasets released in the Universal Dependencies project (Nivre et al., 2018), which are automatically converted to the UniMorph Schema (McCarthy et al., 2018). In total, we evaluate our model on 107 datasets, covering 66 languages.

After empirically looking at the trade-off between data-size and training time, we decided to limit each dataset to its first 250,000 tokens for all experiments. This speeded up the training considerably, with almost no loss in performance.

For the tuning of our model, we selected a sub-set of datasets from the main benchmark. More specifically, we aimed to get a diversion of language-family, size, and morphological richness (here proxied by the average amount of morphological tags per word). To ensure we do not overfit on a specific dataset/annotation, we selected two datasets for each of these languages. The selected datasets are shown in Table 3.

5.2 Baseline

The baseline consists of two separate parts: a morphological tagger and a lemmatizer. The morphological tagger, which predicts a set of morphological features (as one tag) for each word, is a biLSTM model with character level layers. The k-best predicted morphological tags are then used

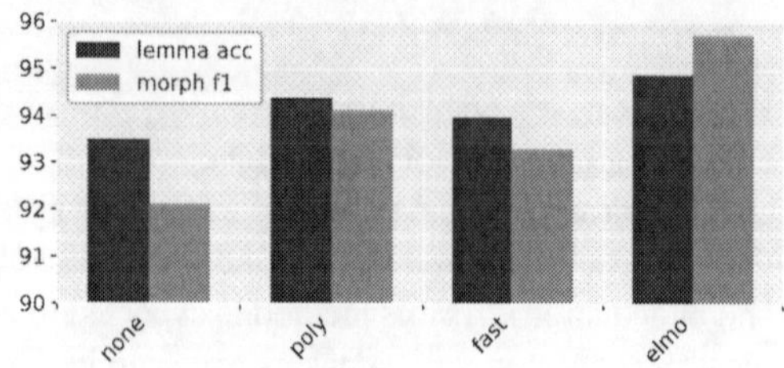

Figure 4: Results of our model when using a variety of types of external embeddings.

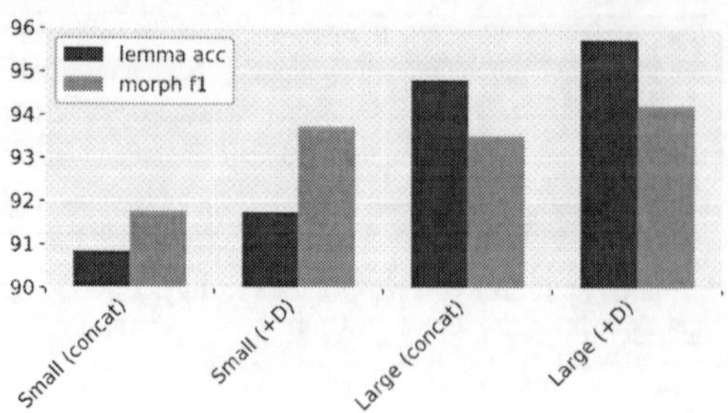

Figure 5: Average results of our model when using simple dataset concatenation versus using dataset embeddings (+D) on 4 small datasets and 4 large datasets

as extra information to improve the lemmatization. The lemmatizer, which is based on Wu et al. (2018), uses a hard attention mechanism within an encoder-decoder model. Unlike the previous models, the morphological tags are explicitly given to the lemmatizer to indicate the morpho-syntactic features of words. The lemmatizer combines the given morphological tags with a character encoding to predict the lemma.

5.3 External Embeddings

In Figure 4, we plotted the average performance of our model when the different types of embeddings are used to initialize the word-surface embeddings (detailed results are in Appendix B). The results show that a performance boost of approximately 2.5% can be obtained for lemmatization and 5% for morphological tagging. Especially the ELMo embeddings perform very well, and result in an improvement of 3.77 and 6.35 percentage points. The Polyglot embeddings perform surprisingly well, considering they only have an embedding size of 64. In addition to the reported settings, we also experimented with concatenating the vectors from all types of external embeddings. However, our empirical results showed that this performed worse compared to using any of the embeddings in isolation.

Because not all types of embeddings are available for all languages, we use fallback options for the test data. We choose embeddings in the following order: ELMo, Polyglot, FastText. After this selection, three languages still have no embeddings (Akkadian, Coptic and Naija), we omitted datasets in these languages from the external embedding experiments.

5.4 Dataset Embeddings

To test whether the dataset embeddings are necessary, we compare them with a naive approach to combine datasets: simply training on the concatenation of both datasets. The average results on 4 small datasets and 4 large datasets which are given in Table 3, are compared separately in Figure 5. In both small and large settings, using dataset embeddings improves the performance in both morphological tagging and lemmatization, however the effect of dataset embeddings is higher on small datasets, especially in the morphological tagging task. For the detailed results on our tune datasets, we refer to Appendix C.

6 Results

In this section, we will compare our final results for two settings with the baseline. In general, we compare two setups: use of external data (external embeddings, +E) and a constrained setup (-E), which only uses training data. For the dataset embeddings, we could only run for the smallest 50 datasets because of time limitations, so for the development data, we only report results for these datasets. For the test data, we used dataset embeddings for datasets for which they have shown to be beneficial on the development data. Our average results are shown in Table 7. For the results for all

Dataset	Language Family	Sents	words	tag/word
en_ewt	IE,Germanic	13,297	204,857	1.95
en_pud	IE,Germanic	800	16,927	1.88
tr_imst	Turkic,Southwestern	4,508	46,417	3.58
tr_pud	Turkic,Southwestern	800	13,380	2.78
zh_cfl	Sino-Tibetan	360	5,688	1.00
zh_gsd	Sino-Tibetan	3,997	98,734	1.06
fi_pud	Uralic,Finnic	800	12,556	2.97
fi_ftb	Uralic,Finnic	14,978	127,536	3.07

Table 3: The datasets which we used to tune our models, with data properties based on the training split. IE: Indo-European

four settings per dataset, we refer to Appendix D; here we see that the best setting is generally to use dataset embeddings when available.

6.1 Morphological Tagging

For the morphological tagging task, external embeddings show to be more beneficial for the tagging task, whereas the dataset embeddings are particularly beneficial for lemmatization, but combining them leads to the best scores for both tasks. Furthermore, our model outperforms the baseline by a large margin. This is because, while the baseline has a separate component for morphological tagging, our model learns both tasks jointly. This approach implicitly enables the decoder to access lemma information for morphological tagging. Besides, we use a multi-attention strategy which combines word level and character level attentions which improves the tagging performance.

6.2 Lemmatization

In contrast to the results on the development data, the baseline outperforms our model on the test data (Table 7). Especially on small datasets which are not paired with another dataset, such as UD_Akkadian-PISANDUB, the baseline performs better with a large margin.

There are two main reasons for this performance difference. First, the baseline uses a hard attention to model alignment distribution explicitly, whereas, our model uses soft attention for both tasks. The results show that a hard attention mechanism performs better on the lemmatization, confirming the findings of Wu et al. (2018). Integrating a lemma decoder having hard attention with a morphological tag decoder which employs soft attention, could be explored in future studies. Second, as explained in the previous section, we optimize for both tasks jointly without any weighting. Although this is more elegant, as only one model is trained, it might not lead to the most optimal performance.

7 Conclusion

In this paper, we presented our model for the Sigmorphon 2019 Task 2 on morphological analysis and lemmatization. We use an encoder-decoder model by utilizing multi-task learning approach. A shared encoder runs on the character and sentence level and two separate decoders jointly learn to generate morphological tags and the lemma for

Models	Morph. tags		Lemma	
	Acc	F1	Acc	Lev
dev (small)				
base	69.66	85.38	91.53	0.19
-E -D	83.16	89.45	86.75	0.29
+E -D	85.84	91.54	87.65	0.28
-E+D	85.58	91.26	89.70	0.27
+E+D	88.03	92.96	91.29	0.24
test (all)				
base	73.16	87.92	94.17	0.13
-E	89.00	93.35	93.05	0.16
+E	90.61	94.57	93.94	0.15

Table 7: Average results for all evaluation metrics for development and test data. +E: use external embeddings for initialization, +D: use dataset embedding strategy. On the development data, we report the average over the datasets where predictions of all settings were available.

each word.

Our system achieved an average morphological tagging F1 score of 94.57 and an average lemma accuracy score of 93.94 on the test data. The experimental analysis showed that:

- Employing a multi-task achitecture having multiple levels of attention mechanism improved the morphological tagging over the baseline strategy.

- Using the pre-trained embeddings substantially improved our scores for both tasks.

- Applying a multi-lingual/dataset strategy by learning special embeddings also improved our scores, specifically for small datasets. On 50 datasets (Table 7), the multi-dataset strategy improved the performance of our model substantially, by 2.95 (accuracy) on lemmatization and 1.81 (F1) on morphological tagging.

- Furthermore, these improvements are highly complementary: using dataset embeddings simultaneously with external embeddings leads to superior performance.

The code to re-run all experiments can be found on: https://bitbucket.org/ahmetustunn/morphology_in_context

Dataset	Lemma Acc.	Lemma Lev.	Morph. tags F1	Morph. tags Acc.	+E	+D	Dataset	Lemma Acc.	Lemma Lev.	Morph. tags F1	Morph. tags Acc.	+E	+D
af_afribooms	96.44	0.10	98.05	98.45	+	+	it_postwita	95.20	0.18	95.42	96.64	+	-
akk_pisandub	47.52	1.35	76.24	75.84	-	+	it_pud	97.11	0.06	93.73	96.96	-	+
am_att	98.49	0.02	87.81	91.52	-	-	ja_gsd	98.98	0.01	98.00	97.76	+	+
ar_padt	94.65	0.14	94.16	96.90	+	+	ja_modern	96.87	0.04	96.74	96.80	-	+
ar_pud	82.53	0.41	83.61	94.16	+	+	ja_pud	99.01	0.02	98.56	98.39	+	+
be_hse	90.28	0.18	82.20	91.52	+	+	kmr_mg	91.31	0.14	83.51	89.44	+	-
bg_btb	97.19	0.08	97.27	98.79	+	-	ko_gsd	90.09	0.21	95.93	95.35	+	-
bm_crb	87.47	0.21	91.42	93.77	+	-	ko_kaist	94.62	0.09	96.84	96.46	+	-
br_keb	92.24	0.18	86.57	89.50	+	+	ko_pud	99.13	0.01	92.38	95.59	+	+
bxr_bdt	87.12	0.31	83.65	86.57	+	+	kpv_ikdp	85.94	0.26	66.41	75.96	-	+
ca_ancora	99.00	0.02	97.94	99.04	+	-	kpv_lattice	81.87	0.46	69.23	82.21	+	+
cop_scriptorium	96.13	0.08	94.67	96.31	-	-	la_ittb	98.33	0.04	95.01	97.77	+	-
cs_cac	98.39	0.03	95.21	98.36	+	-	la_perseus	92.73	0.15	83.75	93.01	+	+
cs_cltt	97.60	0.29	93.30	97.59	+	+	la_proiel	96.76	0.07	90.28	96.60	+	-
cs_fictree	97.78	0.04	93.84	97.57	+	-	lt_hse	80.14	0.46	67.23	83.26	+	+
cs_pdt	97.94	0.04	94.36	97.97	+	-	lv_lvtb	95.02	0.09	92.96	96.91	+	+
cs_pud	96.84	0.05	91.19	97.21	+	+	mr_ufal	72.63	0.67	62.33	76.02	+	+
cu_proiel	95.54	0.10	88.67	95.48	-	-	nl_alpino	96.25	0.08	95.10	96.05	+	-
da_ddt	96.96	0.05	96.05	97.49	+	+	nl_lassysmall	94.30	0.12	93.45	94.26	-	-
de_gsd	95.24	0.10	84.99	93.71	+	-	no_bokmaal	97.72	0.04	95.21	97.05	+	-
el_gdt	94.64	0.11	92.79	97.47	+	+	no_nynorsk	95.86	0.08	94.05	96.27	-	-
en_ewt	98.39	0.08	96.18	97.24	+	+	no_nynorsklia	97.58	0.04	94.53	96.62	+	+
en_gum	97.85	0.04	95.95	96.95	+	+	pcm_nsc	99.48	0.02	94.79	93.01	+	+
en_lines	97.96	0.04	96.45	97.32	+	-	pl_lfg	97.06	0.06	94.55	97.76	+	+
en_partut	97.97	0.03	95.40	96.27	+	+	pl_sz	97.11	0.05	90.88	96.56	+	+
en_pud	97.20	0.04	95.44	96.85	+	+	pt_bosque	98.24	0.03	94.83	97.53	+	-
es_ancora	99.03	0.02	97.83	98.91	+	-	pt_gsd	98.14	0.10	98.24	98.37	+	-
es_gsd	98.75	0.02	94.60	97.37	-	+	ro_nonstandard	96.44	0.07	92.74	96.18	-	+
et_edt	95.07	0.11	94.51	97.24	+	-	ro_rrt	98.29	0.03	97.47	98.42	+	-
eu_bdt	96.03	0.09	90.15	95.38	+	-	ru_gsd	96.79	0.05	90.69	96.05	+	-
fa_seraji	95.20	0.23	97.76	98.23	+	-	ru_pud	94.31	0.10	87.93	95.50	+	+
fi_ftb	94.65	0.12	95.17	97.37	+	-	ru_syntagrus	96.76	0.07	95.10	97.71	+	-
fi_pud	89.35	0.28	95.24	97.51	+	+	ru_taiga	93.44	0.15	86.33	93.83	+	+
fi_tdt	93.61	0.14	95.31	97.52	+	-	sa_ufal	52.26	1.18	42.21	64.45	+	+
fo_oft	85.59	0.29	80.60	90.62	-	+	sk_snk	95.61	0.08	91.49	96.75	+	-
fr_gsd	98.12	0.04	97.31	98.43	+	-	sl_ssj	97.84	0.03	93.65	97.13	+	-
fr_partut	96.54	0.05	94.96	97.71	+	+	sl_sst	96.24	0.07	90.72	95.09	+	+
fr_sequoia	98.27	0.03	97.18	98.77	+	-	sme_giella	87.54	0.27	86.22	91.38	+	+
fr_spoken	99.52	0.01	98.15	98.18	+	+	sr_set	96.09	0.07	92.38	96.27	+	-
ga_idt	89.07	0.26	83.95	90.82	+	-	sv_lines	96.43	0.08	93.13	97.03	+	-
gl_ctg	98.31	0.03	97.80	97.59	+	-	sv_pud	94.19	0.11	94.97	97.09	+	+
gl_treegal	96.56	0.06	93.97	96.93	+	-	sv_talbanken	96.65	0.07	96.32	98.20	+	-
got_proiel	95.04	0.10	85.99	94.39	-	-	ta_ttb	88.17	0.28	81.14	91.29	+	-
grc_perseus	92.42	0.18	88.90	95.69	+	-	tl_trg	75.68	2.24	86.49	91.30	+	+
grc_proiel	96.70	0.08	91.15	97.37	+	-	tr_imst	96.09	0.07	90.79	95.52	+	+
he_htb	96.61	0.06	95.86	97.35	+	-	tr_pud	86.46	0.34	87.63	94.96	+	+
hi_hdtb	98.61	0.02	91.80	97.30	+	-	uk_iu	95.45	0.09	91.92	96.42	+	-
hr_set	94.18	0.11	89.41	96.02	+	-	ur_udtb	95.91	0.07	77.31	92.02	+	-
hsb_ufal	87.11	0.21	77.12	86.73	+	+	vi_vtb	99.20	0.03	89.55	88.18	-	+
hu_szeged	94.17	0.12	87.95	96.22	+	+	yo_ytb	98.06	0.02	92.64	93.27	-	-
hy_armtdp	92.15	0.15	84.64	91.66	+	+	yue_hk	99.29	0.01	92.32	90.23	-	+
id_gsd	99.09	0.02	89.32	93.04	-	-	zh_cfl	96.57	0.04	91.61	90.35	+	+
it_isdt	97.83	0.04	96.78	98.01	-	-	zh_gsd	99.02	0.01	94.61	94.59	+	+
it_partut	98.25	0.04	97.30	98.45	-	+	average	93.94	0.15	90.61	94.57		

Table 6: All four evaluation metrics for the test data of our best system. E: use of external embeddings. D: use of dataset embeddings. Results might be different compared to the ones in the overview paper, as we did not have enough time to run all experiments before the deadline. +E: whether external embeddings were used. +D: whether dataset embeddings were used.

Acknowledgements

We would like to thank all our colleagues and the anonymous reviewers. Furthermore, we would like to thank the Center for Information Technology of the University of Groningen for their support and for providing access to the Peregrine high performance computing cluster.

References

Rami Al-Rfou, Bryan Perozzi, and Steven Skiena. 2013. Polyglot: Distributed word representations for multilingual NLP. In *Proceedings of the Seventeenth Conference on Computational Natural Language Learning*, pages 183–192, Sofia, Bulgaria. Association for Computational Linguistics.

Waleed Ammar, George Mulcaire, Miguel Ballesteros, Chris Dyer, and Noah A Smith. 2016. Many languages, one parser. *Transactions of the Association for Computational Linguistics*, 4:431–444.

Dzmitry Bahdanau, Kyunghyun Cho, and Yoshua Bengio. 2014. Neural machine translation by jointly learning to align and translate. *arXiv preprint arXiv:1409.0473*.

Piotr Bojanowski, Edouard Grave, Armand Joulin, and Tomas Mikolov. 2017. Enriching word vectors with subword information. *Transactions of the Association for Computational Linguistics*, 5:135–146.

Wanxiang Che, Yijia Liu, Yuxuan Wang, Bo Zheng, and Ting Liu. 2018. Towards better UD parsing: Deep contextualized word embeddings, ensemble, and treebank concatenation. In *Proceedings of the CoNLL 2018 Shared Task: Multilingual Parsing from Raw Text to Universal Dependencies*, pages 55–64, Brussels, Belgium. Association for Computational Linguistics.

Kyunghyun Cho, Bart van Merrienboer, Caglar Gulcehre, Dzmitry Bahdanau, Fethi Bougares, Holger Schwenk, and Yoshua Bengio. 2014. Learning phrase representations using rnn encoder–decoder for statistical machine translation. In *Proceedings of the 2014 Conference on Empirical Methods in Natural Language Processing (EMNLP)*, pages 1724–1734.

Costanza Conforti, Matthias Huck, and Alexander Fraser. 2018. Neural morphological tagging of lemma sequences for machine translation. In *Proceedings of the 13th Conference of the Association for Machine Translation in the Americas (Volume 1: Research Papers)*, volume 1, pages 39–53.

Ryan Cotterell, Christo Kirov, John Sylak-Glassman, Géraldine Walther, Ekaterina Vylomova, Arya D McCarthy, Katharina Kann, Sebastian Mielke, Garrett Nicolai, Miikka Silfverberg, et al. 2018. The conll–sigmorphon 2018 shared task: Universal morphological reinflection. *arXiv preprint arXiv:1810.07125*.

Ryan Cotterell, Christo Kirov, John Sylak-Glassman, Géraldine Walther, Ekaterina Vylomova, Patrick Xia, Manaal Faruqui, Sandra Kübler, David Yarowsky, Jason Eisner, et al. 2017. Conll-sigmorphon 2017 shared task: Universal morphological reinflection in 52 languages. *arXiv preprint arXiv:1706.09031*.

Ryan Cotterell, Christo Kirov, John Sylak-Glassman, David Yarowsky, Jason Eisner, and Mans Hulden. 2016. The sigmorphon 2016 shared taskmorphological reinflection. In *Proceedings of the 14th SIGMORPHON Workshop on Computational Research in Phonetics, Phonology, and Morphology*, pages 10–22.

Erenay Dayanık, Ekin Akyürek, and Deniz Yuret. 2018. Morphnet: A sequence-to-sequence model that combines morphological analysis and disambiguation. *arXiv preprint arXiv:1805.07946*.

Edouard Grave, Piotr Bojanowski, Prakhar Gupta, Armand Joulin, and Tomas Mikolov. 2018. Learning word vectors for 157 languages. In *Proceedings of the International Conference on Language Resources and Evaluation (LREC 2018)*.

Georg Heigold, Guenter Neumann, and Josef van Genabith. 2017. An extensive empirical evaluation of character-based morphological tagging for 14 languages. In *Proceedings of the 15th Conference of the European Chapter of the Association for Computational Linguistics: Volume 1, Long Papers*, pages 505–513.

Melvin Johnson, Mike Schuster, Quoc V Le, Maxim Krikun, Yonghui Wu, Zhifeng Chen, Nikhil Thorat, Fernanda Viégas, Martin Wattenberg, Greg Corrado, et al. 2017. Googles multilingual neural machine translation system: Enabling zero-shot translation. *Transactions of the Association for Computational Linguistics*, 5:339–351.

Yova Kementchedjhieva, Johannes Bjerva, and Isabelle Augenstein. 2018. Copenhagen at conll–sigmorphon 2018: Multilingual inflection in context with explicit morphosyntactic decoding. *Proceedings of the CoNLL SIGMORPHON 2018 Shared Task: Universal Morphological Reinflection*, pages 93–98.

Diederik P Kingma and Jimmy Ba. 2014. Adam: A method for stochastic optimization. *arXiv preprint arXiv:1412.6980*.

Eliyahu Kiperwasser and Yoav Goldberg. 2016. Simple and accurate dependency parsing using bidirectional LSTM feature representations. *Transactions of the Association for Computational Linguistics*, 4:313–327.

Daniel Kondratyuk, Tomáš Gavenčiak, Milan Straka, and Jan Hajič. 2018. Lemmatag: Jointly tagging and lemmatizing for morphologically rich languages with brnns. In *Proceedings of the 2018 Conference on Empirical Methods in Natural Language Processing*, pages 4921–4928.

Thang Luong, Hieu Pham, and Christopher D Manning. 2015. Effective approaches to attention-based neural machine translation. In *Proceedings of the 2015 Conference on Empirical Methods in Natural Language Processing*, pages 1412–1421.

Chaitanya Malaviya, Shijie Wu, and Ryan Cotterell. 2019. A simple joint model for improved contextual neural lemmatization. *arXiv preprint arXiv:1904.02306*.

Arya D. McCarthy, Miikka Silfverberg, Ryan Cotterell, Mans Hulden, and David Yarowsky. 2018. Marrying Universal Dependencies and Universal Morphology. In *Proceedings of the Second Workshop on Universal Dependencies (UDW 2018)*, pages 91–101, Brussels, Belgium. Association for Computational Linguistics.

Arya D. McCarthy, Ekaterina Vylomova, Shijie Wu, Chaitanya Malaviya, Lawrence Wolf-Sonkin, Garrett Nicolai, Christo Kirov, Miikka Silfverberg, Sebastian Mielke, Jeffrey Heinz, Ryan Cotterell, and Mans Hulden. 2019. The SIGMORPHON 2019 shared task: Crosslinguality and context in morphology. In *Proceedings of the 16th SIGMORPHON Workshop on Computational Research in Phonetics, Phonology, and Morphology*, Florence, Italy. Association for Computational Linguistics.

Hwee Tou Ng, Siew Mei Wu, Ted Briscoe, Christian Hadiwinoto, Raymond Hendy Susanto, and Christopher Bryant. 2014. The conll-2014 shared task on grammatical error correction. In *Proceedings of the Eighteenth Conference on Computational Natural Language Learning: Shared Task*, pages 1–14.

Joakim Nivre, Mitchell Abrams, Željko Agić, Lars Ahrenberg, Lene Antonsen, Katya Aplonova, Maria Jesus Aranzabe, Gashaw Arutie, Masayuki Asahara, Luma Ateyah, Mohammed Attia, Aitziber Atutxa, Liesbeth Augustinus, Elena Badmaeva, Miguel Ballesteros, Esha Banerjee, Sebastian Bank, Verginica Barbu Mititelu, Victoria Basmov, John Bauer, Sandra Bellato, Kepa Bengoetxea, Yevgeni Berzak, Irshad Ahmad Bhat, Riyaz Ahmad Bhat, Erica Biagetti, Eckhard Bick, Rogier Blokland, Victoria Bobicev, Carl Börstell, Cristina Bosco, Gosse Bouma, Sam Bowman, Adriane Boyd, Aljoscha Burchardt, Marie Candito, Bernard Caron, Gauthier Caron, Gülsen Cebiroğlu Eryiğit, Flavio Massimiliano Cecchini, Giuseppe G. A. Celano, Slavomír Čéplö, Savas Cetin, Fabricio Chalub, Jinho Choi, Yongseok Cho, Jayeol Chun, Silvie Cinková, Aurélie Collomb, Çağrı Çöltekin, Miriam Connor, Marine Courtin, Elizabeth Davidson, Marie-Catherine de Marneffe, Valeria de Paiva, Arantza Diaz de Ilarraza, Carly Dickerson, Peter Dirix, Kaja Dobrovoljc, Timothy Dozat, Kira Droganova, Puneet Dwivedi, Marhaba Eli, Ali Elkahky, Binyam Ephrem, Tomaž Erjavec, Aline Etienne, Richárd Farkas, Hector Fernandez Alcalde, Jennifer Foster, Cláudia Freitas, Katarína Gajdošová, Daniel Galbraith, Marcos Garcia, Moa Gärdenfors, Sebastian Garza, Kim Gerdes, Filip Ginter, Iakes Goenaga, Koldo Gojenola, Memduh Gökırmak, Yoav Goldberg, Xavier Gómez Guinovart, Berta Gonzáles Saavedra, Matias Grioni, Normunds Grūzītis, Bruno Guillaume, Céline Guillot-Barbance, Nizar Habash, Jan Hajič, Jan Hajič jr., Linh Hà Mỹ, Na-Rae Han, Kim Harris, Dag Haug, Barbora Hladká, Jaroslava Hlaváčová, Florinel Hociung, Petter Hohle, Jena Hwang, Radu Ion, Elena Irimia, Ọlájídé Ishola, Tomáš Jelínek, Anders Johannsen, Fredrik Jørgensen, Hüner Kasıkara, Sylvain Kahane, Hiroshi Kanayama, Jenna Kanerva, Boris Katz, Tolga Kayadelen, Jessica Kenney, Václava Kettnerová, Jesse Kirchner, Kamil Kopacewicz, Natalia Kotsyba, Simon Krek, Sookyoung Kwak, Veronika Laippala, Lorenzo Lambertino, Lucia Lam, Tatiana Lando, Septina Dian Larasati, Alexei Lavrentiev, John Lee, Phng Lê H`ông, Alessandro Lenci, Saran Lertpradit, Herman Leung, Cheuk Ying Li, Josie Li, Keying Li, KyungTae Lim, Nikola Ljubešić, Olga Loginova, Olga Lyashevskaya, Teresa Lynn, Vivien Macketanz, Aibek Makazhanov, Michael Mandl, Christopher Manning, Ruli Manurung, Cătălina Mărănduc, David Mareček, Katrin Marheinecke, Héctor Martínez Alonso, André Martins, Jan Mašek, Yuji Matsumoto, Ryan McDonald, Gustavo Mendonca, Niko Miekka, Margarita Misirpashayeva, Anna Missilä, Cătălin Mititelu, Yusuke Miyao, Simonetta Montemagni, Amir More, Laura Moreno Romero, Keiko Sophie Mori, Shinsuke Mori, Bjartur Mortensen, Bohdan Moskalevskyi, Kadri Muischnek, Yugo Murawaki, Kaili Müürisep, Pinkey Nainwani, Juan Ignacio Navarro Horñiacek, Anna Nedoluzhko, Gunta Nešpore-Bērzkalne, Lng Nguy~ên Thị, Huy`ên Nguy~ên Thị Minh, Vitaly Nikolaev, Rattima Nitisaroj, Hanna Nurmi, Stina Ojala, Adédayọ Olúòkun, Mai Omura, Petya Osenova, Robert Östling, Lilja Øvrelid, Niko Partanen, Elena Pascual, Marco Passarotti, Agnieszka Patejuk, Guilherme Paulino-Passos, Siyao Peng, Cenel-Augusto Perez, Guy Perrier, Slav Petrov, Jussi Piitulainen, Emily Pitler, Barbara Plank, Thierry Poibeau, Martin Popel, Lauma Pretkalnina, Sophie Prévost, Prokopis Prokopidis, Adam Przepiórkowski, Tiina Puolakainen, Sampo Pyysalo, Andriela Rääbis, Alexandre Rademaker, Loganathan Ramasamy, Taraka Rama, Carlos Ramisch, Vinit Ravishankar, Livy Real, Siva Reddy, Georg Rehm, Michael Rießler, Larissa Rinaldi, Laura Rituma, Luisa Rocha, Mykhailo Romanenko, Rudolf Rosa, Davide Rovati, Valentin Roca, Olga Rudina, Jack Rueter, Shoval Sadde, Benoît Sagot, Shadi Saleh, Tanja Samardžić, Stephanie Samson, Manuela Sanguinetti, Baiba Saulīte, Yanin Sawanakunanon, Nathan Schneider, Sebastian Schuster, Djamé Seddah, Wolfgang Seeker, Mojgan Seraji, Mo Shen, Atsuko Shimada, Muh Shohibussirri, Dmitry Sichinava, Natalia Silveira, Maria Simi, Radu Simionescu, Katalin Simkó, Mária Šimková, Kiril Simov, Aaron Smith, Isabela Soares-Bastos, Carolyn Spadine, Antonio Stella, Milan Straka, Jana Strnadová, Alane Suhr, Umut Sulubacak, Zsolt Szántó, Dima Taji, Yuta Takahashi, Takaaki Tanaka, Isabelle Tellier, Trond Trosterud, Anna Trukhina, Reut Tsarfaty, Francis Tyers, Sumire Uematsu, Zdeňka Urešová, Larraitz Uria, Hans Uszkoreit, Sowmya Vajjala, Daniel van Niekerk, Gertjan van Noord, Viktor Varga, Eric Villemonte de la Clergerie, Veronika Vincze, Lars Wallin, Jing Xian Wang, Jonathan North Washington, Seyi Williams, Mats Wirén, Tsegay Woldemariam, Tak-sum Wong, Chunxiao Yan, Marat M. Yavrumyan, Zhuoran Yu, Zdeněk Žabokrtský, Amir Zeldes, Daniel Zeman, Manying Zhang, and Hanzhi Zhu. 2018. Universal dependencies 2.3. LINDAT/CLARIN digital library at the Institute of Formal and Applied Linguistics (ÚFAL), Faculty of Mathematics and Physics, Charles University.

Matthew Peters, Mark Neumann, Mohit Iyyer, Matt Gardner, Christopher Clark, Kenton Lee, and Luke Zettlemoyer. 2018. Deep contextualized word representations. In *Proceedings of the 2018 Conference of the North American Chapter of the Association for Computational Linguistics: Human Language Technologies, Volume 1 (Long Papers)*, pages 2227–2237, New Orleans, Louisiana. Association for Computational Linguistics.

Barbara Plank, Anders Søgaard, and Yoav Goldberg. 2016. Multilingual part-of-speech tagging with bidirectional long short-term memory models and auxiliary loss. *arXiv preprint arXiv:1604.05529*.

Aaron Smith, Bernd Bohnet, Miryam de Lhoneux, Joakim Nivre, Yan Shao, and Sara Stymne. 2018. 82 treebanks, 34 models: Universal dependency parsing with multi-treebank models. In *Proceedings of the CoNLL 2018 Shared Task: Multilingual Parsing from Raw Text to Universal Dependencies*, pages 113–123, Brussels, Belgium. Association for Computational Linguistics.

Anders Søgaard and Yoav Goldberg. 2016. Deep multi-task learning with low level tasks supervised at lower layers. In *Proceedings of the 54th Annual Meeting of the Association for Computational Linguistics (Volume 2: Short Papers)*, volume 2, pages 231–235.

Ilya Sutskever, Oriol Vinyals, and Quoc V Le. 2014. Sequence to sequence learning with neural networks. In *Advances in neural information processing systems*, pages 3104–3112.

Shijie Wu, Pamela Shapiro, and Ryan Cotterell. 2018. Hard non-monotonic attention for character-level transduction. In *Proceedings of the 2018 Conference on Empirical Methods in Natural Language Processing*, pages 4425–4438, Brussels, Belgium. Association for Computational Linguistics.

Daniel Zeman, Jan Hajič, Martin Popel, Martin Potthast, Milan Straka, Filip Ginter, Joakim Nivre, and Slav Petrov. 2018. CoNLL 2018 shared task: Multilingual parsing from raw text to universal dependencies. In *Proceedings of the CoNLL 2018 Shared Task: Multilingual Parsing from Raw Text to Universal Dependencies*, pages 1–21, Brussels, Belgium. Association for Computational Linguistics.

A Matching of Datasets

Src Data	Additional	Emb. type	Src Data	Additional	Emb. type
af_afribooms	nl_alpino	poly	it_postwita	it_isdt	elmo
akk_pisandub	cs_pdt	elmo	it_pud	it_isdt	elmo
am_att			ja_gsd	ja_pud	elmo
ar_padt	ar_pud	elmo	ja_modern	ja_gsd	elmo
ar_pud	ar_padt	elmo	ja_pud	ja_gsd	elmo
be_hse	ru_syntagrus	poly	kmr_mg	es_gsd	poly
bg_btb	ru_syntagrus	elmo	ko_gsd	ko_kaist	elmo
bm_crb	cs_pdt	fast	ko_kaist	ko_gsd	elmo
br_keb	no_bokmaal	poly	ko_pud	ko_kaist	elmo
bxr_bdt	ru_syntagrus	fast	kpv_ikdp	ru_syntagrus	fast
ca_ancora	es_ancora	elmo	kpv_lattice	ru_syntagrus	fast
cop_scriptorium			la_ittb	la_proiel	elmo
cs_cac	cs_pdt	elmo	la_perseus	la_proiel	elmo
cs_cltt	cs_pdt	elmo	la_proiel	la_ittb	elmo
cs_fictree	cs_pdt	elmo	lt_hse	lv_lvtb	poly
cs_pdt	cs_cac	elmo	lv_lvtb	hr_set	elmo
cs_pud	cs_pdt	elmo	mr_ufal	hi_hdtb	poly
cu_proiel	ru_syntagrus	elmo	nl_alpino	nl_lassysmall	elmo
da_ddt	no_bokmaal	elmo	nl_lassysmall	nl_alpino	elmo
de_gsd	fr_gsd	elmo	no_bokmaal	no_nynorsk	elmo
el_gdt	grc_proiel	elmo	no_nynorsk	no_bokmaal	elmo
en_ewt	en_gum	elmo	no_nynorsklia	no_nynorsk	elmo
en_gum	en_ewt	elmo	pcm_nsc	en_ewt	elmo
en_lines	en_ewt	elmo	pl_lfg	pl_sz	elmo
en_partut	en_ewt	elmo	pl_sz	pl_lfg	elmo
en_pud	en_ewt	elmo	pt_bosque	pt_gsd	elmo
es_ancora	es_gsd	elmo	pt_gsd	pt_bosque	elmo
es_gsd	es_ancora	elmo	ro_nonstandard	ro_rrt	elmo
et_edt	cs_pdt	elmo	ro_rrt	ro_nonstandard	elmo
eu_bdt	es_ancora	elmo	ru_gsd	ru_syntagrus	elmo
fa_seraji	ur_udtb	elmo	ru_pud	ru_syntagrus	elmo
fi_ftb	fi_tdt	elmo	ru_syntagrus	ru_gsd	elmo
fi_pud	fi_tdt	elmo	ru_taiga	ru_syntagrus	elmo
fi_tdt	fi_ftb	elmo	sa_ufal	hi_hdtb	poly
fo_oft	no_nynorsk	poly	sk_snk	cs_pdt	elmo
fr_gsd	fr_sequoia	elmo	sl_ssj	hr_set	elmo
fr_partut	fr_gsd	elmo	sl_sst	sl_ssj	elmo
fr_sequoia	fr_gsd	elmo	sme_giella	no_nynorsk	poly
fr_spoken	fr_gsd	elmo	sr_set	hr_set	poly
ga_idt	cs_pdt	elmo	sv_lines	sv_talbanken	elmo
gl_ctg	es_ancora	elmo	sv_pud	sv_talbanken	elmo
gl_treegal	gl_ctg	elmo	sv_talbanken	sv_lines	elmo
got_proiel	no_nynorsk	none	ta_ttb		
grc_perseus	grc_proiel	elmo	tl_trg	es_gsd	poly
grc_proiel	grc_perseus	elmo	tr_imst	tr_pud	elmo
he_htb	ru_gsd	elmo	tr_pud	tr_imst	elmo
hi_hdtb	mr_ufal	poly	uk_iu	ru_syntagrus	elmo
hr_set	sr_set	poly	ur_udtb	fa_seraji	elmo
hsb_ufal	cs_pdt	poly	vi_vtb	en_ewt	elmo
hu_szeged	et_edt	elmo	yo_ytb	es_gsd	poly
hy_armtdp	ru_pud	poly	yue_hk	zh_gsd	poly
id_gsd	es_gsd	elmo	zh_cfl	zh_gsd	elmo
it_isdt	it_partut	elmo	zh_gsd	ja_gsd	elmo
it_partut	it_isdt	elmo			

Table 8: This shows for each dataset, with which dataset it has the highest word overlap, and what their best common embeddings type is. Three datasets could not be paired, as they had 0% overlap with all other datasets (ignoring punctuation and numericals).

B   External Embeddings per Dataset

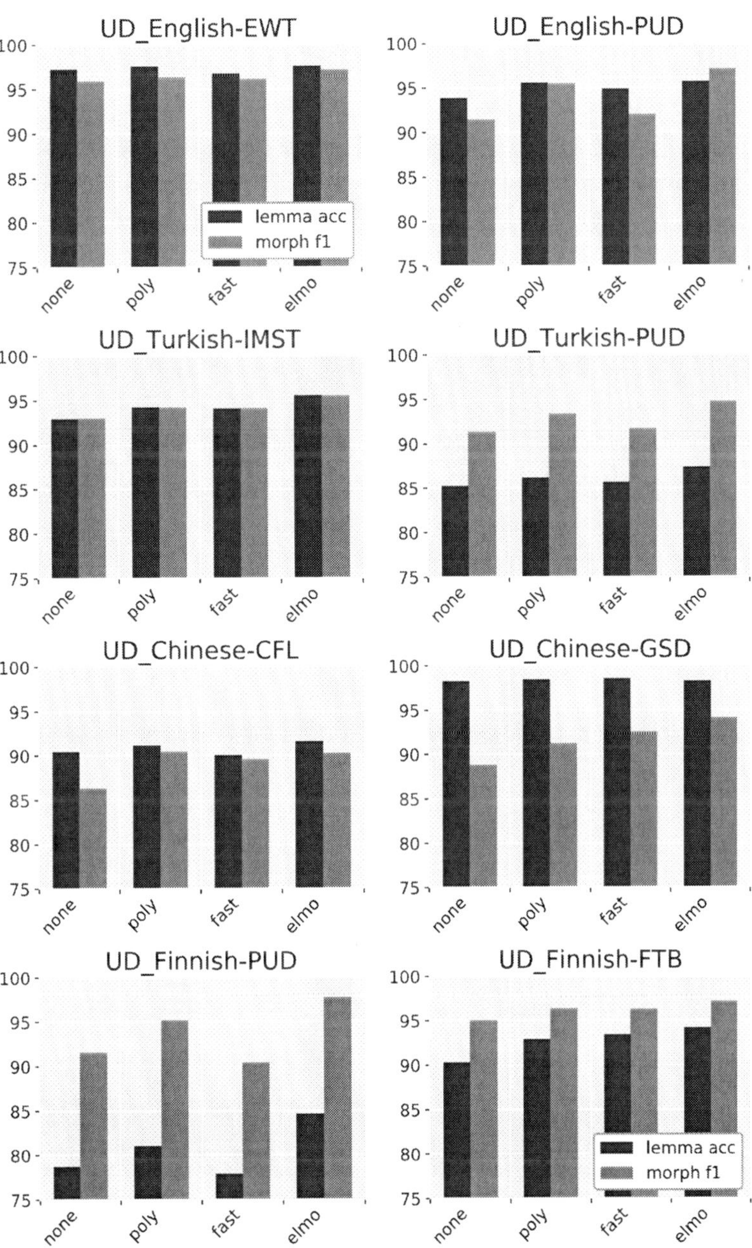

Figure 6: Results of different types of embeddings on the development splits of our tune datasets.

C Dataset Embeddings per Dataset

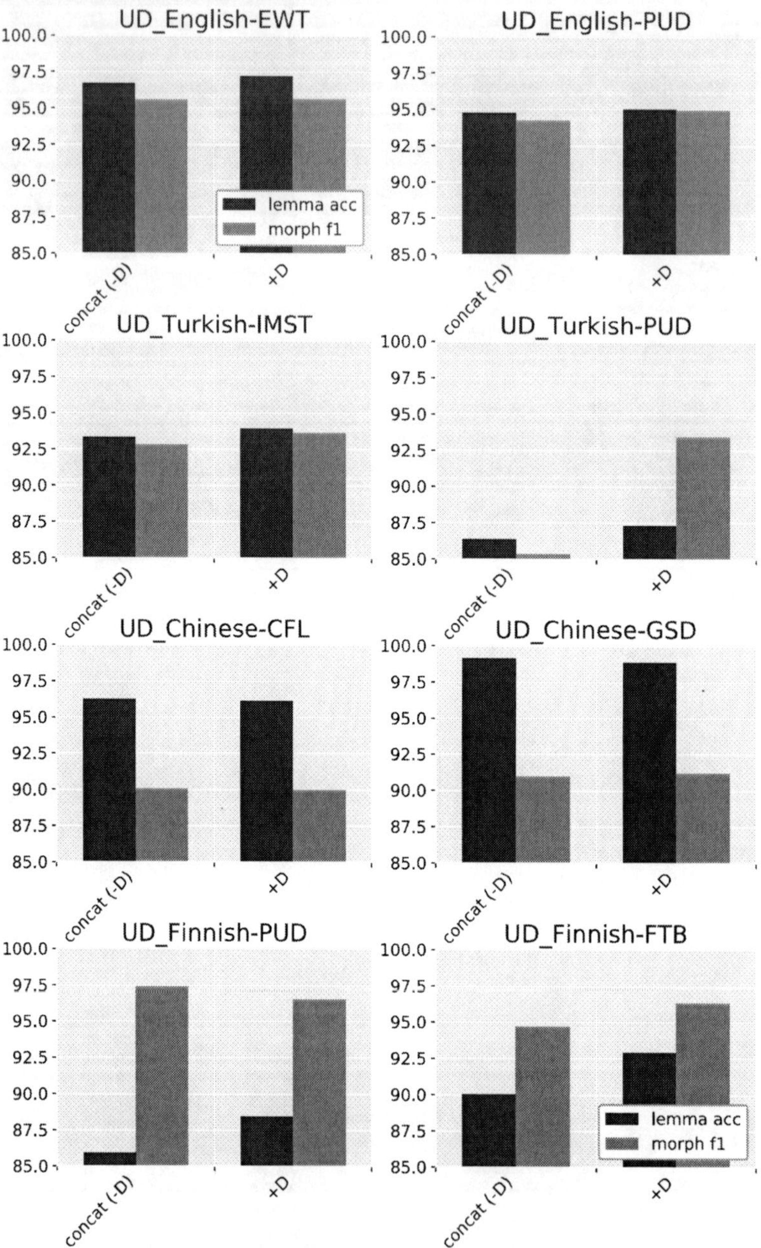

Figure 7: Results of dataset embeddings on the development splits of our tune datasets. We compare the dataset embeddings with a simple concatenation of the datasets.

D Results of External and Treebank Embeddings on Development Data

Dataset	Base	-E-D	-E+D	+E-D	+E+D	Lem	Mor	Dataset	Base	-E-D	-E+D	+E-D	+E+D	Lem	Mor
af_afribooms	95.48	95.14	95.95	96.63	**97.03**	96.49	97.57	it_postwita	92.19	95.12	0.00	**96.19**	0.00	95.24	97.14
akk_pisandub	74.76	63.65	**64.76**	59.64	63.07	46.67	82.85	it_pud	94.14	94.06	**97.02**	90.29	96.80	97.25	96.79
am_att	93.53	**95.51**	0.00	93.77	0.00	98.90	92.12	ja_gsd	93.98	96.96	97.27	98.08	**98.21**	98.91	97.52
ar_padt	93.40	93.74	90.05	93.93	**95.92**	94.90	96.94	ja_modern	94.26	94.61	**96.55**	94.19	96.47	96.45	96.65
ar_pud	86.58	84.28	76.56	88.02	**88.65**	82.70	94.60	ja_pud	92.91	95.16	98.34	97.02	**99.02**	99.46	98.59
be_hse	84.82	80.69	88.10	81.32	**89.13**	87.48	90.78	kmr_mg	89.17	87.36	0.00	**87.81**	0.00	88.57	87.06
bg_btb	95.57	97.43	0.00	**97.97**	0.00	97.15	98.79	ko_gsd	89.38	91.49	0.00	**92.82**	0.00	90.45	95.19
bm_crb	88.86	91.34	0.00	**91.50**	0.00	88.70	94.30	ko_kaist	91.99	94.89	0.00	**95.57**	0.00	94.69	96.45
br_keb	91.00	86.51	0.00	89.14	**91.39**	91.49	91.29	ko_pud	93.89	94.02	96.57	96.32	**97.55**	98.80	96.30
bxr_bdt	83.66	83.46	86.34	84.33	**86.36**	86.83	85.89	kpv_ikdp	67.44	61.19	**73.16**	60.82	72.83	71.08	75.24
ca_ancora	96.91	98.43	0.00	**99.08**	0.00	99.11	99.06	kpv_lattice	75.14	63.65	74.16	62.89	**76.29**	78.57	74.01
cop_scriptorium	94.53	**95.53**	0.00	94.54	0.00	95.12	95.94	la_ittb	95.85	97.89	0.00	**98.17**	0.00	98.39	97.94
cs_cac	95.86	97.31	0.00	**98.30**	0.00	98.34	98.26	la_perseus	83.11	82.97	89.34	87.26	**91.25**	90.80	91.70
cs_cltt	95.53	94.32	97.20	93.19	**97.67**	97.82	97.51	la_proiel	94.03	95.05	0.00	**96.74**	0.00	96.88	96.59
cs_fictree	94.10	96.09	0.00	**97.85**	0.00	97.99	97.72	lt_hse	76.09	70.49	74.93	76.93	**81.48**	80.69	82.27
cs_pdt	95.26	96.96	0.00	**98.00**	0.00	98.02	97.98	lv_lvtb	92.38	93.88	0.00	95.67	**95.70**	94.73	96.67
cs_pud	89.85	88.22	96.04	94.17	**96.94**	97.05	96.83	mr_ufal	76.22	74.79	76.64	74.80	**77.87**	76.71	79.02
cu_proiel	93.47	**94.94**	0.00	94.78	0.00	95.00	94.87	nl_alpino	94.25	95.77	0.00	**96.17**	0.00	96.35	95.99
da_ddt	93.74	91.53	95.66	97.19	**97.35**	97.01	97.68	nl_lassysmall	92.62	**95.05**	0.00	94.19	0.00	95.16	94.95
de_gsd	0.00	93.59	94.35	**94.44**	0.00	95.23	93.64	no_bokmaal	95.53	97.45	0.00	**97.62**	0.00	97.91	97.32
el_gdt	95.23	95.83	95.36	95.76	**96.00**	94.50	97.50	no_nynorsk	0.00	**97.23**	0.00	96.26	0.00	97.34	97.13
en_ewt	93.99	94.49	96.41	97.66	**97.78**	98.26	97.29	no_nynorsklia	91.80	95.52	95.25	95.61	**96.99**	97.79	96.18
en_gum	93.74	92.04	96.04	93.90	**97.53**	97.80	97.26	pcm_nsc	89.24	95.87	96.10	95.86	**96.17**	100.00	92.35
en_lines	94.61	96.24	0.00	**97.60**	0.00	98.01	97.20	pl_lfg	92.07	95.56	95.66	96.82	**97.43**	97.03	97.84
en_partut	93.33	95.15	96.05	96.11	**97.24**	98.24	96.25	pl_sz	91.10	93.78	95.00	96.15	**97.09**	97.37	96.80
en_pud	91.62	92.70	95.00	96.23	**97.07**	97.20	96.94	pt_bosque	94.88	97.08	0.00	**97.91**	0.00	98.32	97.50
es_ancora	96.87	98.27	98.38	**98.89**	0.00	98.96	98.83	pt_gsd	0.00	97.44	0.00	**98.14**	0.00	97.94	98.35
es_gsd	0.00	97.62	**98.14**	98.13	0.00	98.68	97.59	ro_nonstandard	93.62	95.73	**96.20**	96.11	0.00	96.32	96.09
et_edt	93.31	94.50	0.00	**96.20**	0.00	94.99	97.42	ro_rrt	95.56	97.39	97.46	**98.20**	0.00	98.23	98.16
eu_bdt	91.94	94.76	0.00	**95.80**	0.00	96.03	95.57	ru_gsd	55.99	94.85	0.00	**96.93**	0.00	97.10	96.75
fa_seraji	0.00	95.90	0.00	**96.61**	0.00	95.27	97.96	ru_pud	89.25	88.21	94.70	94.07	**95.94**	95.06	96.82
fi_ftb	92.27	94.23	94.65	**96.13**	0.00	94.81	97.45	ru_syntagrus	94.37	96.66	0.00	**97.25**	0.00	96.75	97.75
fi_pud	88.69	86.82	92.50	90.42	**93.12**	87.97	98.27	ru_taiga	85.09	85.38	92.94	91.17	**94.70**	94.28	95.13
fi_tdt	89.32	94.30	94.31	**95.56**	0.00	93.43	97.70	sa_ufal	68.45	61.87	64.32	62.96	**67.69**	63.92	71.46
fo_oft	88.93	88.18	**89.65**	87.98	89.28	88.11	91.19	sk_snk	92.44	93.12	0.00	**96.52**	0.00	96.20	96.85
fr_gsd	96.43	97.93	97.73	**98.30**	0.00	98.13	98.47	sl_ssj	92.97	95.59	0.00	**97.35**	0.00	97.60	97.09
fr_partut	94.09	94.62	96.89	96.54	**97.47**	97.10	97.83	sl_sst	89.78	89.19	94.26	93.20	**95.98**	96.89	95.06
fr_sequoia	95.59	96.64	97.98	**98.49**	0.00	98.43	98.54	sme_giella	89.69	89.60	87.56	88.27	**90.44**	88.32	92.56
fr_spoken	96.34	96.71	97.92	97.94	**98.63**	99.41	97.84	sr_set	93.82	95.64	0.00	**95.91**	0.00	95.84	95.98
ga_idt	86.92	84.13	0.00	**90.14**	0.00	89.15	91.13	sv_lines	93.54	93.97	95.07	**96.98**	0.00	96.90	97.07
gl_ctg	95.09	97.48	97.97	**98.15**	0.00	98.38	97.92	sv_pud	91.08	89.84	93.61	95.03	**95.68**	94.48	96.88
gl_treegal	92.77	93.38	95.64	**96.29**	94.91	96.03	96.55	sv_talbanken	0.00	96.13	95.95	**97.61**	0.00	96.85	98.38
got_proiel	94.19	**95.40**	0.00	95.00	0.00	95.63	95.17	ta_ttb	93.31	89.73	0.00	**91.46**	0.00	91.15	91.76
grc_perseus	0.00	93.48	0.00	**94.02**	0.00	92.46	95.57	tl_trg	68.66	73.36	70.36	69.13	**78.62**	76.00	81.25
grc_proiel	0.00	95.73	0.00	**97.06**	0.00	96.72	97.41	tr_imst	90.73	93.46	93.81	95.40	**95.43**	95.50	95.35
he_htb	94.31	95.82	96.55	**96.87**	0.00	96.47	97.27	tr_pud	87.86	88.63	90.39	90.83	**91.74**	87.96	95.52
hi_hdtb	96.36	97.43	97.55	**97.93**	97.71	98.53	97.32	uk_iu	91.39	92.41	94.06	**95.75**	0.00	95.24	96.25
hr_set	93.21	93.27	0.00	**95.25**	0.00	94.20	96.30	ur_udtb	92.12	92.85	0.00	**93.59**	0.00	95.61	91.57
hsb_ufal	84.64	82.83	82.98	84.67	**84.79**	86.28	83.31	vi_vtb	89.39	93.37	**94.48**	94.13	0.00	99.40	89.56
hu_szeged	91.06	91.65	91.03	90.94	**94.70**	93.42	95.98	yo_ytb	88.72	**92.41**	91.38	89.07	0.00	94.40	90.42
hy_armtdp	0.00	92.02	0.00	92.69	**93.08**	93.16	93.01	yue_hk	85.19	90.97	**94.10**	89.32	93.94	98.97	89.22
id_gsd	92.75	**96.05**	0.00	95.89	0.00	99.08	93.03	zh_cfl	85.31	89.34	93.05	91.33	**93.86**	96.26	91.46
it_isdt	95.73	**97.83**	97.62	97.12	97.80	97.63	98.02	zh_gsd	91.34	94.15	95.04	96.57	**96.79**	99.06	94.52
it_partut	95.36	95.59	**98.11**	97.84	97.73	97.85	98.37								

Table 9: Results on all development datasets. The average of lemma accuracy and morphological F1 score is used as main metric. base: baseline. E: external embeddings. D: dataset embeddings. Bold indicates which model is used on the test data. Lem: lemma accuracy of the bold model. Mor: morphologic tagging F1 score of bold model. A score of 0.00 means that we did not have time to run the model for this setting.

IT–IST at the SIGMORPHON 2019 Shared Task: Sparse Two-headed Models for Inflection

Ben Peters[†] and **André F.T. Martins**[†‡]

[†]Instituto de Telecomunicações, Lisbon, Portugal

[‡]Unbabel, Lisbon, Portugal

benzurdopeters@gmail.com, andre.martins@unbabel.com

Abstract

This paper presents the Instituto de Telecomunicações–Instituto Superior Técnico submission to Task 1 of the SIGMORPHON 2019 Shared Task. Our models combine sparse sequence-to-sequence models with a two-headed attention mechanism that learns separate attention distributions for the lemma and inflectional tags. Among submissions to Task 1, our models rank second and third. Despite the low data setting of the task (only 100 in-language training examples), they learn plausible inflection patterns and often concentrate all probability mass into a small set of hypotheses, making beam search exact.

1 Introduction

Morphological inflection is the task of producing an inflected form, given a lemma and a set of inflectional tags. A widespread approach to the task is the attention-based sequence-to-sequence model (*seq2seq*; Bahdanau et al., 2015; Kann and Schütze, 2016); such models perform well but are difficult to interpret. To mitigate this shortcoming, we employ an alternative architecture which combines sparse *seq2seq* modeling (Peters et al., 2019) with two-headed attention that attends separately to the lemma and inflectional tags (Ács, 2018). The attention and output distributions are computed with the sparsemax function and models are trained to minimize sparsemax loss (Martins and Astudillo, 2016). Sparsemax, unlike softmax, can assign exactly zero attention weight to irrelevant source tokens and exactly zero probability to implausible hypotheses. We apply our models to Task 1 at the SIGMORPHON 2019 Shared Task (McCarthy et al., 2019), which extends morphological inflection to a cross-lingual setting. We present two sparse *seq2seq* architectures:

- DOUBLEATTN (`it-ist-01-1`) is a reimplementation of the two-headed attention model (Ács, 2018) which substitutes sparsemax and its loss for softmax and cross entropy loss. It uses separate encoders and attention heads for the lemma and inflections, and concatenates the outputs of the attention heads.

- GATEDATTN (`it-ist-02-1`) replaces the attention concatenation with a sparse gate which interpolates the lemma and inflection attention. The intuition is that the lemma and inflectional tags are not likely to be equally important at all time steps. For example, in a suffixing language, the first several generated characters are likely to be identical to the lemma; inflectional tags are not relevant. The sparse gate allows the model to learn to shift focus between the two attentions while ignoring the other at a given time step.

GATEDATTN and DOUBLEATTN rank second and third, respectively, among submissions to Task 1. In addition, their behavior is highly interpretable: they mostly learn to attend to a single lemma hidden state at a time, progressing monotonically from left to right, while their inflection attention learns patterns which reflect underlying morphological structure. The sparse output layer often allows the model to concentrate all probability mass into a single hypothesis, providing a certificate that decoding is exact. Our analysis shows that sparsity is also highly predictive of performance on the shared task metrics, showing that the models "know what they know".

2 Models

Our architecture is mostly the same as a standard RNN-based *seq2seq* model with attention. In this section, we outline the changes needed to extend this model to use sparsemax and two-headed attention in a multilingual setting.

Proceedings of the 16th Workshop on Computational Research in Phonetics, Phonology, and Morphology, pages 50–56
Florence, Italy. August 2, 2019 ©2019 Association for Computational Linguistics

2.1 Sparsemax

Our models' sparsity comes from the sparsemax function (Martins and Astudillo, 2016), which computes the Euclidean projection of a vector $z \in \mathbb{R}^n$ onto the n–dimensional probability simplex $\triangle^n := \{p \in \mathbb{R}^n : p \geq 0, \mathbf{1}^\top p = 1\}$:

$$\text{sparsemax}(z) := \underset{p \in \triangle^n}{\text{argmin}} \|p - z\|^2 \quad (1)$$

Like softmax, sparsemax converts an arbitrary real-valued vector into a probability distribution. The critical difference is that sparsemax can assign exactly zero probability, whereas softmax is strictly positive. Sparsemax is differentiable almost everywhere and can be computed quickly, allowing its use as a drop-in replacement for softmax. It has previously been used in *seq2seq* for computing both attention weights (Malaviya et al., 2018) and output probabilities (Peters et al., 2019). Sparse attention is attractive in morphological inflection because it resembles hard attention, which has been successful on the task (Aharoni and Goldberg, 2017; Wu et al., 2018).

2.2 Encoder–Decoder Model

Multilingual embeddings Each encoder and decoder uses an embedding layer to convert one-hot token representations into dense embeddings. To account for the bilingual nature of Task 1, each of our embedding layers contains two look-up tables: one for the sequence of input tokens, and the other for the language of the sequence. At each time step, the current token's embedding is concatenated to a language embedding.[1] Each encoder and decoder uses a separate embedding layer; no weights are tied. Characters and inflectional tags use embeddings of size D_c, while language embeddings are of size D_ℓ. Thus the total embedding size is $D = D_c + D_\ell$.

Encoders The lemma and inflection encoders are both bidirectional LSTMs (Graves and Schmidhuber, 2005). An encoder's forward and backward hidden states are concatenated, forming a sequence of source hidden states. We set the size of these hidden states as D in all experiments.

Decoder The decoder is a unidirectional LSTM (Hochreiter and Schmidhuber, 1997) with input

feeding (Luong et al., 2015). At time step t, it computes a hidden state $s_t \in \mathbb{R}^D$. Conditioned on s_t and the hidden state sequences from the lemma and inflection encoders, a two-headed attention mechanism then computes an attentional hidden state $\tilde{s}_t \in \mathbb{R}^D$. The decoder LSTM is initialized only with the lemma encoder's state.

Attention head At time t, an attention head computes a context vector $c_t \in \mathbb{R}^D$ conditioned on the decoder state s_t and an encoder state sequence $H = [h_1, \ldots, h_J]$. A head consists of two modular components:

1. **Alignment** Compute a vector $a \in \mathbb{R}^J$ of alignment scores between s_t and H. We use the general attention scorer (Luong et al., 2015), which computes $a_j := s_t^\top W_a h_j$.

2. **Context** Compute the context vector c_t as a weighted sum of H: $c_t := \sum_{j=1}^J \pi_j h_j$, where $\pi = \text{sparsemax}(a)$ is a sparse vector of alignment scores in the simplex.

In Luong et al.'s single-headed attention, the attentional hidden state $\tilde{s}_t = \tanh(W_s[c_t; s_t])$ is computed by a concatenation layer from the context vector and pre-attention hidden state. However, our two-headed attention mechanism produces two context vectors and so must be computed differently. We use two different formulations, which we describe next.

DOUBLEATTN uses the same strategy for combining multiple context vectors as Ács (2018): the lemma and inflection context vectors u_t and v_t and the target hidden state s_t are inputs to a concatenation layer:

$$\tilde{s}_t = \tanh(W_d[u_t; v_t; s_t]) \quad (2)$$

where $W_d \in \mathbb{R}^{D \times 3D}$.

GATEDATTN, on the other hand, computes separate candidate attentional hidden states for the two context vectors:

$$\tilde{s}_{ut} = \tanh(W_u[u_t; s_t]) \quad (3)$$
$$\tilde{s}_{vt} = \tanh(W_v[v_t; s_t]) \quad (4)$$

where $W_u, W_v \in \mathbb{R}^{D \times 2D}$. We define gate weights $W_g \in \mathbb{R}^{2 \times 3D}$ and gate bias $b_g \in \mathbb{R}^2$ and

---

[1]The language embedding is the same at all time steps within an example; there is no code-switching in this task.

Model	Acc. ↑	Lev. Dist. ↓
DOUBLEATTN	48.999	1.2918
GATEDATTN	50.179	1.3209
Baseline (Wu and Cotterell, 2019)	48.549	1.3281

Table 1: Task 1 test results on the SIGMORPHON 2019 Shared Task, averaged across language pairs.

use a sparse gate to compute weights $p_t \in \triangle^2$ for the two candidate states:

$$p_t = \mathrm{sparsemax}(W_g[u_t; v_t; s_t] + b_g) \quad (5)$$

We then stack the two candidate states $\tilde{s}_{ut}$ and $\tilde{s}_{vt}$ into a matrix $\tilde{S}_t \in \mathbb{R}^{2 \times D}$ and use the gate weights to compute $\tilde{s}_t$ as a weighted sum of them:

$$\tilde{s}_t = p_t \tilde{S} \quad (6)$$

Just as a two-dimensional softmax is equivalent to a sigmoid, this two-dimensional sparsemax is a hard sigmoid, as was pointed out by Martins and Astudillo (2016). It provides extra interpretability in the form of a three-way answer about what is relevant at a time step: the lemma, the inflections, or both.

Sparse outputs After the attentional hidden state is computed, an output layer computes scores for each output type $z = W_z \tilde{s} + b_z$. These are then converted into a sparse probability distribution $p^\star = \mathrm{sparsemax}(z)$. The model is trained to minimize the sparsemax loss (Martins and Astudillo, 2016), defined as

$$\mathsf{L}_{\mathsf{sparsemax}}(y, z) := \frac{1}{2}(\|e_y - z\|^2 - \|p^\star - z\|^2) \quad (7)$$

where y is the index of the gold target and e_y is a one-hot vector. The sparsemax loss is differentiable, convex, and has a margin, and its gradient is sparse. Although softmax-based models use the cross entropy loss, this is not possible for our models because the cross entropy loss is infinite when the model assigns zero probability to the gold target.

3 Results

Our test results are shown in Table 1. Our two models ranked second and third among official submissions to Task 1.

Hyperparameter	Value
Character embedding size	180
Tag embedding size	180
Language embedding size	20
RNN size	200
Lemma encoder layers	2
Inflection encoder layers	$\{1, 2\}$
Dropout	$\{0.3, 0.4, 0.5\}$

Table 2: Hyperparameters for all models. Bracketed values were tuned individually for each language pair.

3.1 Experimental set-up

Each model was trained with early stopping for a maximum of 30 epochs with a batch size of 64. We used the Adam optimizer (Kingma and Ba, 2015) with a learning rate of 10^{-3}, which was halved when validation accuracy failed to improve for three consecutive epochs. We tuned the dropout and the number of inflection encoder layers on a separate grid for each language pair. Our hyperparameter ranges are shown in Table 2. At test time, we decoded with a beam size of 5. We oversampled the low resource training data 100 times and did not use synthetic data or filter the corpora. We implemented our models in PyTorch (Paszke et al., 2017) with a codebase derived from OpenNMT-py (Klein et al., 2017).[2]

Hyperparameters for Uzbek The Uzbek training set contains only 1060 examples, much smaller than the other high resource corpora, and initial results with Uzbek language pairs were poor. We improved performance by oversampling the Uzbek data 10 times (yielding roughly the same high-low balance as the other pairs) and reducing the initial learning rate to 10^{-4}.

4 Analysis

Next we interpret our models' behavior on a selection of language pairs from Task 1.

4.1 Sparse Attention

Table 3 shows the sparsity of our attention mechanisms, averaged across language families. The attention is extremely sparse, especially over the lemma: models attend to fewer than 1.1 lemma characters per target character on average. Sparsity is more varied between language families in the inflection attention. This may be explained by

---

Family	DOUBLEATTN		GATEDATTN			#Langs
	Lemma	Infl.	Lemma	Infl.	Total	
Afro-Asiatic	1.11	1.55	1.14	1.27	1.62	5
Baltic	1.02	1.33	1.02	1.34	1.54	1
Celtic	1.23	1.54	1.20	1.59	2.00	12
Dravidian	1.69	1.42	1.86	1.35	1.95	1
Germanic	1.05	1.56	1.05	1.39	1.61	17
Greek	1.15	1.52	1.18	1.62	2.11	1
Indo-Iranian	1.10	1.35	1.11	1.37	1.67	7
Murrinhpatha	1.16	1.28	1.15	1.35	1.71	1
Niger-Congo	1.07	1.30	1.04	1.09	1.11	1
NW Caucasian	1.02	1.08	1.02	1.20	1.25	2
Quechua	1.24	1.19	1.09	1.23	1.42	1
Romance	1.01	1.27	1.02	1.30	1.39	10
Slavic	1.08	1.31	1.07	1.35	1.55	9
Turkic	1.06	1.09	1.08	1.15	1.35	20
Uralic	1.03	1.21	1.04	1.31	1.48	12
Overall	1.09	1.33	1.09	1.33	1.56	100

Table 3: Average number of positions with nonzero attention per target time step on the Task 1 development sets, grouped by the family of the low resource language. For DOUBLEATTN, this is simply averaged over all target time steps. For GATEDATTN, the lemma attention nonzeros are summed only over time steps in which the gate is active for the lemma, and similarly for the inflection attention nonzeros. The 'Total' column for GATEDATTN indicates the average number of nonzeros over all time steps after accounting for the gate.

typological differences between languages, which we next analyze in detail.

Turkic languages are characterized by concatenative inflections (Bickel and Nichols, 2013b) which represent individual features (monoexponence; Bickel and Nichols, 2013a). Monoexponence should allow the inflection attention to concentrate on a single tag at a time, and Table 3 confirms that Turkic inflection attention is among the sparsest for both DOUBLEATTN and GATEDATTN models. The Azeri attention plot in Figure 1 illustrates that the inflection attention usually focuses on a single morpheme at a time, with some discrepancies at morpheme boundaries, where other tags may be relevant because of voicing assimilation rules. Furthermore, the sparse gate generally allows the model to focus on only one attention head at a time: in the Azeri example, there is only one position at which both attention heads are used. This position is the final consonant of the lemma, which appears to change because of a phonological environment created by the suffix. The shared task results suggest that sparse inflection attention is a good inductive bias for agglutinative languages: one of our models has the best

test accuracy among task submissions on 11 of 20 pairs where the low resource language is Turkic and 11 of 12 pairs in the typologically similar Uralic languages.

Germanic languages present different challenges, which may explain our models' less sparse inflection attention. Often several inflections are fused into a single affix; a familiar example is the German suffix *st*, which marks a verb as present tense, second person, and singular, but has no separable parts that represent these features individually. The North Frisian plot in Figure 1 demonstrates the less sparse nature of Germanic inflection attention. Producing "wulst" from the lemma "wel" requires both a suffix and a change to the lemma, and multiple inflectional tags are attended to at several time steps. The fusional nature of the morphology means there is not a clear alignment between the inflected sequence and the tags. This in reflected in the fact that at many time steps, DOUBLEATTN and GATEDATTN disagree about which tags to attend to. Unlike in the Turkic example, GATEDATTN's gate usually gives weight to both attention heads. This makes sense because the inflection requires a change to the lemma, not

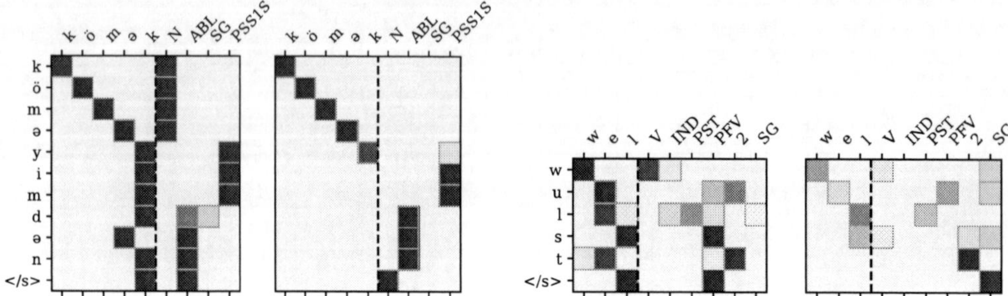

Figure 1: Pairs of attention plots for Azeri (left) and North Frisian (right) words with models trained on the Turkish–Azeri and Danish–North Frisian language pairs. Within each pair, the left plot comes from the DOUBLEATTN model and the right plot from GATEDATTN. Gray squares have zero attention weight. The dashed vertical line separates the lemma and inflection attention heads. Attention values in the GATEDATTN plots are scaled by gate weights, which is why there is no inflection attention for the first several positions of the Azeri word.

just a suffix that follows it.

4.2 Sparse Output Layer

Sparse output probabilities provide tools for analysis that are not available to softmax-based models: when no hypotheses are pruned, they provide a certificate that beam search is exact; when only one hypothesis is possible, this gives an indication of the model's certainty; and when probability is distributed among a small set of hypotheses, it is easy to reason about what phenomena continue to confuse the model.

Certainty When the probability distribution is completely concentrated at each time step, the model will be able to generate only one hypothesis, regardless of the beam width. When this happens for a particular input, the model can be said to be **certain** for that input. This also trivially guarantees that beam search is exact because no hypotheses have been pruned. As Figure 2 shows, certainty is a strong indication of performance. This suggests future work using certainty as a validation metric alternative to accuracy and loss.

Interpretable ambiguity Our Turkish–Azeri GATEDATTN model demonstrates that there is also useful information to be gleaned from the cases where the model produces multiple hypotheses. Of the 100 examples in the development set, GATEDATTN concentrated all probability mass into a single hypothesis for 79 of them, but the other 21 examples exhibit ambiguities that have linguistically plausible interpretations:

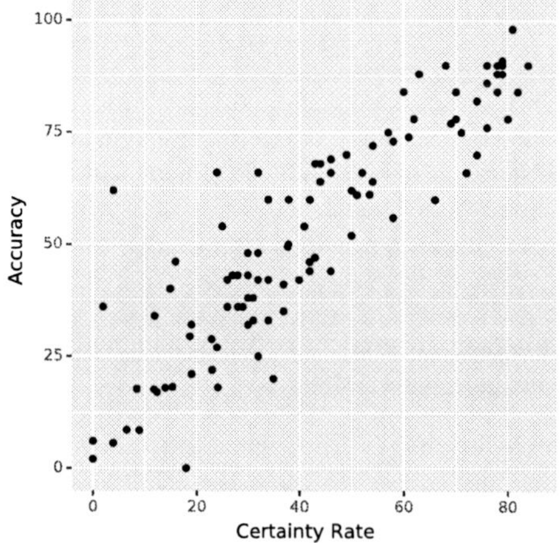

Figure 2: Percentage of inputs for which the selected GATEDATTN model concentrates all probability into a single hypothesis compared to the word-level accuracy on the development set. Each point is a language pair.

- **Consonant alternations** In 13 of the 21 examples, the hypotheses differ in their treatment of stop consonants, which have very similar phonological alternations in the two languages that are represented in orthography. The ambiguity is a sign that the model has not mastered Azeri phonological rules. Nine of the examples concern lemma-final "k" and "q", which have slightly different rules in Azeri than Turkish.[3]

---

[3]This judgment is based on inspection of the Azeri data and prior knowledge of Turkish.

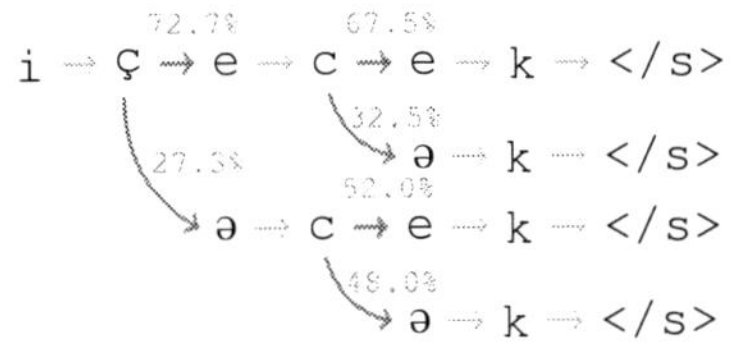

Figure 3: The Turkish–Azeri GATEDATTN model's full beam search for the Azeri lemma "içmek" and the tags V 3 SG FUT. All other sequences have zero probability. The correct form is "içəcək", while the model prefers "içecek", which would be correct with Turkish vowel harmony rules.

- **Vowel harmony** In two other examples, the model produced multiple guesses for the vowels in the future tense marker. One of these examples is shown in Figure 3. In both instances, Azeri vowel harmony rules would generate "ə" in the suffix, but the model instead produced "e", which is correct with Turkish vowel harmony. This shows the influence of the high resource language.

- **Other cases** The last six non-certain examples consist of a loanword with an unusual character sequence, two instances where one hypothesis has the wrong possessive suffix, and two where a hypothesis inserts or drops a character. The top prediction was nonetheless correct in all six.

This sort of analysis is not possible with traditional dense models because probability can never become concentrated in a small set of hypotheses and it is impossible to separate legitimate ambiguities from the long tail of implausible hypotheses.

Paradigm completion Figure 3 suggests that our models do a good job of concentrating probability in a small number of hypotheses. This raises the question of whether, by underspecifying the inflectional tags, the set of possible hypotheses in the beam can be made to resemble a lemma's complete paradigm. To investigate, we trained monolingual models with the English, German, and Turkish data from the high resource setting of Task 1 of the CoNLL–SIGMORPHON 2018 Shared Task (Cotterell et al., 2018). We used mostly the same hyperparameters as for this year's submission, except that there are no language embeddings, and the inflection tags are not used and the models have single-headed attention over the lemma sequences. We increased the beam width to 10 in order to accomodate the models' greater uncertainty. With English, this often works well: for the regular verb "jitter", the model's only possible hypotheses are "jittered", "jittering", "jitters", and "jitter", which is the complete paradigm. Irregular verbs often have a handful of other hypotheses, and sometimes the beam gives some probability to misspellings. Something similar can be seen in German, although the beam rarely contains all surface forms. For German nouns, the beam often shows uncertainty about plural formation: the hypotheses for "Nadelbaum" include "Nadelbaume", "Nadelbäume", and "Nadelbäumer", all of which are plausible German plurals. Turkish has very large paradigms, so in general it is not possible to fit all forms into a beam of any reasonable size. However, the hypotheses in the beam do typically correspond to correct forms.

5 Conclusion

We presented a new style of *seq2seq* model which brings together two-headed attention (Ács, 2018) and sparse modeling for morphological inflection (Peters et al., 2019). Our models learn sparse attention distributions in both attention heads. Their sparse probability distribution over hypotheses often allows beam search to become exact, while the remaining ambiguities often have a clear linguistic interpretation. The two versions of our model rank second and third among submissions to Task 1.

Acknowledgments

This work was supported by the European Research Council (ERC StG DeepSPIN 758969), and by the Fundação para a Ciência e Tecnologia through contracts UID/EEA/50008/2019 and CMUPERI/TIC/0046/2014 (GoLocal). We thank Gonçalo Correia, Aitor Egurtzegi, Erick Fonseca, Pedro Martins, Tsvetomila Mihaylova, Vlad Niculae, Marcos Treviso, and the anonymous reviewers, for helpful discussion and feedback.

References

Judit Ács. 2018. BME-HAS system for CoNLL–SIGMORPHON 2018 shared task: Universal morphological reinflection. *Proceedings of the CoNLL SIGMORPHON 2018 Shared Task: Universal Morphological Reinflection*, pages 121–126.

Roee Aharoni and Yoav Goldberg. 2017. Morphological inflection generation with hard monotonic attention. In *Proc. ACL*.

Dzmitry Bahdanau, Kyunghyun Cho, and Yoshua Bengio. 2015. Neural machine translation by jointly learning to align and translate. In *Proc. ICLR*.

Balthasar Bickel and Johanna Nichols. 2013a. Exponence of selected inflectional formatives. In Matthew S. Dryer and Martin Haspelmath, editors, *The World Atlas of Language Structures Online*. Max Planck Institute for Evolutionary Anthropology, Leipzig.

Balthasar Bickel and Johanna Nichols. 2013b. Fusion of selected inflectional formatives. In Matthew S. Dryer and Martin Haspelmath, editors, *The World Atlas of Language Structures Online*. Max Planck Institute for Evolutionary Anthropology, Leipzig.

Ryan Cotterell, Christo Kirov, John Sylak-Glassman, Gėraldine Walther, Ekaterina Vylomova, Arya D McCarthy, Katharina Kann, Sebastian Mielke, Garrett Nicolai, Miikka Silfverberg, David Yarowsky, Jason Eisner, and Mans Hulden. 2018. The CoNLL–SIGMORPHON 2018 shared task: Universal morphological reinflection. *Proc. CoNLL–SIGMORPHON*.

Alex Graves and Jürgen Schmidhuber. 2005. Framewise phoneme classification with bidirectional LSTM and other neural network architectures. *Neural Networks*, 18(5-6):602–610.

Sepp Hochreiter and Jürgen Schmidhuber. 1997. Long short-term memory. *Neural Computation*, 9(8):1735–1780.

Katharina Kann and Hinrich Schütze. 2016. Single-Model Encoder-Decoder with Explicit Morphological Representation for Reinflection. In *Proc. ACL*.

Diederik Kingma and Jimmy Ba. 2015. Adam: A method for stochastic optimization. In *Proc. ICLR*.

Guillaume Klein, Yoon Kim, Yuntian Deng, Jean Senellart, and Alexander M Rush. 2017. OpenNMT: Open-source toolkit for neural machine translation. *arXiv e-prints*.

Minh-Thang Luong, Hieu Pham, and Christopher D Manning. 2015. Effective approaches to attention-based neural machine translation. In *Proc. EMNLP*.

Chaitanya Malaviya, Pedro Ferreira, and André FT Martins. 2018. Sparse and constrained attention for neural machine translation. In *Proc. ACL*.

André FT Martins and Ramón Fernandez Astudillo. 2016. From softmax to sparsemax: A sparse model of attention and multi-label classification. In *Proc. of ICML*.

Arya D. McCarthy, Ekaterina Vylomova, Shijie Wu, Chaitanya Malaviya, Lawrence Wolf-Sonkin, Garrett Nicolai, Christo Kirov, Miikka Silfverberg, Sebastian Mielke, Jeffrey Heinz, Ryan Cotterell, and Mans Hulden. 2019. The SIGMORPHON 2019 shared task: Crosslinguality and context in morphology. In *Proceedings of the 16th SIGMORPHON Workshop on Computational Research in Phonetics, Phonology, and Morphology"*, Florence, Italy. Association for Computational Linguistics.

Adam Paszke, Sam Gross, Soumith Chintala, Gregory Chanan, Edward Yang, Zachary DeVito, Zeming Lin, Alban Desmaison, Luca Antiga, and Adam Lerer. 2017. Automatic differentiation in PyTorch. In *Proc. NeurIPS Autodiff Workshop*.

Ben Peters, Vlad Niculae, and André FT Martins. 2019. Sparse Sequence-to-Sequence Models. In *Proc. ACL*.

Shijie Wu and Ryan Cotterell. 2019. Exact Hard Monotonic Attention for Character-Level Transduction. *Proc. ACL*.

Shijie Wu, Pamela Shapiro, and Ryan Cotterell. 2018. Hard non-monotonic attention for character-level transduction. In *Proc. EMNLP*.

CMU-01 at the SIGMORPHON 2019 Shared Task on Crosslinguality and Context in Morphology

Aditi Chaudhary   Elizabeth Salesky   Gayatri Bhat
David R. Mortensen   Jaime G. Carbonell   Yulia Tsvetkov
{aschaudh, esalesky, gbhat, dmortens, jgc, ytsvetko}@cs.cmu.edu
Language Technologies Institute
Carnegie Mellon University

Abstract

This paper presents the submission by the CMU-01 team to the SIGMORPHON 2019 task 2 of Morphological Analysis and Lemmatization in Context. This task requires us to produce the lemma and morpho-syntactic description of each token in a sequence, for 107 treebanks. We approach this task with a hierarchical neural conditional random field (CRF) model which predicts each coarse-grained feature (eg. POS, Case, etc.) independently. However, most treebanks are under-resourced, thus making it challenging to train deep neural models for them. Hence, we propose a multi-lingual transfer training regime where we transfer from multiple related languages that share similar typology.[1]

1 Introduction

Morphological analysis (Hajic and Hladká, 1998; Oflazer and Kuruöz, 1994) is the task of predicting morpho-syntactic properties along with the lemma of each token in a sequence, with several downstream applications including machine translation (Vylomova et al., 2017), named entity recognition (Güngör et al., 2018) and semantic role labeling (Strubell et al., 2018). Advances in deep learning have enabled significant progress for the task of morphological tagging (Müller and Schuetze, 2015; Heigold et al., 2017) and lemmatization (Malaviya et al., 2019) under large amounts of annotated data. However, most languages are under-resourced and often exhibit diverse linguistic phenomena, thus making it challenging to generalize existing state-of-the-art models for all languages.

In order to tackle the issue of data scarcity, recent approaches have coupled deep learning with cross-lingual transfer learning (Malaviya et al., 2018; Cotterell and Heigold, 2017; Kondratyuk,

2019) and have shown promising results. Previous works (e.g., Cotterell and Heigold, 2017) combine the set of morphological properties into a single monolithic tag and employ multi-sequence classification. This runs the risk of data sparsity and exploding output space for morphologically rich languages. Malaviya et al. (2018) instead predict each coarse-grained feature, such as part-of-speech (POS) or Case, separately by modeling dependencies between these features and also between the labels across the sequence using a factorial conditional random field (CRF). However, this results in a large number of factors leading to a slower training time (over 24h).

To address the issues of both data sparsity and having a tractable computation time, we propose a hierarchical neural model which predicts each coarse-grained feature independently, but without modeling the pairwise interactions within them. This results in a time-efficient computation (5–6h) and substantially outperforms the baselines. To more explicitly incorporate syntactic knowledge, we embed POS information in an encoder which is shared with all feature decoders. To address the issue of data scarcity, we present two multi-lingual transfer approaches where we train on a group of typologically related languages and find that language-groups with shallower time-depths (i.e., period of time during which languages diverged to become independent) tend to benefit the most from transfer. We focus on the task of contextual morphological analysis and use the provided baseline model for the task of lemmatization (Malaviya et al., 2019).

This paper makes the following contributions:

1. We present a hierarchical neural model for contextual morphological analysis with a shared encoder and independent decoders for each coarse-grained feature. This provides us with the flexibility to produce any combination of features.

[1] The code is available at https://github.com/Aditi138/MorphologicalAnalysis/.

57

Proceedings of the 16th Workshop on Computational Research in Phonetics, Phonology, and Morphology, pages 57–70
Florence, Italy. August 2, 2019 ©2019 Association for Computational Linguistics

2. We analyze the dependencies among different morphological features to inform model choices, and find that adding POS information to the encoder significantly improves prediction accuracy by reducing errors across features, particularly Gender errors.

3. We evaluate our proposed approach on 107 treebanks and achieve +14.76 (accuracy) average improvement over the shared task baseline (McCarthy et al., 2019) for morphological analysis.

2 Contextual Morphological Analysis

In this section, we formally define the task (§2.1) and describe our proposed approach (§2.2).

2.1 Task Formulation

Formally, we define the task of contextual morphological analysis as a sequence tagging problem. Given a sequence of tokens $\mathbf{x} = x_1, x_2, \cdots, x_n$, the task is to predict the morphological tagset $\mathbf{y} = y_1, y_2, \cdots, y_n$ where the target label y_i for a token x_i constitutes the fine-grained morpho-syntactic traits $\{N;PL;NOM;FEM\}$.

2.2 Our Method

In line with Malaviya et al. (2018), we formulate morphological analysis as a feature-wise sequence prediction task, where we predict the fine-grained labels (e.g N, NOM, ...) for the corresponding coarse-grained features $F =\{POS,Case,...\}$ as shown in Figure 1. However, we only model the transition dependencies between the labels of a feature. This is done for two reasons: 1) As per Malaviya et al. (2018)'s analysis, the removal of pairwise dependencies led to only a -0.93 (avg.) decrease in the F1 score. We further observe in our experiments that our formulation performs better even without explicitly modeling pairwise dependencies; 2) The factorial CRF model gets computationally expensive to train with pairwise dependencies since loopy belief propagation is used for inference.

Therefore, we propose a feature-wise hierarchical neural CRF tagger (Lample et al., 2016; Ma and Hovy, 2016; Yang et al., 2016) with independent predictions for each coarse-grained feature for a given time-step, without explicitly modeling the pairwise dependencies.

2.2.1 Hierarchical Neural CRF model

The hierarchical neural CRF model comprises of two major components, an *encoder* which combines character and word-level features into a continuous representation and a multi-class multi-label *decoder*. Given an unlabeled sequence x, the *encoder* computes the context-sensitive hidden representations for each token x_i. These representations are shared across $|F|$ independent linear-chain CRFs for inference. We refer to this model as MDCRF.

Decoder: Our decoder comprises of $|F|$ independent feature-wise CRFs whose objective function is given as follows:

$$p(\mathbf{y}|\mathbf{x}) = \prod_{j=1}^{F} p_f(\mathbf{y_f}|\mathbf{x})$$

$$p_f(\mathbf{y_f}|\mathbf{x}) = \frac{\prod_{t=1}^{n} \psi_i(y_{f,t-1}, y_{f,t}, \mathbf{x}, t)}{Z(\mathbf{x})}$$

where $F = \{POS, Case, Gender,...\}$ is the set of coarse-grained features observed in the training dataset. $p_f(\mathbf{y_f}|\mathbf{x})$ is a feature-wise CRF tagger with $\psi_i(y_{t-1}, y_t, \mathbf{x}) = \exp(\mathbf{W_f}_{y_{f,t-1},y_{f,t}}^{T}\mathbf{x}_i + \mathbf{b_f}_{y_{f,t-1},y_{f,t}})$ being the energy function for each feature f. During inference the predictions from each feature-wise decoder is concatenated together to output the complete morphological analysis of the sequence x.

Encoder: We adopt a standard hierarchical sequence encoder which is shared among all the $|F|$ feature-wise decoders. It consists of a character-level bi-LSTM that computes hidden representations for each token in the sequence. These subword representations help in capturing information about morphological inflections. To further enforce this signal, we add a layer of self-attention (Vaswani et al., 2017) on top of the character-level bi-LSTM. Self-attention provides each character with a context from all the characters in the token. A bi-LSTM modeling layer is added on top of the self-attention layer which produces a token-level representation. These representations are then concatenated with a word embedding vector and fed to another bi-LSTM to produce context sensitive token representations which are then fed to all the $|F|$ CRFs for inference.

2.2.2 Adding Linguistic Knowledge

Part-of-speech (POS) is perhaps the most important coarse-grained feature. Not only is every token annotated for POS, but most other features depend on it. For instance, verbs do not have Case,

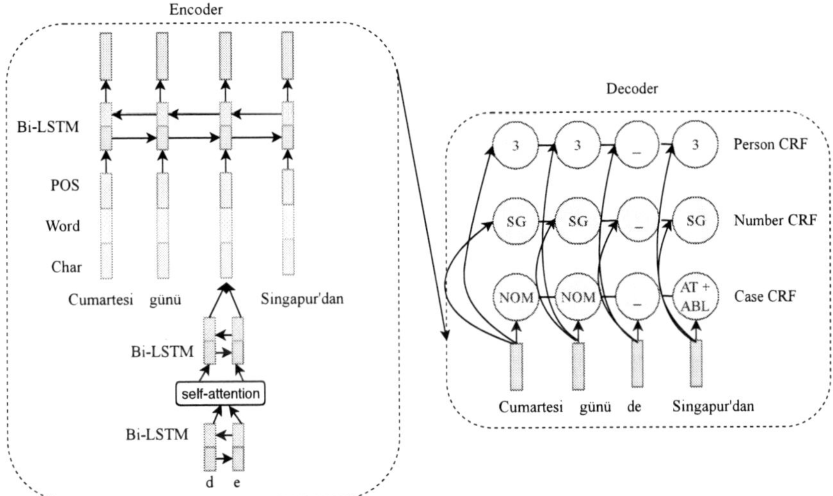

Figure 1: Hierarchical neural model for contextual morphological analysis with independent CRF decoders for each coarse-grained feature F. For the model MDCRF+POS, POS embeddings are concatenated to the word and char-level representations as depicted above. This model has $|F|$-1 decoders since POS tagger is run separately as a prior step. MDCRF refers to the above model without POS embeddings having all $|F|$ decoders.

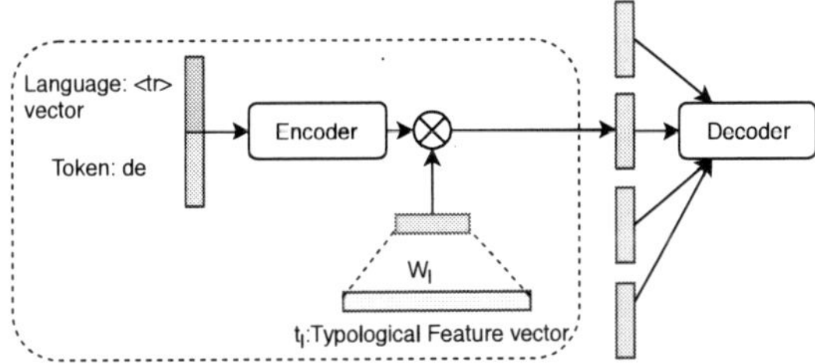

Figure 2: Polyglot model being used for the token "de" in Turkish, denoted by language vector <tr>.

nouns do not have Tense. In order to leverage these linguistic constraints, we incorporate POS information for each token into our shared encoder. We refer to this variant of the model as MDCRF+POS, as shown in Figure 1.

Since POS tags are not available as input, we first run a separate hierarchical neural CRF tagger for POS alone and use the model predictions as input to the MDCRF+POS. For each token, we encode its predicted POS tag into a continuous representation and concatenate it with the character and word-level token representations. Finally, these concatenated representations are fed to the word-level bi-LSTM and inference is performed using $|F|$-1 decoders, excluding the POS decoder. Going forward, we use this model architecture for all our experiments unless otherwise noted.

2.2.3 Multi-lingual Transfer

So far, we have described our model architecture for a monolingual setting. However, the performance of neural models is highly dependent on the availability of large amounts of annotated data, making it challenging to generalize to low-resource languages. Cross-lingual transfer learning attempts to alleviate this challenge by transferring knowledge from high-resource languages. Prior work (Cotterell and Heigold, 2017; Malaviya et al., 2018; Buys and Botha, 2016) has shown the benefits of cross-lingual transfer for morphological tagging. Malaviya et al. (2018) restrict to transferring from one language, whereas Cotterell and Heigold (2017) show that multi-source transfer performs better than single-source. Inspired by this, we experiment with two approaches for multi-lingual transfer learning.

MULTI-SOURCE: In this method, we augment the training data from related languages with the target language data. Similar to Cotterell and Heigold (2017), we perform a hard clustering of languages based on the typological and orthographic similarity of the source languages with the target language. For instance, we construct a language cluster Indo-Aryan, which comprises of all the languages in the dataset that belong to the Indo-Aryan language family which are Hindi, Marathi and Sanskrit. For some larger language families such as Germanic and Slavic, we construct language clusters from a subset of languages. For instance, the North-Germanic language cluster comprises of treebanks from German, Norwegian, Swedish and Danish. Some languages such as Urdu, Tamil are the only representative languages of their respective language families in the dataset. For these languages, we create a cluster with the next closest language with respect to typology or orthography. For Urdu, we add Hindi because of typological similarity. For other such isolates, we add Turkish because of its extensive agglutination. A total of 24 language clusters were defined based on the literature and with help from a linguist, the details of which can be seen in the Appendix Section §6.

Given a language cluster, all the training data from each language within it is first concatenated together. Then, for each language we concatenate the language embedding vector with the token representation in the encoder by adding the language id <LANG ID> at the beginning and end of each sequence. Given a sequence x, the encoder produces contextualized hidden representation h_i for each token x_i:

$$h_i = W_{encoder}(e_i, c_i, p_i, l_i)$$

where e_i is the word embedding vector, c_i is the character-level representation, p_i is the POS embedding and l_i is the language embedding vector. This is done to help the model disambiguate languages as often same tokens have different morpho-syntactic description across languages. For example, the token " तो " is a part of both Hindi and Marathi vocabulary. In Hindi it denotes a CONJ whereas in Marathi it is a pronoun with the following description: 3;MASC;PRO;NOM;SG.

POLYGLOT: Languages are often related to multiple languages along different dimensions. For instance, Swedish is lexically similar to German, but it is morpho-syntactically closer to English. To enable a model to utilize these relationships, we feed explicit typological information to the encoder, drawing inspiration from the polyglot model proposed by Tsvetkov et al. (2016). In this multilingual model, we first concatenate all the training data from the source languages, similar to the MULTI-SOURCE setting and compute h_i for each token. Then context vector h_i is factored by the typology feature vector t_l to integrate these

manually defined features as follows:

$$f_l = \tanh(W_l t_l + b_l)$$

$$g_i^l = h_i \otimes f_l^T$$

where W_l, b_l are language-specific parameters which project the typology vector into a low-dimensional space. Finally, g_i^l computes the global-context language matrix which is vectorized into a column vector and fed to the decoder, as shown in Figure 2.

Tsvetkov et al. (2016) derive their typology vectors from the URIEL database (Littell et al., 2017). We consider a subset of these typology features which are most relevant to the task of morpho-syntactic analysis and obtain 18 Syntax-WALS features.[2] However, we observed that for most language clusters, these typology feature values within a cluster were not discriminating, which defeats the purpose of using POLYGLOT for disambiguating languages across typological dimensions. Therefore, we construct custom typological vector per each language cluster based on the training data global statistics.

For every coarse-grained feature, this constructed vector contains the proportion of words in the training data that are annotated with that feature. We also experiment with calculating these proportions separately for words for each POS label (N, V, ...). Given the importance of POS, we also include the number of fine-grained POS labels that the most frequent coarse-grained features (Gender, Number, Person, Case) can take. This results in bi-gram features such as N-FEM, N-NOM, N-SG. We remove features which do not occur within a given cluster to avoid sparse features. Table 1 shows a portion of the example vector constructed for the Indo-Aryan cluster. From the table we can see that, some features such as ADJ-Gender-FEM and V-Person-1 are present in all the three languages within the cluster. Whereas some features such as ADJ-Gender-NEUT is absent from Hindi because Hindi only has two genders which are MASC and FEM.

---

[2]S-SVO, S-SOV, S-VSO, S-VOS, S-OVS, S-OSV, S-SUBJECT-BEFORE-VERB, S-SUBJECT-AFTER-VERB, S-OBJECT-AFTER-VERB, S-OBJECT-BEFORE-VERB, S-SUBJECT-BEFORE-OBJECT, S-SUBJECT-AFTER-OBJECT,S-ADPOSITION-BEFORE-NOUN, S-ADPOSITION-AFTER-NOUN, S-POSSESSOR-BEFORE-NOUN, S-POSSESSOR-AFTER-NOUN, S-ADJECTIVE-BEFORE-NOUN, S-ADJECTIVE-AFTER-NOUN

Feature	Hindi	Marathi	Sanskrit
ADJ-Gender-FEM	0.054	0.144	0.080
V-Person-1	0.004	0.037	0.0736
ADJ-Gender-NEUT	0.0	0.144	0.159
ADJ-Case-DAT/GEN	0.0002	0.0	0.0

Table 1: Example of manually constructed typology features for the Indo-Aryan cluster.

Training Regime: For both the multi-lingual transfer methods, we train one model per language cluster and fine-tune this model for each individual language. which saves time and compute for training 107 individual models from scratch. Furthermore, since a language cluster can have multiple high-resource languages, we take *min (5000, #training data-points)* for each language to have a tractable training time. We up-sample the low-resource languages to match the number of training data-points of the high-resource languages.

3 Contextual Lemmatization

We use the neural model from Malaviya et al. (2019) for contextual lemmatization. This is a neural sequence-to-sequence model with hard attention, which takes both the inflected form and morphological tag set for a token as input and produces a lemma, both at the character level. The decoder uses the concatenation of the previous character and the tag set to produce the next character in the lemma. The lemmatization model is jointly trained with an LSTM-based tagger using jackknifing to reduce exposure bias in training: Malaviya et al. (2019) report significantly lower lemmatization results training with gold tags and using predicted tags only at test time. We use their tagger for training and our contextual morphological analysis models' predicted tags at evaluation time. This model served as the baseline lemmatizer for Task 2; we refer readers to the shared task paper for model details (McCarthy et al., 2019).

4 Experiments

We conduct the following experiments: We compare our multi-lingual transfer approach with the baselines Malaviya et al. (2018) and Cotterell and Heigold (2017) under the same experimental settings. Next, we compare our approach with the shared task baseline (McCarthy et al., 2019). Finally, we analyze the contributions of different components of our proposed method.

Baselines: Cotterell and Heigold (2017) formulate this task as a sequence prediction problem with the output space being the set of all possible tagsets seen in the training data. Specifically, they construct a neural network based multi-class classifier where each tagset {*N;PL;NOM;FEM*} forms a class. Since the output space is only restricted to the tagsets seen in the training data, this method cannot generalize to unseen tagsets. Furthermore, for morphologically rich languages such as Russian or Turkish, the output space of the tagset is huge leading to sparse training data. (McCarthy et al., 2019) follow a similar approach.

To overcome these drawbacks Malaviya et al. (2018) consider a feature-wise model which predicts fine-grained labels for corresponding coarse categories {POS,Case,...}. Since morpho-syntactic properties are often correlated, they model these inter-dependencies using a factorial CRF and define two inter-dependencies: 1) a *pairwise* dependency, which models correlations between the morpho-syntactic properties within a token, and 2) a *transition* dependency, which models label correlations across all tokens in a sequence. Although this formulation provides the flexibility to produce any combination of tagsets, this model is computationally expensive to train since the factors model dependencies between all labels of all coarse-grained features, leading to >20k factors.

Data processing: We use the train/dev/test split provided in the shared task (McCarthy et al., 2018).[3] Since we model feature-wise prediction for each coarse-grained feature, our model requires the provided data to be annotated for coarse-grained features. Therefore, we construct a feature-label dictionary based on the UM documentation[4] to map the individual fine-grained traits, which are in the UM schema, to their respective coarse-grained categories. This transforms the tagset {N;PL;NOM;FEM} as {*POS=N;Number=PL;Case=NOM;Gender=FEM*}. We note that usually a token has a subset of the coarse-grained categories, therefore we extend the morphological tagset for each token by adding the remaining features observed in the training set and assigning them a special value "_" which denotes null.

---

[3] https://github.com/sigmorphon/2019/tree/master/task2
[4] https://unimorph.github.io/doc/unimorph-schema.pdf

Language	Model	tgt-size=100			tgt-size=1,000		
		Accuracy	F1-Macro	F1-Micro	Accuracy	F1-Macro	F1-Micro
RU/BG	MDCRF + POS + MULTI-SOURCE	**69.13**	**85.78**	**85.86**	**82.72**	**92.15**	**92.17**
	(Malaviya et al., 2018)	46.89	64.75	64.46	67.56	82.06	82.11
	(Cotterell and Heigold, 2017)	52.76	58.23	58.41	71.90	77.89	77.97
FI/HU	MDCRF + POS + MULTI-SOURCE	**57.32**	**80.11**	**78.86**	**70.24**	**85.44**	**84.86**
	(Malaviya et al., 2018)	45.41	68.63	68.07	63.93	85.06	84.12
	(Cotterell and Heigold, 2017)	51.74	68.15	66.82	61.8	75.96	76.16

Table 2: Comparing our model for bilingual transfer with previous baselines.

Hyper-parameters: We use a hidden size of 200 for each direction of the LSTM with a dropout of 0.5. For the character-level bi-LSTM we use a hidden size of 25. We use 100 dimentional size for word and language embeddings with 64 dimensional POS embeddings, all randomly initialized. SGD was used as the optimizer with learning rate of 0.015. The models were trained until convergence. For POLYGLOT, we project the constructed typology vector into 20 dimension hidden size.

5 Results and Discussion

Table 2 shows the comparison results of our proposed approach with the baselines (Malaviya et al., 2018; Cotterell and Heigold, 2017) using cross-lingual transfer. Here MDCRF+POS refers to our model architecture and MULTI-SOURCE refers to our multilingual transfer approach. Malaviya et al. (2018) and Cotterell and Heigold (2017) test their approach on UD v2.1 (Nivre et al., 2017) under two settings: *tgt size* = 100 and *tgt size* = 1000, where *tgt size* denotes the number of target language data-points used during training. Malaviya et al. (2018) transfer from one related high-resource language. We use the same experimental resources for comparison and for a fair comparison we do not fine-tune on the target language. Of the four language pairs tested by Malaviya et al. (2018), we choose RU/BG and FI/HU for comparison, where BG and HU are the target languages and RU and FI are the respective transfer languages, since these languages are morphologically challenging. We see that under both settings our approach outperforms the baselines by a significant margin for both the language pairs.

Next, we compare our multi-lingual transfer approaches MULTI-SOURCE and MULTI-SOURCE + POLYGLOT in order to decide the model for our final submission. We conduct experiments on three low-resource languages: Marathi (*mr-ufal*), Sanskrit (*sa-ufal*) and Belarusian (*be-hse*), all of which have

< 400 training data-points. The italicized text denotes the treebank used in the experiments. For *mr-ufal* and *sa-ufal*, we transfer from a related high-resource language of Hindi (*hi-hdtb*). For *be-hse*, we transfer from two related languages, Russian (*ru-gsd*) and Ukrainian (*uk-iu*). However, from Table 3, we see that the performance of the two models is comparable. Therefore, for our final submission we use only MULTI-SOURCE which is much faster to train than the MULTI-SOURCE + POLYGLOT. We discuss their comparative performance in greater detail in Section §5.1.

Model	mr-ufal	sa-ufal	be-hse
MULTI-SOURCE	**63.52 / 78.22**	42.78 / **67.64**	**77.07** / 82.89
+POLYGLOT	61.18 / 77.42	**43.81** / 65.94	76.51 / **83.27**

Table 3: Multi-lingual comparison results for Marathi (*mr-ufal*), Sanskrit (*sa-ufal*) and Belarusian (*be-hse*) on the validation set.

Finally, we compare our approach with the shared task baseline. Table 5, 6 in the Appendix shows our results for all 107 treebanks. We observe that out system achieves an average improvement of +14.70 (accuracy) and +4.63 (F1) over the provided baseline (McCarthy et al., 2019). We note that for the shared task submission, we did not use self-attention over the character-level representations. Therefore, we additionally show the results after adding self-attention. We observe that the addition gives an average improvement of +0.60 (accuracy) and +0.30 (F1) over our previous best submission.

5.1 Analysis

Here we analyze the different components of our model in an effort to understand what it is learning.

Why does adding POS help? As discussed earlier (§2), we explicitly add the POS feature in the form of embeddings into the shared encoder. To evaluate the contribution of POS alone, we conduct monolingual experiments without concatenating the POS embeddings with the token-level representations. Table 4 outlines the ablation results for three treebanks with varying training size. We observe that our monolingual model MDCRF significantly outperforms the baseline (McCarthy et al., 2019) by +13.72 accuracy and +3.82 F1 (avg). On adding POS, we further gain +3.56 accuracy and +0.71 F1 over MD-CRF across the three treebanks. We note that this improvement is more pronounced for the low-medium resource languages of Marathi (+6.12 accuracy) and Ukrainian (+3.57 accuracy).

Model	mr-ufal	uk-iu	hi-hdtb
MDCRF+POS	**64.71 / 79.40**	**84.79 / 92.03**	**90.46** / 96.69
MDCRF	58.59 / 77.91	81.22 / 91.35	89.45 / **96.73**
McCarthy et al. (2019)	43.76 / 73.38	63.36 / 87.01	80.96 / 94.14

Table 4: Ablation results for Marathi (*mr-ufal*), Ukrainian (*uk-iu*) and Hindi (*hi-hdtb*) with training size of 373, 5441, 13381 respectively on the validation set.

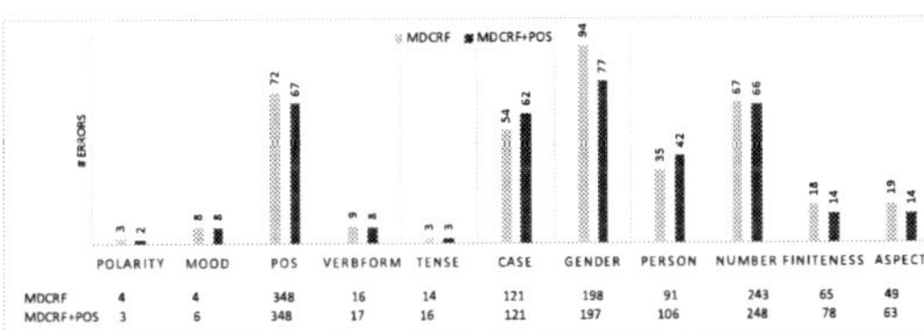

Figure 3: Number of errors per coarse-grained feature for Marathi comparing the addition of POS to the encoder. The rows at the bottom denote the total number of predictions per each feature for both the models.

To understand where the addition of POS helps, we analyse the number of errors made per each coarse-grained feature. For the example of Marathi, POS helped the most in reducing Gender errors (Figure 3). For some word forms, the gender may be inferred from inflectional form alone, but for others, this information may be insufficient, e.g. "किंमत" (price.N.FEM.SG.ACC) in Marathi which does not have the traditional female suffix "ई". We observe that this behavior corresponds to POS: verbs and adjectives are more predictable from surface forms alone than nouns. The addition of POS information in the encoder helps the model learn to weigh different encoded information more heavily when assigning gender to different parts of speech. For Ukrainian and Sanskrit, POS information also helped reduce errors in Case and Number. More details can be found in Appendix Section §6.

Tkachenko and Sirts (2018) also model dependence on POS with a POS-dependent context vector in the decoder. However, they observe no significant improvement; we hypothesize that incorporating POS information into the shared encoder instead provides the model with a stronger signal.

What is the model learning? One of the major advantages of our model's use of self-attention is that it enables us to provide insights into what the model has learned. As seen in Figure 4, we found evidence of the model learning language-specific inflectional properties. Both Marathi and Belarusian display morphological inflections predominantly in the form of suffix and the attention maps for both these languages demonstrate the same. For the Marathi example, the last three characters denote the ergative case and we can see that the attention weights are concentrated on these three characters. Similarly for the Belarusian example, the last two characters denote the genitive case with plural number and is the focus of the attention. For Indonesian, inflections can be also found as circumfixes where the affix is attached at both the beginning and end of the token. For instance, both *ke-* and *-an* affixes are appended to form nouns and we can see from Figure 4 that the attention is focused both on the prefix and the suffix. Interestingly for Indonesian, the model seems to have also discovered the stem *camat*, as evidenced from the attention pattern.

Does *time-depth* matter for transfer learning? As discussed earlier, we train one model per language cluster for multi-lingual transfer learning. We compare different clusters to see if *time-depth* of the languages within a cluster affects the extent of transfer. *Time depth* is the period of time that has elapsed since all languages in the group were a single language (in other words, the time since divergence). We consider the following three clusters: Hindi-Marathi-Sanskrit (Indo-Aryan), Russian-Ukrainian-Belarusian (Slavic) and Arabic-Hebrew-Amharic-Akkadian (Semitic). These three clusters were chosen because the languages in them became separate languages at varying time-depths. For instance, in the Semitic cluster the languages diverged roughly 5000 years ago, whereas for the Slavic cluster the time-depth is <1000 years. Therefore, we expect transfer to help more for languages where the time-depth is more recent. In Figure 5, we compare the MULTI-SOURCE model with our best mono-

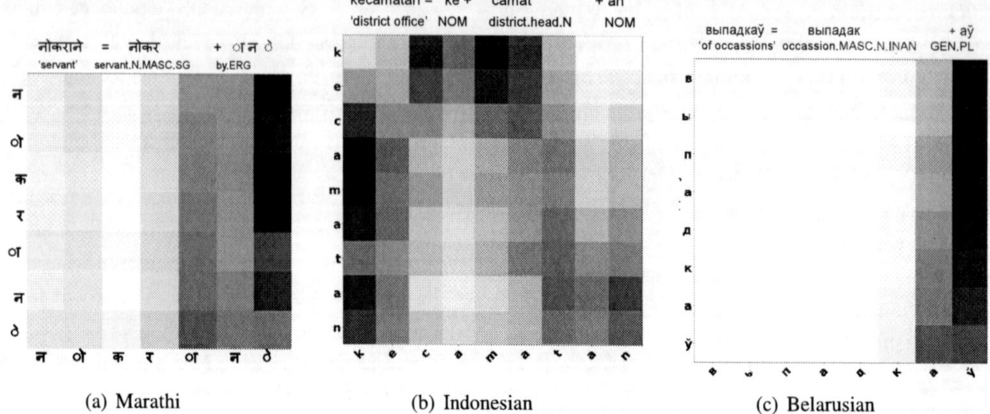

(a) Marathi   (b) Indonesian   (c) Belarusian

Figure 4: Character-level attention maps for three typologically different languages. Marathi and Belarusian display morphological inflections pre-dominantly as suffix. Indonesian displays inflections in the form of prefix, suffix and circumfix where the affix is found both at the beginning and end of a token.

lingual model MDCRF+POS and we see that transfer helps most for the Slavic cluster by +2.9 accuracy. For the Indo-Aryan cluster it helps by +0.32 accuracy and for the Semitic cluster we observe a slight negative effect with transfer (-0.0176 accuracy). This supports our hypothesis that *time-depth* does affect the extent of transfer learning with language clusters having lower *time-depths* benefiting the most.

One particular advantage that the Slavic cluster has over both the Indo-Aryan and Semitic clusters is the similarity of script. Russian, Belarusian, and Ukrainian use variants of the same script; Hindi, Sanskrit, and Marathi do, as well, but the Semitic languages all use different scripts. This is also attributed to the shallower time-depths of the Slavic and Indo-Aryan clusters. Therefore, as suggested by the anonymous reviewers, we add Czech and Polish to the Slavic cluster and see to what extent the scripts are confusing the model. Czech and Polish use different script as compared to Russian, Belarusian, and Ukrainian. We observe that MULTI-SOURCE model like before, achieves similar improvements over the monolingual models for Belarusian (+8.17 accuracy) and Ukrainian (+1.2 accuracy). However, a slight decrease is observed for Russian (-0.45 accuracy). This suggests that the MULTI-SOURCE model is robust to scriptal changes and benefits the low-resource languages by learning from typologically similar languages, more so for language clusters with shallow time-depths.

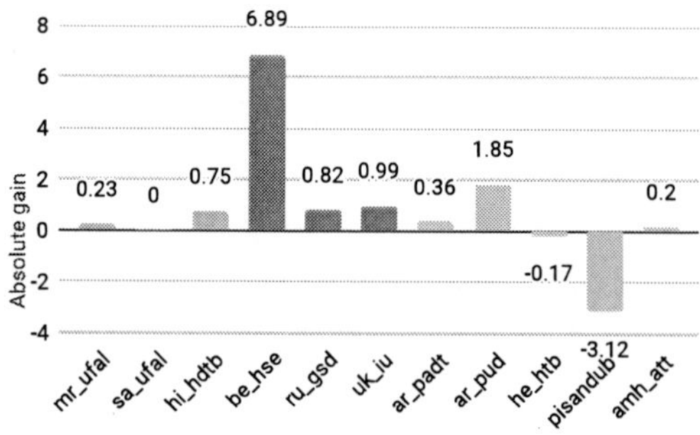

Figure 5: Absolute gain of multi-lingual transfer over monolingual models. Blue denotes the *Indo-Aryan* cluster, pink the *Slavic*, and yellow the *Semitic*.

Why did POLYGLOT not help further? We hypothesize that one reason why POLYGLOT did not help over MULTI-SOURCE is because the language embedding vector probably learns the same typological information which the typology vector encodes. Hence, the typological vector doesn't seem to add any new information. As evidence, we look at the transition weights learned in both the models; as shown in Figure 7, we see that the transition weights learned for the Case feature are very similar for both MULTI-SOURCE and MULTI-SOURCE + POLYGLOT. In the future, we plan to explore the contextual parameter generation method (Platanios et al., 2018) for leveraging the typology vectors to inform the decoders during inference.

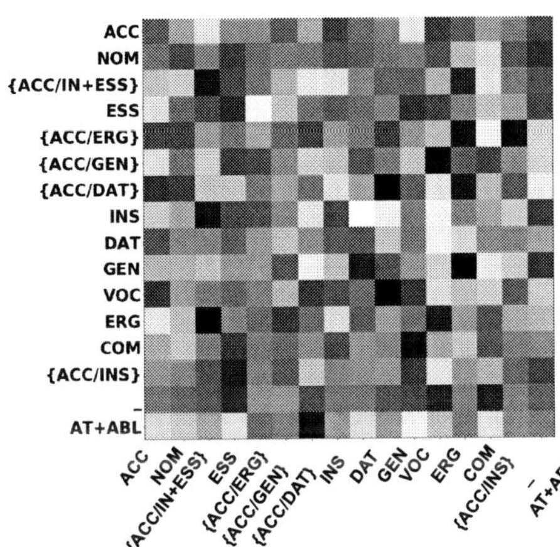 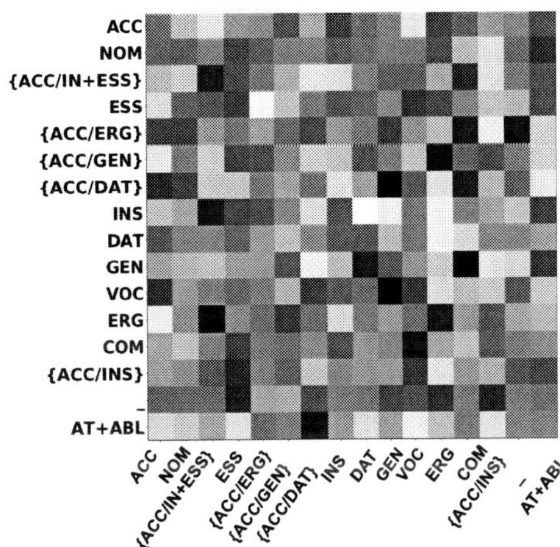

Figure 6: Transition weights for the *Case* feature for Hindi across MULTI-SOURCE (left) and MULTI-SOURCE + POLYGLOT (right) models trained with Hindi (*hi-hdtb*), Marathi (*mr-ufal*) and Sanskrit (*sa-ufal*).

5.2 Error Analysis

In this section, we analyze the major error categories for the MULTI-SOURCE model for the Indo-Aryan cluster. We observe that Gender, Case, Number, Person features account for the most number of errors (65% for Marathi, 49% for Sanskrit). One reason for this is the non-overlapping output label space across the languages within a cluster. For instance, in the Indo-Aryan cluster, Hindi is a high-resource language ($> 13k$ training sentences) with Marathi (373) and Sanskrit (184) being the low-resource languages. We observe that the label space for Case, Gender, Number overlap the least among the three languages. Marathi and Sanskrit have three genders: *NEUT, FEM, MASC* whereas Hindi only has *FEM, MASC*. Furthermore, only two Hindi Case labels (*ACC, NOM*) overlap with Marathi and Sanskrit because in Hindi the labels often have alternatives such as *ACC/ERG, ACC/DAT*. These differences in the output space negatively affect the transfer. For the Slavic cluster, we observe that almost all the feature labels overlap nicely for the languages therein, which is probably another reason why we see a gain of +6.89 for Belarusian in Figure 5 and only +0.32 increase for Marathi.

We also note that for some languages such as Belarusian and Russian, the POS errors increased by 25.3% and 4.4% respectively for the MDCRF+POS model. This suggests that decoupling POS feature from the other feature decoders harmed the model. In future, we plan to improve the MDCRF+POS model by jointly training POS decoder with the other fea-ture decoders which use the latent representation of POS in an end-to-end fashion.

6 Conclusion and Future Work

We implement a hierarchical neural model with independent decoders for each coarse-grained morphological feature and show that incorporating POS information in the shared encoder helps improve prediction for other features. Furthermore, our multilingual transfer methods not only help improve results for related languages but also eliminate the need of training individual models for each dataset from scratch. In future, we plan to explore the use of pre-trained multi-lingual word embeddings such as BERT (Devlin et al., 2019), in our encoder.

Acknowledgement

We are thankful to the anonymous reviewers for their valuable suggestions.

References

Jan Buys and Jan A. Botha. 2016. Cross-lingual morphological tagging for low-resource languages. In *Proc. of ACL*, pages 1954–1964.

Ryan Cotterell and Georg Heigold. 2017. Cross-lingual character-level neural morphological tagging. In *Proc. of EMNLP*, pages 748–759.

Jacob Devlin, Ming-Wei Chang, Kenton Lee, and Kristina Toutanova. 2019. BERT: Pre-training of deep bidirectional transformers for language understanding. In *Proc. of NAACL*, pages 4171–4186.

Onur Güngör, Suzan Üsküdarlı, and Tunga Güngör. 2018. Improving named entity recognition by jointly learning to disambiguate morphological tags. *arXiv preprint arXiv:1807.06683*.

Jan Hajic and Barbora Hladká. 1998. Tagging inlective languages: Prediction of morphological categories for a rich structured tagset. In *Proc. of ACL*, volume 1.

Georg Heigold, Guenter Neumann, and Josef van Genabith. 2017. An extensive empirical evaluation of character-based morphological tagging for 14 languages. In *Proc. of EACL*, pages 505–513.

Daniel Kondratyuk. 2019. 75 languages, 1 model: Parsing universal dependencies universally. *arXiv preprint arXiv:1904.02099*.

Guillaume Lample, Miguel Ballesteros, Sandeep Subramanian, Kazuya Kawakami, and Chris Dyer. 2016. Neural architectures for named entity recognition. In *Proc. of NAACL*, pages 260–270.

Patrick Littell, David R Mortensen, Ke Lin, Katherine Kairis, Carlisle Turner, and Lori Levin. 2017. Uriel and lang2vec: Representing languages as typological, geographical, and phylogenetic vectors. In *Proc. of EACL*, volume 2, pages 8–14.

Xuezhe Ma and Eduard Hovy. 2016. End-to-end sequence labeling via bi-directional LSTM-CNNs-CRF. In *Proc. of ACL*, pages 1064–1074.

Chaitanya Malaviya, Matthew R. Gormley, and Graham Neubig. 2018. Neural factor graph models for cross-lingual morphological tagging. In *Proc. of ACL*, pages 2653–2663.

Chaitanya Malaviya, Shijie Wu, and Ryan Cotterell. 2019. A simple joint model for improved contextual neural lemmatization. *arXiv preprint arXiv:1904.02306v2*.

Arya D. McCarthy, Miikka Silfverberg, Ryan Cotterell, Mans Hulden, and David Yarowsky. 2018. Marrying Universal Dependencies and Universal Morphology. In *Proceedings of the Second Workshop on Universal Dependencies (UDW 2018)*, pages 91–101.

Arya D. McCarthy, Ekaterina Vylomova, Shijie Wu, Chaitanya Malaviya, Lawrence Wolf-Sonkin, Garrett Nicolai, Christo Kirov, Miikka Silfverberg, Sebastian Mielke, Jeffrey Heinz, Ryan Cotterell, and Mans Hulden. 2019. The SIGMORPHON 2019 shared task: Crosslinguality and context in morphology. In *Proceedings of the 16th SIGMORPHON Workshop on Computational Research in Phonetics, Phonology, and Morphology*.

Thomas Müller and Hinrich Schuetze. 2015. Robust morphological tagging with word representations. In *Proc. of NAACL*, pages 526–536.

Joakim Nivre, Željko Agić, Lars Ahrenberg, Lene Antonsen, Maria Jesus Aranzabe, Masayuki Asahara, Luma Ateyah, Mohammed Attia, Aitziber Atutxa, Liesbeth Augustinus, et al. 2017. Universal dependencies 2.1.

Kemal Oflazer and Ilker Kuruöz. 1994. Tagging and morphological disambiguation of turkish text. In *Proc. of ANLP*, pages 144–149.

Emmanouil Antonios Platanios, Mrinmaya Sachan, Graham Neubig, and Tom Mitchell. 2018. Contextual parameter generation for universal neural machine translation. In *Proc. of EMNLP*, pages 425–435.

Emma Strubell, Patrick Verga, Daniel Andor, David Weiss, and Andrew McCallum. 2018. Linguistically-informed self-attention for semantic role labeling. In *Proc. of EMNLP*, pages 5027–5038.

Alexander Tkachenko and Kairit Sirts. 2018. Modeling composite labels for neural morphological tagging. *arXiv preprint arXiv:1810.08815*.

Yulia Tsvetkov, Sunayana Sitaram, Manaal Faruqui, Guillaume Lample, Patrick Littell, David Mortensen, Alan W. Black, Lori Levin, and Chris Dyer. 2016. Polyglot neural language models: A case study in cross-lingual phonetic representation learning. In *Proc. of NAACL*, pages 1357–1366.

Ashish Vaswani, Noam Shazeer, Niki Parmar, Jakob Uszkoreit, Llion Jones, Aidan N Gomez, Łukasz Kaiser, and Illia Polosukhin. 2017. Attention is all you need. In *Proc. of NIPS*, pages 5998–6008.

Ekaterina Vylomova, Trevor Cohn, Xuanli He, and Gholamreza Haffari. 2017. Word representation models for morphologically rich languages in neural machine translation. In *Proceedings of the First Workshop on Subword and Character Level Models in NLP*, pages 103–108.

Zhilin Yang, Ruslan Salakhutdinov, and William Cohen. 2016. Multi-task cross-lingual sequence tagging from scratch. *arXiv preprint arXiv:1603.06270*.

Appendix

Comprehensive Results

Table 5 and 6 document the comprehensive results of our submissions. MULTI-SOURCE was our previous submission to the shared task. We conducted additional experimentas with the addition of self-attention and also report the results for MULTI-SOURCE+SELF-ATTENTION. We report both the accuracy and F1 metric.

Language Clusters

We train one model per language cluster for the multi-lingual transfer learning. Each language cluster was constructed based on the typological similarity of the languages therein. Table 5, 6 show the language clusters.

Analysis

In order to understand where the addition of POS helps, we plot the number of errors per each coarse-grained feature for three languages in Figure 7. For Sanskrit and Ukrainian we see that POS generally helps reduce the errors predominantly for the features: Case, Gender, Number. For Belarusian, we did not observe a clear trend since the POS accuracy actually decreased for MDCRF+POS.

Language Cluster	Target	MULTI-SOURCE + SELF-ATTENTION Accuracy / F1	MULTI-SOURCE Accuracy / F1	(McCarthy et al., 2019) Accuracy / F1	# Training Sentences
armenian	UD-Armenian-ArmTDP	83.74 / **88.54**	**83.83** / 88.17	- / -	825
austronesian	UD-Indonesian-GSD	**90.05 / 93.13**	90.01 / 93.11	71.49 / 86.02	4475
baltic	UD-Latvian-LVTB	89.0 / 93.04	**89.0 / 93.08**	70.21 / 89.53	7937
	UD-Lithuanian-HSE	**70.29 / 76.38**	68.08 / 74.56	43.13 / 67.41	211
celtic	UD-Breton-KEB	**85.97 / 88.78**	85.07 / 88.07	77.41 / 88.58	711
	UD-Irish-IDT	**76.75 / 84.1**	76.5 / 84.11	67.45 / 81.72	817
dravidian	UD-Tamil-TTB	**82.92 / 89.91**	82.48 / 89.77	75.64 / **90.23**	481
egyptian	UD-Coptic-Scriptorium	92.02 / 95.28	**92.17 / 95.33**	87.99 / 93.78	673
germanic	UD-Afrikaans-AfriBooms	96.92 / **97.37**	**96.94** / 97.35	84.05 / 92.32	1548
	UD-Dutch-Alpino	**94.85 / 95.69**	94.35 / 95.4	82.15 / 91.26	10867
	UD-Dutch-LassySmall	93.48 / 94.08	**93.53 / 94.2**	76.24 / 88.13	5873
	UD-English-EWT	94.08 / **95.46**	**93.9** / 95.4	79.19 / 90.46	13298
	UD-English-GUM	93.44 / 94.38	**93.56 / 94.47**	79.63 / 90.04	3520
	UD-English-LinES	**94.37 / 95.19**	93.75 / 94.93	81.03 / 90.99	3652
	UD-English-ParTUT	**92.01 / 92.69**	91.95 / 92.61	79.57 / 89.04	1673
	UD-English-PUD	89.41 / 91.42	**89.8 / 91.6**	78.85 / 88.8	801
	UD-Faroese-OFT	**80.6 / 89.27**	77.52 / 87.87	67.11 / 87.27	967
	UD-Gothic-PROIEL	**84.53 / 92.93**	83.0 / 92.47	83.01 / 91.3	4321
north-germanic	UD-German-GSD	**83.72 / 92.73**	82.82 / 92.5	- / -	12473
	UD-Danish-DDT	**91.78 / 93.72**	91.34 / 93.61	77.89 / 90.89	4410
	UD-Norwegian-Nynorsk	**94.39 / 96.35**	94.29 / 96.33	71.8 / 88.16	14061
	UD-Norwegian-NynorskLIA	93.03 / 94.55	**93.75 / 94.89**	- / -	1117
	UD-Swedish-LinES	**89.92 / 93.61**	89.62 / 93.59	77.97 / 91.02	3652
	UD-Swedish-PUD	**87.72 / 90.01**	87.13 / 89.8	77.78 / 89.32	801
hellenic	UD-Ancient-Greek-Perseus	**84.79 / 92.1**	84.27 / 91.88	- / -	11136
	UD-Ancient-Greek-PROIEL	**88.1 / 95.55**	86.01 / 94.67	- / -	13665
	UD-Greek-GDT	**91.15 / 96.23**	90.73 / 96.0	78.14 / 93.49	2017
indo-iranian	UD-Urdu-UDTB	77.77 / 92.12	**78.05 / 92.16**	67.99 / 88.42	4105
indoaryan	UD-Hindi-HDTB	90.76 / 96.77	**91.05 / 96.85**	80.96 / 94.14	13318
	UD-Marathi-UFAL	**57.99 / 73.54**	57.72 / 73.04	43.76 / 73.38	373
	UD-Sanskrit-UFAL	43.72 / 64.9	**46.73** / 68.08	44.33 / **68.34**	185
isolate	UD-Basque-BDT	**75.2 / 88.07**	75.14 / 87.91	67.61 / 87.63	7195
italic	UD-Latin-ITTB	**94.57 / 97.26**	94.25 / 97.11	77.62 / 93.19	16809
	UD-Latin-Perseus	**76.17 / 86.32**	75.76 / 85.92	53.23 / 77.5	1819
	UD-Latin-PROIEL	**86.78 / 94.39**	86.18 / 94.19	82.27 / 91.38	14721
jako	UD-Japanese-GSD	**96.8 / 96.4**	96.8 / 96.4	85.25 / 90.31	6557
	UD-Japanese-Modern	**95.27 / 95.32**	95.27 / 95.32	94.29 / 95.2	658
	UD-Japanese-PUD	**95.94 / 95.44**	95.94 / 95.44	84.73 / 89.63	801
	UD-Komi-Zyrian-IKDP	**51.56** / 61.03	51.56 / 62.27	33.73 / **62.59**	70
	UD-Komi-Zyrian-Lattice	53.85 / 64.85	**54.4** / 65.23	45.6 / **70.61**	153
	UD-Korean-GSD	**92.56 / 91.68**	92.56 / 91.68	80.18 / 86.08	5072
	UD-Korean-Kaist	**95.54 / 94.99**	95.54 / 94.99	84.32 / 89.4	21891
	UD-Korean-PUD	84.27 / 89.02	**84.46** / 89.28	81.6 / **91.15**	801
	UD-Kurmanji-MG	80.82 / 87.79	**80.82 / 87.81**	70.2 / 85.85	604
niger-congo	UD-Bambara-CRB	91.65 / 94.76	**92.41 / 94.86**	78.86 / 89.41	821
	UD-Naija-NSC	**94.56 / 92.71**	94.56 / 92.71	68.66 / 78.96	759
	UD-Yoruba-YTB	93.41 / 93.88	**93.8 / 94.19**	71.2 / 81.83	81
persian	UD-Persian-Seraji	96.15 / **96.85**	**95.95** / 96.69	- / -	4798
phillipine	UD-Tagalog-TRG	83.78 / 92.09	**83.78 / 92.75**	44.0 / 69.31	45
sinotibetan	UD-Cantonese-HK	**89.64 / 86.82**	89.64 / 86.82	70.15 / 77.76	521
	UD-Chinese-CFL	**88.65 / 86.96**	88.65 / 86.96	74.65 / 79.91	361
	UD-Chinese-GSD	90.83 / 90.54	**90.9 / 90.56**	76.81 / 84.35	3998
	UD-Vietnamese-VTB	**90.1 / 88.84**	90.1 / 88.84	70.71 / 79.01	2401
semitic	UD-Akkadian-PISANDUB	79.21 / 78.65	79.21 / 78.65	**84.0 / 84.19**	81
	UD-Amharic-ATT	87.24 / **91.13**	**86.58** / 90.91	76.0 / 88.16	860
	UD-Arabic-PADT	91.77 / **95.44**	**91.52** / 95.36	77.03 / 92.03	6132
	UD-Arabic-PUD	77.63 / **89.06**	**77.89** / 89.0	63.81 / 86.29	801
	UD-Hebrew-HTB	**94.33 / 95.81**	94.03 / 95.65	81.59 / 91.84	4973

Table 5: Comprehensive results

Cluster	Target	MULTI-SOURCE + SELF-ATTENTION Accuracy / F1	MULTI-SOURCE Accuracy / F1	(McCarthy et al., 2019) Accuracy / F1	# Training Sentences
turkic	UD-Turkish-IMST	**85.68 / 90.64**	85.02 / 90.43	62.04 / 85.33	4509
	UD-Turkish-PUD	**79.78 / 90.88**	79.33 / 90.54	66.92 / 88.05	801
romance	UD-Catalan-AnCora	textbf96.68 / **98.26**	96.63 / 98.24	85.77 / 95.7	13343
	UD-French-GSD	96.19 / **97.51**	95.76 / 97.32	84.44 / 94.81	13074
	UD-French-ParTUT	93.04 / 96.05	**93.04 / 96.12**	81.32 / 92.08	817
	UD-French-Sequoia	**95.08** / 96.95	94.96 / **96.96**	82.64 / 93.42	2480
	UD-French-Spoken	**96.05 / 96.08**	96.05 / 96.08	94.57 / 94.85	2229
	UD-Galician-CTG	96.65 / 96.31	**96.66 / 96.32**	87.23 / 91.81	3195
	UD-Galician-TreeGal	**89.69** / 93.2	89.3 / **93.25**	76.85 / 90.05	801
	UD-Italian-ISDT	95.91 / 97.24	**95.96 / 97.27**	83.62 / 94.34	11334
	UD-Italian-ParTUT	**95.0** / 96.39	94.87 / 96.39	84.03 / 93.42	1673
	UD-Italian-PoSTWITA	**92.13 / 93.13**	92.03 / 93.02	70.23 / 88.18	5371
	UD-Italian-PUD	**87.55** / 92.4	87.38 / **92.46**	80.89 / **92.66**	801
	UD-Portuguese-Bosque	**92.28 / 95.57**	92.06 / 95.5	63.14 / 86.12	7493
	UD-Portuguese-GSD	**97.33 / 97.54**	97.33 / 97.54	- / -	9663
	UD-Romanian-Nonstandard	**91.13 / 95.33**	91.07 / 95.29	74.31 / 91.5	8056
	UD-Romanian-RRT	94.67 / 96.58	**94.82 / 96.63**	81.45 / 93.96	7620
	UD-Spanish-AnCora	**96.97 / 98.25**	96.86 / 98.22	84.27 / 95.3	14145
	UD-Spanish-GSD	94.05 / 97.08	**94.07 / 97.1**	- / -	12811
slavic	UD-Belarusian-HSE	**79.63 / 85.37**	77.28 / 84.11	54.99 / 79.07	315
	UD-Bulgarian-BTB	**94.22 / 96.44**	93.99 / 96.37	79.75 / 93.91	8911
	UD-Buryat-BDT	**78.85 / 81.24**	75.96 / 78.66	63.26 / 78.53	742
	UD-Old-Church-Slavonic-PROIEL	87.22 / **94.13**	86.94 / 94.03	82.86 / 90.34	5070
	UD-Russian-GSD	**84.26 / 91.91**	83.25 / 91.55	64.42 / 88.77	4025
	UD-Russian-PUD	76.77 / **87.55**	**77.25** / 87.49	63.15 / 85.52	801
	UD-Russian-SynTagRus	91.65 / 95.96	**92.74 / 96.5**	73.9 / 92.84	49512
	UD-Russian-Taiga	74.14 / 80.23	**75.24 / 81.25**	52.99 / 78.71	1412
	UD-Ukrainian-IU	**86.02 / 92.41**	85.33 / 92.2	63.36 / 87.01	5441
	UD-Upper-Sorbian-UFAL	**74.04 / 82.45**	70.12 / 81.21	55.66 / 78.3	517
ugric	UD-Estonian-EDT	87.71 / 94.58	**88.47 / 94.93**	74.56 / 91.71	24579
	UD-Finnish-FTB	83.24 / 90.38	**83.63 / 90.7**	73.16 / 89.51	14979
	UD-Finnish-PUD	77.05 / 86.33	**77.49 / 86.77**	71.65 / **88.87**	801
	UD-Hungarian-Szeged	**80.57 / 90.88**	79.16 / 90.13	63.72 / 87.29	1441
	UD-North-Sami-Giella	**84.35 / 88.8**	83.78 / 88.65	67.04 / 85.6	2498
	UD-Norwegian-Bokmaal	**94.97 / 96.68**	94.58 / 96.51	81.44 / 93.19	16037
	UD-Swedish-Talbanken	**93.94 / 96.01**	93.64 / 95.9	- / -	4821
	UD-Finnish-TDT	**86.51 / 92.63**	85.55 / 92.2	75.13 / 90.92	12109
westslavic	UD-Croatian-SET	**87.23 / 94.04**	86.88 / 93.91	72.71 / 90.99	7112
	UD-Czech-CAC	90.66 / 96.72	**91.38 / 96.99**	77.15 / 93.92	19768
	UD-Czech-CLTT	**91.29** / 96.15	91.07 / **96.22**	73.92 / 92.37	901
	UD-Czech-FicTree	90.05 / 95.42	**90.0 / 95.49**	68.28 / 90.37	10209
	UD-Czech-PDT	**89.78 / 96.37**	54.13 / 73.56	76.69 / 94.28	70331
	UD-Czech-PUD	75.65 / 88.19	**77.72 / 89.37**	59.54 / 85.5	801
	UD-Polish-LFG	87.76 / 93.7	**87.81 / 93.65**	- / -	13797
	UD-Polish-SZ	**82.27 / 91.38**	81.01 / 90.88	65.58 / 88.29	6582
	UD-Serbian-SET	**91.89 / 95.46**	91.35 / 95.29	75.73 / 91.19	3113
	UD-Slovak-SNK	**85.59 / 93.12**	84.99 / 92.83	64.24 / 88.16	8484
	UD-Slovenian-SSJ	**89.05 / 94.03**	87.92 / 93.55	73.73 / 89.95	6401
	UD-Slovenian-SST	85.13 / **90.16**	**85.51** / 90.02	73.4 / 84.74	2551

Table 6: Comprehensive results

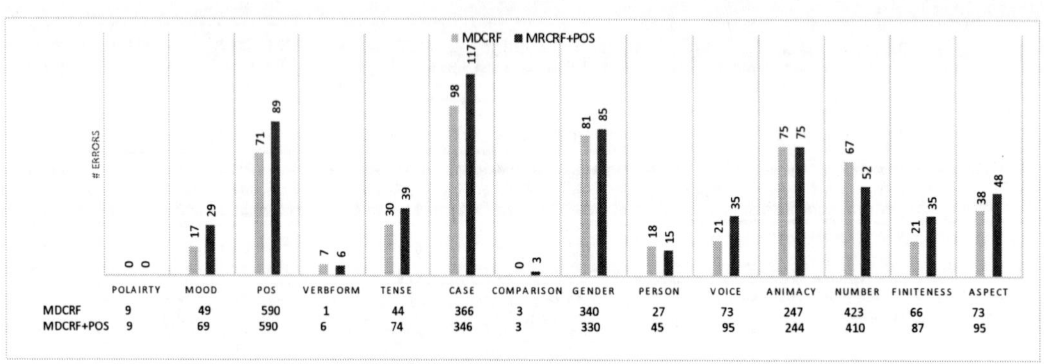

(a) Belarusian (be-hse)

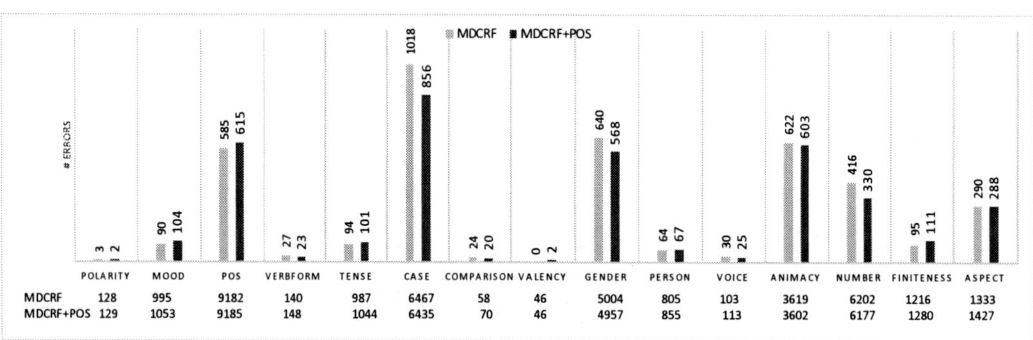

(b) Ukrainian (uk-iu)

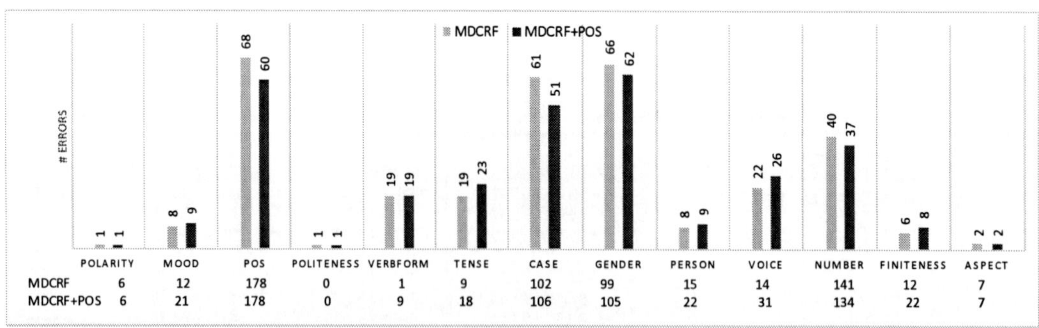

(c) Sanskrit (sa-ufal)

Figure 7: Number of errors per coarse-grained feature for models comparing the addition of POS to the encoder. The rows at the bottom denote the total number of predictions per each feature for both the models.

Cross-lingual morphological inflection with explicit alignment

Çağrı Çöltekin
University of Tübingen
Department of Linguistics
`ccoltekin@sfs.uni-tuebingen.de`

Abstract

This paper describes two related systems for cross-lingual morphological inflection for SIGMORPHON 2019 Shared Task participation. Both sets of results submitted to the shared task for evaluation are obtained using a simple approach of predicting transducer actions based on initial alignments on the training set, where cross-lingual transfer is limited to only using the high-resource language data as additional training set. The performance of the system does not reach the performance of the top two systems in the competition. However, we show that results can be improved with further tuning. We also present further analyses showing that the cross-lingual gain is rather modest.

1 Introduction

Morphological inflection generation is the task of generating a word based on its lemma and morphological features. For example, given the German lemma *aufgeben* 'to give up' and the morphological tags {V.PTCP, PST}, the task is to predict the inflected form *aufgegeben* (morphological tags are described in McCarthy et al., 2019; Kirov et al., 2018). Traditionally, finite-state methods (Koskenniemi, 1985) are used for morphological generation (and analysis). Since such systems typically require man-months of expert work, and difficult to maintain and adapt to changes in the language, data driven approaches to inflection generation have recently become popular (Durrett and DeNero, 2013; Nicolai et al., 2015; Ahlberg et al., 2015; Faruqui et al., 2016). The task is further popularized by the past three SIGMOR-PHON morphological (re)inflection shared tasks (Cotterell et al., 2016, 2017, 2018). The primary focus of the task tackled in this paper, the task 1 of the present SIGMORPHON shared task (Mc-Carthy et al., 2019), is the cross-lingual transfer learning of the inflection generation.

The dominant approach to morphological inflection has been sequence-to-sequence neural networks with attention (e.g., Kann and Schütze, 2016; Makarov et al., 2017; Makarov and Clematide, 2018). Furthermore, there seems to be a shift from soft attention models towards models with monotonic attention (Ahlberg et al., 2015; Makarov and Clematide, 2018; Wu and Cotterell, 2019), which indicate that the predictions of the decoder benefit most from a (short) window in the output. Although we do not use an encoder-decoder architecture, the simple systems presented here are similar to hard-monotonic attention models in the sense that they predict the transduction actions based on a window on the input and output. The method presented here is much simpler, however. The predictions are not conditioned on any hidden (continuous or discrete) state or variable.

A particular reason of interest for data-driven approaches to morphological inflection generation is to avoid the considerable amount of expert time required for building rule-based finite-state systems. This is particularly important for low-resource languages, where experts, and maybe even native speakers, are hard to come by. As past SIGMORPHON shared tasks demonstrated, however, satisfactory results in the morphological inflection task requires relatively large amount of data. The low-resource settings in earlier SIG-MORPHON shared tasks often resulted in much worse accuracy compared to the high-resource settings. A potential solution to this problem, the focus of the current inflection shared task, is cross-lingual or transfer learning, which has been demonstrated to be useful a number of language processing tasks (e.g., Yarowsky et al., 2001; Faruqui and Kumar, 2015; Johnson et al., 2017; Barnes et al., 2018). In cross-lingual learn-

Proceedings of the 16th Workshop on Computational Research in Phonetics, Phonology, and Morphology, pages 71–79
Florence, Italy. August 2, 2019 ©2019 Association for Computational Linguistics

ing, the data or resources that exist for a related language are leveraged to improve the learning in low-resource setting. The method we use for cross-lingual learning is rather simple. We only use the (related) high-resource language as additional training data.

2 The method

The inflection systems in this study operate by predicting a number of transduction actions based on current position in the lemma, morphological tags, and the output produced so far. The general idea is similar to transition-based parsers (Yamada and Matsumoto, 2003; Nivre et al., 2004) where the aim is to predict the parsing action in a given state of the parser. The similar ideas were used in the past for morphological inflection generation as well. The system presented here is most similar to the baseline system of SIGMORPHON 2016 shared task (Cotterell et al., 2016), and also shares many aspects of the inflection generation systems that follow an align-and-transduce strategy in the earlier SIGMORPHON shared tasks (e.g., Alegria and Etxeberria, 2016; Nicolai et al., 2016; Liu and Mao, 2016). Our current models do not make use of any hidden representations, such as the parser state in transition based parsing, or hidden representations learned in a recurrent neural network.

2.1 Alignment

During training, we need to determine the gold-standard transduction actions, which requires aligning the lemmas and word forms. Better sequence alignment is one of the concerns for the similar inflection systems cited above, as well as the sequence-to-sequence models that operate with hard monotonic attention. Better alignments are also a common concern and studied extensively in other areas of computational linguistics such as dialectometry (Wieling et al., 2009; Prokić, 2010) and historical linguistics (List, 2012; Jäger, 2013). Standard alignment algorithms that use equal penalties for edit operations often fail to capture the similarities and differences between characters (or phonetic segments). As a result, often a weighted method is used such that similar characters in one of the sequences are more likely to be aligned with the similar characters in the other. The weights are most often learned from the data using an unsupervised method. The data-driven weights are found to be more effective than manu-

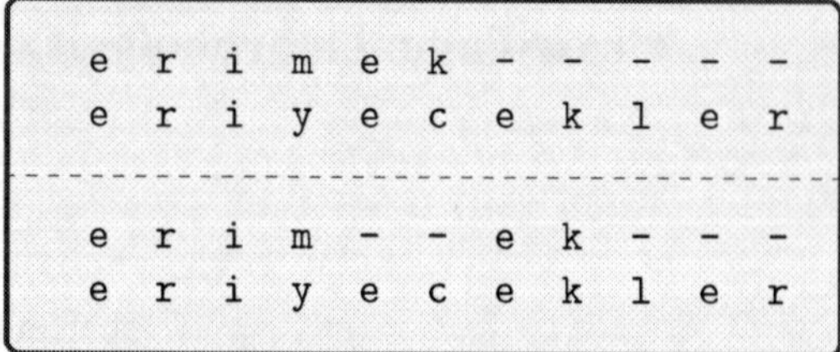

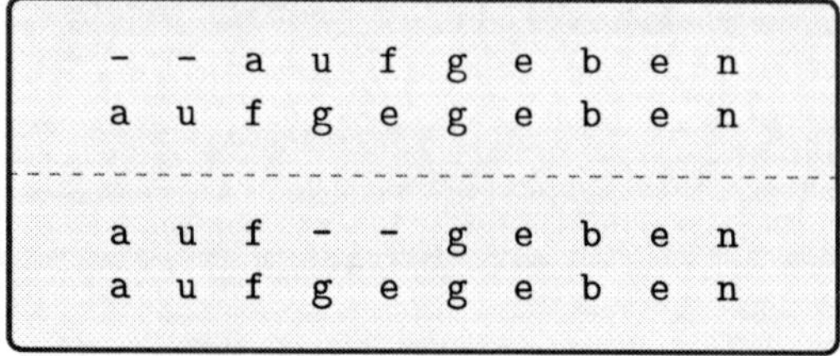

Figure 1: Example alignments of two lemma–form pairs from Turkish (top) and German (bottom). In each box, upper part shows the alignment based on longest common substring, while lower part shows minimum edit distance solution.

ally assigned weights based on linguistic knowledge/intuitions (Sofroniev and Çöltekin, 2018). We tried a few of these more informed weighted alignment methods. However, in preliminary experiments, a simple alignment mechanism based on longest common substring (LCS) worked best. Hence, in all the experiments reported here, alignments are performed first by finding the longest common substring of lemma and the word from, and aligning the two strings such that the LCS is aligned correctly. The rest of the characters are aligned disregarding whether they match or not. The method introduces gaps only at the beginning and end of the sequences. If there are two matching substrings of equal length, we pick the first sequence.

Figure 1 presents two example alignments based on the LCS and the edit distance. In the first example (top figure), minimum edit distance aligns substring ek, part of the infinitive marker mek used in verbal lemmas in the data set, to a substring string that matches accidentally in the word form. The intuition here is that even if we do not have a good reason for aligning the infinitive marker mek with the initial part of the suffix, doing this consistently facilitates learning. The example from German (and in general infixes) is a potentially problematic case for the LCS-based aligner. Minimum edit distance here produces an alignment that is intuitively better. However, since in most cases we expect a

Lemma (input)	Form (output)	Action
s	s	copy
c	c	copy
h	h	copy
r	r	copy
e	i	replace(i)
i	e	replace(e)
b	b	copy
e	e	copy
n	s	replace(s)
#	t	insert(t)
#	#	copy

Table 1: The sequence of actions mapping the German lemma *schreiben* 'to write' to its second person singular past form *schriebst*.

limited number prefixes to precede 'infixed' material, the LCS solution still provides reasonably regular patterns to predict.

2.2 Transduction actions

The inflection systems use four character-to-character transduction actions:

copy copies the current character of the lemma to the word form, and advances to the next character on the lemma

replace(c) inserts the character c to the word form, and advances to the next character on the lemma

insert(c) inserts the character c to the word form, without advancing the current lemma pointer

delete deletes the current character of the lemma, and advances to the next character on the lemma

All actions are character-to-character operations based on one-to-one alignments, and each action is represented individually, i.e., we do not compress consecutive actions of the same type to a single complex action. Table 1 demonstrates the series of transductions for an example lemma–word form pair. Both lemmas and words are appended with a special end-of-sequence symbol (indicated with '#' in Table 1). The decoding stops when any of the actions predict the end-of-sequence symbol.

2.3 Classifiers

Given the gold standard action sequences extracted from a training set as described above, we can use any multi-class classification method for predicting the next action. We experimented both with traditional linear classifiers, in particular SVMs, and feed-forward neural network classifiers. Regardless of the classification method, however, the features are based on the morphological tags, characters within a local window around the current lemma character, and the last few (predicted) characters of the word form. During training we use the gold-data for extracting features from the word forms.

Since the linear methods cannot represent non-linear combinations of the features, we use the following feature (combinations).

- The current lemma character.

- The varying-length, overlapping n-grams to the left and right of the current lemma character. For example, at the fourth step in Table 1, with current lemma character r, and assuming a window size of three, we include h, ch, and sch as n-grams before the current point, and e, ei, and eib as n-grams after the current point.

- The varying-length, overlapping n-grams of the last part of the output already predicted. For the same position, this would amount to n-grams h, ch, and sch.

- Morphological tags, including a special tag indicating the language, and all binary combination of tags. For example, with input tags {V, PST, S} we also include {V-PST, V-S, PST-S} as additional tag features.

- Cross product of all tag features with the other features.

All features for the linear classifiers are combined as a single sparse feature vector. The features are weighted using TF-IDF, but no pruning or any other feature selection step is employed.

As well as the choice of the window size, the choice of the features and feature combinations clearly is important for the linear models. Variations on this feature scheme, e.g., also including interactions between the n-grams, and including skip-grams may improve model's predictions.

However, they also increase the feature set size, resulting in an increases in the time it takes to tune the classifiers. The choice above was a compromise between accuracy and demands on computation (which may be an important factor when tuning models for 100 language pairs).

Intuitively, and also shown in similar tasks earlier, the neural models here have an expected advantage as they can learn useful combinations of arbitrary features automatically. The features for the neural classifier used in this study are based on the same set of characters and the tags, but without explicit combinations of the features.

For both type classifiers, a straightforward option is to train a single multi-class classifier is predicting all possible actions (including the composite actions such as replace(i)). Alternatively, one can first predict one of the four action types, and then predict the parameter of the action if the action is replace or insert. For the linear classifier, this means training three separate classifiers, and applying two of them in correct order at prediction time. For the neural model, a similar approach is used. The model first predicts the action, and then the parameter of the action, for which action is also given as an additional predictor. The different parts of the network are trained jointly, and share some of the weights which may provide additional benefits. We experimented with both approaches. Initial experiments produced mixed results, one or the other option performing better in different data sets. The results presented here are based on the two-level classifiers, chosen somewhat arbitrarily.

At prediction time we decode the sequence greedily, choosing the single-best action according to the model at each step. However, both systems can produce multiple outputs with minor modification to the decoding algorithm.

2.4 Cross lingual transfer

The main focus of the present task is cross-lingual transfer. Although we entertained a few ideas, including the use of cross-lingual character embeddings and translation of transition sequences, the approach used at the end was straightforward inclusion of the high-resource language data in training the models. During cross-lingual training, however, we include an additional hyperparameter that determines the weight training instances belonging to the source language. This way the model also learns 'how much to learn from the source language' during tuning.

Since a sizable number of language pairs do not use the same writing system, a learner relying on categorical character inputs cannot learn from the source language data. Even when the script used by both languages are the same, there are often differences in the writing traditions that make the transfer difficult. Without success from our preliminary experiments with cross-lingual character embeddings, we used the inputs as is, only experimenting with transliteration of the source language input to the target language input for a limited set of language pairs.

Performing the correct, or useful, transliterations for this task seems difficult. There are no standard transliteration methods defined for most language pairs in the data. The standard transliteration methods for some languages exists, where the standard typically defines how to transliterate a language written with a non-Latin script to some version of the Latin script. However, the standard methods are often designed for easy reading/phonetization by English speakers. Even in cases of target languages that use a version of the Latin script, there are significant differences to hinder cross-lingual learning considerably. As a result, we report below some of the experiments with transliterations between Latin and Cyrillic scripts for only eight language pairs (all Turkic languages) to demonstrate the potential gains that can be obtained with transliteration. The transliteration method follows Çöltekin and Barnes (2019). The method does not follow any transliteration standards (e.g., one set by ISO), but tries to maximize the similarities of the writing traditions in these particular languages.

3 Experimental setup

3.1 Data and preprocessing

The shared task data used in this study consists of 100 language pairs, which is described in detail in McCarthy et al. (2019). Here we only provide a basic overview that is relevant to our discussion below. All language pairs feature a high-resource training set from the source language, a low-resource training set and a development set, both from the target language. Number of unique source and target languages are both 44. The number of source languages for a target language, and number of target languages for a source language differ. Some languages also appear as both source and target languages in different pairs. Most source languages have 10 000 training instances, with a few exceptions (notably Uzbek with only 1 060 word forms). The number of training instances for all target languages is 100, with a single exception of Telugu with 61 word forms. Development set sizes vary more between 50, 100 and 1 000 word forms. The number of unique lemmas and tag combinations also vary among different training and development sets.

The relation of language pairs also differ. Most pairs have shared ancestry, ranging from very close (e.g., Turkish–Azeri) to rather far modern relatives (e.g., Russian–Portuguese), or historical relatives (e.g., Polish–Old Church Slavonic). There are also a few pairs where the relation is rather through geographical contact (e.g., Italian–Maltese). As noted above, one obstacle for cross-lingual learning is the different writing systems used in these languages. The data set includes 11 different scripts, and 30 of language pairs do not use the same script. It should be noted, however, that the use of common script does not necessarily solve all the problems regarding mapping character sequences across languages reliably. Even when they use the same script, e.g., Latin or Cyrillic, the differences adopted in the writing tradition of each languages may still introduce difficulties.

To overcome the differences in scripts, we transliterated source language data in eight pairs (Bashkir–Azeri, Bashkir–Crimean-Tatar, Bashkir–Tatar, Bashkir–Turkmen, Turkish–Kazakh, Turkish–Khakas, Uzbek–Kazakh, and Uzbek–Khakas) into the script used by the target language. The transliteration method used tries to maximize the similarity of the transliterations with the writing system of the target language.

3.2 Classifier tuning

For both classifiers we performed a random search through the hyperparameter space, which included the weight of the source language instances. Hence, both classifiers are tuned to make use of the source language based on their usefulness. The other common parameter for both the linear and the neural classifier included window size, which determines the number of characters to the left and right of the current lemma position, the number of characters from the end of the word form predicted so far. For linear models the only other hyperparameter we tune is the regularization constant.

For the neural model we fixed the architecture after some initial experimentation, where the ac-

tion classifier had two hidden layers of 100 units with ReLU activation, followed by a softmax classifier. The part of the network that predict the parameter of insert and replace actions had one layer with ReLU activation followed by a softmax classifier. The input to the parameter classifier was the output of the hidden layer of the activity classifier, as well as the activity prediction. We used early stopping, stopping when the mean edit distance on the development set did not improve. We use only a single-best system, without any weight averaging or ensembling.

Both models are tuned on the training sets of target language, and both source and target combination with a parameter controlling the weight of the source language instances. Random search for transfer model includes the best model parameters tuned on mono-lingual low-resource setting with a source weight parameter set to 0. Hence, the transfer models for each language pair does at

All linear models were implemented in scikit-learn Python library (Pedregosa et al., 2011) using liblinear back end (Fan et al., 2008). The neural model was implemented with Tensorflow (Abadi et al., 2015) using Keras API (Chollet et al., 2015).

4   Results

The official results obtained by our linear and neural model alongside the best and worst baseline results published by the organizers presented in Table 2. The organizers offer a large number of baseline results. We only present the best (unpublished transformer model) and the worst ('untuned' monotonic alignment model). The best system in the competition (CMU-03) achieves an accuracy of 58.79 and mean edit distance of 1.52.

Besides the official results, we also present results obtained after the competition in Table 2. The row labeled '*Linear' presents the results obtained with the same linear classifier after fixing a bug in feature extraction and further tuning. The row marked as 'target only', presents results that are obtained using only the target language, without any attempt of cross-lingual learning. Both scores are obtained using the official evaluation script on the test data released after the end of the evaluation period.

The neural predictor performed worse than the linear predictor, within the (rather limited) effort and computational resources put into developing it. Although the performance is still below the top

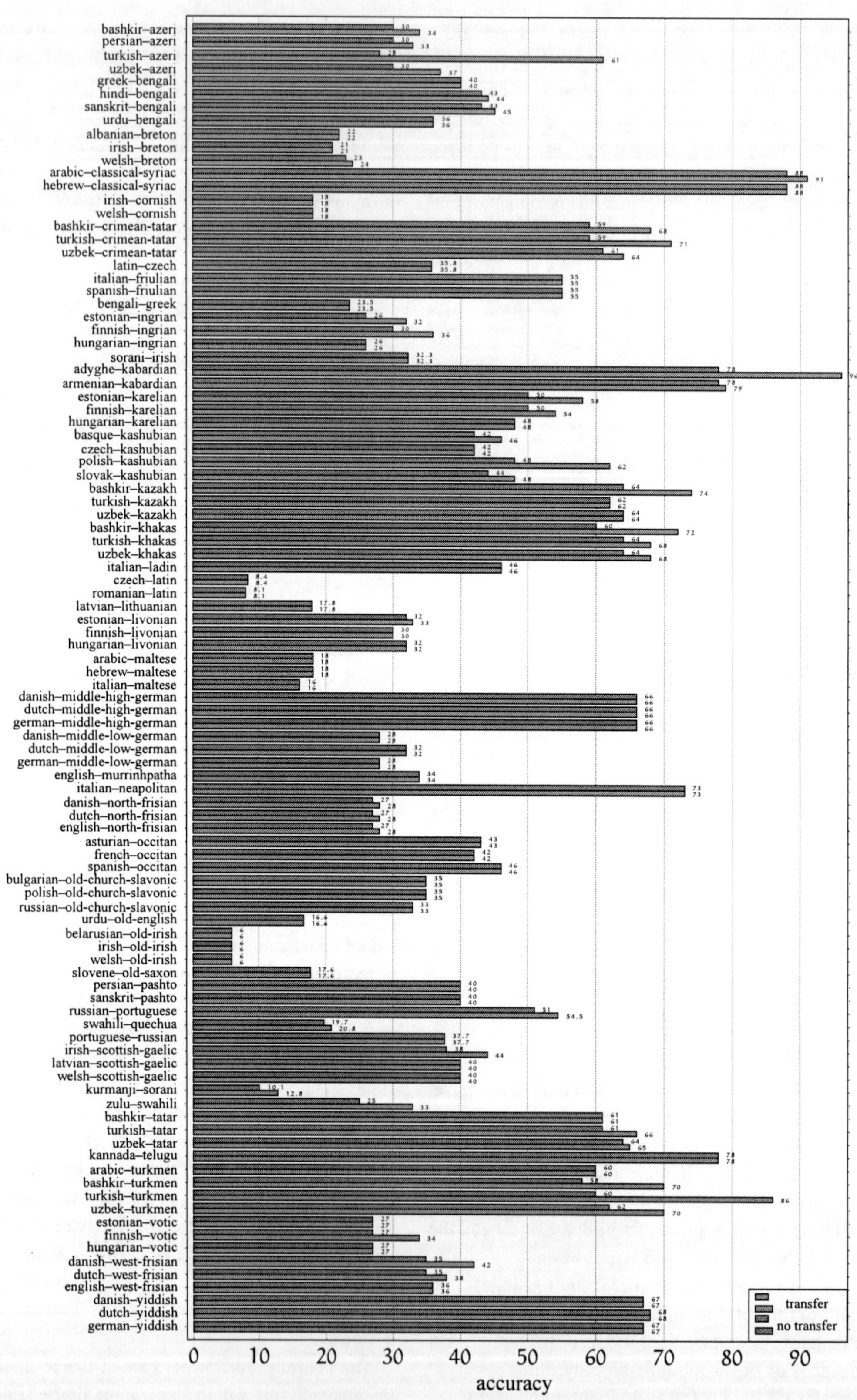

Figure 2: Detailed accuracy scores obtained using the linear predictor with and without source language data. The language pairs are sorted by the target language.

System	Accuracy	MED
Linear	34.49	1.88
Neural	20.86	2.36
*Linear	43.67	1.43
*Linear, target only	41.00	1.50
Baseline (worst)	28.76	2.07
Baseline (best)	54.25	1.13

Table 2: Overall results obtained by our systems in comparison to the official state-of-the-art baseline (Wu and Cotterell, 2019). The scores are word-form accuracy and mean edit distance (MED) averaged over all 100 language pairs. The rows marked with asterisk indicate post-evaluation scores obtained using the linear predictor, after fixing a bug and further tuning.

performing systems, the post-evaluation fixes and tuning results in a dramatic increase in the performance of the linear model. The more interesting result, however, is the small difference between the transfer learning results and the 'target only' results. We present the target-only and transfer accuracy scores for each language pair in Figure 2. In general, the gains from cross-lingual learning are modest. There is no improvement at all for 59 of the language pairs. As expected, this includes all 30 pairs with writing system mismatch, excluding some of the language pairs for which we transliterated the source data. The effect of transliteration is rather modest as well, yielding an improvement between 4 to 12 percentage points of accuracy for four of the eight language pairs where it was used. The effect of the transliteration to the overall score is a $0.29\,\%$ increase in accuracy. Not surprisingly, the highest increases due to cross-lingual learning are obtained when source and target languages are closely related. The highest increase is obtained from Turkish to Azeri with $33\,\%$, followed by Turkish–Turkmen and Adyghe–Kabardian with $26\,\%$ and $18\,\%$ respectively.

5 Summary and outlook

We presented a simple inflection system based on predicting transduction actions. Of the predictors we tried, the linear predictor performs reasonably well. Although its performance is lower than the top performing systems in the shared task, the system is far from being well-tuned, and as demonstrated above simple improvements may have a major effects on the performance. Furthermore,

the linear predictor has the advantage of requiring relatively less computational resources, which may be advantageous in some cases. One further advantage is the ease of analyses of linear learners. What the linear model learns is often much simpler to understand and interpret, and although the need for crafting feature combinations is one of its weaknesses, it may also provide further insight through more interpretable ablation studies. Our neural predictor did not perform as well as the linear predictor. This, however, is by no means a conclusive result. If tuned well, neural networks should in fact work well in this task because of their capability of learning arbitrary combinations of their inputs.

On the cross-lingual side of the problem, the improvements we get are rather modest. In fact, there is a only small overall improvement due to cross-lingual learning over learning only from low-resource target language. Since our relatively simple system can get up to $40\,\%$ accuracy by learning only from the small target language training sets, there is also a good chance that more successful systems are also relying more on the target language data rather than benefiting from transfer learning. Some of the reasons for low success is probably the make up of the data. Not all language pairs are close enough to facilitate the transfer learning. However, there are many possible directions for exploiting the cross-lingual signal better. The simple method used in this study can be improved in many ways. Although our initial experiments were not successful. We believe cross-lingual character embeddings, and 'translating' transduction actions from source language to target language may be potential ways to get a better cross-lingual input.

Acknowledgments

Some of the experiments reported here were run on a Titan Xp donated by the NVIDIA Corporation.

References

Martín Abadi, Ashish Agarwal, Paul Barham, Eugene Brevdo, Zhifeng Chen, Craig Citro, Greg S. Corrado, Andy Davis, Jeffrey Dean, Matthieu Devin, Sanjay Ghemawat, Ian Goodfellow, Andrew Harp, Geoffrey Irving, Michael Isard, Yangqing Jia, Rafal Jozefowicz, Lukasz Kaiser, Manjunath Kudlur, Josh Levenberg, Dan Mané, Rajat Monga, Sherry Moore, Derek Murray, Chris Olah, Mike Schuster, Jonathon Shlens, Benoit Steiner, Ilya Sutskever, Kunal Talwar, Paul Tucker, Vincent Vanhoucke, Vijay Vasudevan, Fernanda Viégas, Oriol Vinyals, Pete Warden, Martin Wattenberg, Martin Wicke, Yuan Yu, and Xiaoqiang Zheng. 2015. TensorFlow: Large-scale machine learning on heterogeneous systems. Software available from tensorflow.org.

Malin Ahlberg, Markus Forsberg, and Mans Hulden. 2015. Paradigm classification in supervised learning of morphology. In *Proceedings of the 2015 Conference of the North American Chapter of the Association for Computational Linguistics: Human Language Technologies*, pages 1024–1029, Denver, Colorado. Association for Computational Linguistics.

Iñaki Alegria and Izaskun Etxeberria. 2016. EHU at the SIGMORPHON 2016 shared task. a simple proposal: Grapheme-to-phoneme for inflection. In *Proceedings of the 14th SIGMORPHON Workshop on Computational Research in Phonetics, Phonology, and Morphology*, pages 27–30, Berlin, Germany. Association for Computational Linguistics.

Jeremy Barnes, Roman Klinger, and Sabine Schulte im Walde. 2018. Bilingual sentiment embeddings: Joint projection of sentiment across languages. In *Proceedings of the 56th Annual Meeting of the Association for Comutational Linguistics (Volume 1: Long Papers)*, pages 2483–2493.

François Chollet et al. 2015. Keras. `https://github.com/fchollet/keras`.

Çağrı Çöltekin and Jeremy Barnes. 2019. Neural and linear pipeline approaches to cross-lingual morphological analysis. In *Proceedings of the Sixth Workshop on NLP for Similar Languages, Varieties and Dialects*, pages 153–164, TOBEFILLED-Ann Arbor, Michigan. Association for Computational Linguistics.

Ryan Cotterell, Christo Kirov, John Sylak-Glassman, Géraldine Walther, Ekaterina Vylomova, Arya D. McCarthy, Katharina Kann, Sebastian Mielke, Garrett Nicolai, Miikka Silfverberg, David Yarowsky, Jason Eisner, and Mans Hulden. 2018. The CoNLL–SIGMORPHON 2018 shared task: Universal morphological reinflection. In *Proceedings of the CoNLL SIGMORPHON 2018 Shared Task: Universal Morphological Reinflection*, pages 1–27. Association for Computational Linguistics.

Ryan Cotterell, Christo Kirov, John Sylak-Glassman, Géraldine Walther, Ekaterina Vylomova, Patrick Xia, Manaal Faruqui, Sandra Kübler, David Yarowsky, Jason Eisner, and Mans Hulden. 2017. CoNLL-SIGMORPHON 2017 shared task: Universal morphological reinflection in 52 languages. In *Proceedings of the CoNLL SIGMORPHON 2017 Shared Task: Universal Morphological Reinflection*, pages 1–30. Association for Computational Linguistics.

Ryan Cotterell, Christo Kirov, John Sylak-Glassman, David Yarowsky, Jason Eisner, and Mans Hulden.

2016. The SIGMORPHON 2016 shared Task—Morphological reinflection. In *Proceedings of the 14th SIGMORPHON Workshop on Computational Research in Phonetics, Phonology, and Morphology*, pages 10–22, Berlin, Germany. Association for Computational Linguistics.

Greg Durrett and John DeNero. 2013. Supervised learning of complete morphological paradigms. In *Proceedings of the 2013 Conference of the North American Chapter of the Association for Computational Linguistics: Human Language Technologies*, pages 1185–1195, Atlanta, Georgia. Association for Computational Linguistics.

Rong-En Fan, Kai-Wei Chang, Cho-Jui Hsieh, Xiang-Rui Wang, and Chih-Jen Lin. 2008. LIBLINEAR: A library for large linear classification. *Journal of Machine Learning Research*, 9:1871–1874.

Manaal Faruqui and Shankar. Kumar. 2015. Multilingual open relation extraction using cross-lingual projection. In *Proceedings of the 2016 Conference of the North American Chapter of the Association for Computational Linguistics: Human Language Technologies*, Proceedings of the 2018 Conference of the North American Chapter of the Association for Computational Linguistics: Human Language Technologies, Volume 2 (Short Papers), pages 1351–1356.

Manaal Faruqui, Yulia Tsvetkov, Graham Neubig, and Chris Dyer. 2016. Morphological inflection generation using character sequence to sequence learning. In *Proceedings of the 2016 Conference of the North American Chapter of the Association for Computational Linguistics: Human Language Technologies*, pages 634–643, San Diego, California. Association for Computational Linguistics.

Melvin Johnson, Mike Schuster, Quoc V. Le, Maxim Krikun, Yonghui Wu, Zhifeng Chen, Nikhil Thorat, Fernanda Viégas, Martin Wattenberg, Greg Corrado, Macduff Hughes, and Jeffrey Dean. 2017. Google's multilingual neural machine translation system: Enabling zero-shot translation. *Transactions of the Association for Computational Linguistics*, 5:339–351.

Gerhard Jäger. 2013. Phylogenetic Inference from Word Lists Using Weighted Alignment with Empirically Determined Weights. *Language Dynamics and Change*, 3(2):245–291.

Katharina Kann and Hinrich Schütze. 2016. MED: The LMU system for the SIGMORPHON 2016 shared task on morphological reinflection. In *Proceedings of the 14th SIGMORPHON Workshop on Computational Research in Phonetics, Phonology, and Morphology*, pages 62–70, Berlin, Germany. Association for Computational Linguistics.

Christo Kirov, Ryan Cotterell, John Sylak-Glassman, Géraldine Walther, Ekaterina Vylomova, Patrick

Xia, Manaal Faruqui, Sebastian J. Mielke, Arya Mc-
Carthy, Sandra Kübler, David Yarowsky, Jason Eisner, and Mans Hulden. 2018. UniMorph 2.0: Universal Morphology. In *Proceedings of the 11th
Language Resources and Evaluation Conference*,
Miyazaki, Japan. European Language Resource Association.

Kimmo Koskenniemi. 1985. Compilation of automata
from morphological two-level rules. In *Papers from
the Fifth Scandinavian Conference of Computational
Linguistics*, page 143–149.

Johann-Mattis List. 2012. SCA: Phonetic Alignment
based on sound classes. *New Directions in Logic,
Language and Computation*, pages 32–51.

Ling Liu and Lingshuang Jack Mao. 2016. Morphological reinflection with conditional random fields
and unsupervised features. In *Proceedings of the
14th SIGMORPHON Workshop on Computational
Research in Phonetics, Phonology, and Morphology*, pages 36–40, Berlin, Germany. Association for
Computational Linguistics.

Peter Makarov and Simon Clematide. 2018. UZH at
CoNLL–SIGMORPHON 2018 shared task on universal morphological reinflection. In *Proceedings
of the CoNLL–SIGMORPHON 2018 Shared Task:
Universal Morphological Reinflection*, pages 69–75,
Brussels. Association for Computational Linguistics.

Peter Makarov, Tatiana Ruzsics, and Simon Clematide.
2017. Align and copy: UZH at SIGMORPHON
2017 shared task for morphological reinflection. In
*Proceedings of the CoNLL SIGMORPHON 2017
Shared Task: Universal Morphological Reinflection*,
pages 49–57, Vancouver. Association for Computational Linguistics.

Arya D. McCarthy, Ekaterina Vylomova, Shijie Wu,
Chaitanya Malaviya, Lawrence Wolf-Sonkin, Garrett Nicolai, Christo Kirov, Miikka Silfverberg, Sebastian Mielke, Jeffrey Heinz, Ryan Cotterell, and
Mans Hulden. 2019. The SIGMORPHON 2019
shared task: Crosslinguality and context in morphology. In *Proceedings of the 16th SIGMORPHON
Workshop on Computational Research in Phonetics,
Phonology, and Morphology*, Florence, Italy. Association for Computational Linguistics.

Garrett Nicolai, Colin Cherry, and Grzegorz Kondrak.
2015. Inflection generation as discriminative string
transduction. In *Proceedings of the 2015 Conference
of the North American Chapter of the Association for
Computational Linguistics: Human Language Technologies*, pages 922–931, Denver, Colorado. Association for Computational Linguistics.

Garrett Nicolai, Bradley Hauer, Adam St Arnaud, and
Grzegorz Kondrak. 2016. Morphological reinflection via discriminative string transduction. In *Proceedings of the 14th SIGMORPHON Workshop on
Computational Research in Phonetics, Phonology,*

and Morphology, pages 31–35, Berlin, Germany.
Association for Computational Linguistics.

Joakim Nivre, Johan Hall, and Jens Nilsson. 2004.
Memory-based dependency parsing. In *Proceedings of the 8th Conference on Computational Natural Language Learning (CoNLL)*, pages 49–56.

F. Pedregosa, G. Varoquaux, A. Gramfort, V. Michel,
B. Thirion, O. Grisel, M. Blondel, P. Prettenhofer,
R. Weiss, V. Dubourg, J. Vanderplas, A. Passos,
D. Cournapeau, M. Brucher, M. Perrot, and E. Duch-
esnay. 2011. Scikit-learn: Machine learning in
Python. *Journal of Machine Learning Research*,
12:2825–2830.

Jelena Prokić. 2010. *Families and resemblances*. Ph.D.
thesis, University of Groningen.

Pavel Sofroniev and Çağrı Çöltekin. 2018. Phonetic
vector representations for sound sequence alignment. In *Proceedings of the Fifteenth Workshop
on Computational Research in Phonetics, Phonology, and Morphology*, pages 111–116, Brussels, Belgium. Association for Computational Linguistics.

Martijn Wieling, Jelena Prokić, and John Nerbonne.
2009. Evaluating the pairwise string alignment of
pronunciations. In *Proceedings of the EACL 2009
workshop on language technology and resources for
cultural heritage, social sciences, humanities, and
education*, pages 26–34.

Shijie Wu and Ryan Cotterell. 2019. Exact hard
monotonic attention for character-level transduction.
arXiv preprint arXiv:1905.06319v1.

Hiroyasu Yamada and Yuji Matsumoto. 2003. Statistical dependency analysis with support vector machines. In *Proceedings of 8th international workshop on parsing technologies (IWPT)*, pages 195–
206.

David Yarowsky, Grace Ngai, and Richard Wicen-
towski. 2001. Inducing multilingual text analysis
tools via robust projection across aligned corpora.
In *Proceedings of the first international conference
on Human language technology research*, pages 1–8.
Association for Computational Linguistics.

THOMAS: The Hegemonic OSU Morphological Analyzer using Seq2seq

Byung-Doh Oh[1]*   **Pranav Maneriker**[2]*   **Nanjiang Jiang**[1]*

[1]Department of Linguistics, The Ohio State University
[2]Department of Computer Science and Engineering, The Ohio State University
`{oh.531, maneriker.1, jiang.1879}@osu.edu`

Abstract

This paper describes the OSU submission to the SIGMORPHON 2019 shared task, *Crosslinguality and Context in Morphology*. Our system addresses the *contextual morphological analysis* subtask of Task 2, which is to produce the morphosyntactic description (MSD) of each fully inflected word within a given sentence. We frame this as a sequence generation task and employ a neural encoder-decoder (seq2seq) architecture to generate the sequence of MSD tags given the encoded representation of each token. Follow-up analyses reveal that our system most significantly improves performance on morphologically complex languages whose inflected word forms typically have longer MSD tag sequences. In addition, our system seems to capture the structured correlation between MSD tags, such as that between the verb V tag and TAM-related tags.

1 Introduction

For many natural language processing (NLP) applications such as parsing and machine translation, correctly analyzing the part-of-speech and fine-grained morphological information (e.g. tense, mood, and aspect) of a given string of words is crucial for satisfactory performance. This task depends on the system's ability to learn reliable representations of the sequence on two distinct levels – one at the character-level, which is indicative of the morphosyntactic values of the word, and the other at the word-level, which is informative of subsequent words that are likely to appear in the sequence. In addition, the system needs to have representational flexibility in order to be used in a cross-linguistic setting, as languages with typologically distinct morphological systems (e.g. isolating, agglutinative, and fusional) have different methods of realizing morphological information.

Input	They buy and sell books .
MSD tags	N;NOM;PL | V;SG;1;PRS | CONJ | V;PL;3;PRS | N;PL | PUNCT

Table 1: Example English contextual morphological analysis problem from SIGMORPHON 2019 Shared Task 2 (McCarthy et al., 2019).

Task 2 of the SIGMORPHON 2019 Shared Task, *Morphological Analysis and Lemmatization in Context* (McCarthy et al., 2019), provides an appropriate setting to examine the applicability of morphological analyzers on typologically distinct languages. As mentioned on the shared task webpage,[1] the goal of the *contextual morphological analysis* subtask of Task 2 is to produce the morphosyntactic description (MSD) of each word within a given sentence (i.e. "context," see Table 1 for example).[2] The system's performance is evaluated on a total of 107 treebanks from the UniMorph dataset (McCarthy et al., 2018), which covers more than 70 languages. Again, this requires the system to generalize across typologically different languages without being biased towards a particular morphological system.

In this paper, we present our approach of treating contextual morphological analysis as the generation of the correct sequence of MSD tag dimensions. To address the task, we take a similar approach as the shared task baseline system (Malaviya et al., 2019) in encoding each word in the sequence with a representation learned by a

---

*First authors. Ordering determined by dice roll.

[1] `https://sigmorphon.github.io/sharedtasks/2019/task2/`

[2] For the other subtask of *contextual lemmatization*, the goal of which is to return the correct lemmata of the fully inflected forms, we generated the predictions using the pretrained shared task baseline lemmatizer (Malaviya et al., 2019). As the baseline system conducts lemmatization by conditioning on predicted MSD tags, we provided the system with the predictions from our seq2seq model as input.

Proceedings of the 16th Workshop on Computational Research in Phonetics, Phonology, and Morphology, pages 80–86
Florence, Italy. August 2, 2019 ©2019 Association for Computational Linguistics

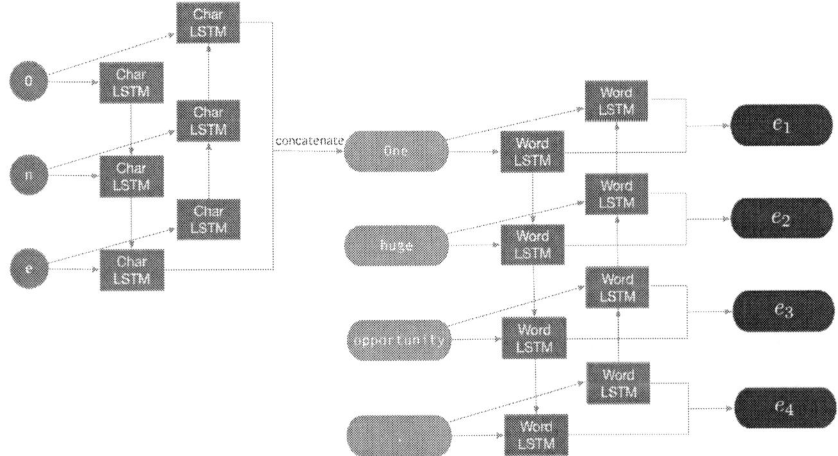

Figure 1: The encoder based on bidirectional LSTM for the baseline, binary relevance, and seq2seq models.

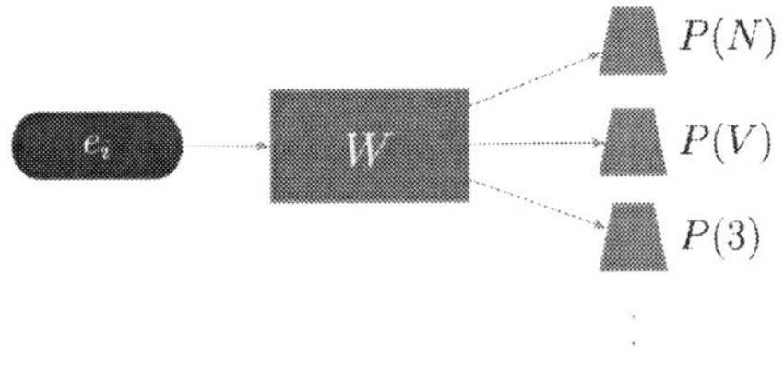

(a) The decoder of the binary relevance model, which makes independent binary decisions for each possible tag dimension.

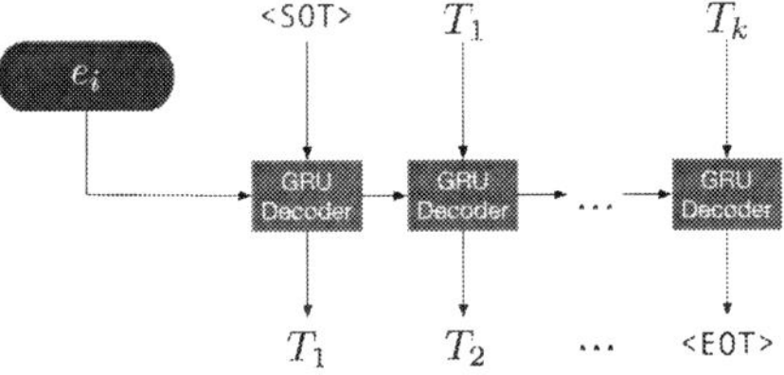

(b) The GRU decoder of the seq2seq model, which predicts the next tag dimension given the encoder representation and the prediction at the previous timestep.

Figure 2: Overview of the decoder architectures.

character-level recurrent neural network (RNN). With the baseline system that treats each possible combination of MSD tag dimensions separately and chooses the most likely combination, we first demonstrate that modifying the system to make multiple independent binary decisions over each possible tag dimension results in higher performance. Furthermore, we present an encoder-decoder (seq2seq) model that decodes the representation of each input word into a sequence of MSD tag dimensions. The use of the seq2seq model further improves model performance, espe-

cially in terms of exact match accuracy for tokens that have long sequences of MSD tag dimensions. Our best-performing model outperforms the official baseline by 14.25 on exact match accuracy and by 4.6 on micro-averaged F1.

2 Model Description

Baseline model The baseline model takes as input each sentence in the training data, and uses a bidirectional LSTM (Long Short-Term Memory, Hochreiter and Schmidhuber, 1997) to learn a representation for each word by attending to its individual characters. The learned representation is then subsequently fed into a fully connected linear layer, which maps the representation of the word to the space of every observed combination of MSD tag dimensions. The network is updated based on the cross-entropy loss between the model's prediction and the correct combination of MSD tag dimensions.

Binary relevance model An obvious limitation to the above baseline approach is that the number of observed combinations of MSD tag dimensions is typically large for most languages, and especially for agglutinative and fusional languages whose words contain relatively more morphological information than those of other languages (see Table 2). In addition, treating each combination separately prevents the model from generalizing to other instances of the same MSD tag dimension that might simply appear in a different combination. We hypothesize that this would most unfavorably impact system performance on

	Sents	Tokens	Tags	Combinations
en	13297	204857	36	178
es	14144	439925	40	419
hi	13317	281948	43	1508
ru	4024	79989	47	1385
tr	4508	46417	55	1896
zh	3997	98734	21	39

Table 2: Descriptive statistics for the six UniMorph treebanks used for training. Number of tags refers to the number of different MSD tag dimensions, and the number of combinations refers to the number of different MSD tag combinations present in each training set.

	Baseline		Bin. Rel.		Seq2seq	
	Acc.	F1	Acc.	F1	Acc.	F1
en	80.17	90.91	92.53	**95.75**	**93.72**	95.41
es	84.35	95.35	96.39	**98.42**	**96.77**	98.31
hi	80.60	93.92	87.59	**96.37**	**88.13**	95.99
ru	63.37	87.49	81.42	**92.92**	**84.92**	**92.92**
tr	62.94	86.10	84.15	**93.87**	**87.08**	93.84
zh	75.97	83.79	89.61	91.18	**91.57**	**91.35**

Table 3: Exact match accuracy and micro-averaged F1 scores of the models evaluated on the test portion of each respective UniMorph treebank. For each dataset, the best results under each metric are in bold.

agglutinative languages, which typically have a clear correspondence between surface string and MSD tag dimension. In order to mitigate this issue, we mapped the learned representation of each word to the space of individual MSD tag dimensions, where independent binary decisions about the presence of each tag dimension are made.

Encoder-decoder (seq2seq) model[3] Nonetheless, given the fact that particular MSD tag dimensions tend to co-occur within a same word (e.g. the "verb" tag dimension frequently co-occurs with tense- or aspect-related tag dimensions), the independence assumption between individual tag dimensions made in the binary relevance model may be too strong to capture this inherent structure. To account for the potential dependence between predicted tag dimensions, we feed the encoded representation of each word as the initial hidden states of a GRU (Gated Recurrent Unit, Cho et al., 2014) decoder, which is then trained to predict one tag dimension at each decoding timestep. The use of such a seq2seq model is also partly motivated by its state-of-the-art performance in various NLP tasks such as machine translation (Bahdanau et al., 2015; Luong et al., 2015), document classification (Nam et al., 2017; Yang et al., 2018), morphological reinflection (Kann and Schütze, 2016; Kann et al., 2017), and morphological analysis like the current shared task (Tkachenko and Sirts, 2018). Our seq2seq model resembles Tkachenko and Sirts's (2018) SEQ model, with the primary difference being the use of a GRU decoder (instead of their unidirectional LSTM) and the sorting of tag dimensions in decreasing order of frequency

during training. An overview of our model architecture is presented in Figures 1 and 2.

Our seq2seq model strongly outperforms the official baseline, scoring 14.25 and 4.6 points higher on average across 107 datasets on exact match accuracy and micro-averaged F1 scores respectively. For an in-depth analysis of each model, we focus on 6 languages and compare the performance of our two models (binary relevance and seq2seq) to that of the baseline model.

3 Experimental Design

Training data Following the shared task guidelines, six different treebanks from the UniMorph dataset (McCarthy et al., 2018) provided the data for training and evaluating the model. The six treebanks – English-EWT, Spanish-Ancora, Hindi-HDTB, Russian-GSD, Turkish-IMST, and Chinese-GSD – cover a wide spectrum of morphological typology, thus making it suitable to assess the generalizability of each morphological analysis system. The descriptive statistics of each training set are outlined in Table 2.

Training and evaluation procedure For the binary relevance model, most of the hyperparameters followed the default settings of the baseline system code[4]; characters were embedded into 128-dimension representations, and the character-level biLSTM was trained to output a 256-dimension representation. Adam (Kingma and Ba, 2015) was used as the optimizer, using the default settings of the PyTorch deep learning library (Paszke et al., 2017). The model was trained for five epochs using batches of size 16, with early stopping.[5] The same hyperparameters were used

---

[3] The predictions from this model were submitted to the shared task. The code repository can be found at `https://github.com/njjiang/THOMAS`

[4] `https://github.com/sigmorphon/contextual-analysis-baseline`

[5] As the task organizers do not explicitly mention the hyperparameters used to train the baseline models, it is assumed

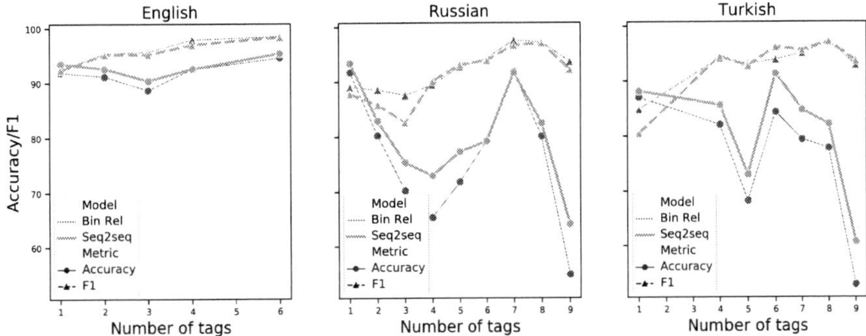

Figure 3: Exact match accuracy and micro-averaged F1 scores of the models on tokens with different numbers of MSD tag dimensions.

	Bin. Rel.	Seq2seq
en	459	89
es	559	70
hi	439	199
ru	423	166
tr	124	63
zh	117	0

Table 4: Number of instances where two tag dimensions that do not co-occur in the test portion of the dataset were predicted together by each model.

to train the encoder portion of the seq2seq model.

As for the GRU decoder, the maximum sequence length was fixed as the maximum sequence length seen during training. Following prior work (Yang et al., 2018), the order of the output tags was fixed to be in decreasing order of frequency of occurrence in the training set. Decoding took place in a greedy manner, and only the highest scoring hypothesis at the previous timestep was further pursued. The model was trained without any teacher forcing, as preliminary results showed that a teacher forcing ratio of 0.5 resulted in a decrease in model performance.

After training was complete, the models' accuracy was evaluated on the held-out test portion of the six treebanks that were used to train the models. As per the shared task guidelines, the exact match accuracy and micro-averaged F1 scores were calculated for each of the trained models.

4 Results and Discussion

As can be seen in Table 3, having the model make independent binary decisions for each possible MSD tag dimension (i.e. the binary relevance model) significantly increases model performance. This is most likely the result of having narrowed down the output space and thereby allowing the model to generalize over instances of the same tag dimension that appear in different combinations. In addition, using a neural decoder to generate a sequence of tag dimensions further improves model performance in terms of exact match accuracy, which is sensitive to predicting the correct number of tag dimensions. This corroborates the results of Tkachenko and Sirts (2018), who found that their sequence generation model outperformed other neural classifiers in terms of accuracy on most languages. The increase in performance is especially salient in Russian and Turkish, which typically have more tag dimensions per word than other languages. An analysis of the distribution of predicted tag dimensions (Table 4) shows that the seq2seq model predicts significantly less "invalid" combinations that are not attested in the gold test set,[6] indicating that the seq2seq model is more capable of capturing the structured dependence compared to the binary relevance model.

Lengths of tag sequences To further examine where the seq2seq model makes significant improvement, the exact match accuracy and micro-averaged F1 scores were calculated according to

---

that the default settings of the code were used to train them. The only changes to the default settings when training the binary relevance model were in the training epochs (default 10 epochs) and batch size (not implemented, therefore default size 1).

[6]These include combinations of tag dimensions that are either in complementary distribution (e.g. the singular SG and plural PL tags) or linguistically irrelevant (e.g. the noun N tag and tense-related tags).

en	Bin. Rel.			Seq2seq		
	P < G	**P = G**	**P > G**	**P < G**	**P = G**	**P > G**
0	-	3199	14	-	3201	12
1	0	7819	252	0	7872	199
2	386	9296	164	165	9605	76
3	61	1017	44	58	1037	27
4	125	1995	20	150	1986	4
5	3	384	2	1	386	2
6	27	704	6	20	716	1
ru	**P < G**	**P = G**	**P > G**	**P < G**	**P = G**	**P > G**
0	-	1712	1	-	1712	1
1	0	1751	91	0	1770	72
2	11	165	17	3	176	14
3	21	126	11	4	138	16
4	48	341	29	3	381	34
5	448	3906	235	48	4512	29
6	12	89	0	7	90	4
7	19	386	2	14	389	4
8	11	191	4	4	202	0
9	40	97	5	17	124	1
tr	**P < G**	**P = G**	**P > G**	**P < G**	**P = G**	**P > G**
0	-	1034	0	-	1034	0
1	0	1198	87	0	1183	102
4	175	1382	35	63	1484	45
5	143	477	10	81	538	11
6	28	209	6	9	225	9
7	81	470	26	36	506	35
8	53	257	10	29	279	12
9	24	27	0	18	33	0

Table 5: Comparison of the number of MSD tag dimensions predicted by each model and that in the gold annotation, sorted according to the number of tags in the gold annotation. P refers to the number of tags predicted by the model, and G refers to the number of tags that are in the gold annotation.

Tag	Freq.	Bin. Rel.		Seq2seq	
		Acc.	**F1**	**Acc.**	**F1**
COND	18	27.78	86.09	**66.67**	**94.82**
FUT	62	**72.58**	**95.85**	69.35	93.72
HAB	106	75.47	**94.74**	**77.36**	92.67
IMP	32	59.38	77.34	**75.0**	**84.79**
IND	1022	81.12	96.08	**85.71**	**96.51**
OPT	14	71.43	88.4	**85.71**	**95.24**
PFV	944	78.18	94.93	**84.43**	**95.98**
POT	56	**67.86**	**96.91**	62.5	94.19
PROG	134	88.81	98.98	**90.3**	**99.13**
PROSP	3	66.67	95.24	**100.0**	**100.0**
PRS	646	75.54	93.29	**82.82**	**94.47**
PST	439	84.28	98.11	**87.7**	**98.39**
PST+PRF	38	89.47	97.95	**97.37**	**99.26**
FUT/PST	3	66.67	95.24	**100.0**	**100.0**

Table 6: Performance of the two models on TAM-related tokens in the Turkish test set. For each TAM-related tag dimension, the best results under each metric are in bold.

the number of MSD tag dimensions in the test portion of the dataset. In Figure 3, the scores are presented for English, Russian, and Turkish.[7] Additionally, we compared the number of tag dimensions predicted by each model to that of the gold annotation in order to investigate whether there was a tendency for the models to over- or under-predict the correct number of tag dimensions (Table 5). Although there is no clear pattern as to sequences of what length (i.e. short or long) the seq2seq model helps the most, it is clear from the scores that the seq2seq model has the capability to reproduce longer sequences of tag dimensions in comparison to the binary relevance model. Furthermore, while both models predict the correct number of tag dimensions for the vast majority of test examples, the seq2seq model makes more accurate predictions across sequences of nearly

all lengths. There is also a general tendency for the two models to under-predict rather than over-predict distinct tag dimensions, with the exception of the seq2seq model on Russian examples with four tag dimensions or less.

Dependence between tag dimensions We hypothesize that the neural decoder of the seq2seq model helped it correctly predict tag dimensions that are low in frequency but often co-occur with a more frequent tag dimension. Such highly dependent examples can be found in the verbal paradigm of a language, where tag dimensions that indicate a particular tense, aspect, and mood (TAM; e.g. present, progressive, indicative) always co-occur with the verb (V) tag dimension. We expect that the prediction of the higher-frequency V tag dimension during decoding would have helped the model accurately predict these specific TAM-related tag dimensions. As a case study testing this hypothesis, we compared the performance of the two models on TAM-related tokens present in the Turkish test set. The results in Table 6 reveal that the seq2seq model generally outperforms the binary relevance model, indicating that the seq2seq model captures the dependence between the V tag dimension and TAM-related tag dimensions.

While the above analyses clearly demonstrate that the seq2seq model learns the structure behind MSD tag dimensions and thus predicts more linguistically plausible sequences in comparison to

---

[7]There was only one token each with two or three tag dimensions in the test portion of the Turkish dataset (and none in the development portion). As such, the scores for tokens with two or three tag dimensions were omitted in the figure.

Gold	Prediction
INAN;GEN;PL;V;IPFV;PRS;V.PTCP;PASS	INAN;GEN;PL;ADJ
PL;V;FIN;IND;IPFV;PRS;2	SG;INAN;N;FEM;DAT
PL;V;FIN;IND;IPFV;PRS;2	SG;V;FIN;PFV;2;IMP
PL;V;FIN;IND;IPFV;PRS;MID;2	SG;V;FIN;IND;IPFV;3;PRS
PL;V;FIN;IND;PFV;1;FUT	SG;INAN;MASC;N;NOM
PL;V;FIN;IPFV;MID;2;IMP	SG;N;NOM;FEM;V
SG;INAN;FEM;V;ESS;IPFV;PRS;V.PTCP;PASS	SG;INAN;N;NEUT;ESS
SG;INAN;GEN;FEM;V;PST;PFV;V.PTCP;PASS	SG;INAN;GEN;FEM;ADJ
SG;INAN;NOM;V;NEUT;PST;PFV;V.PTCP;PASS	SG;INAN;N;NOM;NEUT
SG;MASC;NOM;ANIM;V;PST;PFV;V.PTCP;PASS	SG;MASC;N;NOM;ANIM
SG;MASC;V;FIN;IND;PST;PFV	SG;MASC;N;NOM;ANIM;PST;PFV;V.PTCP;PASS
SG;V;FIN;IND;IPFV;PRS;1	SG;N;NOM;V;FIN

Table 7: Representative errors from the seq2seq model on Russian test examples with seven or more tag dimensions in the gold annotation.

the binary relevance model, the binary relevance model slightly outperforms the seq2seq model in terms of micro-averaged F1 score. We conjecture that this is due to the nature of the decoder employed in the seq2seq model. Because the decoder conditions on its prediction at the previous timestep, once the decoder predicts an erroneous tag dimension, it is likely to continue to deviate from the correct sequence. This will result in predictions that do not have many tag dimensions in common with the gold annotation. On the other hand, as the binary relevance model is optimized to predict each individual tag dimension independently, it is more likely to generate "partially correct" sequences that are penalized less severely by the F1 score. Representative errors from the seq2seq model on the Russian test set presented in Table 7 demonstrate this tendency; in general, the prediction of an incorrect tag dimension results in predictions that have little overlap with the gold annotation.

In order to alleviate such decoding errors of the seq2seq model, a beam search could be conducted to pursue multiple hypotheses simultaneously. This could help the model recover from an initial erroneous prediction, albeit at the cost of computational efficiency. Furthermore, to explicitly incorporate the underlying structure between MSD tag dimensions, the binary relevance model could be extended to a multiclass multilabel classifier, which selects one tag among those that are in complementary distribution for each morphological category (e.g. part-of-speech, case, number) as in Tkachenko and Sirts (2018). Finally, a more rigorous search for the optimal hyperparameters (e.g. hidden state sizes, training epochs, learning rate) of each model could further enhance their performance. We leave these directions to future work.

5 Conclusion

In this paper, we present our approach to the SIGMORPHON 2019 *contextual morphological analysis* shared task. Expanding from the baseline model that chooses the most likely combination from all those present in the training data, we demonstrate that having the model make independent binary decisions over each tag dimension alleviates data sparsity and improves model performance. Furthermore, based on the linguistic insight that certain tag dimensions often co-occur together, we employed a neural decoder to turn contextual morphological analysis into a sequence generation task and aimed to capture this dependence. This again improved model performance in terms of exact match accuracy, especially for morphologically rich languages that generally have more MSD tag dimensions for every token. A follow-up case study of Turkish verbal inflections demonstrates that the seq2seq model captures the correlation between the more frequent V tag dimension and the less frequent TAM-related tag dimensions.

Acknowledgement

We thank Micha Elsner for all his valuable advice throughout the course of this project.

References

Dzmitry Bahdanau, Kyunghyun Cho, and Yoshua Bengio. 2015. Neural machine translation by jointly learning to align and translate. In *3rd International Conference on Learning Representations, ICLR 2015, San Diego, CA, USA, May 7-9, 2015, Conference Track Proceedings*.

Kyunghyun Cho, Bart van Merrienboer, Caglar Gulcehre, Dzmitry Bahdanau, Fethi Bougares, Holger Schwenk, and Yoshua Bengio. 2014. Learning phrase representations using RNN encoder–decoder for statistical machine translation. In *Proceedings of the 2014 Conference on Empirical Methods in Natural Language Processing (EMNLP)*, pages 1724–1734, Doha, Qatar. Association for Computational Linguistics.

Sepp Hochreiter and Jürgen Schmidhuber. 1997. Long short-term memory. *Neural Computation*, 9(8):1735–1780.

Katharina Kann, Ryan Cotterell, and Hinrich Schütze. 2017. Neural multi-source morphological reinflection. In *Proceedings of the 15th Conference of the European Chapter of the Association for Computational Linguistics: Volume 1, Long Papers*, pages 514–524, Valencia, Spain. Association for Computational Linguistics.

Katharina Kann and Hinrich Schütze. 2016. MED: The LMU system for the SIGMORPHON 2016 shared task on morphological reinflection. In *Proceedings of the 14th SIGMORPHON Workshop on Computational Research in Phonetics, Phonology, and Morphology*, pages 62–70, Berlin, Germany. Association for Computational Linguistics.

Diederik P. Kingma and Jimmy Ba. 2015. Adam: A method for stochastic optimization. In *3rd International Conference on Learning Representations, ICLR 2015, San Diego, CA, USA, May 7-9, 2015, Conference Track Proceedings*.

Thang Luong, Hieu Pham, and Christopher D. Manning. 2015. Effective approaches to attention-based neural machine translation. In *Proceedings of the 2015 Conference on Empirical Methods in Natural Language Processing*, pages 1412–1421, Lisbon, Portugal. Association for Computational Linguistics.

Chaitanya Malaviya, Shijie Wu, and Ryan Cotterell. 2019. A simple joint model for improved contextual neural lemmatization. *arXiv preprint arXiv:1904.02306v2*.

Arya D. McCarthy, Miikka Silfverberg, Ryan Cotterell, Mans Hulden, and David Yarowsky. 2018. Marrying Universal Dependencies and Universal Morphology. In *Proceedings of the Second Workshop on Universal Dependencies (UDW 2018)*, pages 91–101, Brussels, Belgium. Association for Computational Linguistics.

Arya D. McCarthy, Ekaterina Vylomova, Shijie Wu, Chaitanya Malaviya, Lawrence Wolf-Sonkin, Garrett Nicolai, Christo Kirov, Miikka Silfverberg, Sebastian Mielke, Jeffrey Heinz, Ryan Cotterell, and Mans Hulden. 2019. The SIGMORPHON 2019 shared task: Crosslinguality and context in morphology. In *Proceedings of the 16th SIGMORPHON Workshop on Computational Research in Phonetics, Phonology, and Morphology*, Florence, Italy. Association for Computational Linguistics.

Jinseok Nam, Eneldo Loza Mencía, Hyunwoo J Kim, and Johannes Fürnkranz. 2017. Maximizing subset accuracy with recurrent neural networks in multi-label classification. In I. Guyon, U. V. Luxburg, S. Bengio, H. Wallach, R. Fergus, S. Vishwanathan, and R. Garnett, editors, *Advances in Neural Information Processing Systems 30*, pages 5413–5423. Curran Associates, Inc.

Adam Paszke, Sam Gross, Soumith Chintala, Gregory Chanan, Edward Yang, Zachary DeVito, Zeming Lin, Alban Desmaison, Luca Antiga, and Adam Lerer. 2017. Automatic differentiation in PyTorch. In *NIPS-W*.

Alexander Tkachenko and Kairit Sirts. 2018. Modeling composite labels for neural morphological tagging. In *Proceedings of the 22nd Conference on Computational Natural Language Learning*, pages 368–379, Brussels, Belgium. Association for Computational Linguistics.

Pengcheng Yang, Xu Sun, Wei Li, Shuming Ma, Wei Wu, and Houfeng Wang. 2018. SGM: Sequence generation model for multi-label classification. In *Proceedings of the 27th International Conference on Computational Linguistics*, pages 3915–3926, Santa Fe, New Mexico, USA. Association for Computational Linguistics.

Sigmorphon 2019 Task 2 system description paper: Morphological analysis in context for many languages, with supervision from only a few

Jared Kelly[*] **Brad Aiken**[**] **Alexis Palmer**[*]
Suleyman Olcay Polat[**] **Taraka Rama**[*] **Rodney Nielsen**[**]

[*]Department of Linguistics, University of North Texas
{jared.kelly,alexis.palmer}@unt.edu, tarakark@ifi.uio.no
[**]Department of Computer Science and Engineering, University of North Texas
{bradfordaiken,suleymanolcaypolat}@my.unt.edu, rodney.nielsen@unt.edu

Abstract

This paper presents the UNT HiLT+Ling system for the Sigmorphon 2019 shared Task 2: Morphological Analysis and Lemmatization in Context. Our core approach focuses on the morphological tagging task; part-of-speech tagging and lemmatization are treated as secondary tasks. Given the highly multilingual nature of the task, we propose an approach which makes minimal use of the supplied training data, in order to be extensible to languages without labeled training data for the morphological analysis task. Specifically, we use a parallel Bible corpus to align contextual embeddings at the verse level. The aligned verses are used to build cross-language translation matrices, which in turn are used to map between embedding spaces for the various languages. Finally, we use sets of inflected forms, primarily from a high-resource language, to induce vector representations for individual UniMorph tags. Morphological tagging is performed by matching vector representations to embeddings for individual tokens. While our system results are dramatically below the average system submitted for the shared task evaluation campaign, our method is (we suspect) unique in its minimal reliance on labeled training data.

1 Introduction

This paper describes the UNT HiLT+Ling system submission for the Sigmorphon shared task on morphological analysis and lemmatization in context (McCarthy et al., 2019). We focus primarily on the morphological tagging task, treating part-of-speech tagging and lemmatization as secondary tasks. We approach morphological analysis from the perspective of low-resource languages, aiming to develop an approach which exploits existing language resources in order to make morphological analysis in context feasible for languages

without annotated training data. We propose a model to perform morphosyntactic annotation for any language with a translation of the Bible. According to Wycliffe[1], there are currently 683 languages in the world which contain a translation of the entire Bible, and an additional 1534 languages for which the entire New Testament, and sometimes other sections, are available.

We train contextual word representations using ELMo (Peters et al., 2018) and align embedding spaces for language pairs using Bible verse numbers as an alignment signal. We then compute vector representations for UniMorph tags in English and project those representations into the target language. The projected morpheme tag embeddings are used to identify morphological features and label tokens in context with UniMorph tags.

We give a system overview in Section 2, with more detailed model descriptions in Section 5. The system's performance is currently poor; we outline known limitations and make some suggestions for improvement.

2 System Overview

The system we developed for Sigmorphon 2019 Task 2 can be divided into two parts: the core model and two additional non-core components. The core model is responsible for the morphological tagging task, our main focus. The two non-core components are part-of-speech tagging and lemmatization.

Core model: Minimally-supervised morphological analysis in context. Following task specifications, we aim to predict UniMorph tags for words in context. Our approach is designed to work on new languages with minimal supervision. Specifically, the base model uses the following forms of supervision: a) multilingual bible

---

[1]http://www.wycliffe.net/statistics

87

Proceedings of the 16th Workshop on Computational Research in Phonetics, Phonology, and Morphology, pages 87–94
Florence, Italy. August 2, 2019 ©2019 Association for Computational Linguistics

data, verse-aligned; and b) roughly twenty words per from the training data per UniMorph tag. Once this model has been developed, it can be applied for a new language with no annotated training data for the task; the only data needed is a Bible in that language.

The steps in the process (explained in detail in Section 5.1) are as follows:

1. Learn sentence-level ELMO embeddings (Peters et al., 2018) for each language.
2. Use verse-aligned data to learn a vector translation matrix (following Mikolov et al., 2013a) between each language and English.
3. Compute a vector representation for each UniMorph tag.
4. For UniMorph tags found in English, map tag vectors into the other languages which use the tag, by way of the relevant translation matrix. For tags not found in English, compute vector representations for each tag in the language-specific space.
5. Identify all UniMorph tags represented in the embedding for a given word, treating morphological analysis in the style of analogy tasks (Mikolov et al., 2013b).

POS tagging and lemmatization. POS tagging and lemmatization are treated as non-core components of the model. In other words, we incorporate these tasks into our model in order to meet the requirements of the competition. For these two tasks, greater supervision is allowed, and models are learned from the training data provided. The POS tagger in our system is a straightforward HMM model, and lemmatization is done with a seq2seq neural architecture. See Section 5.2 for more detailed descriptions of the models.

3   Related Work

The core idea of using the Bible as parallel data in low-resource settings is largely inspired by previous work. The Bible has been used as a means of alignment for cross-lingual projection, both for POS tagging (Agic et al., 2015) and for dependency parsing (Agic et al., 2016), as well as for base noun-phrase bracketing, named-entity tagging, and morphological analysis (Yarowsky et al., 2001) with promising results.

Peters et al. (2018) introduce ELMo embeddings, contextual word embeddings which incorporate character-level information using a CNN.

Both of these properties - sensitivity to context and the ability to capture sub-word information - make contextual embeddings suitable for the task at hand.

In order to make embeddings useful across languages, we need a method for aligning embedding spaces across languages. Ruder et al. (2017) provide an excellent survey of methods for aligning embedding spaces. Mikolov et al. (2013a) introduce a translation matrix for aligning embeddings spaces in different languages and show how this is useful for machine translation purposes. We adopt this approach to do alignment at the verse level. Alignment with contextual embeddings is more complicated, since the embeddings are dynamic by their very nature (different across different contexts). In order to align these dynamic embeddings, Schuster et al. (2019) introduce a number of methods, however they all require either a supervised dictionary for each language, or access to the MUSE framework for alignment, neither of which we assume in our work.

The UniMorph 2.0 data-set (Kirov et al., 2018) provides resources for morphosyntactic analysis across 111 different languages. The work described here uses the tag set from UniMorph.

4   Data

This section describes the data resources used for training and evaluating the system.

4.1   Bible data

The main data used for building our core model is a multilingual Bible corpus. For as many of the shared task languages as possible (41), we use the corpus from Christodouloupoulos and Steedman (2015). Bibles for an additional 19 languages were sourced elsewhere. Of the remaining 11 languages, we use proxy languages (Section 4.2) for 9. For two languages (Akkadian and Sanskrit), we were unable to locate a suitable Bible in time. Where there are multiple data sets for a given language, we use the same Bible for all data sets.

For some languages we have access to the entire Bible, and for others only the New Testament (NT). This introduces discrepancies in the amount of data used to train embeddings from language to language, as the Old Testament is much longer than the New Testament.

The Bible is a natural source of parallel data, as it is available (either in whole or in parts) in

Shared task language	ISO code	Proxy language	ISO code
UD_Belarusian-HSE	bel	Russian	rus
UD_Breton-KEB	bre	Irish Gaelic	gle
UD_Galician-CTG	glg	Portuguese	por
UD_Galician-TreeGal	glg	Portuguese	por
UD_Gothic-PROIEL	got	Icelandic	isl
UD_Norwegian-Nynorsk	nno	Icelandic	isl
UD_Norwegian-NynorskLIA	nno	Icelandic	isl
UD_Upper_Sorbian-UFAL	hsb	Czech	ces
		Dialect	
UD_Armenian-ArmTDP	hy	Eastern Armenian	hye
UD_Irish-IDT	ga	Irish Gaelic	gle
UD_Persian-Seraji	fa	Western Persian	pes
		No Bible	
UD_Akkadian-PISANDUB	akk		
UD_Sanskrit-UFAL	san		

Table 1: Shared task languages for which a proxy language or close dialect was used, and languages for which no Bible was used.

over one thousand languages, including many low-resource languages. One advantage of using the Bible, beyond its wide availability in translation for free, is that its verses are fairly well-aligned in meaning across languages (unlike words or even sentences). One drawback to using Bible data is the archaic nature of the language. For example, even if we use a modern translation, the English Bible contains fewer than 15,000 different word types, and no occurrences of modern words (e.g. *Republican*, *computer*, or *NASA*).

The limited domain of the text offers both advantages and disadvantages. On the one hand, much of the vocabulary found in the shared task evaluation data does not occur in the Bible. Using embeddings trained on the Bible, then, results in an extremely large number of out-of-vocabulary tokens at test time. On the other, the semantic territory covered by the embedding spaces varies remarkably little from language to language, increasing the feasibility of aligning embedding spaces across multiple languages.

4.2 Proxy languages

In order to do morphological analysis for a given language, our method requires access to a digitally-available version of at least portions of the Bible for that language. At the time the model was developed, we did not have access to Bibles for all shared task languages. For each missing

language, we select a proxy language (Table 1). For example, we don't have a Bible for Galician, so at every stage in the process where the Galician Bible would be used, we substitute the Portuguese Bible, treating Portuguese as pseudo-Galician. We identify two different cases of proxy language substitution. In some cases, we are able to select a closely-related dialect for the target language. In others, the proxy language is selected based on a combination of morphological similarity (typologically speaking) and language relatedness.[2]

4.3 Sigmorphon data

We use the provided training data (McCarthy et al., 2018) primarily to train a part-of-speech tagger and lemmatizer for each shared task data set, and the provided test data is used to evaluate the system. We use portions of the training data for three other purposes: a) to build contrasting sets of words for each UniMorph tag (Section 5.1.3); b) to build lists of UniMorph tags relevant for each language; and c) to create a simple baseline for the two languages for which we have no Bible, proxy language or otherwise.

---

[2]In an early experiment, we investigated the effectiveness of similarity measures over language vectors (Malaviya et al., 2017; Littell et al., 2017) for selecting proxy languages. The results were mixed, so we opted for expert selection of proxy languages instead. Lin et al. (2019) discusses some of the issues involved.

5 Models

The model description consists of two parts: the core model, for morphological analysis, and two non-core components, for part-of-speech tagging and lemmatization.

5.1 Core model: morphological analysis

Our core system addresses the task of morphological analysis with minimal supervision from labeled training data. The approach exploits parallel data in the form of a multilingual Bible corpus.

5.1.1 Contextual embeddings for every Bible

Prior research has shown embedded word vector representations are capable of capturing contextual nuances in meaning beyond one sense per word (Arora et al., 2018, for example). Because context variance is an important factor affecting morphological analysis, we use ELMo embeddings (Peters et al., 2018) as our base representation. As a first step, we train separate ELMo models on each of the Bible translations in our corpus. For each language, we hold out four books (Mark, Ephesians, 2 Timothy, and Hebrews) for model evaluation and train on all remaining books. Models are trained at the sentence level, using default parameter settings and following recommendations from the AllenNLP `bilm-tf` repository.[3]

5.1.2 Verse alignment for embedding projection

The next step is to use the natural verse alignment of the Bible to learn projections from one embedding space to another, treating English as the source language and learning projections into the embedding spaces for each of our non-English Bible languages in turn.

Mikolov et al. (2013a) show that type-level embedding spaces (e.g. word2vec) can be projected across languages by calculating a translation matrix from a set of type-level translation word pairs. The translation matrix is a vector of dimension-wise factors by which word representations from a source language can be multiplied to transform them into parallel word representations in the target language embedding space.

Aligning contextual representations such as ELMo is more complicated, as there is no good way of aligning words between two language embedding spaces without a dictionary and without

losing the encoded information about contextual polysemy, for which ELMo is particularly useful.

Schuster et al. (2019) propose using context-free anchors to align contextually-dependent embedding spaces (such as ELMo). We propose instead to calculate translation matrices at the verse level, computing the representation for each verse as the unweighted average of its constituent contextual word embeddings.

First, we compute ELMo embeddings for each token in a small subset of the Bible: Psalms (OT) and Romans (NT). For a given language pair, we compute a verse embedding for each verse that appears in both Bibles (some verses are missing in some languages, and some languages have extra verses)[4] and derive the translation matrix for that language pair using the standard method, as introduced by Mikolov et al. (2013a).

Given pairs of verse vectors in a source and target language $\{x_i, z_i\}_{i=1}^{n}$ respectively, we calculate the translation matrix (W) between the two languages utilizing gradient descent, as follows:

$$\min_{W} \sum_{i=1}^{n} \parallel W x_i - z_i \parallel^2$$

5.1.3 Inducing vectors for UniMorph tags

In lieu of using supervised, annotated data for training the model with morphological information, we work from the hypotheses that each of the 42 UniMorph tags can be isolated in the embedding space and that we can derive a vector representation for each tag, applying a process similar to the well-known analogy tasks of Mikolov et al. (2013b). For this purpose, we build small hand-curated data sets (only in English), with contrasting sets of words for each tag. In other words, for each UniMorph tag found in English, we collect from the training data one set of words with the tag and a parallel set without it. The word sets do not necessarily contain minimal pairs, but rather groups of words that are matched for part-of-speech. For example, for the plural tag PL, we build a list of 10 plural tokens (e.g. [*women*, *cats*, *dogs*, *deer*, ...]) and another list of 10 singular tokens (e.g. [*man*, *car*, *dog*, *apple*, ...]). The (vectors for) the set of words with the tag are subtracted

---

[3] https://github.com/allenai/bilm-tf

[4] Even though the differences of diverse and distant languages result in occasional discrepancies in the verse alignment, we believe that verse-level alignment offers closer semantic matching than unsupervised sentence-level alignment could achieve. Across the 60 languages for which we have Bibles, the average ratio of sentences to verses is 1.27 to 1.

from (vectors for) the set of words without the tag. More precisely, we take the weighted average of both sets of words, in which those with the tag are weighted 1, and those without it are weighted -1.

Having derived a vector representation for each UniMorph tag, these vectors can now be projected from English into the target language using the respective translation matrix. Rather than projecting every tag into every language, we project only the tags that are seen in a given language's training data.

Of course, only a subset of all UniMorph tags are found in English. For those which do not appear in the English data (e.g. Ergative), an additional method was developed using the Sigmorphon training data in other languages. When tagging a language that has the tag ERG in the training data, we build new word list pairs specific to that language and calculate the UniMorph tag representation as described above.

5.1.4   Morphological analysis

To assign UniMorph tags to words at test time, a sequence of tokens in context (one sentence at a time) is fed into ELMo using the target language ELMo model, generating contextual embeddings for each word in the sequence. Next, for each token, we iteratively subtract each of the target language's possible UniMorph vectors and search for another word in the target language whose embedding is within 0.1 cosine distance of the resulting vector. For example, when tagging the German word *Kinder* (children), subtracting the vector representation for the Plural tag should result in a vector that is close to that for *Kind* (child). This subtraction process is applied to every word, for every UniMorph tag found in the language. Whenever a word is found within the threshold of the derived embedding, the tag that resulted in the successful transformation is assigned to that token. In the example above, *Kinder* gets tagged with PL.

Intuitively, this method is plausible because words, their inflected forms, synonyms, and closely related terms tend to occur in tight clusters in embedding spaces. Therefore, subtracting the embedding for the PL tag from the embedding for *the* should not produce a close match in English, since the plural tag is never associated with *the*. This would not be a grammatically meaningful transformation.

5.1.5   Baselines

We use two different baselines for the morphological analysis task.

No-embedding baseline.   This method is used to tag the two languages for which we have no Bible, not even for a proxy language, and thus have no Bible-trained word embeddings for the language. Under this approach, each word is simply labeled with all tags it has been seen with in the training data.

Embedding baseline.   This method makes use of the verse embeddings described above and was deployed to do tagging where time constraints prohibited implementation of the full model for a given language.

The contextualized word representations built to support the embedding projection process are collected into a set of dictionaries (one for each language) of seen tokens and their associated vectors. In this setting, instead of re-training the ELMo model on test data in context, we retrieve stored vectors for tokens to be tagged. This method has clear shortcomings, both with respect to coverage of the model and regarding the handling of polysemous tokens.

5.2   Non-core components: POS tagging and lemma generation

For part-of-speech tagging, we implement a Hidden Markov Model Viterbi algorithm trained on the Sigmorphon training and development datasets. Given our interest in methods which reduce the need for large labeled corpora and supervised learning, we additionally implemented some simple heuristics based on previously-generated morpheme tags.

For example, a word is given a higher probability of being tagged as a verb if it has a modal, tense, or other conjugative tag already assigned to it (e.g., V.PTCP or PRS). These heuristics were designed to be entirely language-neutral, generalizing to the full set of test languages.

As a final task, we perform lemma generation using a joint neural model following Malaviya et al. (2019)'s proposed method. The joint model consists of a simple LSTM-based tagger to recover the morphology of a sentence and a sequence-to-sequence model with hard attention mechanism as a lemmatizer. The lemmatization model trains over words and their morphological information

	Lemma Accuracy	Lemma Levenshtein	Morph Accuracy	Morph F1
Mean	83.143	0.5511	15.689	51.870
Median	90.66	0.16	13.98	55.18

Table 2: Shared task results for our models, across all languages.

	Morph Accuracy	Morph F1
Full Bible (n=77)	16.08	52.64
NT only (n=17)	13.12	48.68
Bible from close dialect (n=3; 2 NT, 1 full)	20.55	57.06
Bible from proxy language, (n=8; all full Bible)	12.88	51.57
No Bible	26.6	42.23

Table 3: Morphological analysis results. Macro-average for subgroups of data sets, categorized according to resources available for embedding training, alignment, and projection.

recovered with the tagger. To counter exposure bias, all training is done with Jackknifing.

5.3 Limitations - there are many

The models as described above are subject to many limitations, and we have many ideas for improving the system.

First, the model is computationally intensive and time intensive, to an extent that meant we only applied the full model to a fraction of the data.

Because producing ELMo embeddings on-the-fly is so time consuming, we took some shortcuts in order to get results in time for submission. Word types already tagged were stored together with their tags after the first encounter, and the tags retrieved for later occurrences. Also, only a subset of the test sentences were in fact tagged with the ELMo approach at all. These two things together resulted in many false positives and redundant tags (e.g. the same noun tagged as both nominative and accusative). We feel confident that a full run of the system, however long it takes, will result in much better performance.

Second, our method for tagging words with UniMorph tags does nothing to constrain the set of possible tags, allowing multiple conflicting tags to be simultaneously assigned. Application of output constraints could go a long way toward solving this issue.

Third, we would like to rework our method for collecting pairs of word lists for derivation of vector representations for UniMorph tags. A problem with the current method is that it assumes the existence of inflected/non-inflected word pairs for all tags, and in all languages. In fact, many morphological paradigms do not consist of contrasts between inflected and un-inflected forms (these are perhaps more common in English than in most languages), but rather of sets of inflectional options, one of which is likely to occur. Our model does not currently account well for this aspect of morphology.

For example, when tagging the German article *dem* (definite, masculine, **dative**), subtracting the vector representation for the Dative tag under our current model results in an ill-defined form; there is no article that is definite and masculine and with undefined case. Instead, we would like for the process to yield a set of vectors, close to those for the articles *der* (definite, masculine, **nominative**); *den* (definite, masculine, **accusative**); and *des* (definite, masculine, **genitive**).

Fourth, the system is very bad at handling morphological analysis for out-of-vocabulary tokens, and there are many out-of-vocabulary tokens.

6 Results

Table 2 provides an overview of our system results. Additional discussion of results can be found in McCarthy et al. (2019). The results are uncontroversially bad, particularly for the morphological analysis task. For this portion of the task, our accuracies are dramatically lower than all other teams (at least 50% worse than every other team, on most languages). Some of this performance gap surely can be attributed to the fact that we make very minimal use of the training data supplied, but not all of it! We strongly believe that the limitations described in Section 5.3 have severely decreased our results, and we look forward to giving our method a true test in the near future.

For lemmatization, we come closer to average performance, coming in at roughly 12 percent less accurate on average (across languages) than the top-performing submitted system.

Table 3 looks at results compared to the amount and type of Bible data used to train embeddings for each language. Performance suffers when training on only the New Testament, compared to the full Bible. Surprisingly, proxy language training shows only a slightly lower average performance compared to training and testing on the same language. Of course, all results need to be interpreted with respect to the limitations previously discussed.

7 Discussion

In addition to the model and implementation limitations discussed in Section 5.3, there are a number of extensions which could be considered for improving the model.

Our current model allows a mismatch between granularity for training of the embedding spaces (sentences) and granularity for alignment of the embedding spaces (verses). We'd like to experiment with verse-trained models as well.

We would also like to train on all of our Bible data, without holding out any data for evaluation of the embedding space (i.e. the four books mentioned in Section 4). For languages for which we don't have a Bible, we will investigate new methods for identifying transfer languages (Lin et al., 2019).

Even though our models as implemented prior to submission failed to attain reasonable accuracy on the morphological analysis task, we believe that performance can be improved and that the general architecture deserves further exploration. Ideally, our model could extend to any of the 800 (or more) languages that has a translation of the entire bible, opening new frontiers for minimally-supervised morphological analysis.

Acknowledgments

Thanks to the reviewers for helpful feedback. Computational resources were provided by UNT office of High-Performance Computing.

References

Zeljko Agic, Dirk Hovy, and Anders Sgaard. 2015. If all you have is a bit of the Bible: Learning POS taggers for truly low-resource languages. In *Proceedings of the 53rd Annual Meeting of the Association for Computational Linguistics and the 7th International Joint Conference on Natural Language Processing*, pages 268–272.

Zeljko Agic, Anders Johannsen, Barbara Plank, Hctor Martnez Alonso, Natalie Schluter, and Anders Sgaard. 2016. Multilingual Projection for Parsing Truly Low-Resource Languages. *Transactions of the Association for Computational Linguistics*, 4:301–312.

Sanjeev Arora, Yuanzhi Li, Yingyu Liang, Tengyu Ma, and Andrej Risteski. 2018. Linear algebraic structure of word senses, with applications to polysemy. *Transactions of the Association of Computational Linguistics*, 6:483–495.

Christos Christodouloupoulos and Mark Steedman. 2015. A massively parallel corpus: the Bible in 100 languages. *Language Resources and Evaluation*, 49(2):375–395.

Christo Kirov, Ryan Cotterell, John Sylak-Glassman, Géraldine Walther, Ekaterina Vylomova, Patrick Xia, Manaal Faruqui, Sebastian J. Mielke, Arya D. McCarthy, Sandra Kübler, David Yarowsky, Jason Eisner, and Mans Hulden. 2018. UniMorph 2.0: Universal Morphology. *CoRR*, abs/1810.11101.

Yu-Hsiang Lin, Chian-Yu Chen, Jean Lee, Zirui Li, Yuyan Zhang, Mengzhou Xia, Shruti Rijhwani, Junxian He, Zhisong Zhang, Xuezhe Ma, Antonios Anastasopoulos, Patrick Littell, and Graham Neubig. 2019. Choosing transfer languages for cross-lingual learning. In *Proceedings of ACL 2019*

Patrick Littell, David R Mortensen, Ke Lin, Katherine Kairis, Carlisle Turner, and Lori Levin. 2017. Uriel and lang2vec: Representing languages as typological, geographical, and phylogenetic vectors. In *Proceedings of the 15th Conference of the European Chapter of the Association for Computational Linguistics: Volume 2, Short Papers*, volume 2, pages 8–14.

Chaitanya Malaviya, Graham Neubig, and Patrick Littell. 2017. Learning language representations for typology prediction. In *Conference on Empirical Methods in Natural Language Processing (EMNLP)*, Copenhagen, Denmark.

Chaitanya Malaviya, Shijie Wu, and Ryan Cotterell. 2019. A simple joint model for improved contextual neural lemmatization. *CoRR*, abs/1904.02306.

Arya D. McCarthy, Miikka Silfverberg, Ryan Cotterell, Mans Hulden, and David Yarowsky. 2018. Marrying Universal Dependencies and Universal Morphology. In *Proceedings of the Second Workshop*

on Universal Dependencies (UDW 2018), pages 91–
101, Brussels, Belgium. Association for Computational Linguistics.

Arya D. McCarthy, Ekaterina Vylomova, Shijie Wu,
Chaitanya Malaviya, Lawrence Wolf-Sonkin, Garrett Nicolai, Christo Kirov, Miikka Silfverberg, Sebastian Mielke, Jeffrey Heinz, Ryan Cotterell, and
Mans Hulden. 2019. The SIGMORPHON 2019
shared task: Crosslinguality and context in morphology. In *Proceedings of the 16th SIGMORPHON
Workshop on Computational Research in Phonetics,
Phonology, and Morphology*, Florence, Italy. Association for Computational Linguistics.

Tomas Mikolov, Quoc V. Le, and Ilya Sutskever. 2013a.
Exploiting Similarities among Languages for Machine Translation. *CoRR*, abs/1309.4168.

Tomas Mikolov, Wen-tau Yih, and Geoffrey Zweig.
2013b. Linguistic regularities in continuous space
word representations. In *Proceedings of the 2013
Conference of the North American Chapter of the
Association for Computational Linguistics: Human
Language Technologies*, pages 746–751.

Matthew E. Peters, Mark Neumann, Mohit Iyyer, Matt
Gardner, Christopher Clark, Kenton Lee, and Luke
Zettlemoyer. 2018. Deep contextualized word rep-
resentations. *CoRR*, abs/1802.05365.

Sebastian Ruder, Ivan Vulić, and Anders Søgaard.
2017. A survey of cross-lingual embedding models.
CoRR, abs/1706.04902.

Tal Schuster, Ori Ram, Regina Barzilay, and
Amir Globerson. 2019. Cross-Lingual Alignment
of Contextual Word Embeddings, with Applications to Zero-shot Dependency Parsing. *CoRR*,
abs/1902.09492.

David Yarowsky, Grace Ngai, and Richard Wicen-
towski. 2001. Inducing Multilingual Text Analysis Tools via Robust Projection Across Aligned Corpora. In *Proceedings of the First International Conference on Human Language Technology Research*,
HLT '01, pages 1–8, Stroudsburg, PA, USA. Association for Computational Linguistics.

UDPipe at SIGMORPHON 2019: Contextualized Embeddings, Regularization with Morphological Categories, Corpora Merging

Milan Straka and **Jana Straková** and **Jan Hajič**
Charles University
Faculty of Mathematics and Physics
Institute of Formal and Applied Linguistics
`{straka,strakova,hajic}@ufal.mff.cuni.cz`

Abstract

We present our contribution to the *SIGMOR-PHON 2019 Shared Task: Crosslinguality and Context in Morphology*, Task 2: contextual morphological analysis and lemmatization.

We submitted a modification of the *UDPipe 2.0*, one of best-performing systems of the *CoNLL 2018 Shared Task: Multilingual Parsing from Raw Text to Universal Dependencies* and an overall winner of the *The 2018 Shared Task on Extrinsic Parser Evaluation*.

As our first improvement, we use the pretrained contextualized embeddings (BERT) as additional inputs to the network; secondly, we use individual morphological features as regularization; and finally, we merge the selected corpora of the same language.

In the lemmatization task, our system exceeds all the submitted systems by a wide margin with lemmatization accuracy 95.78 (second best was 95.00, third 94.46). In the morphological analysis, our system placed tightly second: our morphological analysis accuracy was 93.19, the winning system's 93.23.

1 Introduction

This work describes our participant system in the *SIGMORPHON 2019 Shared Task: Crosslinguality and Context in Morphology*. We contributed a system in Task 2: contextual morphological analysis and lemmatization.

Given a segmented and tokenized text in a CoNLL-U format with surface forms (column 2) as in the following example:

```
# sent-id = 1
# text = They buy and sell books.
1   They    _       _   _   _       ...
2   buy     _       _   _   _       ...
3   and     _       _   _   _       ...
4   sell    _       _   _   _       ...
5   books   _       _   _   _       ...
6   .       _       _   _   _       ...
```

the task is to infer lemmas (column 3) and morphological analysis (column 6) in the form of concatenated morphological features:

```
# sent-id = 1
# text = They buy and sell books.
1   They    they    _   _   N;NOM;PL      ...
2   buy     buy     _   _   V;SG;1;PRS    ...
3   and     and     _   _   CONJ          ...
4   sell    sell    _   _   V;PL;3;PRS    ...
5   books   book    _   _   N;PL          ...
6   .       .       _   _   PUNCT         ...
```

The *SIGMORPHON 2019* data consists of 66 distinct languages in 107 corpora (McCarthy et al., 2018).

We submitted a modified *UDPipe 2.0* (Straka, 2018), one of the three winning systems of the *CoNLL 2018 Shared Task: Multilingual Parsing from Raw Text to Universal Dependencies* (Zeman et al., 2018) and an overall winner of the *The 2018 Shared Task on Extrinsic Parser Evaluation* (Fares et al., 2018).

Our improvements to the *UDPipe 2.0* are three-fold:

- We use the pretrained contextualized embeddings (BERT) as additional inputs to the network (described in Section 3.3).
- Apart from predicting the whole POS tag, we regularize the model by also predicting individual morphological features (Section 3.4).
- In some languages, we merge all the corpora of the same language (Section 3.5).

Our system placed first in lemmatization and closely second in morphological analysis.

We give an overview of the related work in Section 2, we describe our methodology in Section 3, the results with ablation experiments are given in Section 4 and we conclude in Section 5.

2 Related Work

A new type of deep contextualized word representation was introduced by Peters et al. (2018).

Proceedings of the 16th Workshop on Computational Research in Phonetics, Phonology, and Morphology, pages 95–103
Florence, Italy. August 2, 2019 ©2019 Association for Computational Linguistics

The proposed embeddings, called ELMo, were obtained from internal states of deep bidirectional language model, pretrained on a large text corpus. The idea of ELMos was extended by Devlin et al. (2018), who instead of a bidirectional recurrent language model employ a Transformer (Vaswani et al., 2017) architecture.

The *Universal Dependencies* project (Nivre et al., 2016) seeks to develop cross-linguistically consistent treebank annotation of morphology and syntax for many languages. In 2017 and 2018 CoNLL Shared Tasks *Multilingual Parsing from Raw Text to Universal Dependencies* (Zeman et al., 2017, 2018), the goal was to process raw texts into tokenized sentences with POS tags, lemmas, morphological features and dependency trees of Universal Dependencies. Straka (2018) was one of the winning systems of the 2018 shared task, performing the POS tagging, lemmatization and dependency parsing jointly. Another winning system of Che et al. (2018) employed manually trained ELMo-like contextual word embeddings and ensembling, reporting 7.9% error reduction in LAS parsing performance.

The Universal Morphology (UniMorph) is also a project seeking to provide annotation schema for morphosyntactic details of language (Sylak-Glassman, 2016). Each POS tag consists of a set of morphological features, each belonging to a morphological category (also called a dimension of meaning).

3 Methods

3.1 Architecture Overview

Our **baseline** is the *UDPipe 2.0* (Straka, 2018). The original *UDPipe 2.0* is available at `http://github.com/CoNLL-UD-2018/UDPipe-Future`. Here, we describe the overall architecture, focusing on the modifications made for the *SIGMORPHON 2019*. The resulting model is presented in Figure 1.

In short, *UDPipe 2.0* is a multi-task model predicting POS tags, lemmas and dependency trees. For the *SIGMORPHON 2019*, we naturally train and predict only the POS tags (morphosyntactic features) and lemmas. After embedding input words, three shared bidirectional LSTM (Hochreiter and Schmidhuber, 1997) layers are performed. Then, softmax classifiers process the output and generate the lemmas and POS tags (morphosyntactic features).

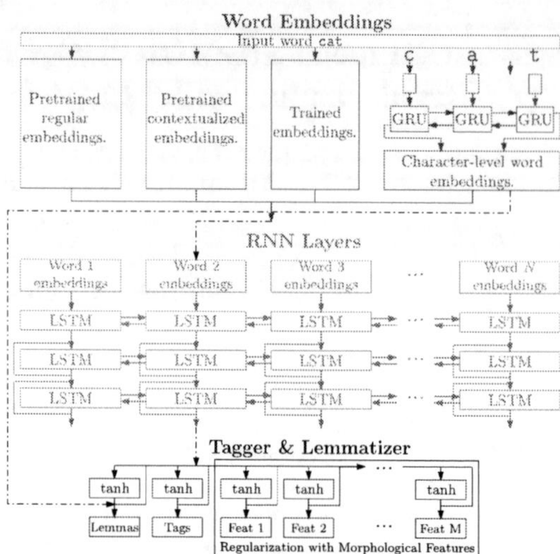

Figure 1: The overall system architecture

The lemmas are generated by classifying into a set of edit scripts which process input word form and produce lemmas by performing character-level edits on the word prefix and suffix. The lemma classifier additionally takes the character-level word embeddings as input. The lemmatization is further described in Section 3.2.

The input word embeddings are the same as in the *UDPipe 2.0* (Straka, 2018):

- **end-to-end word embeddings**,
- **word embeddings (WE):** We use FastText word embeddings (Bojanowski et al., 2017) of dimension 300, which we pretrain for each language on plain texts provided by CoNLL 2017 UD Shared Task, using segmentation and tokenization trained from the UD data.[1] For languages not present in the CoNLL 2017 UD Shared Task, we use pretrained embeddings from (Grave et al., 2018), if available.
- **character-level word embeddings (CLE):** We employ bidirectional GRUs (Cho et al., 2014; Graves and Schmidhuber, 2005) of dimension 256 in line with (Ling et al., 2015): we represent every Unicode character with a vector of dimension 256, and concatenate GRU output for forward and reversed word characters. The character-level word embeddings are trained together with UDPipe network.

We refer the readers for detailed description of the architecture and the training procedure to

---

[1] We use `-minCount 5 -epoch 10 -neg 10` **options**.

Lemma Rule	Casing Script	Edit Script	Most Frequent Examples
`↓0;d¦`	all lowercase	do nothing	the→the to→to and→and
`↑0¦↓1;d¦`	first upper, then lower	do nothing	Bush→Bush Iraq→Iraq Enron→Enron
`↓0;d¦-`	all lowercase	remove last character	your→you an→a years→year
`↓0;abe`	all lowercase	ignore form, use be	is→be was→be 's→be
`↑0;d¦`	all uppercase	do nothing	I→I US→US NASA→NASA
`↓0;d¦--`	all lowercase	remove last 2 chars	been→be does→do called→call
`↓0;d¦---`	all lowercase	remove last 3 chars	going→go being→be looking→look
`↓0;d--+b¦`	all lowercase	change first 2 chars to b	are→be 're→be Are→be
`↓0;d¦-+v+e`	all lowercase	change last char to ve	has→have had→have Has→have
`↓0;d¦---+e`	all lowercase	change last 3 chars to e	having→have using→use making→make
`↓0;d¦-+o→`	all lowercase	change last but 1 char to o	n't→not knew→know grew→grow

Table 1: Eleven most frequent lemma rules in English EWT corpus, ordered from the most frequent one.

Straka (2018).

The main modifications to the *UDPipe 2.0* are the following:

- **contextualized embeddings (BERT)**: We add pretrained contextual word embeddings as another input to the neural network. We describe this modification in Section 3.3.
- **regularization with individual morphological features**: We predict not only the full POS tag, but regularize the model by also predicting individual morphological features, which is described in Section 3.4.
- **corpora merging**: In some cases, we merge the corpora of the same language. We describe this step in Section 3.5.

Furthermore, we also employ model ensembling, which we describe in Section 3.6.

3.2 Lemmatization

The lemmatization is modeled as a multi-class classification, in which the classes are the complete rules which lead from input forms to the lemmas. We call each class encoding a transition from input form to lemma a *lemma rule*. We create a lemma rule by firstly encoding the correct casing as a *casing script* and secondly by creating a sequence of character edits, an *edit script*.

Firstly, we deal with the casing by creating a *casing script*. By default, word form and lemma characters are treated as lowercased. If the lemma however contains upper-cased characters, a rule is added to the casing script to uppercase the corresponding characters in the resulting lemma. For example, the most frequent casing script is "keep the lemma lowercased (don't do anything)" and the second most frequent casing script is "uppercase the first character and keep the rest lowercased".

As a second step, an *edit script* is created to convert input lowercased form to lowercased lemma. To ensure meaningful editing, the form is split to three parts, which are then processed separately: a prefix, a root (stem) and a suffix. The root is discovered by matching the longest substring shared between the form and the lemma; if no matching substring is found (e.g., form *went* and lemma *go*), we consider the word irregular, do not process it with any edits and directly replace the word form with the lemma. Otherwise, we proceed with the edit scripts, which process the prefix and the suffix separately and keep the root unchanged. The allowed character-wise operations are character copy, addition and deletion.

The resulting *lemma rule* is a concatenation of a casing script and an edit script. The most common lemma rules in English EWT corpus are presented in Table 1, and the number of lemma rules for every language is displayed in Tables 5 and 6.

Using the generated lemma rules, the task of lemmatization is then reduced to a multiclass classification task, in which the artificial neural network predicts the correct lemma rule.

3.3 Contextual Word Embeddings (BERT)

We add pretrained contextual word embeddings as another input to the neural network. We use the pretrained contextual word embeddings called BERT (Devlin et al., 2018).[2] For English, we use the native English model (`BERT-Base English`), for Chinese use use the native Chinese model (`BERT-Base Chinese`) and for all other languages, we use the Multilingual model (`BERT-Base Uncased`). All models provide contextualized embeddings of dimension 768.

---

[2] `https://github.com/google-research/bert`

We average the last four layers of the BERT model to produce the embeddings. Because BERT utilizes word pieces, we decompose words into appropriate subwords and then average the generated embeddings over subwords belonging to the same word.

Contrary to finetuning approach used by the BERT authors (Devlin et al., 2018), we never finetune the embeddings.

3.4 Regularization with Individual Morphological Features

Our model predicts the POS tags as a unit, i.e., the whole set of morphological features at once. There are other possible alternatives – for example, we could predict the morphological features individually. However, such a prediction needs to decide which morphological categories to use and should use a classifier capable of handling dependencies between the predicted features, and all our attempts to design such a classifier resulted in systems with suboptimal performance. Using a whole-set classifier alleviates the need for finding a correct set of categories for a word and handling the feature dependencies, but suffers from the curse of dimensionality, especially on smaller corpora with richer morphology.

Nevertheless, the performance of a whole-set classifier can be improved by regularizing with the individual morphological feature prediction. Similarly to Kondratyuk et al. (2018), our model predicts not only the full set of morphological features at once, but also the individual features. Specifically, we employ as many additional softmax output layers as the number of morphological categories used in the corpus, each predicting the corresponding feature or a special value of None. The averaged cross-entropy loss of all predicted categories multiplied by a weight w is added to the training loss. The predicted features are not used in any way during inference and act only as model regularization.

The number of full POS tags (complete sets of morphological features), individual morphological features and number of used morphological categories for every corpus is provided in Tables 5 and 6.

3.5 Corpora Merging

Given that the shared task data consists of multiple corpora for some of the languages, it is a natural approach to concatenate all corpora of the same language and use the resulting so-called *merged model* for prediction on individual corpora.

In theory, concatenating all corpora of the same language should be always beneficial considering the universal scheme used for annotation. Nonetheless, the merged model exhibits worse performance in many cases, compared to a specialized model trained on the corpus training data only, supposedly because of systematically different annotation. We consequently improve the merged model performance during inference by allowing only such lemma rules and morphological feature sets that are present in the training data of the predicted corpus.

3.6 Model Ensembling

For every corpus, we consider three model configurations – the regular model with BERT embeddings trained only on the corpus data, the merged model with BERT embeddings trained on all corpora of the corresponding language, and the no-BERT model trained only on the corpus data.

To allow automatic model selection and to obtain highest performance, we use ensembling. Namely, we train three models for every model configuration, obtaining nine models for every language. Then, we choose a model subset whose ensemble achieves the highest performance on the development data. The chosen subsets then formed the competition entry of our system.

However, post-competition examination using half of development data for ensemble selection and the other for evaluation revealed that the model selection can overfit, sometimes choosing one or two models with high performance caused by noise instead of high-quality generalization. Therefore, we also consider another model selection method – we ensemble the three models for every configuration, and choose the best configuration out of three ensembles on the development data. This second system has been submitted as a post-competition entry.

4   Results

4.1   *SIGMORPHON 2019* Test Results

Table 2 shows top 5 results in lemma accuracy, lemma Levenshtein, morphological accuracy and morphological F1 in Task 2 of the *SIGMORPHON 2019*, averaged over all 107 corpora. Our system is called UFALPRAGUE-01.

Lemma Accuracy		Morph Accuracy	
UFALPRAGUE-01	**95.78**	CHARLES-SAARLAND-02	93.23
CHARLES-SAARLAND-02	95.00	**UFALPRAGUE-01**	**93.19**
ITU-01	94.46	RUG-01	90.53
baseline-test-00	94.17	EDINBURGH-01	88.93
CBNU-01	94.07	RUG-02	88.80
Lemma Levenshtein		Morph F1	
UFALPRAGUE-01	**0.098**	CHARLES-SAARLAND-02	96.02
CHARLES-SAARLAND-02	0.108	**UFALPRAGUE-01**	**95.92**
ITU-01	0.108	RUG-01	94.54
CBNU-01	0.127	RUG-02	93.22
baseline-test-00	0.129	EDINBURGH-01	92.89

Table 2: Top 5 results in lemma accuracy, lemma Levenshtein, morphological accuracy and morphological F1.

Word Embeddings	BERT	Feature Regularization	Lemma		Morph	
			Acc	Lev	Acc	F1
✗	✗	✗	94.251	0.168	90.506	93.585
✓ FT only	✗	✗	95.229	0.109	91.704	94.745
✓	✗	✗	95.294	0.107	91.828	94.849
✗	✓	✗	95.440	0.106	92.789	95.614
✓	✓	✗	95.534	0.104	92.980	95.755
✗	✗	✓ $w = 1$	95.120	0.111	91.468	94.672
✓	✗	✓ $w = 1$	95.365	0.104	92.135	95.189
✓	✓	✓ $w = 1$	95.516	0.105	93.148	95.957
✓	✓	✓ $w = 0.5$	95.534	0.105	93.172	95.939
✓	✓	✓ $w = 2$	95.539	0.105	93.175	95.965

Table 3: Lemma accuracy, lemma Levenshtein, morphological accuracy, and morphological F1 results of ablation experiments. For comparison, the *FT only* embeddings denote the pretrained embeddings of (Grave et al., 2018).

Regular Model	Merged Model	Without BERT	Ensembling	Lemma		Morph	
				Acc	Lev	Acc	F1
✓	✗	✗	✗	95.516	0.105	93.148	95.957
✓	✓	✗	✗	95.702	0.101	93.322	96.081
✓	✗	✓	✗	95.524	0.104	93.177	95.966
✓	✓	✓	✗	95.709	0.100	93.353	96.090
✓	✗	✗	✓ Every model	95.606	0.102	93.257	95.997
✓	✓	✗	✓ configuration	95.785	0.098	93.422	96.123
✓	✗	✓	✓ has independent	95.598	0.102	93.300	96.035
✓	✓	✓	✓ 3-model ensemble	95.776	0.099	93.464	96.160
The competition entry, which allows ensembling any combination of the 9 models							
✓	✓	✓	✓ Any combination	95.776	0.098	93.186	95.924

Table 4: Lemma accuracy, lemma Levenshtein, morphological accuracy, and morphological F1 results of model combinations. When not specified otherwise, all models utilize pretrained word embeddings, BERT, and feature regularization with weight $w = 1$.

Our participant system placed as one of the winning systems of the shared task. In the lemmatization task, our system exceeds all the submitted systems by a wide margin with lemmatization accuracy 95.78 (second best was 95.00, third 94.46). In the morphological analysis, our system placed tightly second: our morphological analysis accuracy was 93.19, the winning system's 93.23.

4.2 Ablation Experiments

The effect of pretrained word embeddings, BERT contextualized embeddings and regularization with morphological features is evaluated in Table 3. Even the baseline model without any of the mentioned enhancements achieves relatively high performance and would place third in both lemmatization and tagging accuracy (when not considering our competition entry).

Pretrained word embeddings improve the performance of both the lemmatizer and the tagger by a substantial margin. For comparison with the embeddings we trained on CoNLL 2017 UD Shared Task plain texts, we also evaluate the embeddings provided by Grave et al. (2018), which achieve only slightly lower performance than our embeddings – we presume the difference is caused mostly by different tokenization, given that the training data comes from Wikipedia and CommonCrawl in both cases.

BERT contextualized embeddings further considerably improve POS tagging performance, and have minor impact on lemmatization improvement.

When used in isolation, the regularization with morphological categories provides quite considerable gain for both lemmatization and tagging, nearly comparable to the effect of adding precomputed word embeddings. Combining all the enhancements together then produces a model with the highest performance.

4.3 Model Combinations

For every corpus, we consider three model configurations – a regular model, then a model trained on the merged corpora of a corresponding language, and a model without BERT embeddings (which we consider since even if BERT embeddings can be computed for any language, the results might be misleading if the language was not present in the BERT training data). For every model configuration, we train three models using different random initialization.

The test set results of choosing the best model configuration on a development set are provided in Table 4. Employing the merged model in addition to the regular model increases the performance slightly, and the introduction of no-BERT model results in minimal gains. Finally, ensembling the models of a same configuration provides the highest performance.

As discussed in Section 3.6, our competition entry selected the ensemble using arbitrary subset of all the nine models which achieved best performance on the development data. This choice resulted in overfitting on POS tag prediction, with results worse than no ensembling.

4.4 Detailed Results

Tables 5 and 6 present detailed results of our best system from Table 4. Note that while this system is not our competition entry, it utilizes the same models as the competition entry, only combined in a different way. Furthermore, because one model configuration was chosen for every language, we can examine which configuration performed best, and quantify what the exact effect of corpora merging and BERT embeddings are.

5 Conclusions

We described our system which participated in the *SIGMORPHON 2019 Shared Task: Crosslinguality and Context in Morphology*, Task 2: contextual morphological analysis and lemmatization, which placed first in lemmatization and closely second in morphological analysis. The contributed architecture is a modified *UDPipe 2.0* with three improvements: addition of pretrained contextualized BERT embeddings, regularization with morphological categories and corpora merging in some languages. We described these improvements and published the related ablation experiment results.

Acknowledgements

The work described herein has been supported by OP VVV VI LINDAT/CLARIN project of the Ministry of Education, Youth and Sports of the Czech Republic (project CZ.02.1.01/0.0/0.0/16_013/0001781) and it has been supported and has been using language resources developed by the LINDAT/CLARIN project of the Ministry of Education, Youth and Sports of the Czech Republic (project LM2015071).

Treebank	Words	Lemma Rules	POS Tags	Feats/ /Cats	Lemma Acc	Lev	Morph Acc	F1	R	M	N	Merged Δ LAcc	MAcc	BERT Δ LAcc	MAcc	BT
Afrikaans-AfriBooms	38 843	185	41	29/ 9	99.10	0.01	99.26	99.40	✓	✗	✗			0.15	0.64	✓
Akkadian-PISANDUB	1 425	548	12	11/ 1	55.94	1.50	86.63	86.46	✗	✗	✓			0.99	-4.45	✗
Amharic-ATT	7 952	1	54	35/10	100.00	0.00	89.70	93.24	✓	✗	✗			0.00	0.57	✓
Ancient Greek-PROIEL	171 478	6 843	887	49/14	94.04	0.15	92.99	97.92	✗	✓	✗	0.65	0.30	-0.04	-0.01	✗
Ancient Greek-Perseus	162 164	9 088	795	44/11	91.91	0.21	91.91	96.74	✗	✓	✗	0.78	0.26	-0.05	0.01	✗
Arabic-PADT	225 494	3 174	287	35/12	96.09	0.11	95.38	97.48	✓	✗	✗	-0.09	0.02	0.35	0.66	✓
Arabic-PUD	16 845	3 919	371	39/12	79.26	0.78	86.52	95.30	✓	✗	✗			0.46	3.22	✓
Armenian-ArmTDP	18 595	277	360	65/16	95.91	0.08	93.63	96.54	✓	✗	✗			0.62	1.90	✓
Bambara-CRB	11 205	311	43	32/ 9	92.10	0.12	94.00	95.62	✓	✗	✗			-0.84	0.07	✗
Basque-BDT	97 336	1 168	865	136/15	97.14	0.06	93.56	96.47	✓	✗	✗			0.53	4.37	✓
Belarusian-HSE	6 541	229	291	46/14	92.39	0.15	90.28	95.24	✓	✗	✗			0.00	3.16	✓
Breton-KEB	8 062	329	87	36/13	93.03	0.15	91.44	93.95	✓	✗	✗			0.09	0.89	✓
Bulgarian-BTB	124 749	605	316	44/15	98.34	0.05	97.84	99.03	✓	✗	✗			0.25	0.21	✓
Buryat-BDT	8 029	132	167	41/12	90.38	0.23	87.98	89.94	✓	✗	✗			0.76	1.35	✗
Cantonese-HK	5 121	17	13	12/ 1	100.00	0.00	91.25	88.86	✓	✗	✗			0.00	0.54	✓
Catalan-AnCora	427 672	579	145	41/13	99.32	0.01	98.66	99.35	✓	✗	✗			0.09	0.34	✓
Chinese-CFL	5 688	14	13	12/ 1	99.76	0.00	94.21	93.34	✓	✗	✗	0.00	-0.12	0.00	3.43	✓
Chinese-GSD	98 734	26	27	21/ 8	99.98	0.00	96.64	96.51	✓	✗	✗	0.00	0.11	-0.01	2.61	✓
Coptic-Scriptorium	17 624	181	53	26/ 9	97.31	0.06	95.85	96.82	✓	✗	✗			-0.05	-0.56	✗
Croatian-SET	157 446	578	818	51/16	97.45	0.05	94.16	97.67	✓	✗	✗			0.22	0.83	✓
Czech-CAC	395 043	929	960	57/15	99.31	0.01	97.78	99.20	✓	✗	✗	-0.18	-0.37	0.06	0.73	✓
Czech-CLTT	28 649	229	350	48/15	99.22	0.02	95.42	98.30	✗	✓	✗	0.11	-0.06	0.37	1.00	✓
Czech-FicTree	133 300	692	971	53/15	98.80	0.02	96.30	98.53	✓	✗	✗	0.36	-0.23	0.12	0.65	✓
Czech-PDT	1 207 922	1 661	1 123	57/15	99.37	0.01	98.02	99.25	✓	✗	✗	-0.05	-0.15	0.04	0.44	✓
Czech-PUD	14 814	349	549	56/15	98.13	0.03	94.46	98.14	✗	✓	✗	2.59	3.94	0.77	3.84	✓
Danish-DDT	80 964	426	128	41/14	98.30	0.03	97.76	98.49	✓	✗	✗			0.44	0.84	✓
Dutch-Alpino	167 187	631	43	33/10	98.45	0.03	97.59	98.20	✗	✓	✗	-0.03	-0.03	0.12	0.39	✓
Dutch-LassySmall	78 638	527	41	31/10	98.34	0.03	97.86	98.29	✗	✓	✗	0.28	0.18	0.07	0.56	✓
English-EWT	204 839	235	76	36/12	99.01	0.02	97.53	98.27	✓	✗	✗	-0.18	-0.38	0.30	0.99	✓
English-GUM	63 862	160	74	37/12	98.53	0.02	97.29	98.01	✓	✗	✗	-0.84	-1.23	0.26	1.23	✓
English-LinES	66 428	166	78	36/12	98.62	0.02	97.52	98.14	✓	✗	✗	-0.83	-1.13	0.22	0.87	✓
English-PUD	16 921	70	66	35/12	97.79	0.03	96.32	97.28	✓	✗	✗	-1.76	-0.54	0.83	2.55	✓
English-ParTUT	39 302	115	83	33/10	98.37	0.03	96.25	96.92	✓	✗	✗	-0.48	-2.36	0.21	1.19	✓
Estonian-EDT	346 986	3 294	494	52/14	96.59	0.06	96.72	98.37	✓	✗	✗			0.35	0.44	✓
Faroese-OFT	7 994	297	234	36/13	90.30	0.18	88.28	94.29	✓	✗	✗			1.64	2.11	✗
Finnish-FTB	127 536	1 211	660	53/12	96.05	0.08	96.55	97.98	✓	✗	✗			0.37	0.44	✓
Finnish-PUD	12 553	889	284	50/12	88.90	0.19	96.58	98.33	✗	✓	✗	2.15	1.97	1.21	2.09	✓
Finnish-TDT	161 582	2 650	565	51/12	95.91	0.08	96.81	98.21	✓	✗	✗	-0.20	-0.08	0.34	0.39	✓
French-GSD	320 404	736	134	40/13	98.82	0.02	97.82	98.71	✓	✗	✗	0.01	-0.15	0.11	0.38	✓
French-ParTUT	22 627	219	111	34/10	96.66	0.06	95.84	98.02	✓	✗	✗			0.12	0.88	✓
French-Sequoia	56 484	317	126	35/12	99.01	0.02	98.15	99.13	✓	✗	✗			0.14	0.56	✓
French-Spoken	28 182	208	13	12/ 1	98.91	0.02	98.12	98.15	✓	✗	✗			0.14	0.25	✓
Galician-CTG	111 034	160	14	13/ 2	98.87	0.02	98.28	98.12	✓	✗	✗	0.00	-0.04	0.11	0.29	✓
Galician-TreeGal	20 566	147	161	44/13	98.49	0.03	95.71	97.63	✓	✗	✗	-0.03	-11.16	0.38	1.27	✓
German-GSD	234 161	841	600	41/12	97.70	0.05	89.89	95.64	✓	✗	✗			0.21	0.79	✓
Gothic-PROIEL	44 660	1 130	540	43/13	95.61	0.09	90.50	96.39	✗	✗	✓			-0.04	-0.13	✗
Greek-GDT	50 567	1 285	243	40/12	96.85	0.08	95.89	98.36	✓	✗	✗			0.09	0.86	✓
Hebrew-HTB	129 425	387	236	38/13	98.18	0.03	97.51	98.24	✓	✗	✗			0.19	0.45	✓
Hindi-HDTB	281 948	286	738	49/12	98.89	0.01	93.23	97.83	✓	✗	✗			0.07	0.53	✓
Hungarian-Szeged	33 463	329	427	59/14	97.45	0.05	95.22	98.32	✓	✗	✗			0.25	2.21	✓
Indonesian-GSD	97 213	65	129	27/ 9	99.62	0.01	92.06	94.75	✓	✗	✗			0.05	0.67	✓
Irish-IDT	18 996	476	163	37/12	92.06	0.18	86.41	91.51	✓	✗	✗			0.00	0.49	✓
Italian-ISDT	239 381	321	142	38/11	98.86	0.02	98.30	99.03	✗	✓	✗	0.01	0.19	0.13	0.33	✓
Italian-PUD	18 834	167	159	38/14	97.57	0.05	96.33	98.34	✓	✗	✗	0.41	-11.18	0.46	2.19	✓
Italian-ParTUT	44 556	194	110	34/11	99.26	0.02	98.66	99.16	✗	✓	✗	0.78	0.85	0.04	0.58	✓
Italian-PoSTWITA	99 067	945	122	33/10	97.82	0.05	96.52	97.49	✓	✗	✗	-0.13	-0.10	0.33	0.67	✓

Table 5: For every corpus, its size, the number of unique lemma rules, the number of unique POS tags, and the number of morphological features and morphological categories is presented. Then the test set results of lemma accuracy, lemma Levenshtein, morphological accuracy and morphological F1 follow, using a model achieving best score on the development set. We consider the regular model R, or a model on the merged corpus M and a model without BERT embeddings N. Finally, we show the increase of the merged model to the regular model, the increase of the regular model to the no-BERT model, and indicate if the language is present in BERT training data (BT).

Treebank	Words	Lemma Rules	POS Tags	Feats/Cats	Lemma Acc	Lemma Lev	Morph Acc	Morph F1	R	M	N	Merged Δ LAcc	Merged Δ MAcc	BERT Δ LAcc	BERT Δ MAcc	BT
Japanese-GSD	147 897	104	13	12/ 1	99.65	0.00	98.14	97.91	✗	✓	✗	0.03	-0.02	-0.01	0.23	✓
Japanese-Modern	11 556	44	14	12/ 2	98.67	0.01	96.80	96.87	✓	✗	✗	-0.14	-0.20	-0.20	0.33	✓
Japanese-PUD	21 650	51	12	11/ 1	99.77	0.00	99.32	99.25	✗	✓	✗	0.64	0.99	0.19	0.34	✓
Komi Zyrian-IKDP	847	85	114	40/11	85.94	0.25	76.56	86.19	✗	✓	✗	2.35	0.78	1.56	5.47	✗
Komi Zyrian-Lattice	1 653	58	184	46/13	87.36	0.28	73.63	85.36	✗	✓	✗	1.10	3.85	0.55	1.10	✗
Korean-GSD	64 311	1 470	13	12/ 1	93.77	0.12	96.47	95.92	✓	✗	✗	-0.63	-5.78	0.59	1.08	✓
Korean-Kaist	280 494	3 137	13	12/ 1	95.65	0.07	97.31	96.98	✓	✗	✗	-0.03	-0.23	0.17	0.31	✓
Korean-PUD	13 306	9	109	29/11	99.07	0.01	94.06	96.23	✓	✗	✗	-10.90	-16.72	0.06	2.67	✓
Kurmanji-MG	8 077	275	148	41/14	94.71	0.10	85.57	91.52	✓	✗	✗			0.09	0.80	✗
Latin-ITTB	281 652	726	539	46/12	98.99	0.02	96.85	98.49	✓	✗	✗	0.10	0.02	0.04	0.13	✓
Latin-PROIEL	160 257	1 555	872	48/13	97.28	0.06	92.40	97.23	✗	✓	✗	0.07	0.12	0.02	0.06	✓
Latin-Perseus	23 339	879	427	43/11	93.32	0.14	86.97	94.28	✗	✓	✗	2.99	2.60	0.17	0.48	✓
Latvian-LVTB	121 760	677	644	49/15	97.22	0.05	95.48	97.74	✓	✗	✗			0.04	0.22	✓
Lithuanian-HSE	4 301	209	337	45/13	87.27	0.26	82.34	89.59	✓	✗	✗			0.68	2.88	✓
Marathi-UFAL	3 055	236	222	45/11	76.42	0.66	67.21	79.00	✓	✗	✗			-0.54	0.54	✓
Naija-NSC	10 280	7	13	12/ 1	99.93	0.00	96.28	95.06	✓	✗	✗			0.00	0.45	✗
North Sami-Giella	21 380	1 019	314	51/13	92.18	0.16	91.78	94.96	✓	✗	✗			-0.25	0.04	✗
Norwegian-Bokmaal	248 922	445	142	42/14	99.14	0.01	97.88	98.77	✓	✗	✗			0.03	0.31	✓
Norwegian-Nynorsk	241 028	478	138	40/12	98.96	0.02	97.48	98.49	✗	✓	✗	0.05	-0.01	0.11	0.43	✓
Norwegian-NynorskLIA	10 843	111	100	37/14	98.15	0.03	96.30	97.25	✗	✓	✗	0.35	0.35	-0.07	0.43	✓
Old Church Slavonic -PROIEL	45 894	1 796	726	48/13	94.71	0.11	92.92	97.06	✓	✗	✗			-0.07	0.13	✗
Persian-Seraji	122 574	772	104	31/10	96.86	0.16	98.30	98.67	✓	✗	✗			0.27	0.60	✓
Polish-LFG	104 730	819	609	50/14	97.79	0.04	96.42	98.55	✓	✗	✗	-0.07	-0.89	0.18	0.72	✓
Polish-SZ	66 430	695	717	51/15	97.45	0.04	94.61	97.89	✓	✗	✗			0.34	1.94	✓
Portuguese-Bosque	180 773	402	247	43/12	98.70	0.02	96.09	98.18	✓	✗	✗	-4.84	-5.27	0.19	0.76	✓
Portuguese-GSD	255 690	175	19	17/ 5	99.07	0.05	98.88	98.96	✓	✗	✗	-2.49	-0.62	0.19	0.49	✓
Romanian-Nonstandard	156 320	2 094	288	45/14	96.78	0.06	94.62	97.27	✗	✓	✗	0.02	-0.02	0.23	0.38	✓
Romanian-RRT	174 747	678	254	47/14	98.50	0.03	97.97	98.68	✓	✗	✗	-0.03	-0.05	0.15	0.30	✓
Russian-GSD	79 989	553	668	47/14	97.93	0.04	94.38	97.64	✓	✗	✗			0.89	4.05	✓
Russian-PUD	15 433	309	525	46/15	94.69	0.09	90.24	96.45	✓	✗	✗	0.96	-7.25	1.88	7.14	✓
Russian-SynTagRus	886 711	1 744	678	48/13	98.92	0.02	98.05	99.05	✓	✗	✗	-0.04	-0.08	0.24	1.02	✓
Russian-Taiga	16 762	434	383	47/13	95.33	0.10	89.36	94.74	✗	✓	✗	2.64	-0.40	2.14	7.02	✓
Sanskrit-UFAL	1 450	244	232	54/14	64.82	0.89	50.25	68.99	✗	✗	✓			0.00	0.00	✗
Serbian-SET	68 933	359	421	39/12	98.27	0.03	96.68	98.40	✓	✗	✗			0.50	1.04	✓
Slovak-SNK	85 257	598	830	52/15	97.49	0.04	94.96	97.96	✓	✗	✗			0.28	1.30	✓
Slovenian-SSJ	112 136	369	744	52/15	98.84	0.02	96.99	98.59	✗	✓	✗	0.06	0.14	0.28	1.03	✓
Slovenian-SST	23 759	214	473	49/14	97.74	0.05	93.52	95.96	✗	✓	✗	1.53	1.68	0.35	0.66	✓
Spanish-AnCora	439 925	594	173	42/13	99.48	0.01	98.63	99.28	✓	✗	✗	-0.24	-0.19	0.17	0.35	✓
Spanish-GSD	345 545	310	239	52/14	99.31	0.01	95.67	97.97	✓	✗	✗	-0.27	-0.50	0.05	0.26	✓
Swedish-LinES	63 365	332	135	38/11	98.05	0.04	94.66	97.47	✓	✗	✗	-0.19	-0.56	-0.02	0.57	✓
Swedish-PUD	14 952	171	94	36/11	95.85	0.07	95.39	97.25	✗	✓	✗	0.00	-0.04	0.74	2.21	✓
Swedish-Talbanken	77 238	291	119	38/11	98.60	0.02	97.84	98.87	✓	✗	✗	-0.16	-0.21	0.08	0.69	✓
Tagalog-TRG	230	19	33	31/11	91.89	0.30	91.89	95.04	✓	✗	✗			-5.41	0.00	✓
Tamil-TTB	7 634	99	172	47/13	96.65	0.07	91.85	96.11	✓	✗	✗			1.45	2.01	✓
Turkish-IMST	46 417	211	985	56/13	96.84	0.06	92.83	96.60	✓	✗	✗	-0.31	-0.83	0.15	0.82	✓
Turkish-PUD	13 380	103	503	62/13	88.02	0.30	88.69	95.07	✓	✗	✗	1.23	-2.39	0.33	2.67	✓
Ukrainian-IU	93 264	629	597	49/14	97.84	0.04	95.40	97.93	✓	✗	✗			0.25	1.51	✓
Upper Sorbian-UFAL	8 959	222	417	49/14	93.46	0.11	87.11	93.71	✓	✗	✗			0.56	2.89	✗
Urdu-UDTB	110 682	448	740	49/12	97.10	0.05	80.95	93.44	✓	✗	✗			0.34	0.82	✓
Vietnamese-VTB	35 237	51	13	11/ 2	99.91	0.00	93.49	92.71	✓	✗	✗			0.05	1.06	✓
Yoruba-YTB	2 158	3	29	19/ 4	97.67	0.02	91.86	92.66	✓	✗	✗			0.00	0.00	✓

Table 6: For every corpus, its size, the number of unique lemma rules, the number of unique POS tags, and the number of morphological features and morphological categories is presented. Then the test set results of lemma accuracy, lemma Levenshtein, morphological accuracy and morphological F1 follow, using a model achieving best score on the development set. We consider the regular model R, or a model on the merged corpus M and a model without BERT embeddings N. Finally, we show the increase of the merged model to the regular model, the increase of the regular model to the no-BERT model, and indicate if the language is present in BERT training data (BT).

References

Piotr Bojanowski, Edouard Grave, Armand Joulin, and Tomas Mikolov. 2017. Enriching Word Vectors with Subword Information. *Transactions of the Association for Computational Linguistics*, 5:135–146.

Wanxiang Che, Yijia Liu, Yuxuan Wang, Bo Zheng, and Ting Liu. 2018. Towards better UD parsing: Deep contextualized word embeddings, ensemble, and treebank concatenation. In *Proceedings of the CoNLL 2018 Shared Task: Multilingual Parsing from Raw Text to Universal Dependencies*, pages 55–64, Brussels, Belgium. Association for Computational Linguistics.

KyungHyun Cho, Bart van Merrienboer, Dzmitry Bahdanau, and Yoshua Bengio. 2014. On the Properties of Neural Machine Translation: Encoder-Decoder Approaches. *CoRR*.

Jacob Devlin, Ming-Wei Chang, Kenton Lee, and Kristina Toutanova. 2018. BERT: Pre-training of Deep Bidirectional Transformers for Language Understanding.

Murhaf Fares, Stephan Oepen, Lilja Øvrelid, Jari Björne, and Richard Johansson. 2018. The 2018 Shared Task on Extrinsic Parser Evaluation: On the Downstream Utility of English Universal Dependency Parsers. In *Proceedings of the CoNLL 2018 Shared Task: Multilingual Parsing from Raw Text to Universal Dependencies*, pages 22–33. Association for Computational Linguistics.

Edouard Grave, Piotr Bojanowski, Prakhar Gupta, Armand Joulin, and Tomas Mikolov. 2018. Learning word vectors for 157 languages. In *Proceedings of the International Conference on Language Resources and Evaluation (LREC 2018)*.

Alex Graves and Jürgen Schmidhuber. 2005. Framewise phoneme classification with bidirectional lstm and other neural network architectures. *Neural Networks*, pages 5–6.

Sepp Hochreiter and Jürgen Schmidhuber. 1997. Long Short-Term Memory. *Neural Comput.*, 9(8):1735–1780.

Daniel Kondratyuk, Tomas Gavenciak, Milan Straka, and Jan Hajic. 2018. Lemmatag: Jointly tagging and lemmatizing for morphologically rich languages with brnns. In *Proceedings of the 2018 Conference on Empirical Methods in Natural Language Processing, Brussels, Belgium, October 31 - November 4, 2018*, pages 4921–4928. Association for Computational Linguistics.

Wang Ling, Tiago Luís, Luís Marujo, Ramón Fernandez Astudillo, Silvio Amir, Chris Dyer, Alan W. Black, and Isabel Trancoso. 2015. Finding Function in Form: Compositional Character Models for Open Vocabulary Word Representation. *CoRR*.

Arya D. McCarthy, Miikka Silfverberg, Ryan Cotterell, Mans Hulden, and David Yarowsky. 2018. Marrying Universal Dependencies and Universal Morphology. In *Proceedings of the Second Workshop on Universal Dependencies (UDW 2018)*, pages 91–101, Brussels, Belgium. Association for Computational Linguistics.

Joakim Nivre, Marie-Catherine de Marneffe, Filip Ginter, Yoav Goldberg, Jan Hajič, Christopher Manning, Ryan McDonald, Slav Petrov, Sampo Pyysalo, Natalia Silveira, Reut Tsarfaty, and Daniel Zeman. 2016. Universal Dependencies v1: A multilingual treebank collection. In *Proceedings of the 10th International Conference on Language Resources and Evaluation (LREC 2016)*, pages 1659–1666, Portorož, Slovenia. European Language Resources Association.

Matthew Peters, Mark Neumann, Mohit Iyyer, Matt Gardner, Christopher Clark, Kenton Lee, and Luke Zettlemoyer. 2018. Deep Contextualized Word Representations. In *Proceedings of the 2018 Conference of the North American Chapter of the Association for Computational Linguistics: Human Language Technologies, Volume 1 (Long Papers)*, pages 2227–2237. Association for Computational Linguistics.

Milan Straka. 2018. UDPipe 2.0 Prototype at CoNLL 2018 UD Shared Task. In *Proceedings of CoNLL 2018: The SIGNLL Conference on Computational Natural Language Learning*, pages 197–207, Stroudsburg, PA, USA. Association for Computational Linguistics.

John Sylak-Glassman. 2016. The composition and use of the universal morphological feature schema (unimorph schema).

Ashish Vaswani, Noam Shazeer, Niki Parmar, Jakob Uszkoreit, Llion Jones, Aidan N. Gomez, Lukasz Kaiser, and Illia Polosukhin. 2017. Attention is all you need. *CoRR*, abs/1706.03762.

Daniel Zeman, Filip Ginter, Jan Hajič, Joakim Nivre, Martin Popel, and Milan Straka. 2018. CoNLL 2018 Shared Task: Multilingual Parsing from Raw Text to Universal Dependencies. In *Proceedings of the CoNLL 2018 Shared Task: Multilingual Parsing from Raw Text to Universal Dependencies*, Brussels, Belgium. Association for Computational Linguistics.

Daniel Zeman, Martin Popel, Milan Straka, Jan Hajič, Joakim Nivre, Filip Ginter, et al. 2017. CoNLL 2017 Shared Task: Multilingual Parsing from Raw Text to Universal Dependencies. In *Proceedings of the CoNLL 2017 Shared Task: Multilingual Parsing from Raw Text to Universal Dependencies*, pages 1–19, Vancouver, Canada. Association for Computational Linguistics.

CUNI-Malta system at SIGMORPHON 2019 Shared Task on Morphological Analysis and Lemmatization in context: Operation-based word formation

Ronald Cardenas[♣♠] **Claudia Borg**[♠] **Daniel Zeman**[♣]
[♣] Institute of Formal and Applied Linguistics, Charles University in Prague
[♠] Department of Artificial Intelligence, Faculty of ICT, University of Malta
`ronald.cardenas@matfyz.cz claudia.borg@um.edu.mt`
`zeman@ufal.mff.cuni.cz`

Abstract

This paper presents the submission by the Charles University-University of Malta team to the SIGMORPHON 2019 Shared Task on Morphological Analysis and Lemmatization in context. We present a lemmatization model based on previous work on neural transducers (Makarov and Clematide, 2018b; Aharoni and Goldberg, 2016). The key difference is that our model transforms the whole word form in every step, instead of consuming it character by character. We propose a merging strategy inspired by Byte-Pair-Encoding that reduces the space of valid operations by merging frequent adjacent operations. The resulting operations not only encode the actions to be performed but the relative position in the word token and how characters need to be transformed. Our morphological tagger is a vanilla biLSTM tagger that operates over operation representations, encoding operations and words in a hierarchical manner. Even though relative performance according to metrics is below the baseline, experiments show that our models capture important associations between interpretable operation labels and fine-grained morpho-syntax labels.

1 Introduction

Tasks related to morphological analysis have been traditionally formulated as string transduction problems tackled by weighted finite state transducers (Mohri, 2004; Eisner, 2002). More recently, however, the problem has been tackled with neural architectures featuring sequence-to-sequence architectures (Kann and Schütze, 2016) and neural transducers (Aharoni and Goldberg, 2016; Makarov and Clematide, 2018b,a).

In this paper we describe our submission for the SIGMORPHON 2019 Shared Task related to morphological analysis and lemmatization in context (McCarthy et al., 2019). We focus on an operation-based word formation process using a neural transducer which consumes more than one character at a time. Our main motivation for this approach stems from neural transducers that normally consume one character at a time using context-enriched representation of characters.[1] In language modelling, character-based RNNs have a difficulty capturing long dependencies between characters, especially dependencies in words which are separated by several tokens. This can be a crucial piece of information for morphological analysis in context. This type of approach has already been extend effectively to Neural Machine Translation by (Sennrich et al., 2016), who employ simple character n-gram models and a segmentation based on the *byte pair encoding* (BPE) compression algorithm.

2 Related Work

In the last few years, efforts on the analysis of endangered low-resourced languages and the development of basic language tools for them (Rios, 2016; Pereira-Noriega et al., 2017; Cardenas and Zeman, 2018) have once more brought attention into the latent necessity for research of less language-dependent models that are not unreasonably data hungry.

On the other hand, more recent efforts have proposed combined strategies to bring together the transducer paradigm and neural architectures (Rastogi et al., 2016; Aharoni and Goldberg, 2016; Lin et al., 2019). For example, the neural transducer proposed by (Aharoni and Goldberg, 2016) presents a sequence to sequence architecture that decodes one character at a time while attending at the input character under a hard-monotonic constrain. However, their method relies on out-of-

---

[1] We release our code at `https://github.com/ronaldahmed/morph-bandit`

Proceedings of the 16th Workshop on Computational Research in Phonetics, Phonology, and Morphology, pages 104–112
Florence, Italy. August 2, 2019 ©2019 Association for Computational Linguistics

the-pipeline alignment of the input and output string at the character level. Subsequent work by Makarov and Clematide (2018b) proposed a transition-based architecture instead, although still operating under the same conditions, i.e. consuming one character at a time and relying on pre-alignment. More recently, however, Makarov and Clematide (2018a) proposed to learn alignment lattices along the transduction mechanism under an imitation learning framework, hence eliminating the need for single, noisy alignments.

In this work, we propose a neural architecture that encodes more expressive, interpretable transducer operations. We relax the condition of consuming one character at a time, and derive operations meant to be applied at the word level instead. These operations are obtained by merging initial character-level operations using the BPE algorithm (Gage, 1994).

3 Task Description

The SIGMORPHON 2019 Shared Task (McCarthy et al., 2019) features three main tasks: (i) cross-lingual transfer for inflection generation, (ii) morphological analysis and lemmatization in context, and (iii) an open challenge over past editions of the shared tasks.

We participated in Task II for which a complete sentence of word forms is presented and lemmas and feature bundles (morpho-syntactic description labels) are to be predicted for each token. This task features an outstanding diverse pool of 66 languages from a total of 107 treebanks. Data (forms, lemmas, and feature bundles) are obtained from UniversalDependencies v.2.3 treebanks (Nivre et al., 2018). However, the feature bundles are translated into the UniMorph tagset (Kirov et al., 2018) using the mapping strategy proposed by McCarthy et al. (2018).

4 Problem Formulation

Let $w \in V$ and $z \in V^L$ be a word type and its corresponding lemma; and let $\mathcal{A}$ be a set of string transformation actions. We define the function $T : V \times \mathcal{A}^m \mapsto V^L$ that receives as input a word form w and a sequence of string transformations $a = \langle a_0, ., a_i, .., a_m \rangle$. T iteratively applies the transformations one at a time and returns the resulting string. The objective is to obtain a sequence of actions a such that a form w gets transformed into its lemma z, i.e. $T(w, a) = z$.

4.1 String transformations at the word level

We encode every string transformation - henceforth, action- $a_i \in \mathcal{A}$ as follows: $\langle \texttt{operation-position-segment} \rangle$. The additional information encoded such as position and segment (characters) involved, allows actions to operate at the word level and act upon a segment of characters instead of a single character. This is a key difference between $\mathcal{A}$ and the action sets of most previously proposed neural transducers (Aharoni and Goldberg, 2017; Makarov and Clematide, 2018b,c) which only encode the operation to perform and consume one character at a time.

4.2 Obtaining gold action sequences

We discuss now how to deterministically populate $\mathcal{A}$. We start off with operations that act upon one character at a time. We derive these operations with the Damerou-Levenshtein (DL) distance algorithm which adds the *transposition* operation in addition to the traditional set of the edit distance algorithm. However, the set $\mathcal{A}$ of the form $\langle \texttt{operation-position-segment} \rangle$ directly derived by this algorithm is too large and sparse to be learned effectively, especially because of the `position` component.

Hence, we simplify $\mathcal{A}$ by merging the k most frequent operations performed at adjacent positions by using Byte-Pair-Encoding (BPE) (Gage, 1994). Furthermore, we replace the `position` component of actions performed at the beginning of a token with the label _A, indicating that it is a prefixing action. Analogously, we use the label A_ to indicate it is a suffixing action. Table 1 presents a description of the licensed values of each component, including the operation set considered.

Finally, actions are sorted so that prefix actions are performed first, followed by inner-word actions (positions _i_), and lastly, suffix actions. In addition, prefix and suffix actions are sorted so that T would process the word form from the outside in. Consider the example presented in Table 2, a sequence of suffix actions. The form *visto* (Spanish for 'seen', past participle) is transformed into the lemma *ver* ('to see'), with all actions operating at the right border of the current token.

5 System Description

In this section we describe the models presented for Task 2 on morphological tagging and lemma-

Component	Label	Description
operation	INS	insert
	DEL	delete
	SUBS	substitute
	TRSP	transpose
	STOP	stop
position	_A	at the beginning (prefix)
	A_	at the end (suffix)
	_i_	at position i
segment	c	$c \in \Sigma^* \backslash \{\emptyset\}$

Table 1: Description of components encoded in action labels. Σ: set of characters observed in the training data.

Token	Action
visto	DEL-A_-o
vist	DEL-A_-t
vis	SUBS-A_-er
ver	STOP
visto DEL-A_-o DEL-A_-t SUBS-A_-er STOP	

Table 2: Example of step-by-step transformation from form *visto* (Spanish for 'seen', past participle) to lemma *ver* ('to see'). Bottom row presents the final token representation as the initial form followed by the action sequence.

tization in context. We tackle the tasks of lemmatization and analysis with two separate, pipelined models, as follows.

5.1 Lemmatization Model

We posit the task of lemmatization as a language modelling problem over action sequences. Let $w = \langle w^0, ..., w^i, ..., w^n \rangle$ be a sequence of word tokens, $z = \langle z^0, ..., z^i, ..., z^n \rangle$ the lemma sequence associated with w, and $a^i = \langle a_0^i, ..., a_j^i, ... a_m^i \rangle$ the action sequence such that $T(w^i, a^i) = z^i$. We encode a^i using an RNN with an LSTM cell (Hochreiter and Schmidhuber, 1997), as follows

$$h_j^i = LSTM(e_j^i, h_{j-1}^i)$$

where e_j^i is the embedding of action a_j^i. Then, the probability of action a_j^i is defined as

$$P(a_j^i|a_{1:j-1}^i, \theta) = softmax(g(W * h_j + b)) \quad (1)$$

where $g(x)$ is the ReLU activation function, and W and b are network parameters. As a way to introduce the original word form into the encoded sequence, we prepend w^i to a^i. Hence, the probability of the first action is determined by $h_0 = LSTM(e_0^i, h_m^{i-1})$ where h_m^{i-1} is the last state of the encoded action sequence of the previous word w^{i-1}, and e_0^i is the embedding of word w^i.

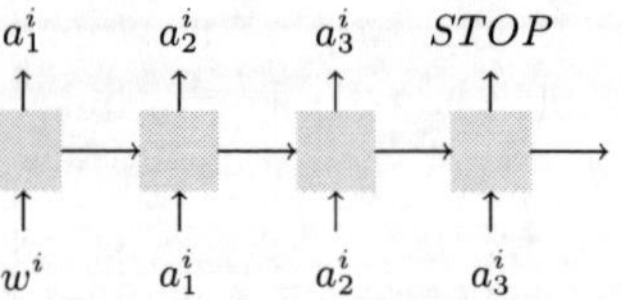

Figure 1: Architecture of the lemmatization model posited as a language model over action sequences.

The network is then optimized by minimizing the negative log-likelihood of the action sequences, as follows,

$$\mathcal{L}(W, \theta) = - \sum_{w \in W} \sum_{i=0}^{n} P(w^i|\theta) \cdot$$

$$\sum_{j=1}^{m} P(a_j^i|a_{1:j-1}^i, \theta)$$

where W is the set of all sentences in the training set and θ represents the parameters of the network. Figure 1 presents a representation of the lemmatizer model architecture. Note that a_m^i is the special action label $STOP$. During decoding, we construct the lemma z^i by running T over the predicted action sequence of w^i.

5.2 Morphological Tagging Model

Let $F^i = \{f_0^i, ..., f_k^i, f_K^i\}$ be the morpho-syntactic description (MSD) label associated with word form w^i, defined as the concatenation of all individual features f_k such as N or Pl, and F^i. We tackle the task of morphological tagging as a sequence labeling problem over aggregated representations of word forms.

We starts off by encoding the action sequence using a bidirectional LSTM (Graves et al., 2013) in order to obtain a word level representation $x^i = [f_m; b_0]$, where f_m is the the last forward state and b_0 is the first backward state. We use action embeddings trained by the lemmatizer and we freeze them during training.

Then, the sequence $x^0, .., x^n$, $u^i = biLSTM(x^i, u^{i-1})$ is encoded by a word-level biLSTM

$$u^i = biLSTM(x^i, u^{i-1})$$ Then, the probablity of feature label F^i is given by

$$P(F^i|x^{1:i-1}, \theta) = softmax(g(W * u^i + b)) \quad (2)$$

where $g(x)$ is a ReLU activation function, and W and b are network parameters. The network is optimized using cross-entropy loss.

6 Experimental Setup

We follow a two step approach to morphological analysis by first obtaining the action sequence using the lemmatizer model, and then obtaining the feature label sequence over these action representations. All models were implemented and trained using PyTorch 1.0.0. [2]

6.1 Action sequence preprocessing

We lowercase forms and lemmas before running the DL-distance algorithm. Following the BPE training procedure described by Sennrich et al. (2016), we obtain the list of merged operations from the action sequences derived from the training data. We limit the number of merges to 50. Then, these merges are applied to action sequences on the development and test data.

6.2 Training and optimization of details

Both the lemmatizer and analyzer models were trained using Adam (Kingma and Ba, 2017), regularized using dropout (Srivastava et al., 2014), and employing an early stopping strategy. We tune the hyper-parameters of both models over the development set of Spanish (*es_ancora*)[3] and then we use the optimal configuration to train on all treebanks except *kpv_ikdp*, *kpv_lattice*, and *sa_ufal*. Preliminary experiments showed that these treebanks needed a smaller analyzer model to perform well. In this case, we choose *kpv_ikdp* as our reference to obtain an optimal hyper-parameter configuration.

In each case, hyper-parameters were optimized over 30 iterations of random search guided by a Tree-structured Parzen Estimator (TPE).[4] Table 3 presents the hyper-parameters for the lemmatizer, analyzer, and the small version of the analyzer.

For decoding of lemmas, we follow a greedy approach to action sequence decoding. We also experimented with beam search but the improvements were not significant. Furthermore, we implement heuristics to prune a predicted sequence of actions. In addition to the heuristic of halting decoding if a PAD or STOP action is found, we halt if the action is not valid given the current string. For example, the action `DEL-_5_-o` cannot be applied to string `who` for the simple reason

---

[2] https://pytorch.org/

[3] We wanted to use a language that is morphologically more complex than English as our reference.

[4] We use HyperOpt library (http://hyperopt.github.io/hyperopt/)

Hyper-parameter	Lem	Anlz	Anlz-small
Batch size	128	24	40
Learning rate	6.90E-05	1.00E-04	0.01
Dropout	0.19	0.05	0.07
Epochs / patience	20 / 5	100 / 30	100 / 30
Action embedding	140	140	140
Action-LSTM cell	100	100	10
Word-LSTM cell	-	100	40
FF layer size	100	100	100
Clipping threshold	-	-	0.38

Table 3: Hyper-parameters of all models proposed. Lem = Lemmatizer; Anlz = Analyzer

that the string is not long enough and, hence, the action is not valid.

6.3 Baseline model

We consider the baseline neural model provided by the organizers of the shared task. The architecture, proposed by Malaviya et al. (2019), performs lemmatization and morphological tagging jointly. The morphological tagging module of the model employs an LSTM-based tagger (Heigold et al., 2017), whilst the lemmatizer module employs a sequence-to-sequence architecture with hard attention mechanism (Xu et al., 2015).

6.4 Co-occurrence of actions and morphological features

We further investigate the co-occurrence of action labels with individual morphological features. Given the word form w^i and its associated morphological tag $F^i = \{f_0^i, ..., f_k^i, f_K^i\}$ and action sequence $a^i = \langle a_0, ..., a_j, ..., a_m \rangle$, let us define the joint probability distribution between individual features and action labels, as

$$p(f_k^i, a_j^i) = P(f_k^i | x_{1:i}) \cdot P(a_j^i | a_{1:j-1}^i) \quad (3)$$

We consider $P(F^i | x_{1:i}) = P(f_k^i | x_{1:i}), \forall f_k^i \in F^i$. Note that $P(F^i | x_{1:i})$ and $P(a_j^i | a_{1:j-1}^i)$ are the probabilities obtained by the lemmatizer and tagger in equations 1 and 2, respectively.

7 Results and Discussion

7.1 Lemmatization and Morphological Tagging

Table 4 presents results on all metrics for the top 5 and bottom 5 scored treebanks according to the MSD-F1 scores on the official test evaluation. Results for the development set are presented as averaged over 10 runs with standard deviation value in parenthesis.

In lemmatization, our model underperforms the baseline for most treebanks, incurring in an error increase ranging from 0.27% to 35.14% in lemma accuracy. However, we improve over the baseline on the following languages: Tagalog *(tl_trg)*, Chinese *(zh_gsd, zh_cfl)*, Cantonese *(yue_hk)*, and Amharic *(am_att)*.

We hypothesize that the relative poor performance in lemmatization stems from the input representation, i,e. the action sequences. Combinations of `position` information inside the token *(_i_)* and `segment` characters produces an action set $\mathcal{A}$ that is too fine-grained and sparse, even after the BPE merging of adjacent actions.

In morphological tagging, we observe an error increase ranging from 0.31% to 7.34% in MSD-F1 score. The exception were Russian *(ru_gsd)* and Finnish *(fi_tdt)* for which we obtain an error decrease of 34.88% and 46.71% in MSD-accuracy,[5] respectively.

7.2 Actions and Morphological Features

Figure 2 shows the distribution of individual morphological features over action labels, as defined in Eq.3 for Czech *(cs_pdt)*. Every row represents how likely a fine-grained feature label is to co-occur with an action performed during lemmatization of a token. On the left, we have co-occurrence distributions of gold actions and gold feature labels. On the right, we have co-occurrence distributions of predicted actions and predicted feature labels. For ease of visualization, we only plot the 20 most frequent action labels and the 30 most frequent features in the development set. We can observe the lemmatizer and tagger succeed in fitting the gold distribution. This is to be expected since the distribution in Eq.3 depends on $P(F^i|x_{1:i})$ and $P(a_j|a_{1:j})$, which are directly optimized by our models. We obtain similar plots for Spanish, English, Turkish, German, and Arab.

This analysis also sheds light on which actions and morphological features the model learns to associate. For example, action `del-A_-y` is strongly associated with features PL, N, and MASC, in accordance with the suffix *y* being a plural marker. Another notable example is that of the prefix *ne* which negates a verb. We observe that action `del-_A-ne` is strongly associated with feature V. We also observe ubiquitous

features such as POS (positive polarity), which shows an annotation preference unless the bound morpheme of negation is observed *(ne)*.

8 Limitations

8.1 Fixed gold action sequences

Obtaining gold action sequences as a previous, independent step presents a drawback, as pointed out by Makarov and Clematide (2018a). The optimal action sequence obtained for certain word-lemma pair might not be unique. Hence, if the lemmatizer predicts an alternative valid action sequence, the loss function would still penalize it during training. Given that we consider only one optimal sequence per word-lemma pair, our model cannot take advantage of all the possible valid alternative gold sequences.

8.2 Monotonic correspondence assumption

Previous work on neural transducers for morphology tasks (Aharoni and Goldberg, 2017; Makarov and Clematide, 2018b,a) rely on the fact that an almost monotonic alignment of input and output characters exists. This assumption also includes that both words and lemmas are presented in the same writing system (*same-script condition*), if no off-the-shelf character mapper is used. Our action sequencer relies on the same-script condition in order to not produce too long sequences and in turn, our lemmatizer relies on it to learn meaningful sequences.

However, upon inspection, we identify a couple of treebanks that violate this condition. In the first one, Arabic-PUD *(ar_pud)*, lemmas are romanized, i.e. presented in Latin rather than Arabic script. For the second one, Akkadian-PISANDUB *(akk_pisandub)*, different writing systems (ideographic vs. syllabic) are encoded in the forms but are not preserved in the lemmas. This encoding includes extra symbols such as hyphens and square brackets as well as capitalization of continuous segments. This kind of mismatch between word forms and lemmas forces our lemmatizer to learn action sequences that transform one character at a time, leading to poor performance given our architecture (16.75% and 14.36% on lemmata accuracy for *ar_pud* and *akk_pisandub*, respectively).

8.3 Lemmatizer biased to copy word forms

Languages with little to no morphology such as Chinese or Vietnamese will bias a transducer into

---

Treebank	Dev				Test			
	LAcc	Lev-Dist	MAcc	M-F1	LAcc	Lev-Dist	MAcc	M-F1
UD_Catalan-AnCora	83.25(0.46)	0.27(0.01)	80.56(0.44)	85.59(0.35)	83.47	0.26	81.94	86.79
UD_Spanish-GSD	93.78(0.34)	0.11(0.01)	77.58(0.31)	84.64(0.18)	93.83	0.10	78.44	85.06
UD_Spanish-AnCora	85.68(0.28)	0.23(0.01)	78.42(0.24)	84.07(0.16)	84.68	0.24	79.66	84.72
UD_French-GSD	86.49(0.45)	0.23(0.01)	79.95(0.16)	85.44(0.17)	86.85	0.21	78.59	84.51
UD_Hindi-HDTB	92.73(0.26)	0.15(0.01)	69.02(0.42)	84.35(0.20)	92.92	0.15	69.43	84.38
UD_Latin-Perseus	57.14(0.65)	1.12(0.01)	31.97(0.86)	33.77(1.46)	56.02	1.14	30.96	32.14
UD_Lithuanian-HSE	49.47(0.58)	1.13(0.03)	22.53(6.82)	24.87(4.19)	35.82	1.24	21.39	28.57
UD_Cantonese-HK	98.68(0.19)	0.02(0.00)	23.23(0.18)	25.11(0.17)	98.57	0.01	23.57	25.76
UD_Chinese-CFL	100.00(0.00)	0.00(0.00)	24.21(0.06)	25.73(0.05)	99.53	0	23.29	24.71
UD_Yoruba-YTB	96.80(0.00)	0.03(0.00)	24.40(0.31)	22.06(0.96)	96.12	0.04	20.54	17.5
Mean	74.39	0.62	44.07	53.79	74.94	0.62	50.37	58.81
Median	78.46	0.43	45.96	55.13	78.42	0.44	52.77	62.26

Table 4: Results on Task2 for the best and worst 5 treebanks. Scores over the development set are presented as mean (std) values over 10 runs. Scores over test set are taken from the official results. LAcc = lemmatization accuracy; Lev-Dist = Levenshtein distance of lemmas; MAcc = accuracy of morphosyntactic descriptions (features); M-F1 = F_1 score of morphosyntactic descriptions.

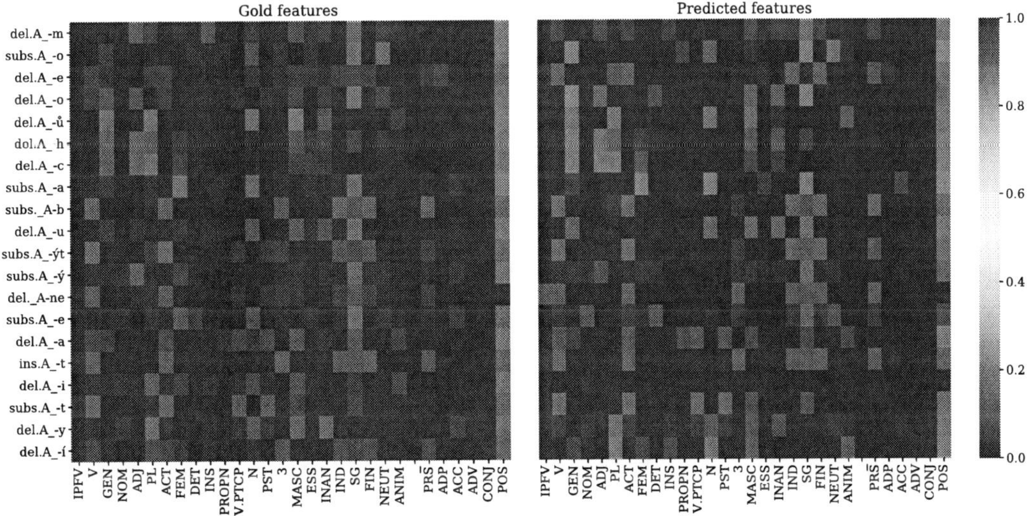

Figure 2: Probability distribution of gold and predicted morphological features given a certain action label, for the Czech-PDT treebank (cs_pdt). For ease of visualization, we only plot the 20 most frequent action labels and the 30 most frequent features in the development set.

copying the whole input to the output, as pointed out by Makarov and Clematide (2018b). Our proposed lemmatizer exhibits the same kind of bias, obtaining up to 99.53% of lemmata accuracy for Chinese-CFL and Levenshtein distance of 0.0 in test set and 100% and 0.0 in the development set. Other languages benefit from this bias also, as can be observed in Figure 3. We note that, on average, the lemmatizer predicts no more than 3 actions before halting.

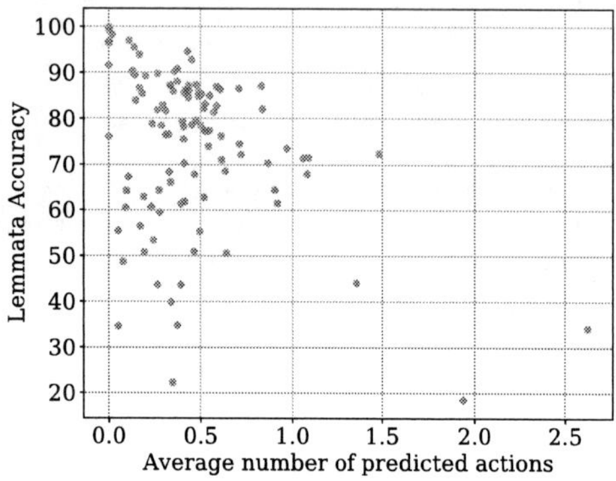

Figure 3: Average number of predicted actions over development set, not including the STOP operation, one data point per treebank.

9   Conclusions

We presented our submission to the SIGMOR-PHON 2019 Shared Task on Morphological Analysis and Lemmatization in context. We presented a lemmatization strategy based on word formation operations derived from extended edit-distance operations that operate at the word level instead of at the character leve. These operations are merged using a BPE-inspired algorithm in order to encode segment (prefix, suffix) information in addition to the action to perform. Most notably, the proposed models are capable of associate the derived interpretable operations with morpho-syntactic feature labels. We find that the proposed architectures underperform the shared task baseline for most treebanks, showing plenty of room for improvement in this regard.

References

Roee Aharoni and Yoav Goldberg. 2016. Morphological inflection generation with hard monotonic attention. *arXiv preprint arXiv:1611.01487.*

Roee Aharoni and Yoav Goldberg. 2017. Morphological inflection generation with hard monotonic attention. In *Proceedings of the 55th Annual Meeting of the Association for Computational Linguistics (Volume 1: Long Papers)*, pages 2004–2015, Vancouver, Canada. Association for Computational Linguistics.

Ronald Cardenas and Daniel Zeman. 2018. A morphological analyzer for shipibo-konibo. *SIGMOR-PHON 2018*, page 131.

Jason Eisner. 2002. Parameter estimation for probabilistic finite-state transducers. In *Proceedings of the 40th Annual Meeting of the Association for Computational Linguistics.*

Philip Gage. 1994. A new algorithm for data compression. *The C Users Journal*, 12(2):23–38.

Alex Graves, Abdel-rahman Mohamed, and Geoffrey Hinton. 2013. Speech recognition with deep recurrent neural networks. In *2013 IEEE international conference on acoustics, speech and signal processing*, pages 6645–6649. IEEE.

Georg Heigold, Guenter Neumann, and Josef van Genabith. 2017. An extensive empirical evaluation of character-based morphological tagging for 14 languages. In *Proceedings of the 15th Conference of the European Chapter of the Association for Computational Linguistics: Volume 1, Long Papers*, pages 505–513.

Sepp Hochreiter and Jürgen Schmidhuber. 1997. Long short-term memory. *Neural computation*, 9(8):1735–1780.

Katharina Kann and Hinrich Schütze. 2016. Single-model encoder-decoder with explicit morphological representation for reinflection. *arXiv preprint arXiv:1606.00589.*

Diederik P Kingma and Jimmy Ba. 2017. Adam: A method for stochastic optimization. *arXiv preprint arXiv:1412.6980.*

Christo Kirov, Ryan Cotterell, John Sylak-Glassman, Géraldine Walther, Ekaterina Vylomova, Patrick Xia, Manaal Faruqui, Sebastian J. Mielke, Arya McCarthy, Sandra Kübler, David Yarowsky, Jason Eisner, and Mans Hulden. 2018. UniMorph 2.0: Universal Morphology. In *Proceedings of the 11th Language Resources and Evaluation Conference*, Miyazaki, Japan. European Language Resource Association.

Chu-Cheng Lin, Hao Zhu, Matthew R. Gormley, and Jason Eisner. 2019. Neural finite-state transducers: Beyond rational relations. In *Proceedings of the 2019 Conference of the North American Chapter of the Association for Computational Linguistics: Human Language Technologies, Volume 1 (Long and Short Papers)*, pages 272–283, Minneapolis, Minnesota. Association for Computational Linguistics.

Peter Makarov and Simon Clematide. 2018a. Imitation learning for neural morphological string transduction. In *Proceedings of the 2018 Conference on Empirical Methods in Natural Language Processing*, pages 2877–2882.

Peter Makarov and Simon Clematide. 2018b. Neural transition-based string transduction for limited-resource setting in morphology. In *Proceedings of the 27th International Conference on Computational Linguistics*, pages 83–93.

Peter Makarov and Simon Clematide. 2018c. Uzh at conll-sigmorphon 2018 shared task on universal morphological reinflection. *Proceedings of the CoNLL SIGMORPHON 2018 Shared Task: Universal Morphological Reinflection*, pages 69–75.

Chaitanya Malaviya, Shijie Wu, and Ryan Cotterell. 2019. A simple joint model for improved contextual neural lemmatization. In *Proceedings of the 2019 Annual Conference of the North American Chapter of the Association for Computational Linguistics (NAACL)*.

Arya D. McCarthy, Miikka Silfverberg, Ryan Cotterell, Mans Hulden, and David Yarowsky. 2018. Marrying Universal Dependencies and Universal Morphology. In *Proceedings of the Second Workshop on Universal Dependencies (UDW 2018)*, pages 91–101, Brussels, Belgium. Association for Computational Linguistics.

Arya D. McCarthy, Ekaterina Vylomova, Shijie Wu, Chaitanya Malaviya, Lawrence Wolf-Sonkin, Garrett Nicolai, Christo Kirov, Miikka Silfverberg, Sebastian Mielke, Jeffrey Heinz, Ryan Cotterell, and Mans Hulden. 2019. The SIGMORPHON 2019 shared task: Crosslinguality and context in morphology. In *Proceedings of the 16th SIGMORPHON Workshop on Computational Research in Phonetics, Phonology, and Morphology*, Florence, Italy. Association for Computational Linguistics.

Mehryar Mohri. 2004. Weighted finite-state transducer algorithms. an overview. In *Formal Languages and Applications*, pages 551–563. Springer.

Joakim Nivre, Mitchell Abrams, Željko Agić, Lars Ahrenberg, Lene Antonsen, Katya Aplonova, Maria Jesus Aranzabe, Gashaw Arutie, Masayuki Asahara, Luma Ateyah, Mohammed Attia, Aitziber Atutxa, Liesbeth Augustinus, Elena Badmaeva, Miguel Ballesteros, Esha Banerjee, Sebastian Bank, Verginica Barbu Mititelu, Victoria Basmov, John Bauer, Sandra Bellato, Kepa Bengoetxea, Yevgeni Berzak, Irshad Ahmad Bhat, Riyaz Ahmad Bhat, Erica Biagetti, Eckhard Bick, Rogier Blokland, Victoria Bobicev, Carl Börstell, Cristina Bosco, Gosse Bouma, Sam Bowman, Adriane Boyd, Aljoscha Burchardt, Marie Candito, Bernard Caron, Gauthier Caron, Gülşen Cebiroğlu Eryiğit, Flavio Massimiliano Cecchini, Giuseppe G. A. Celano, Slavomír Čéplö, Savas Cetin, Fabricio Chalub, Jinho Choi, Yongseok Cho, Jayeol Chun,

Silvie Cinková, Aurélie Collomb, Çağrı Çöltekin, Miriam Connor, Marine Courtin, Elizabeth Davidson, Marie-Catherine de Marneffe, Valeria de Paiva, Arantza Diaz de Ilarraza, Carly Dickerson, Peter Dirix, Kaja Dobrovoljc, Timothy Dozat, Kira Droganova, Puneet Dwivedi, Marhaba Eli, Ali Elkahky, Binyam Ephrem, Tomaž Erjavec, Aline Etienne, Richárd Farkas, Hector Fernandez Alcalde, Jennifer Foster, Cláudia Freitas, Katarína Gajdošová, Daniel Galbraith, Marcos Garcia, Moa Gärdenfors, Sebastian Garza, Kim Gerdes, Filip Ginter, Iakes Goenaga, Koldo Gojenola, Memduh Gökırmak, Yoav Goldberg, Xavier Gómez Guinovart, Berta Gonzáles Saavedra, Matias Grioni, Normunds Grūzītis, Bruno Guillaume, Céline Guillot-Barbance, Nizar Habash, Jan Hajič, Jan Hajič jr., Linh Hà Mỹ, Na-Rae Han, Kim Harris, Dag Haug, Barbora Hladká, Jaroslava Hlaváčová, Florinel Hociung, Petter Hohle, Jena Hwang, Radu Ion, Elena Irimia, Ọlájídé Ishola, Tomáš Jelínek, Anders Johannsen, Fredrik Jørgensen, Hüner Kaşıkara, Sylvain Kahane, Hiroshi Kanayama, Jenna Kanerva, Boris Katz, Tolga Kayadelen, Jessica Kenney, Václava Kettnerová, Jesse Kirchner, Kamil Kopacewicz, Natalia Kotsyba, Simon Krek, Sookyoung Kwak, Veronika Laippala, Lorenzo Lambertino, Lucia Lam, Tatiana Lando, Septina Dian Larasati, Alexei Lavrentiev, John Lee, Phng Lê H`ông, Alessandro Lenci, Saran Lertpradit, Herman Leung, Cheuk Ying Li, Josie Li, Keying Li, KyungTae Lim, Nikola Ljubešić, Olga Loginova, Olga Lyashevskaya, Teresa Lynn, Vivien Macketanz, Aibek Makazhanov, Michael Mandl, Christopher Manning, Ruli Manurung, Cătălina Mărănduc, David Mareček, Katrin Marheinecke, Héctor Martínez Alonso, André Martins, Jan Mašek, Yuji Matsumoto, Ryan McDonald, Gustavo Mendonça, Niko Miekka, Margarita Misirpashayeva, Anna Missilä, Cătălin Mititelu, Yusuke Miyao, Simonetta Montemagni, Amir More, Laura Moreno Romero, Keiko Sophie Mori, Shinsuke Mori, Bjartur Mortensen, Bohdan Moskalevskyi, Kadri Muischnek, Yugo Murawaki, Kaili Müürisep, Pinkey Nainwani, Juan Ignacio Navarro Horñiacek, Anna Nedoluzhko, Gunta Nešpore-Bērzkalne, Lng Nguy~ên Thị, Huy`ên Nguy~ên Thị Minh, Vitaly Nikolaev, Rattima Nitisaroj, Hanna Nurmi, Stina Ojala, Adédayọ Olúòkun, Mai Omura, Petya Osenova, Robert Östling, Lilja Øvrelid, Niko Partanen, Elena Pascual, Marco Passarotti, Agnieszka Patejuk, Guilherme Paulino-Passos, Siyao Peng, Cenel-Augusto Perez, Guy Perrier, Slav Petrov, Jussi Piitulainen, Emily Pitler, Barbara Plank, Thierry Poibeau, Martin Popel, Lauma Pretkalniņa, Sophie Prévost, Prokopis Prokopidis, Adam Przepiórkowski, Tiina Puolakainen, Sampo Pyysalo, Andriela Rääbis, Alexandre Rademaker, Loganathan Ramasamy, Taraka Rama, Carlos Ramisch, Vinit Ravishankar, Livy Real, Siva Reddy, Georg Rehm, Michael Rießler, Larissa Rinaldi, Laura Rituma, Luisa Rocha, Mykhailo Romanenko, Rudolf Rosa, Davide Rovati, Valentin Roca, Olga Rudina, Jack Rueter, Shoval Sadde,

Benoît Sagot, Shadi Saleh, Tanja Samardžić, Stephanie Samson, Manuela Sanguinetti, Baiba Saulīte, Yanin Sawanakunanon, Nathan Schneider, Sebastian Schuster, Djamé Seddah, Wolfgang Seeker, Mojgan Seraji, Mo Shen, Atsuko Shimada, Muh Shohibussirri, Dmitry Sichinava, Natalia Silveira, Maria Simi, Radu Simionescu, Katalin Simkó, Mária Šimková, Kiril Simov, Aaron Smith, Isabela Soares-Bastos, Carolyn Spadine, Antonio Stella, Milan Straka, Jana Strnadová, Alane Suhr, Umut Sulubacak, Zsolt Szántó, Dima Taji, Yuta Takahashi, Takaaki Tanaka, Isabelle Tellier, Trond Trosterud, Anna Trukhina, Reut Tsarfaty, Francis Tyers, Sumire Uematsu, Zdeňka Urešová, Larraitz Uria, Hans Uszkoreit, Sowmya Vajjala, Daniel van Niekerk, Gertjan van Noord, Viktor Varga, Eric Villemonte de la Clergerie, Veronika Vincze, Lars Wallin, Jing Xian Wang, Jonathan North Washington, Seyi Williams, Mats Wirén, Tsegay Woldemariam, Tak-sum Wong, Chunxiao Yan, Marat M. Yavrumyan, Zhuoran Yu, Zdeněk Žabokrtský, Amir Zeldes, Daniel Zeman, Manying Zhang, and Hanzhi Zhu. 2018. Universal dependencies 2.3. LINDAT/CLARIN digital library at the Institute of Formal and Applied Linguistics (ÚFAL), Faculty of Mathematics and Physics, Charles University.

José Pereira-Noriega, Rodolfo Mercado-Gonzales, Andrés Melgar, Marco Sobrevilla-Cabezudo, and Arturo Oncevay-Marcos. 2017. Ship-lemmatagger: Building an nlp toolkit for a peruvian native language. In *International Conference on Text, Speech, and Dialogue*, pages 473–481. Springer.

Pushpendre Rastogi, Ryan Cotterell, and Jason Eisner. 2016. Weighting finite-state transductions with neural context. In *Proceedings of the 2016 Conference of the North American Chapter of the Association for Computational Linguistics: Human Language Technologies*, pages 623–633.

Annette Rios. 2016. A basic language technology toolkit for quechua. *Procesamiento del Lenguaje Natural*, (56):91–94.

Rico Sennrich, Barry Haddow, and Alexandra Birch. 2016. Neural machine translation of rare words with subword units. In *Proceedings of the 54th Annual Meeting of the Association for Computational Linguistics (Volume 1: Long Papers)*, pages 1715–1725, Berlin, Germany. Association for Computational Linguistics.

Nitish Srivastava, Geoffrey Hinton, Alex Krizhevsky, Ilya Sutskever, and Ruslan Salakhutdinov. 2014. Dropout: a simple way to prevent neural networks from overfitting. *The Journal of Machine Learning Research*, 15(1):1929–1958.

Kelvin Xu, Jimmy Lei Ba, Ryan Kiros, Kyunghyun Cho, Aaron Courville, Ruslan Salakhutdinov, Richard S. Zemel, and Yoshua Bengio. 2015. Show, attend and tell: Neural image caption generation with visual attention. In *Proceedings of the 32Nd International Conference on International Conference on Machine Learning - Volume 37*, ICML'15, pages 2048–2057. JMLR.org.

Acknowledgments

This research is supported by the Erasmus Mundus European Masters Program in Language and Communication Technologies (LCT).

A Little Linguistics Goes a Long Way:
Unsupervised Segmentation with Limited Language Specific Guidance

Alexander Erdmann, Salam Khalifa, Mai Oudah, Nizar Habash and Houda Bouamor[†]
Computational Approaches to Modeling Language Lab
New York University Abu Dhabi, UAE
[†]Carnegie Mellon University in Qatar, Qatar
`{ae1541,salamkhalifa,mai.oudah,nizar.habash}@nyu.edu`
`hbouamor@cmu.edu`

Abstract

We present de-lexical segmentation, a linguistically motivated alternative to greedy or other unsupervised methods, requiring language specific knowledge, but no direct supervision. Our technique involves creating a small grammar of closed-class affixes which can be written in a few hours. The grammar over generates analyses for word forms attested in a raw corpus which are disambiguated based on features of the linguistic base proposed for each form. Extending the grammar to cover orthographic, morphosyntactic or lexical variation is simple, making it an ideal solution for challenging corpora with noisy, dialect-inconsistent, or otherwise non-standard content. We demonstrate the utility of de-lexical segmentation on several dialects of Arabic. We consistently outperform competitive unsupervised baselines and approach the performance of state-of-the-art supervised models trained on large amounts of data, providing evidence for the value of linguistic input during preprocessing.

1 Introduction

Non-standard domains, dialectal variation, and unstandardized spelling make segmentation challenging, though morphologically rich languages require good segmentation to enable downstream applications from syntactic parsing to machine translation (MT). For domains lacking sufficient annotated data to train segmenters, one must resort to language specific greedy techniques or language agnostic unsupervised techniques. Greedy techniques use maximum matching to identify base words, leveraging large dictionaries (Guo, 1997). Yet such dictionaries are often unavailable or too expensive for low resource languages. Language agnostic unsupervised options like MORFESSOR (Creutz and Lagus, 2005) and byte pair encoding (BPE) (Sennrich et al., 2016) assume no resources beyond raw text but can yield lower performance on downstream tasks (Vania and Lopez, 2017; Kann et al., 2018). They also suffer from typological biases and favor intended applications at the expense of others.

To this end, we present *De-lexical Segmentation* (DESEG), a slightly more expensive but powerful alternative to language agnostic morphological segmentation, realizing most of the benefits of supervised segmentation at far less a cost. DESEG requires language specific input in the form of a small grammar describing the combinatorics of closed-class affixes. We demonstrate that such a grammar can be constructed easily and rapidly for a new language or dialect. Hence, DESEG addresses the scenario in which there is no supervised segmenter available for a given language or dialect (or no segmenter trained on a domain with sufficient lexical overlap with the target domain in its training data), but the user does have linguistic knowledge of the target language/dialect.

The user-provided grammar is employed in conjunction with a large, raw corpus. The grammar over generates analyses for all words therein, allowing for maximal recall not only of the possible affix combinations, but also variant spellings and dialectal idiosyncrasies. The preferred analysis is disambiguated based on the fertility with which its proposed base attaches to different affixes in analyses of other words throughout the corpus. This follows from the logic that valid bases are more likely to productively combine with more exponents[1] (Bertram et al., 2000). By leveraging language specific resources but learning to disambiguate empirically without supervision, we mitigate much of the sparsity inherent in processing

---

[1]Exponents refer to recurring means by which morphosyntactic properties are realized within classes of words, e.g., adding suffix *+s* to get the third person singular present tense for verbs like WALK, TALK, and SKIP.

113

Proceedings of the 16th Workshop on Computational Research in Phonetics, Phonology, and Morphology, pages 113–124
Florence, Italy. August 2, 2019 ©2019 Association for Computational Linguistics

non-standard domains.

Using a corpus of several Arabic dialects exhibiting rich and complex morphology, unstandardized spelling, and variation bordering on mutual unintelligibility, we evaluate DESEG intrinsically on language modeling (LM) and extrinsically on MT. DESEG consistently outperforms MORFESSOR and BPE while only costing a few hours of grammar-building labor; and in some environments it outperforms state-of-the-art supervised Arabic tokenizers MADAMIRA (Pasha et al., 2014) and FARASA (Abdelali et al., 2016). The success of such a simple model is strong evidence for the value of linguistic input during preprocessing. DESEG is publicly available at `github.com/CAMeL-Lab/deSeg`.

2   Related Work

Many morphologically rich languages lack crucial preprocessing resources like morphological analyzers or segmenters. Even well resourced languages often lack such resources for non-standard dialects and domains. There have been many approaches to address this problem, varying along a number of dimensions: the degree of language independence or specificity, the required amount of machine learning supervision, the degree of depth and richness of the morphological representations.

Language agnostic unsupervised models There are many works using minimally supervised to unsupervised models of morphology for connecting morphologically related words and identifying optimal (and at times application dependent) segmentations (Smith and Eisner, 2005; Creutz and Lagus, 2005; Snyder and Barzilay, 2008; Poon et al., 2009; Dreyer and Eisner, 2011; Stallard et al., 2012; Sirts and Goldwater, 2013; Narasimhan et al., 2015; Sennrich et al., 2016; Eskander et al., 2016b; Ataman et al., 2017; Ataman and Federico, 2018; Eskander et al., 2018). In this paper, we compare to two popular language agnostic segmentation systems: MORFESSOR (Creutz and Lagus, 2005) and BPE (Sennrich et al., 2016). Both train on large corpora of unannotated text in an unsupervised manner.

Standard Arabic models Modern Standard Arabic (MSA) morphological analysis, disambiguation and tokenization has been the focus of a large number of efforts. Khoja and Garside (1999) was one of the earliest published efforts on automatic shallow and deterministic segmentation for MSA. Darwish (2002) used limited resources and greedy techniques to automatically learn rules and statistics to build a shallow morphological analyzer. There are many MSA morphological analyzers with rich representations and good coverage that required very intensive efforts to create (Beesley, 1998; Buckwalter, 2004; Attia, 2006, 2007; Smrž, 2007; Boudchiche et al., 2017). Buckwalter (2004) is perhaps the most commonly used among them, as it contributed the representations for the Penn Arabic treebank (PATB) (Maamouri and Bies, 2004). The PATB has been the most used resource for supervised morphological disambiguation (Diab et al., 2004; Habash and Rambow, 2005; Pasha et al., 2014; AlGahtani and McNaught, 2015; Zalmout and Habash, 2017). Some efforts have used other annotated resources and/or large unannotated data sets (Lee et al., 2003; Abdelali et al., 2016; Freihat et al., 2018). More closely related to this paper, Erdmann and Habash (2018) demonstrated that de-lexicalized information provides a cheap means of inducing morphological knowledge and thereby predicting lexical information in MSA. They employ a de-lexicalized grammar which is similar to ours, but they do not handle dialectal variants or spelling variation. They also do not use the grammar for segmentation, but for pruning word embedding clusters in order to predict the paradigm membership of forms encountered in raw text.

Dialectal Arabic models Work on dialectal Arabic morphology and tokenization is relatively newer than work on MSA. Some of the earlier efforts worked on rule-based approaches to model dialectal morphology directly (Habash and Rambow, 2006; Habash et al., 2012), or exploiting existing MSA resources (Salloum and Habash, 2014). Later, a number of annotation efforts have led to the creation of varying sizes of dialectal annotated corpora following the style of the PATB (Maamouri et al., 2014; Jarrar et al., 2016; Al-Shargi et al., 2016; Khalifa et al., 2018; Alshargi et al., 2019). The created annotations supported models for dialectal Arabic analysis, disambiguation and tokenization building on the same successful approaches in MSA (Eskander et al., 2016a; Habash et al., 2013; Pasha et al., 2014; Zalmout et al., 2018; Zalmout and Habash, 2019). More closely related to this paper, Eldesouki et al. (2017) used de-lexicalized analysis strategy for four colloquial varieties of Arabic, though they also use minimal training data and extract features from an open class lexicon to learn either an SVM or bi-LSTM-CRF disambiguation model. They further show that domain adaptation from existing MSA training data is beneficial. Also, Samih et al. (2017) applied a related model to segmentation, allowing different Arabic dialects to inform one another, thus avoiding the need to perform dialect identification during preprocessing.

We compare our model to MADAMIRA (Pasha et al., 2014) and FARASA (Abdelali et al., 2016), which represent the fully supervised state of the art for segmenting Arabic in the standard domain, but have limited support for multiple colloquial variants of the language.

Finally, we note that, linguistically, our work is inspired by Bertram et al. (2000) who find that *prolific* stems with large derivational families are accessed more quickly. Their work suggests that stem *fertility*—or the productivity with which a stem can combine with different affixes—is cognitively relevant to morphological organization.

3   De-lexical Segmentation for Arabic

In this section, we introduce a case study on segmenting a multi-dialect Arabic corpus and explain the linguistic challenges it presents for popular approaches to segmentation. Furthermore, we discuss the construction of DESEG's grammar and its disambiguation algorithm.

3.1   Arabic and its Dialects

Arabic is highly diaglossic (Ferguson, 1959), with the relatively consistent high register of Modern Standard Arabic being learned in schools across the Arab World. Meanwhile the often mutually unintelligible low register variants—collectively known as dialectal Arabic (DA)—are spoken colloquially. The phonological, morpho-syntactic, and lexical variation within the Arabic sprachbund is comparable to that among Romance languages (Chiang et al., 2006; Rouchdy, 2013; Erdmann et al., 2017), leading to problematic noise in multi-dialect corpora (Erdmann et al., 2018). Furthermore, lack of spelling conventions in DA exacerbates data sparsity, as does a rich morphology featuring templatic phenomena and robust cliticization, making it challenging to train quality segmenters even with much supervised data.

3.2   Data

To demonstrate how our model handles such challenging phenomena, we apply it to the CORPUS6 subset of the MADAR-BTEC (Takezawa et al., 2002) corpus of Arabic dialects (Salameh et al., 2018). This consists of 12,000 sentences in the travel domain (9,000 for training) parallel between English, MSA, and the DA varieties spoken in Beirut, Cairo, Doha, Rabat, and Tunis. This comprises a representative sample of the breadth of intra-DA variation (Bouamor et al., 2018).

In addition to CORPUS6, we also use large amounts of raw monolingual data to train our segmenter and the unsupervised baselines. To avoid introducing even more noise, we restrict our monolingual datasets as much as possible to similar domains. For DA, we use the four subsets of Almeman and Lee (2013)'s web crawl of forums, comments and blogs, consisting of over 10 million words for each subset's dialect region. It is worth noting however, that the granularity of their dialect regions is coarser than the granularity of CORPUS6. Hence, their Maghrebi dialect corresponds to two dialects in CORPUS6, Tunis and Rabat, while the remaining three dialect regions have rather obvious one-to-one correspondences with CORPUS6, i.e., Egyptian to Cairo, Levantine to Beirut, and Gulf to Doha. For MSA, which rarely occurs consistently (i.e., outside of brief instances of code-mixing) in such casual domains, we used the TED corpus (Cettolo and Girardi, 2012) for our monolingual data set, finding a compromise between domain relevance and corpus size. It contains about 2.5 million words.

Obviously, CORPUS6 is small relative to other MT corpora, but this is exactly why it is a meaningful evaluation corpus. Larger parallel corpora are often only available for better resourced languages/domains where fully supervised segmenters are also more likely to be available, negating the need to build one's own segmenter. Furthermore, as parallel data becomes less sparse, tokenization necessarily has less of an effect since models can memorize and effectively use longer sequences. With that said, CORPUS6 is commissioned, and in future work we would like to also test DESEG's performance on natural corpora.

3.3   De-lexical Analysis

The DESEG grammar provides all possible *delexical* analyses of words by assuming any n-gram

(A)

Morph.Feat.	Prefix	Suffix
PV.1US	∅	+t ت+
PV.1UP	∅	+nA نا+
PV.2MS	∅	+t ت+
PV.2FS	∅	+t/ty ت/تي+
PV.2US	∅	+ty تي+
PV.2UP	∅	+twA توا+
PV.3MS	∅	∅
PV.3FS	∅	+t ت+
PV.3UP	∅	+wA وا+
IV.1US	A/n+ ا/ن+	∅
IV.1UP	n+ ن+	+wA/∅ وا/∅+
IV.2MS	t+ ت+	∅
IV.2FS	t+ ت+	+y/yn/∅ ي/ين/∅+
IV.2UP	t+ ت+	+wA/wn وا/ون+
IV.3MS	y+ ي+	∅
IV.3FS	t+ ت+	∅
IV.3UP	y+ ي+	+wA/wn وا/ون+
CV.2MS	∅	∅
CV.2FS	∅	+y/∅ ي/∅+
CV.2UP	∅	+wA وا+
NOM.MS	∅	∅
NOM.FS	∅	+ħ ة+
NOM.MD	∅	+yn ين+
NOM.FD	∅	+tyn تين+
NOM.MP	∅	+yn ين+
NOM.FP	∅	+At ات+
PART	∅	∅

(B)

Proclitics	Orth	POS
ART	Al+ ال+	DET
ART	h+Al+ ه+ال+	DEM_PART+DET
$PART_n$	š+ ش+	INTERROG_PART
$PART_n$	ς+ ع+	PREP
$PART_n$	b+ ب+	PREP
$PART_n$	d+ د+	PREP
$PART_n$	f+ ف+	PREP
$PART_n$	k+ ك+	PREP
$PART_n$	w+ و+	PREP
$PART_n$	yA+ يا+	VOC_PART
$PART_n$	Ā/A+ الآ+	VOC_PART
$PART_n$	l+ ل+	PREP
$PART_v$	H+ ح+	FUT_PART
$PART_v$	b/m+ ب/م+	PROG_PART
$PART_v$	b+ ب+	FUT_PART
$PART_v$	g+ غ+	FUT_PART
$PART_v$	h+ ه+	FUT_PART
$PART_v$	k+ ك+	PROG_PART
$PART_v$	t+ ت+	PROG_PART
$PART_v$	l+ ل+	JUS_PART
m_NEG	m/mA+ م/ما+	NEG_PART
CONJ	f+ ف+	CONJ
CONJ	f+ ف+	CONNEC_PART
CONJ	f+ ف+	RC_PART
CONJ	t+ ت+	SUB_CONJ
CONJ	w+ و+	CONJ
CONJ	w+ و+	SUB_CONJ

(C)

Enclitics	Orth	POS
$PRON_{n,v}$	+kw +كو	2UP
$PRON_{n,v}$	+ky +كي	2UP
$PRON_{n,v}$	+km +كم	2MP/2UP
$PRON_{n,v}$	+h/w +ه/و	3MS
$PRON_{n,v}$	+hA +ها	3FS
$PRON_{n,v}$	+hm +هم	3UP
$PRON_{n,v}$	+hn +هن	3FP
$PRON_{n,v}$	+hn/n +ن/هن	3UP
$PRON_{n,v}$	+j +ج	2FS
$PRON_{n,v}$	+k +ك	2MS/2FS
$PRON_{n,v}$	+kn +كن	2UP/2FP
$PRON_{n,v}$	+nA +نا	1UP
$PRON_{n,v}$	+y +ي	1US
$PRON_v$	+ny +ني	1US
IOBJ	+l+h/w +ل+ه/و	PREP+3MS
IOBJ	+l+hA +ل+ها	PREP+3FS
IOBJ	+l+hm +ل+هم	PREP+3MP/3UP
IOBJ	+l+hn/n +ل+هن/ن	PREP+3FP/3UP
IOBJ	+l+j +ل+ج	PREP+2FS
IOBJ	+l+k +ل+ك	PREP+2MS/2FS
IOBJ	+l+km +ل+كم	PREP+2MP/2UP
IOBJ	+l+kn +ل+كن	PREP+2FP/2UP
IOBJ	+l+nA +ل+نا	PREP+1UP
IOBJ	+l+y +ل+ي	PREP+1US
NEG_PART	+š +ش	NEG_PART

(D)

$$
\begin{aligned}
\textbf{WORD} &\rightarrow \textbf{CONJ}?~(\textbf{NOM}|\textbf{VERB}|\textbf{PART}) \\
\textbf{PART} &\rightarrow \textbf{PART}_0~\textbf{PRON}_n? \\
\textbf{NOM} &\rightarrow \textbf{PART}_n?~(\textbf{ART}?~\textbf{NOM}_0|\textbf{NOM}_0~\textbf{PRON}_n?) \\
\textbf{VERB} &\rightarrow \text{m\_NEG}?~\textbf{VERB}_1~\text{NEG\_PART}? \\
\textbf{VERB}_1 &\rightarrow (\textbf{PART}_v?~\textbf{VERB}_{0.iv}|\textbf{VERB}_{0.pv}|\textbf{VERB}_{0.cv})~\textbf{PRON}_v?~\textbf{IOBJ}?
\end{aligned}
$$

Table 1: All the elements needed to build a de-lexicalized morphological analyzer for the five dialects. (A) represents all the abstract meta paradigms for the basic Arabic POS: verbs (perfective (PV), imperfective (IV), and command (CV)), nominals (NOM), and particles (PART). (B) and (C) are the set of clitics along with their respective POS, categorized by their morphological role. The CFG in (D) describes the valencies of the clitics surrounding the base form.

of some minimum length can be an open class base, provided the remaining characters comprise a supported affix pattern. Hence, a simple grammar which only supports words without affixes or with a single suffix, +*s*, would return two analyses for *wugs*: *wugs* and *wug +s*, and one for *foo*: *foo*. To build such a grammar for an Arabic dialect, we target clitic affixation, as this phenomenon is non-templatic with minimal fusional edits, making it easier to model with a smaller grammar, yet it accounts for a great deal of sparsity, as Arabic clitics are as productive as regular inflectional exponents.

We use our grammar to build a de-lexicalized morphological analyzer for all DA dialects targeting the D3 segmentation scheme (Habash, 2010), which separates all clitics and only clitics from the base forms to which they attach. We chose D3

as Sadat and Habash (2006) demonstrate it to be the most effective scheme for low resource Arabic MT. [2] While Arabic exhibits many other non-concatenative, templatic phenomena which complicate segmentation and tokenization, clitics are always concatenated to the outsides of base forms after the templatic pattern has been applied and are thus easier to separate. Occasionally, fusional processes can alter phonemes/graphemes on either side of base–clitic or clitic–clitic boundaries, but no templatic process is ever invoked to alter the internal structure of bases by affixing any clitic.

We follow Khalifa et al. (2017)'s approach to

---

[2] With more data, the more effective schemes are ATB and D2 (Sadat and Habash, 2006). ATB resembles D3 but does not separate the definite article proclitic. D2 resembles ATB but does not separate the pronominal enclitic.

extending paradigms with possible clitic combinations, though we don't require any stem lexical information. Hence, we cheaply enable the grammar to over generate, accommodating more spelling variants and removing the need to construct an open class lexicon. Instead, we simply provide meta paradigms for abstractions over base forms with the same combinatorics. Each cell in a meta paradigm represents a unique exponent, or possible mapping of clitics to positions surrounding the abstract base, such that the inflected form would be valid for any real base represented by that meta paradigm. Considering verbal affixation in English, *walk* and *talk* would be two real bases taking the same meta paradigm with four cells, represented by exponents *_+ing _+s, _,* and *_+ed*. Thus, any two bases exhibiting distinct exponent signatures will belong to distinct meta paradigms.

In Arabic, by contrast, paradigms are enumeratively and integratively more complex than the TALK/WALK meta paradigm (Ackerman and Malouf, 2013). Table 1[3] exemplifies Arabic's enumerative complexity, as verbs, for instance, depending on dialect, can take some 20 affixes according to (A), realizing various combinations of aspect, person, gender, and number.

Having taken an affix, the verb can participate in myriad possible additional combinations with clitics in (B) and (C) as dictated by the bottom two rules in the CFG in (D). Arabic is thus, integratively complex in that rich exponents can be comprised of many interacting morphemes whose meanings are often affected by each other's presence. Furthermore, fusional processes acting on such complex forms results in frequent allomorphy. Allomorphy is mostly limited to internal, non-clitic morphemes, which enables us to greatly reduce sparcity without propagating error by focusing on clitics. Hence, we can represent all verbs with a single meta paradigm which is large, but can be described in two CFG rules. In practice then, each of the 20 possible affixes in (A) will correspond to distinct abstract bases, though this eliminates the need to specify 20 distinct meta paradigms for single lexemes. We target relating these abstract bases to each other via non-concatenative modeling in future work.

In terms of the effort required to create the grammar, there are a total of 98 unique affixes for

[3]POS tags in Table 1 are presented in the Buckwalter scheme used in annotating the Penn Arabic Treebank (PATB) (Maamouri and Bies, 2004)

all dialects. We include the non-clitic affixes in Table 1 (A) in this count as they are used to restrict the set of possible meta paradigms. Of these, 45% appear in at least two dialects and 33% appear in all dialects. The total number of affix–dialect pairs is 288. On average, 88% of each dialect's affixes are shared by at least one other dialect and 45% by all dialects. The average dialect specific list contains 58 affixes and adding a second dialect requires an additional 16. Adding a third, fourth, and fifth dialect requires 10, 8, and 7 additional affixes on average, respectively. Thus, building a single dialect grammar is cheap and adding dialects is even cheaper. Our final grammar contains five meta paradigms, one for each of the basic Arabic parts-of-speech—verbs (PV, IV, and CV), nominals, and particles—compiled into an analyzer like that of Buckwalter (2004).

3.4 Unsupervised Disambiguation

DESEG supports two simple, fast models for disambiguating the grammar's analyses. The first, DESEG_g, greedily selects the maximum match analysis, or that with the smallest base after matching affixes. The second, DESEG_f, selects the analysis with the most fertile base. The fertility of each candidate base is calculated in the raw corpus by counting the possible combinations of adjacent affixes with which it appears over all analyses for all words in which it is proposed as a base.

For example, consider the three-word toy corpus in Table 2. بيقولها *byqwlhA*, correctly segmented as *b+ yqwl +hA*, PROG+ say.3MS +it, 'he is saying it', has six possible analyses, each with a different candidate base. Two candidate bases, *yqwl* and *byqwl*, are also candidate bases for another word, بيقول *byqwl* 'he's not saying', but only *yqwl* exhibits multiple unique adjoining affix sets. In *byqwlhA*, it takes the circumfix *b | hA*, while in *byqwl*, it takes the prefix *b*. The fertility of base *yqwl* suggests it is more likely to be a productive stem in the language, whereas the lack of fertility for the base *byqwl* suggests it is not systematically utilized in the language as a base might be expected to be used, and that it is more likely a simple coincidence that enables the over permissive grammar to allow such a candidate.

The final word in the vocabulary, ييقولي *ybqwly*, correctly segmented as *ybqw +l +y*, remain.3MP +to +me 'they remain for me', is challenging because no other inflection of the lexeme is attested.

Vocabulary		Candidate Segmentations		Candidate Bases		Attested Adjoining Affixes		Fertility	Base Length
byqwlhA	بيقولها	**b+ yqwl +hA**	ب+ يقول +ها	**yqwl**	يقول	**b | Ø , b | hA**	ها | ب , Ø | ب	**2**	**4**
		byqwlhA	بيقولها	byqwlhA	بيقولها			0	7
		b+ yqwlhA	ب+ يقولها	yqwlhA	يقولها	b | Ø	Ø | ب	1	6
		b+ yqw +l +hA	ب+ يقو +ل +ها	yqw	يقو	b | l	ب | ل	1	3
		byqwl +hA	بيقول +ها	byqwl	بيقول	Ø | hA	ها | Ø	1	5
		byqw +l +hA	بيقو +ل +ها	byqw	بيقو	Ø | l	ل | Ø	1	4
byqwl	بيقول	**b+ yqwl**	ب+ يقول	**yqwl**	يقول	**b | Ø , b | hA**	ها | ب , Ø | ب	**2**	**4**
		byqwl	بيقول	byqwl	بيقول	Ø | hA	ها | Ø	1	5
ybqwly	يبقولي	**ybqw +l +y**	يبقو +ل +ي	**ybqw**	يبقو	Ø | l	ل | Ø	1	4
		ybqwly	يبقولي	ybqwly	يبقولي			0	6
		ybqwl +y	يبقول +ي	ybqwl	يبقول	Ø | y	ي | Ø	1	5

Table 2: Calculating fertility in a toy Arabic corpus of three words given all possible candidate analyses of the input corpus vocabulary. Correct analyses are depicted in bold.

Yet, by maximum matching on the affixes, we choose the correct analysis—*ybqw* plus the complex suffix of prepositional *l* followed by object *y*—as the proposed base *ybqw* is shorter than the other candidate base which is produced by erroneously assuming a nominal meta paradigm. The nominal analysis re-analyzes *y* as the first person possessive enclitic and crucially extends the base with *l*, as *l* is not a viable nominal enclitic. Thus, choosing the shortest base can help to eliminate coincidentally feasible analyses.

Each model, DESEG$_f$ and DESEG$_g$, breaks ties using the other. Thus, DESEG$_f$ would correctly segment the entire toy corpus, as the correct analyses in *byqwlhA* and *byqwl* feature the uniquely most fertile candidate bases, and while there is a fertility tie for *ybqwly*, backing off to the candidate segmentation with the smallest base length correctly selects the segmentation with *ybqw* as the base. DESEG$_g$ correctly segments *byqwl* and *ybqwly*, but incorrectly predicts that the stem-final *l* in *byqwlhA* is actually the same enclitic preposition present in *ybqwly* and thus, over segments.

In the event of ties after considering both fertility and base length, both models back off again to the analysis with the base that most frequently occurs as a full word in the raw corpus. Prioritizing this frequency above either fertility or base length minimization always hurt performance, even though it proved quite useful as a feature for Narasimhan et al. (2015). We attribute this seeming discrepancy to the interaction of Arabic's rich morphology with the noise of unstandardized DA data. Many gold bases actually cannot appear as stand-alone words due to the fusional morphology and various writing conventions greatly affect

the frequency with which bases that *can* manifest as stand-alone words *actually do*.

4 Evaluation

We compare DESEG to several alternative segmentation models. We use the CORPUS6 dev set to pick the optimal minimum base length on an intrinsic LM perplexity evaluation, and then perform an extrinsic MT evaluation on the test set.

4.1 Models

We evaluate the following models:

PLAIN This baseline segments only punctuation.

MADAMIRA Egyptian and MSA versions are available for MADAMIRA, which disambiguates a rule-based morphological analyzer's output with an SVM trained on morphologically annotated data. We use the Egyptian version as it is pre-trained on a superset of the MSA data to capture code switching. Thus, performance does not significantly drop when testing on MSA, and performance is significantly greater when testing on DA varietes—even those far outside of Egypt—due to many shared intra-DA linguistic traits not present in MSA (Khalifa et al., 2017). MADAMIRA is a tokenizer in that it not only segments but also mitigates data sparsity due to allomorphy by recovering the canonical underlying morpheme for each segment. We run MADAMIRA in D3 tokenization mode, facilitating comparison with DESEG.

FARASA Similar to MADAMIRA, FARASA is a pre-trained, SVM-based system leveraging gold annotations and external dictionaries. Together, FARASA and MADAMIRA represent the state of

	Invariable			Trainable					
	Rule-based	Pre-trained		Unsupervised		Unsupervised + De-lexical Grammar			
	PLAIN	MADAMIRA	FARASA	BPE	MORFESSOR	DESEG_{g3}	DESEG_{f3}	DESEG_{g2}	DESEG_{f2}
Tokens	42,125	54,559	58,728	53,617	53,509	62823	64708	72644	70704
OOV%	6.8%	3.0%	2.60%	0.7%	2.6%	2.0%	2.1%	1.8%	**1.7%**
Perplexity	163.0	75.0	59	132.2	96.5	52.6	48.0	**33.5**	36.2

Table 3: Out of vocabulary (OOV) and perplexity for all tokenization models in the pooled dialects environment.

Dialects used to Train Segmenter(s)	Dialects used to Train MT System(s)	Invariable			Trainable			
		Rule-based	Pre-trained		Unsupervised		Unsupervised + De-lexical Grammar	
		PLAIN	MADAMIRA	FARASA	BPE	MORFESSOR	DESEG_{g2}	DESEG_{f2}
Pooled	Pooled	29.8	31.5	**32.7**	29.9	30.6	32.0	32.3
Individual	Individual	28.7	**31.4**	31.2	28.4	30.1	30.9	31.3
Individual	Pooled	29.8	31.5	32.7	30.6	31.8	32.5	**32.9**

Table 4: Macro BLEU scores for each tokenization model on CORPUS6 in three environments distinguishing how dialects are pooled or treated separately when training the tokenizer and MT system.

the art for a number of morphological tasks in Arabic. FARASA differs from MADAMIRA in that only one version is publicly available, it segments only, not attempting to tokenize, and the segmentation scheme is linguistically ad hoc, tending to be slightly more granular than D3.

BPE Byte pair encoding uses an algorithm originally designed for file compression to perform unsupervised segmentation. BPE was originally proposed to reduce vocabulary size to make neural MT tractable (Sennrich et al., 2016), as the algorithm's simplicity enables easy application to any language. It separates all characters in the corpus, then performs a pre-determined number of join operations, merging all instances of specified bigrams. Joins are determined such that the resulting corpus will contain as few tokens as possible given the number of join operations allowed. Thus, while the algorithm is unsupervised and easy to apply to any language, it is linguistically naive, assuming that morphological organization is driven solely by enumerative efficiency concerns. Likely for this reason, BPE has not been demonstrated to be particularly useful for applications beyond neural MT (Kann et al., 2018).

MORFESSOR The de facto publicly available unsupervised segmentation system is MORFESSOR. Like BPE, MORFESSOR trains in an unsupervised fashion on large amounts of data and is easily run on any language. Efficient encoding of morphology is also at the center of MORFESSOR's objective function, though it considers not only how compact the corpus can be represented, but also how compact the grammar describing morpheme combinatorics can be represented. Stem morphemes are distinguished from affixal morphemes as the model seeks to limit the number of unique signatures—the sets of unique affixes which can occur with a given stem—that result from the learned segmentation scheme. While MORFESSOR performs well on a number of unsupervised segmentation tasks, it is known to have typological biases toward the languages for which it was originally developed (Kirschenbaum, 2015).

DESEG Our model, described in Section 3, finds a compromise between the convenience of language agnostic unsupervised systems and the performance of systems leveraging language specific resources. DESEG can be run with a minimum base length of either 2 or 3 characters and a priority of base fertility maximization (f) over greedy base length minimization, or vice versa (g). Minimum base length and priority are represented as subscripts in all relevant tables.

4.2 Intrinsic Language Modeling Evaluation

Table 3 shows the LM results for tokenizing CORPUS6 where all trainable segmenters are trained on all of the raw data pooled together instead of training dialect specific tokenizers on relevant subsections of the 40+ million word corpus. To enable pooled DESEG grammars, each dialect's grammar is merged into one highly permissive, over generating pan-Arabic grammar. In the unpooled training scenario, perplexity rankings were consistent with those displayed here. Our model greatly reduces both perplexity and out of vocabulary over all competitive models, though we also exhibit a tendency to over segment. Our best DESEG variants use a minimum base length of two, which is logical because while Arabic features mainly tri-radical roots, gemination causes many base forms to reduce to only two graphemes. In the intrinsic evaluation, it is difficult to tell whether the preference for greed (DESEG_{g2}) or fertility (DESEG_{f2}) is better. Our success is likely due to the fact that we alone cover all the dialects, yet that coverage was achieved in a fraction of the time spent constructing the annotated data upon which state-of-the-art systems rely to cover just a single dialect.

4.3 Extrinsic Machine Translation Evaluation

We conduct MT experiments translating Arabic dialects to English in three environments. Pooled–pooled trains segmenters (only trainable segmenters) on the monolingual corpus with all dialects pooled and the MT system on all the dialects pooled. Individual–individual trains six segmenters on relevant subsections of the monolingual data and six MT systems on the relevant partitions of CORPUS6. Individual–pooled trains individual segmenters but one pan-Arabic MT system, which is reasonable to reduce the over generation of the morphological model but leverage shared information during MT. Neural MT has been used with dialects (Hassan et al., 2017), but given the extreme scarcity of in-domain data, statistical MT (Koehn et al., 2007) is the better choice (Farajian et al., 2017) for comparing quality of segmentation in our setting. DESEG consistently outperforms unsupervised alternatives BPE and MORFESSOR in Table 4 while approaching and even beating state-of-the-art systems FARASA and MADAMIRA in the individual–pooled environment. The Fertility-based model DESEG_{f2} outperforms its greedy counterpart, supporting the argument that base fertility plays a meaningful role in morphological organization.

5   Error Analysis

We performed a quantitative error analysis on 100 sentences randomly selected from CORPUS6 for each variety, creating a *gold* segmentation set. In Table 5, accuracy is computed given the two modes of training DESEG_{f2} (i.e., pooled or individual), and compared with the PLAIN input base-line. Average segmentation accuracy over all varieties correlates with the extrinsic evaluation for both modes of training DESEG_{f2}. In both modes, the best performance is on MSA and the worst is on Rabat then Tunis.

In individual mode, the poor performance of Rabat and Tunis is expected as we could not obtain sufficiently large monolingual data sets that distinguish these two quite linguistically distinct North African varieties. Thus, we were forced to train both grammars' disambiguators on the same data, propagating error whenever a form occurred in the Rabat dialect not analyzable by the Tunis grammar or vice versa. As for pooled mode, careful inspection revealed an exceptional amount of inconsistent spellings in the Tunis and Rabat partitions of CORPUS6 that were not anticipated when constructing the grammar. The definite article proclitic +ال *Al+* for example, frequently appears as its own word, reduced to just ل *l*, or deleted altogether when preceded by another proclitic, especially when the ل *l* assimilates phonologically to the following phoneme. In MSA, by contrast, the definite article is always attached to the following noun, the ل *l* is never deleted, and the ا *A* can only be deleted following the prepositional proclitic +ل *l+*, 'for'. It is not surprising then that MSA performs the best in both modes as there is only negligible inconsistency in MSA spelling, meaning that the grammar need not anticipate an unbounded set of spelling alternatives exacerbating over generation and putting more stress on the disambiguator.

The best DA performance is achieved on Beirut for the pooled mode and Doha for the Individual. Beirut is the least verbose of all dialects in unsegmented space, and also exhibits the lowest ratio of unsegmented tokens to gold segmented tokens, meaning that it rewards over segmenting, which we know DESEG_{f2} is biased toward given its secondary preference for short bases. As for the high performance on Doha, it is worth noting that Doha is also the highest performing dialect on all MT experiments, even recording higher BLEU scores than MSA. It is thus likely that the Doha partition of CORPUS6 is simply more internally consistent than the others, not just in terms of spelling, but also lexical choices and syntactic structure. This could be idiosyncratic to CORPUS6 more than it is characteristic of the Doha dialect, though an independent test corpus would be needed to investigate this further.

While the extrinsic MT results vouch for the effectiveness of pooled grammars when training data cannot be separated by dialect, the pooled training mode consistently fails to outperform PLAIN on the harsh evaluation metric of segmentation accuracy. On average, the pooled mode is 15% less accurate than individual—which does consistently improve over PLAIN—demonstrating that reducing the grammar's capacity to over generate by determining the dialect before segmenting greatly facilitates disambiguation. Indeed, there is a 94% correlation between the verbosity reduction and accuracy increase going from the pooled to individual mode, indicating that the pooled model is over segmenting as more options for mistakenly identifying segmentable clitics become available across different dialects.

This is especially problematic for words like the noun فرد *frd*, 'individual', which contain highly fertile, analyzable bases within their true base. That is, فرد *frd* can also be analyzed out of context as a conjunction followed by a verb ف+ رد *f+ rd* 'so he responded', where the verbal base رد is highly fertile, especially since it is identical to the nominal رد *rd*, 'response' and thus can participate in a large number of clitic combinations as licensed by three feasible meta paradigms (verbal PV, verbal CV, or nominal). Furthermore, the increased uncertainty caused by greater over generation of the analyzer in pooled mode gives the base length minimization back off more influence. Base length minimization as a disambiguation strategy will always over segment by definition if the analyzer permits it. Thus, low frequency or unknown words like the proper name اونو *Awnw*, 'Ono' are frequently over segmented, as occurs in all dialects except Doha and MSA, where the leading or trailing sequences of graphemes happen to not be confusable with any viable clitics according to the grammar.

Considering context will be crucial to improving the model's handling of such cases in future work, as the Cairene sentence هي دي مدام اونو؟ *hy dy mdAm Awnw?*, 'Is this Madame Ono?' provides a blatant clue in the title 'Madame', that اونو *Awnw* is a name and need not be segmented. Similarly, the Beiruti sentence, ازا بتريد صرفلي هالعشرة دولار عخمسة فرد شأفة ... *AzA btryd Srfly hAlςšrħ dwlAr ςxmsħ frd šÂfħ ...*,

	Seg Verbosity			Accuracy			Best
	Input	Pooled	Indiv	Input	Pooled	Indiv	ER
Beirut	0.69	1.22	1.13	56.7	68.7	**79.7**	53
Cairo	0.80	1.29	1.15	77.8	65.9	**81.3**	16
Rabat	0.72	1.30	1.19	66.1	57.9	**70.0**	11
Tunis	0.81	1.32	1.15	**79.4**	62.9	78.5	0
Doha	0.79	1.27	1.11	77.3	67.6	**85.2**	35
MSA	0.80	1.24	1.07	76.3	69.6	**88.3**	50
Average	0.77	1.27	1.13	72.3	65.4	**80.5**	30

Table 5: Segmentation accuracy of DESEG trained on Pooled versus Indiv(idual) dialects/grammars and evaluated on CORPUS6 against the PLAIN input baseline. Seg(mentation) verbosity is the ratio of segmented tokens over gold segmented tokens while accuracy and error reduction (ER) are reported as percentages.

'Please exchange for me this ten dollar [bill] for a single five...' indicates that a noun should follow the numerical modifier خمسة *xmsħ*, 'five', not the proclitic conjunction ف+ *f+*, 'so'.

6 Conclusion and Future Work

We present an effective unsupervised means of introducing linguistic information for segmentation that greatly improves performance over other unsupervised systems as evaluated both intrinsically and extrinsically. We target robust handling of rich morphological phenomena and noisy corpora, achieving performance on a multi-dialect Arabic corpus comparable to state-of-the-art supervised systems. The success of our simple system is strong evidence for the value of linguistic input during preprocessing.

In the future, we plan to evaluate our models on natural (uncommissioned) dialectal corpora. We also plan to enhance our delexicalize models with non-concatenative components. And we also in tend to develop models that consider context.

Acknowledgments

We would like to thank three anonymous reviewers for their feedback. This publication was made possible by grant NPRP 7-290-1-047 from the Qatar National Research Fund (a member of the Qatar Foundation). The statements made herein are solely the responsibility of the authors.

References

Ahmed Abdelali, Kareem Darwish, Nadir Durrani, and Hamdy Mubarak. 2016. Farasa: A Fast and Furious

Segmenter for Arabic. In *Proceedings of the Conference of the North American Chapter of the Association for Computational Linguistics (NAACL)*, pages 11–16, San Diego, California.

Farrell Ackerman and Robert Malouf. 2013. Morphological Organization: The Low Conditional Entropy Conjecture. *Language*, 89(3):429–464.

Faisal Al-Shargi, Aidan Kaplan, Ramy Eskander, Nizar Habash, and Owen Rambow. 2016. Morphologically Annotated Corpus and a Morphological Analyzer for Moroccan and San'ani Yemeni Arabic. In *Proceedings of the Language Resources and Evaluation Conference (LREC)*, Portorož, Slovenia.

Shabib AlGahtani and John McNaught. 2015. Joint Arabic segmentation and part-of-speech tagging. In *Proceedings of the Second Workshop on Arabic Natural Language Processing*, Beijing, China.

Khalid Almeman and Mark Lee. 2013. Automatic building of Arabic Multi Dialect Text Corpora by Bootstrapping Dialect Words. In *Proceedings of the International Conference on Communications, Signal Processing, and their Applications (ICCSPA)*, pages 1–6.

Faisal Alshargi, Shahd Dibas, Sakhar Alkhereyf, Reem Faraj, Basmah Abdulkareem, Sane Yagi, Ouafaa Kacha, Nizar Habash, and Owen Rambow. 2019. Morphologically Annotated Corpora for Seven Arabic Dialects: Taizi, Sanaani, Najdi, Jordanian, Syrian, Iraqi and Moroccan. In *Proceedings of the Workshop on Arabic Natural Language Processing*, Florence, Italy.

Duygu Ataman and Marcello Federico. 2018. Compositional Representation of Morphologically-Rich Input for Neural Machine Translation. *arXiv preprint arXiv:1805.02036*.

Duygu Ataman, Matteo Negri, Marco Turchi, and Marcello Federico. 2017. Linguistically Motivated Vocabulary Reduction for Neural Machine Translation from Turkish to English. *The Prague Bulletin of Mathematical Linguistics*, 108(1):331–342.

Mohammed Attia. 2006. An Ambiguity-Controlled Morphological Analyzer for Modern Standard Arabic Modelling Finite State Networks. In *Proceedings of the Conference on the Challenge of Arabic for NLP/MT*, London.

Mohammed Attia. 2007. Arabic Tokenization System. In *Proceedings of the Workshop on Computational Approaches to Semitic Languages (CASL): Common Issues and Resources*, pages 65–72.

Kenneth Beesley. 1998. Arabic morphology using only finite-state operations. In *Proceedings of the Workshop on Computational Approaches to Semitic Languages (CASL)*, pages 50–7, Montereal.

Raymond Bertram, R Harald Baayen, and Robert Schreuder. 2000. Effects of Family Size for Complex Words. *Journal of memory and language*, 42(3):390–405.

Houda Bouamor, Nizar Habash, Mohammad Salameh, Wajdi Zaghouani, Owen Rambow, Dana Abdulrahim, Ossama Obeid, Salam Khalifa, Fadhl Eryani, Alexander Erdmann, and Kemal Oflazer. 2018. The MADAR Arabic Dialect Corpus and Lexicon. In *Proceedings of the Language Resources and Evaluation Conference (LREC)*, Miyazaki, Japan.

Mohamed Boudchiche, Azzeddine Mazroui, Mohamed Ould Abdallahi Ould Bebah, Abdelhak Lakhouaja, and Abderrahim Boudlal. 2017. AlKhalil Morpho Sys 2: A robust Arabic morpho-syntactic analyzer. *Journal of King Saud University - Computer and Information Sciences*, 29(2):141–146.

Tim Buckwalter. 2004. Buckwalter Arabic Morphological Analyzer Version 2.0. LDC catalog number LDC2004L02, ISBN 1-58563-324-0.

Mauro Cettolo and Christian Girardi. 2012. WIT[3]: Web Inventory of Transcribed and Translated Talks. In *Proceedings of the Conference of the European Association for Machine Translation (EAMT)*, pages 261–268, Trento, Italy.

David Chiang, Mona Diab, Nizar Habash, Owen Rambow, and Safiullah Shareef. 2006. Parsing Arabic Dialects. In *Proceedings of the Conference of the European Chapter of the Association for Computational Linguistics (EACL)*, Trento, Italy.

Mathias Creutz and Krista Lagus. 2005. *Unsupervised morpheme segmentation and morphology induction from text corpora using Morfessor 1.0*. Helsinki University of Technology.

Kareem Darwish. 2002. Building a Shallow Arabic Morphological Analyzer in One Day. In *Proceedings of the Workshop on Computational Approaches to Semitic Languages (CASL)*, pages 47–54, Philadelphia, PA, USA.

Mona Diab, Kadri Hacioglu, and Daniel Jurafsky. 2004. Automatic Tagging of Arabic Text: From Raw Text to Base Phrase Chunks. In *Proceedings of the Conference of the North American Chapter of the Association for Computational Linguistics (NAACL)*, pages 149–152, Boston, MA.

Markus Dreyer and Jason Eisner. 2011. Discovering Morphological Paradigms from Plain Text Using A Dirichlet Process Mixture Model. In *Proceedings of the Conference on Empirical Methods in Natural Language Processing (EMNLP)*, pages 616–627, Edinburgh, United Kingdom.

Mohamed Eldesouki, Younes Samih, Ahmed Abdelali, Mohammed Attia, Hamdy Mubarak, Kareem Darwish, and Kallmeyer Laura. 2017. Arabic Multi-Dialect Segmentation: bi-LSTM-CRF vs. SVM. *arXiv preprint arXiv:1708.05891*.

Alexander Erdmann and Nizar Habash. 2018. Complementary Strategies for Low Resourced Morphological Modeling. In *Proceedings of the Workshop on Computational Research in Phonetics, Phonology, and Morphology (SIGMORPHON)*, pages 54–65, Brussels, Belgium.

Alexander Erdmann, Nizar Habash, Dima Taji, and Houda Bouamor. 2017. Low Resourced Machine Translation via Morpho-syntactic Modeling: The Case of Dialectal Arabic. In *Proceedings of the Machine Translation Summit (MT Summit)*.

Alexander Erdmann, Nasser Zalmout, and Nizar Habash. 2018. Addressing noise in multidialectal word embeddings. In *Proceedings of the Conference of the Association for Computational Linguistics (ACL)*, Melbourne, Australia.

Ramy Eskander, Nizar Habash, Owen Rambow, and Arfath Pasha. 2016a. Creating resources for Dialectal Arabic from a single annotation: A case study on Egyptian and Levantine. In *Proceedings of the International Conference on Computational Linguistics (COLING)*, pages 3455–3465, Osaka, Japan.

Ramy Eskander, Owen Rambow, and Smaranda Muresan. 2018. Automatically Tailoring Unsupervised Morphological Segmentation to the Language. In *Proceedings of the Workshop of the Special Interest Group on Computational Morphology and Phonology (SIGMORPHON)*, pages 78–83.

Ramy Eskander, Owen Rambow, and Tianchun Yang. 2016b. Extending the use of adaptor grammars for unsupervised morphological segmentation of unseen languages. In *Proceedings of the International Conference on Computational Linguistics (COLING)*, pages 900–910.

M Amin Farajian, Marco Turchi, Matteo Negri, Nicola Bertoldi, and Marcello Federico. 2017. Neural vs. phrase-based machine translation in a multi-domain scenario. In *Proceedings of the Conference of the European Chapter of the Association for Computational Linguistics (EACL)*, page 280, Valencia, Spain.

Charles F Ferguson. 1959. Diglossia. *Word*, 15(2):325–340.

Abed Alhakim Freihat, Gabor Bella, Hamdy Mubarak, and Fausto Giunchiglia. 2018. A Single-Model Approach for Arabic Segmentation, POS Tagging, and Named Entity Recognition. In *International Conference on Natural Language and Speech Processing (ICNLSP)*, pages 1–8. IEEE.

Jin Guo. 1997. Critical tokenization and its properties. *Computational Linguistics*, 23(4):569–596.

Nizar Habash, Ramy Eskander, and Abdelati Hawwari. 2012. A Morphological Analyzer for Egyptian Arabic. In *Proceedings of the Workshop of the Special Interest Group on Computational Morphology and Phonology (SIGMORPHON)*, pages 1–9, Montréal, Canada.

Nizar Habash and Owen Rambow. 2005. Arabic tokenization, part-of-speech tagging and morphological disambiguation in one fell swoop. In *Proceedings of the Conference of the Association for Computational Linguistics (ACL)*, pages 573–580, Ann Arbor, Michigan.

Nizar Habash and Owen Rambow. 2006. MAGEAD: A morphological analyzer and generator for the Arabic dialects. In *Proceedings of the International Conference on Computational Linguistics and the Conference of the Association for Computational Linguistics (COLING-ACL)*, pages 681–688, Sydney, Australia.

Nizar Habash, Ryan Roth, Owen Rambow, Ramy Eskander, and Nadi Tomeh. 2013. Morphological Analysis and Disambiguation for Dialectal Arabic. In *Proceedings of the Conference of the North American Chapter of the Association for Computational Linguistics (NAACL)*, Atlanta, Georgia.

Nizar Y Habash. 2010. *Introduction to Arabic natural language processing*, volume 3. Morgan & Claypool Publishers.

Hany Hassan, Mostafa Elaraby, and Ahmed Tawfik. 2017. Synthetic Data for Neural Machine Translation of Spoken-Dialects. *arXiv preprint arXiv:1707.00079*.

Mustafa Jarrar, Nizar Habash, Faeq Alrimawi, Diyam Akra, and Nasser Zalmout. 2016. Curras: an annotated corpus for the Palestinian Arabic dialect. *Language Resources and Evaluation*, pages 1–31.

Katharina Kann, Stanislas Lauly, and Kyunghyun Cho. 2018. The NYU System for the CoNLL–SIGMORPHON 2018 Shared Task on Universal Morphological Reinflection. In *Proceedings of the CoNLL–SIGMORPHON 2018 Shared Task: Universal Morphological Reinflection*, pages 58–63, Brussels. Association for Computational Linguistics.

Salam Khalifa, Nizar Habash, Fadhl Eryani, Ossama Obeid, Dana Abdulrahim, and Meera Al Kaabi. 2018. A morphologically annotated corpus of emirati Arabic. In *Proceedings of the Language Resources and Evaluation Conference (LREC)*, Miyazaki, Japan.

Salam Khalifa, Sara Hassan, and Nizar Habash. 2017. A Morphological Analyzer for Gulf Arabic Verbs. In *Proceedings of the Workshop for Arabic Natural Language Processing (WANLP)*, Valencia, Spain.

Shereen Khoja and Roger Garside. 1999. Stemming Arabic text. *Lancaster, UK, Computing Department, Lancaster University*.

Amit Kirschenbaum. 2015. To Split or Not, and If so, Where? Theoretical and Empirical Aspects of Unsupervised Morphological Segmentation. In *International Conference on Intelligent Text Processing and Computational Linguistics*, pages 139–150. Springer.

Philipp Koehn, Hieu Hoang, Alexandra Birch, Chris Callison-Burch, Marcello Federico, Nicola Bertoldi, Brooke Cowan, Wade Shen, Christine Moran, Richard Zens, Chris Dyer, Ondrej Bojar, Alexandra Constantin, and Evan Herbst. 2007. Moses: Open source toolkit for statistical machine translation. In *Proceedings of the Conference of the Association for Computational Linguistics (ACL)*, pages 177–180, Prague, Czech Republic.

Young-Suk Lee, Kishore Papineni, Salim Roukos, Ossama Emam, and Hany Hassan. 2003. Language Model Based Arabic Word Segmentation. In *Proceedings of the Conference of the Association for Computational Linguistics (ACL)*, pages 399–406.

Mohamed Maamouri and Ann Bies. 2004. Developing an Arabic Treebank: Methods, Guidelines, Procedures, and Tools. In *Proceedings of the Workshop on*

Computational Approaches to Arabic Script-based Languages (CAASL), pages 2–9, Geneva, Switzerland.

Mohamed Maamouri, Ann Bies, Seth Kulick, Michael Ciul, Nizar Habash, and Ramy Eskander. 2014. Developing an Egyptian Arabic Treebank: Impact of Dialectal Morphology on Annotation and Tool Development. In *Proceedings of the Language Resources and Evaluation Conference (LREC)*, Reykjavik, Iceland.

Karthik Narasimhan, Regina Barzilay, and Tommi Jaakkola. 2015. An unsupervised method for uncovering morphological chains. *arXiv preprint arXiv:1503.02335*.

Arfath Pasha, Mohamed Al-Badrashiny, Mona Diab, Ahmed El Kholy, Ramy Eskander, Nizar Habash, Manoj Pooleery, Owen Rambow, and Ryan Roth. 2014. Madamira: A fast, comprehensive tool for morphological analysis and disambiguation of Arabic. In *Proceedings of the Language Resources and Evaluation Conference (LREC)*, pages 1094–1101, Reykjavik, Iceland.

Hoifung Poon, Colin Cherry, and Kristina Toutanova. 2009. Unsupervised Morphological Segmentation with Log-Linear Models. In *Proceedings of Human Language Technologies: The 2009 Annual Conference of the North American Chapter of the Association for Computational Linguistics (HLT–NAACL)*, pages 209–217, Boulder, Colorado.

Aleya Rouchdy. 2013. Language Conflict and Identity: Arabic in the American Diaspora. In *Language Contact and Language Conflict in Arabic*, pages 151–166. Routledge.

Fatiha Sadat and Nizar Habash. 2006. Combination of Arabic Preprocessing Schemes for Statistical Machine Translation. In *Proceedings of the International Conference on Computational Linguistics and the Conference of the Association for Computational Linguistics (COLING-ACL)*, pages 1–8, Sydney, Australia.

Mohammad Salameh, Houda Bouamor, and Nizar Habash. 2018. Fine-grained arabic dialect identification. In *Proceedings of the International Conference on Computational Linguistics (COLING)*, pages 1332–1344, Santa Fe, New Mexico, USA.

Wael Salloum and Nizar Habash. 2014. ADAM: Analyzer for Dialectal Arabic Morphology. *Journal of King Saud University - Computer and Information Sciences*, 26(4):372–378.

Younes Samih, Mohamed Eldesouki, Mohammed Attia, Kareem Darwish, Ahmed Abdelali, Hamdy Mubarak, and Laura Kallmeyer. 2017. Learning from Relatives: Unified Dialectal Arabic Segmentation. In *Proceedings of the Conference on Computational Natural Language Learning (CoNLL)*, pages 432–441.

Rico Sennrich, Barry Haddow, and Alexandra Birch. 2016. Neural Machine Translation of Rare Words with Subword Units. In *Proceedings of the Conference of the Association for Computational Linguistics (ACL)*, pages 1715–1725, Berlin, Germany.

Kairit Sirts and Sharon Goldwater. 2013. Minimally-Supervised Morphological Segmentation using Adaptor Grammars. *Transactions of the Association for Computational Linguistics*, 1:255–266.

Noah A. Smith and Jason Eisner. 2005. Contrastive Estimation: Training Log-Linear Models on Unlabeled Data. In *Proceedings of the Annual Meeting of the Association for Computational Linguistics (ACL)*, pages 354–362, Ann Arbor, Michigan.

Otakar Smrž. 2007. *Functional Arabic Morphology. Formal System and Implementation*. Ph.D. thesis, Charles University in Prague, Prague, Czech Republic.

Benjamin Snyder and Regina Barzilay. 2008. Unsupervised Multilingual Learning for Morphological Segmentation. In *Proceedings of the Conference of the Association for Computational Linguistics (ACL)*, pages 737–745, Columbus, Ohio.

David Stallard, Jacob Devlin, Michael Kayser, Yoong Keok Lee, and Regina Barzilay. 2012. Unsupervised Morphology Rivals Supervised Morphology for Arabic MT. In *Proceedings of the Conference of the Association for Computational Linguistics (ACL)*, pages 322–327, Jeju Island, Korea.

Toshiyuki Takezawa, Eiichiro Sumita, Fumiaki Sugaya, Hirofumi Yamamoto, and Seiichi Yamamoto. 2002. Toward a Broad-coverage Bilingual Corpus for Speech Translation of Travel Conversations in the Real World. In *Proceedings of the Language Resources and Evaluation Conference (LREC)*, pages 147–152, Las Palmas, Spain.

Clara Vania and Adam Lopez. 2017. From Characters to Words to in Between: Do We Capture Morphology? In *Proceedings of Annual Meeting of the Association for Computational Linguistics (ACL)*, Vancouver, Canada. Association for Computational Linguistics.

Nasser Zalmout, Alexander Erdmann, and Nizar Habash. 2018. Noise-robust morphological disambiguation for dialectal Arabic. In *Proceedings of the Conference of the North American Chapter of the Association for Computational Linguistics (NAACL)*, New Orleans, Louisiana, USA.

Nasser Zalmout and Nizar Habash. 2017. Don't throw those morphological analyzers away just yet: Neural morphological disambiguation for Arabic. In *Proceedings of the Conference on Empirical Methods in Natural Language Processing (EMNLP)*, pages 704–713, Copenhagen, Denmark.

Nasser Zalmout and Nizar Habash. 2019. Adversarial Multitask Learning for Joint Multi-Feature and Multi-Dialect Morphological Modeling. In *Proceedings of the Conference of the Association for Computational Linguistics (ACL 2019)*, Florence, Italy.

Equiprobable mappings in weighted constraint grammars

Arto Anttila
Stanford University
anttila@stanford.edu

Scott Borgeson
Stanford University
borgeson@stanford.edu

Giorgio Magri
CNRS
magrigrg@gmail.com

Abstract

We show that MaxEnt is so rich that it can distinguish between any two different mappings: there always exists a nonnegative weight vector which assigns them different MaxEnt probabilities. Stochastic HG instead does admit equiprobable mappings and we give a complete formal characterization of them. We compare these different predictions of the two frameworks on a test case of Finnish stress.

1 Introduction

This paper compares two frameworks for probabilistic constraint-based phonology: *Stochastic Harmonic Grammar* (SHG; Boersma and Pater, 2016)[1] and *Maximum Entropy* (ME; Goldwater and Johnson, 2003; Hayes and Wilson, 2008). Recent literature has documented a few realistic quantitative patterns which seem to admit a better fit in ME than in SHG (Smith and Pater, 2017; Zuraw and Hayes, 2017; Hayes, 2017). These findings suggest that ME is a richer probabilistic framework than SHG (relative to the same constraint set). But how much richer? Can these anecdotal observations reported in the literature be systematized into a principled formal comparison between SHG and ME probabilistic typologies? This paper is part of a larger project trying to address this question. In particular, this paper compares ME and SHG from the perspective of their *equiprobable mappings*. That is phonological mappings which are always assigned the same probability and are therefore phonologically equivalent despite being distinguished by the constraint set.

Section 2 motivates this notion of equiprobability within phonological theory. Section 4 then shows that the ME typology is so rich that it admits no equiprobable mappings: for any two mappings distinguished by the constraints, there exists an ME grammar that distinguishes between them, namely assigns them different probabilities. This typological richness is peculiar to ME and does *not* extend to other implementations of probabilistic constraint-based phonology such as SHG. Indeed, Section 5 shows that the equiprobable SHG mappings are exactly those mappings which are indistinguishable by categorical *Harmonic Grammars* (HG; Legendre *et al.*, 1990a,b; Smolensky and Legendre, 2006) and thus provides a complete characterization of SHG equiprobability.

These formal results are presented informally. A detailed proof of the ME result is provided in a final appendix. The proof of the SHG result is analogous and it is omitted for reasons of space (see the longer version of this paper available on the authors' websites). Our discussion rests on some earlier results on uniform SHG and ME probability inequalities from Anttila and Magri (2018), recalled in Section 3.

Is the richness of ME relative to SHG typologies an empirical advantage or a case of unmotivated overgeneration? Section 6 provides some preliminary evidence that the latter might be the case, by looking at the case of Finnish stress. We compute SHG equiprobable mappings using the formal characterization obtained in Section 5. We show that a large corpus of Finnish provides preliminary empirical support for these mappings indeed being equiprobable. Finally, we show that ME breaks up these equiprobabilities in a way that is phonologically counterintuitive.

2 Equiprobability

A typical phonological process applies uniformly to all forms that share some relevant property, but

---

[1] Boersma and Pater (2016) actually use the term "noisy HG" instead of "stochastic HG". We prefer "stochastic HG" to stress the complete analogy with Boersma's (1997; 1998) earlier framework of stochastic OT. Furthermore, we prefer to use "stochastic" to describe a property of the framework, reserving "noisy" to describe a property of the learning scenario (as opposed to noise-free).

Proceedings of the 16th Workshop on Computational Research in Phonetics, Phonology, and Morphology, pages 125–134
Florence, Italy. August 2, 2019 ©2019 Association for Computational Linguistics

ignores the irrelevant ways in which they differ. For example, in Latin, stress targets heavy syllables, but ignores vowel quality; in English, aspiration targets voiceless stops, but ignores place of articulation; in Finnish, vowel harmony targets [±back], but ignores the number of syllables. This means that words with the same distribution of heavy and light syllables are stressed alike; voiceless stops are aspirated alike; and words of any length harmonize alike. These phonological *equivalences* are a key property of phonological systems.

Derivational phonology captures these equivalences straightforwardly: phonological rules are allowed to refer to only the shared property that defines a natural class, ignoring everything else. To illustrate, the Finnish vowel harmony rule can be simply written as $V \rightarrow [\alpha\text{back}]/V[\alpha\text{back}]C_0\_$. This rule directly encodes the fact that harmony targets [±back] but ignores any other properties such as, say, the number of syllables. Thus, the monosyllabic /maa/ 'country' and the disyllabic /kaava/ 'formula' trigger back harmony on the suffix /-nä/ 'ESSIVE' in exactly the same way. In other words, they are equivalent for vowel harmony.

The situation is *prima facie* less obvious in constraint-based phonology. A candidate may contain multiple constraint violations, some relevant, some irrelevant, but all simultaneously visible and potentially interacting. Yet, categorical implementations of constraint-based phonology are well known to readily predict these desired phonological equivalences. To illustrate, consider an HG grammar for Finnish vowel harmony based on the constraints in Table 1, from Ringen and Heinämäki (1999). The back harmony mappings /maa-nä/ $\rightarrow$ [maana] and /kaava-nä/ $\rightarrow$ [kaavana] can be shown to be HG equivalent: no matter the weighting, no HG grammar succeeds on one but fails on the other.

How should phonological equivalence be extended from the categorical to the probabilistic setting? We submit that equiprobability provides an answer to this question. In fact, let us recall that a *probabilistic phonological grammar* is a function which assigns to each underlying representation (UR) x a probability distribution $\mathbb{P}(y \mid x)$ over the corresponding set of candidate surface representations (SRs) y. We consider two mappings (x, y) and $(\widehat{x}, \widehat{y})$ of the two URs $x, \widehat{x}$ to the two SRs $y, \widehat{y}$. We say that these two mappings

*INT[+back]:	No vowel between [+back] and right word edge
*INT[-back]:	No vowel between [-back] and right word edge
IDENT-ROOT:	Be faithful to /a, ä/ in roots
IDENT:	Be faithful to /a, ä/

Table 1: Constraints for Finnish vowel harmony

are *(uniformly) equiprobable* provided there is no probabilistic grammar in the typology considered which assigns a different probability to those two mappings, namely such that $\mathbb{P}(y \mid x) \neq \mathbb{P}(\widehat{y} \mid \widehat{x})$. To illustrate, the equivalence between the two mappings /maa-nä/ $\rightarrow$ [maana] and /kaava-nä/ $\rightarrow$ [kaavana] is captured in a probabilistic setting through the requirement that their probabilities $\mathbb{P}([\text{maana}] \mid /\text{maa-nä}/)$ and $\mathbb{P}([\text{kaavana}] \mid /\text{kaava-nä}/)$ always coincide. In other words, the probability of vowel harmony does not depend on the number of syllables.[2]

As we will see in Section 5, two mappings are equivalent according to categorical HG if and only if they are equiprobable in SHG. This result suggests that equiprobability is indeed the right extension of the notion of phonological equivalence from the categorical to the probabilistic setting. Surprisingly, we will see in Section 4 that ME instead allows for no equiprobable mappings and thus fails to capture the notion of phonological equivalence.

3 Formal background

Our characterization of ME and SHG equiprobability in sections 4-5 rests on some results from Anttila and Magri (2018; A&M) recalled here.

HG A *weight vector* $\mathbf{w} = (w_1, \ldots, w_n)$ assigns nonnegative weights $w_1, \ldots, w_n \geq 0$ to n underlying phonological constraints $C_1, \ldots, C_n$. The phonological quality of a phonological mapping (x, y) of a UR x and a candidate SR y is quantified by its *harmony* $H_{\mathbf{w}}(x, y)$. This quantity is defined as the weighted sum of the constraint vi-

---

[2] Note that this is quite different from the well-known case of Hungarian vowel harmony where suffixes show different degrees of back-front variation after stems with both back and neutral vowels depending on the number of neutral vowels; see, e.g., Hayes and Londe (2006), Hayes et al. (2009), and Zymet (2015). In our Finnish example, all the stem vowels are unambiguously back, yet our Proposition 1 below says that ME fails to guarantee that the suffix harmony is invariably back.

olations multiplied by -1, namely $H_{\mathbf{w}}(\mathsf{x},\mathsf{y}) = -\sum_{k=1}^{n} w_k C_k(\mathsf{x},\mathsf{y})$. Mappings with large harmony have small constraint violations. The HG grammar corresponding to a weight vector $\mathbf{w}$ maps a UR x to the candidate SR y such that the mapping (x,y) has a larger harmony than the mapping (x,z) corresponding to any other candidate z of x. In this case, we say that y is the *winner* while any other candidate z is a *loser*.

HG thus has an intrinsic comparative nature: absolute numbers of violations are irrelevant, what matters is only the comparison between the violations of the loser and those of the winner. To bring out this intuition, we define the *difference vector* $\mathbf{C}(\mathsf{x},\mathsf{y},\mathsf{z})$ for a UR x, an intended winner candidate y, and an intended loser candidate z as in (1). This vector has a component for each constraint C_k defined as the difference between the number $C_k(\mathsf{x},\mathsf{z})$ of violations assigned by C_k to the loser mapping (x,z) minus the number $C_k(\mathsf{x},\mathsf{y})$ of violations assigned to the winner mapping (x,y).

$$\mathbf{C}(\mathsf{x},\mathsf{y},\mathsf{z}) = \begin{bmatrix} C_1(\mathsf{x},\mathsf{z}) - C_1(\mathsf{x},\mathsf{y}) \\ \vdots \\ C_k(\mathsf{x},\mathsf{z}) - C_k(\mathsf{x},\mathsf{y}) \\ \vdots \\ C_n(\mathsf{x},\mathsf{z}) - C_n(\mathsf{x},\mathsf{y}) \end{bmatrix} \qquad (1)$$

SHG and ME are two probabilistic extensions of this underlying categorical HG model.

SHG The SHG probability $\mathbb{P}^{\mathrm{SHG}}_{\mathbf{w}}(\mathsf{y}\,|\,\mathsf{x})$ that a UR x is mapped to a SR y according to the weight vector $\mathbf{w}$ is the probability of sampling n numbers $\epsilon = (\epsilon_1, \ldots, \epsilon_n)$ independently according to a distribution $\mathcal{D}$ in such a way that the HG grammar corresponding to the weight vector $\mathbf{w} + \epsilon = (w_1 + \epsilon_1, \ldots, w_n + \epsilon_n)$ indeed maps x to y. A&M prove the following Lemma 1 about *uniform* probability inequalities in SHG, namely inequalities which hold for every choice of the weight vector.

Lemma 1 *Consider two mappings (x,y) and $(\widehat{\mathsf{x}},\widehat{\mathsf{y}})$. Assume that the UR x comes with only a finite number m of loser candidates $\mathsf{z}_1, \ldots, \mathsf{z}_m$ (besides the winner candidate y) and that the mapping (x,y) is possible in HG (namely, y beats the losers $\mathsf{z}_1, \ldots, \mathsf{z}_m$ relative to some nonnegative weight vector). The SHG probability inequality $\mathbb{P}^{SGH}_{\mathbf{w}}(\mathsf{y}\,|\,\mathsf{x}) \leq \mathbb{P}^{SGH}_{\mathbf{w}}(\widehat{\mathsf{y}}\,|\,\widehat{\mathsf{x}})$ holds uniformly for every choice of the nonnegative weight vector $\mathbf{w}$ if and only if for every loser candidate $\widehat{\mathsf{z}}$ of the UR $\widehat{\mathsf{x}}$, there exist m nonnegative coefficients*

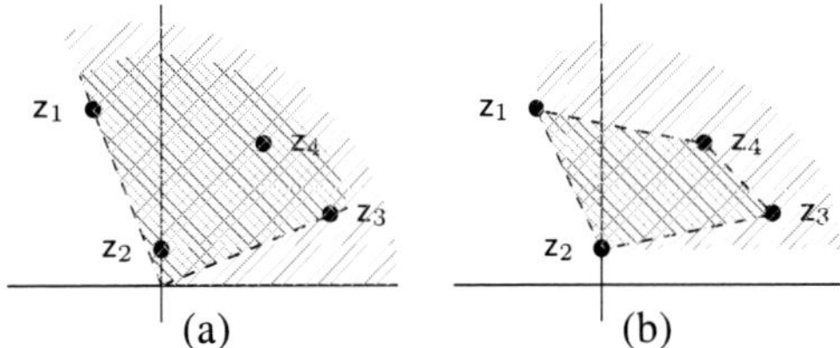

Figure 1: Geometric representation of (a) the SHG Lemma 1 and (b) the ME Lemma 2.

$\lambda_1, \ldots, \lambda_m \geq 0$ *(one for each loser candidate $\mathsf{z}_1, \ldots, \mathsf{z}_m$ of the UR x) such that*

$$\mathbf{C}(\widehat{\mathsf{x}},\widehat{\mathsf{y}},\widehat{\mathsf{z}}) \geq \sum_{i=1}^{m} \lambda_i\, \mathbf{C}(\mathsf{x},\mathsf{y},\mathsf{z}_i) \qquad (2)$$

namely the difference vector $\mathbf{C}(\widehat{\mathsf{x}},\widehat{\mathsf{y}},\widehat{\mathsf{z}})$ is at least as large (constraint by constraint) as the sum of the difference vectors $\mathbf{C}(\mathsf{x},\mathsf{y},\mathsf{z}_i)$ each rescaled by a corresponding nonnegative coefficient λ_i.[3] $\square$

Lemma 1 admits the following geometric interpretation, which will be used below. Suppose there are only $n = 2$ constraints and $m = 4$ losers z_i. The difference vectors $\mathbf{C}(\mathsf{x},\mathsf{y},\mathsf{z}_i)$ which appear on the right hand side of (2) can therefore be represented as the four black dots in Fig. 1. The region $\{\sum_{i=1}^{m} \lambda_i \mathbf{C}(\mathsf{x},\mathsf{y},\mathsf{z}_i) \mid \lambda_i \geq 0\}$ is the *convex cone* generated by these four difference vectors $\mathbf{C}(\mathsf{x},\mathsf{y},\mathsf{z}_i)$, depicted in dark gray in Fig. 1a. The region in light gray singles out the points which are at least as large as some point in this cone. Condition (2) thus says that the difference vector $\mathbf{C}(\widehat{\mathsf{x}},\widehat{\mathsf{y}},\widehat{\mathsf{z}})$ belongs to this light gray region.

ME The ME probability $\mathbb{P}^{\mathrm{ME}}_{\mathbf{w}}(\mathsf{y}\,|\,\mathsf{x})$ that a UR x is mapped to a SR y according to a nonnegative weight vector $\mathbf{w}$ is the exponential of the harmony

---

[3] The two assumptions made by the lemma—that the UR x comes with only a finite number of losers and that the mapping (x,y) is possible in HG—are non-restrictive. In fact, if a mapping (x,y) is impossible in HG, then its SHG probability $\mathbb{P}^{\mathrm{SGH}}_{\mathbf{w}}(\mathsf{y}\,|\,\mathsf{x})$ can be shown to be equal to zero for every choice of the nonnegative weight vector $\mathbf{w}$. The probability inequality $\mathbb{P}^{\mathrm{SGH}}_{\mathbf{w}}(\mathsf{y}\,|\,\mathsf{x}) \leq \mathbb{P}^{\mathrm{SGH}}_{\mathbf{w}}(\widehat{\mathsf{y}}\,|\,\widehat{\mathsf{x}})$ thus holds uniformly, because its left hand side is always equal to zero. The assumption made by the lemma that the mapping (x,y) is possible in HG is therefore non-restrictive. Furthermore, HG has the property that only a finite number of candidates of any given UR win according to some weights (Magri, 2019). All other candidates are redundant because impossible no matter how the weights are chosen. Since HG impossible mappings have zero SHG probability, the candidate set of any underlying form can always be assumed to be finite without loss of generality in SHG. The assumption made by the lemma that the UR x comes with only a finite number of losers is therefore non-restrictive.

$H_\mathbf{w}(x, y)$ of that mapping, normalized through a constant $Z = Z(\mathbf{w}, x)$, namely $\mathbb{P}^{\mathrm{ME}}_\mathbf{w}(y \mid x) = e^{H_\mathbf{w}(x,y)}/Z$. A&M show that also in ME uniform probability inequalities can be characterized in terms of difference vectors, as stated by Lemma 2 below. This ME Lemma is analogous to the SHG Lemma 1 above, but for two differences. The first difference is that condition (2) is only necessary in ME while it is also sufficient in SHG. The second difference is that ME requires the *normalization condition* (3) on the coefficients λ_i.

Lemma 2 *Consider two mappings* (x, y) *and* $(\widehat{x}, \widehat{y})$. *Assume that the UR x comes with a finite number m of loser candidates* $z_1, \ldots, z_m$ *(besides the winner candidate y). If the ME probability inequality* $\mathbb{P}^{ME}_\mathbf{w}(y \mid x) \leq \mathbb{P}^{ME}_\mathbf{w}(\widehat{y} \mid \widehat{x})$ *holds uniformly for every choice of the nonnegative weight vector* $\mathbf{w}$, *then for every loser candidate* $\widehat{z}$ *of the UR* $\widehat{x}$, *there exist m nonnegative coefficients* $\lambda_1, \ldots, \lambda_m \geq 0$ *(one for each loser candidate* $z_1, \ldots, z_m$ *of the UR x) which add up to 1*

$$\lambda_1 + \ldots + \lambda_m = 1 \tag{3}$$

and furthermore satisfy condition (2). □

The normalization condition (3) admits the following geometric interpretation. As seen above, the region $\{\sum_i \lambda_i \mathbf{C}(x, y, z_i) \mid \lambda_i \geq 0\}$ is the convex cone generated by the difference vectors $\mathbf{C}(x, y, z_i)$, represented by the dark gray region in Fig. 1a. The smaller region $\{\sum_i \lambda_i \mathbf{C}(x, y, z_i) \mid \lambda_i \geq 0, \boxed{\sum_i \lambda_i = 1}\}$, which differs for the (boxed) normalization condition (3) on the coefficients λ_i, is instead the *convex hull* generated by the difference vectors $\mathbf{C}(x, y, z_i)$, represented by the smaller dark gray region in Fig. 1b. The effect of the normalization condition (3) is thus to shrink from the larger convex cone to the smaller convex hull. Finally, the region in light gray in Fig. 1b singles out the points which are at least as large as some point in this convex hull. Lemma 2 thus requires the difference vector $\mathbf{C}(\widehat{x}, \widehat{y}, \widehat{z})$ to belong to this light gray region.

4　ME has no equiprobable mappings

Lemmas 1 and 2 say that ME differs from SHG because of the normalization condition (3). This apparently small technical difference has substantial phonological implications. Indeed, this Section shows that the normalization condition (3) makes the ME typology so rich that it can distinguish between any two mappings. In other words,

equiprobability is impossible in ME. The reasoning is presented here informally, split up into three steps formalized in the final appendix.

Step 1 Let us suppose that the two mappings (x, y) and $(\widehat{x}, \widehat{y})$ are equiprobable in ME, namely that the ME probability identity $\mathbb{P}^{\mathrm{ME}}_\mathbf{w}(y \mid x) = \mathbb{P}^{\mathrm{ME}}_\mathbf{w}(\widehat{y} \mid \widehat{x})$ holds for every choice of the nonnegative weight vector $\mathbf{w}$. Let $z_1, \ldots, z_m$ be the loser candidates of the UR x. They define a light gray region as in Fig. 1b, namely the region of points which are at least as large as the points in the convex hull generated by the difference vectors $\mathbf{C}(x, y, z_i)$. Let us denote this light gray region as $LGR^{\mathrm{ME}}(z_1, \ldots, z_m)$. Analogously, let $\widehat{z}_1, \ldots, \widehat{z}_{\widehat{m}}$ be the loser candidates of the other UR $\widehat{x}$. They as well define the light gray region of points which are at least as large as the points in the convex hull generated by the difference vectors $\mathbf{C}(\widehat{x}, \widehat{y}, \widehat{z}_j)$. Let us denote this light gray region as $LGR^{\mathrm{ME}}(\widehat{z}_1, \ldots, \widehat{z}_{\widehat{m}})$.

The probability identity $\mathbb{P}^{\mathrm{ME}}_\mathbf{w}(y \mid x) = \mathbb{P}^{\mathrm{ME}}_\mathbf{w}(\widehat{y} \mid \widehat{x})$ is equivalent to the two reverse inequalities $\mathbb{P}^{\mathrm{ME}}_\mathbf{w}(y \mid x) \leq \mathbb{P}^{\mathrm{ME}}_\mathbf{w}(\widehat{y} \mid \widehat{x})$ and $\mathbb{P}^{\mathrm{ME}}_\mathbf{w}(y \mid x) \geq \mathbb{P}^{\mathrm{ME}}_\mathbf{w}(\widehat{y} \mid \widehat{x})$. By lemma 2 above, the former inequality requires each difference vector $\mathbf{C}(\widehat{x}, \widehat{y}, \widehat{z}_j)$ to belong to $LGR^{\mathrm{ME}}(z_1, \ldots, z_m)$. And the latter inequality requires each difference vector $\mathbf{C}(x, y, z_i)$ to belong to $LGR^{\mathrm{ME}}(\widehat{z}_1, \ldots, \widehat{z}_{\widehat{m}})$. A simple convexity argument deduces from these two facts the identity $LGR^{\mathrm{ME}}(z_1, \ldots, z_m) = LGR^{\mathrm{ME}}(\widehat{z}_1, \ldots, \widehat{z}_{\widehat{m}})$ between the two light gray regions.

Step 2 To proceed, let us suppose for concreteness that $m = 4$ and that the light gray region $LGR^{\mathrm{ME}}(z_1, z_2, z_3, z_4)$ is the one plotted in light gray in Fig. 1b. The difference vectors corresponding to the two losers z_1 and z_2 are *extreme points* (or *vertices*) of this light gray region. In the sense that they crucially contribute to shape it: if these two points were shifted even slightly in any direction, the corresponding light gray region would change. The identity between the two light gray regions established in step 1 thus entails that the two light gray regions share the same set of extreme points. In conclusion, the two difference vectors corresponding to losers z_1 and z_2 which are extreme points of the light gray region in figure Fig. 1b must be shared by the two equiprobable mappings considered. Since these difference vectors are shared by the two equiprobable mappings, they can be "peel off" the two sides of the

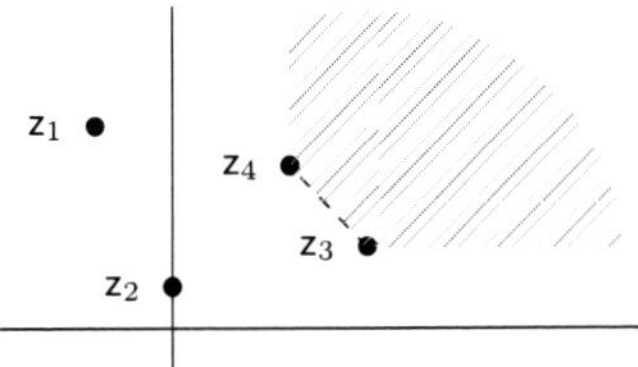

Figure 2: Steps 1-2 for the remaining losers z_3 and z_4.

ME probability identity.

Step 3 We are thus left with the difference vectors corresponding to the other two losers z_3 and z_4 in Fig. 1b. These latter two vectors are not extreme points of the original light gray region but rather sit in the interior of the light gray region. Indeed, they can be shifted around without affecting the shape of the light gray region. Yet, once the two losers z_1 and z_2 have been "peeled off" at step 2, we can repeat the reasoning in steps 1 and 2 ignoring the two losers z_1 and z_2 and instead considering only the other two losers z_3 and z_4.

Thus, we construct the convex hull of the difference vectors corresponding to just these two remaining losers z_3 and z_4. This convex hull is the segment which connects the two corresponding dots. Next, we construct the light gray region of points which are at least as large as some point in that segment, as depicted in Fig. 2. Now the difference vectors corresponding to the two losers z_3 and z_4 are extreme points of the new light gray region. We can therefore repeat the reasoning in steps 1-2 and conclude that these two difference vectors as well must be shared by the two equiprobable mappings considered. And so on.

The reasoning informally sketched above leads to the following Proposition 1, which is the first main result of this paper. It says that two mappings are equiprobable in ME if and only if they share all difference vectors. This entails in particular that the two mappings must have the same number of loser candidates. In other words, the ME typology is so rich that the only case where ME fails to come up with at least one weight vector which assigns different probabilities to the two mappings (x, y) and $(\widehat{x}, \widehat{y})$ is when the two mappings are the same mapping, in the sense that they are indistinguishable by the constraints, as they have the same difference vectors.[4]

[4] To illustrate, suppose that the constraint set only consists of the two constraints NOVOICEDOBSTRUENT and IDENT(voice). The mappings $(x, y) = $ (/mab/, [map]) and $(\widehat{x}, \widehat{y}) = $ (/bam/, [pam]) will always have the same ME proba-

Proposition 1 *Two mappings* (x, y) *and* $(\widehat{x}, \widehat{y})$ *are equiprobable in ME if and only if the corresponding sets of difference vectors coincide.* $\qquad\square$

5   SHG allows for equiprobable mappings

The preceding Section has shown that ME is so rich that it can distinguish between any two different mappings. Crucially, this typological richness is peculiar to ME, not intrinsic to probabilistic constraint-based phonology. In this section, we illustrate this point with the case of SHG. As in the preceding section, the discussion is kept informal. The formalization rests on the same convex geometric tools used for ME in the final appendix. The details are omitted here for reasons of space (see the longer version of this paper available on the authors' website).

Let us consider two mappings (x, y) and $(\widehat{x}, \widehat{y})$. Again, let $z_1, \ldots, z_m$ be the loser candidates of the UR x. They define a light gray region as in Fig. 1a, namely the region of points which are at least as large as the points in the convex cone generated by the difference vectors $\mathbf{C}(x, y, z_i)$. Let us denote this light gray region as $LGR^{\text{SHG}}(z_1, \ldots, z_m)$. This region is different from (and larger than) the light gray region $LGR^{\text{ME}}(z_1, \ldots, z_m)$ considered above for ME, because the latter ME region is restricted through the normalization condition (3) and therefore defined in terms of convex hulls rather than convex cones. Analogously, let $\widehat{z}_1, \ldots, \widehat{z}_{\widehat{m}}$ be the loser candidates of the other UR $\widehat{x}$ and let $LGR^{\text{SHG}}(\widehat{z}_1, \ldots, \widehat{z}_{\widehat{m}})$ be the corresponding SHG light gray region.

Again as in the case of ME, Lemma 1 says that the uniform SHG probability identity $\mathbb{P}_{\mathbf{w}}^{\text{SHG}}(y \mid x) = \mathbb{P}_{\mathbf{w}}^{\text{SHG}}(\widehat{y} \mid \widehat{x})$ entails that the two SHG light gray regions coincide, namely that $LGR^{\text{SHG}}(z_1, \ldots, z_m) = LGR^{\text{SHG}}(\widehat{z}_1, \ldots, \widehat{z}_{\widehat{m}})$. Yet, these SHG light gray regions have different geometric properties than the ME light gray regions. As a result, in the case of SHG the identity between the two light gray regions tells us much less about the difference vectors that generate them than in the case of ME.

To see that concretely, let us consider for instance the SHG light gray region in Fig. 1a. The loser candidates z_2, z_3 and z_4 have difference vectors which sit in the interior of this light gray region. These losers thus contribute nothing to shape

bility, because they and their losers have the same constraint violation profiles.

129

the light gray region: their difference vectors can be shifted around without affecting the shape of the region. Identity of the light gray regions thus tells us nothing about identity of these difference vectors which sit in the interior.

Interestingly, the loser candidates whose difference vectors sit in the interior of the SHG light gray region can be characterized phonologically as those losers which are *HG redundant* given the rest of the losers. In the sense that, for every non-negative weight vector w, if the HG harmony of the winner y is larger than that of the nonredundant losers, then it is in particular larger than the harmony of the redundant losers. In other words, these redundant losers carry no interesting phonological content as they do not in any way affect the weight vectors consistent with the mapping (x, y).

The case of the loser z_1 in Fig. 1a is instead different. Its difference vector sits on the border of the light gray region and therefore contributes to its shape. Yet, its position is not completely determined by the shape of the region. In fact, the shape of the region is not affected if this difference vector is slid closer to or further away from the origin. Equivalently, the shape of the region is not affected if the difference vector corresponding to the nonredundant loser z_1 is rescaled by a nonnegative constant $\lambda \geq 0$. This means that the identity of the two SHG light gray regions does not entail identity of the difference vectors which generate them, not even for those difference vectors which sit on the boundary of the regions and therefore correspond to nonredundant losers. The identity of the two SHG light gray regions only entails that the difference vectors of the nonredundant losers are one the rescaling of the other. This informal reasoning leads to the following Proposition, which is our second main result.

Proposition 2 *Two mappings* (x, y) *and* $(\widehat{x}, \widehat{y})$ *are equiprobable in SHG if and only if each nonredundant difference vector* $C(x, y, z_i)$ *is a rescaling of some nonredundant difference vector* $C(\widehat{x}, \widehat{y}, \widehat{z}_j)$, *namely* $C(x, y, z_i) = \lambda C(\widehat{x}, \widehat{y}, \widehat{z}_j)$ *for some* $\lambda \geq 0$; *analogously, each nonredundant difference vector* $C(\widehat{x}, \widehat{y}, \widehat{z}_j)$ *is a rescaling of some nonredundant difference vector* $C(x, y, z_i)$. $\square$

Interestingly, this characterization of SHG equiprobability coincides with the characterization of equivalence in categorical HG obtained by A&M. We conclude that two mappings are equiprobable in SHG (namely are always assigned

FtBin	Feet are disyllabic.
PkProm	No unstressed light syllables.
Align-L	All feet left.
*Rev	No trochees with sonority reversal.
*Flat	No trochees with a flat sonority profile.
*H.X	No stress next to a heavy syllable.
WSP	No unstressed heavy syllables.
WSP/VV	No unstressed heavies with long vowel.

Table 2: Constraints for foot structure in Finnish nouns

the same probability) if and only if they are equivalent in categorical HG (namely no HG grammar succeeds on one but fails on the other).

6 Equiprobability in Finnish stress

This section brings the preceding formal results to bear on Finnish word stress.

The phonological system The basic generalizations about Finnish word stress can be stated as follows (Carlson, 1978; Hanson and Kiparsky, 1996; Elenbaas, 1999; Elenbaas and Kager, 1999; Karvonen, 2005): (a) primary stress falls on the initial syllable; (b) secondary stress falls on every other syllable after that, (c) except that a light syllable is skipped if the syllable after that is heavy, unless the heavy syllable is final. Examples are íl.moit.tàu.tu.mì.nen 'registering' and íl.moit.tàu.tu.mi.sès.ta 'from registering'.

However, the skipping clause turns out to be a coarse approximation of the actual facts. Skipping is sometimes optional and we find variable stress in cases like pró.fes.so.rìl.la∼pró.fes.sò.ril.la 'professor-ADE', where the basic rule fails at the second variant. This optional pattern turns out to depend on two additional conditions that affect the outcome in a gradient manner (Anttila, 2012): (a) low vowels (/a, ä, o, ö/) attract stress and high vowels (/e, i, u, y/) repel stress; (b) stress is avoided next to a heavy syllable.[5]

In addition to native speaker intuitions about syllable prominence, empirical support for these soft conditions can be obtained from the optional rule of *Stop Deletion* (Keyser and Kiparsky, 1984) which deletes singleton stops in extrametrical syllables (Anttila, 2012). In particular, the /t/ in the partitive suffix /-tA/ is deleted vs. retained

---

[5] The categories "low" and "high" are morphophonemic, not phonetic. In Finnish, low vowels alternate morphophonologically with rounded mid vowels (a ∼ o, ä ∼ ö) and the unrounded high vowel alternates with the unrounded mid vowel (i ∼ e). For this reason we consider o, ö low and e high.

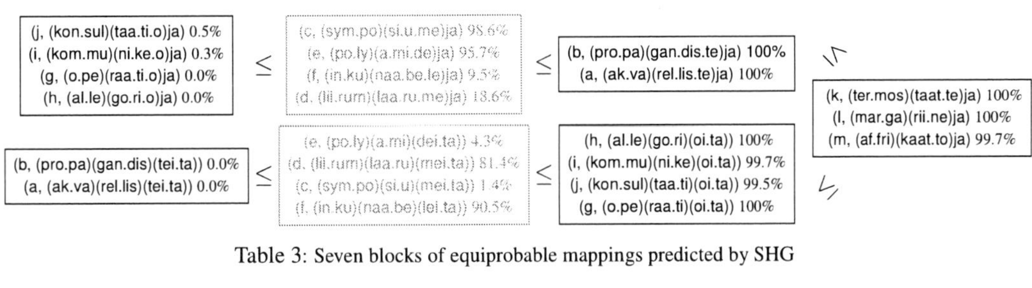

Table 3: Seven blocks of equiprobable mappings predicted by SHG

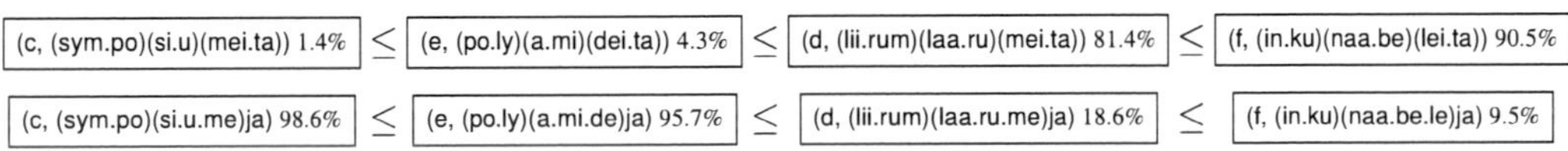

Table 4: SHG's two red blocks are split into two chains of uniform inequalities in ME

depending on the location of secondary stress feet. Given the input /professori-i-tA/ 'professor-PL-PAR' we have two possible foot structures: (pró.fes.so)(rèi.ta) where /t/ falls inside a foot and is retained vs. (pró.fes)(sò.re)ja where /t/ falls outside a foot and is deleted. The metrical free variation is thus reflected in segmental free variation. This provides a valuable diagnostic for foot structure, especially because the segmental variation is present even in the written standard language readily available in large quantities.

The constraints necessary for deriving the foot structure in Finnish nouns are shown in Table 2. These constraints were applied to 48 types of partitive plural nouns, systematically varying stem length, syllable weight, and vowel sonority. All in all, the test set contains 4 types of three-syllable stems, 12 types of 4-syllable stems, and 32 types 5-syllable stems (stem types are briefly denoted as "(a), (b), …" in what follows).

SHG We computed the uniform probability inequalities predicted by SHG for this Finnish stress test case using CoGeTo (Magri and Anttila, 2019), a suite of tools for studying constraint-based typologies of categorical and probabilistic phonological grammars based on their underlying rich convex geometry. The key observation is that SHG predicts seven blocks of equiprobable mappings, shown in Table 3. These blocks are furthermore organized into two chains of uniform probability inequalities. The predicted probabilities increase from left to right. The symbol "≤" between two boxes means that the candidates in the box on the left are predicted to have a probability at most as large as the candidates in the box on the right.

To evaluate the empirical accuracy of the equiprobabilities predicted by SHG, we examined Finnish /t/-deletion in a corpus of approximately 9 million nouns (tokens) harvested from Finnish internet sites on April 12, 2005. The percentages reported in Table 3 represent the token frequency of /t/-retention vs. /t/-deletion variants for each phonologically distinct stem type. The corpus data are consistent with the equiprobability prediction in five out of the seven blocks, namely those in black. These blocks turn out to be empirically nearly categorical, with almost all stems undergoing either /t/-deletion or /t/-retention, consistently with the equiprobability prediction.

However, the two red blocks in Table 3 bundle together the stem types (c)-(f) despite them showing rather different empirical frequencies, providing *prima facie* evidence against SHG's equiprobability prediction. The stem types are illustrated by /symposiumi/ 'symposium', /polyamidi/ 'polyamide', /liirumlaarumi/ 'nonsense', and /inkunaabeli/ 'incunable'. The stems differ in the weight and quality of the preantepenultimate and antepenultimate syllables (heavy vs. light, [+low] vs. [−low]), which results in constraint violation differences, yet HG predicts that all four should undergo /t/-deletion/retention at identical rates. In order to reconcile SHG's equiprobability predictions with corpus frequencies, we make the following observations. First, the difference between types (d) /liirumlaarumi/ and (f) /inkunaabeli/ is not statistically significant ($\chi^2 = 2.9849$, $df = 1$, $p = 0.08404$). Second, type (c) contains only two stems: /symposiumi/ 'symposium' and /imperiumi/ 'empire', both potentially syllabifiable as four-syllable stems, e.g., im.pe.ri.u.mi ∼ im.pe.riu.mi (Anttila and Shapiro, 2017), which is consistent with their unexpectedly high /t/-deletion rate. This leaves us with type (e) /polyamidi/ 'polyamide' (N = 69), again with an unexpectedly high deletion rate for which we have no plausible explanation. We conclude that by and large our Finnish corpus data support SHG's equiprobability predictions.

ME One might wonder whether ME with its ability to make fine-grained distinctions might actually offer a more principled solution to the difficulties just discussed. This turns out *not* to be the case. On the retention side, ME predicts the uniform probability inequalities in the top row of Table 4. For example, the retention probability of /polyamidi/ is predicted to be at most as high as that of /liirumlaarumi/, no matter the choice of the weight vector. That seems initially promising: these inequalities are in fact exactly what we observe in the data. Puzzlingly, on the deletion side, ME reverses the probabilities, yielding the uniform probability inequalities in the bottom row of Table 4. For example, the deletion probability of /polyamidi/ is predicted to be at most as high as that of /liirumlaarumi/. This is exactly the opposite of what we observe in the data. We submit there is simply no way to reconcile ME's predictions with the corpus data. Such counterintuitive probability reversals appear in other blocks as well.

7 Summary and conclusions

We have shown that ME predicts typologies so rich that ME grammars can distinguish between any two different mappings and therefore admit no equiprobable mappings (Proposition 1). This richness does not extend to other implementations of probabilistic constraint-based phonology, such as SHG (Proposition 2), revealing a fundamental difference between the two frameworks.

We have then applied these results to the test case of Finnish word stress. Our corpus data provide preliminary evidence in favor of SHG's equiprobability predictions. In the two blocks where SHG appeared to run into problems, ME did not help refine the analysis empirically, but instead split the SHG equiprobable stem types apart in a counterintuitive fashion. Our study thus provides some preliminary empirical support in favor of SHG, which permits equiprobable mappings, against ME, which does not.

Acknowledgements

For very useful discussion, we would like to thank the participants of the workshop *Analyzing typological structure: from categorical to probabilistic phonology* (Stanford, September 2018; website). The research reported in this paper has been supported by a Collaborative Projects Grant from the France-Stanford Center for Interdisciplinary Studies (project title: *The Mathematics of Language Universals*) as well as by a JCJC grant from the Agence Nationale de la Recherche (project title: *The mathematics of segmental phonotactics*).

A Proof of Proposition 1

We write $\mathbf{c}_i$ and $\widehat{\mathbf{c}}_j$ as shorthands for the difference vectors $\mathbf{C}(x, y, z_i)$ and $\mathbf{C}(\widehat{x}, \widehat{y}, \widehat{z}_j)$ corresponding to the losers z_i and $\widehat{z}_j$. The ME probability inequality $\mathbb{P}^{\mathrm{ME}}_{\mathbf{w}}(x, y) = \mathbb{P}^{\mathrm{ME}}_{\mathbf{w}}(\widehat{x}, \widehat{y})$ can be made explicit as in (4) through some elementary manipulations. As usual, $\mathbf{a}^\top \mathbf{b}$ denotes the scalar product of $\mathbf{a}$ and $\mathbf{b}$.

$$\sum_{i=1}^{m} e^{\mathbf{w}^\top \mathbf{c}_i} = \sum_{j=1}^{\widehat{m}} e^{\mathbf{w}^\top \widehat{\mathbf{c}}_j} \tag{4}$$

Once the ME probability identity $\mathbb{P}^{\mathrm{ME}}_{\mathbf{w}}(x, y) = \mathbb{P}^{\mathrm{ME}}_{\mathbf{w}}(\widehat{x}, \widehat{y})$ is made explicit as in (4), it is obvious that it holds uniformly for every weight vector $\mathbf{w}$ when the two sets of difference vectors coincide, namely $\{\mathbf{c}_1, \ldots, \mathbf{c}_m\} = \{\widehat{\mathbf{c}}_1, \ldots, \widehat{\mathbf{c}}_{\widehat{m}}\}$. To complete the proof of Proposition 1, we thus only have to prove the reverse. We split the proof into three steps, corresponding to those in Section 4.

Step 1. We start from the assumption that the ME probability identity $\mathbb{P}^{\mathrm{ME}}_{\mathbf{w}}(x, y) = \mathbb{P}^{\mathrm{ME}}_{\mathbf{w}}(\widehat{x}, \widehat{y})$ holds uniformly. This means in particular that the probability inequality $\mathbb{P}^{\mathrm{ME}}_{\mathbf{w}}(x, y) \leq \mathbb{P}^{\mathrm{ME}}_{\mathbf{w}}(\widehat{x}, \widehat{y})$ holds uniformly. The necessary condition for this uniform ME inequality provided by Proposition 2 can be rewritten as the inclusion (1). As usual, $\mathbb{R}_+$ is the set of nonnegative real numbers and $A + B = \{\mathbf{a} + \mathbf{b} \mid \mathbf{a} \in A, \mathbf{b} \in B\}$ is the vector sum of two sets A and B of $\mathbb{R}^n$. The region on the right hand side of (1) is the light gray region in Fig. 3.b.

$$(1) \quad \{\widehat{\mathbf{c}}_1, \ldots, \widehat{\mathbf{c}}_{\widehat{m}}\} \subseteq conv(\mathbf{c}_1, \ldots, \mathbf{c}_m) + \mathbb{R}^n_+$$

The set $conv(\mathbf{c}_1, \ldots, \mathbf{c}_m) + \mathbb{R}^n_+$ on the right hand side of (1) is convex because the two sets $conv(\mathbf{c}_1, \ldots, \mathbf{c}_m)$ and $\mathbb{R}^n_+$ are both convex and the sum of two convex sets is convex (Boyd and Vandenberghe, 2004, Section 2.3.2). The inclusion (1) thus extends from the points $\widehat{\mathbf{c}}_1, \ldots, \widehat{\mathbf{c}}_{\widehat{m}}$ to their convex hull $conv(\widehat{\mathbf{c}}_1, \ldots, \widehat{\mathbf{c}}_{\widehat{m}})$, yielding the inclusion $conv(\widehat{\mathbf{c}}_1, \ldots, \widehat{\mathbf{c}}_{\widehat{m}}) \subseteq conv(\mathbf{c}_1, \ldots, \mathbf{c}_m) + \mathbb{R}^n_+$. Finally, by adding $\mathbb{R}^n_+$ at both sides, the latter inclusion entails $conv(\widehat{\mathbf{c}}_1, \ldots, \widehat{\mathbf{c}}_{\widehat{m}}) + \mathbb{R}^n_+ \subseteq conv(\mathbf{c}_1, \ldots, \mathbf{c}_m) + \mathbb{R}^n_+$. Analogously, the reverse probability inequality $\mathbb{P}^{\text{ME}}_{\mathbf{w}}(\widehat{x}, \widehat{y}) \leq \mathbb{P}^{\text{ME}}_{\mathbf{w}}(x, y)$ requires the reverse inclusion $conv(\mathbf{c}_1, \ldots, \mathbf{c}_m) + \mathbb{R}^n_+ \subseteq conv(\widehat{\mathbf{c}}_1, \ldots, \widehat{\mathbf{c}}_{\widehat{m}}) + \mathbb{R}^n_+$, yielding (5).

$$\underbrace{conv(\mathbf{c}_1 \ldots \mathbf{c}_m) + \mathbb{R}^n_+}_{P} = \underbrace{conv(\widehat{\mathbf{c}}_1 \ldots \widehat{\mathbf{c}}_{\widehat{m}}) + \mathbb{R}^n_+}_{\widehat{P}} \quad (5)$$

Step 2. This identity (5) says in particular that the two sets P and $\widehat{P}$ on its left and right hand side have the same set of extreme points, namely $ext(P) = ext(\widehat{P})$. The set $ext(P)$ of extreme points of the set P is nonempty. In fact, a set which is closed, convex, nonempty, and does not contain a line admits at least an extreme point (Bertsekas, 2009, Proposition 2.1.2). Indeed, P is closed, because $conv(\mathbf{c}_1, \ldots, \mathbf{c}_m)$ is compact, $\mathbb{R}^n_+$ is closed, and the sum of a compact set with a closed set is closed (Bertsekas, 2009, Section 1.3). Furthermore, P is convex, because $conv(\mathbf{c}_1, \ldots, \mathbf{c}_m)$ and $\mathbb{R}^n_+$ are both convex and the sum of two convex sets is convex. Finally, P is obviously nonempty and it does not contain a line.

The set $ext(P)$ of extreme points of the set P is a subset of the set of difference vectors $\{\mathbf{c}_1, \ldots, \mathbf{c}_m\}$. In fact, the set of extreme points of the finitely generated polyhedron $conv(\mathbf{c}_1, \ldots, \mathbf{c}_m)$ is a subset of $\{\mathbf{c}_1, \ldots, \mathbf{c}_m\}$ (by the Krein-Milman theorem). The set of extreme points of the pointed cone $\mathbb{R}^n_+$ only consists of the zero vector $\mathbf{0}$. And the set $ext(A + B)$ of extreme points of the vector sum $A + B$ of any two polyhedra A and B is a subset of the vector sum $ext(A) + ext(B)$ of the two sets $ext(A)$ and $ext(B)$ of extreme points of A and B, namely $ext(A + B) \subseteq ext(A) + ext(B)$ (Bertsimas and Tsitsiklis, 1997, exercise 2.22). Analogously, the set $ext(\widehat{P})$ of extreme points of the set $\widehat{P}$ is a nonempty subset of the set $\{\widehat{\mathbf{c}}_1, \ldots, \widehat{\mathbf{c}}_m\}$.

In conclusion, the two sets of difference vectors $\{\mathbf{c}_1, \ldots, \mathbf{c}_m\}$ and $\{\widehat{\mathbf{c}}_1, \ldots, \widehat{\mathbf{c}}_m\}$ share the vectors in the nonempty set $\Omega = ext(P) = ext(\widehat{P})$. Without loss of generality, we assume that these shared vectors are those corresponding to the first $h \geq 1$ losers, so that $\{\mathbf{c}_1, \ldots, \mathbf{c}_m\} = \Omega \cup \{\mathbf{c}_{h+1}, \ldots, \mathbf{c}_m\}$ and $\{\widehat{\mathbf{c}}_1, \ldots, \widehat{\mathbf{c}}_m\} = \Omega \cup \{\widehat{\mathbf{c}}_{h+1}, \ldots, \widehat{\mathbf{c}}_{\widehat{m}}\}$.

Step 3. The terms on the left and the right hand side of the ME probability identity (4) which correspond to the shared difference vectors in Ω cancel out. The ME probability identity thus reduces to $\sum_{i=h+1}^{m} e^{\mathbf{w}^{\mathsf{T}}\mathbf{c}_i} = \sum_{j=h+1}^{\widehat{m}} e^{\mathbf{w}^{\mathsf{T}}\widehat{\mathbf{c}}_j}$, where the sums start at $h + 1$ rather than at 1. The claim

follows by iterating the reasoning above, starting from the latter simplified ME probability identity.

References

Arto Anttila. 2012. Modeling phonological variation. In Abigail C. Cohn, Cécile Fougeron, and Marie Huffman, editors, *The Oxford Handbook of Laboratory Phonology*, pages 76–91. Oxford University Press, Oxford.

Arto Anttila and Giorgio Magri. 2018. Does MaxEnt overgenerate? Implicational universals in Maximum Entropy grammar. In *AMP 2017: Proceedings of the 2017 Annual Meeting on Phonology*, Washington, DC. Linguistic Society of America.

Arto Anttila and Naomi Tachikawa Shapiro. 2017. The interaction of stress and syllabification: Serial or parallel? In *Proceedings of the 34th West Coast Conference on Formal Linguistics*, pages 52–61, Somerville, MA, USA. Cascadilla Proceedings Project.

Dimitri P. Bertsekas. 2009. *Convex Optimization Theory*. Athena Scientific, Belmont, MA, USA.

Dimitris Bertsimas and John N. Tsitsiklis. 1997. *Linear Optimization*. Athena Scientific.

Paul Boersma. 1997. How we learn variation, optionality and probability. In *Proceedings of the Institute of Phonetic Sciences (IFA) 21*, pages 43–58, University of Amsterdam. Institute of Phonetic Sciences.

Paul Boersma. 1998. *Functional Phonology*. Ph.D. thesis, University of Amsterdam, The Netherlands. The Hague: Holland Academic Graphics.

Paul Boersma and Joe Pater. 2016. Convergence properties of a gradual learning algorithm for Harmonic Grammar. In John McCarthy and Joe Pater, editors, *Harmonic Grammar and Harmonic Serialism*. Equinox Press, London.

Stephen Boyd and Lieven Vandenberghe. 2004. *Convex Optimization*. Cambridge University Press.

Lauri Carlson. 1978. Word stress in Finnish. Massachusetts Institute of Technology, Cambridge, Massachusetts.

Nine Elenbaas. 1999. *A unified account of binary and ternary stress. Considerations from Sentani and Finnish*. Ph.D. thesis, LOT: Netherlands Graduate School of Linguistics.

Nine Elenbaas and René Kager. 1999. Ternary rhythm and the lapse constraint. *Phonology*, 16:273–329.

Sharon Goldwater and Mark Johnson. 2003. Learning OT constraint rankings using a Maximum Entropy model. In *Proceedings of the Stockholm Workshop on Variation Within Optimality Theory*, pages 111–120, Stockholm University.

Kristin Hanson and Paul Kiparsky. 1996. A parametric theory of poetic meter. *Language*, 72:287–335.

Bruce Hayes. 2017. Varieties of Noisy Harmonic Grammar. In *Proceedings of the 2016 Annual Meeting in Phonology*, Washington, DC. Linguistic Society of America.

Bruce Hayes and Zsuzsa Cziráky Londe. 2006. Stochastic phonological knowledge: The case of Hungarian vowel harmony. *Phonology*, 23.1:59–104.

Bruce Hayes and Colin Wilson. 2008. A Maximum Entropy model of phonotactics and phonotactic learning. *Linguistic Inquiry*, 39:379–440.

Bruce Hayes, Kie Zuraw, Péter Siptár, and Zsuzsa Londe. 2009. Natural and unnatural constraints in Hungarian vowel harmony. *Language*, 85:822–863.

Dan Karvonen. 2005. *Word Prosody in Finnish*. Ph.D. thesis, University of California, Santa Cruz.

Samuel Jay Keyser and Paul Kiparsky. 1984. Syllable structure in Finnish phonology. In Mark Aronoff and Richard Oehrle, editors, *Language Sound Structure*, pages 7–31. MIT Press, Cambridge, Massachusetts.

Géraldine Legendre, Yoshiro Miyata, and Paul Smolensky. 1990a. Harmonic Grammar: A formal multi-level connectionist theory of linguistic well-formedness: An application. In *Proceedings of the 12th annual conference of the Cognitive Science Society*, pages 884–891, Hillsdale, NJ. Lawrence Erlbaum Associates.

Géraldine Legendre, Yoshiro Miyata, and Paul Smolensky. 1990b. Harmonic Grammar: A formal multi-level connectionist theory of linguistic well-formedness: Theoretical foundations. In *Proceedings of the 12th annual conference of the Cognitive Science Society*, pages 388–395, Hillsdale, NJ. Lawrence Erlbaum.

Giorgio Magri. 2019. Finiteness of optima in constraint-based phonology. Manuscript, CNRS.

Giorgio Magri and Arto Anttila. 2019. CoGeTo: Convex geometry tools for typological analysis in categorical and probabilistic constraint-based phonology (version 1.0). Available at `https://cogeto.stanford.edu`.

Catherine Ringen and Orvokki Heinämäki. 1999. Variation in Finnish vowel harmony. *Natural Language and Linguistc Theory*, 17:303–337.

Brian W. Smith and Joe Pater. 2017. French schwa and gradient cumulativity. Manuscript. University of California, Berkeley and University of Massachusetts, Amherst.

Paul Smolensky and Géraldine Legendre. 2006. *The Harmonic Mind*. MIT Press, Cambridge, MA.

Kie Zuraw and Bruce Hayes. 2017. Intersecting constraint families: an argument for Harmonic Grammar. *Language*, 93.3:497–546.

Jesse Zymet. 2015. Distance-based decay in long-distance phonological processes. In *Proceedings of the 32nd West Coast Conference on Formal Linguistics*, pages 72–81, Somerville, MA. Cascadilla Proceedings Project.

Unbounded Stress in Subregular Phonology

Yiding Hao
Yale University
New Haven, CT, USA
`yiding.hao@yale.edu`

Samuel Andersson
Yale University
New Haven, CT, USA
`samuel.andersson@yale.edu`

Abstract

This paper situates culminative unbounded stress systems within the subregular hierarchy for functions. While Baek (2018) has argued that such systems can be uniformly understood as input tier-based strictly local constraints, we show here that *default-to-opposite-side* and *default-to-same-side* stress systems belong to distinct subregular classes when they are viewed as functions that assign primary stress to underlying forms. While the former system can be captured by *input tier-based input strictly local functions*, a subsequential function class that we define here, the latter system is not subsequential, though it is weakly deterministic according to McCollum et al.'s (2018) non-interaction criterion. Our results motivate the extension of recently proposed subregular language classes to subregular functions and argue in favor of McCollum et al.'s definition of weak determinism over that of Heinz and Lai (2013).

1 Introduction

The treatment of unbounded stress (Baek, 2018), Uyghur backness harmony (Mayer and Major, 2018), and Sanskrit n-retroflexion (Graf and Mayer, 2018) in subregular phonology has given rise to a rich collection of extensions of the *tier-based strictly local* languages (TSL; Heinz et al., 2011) as formal descriptions of the typology of phonotactic dependencies. These language classes formalize the notion of local dependencies defined on tiers. While the TSL languages assume that each segment is either projected to the tier or not, the extensions allow for rich tier-projection schemata that are sensitive to local context.

Meanwhile, the formal study of phonological processes has shown that mappings from underlying representations to surface representations often exhibit a form of locality analogous to the notion captured by TSL languages. This insight is

formalized by the *input strictly local* (ISL; Chandlee, 2014), *output strictly local* (OSL; Chandlee et al., 2015), and *input–output strictly local* (IOSL; Chandlee et al., In prep) functions, proposed as functional counterparts of the TSL languages. Chandlee (2014) argues that most phonological processes are captured by these classes of functions, and of the ones that are not, Heinz and Lai (2013) and McCollum et al. (2018) propose two versions of the *weakly deterministic* functions that describe non-deterministic harmony patterns.

This paper examines culminative unbounded stress systems as string-to-string mappings. Baek (2018) analyzes these systems as phonotactic constraints and shows that they are not TSL in general. To capture them, Baek defines the *tier-based strictly local languages with structural features* (TSL-SF), an extension of TSL in which the tier-projection mechanism is sensitive to the position of segments within prosodic units. The TSL-SF languages were later subsumed by Graf and Mayer's (2018) *input–output tier-based strictly local* (IO-TSL) languages, in which the tier-projection mechanism is implemented by an arbitrary IOSL function. As mappings, we show that *default-to-opposite-side* (DO) stress systems can be captured using a similar approach. Examples of such systems include stressing the leftmost long vowel and assigning rightmost stress in the absence of long vowels. We propose the *input tier-based input strictly local* (I-TISL) functions as a functional analogue of the generalized tier-projection mechanism of the IO-TSL languages. Based on the stress system of Abkhaz, we advocate for a tier projection that is slightly more general than the restricted mechanism used in Baek. Next, we show that *default-to-same-side* (DS) stress systems, such as that of Lhasa Tibetan, are not subsequential. Examples of DS systems include those in which the leftmost long vowel is stressed, and

Proceedings of the 16th Workshop on Computational Research in Phonetics, Phonology, and Morphology, pages 135–143
Florence, Italy. August 2, 2019 ©2019 Association for Computational Linguistics

the leftmost vowel is stressed when all vowels are short. We argue that DS systems can be naturally captured using McCollum et al.'s (2018) definition of weak determinism but not using Heinz and Lai's (2013) definition, therefore arguing in favor of the former definition.

This paper is structured as follows. Section 2 states basic notation and definitions used throughout this paper. Section 3 defines the I-TISL functions and shows that they can capture the DO stress system of Abkhaz. Section 4 considers Lhasa Tibetan and its relation to the two definitions of weak determinism. Section 5 presents a discussion of these results and their connection with analyses of stress based on metrical grid theory. Section 6 concludes.

2 Preliminaries

As usual, $\mathbb{N}$ denotes the set of nonnegative integers. Σ and Γ denote finite alphabets not including the left and right word boundary symbols $\rtimes$ and $\ltimes$, respectively. The length of a string x is denoted by $|x|$, and λ denotes the empty string. Alphabet symbols are identified with strings of length 1, and individual strings are identified with singleton sets of strings. For $k \in \mathbb{N}$, α^k denotes α concatenated with itself k-many times, α^* denotes $\bigcup_{i=0}^{\infty} \alpha^i$, and α^+ denotes $\alpha\alpha^*$. The *longest common prefix* of a set of strings A is the longest string $\mathrm{lcp}(A)$ such that every string in A begins with $\mathrm{lcp}(A)$. The k-*suffix* of a string x, denoted $\mathrm{suff}^k(x)$, is the string consisting of the last k-many symbols of $\rtimes^k x$. The *reverse* of a string $x = x_1 x_2 \ldots x_n$, denoted x^{R}, is the string $x_n x_{n-1} \ldots x_1$. For any functions $f : A \to B$ and $g : B \to C$, the notation $g \circ f$ represents the function given by $(g \circ f)(x) = g(f(x))$. A function $f : \Sigma^* \to \Gamma^*$ is *same-length* if for all $x \in \Sigma^*$, $|f(x)| = |x|$.

2.1 Subsequential Functions

This subsection presents an algebraic definition of the subsequential functions, analogous to the Nerode–Myhill characterization of the regular languages. We use the *translations* of a function f to describe the possible behaviors of a subsequential finite-state transducer (SFST) for f, and we identify each translation of f with a state of the minimal SFST for f.

Definition 1. Let $f : \Sigma^* \to \Gamma^*$. We define the function $f^{\leftarrow} : \Sigma^* \to \Gamma^*$ by

$$f^{\leftarrow}(x) := \mathrm{lcp}\left(\{f(xy)|y \in \Sigma^*\}\right).$$

For any $x, y \in \Sigma^*$, $f_x^{\rightarrow}(y)$ denotes the string such that $f(xy) = f^{\leftarrow}(x)f_x^{\rightarrow}(y)$. We refer to the function $f_x^{\rightarrow}$ as the *translation of f by x* and to $f^{\leftarrow}$ as *f top*.[1]

Intuitively, $f^{\leftarrow}(x)$ refers to the output of the minimal SFST for f after reading the input x, and the translation $f_x^{\rightarrow}$ describes the behavior of the minimal SFST upon reading further input symbols.

Definition 2 (Raney, 1958). A function $f : \Sigma^* \to \Gamma^*$ is *subsequential* if the set $\{f_x^{\rightarrow}|x \in \Sigma^*\}$ is finite. We say that f is *left-subsequential* if it is subsequential and *right-subsequential* if the function $g : \Sigma^* \to \Gamma^*$ defined by $g(x) := f\left(x^{\mathrm{R}}\right)^{\mathrm{R}}$ is subsequential. We say that f is *sequential* or *left-sequential* if f is subsequential and $f = f^{\leftarrow}$. We say that f is *right-sequential* if the function $g : \Sigma^* \to \Gamma^*$ defined by $g(x) := f\left(x^{\mathrm{R}}\right)^{\mathrm{R}}$ is sequential.

The *strictly local functions* are defined by assuming that each translation corresponds to an i-suffix of the input and a j-suffix of the output.

Definition 3 (Chandlee et al., In prep). For $i, j \in \mathbb{N}$, a function $f : \Sigma^* \to \Gamma^*$ is i, j-*input–output strictly local* (i, j-IOSL) if for every $x, y \in \Sigma^*$, if $\mathrm{suff}^{i-1}(x) = \mathrm{suff}^{i-1}(y)$ and $\mathrm{suff}^{j-1}(f^{\leftarrow}(x)) = \mathrm{suff}^{j-1}(f^{\leftarrow}(y))$, then $f_x^{\rightarrow} = f_y^{\rightarrow}$. If the function $g(x) := f\left(x^{\mathrm{R}}\right)^{\mathrm{R}}$ is i, j-IOSL, then f is *right i, j-input–output strictly local* (right i, j-IOSL). A function is *i-input strictly local* (i-ISL) if it is $i, 1$-IOSL and *j-output strictly local* (j-OSL) if it is $1, j$-IOSL. A function is *input–output strictly local* (IOSL), *input strictly local* (ISL), or *output strictly local* (OSL) if if is i, j-IOSL, i-ISL, or j-OSL for some $i, j \in \mathbb{N}$, respectively. A function is *homomorphic* if it is sequential and $1, 1$-IOSL.

Since there are only finitely many possible i-suffixes and j-suffixes, it is clear that all IOSL functions are subsequential.

3 DO Stress and Tier Projection

In culminative unbounded stress systems, primary stress is assigned to either the first or last syllable that fulfills a particular criterion—e.g., having a long vowel. In the absence of such syllables, primary stress is assigned to either the first or last syllable by default. DO stress systems are those

---

[1]This terminology follows Sakarovitch (2009, pp. 692–693). In the transducer inference literature, Oncina et al. (1993) refer to $f_x^{\rightarrow}$ as the *tails of x in f*, and Chandlee et al. (2015) refer to $f^{\leftarrow}$ as the *prefix function associated to f*.

in which qualifying syllables closest to one word edge receive stress, while the syllable closest to the other edge receives stress by default. In DS stress systems, qualifying syllables closest to one word edge receive stress, and the syllable closest to the same edge receives stress by default. For example, in the typology of Hayes (1995), leftmost heavy otherwise rightmost (LHOR) and rightmost heavy otherwise leftmost systems (RHOL) are DO, while leftmost heavy otherwise leftmost (LHOL) and rightmost heavy otherwise rightmost (RHOR) systems are DS.

This section considers the DO stress system of Abkhaz, which we describe in Subsection 3.1. Subsection 3.2 defines the I-TSL functions and shows how they can capture the Abkhaz stress system.

3.1 Abkhaz Stress

Below we illustrate the stress system of the standard Abzhuy variety of Abkhaz ([abk], Northwest Caucasian), as analyzed by Dybo (1977; refined by Spruit, 1986 and Trigo, 1992). The Abkhaz stress system depends on a set of phonologically-contrastive accentual specifications. In the data considered here, every syllable of every morpheme is lexically specified as either dominant (D) or recessive (R; see Spruit, 1986 for accentual specifications which do not align with syllable boundaries). The so-called *Dybo's Rule* for stress states: assign primary stress to the leftmost D not immediately followed by another D (Spruit, 1986, p. 38). We mark dominant syllables by underlining, and hyphens indicate morpheme boundaries. Evidence for accentual specifications can be found in Spruit (1986).

The Abkhaz stress pattern is illustrated in Tables 1–3. When a word contains only a single dominant syllable, it receives the primary stress. When there is a span of multiple dominant syllables which are all adjacent, the rightmost such syllable is stressed. When there are multiple spans of adjacent D syllables, the rightmost D of the leftmost span is stressed. In words with only D syllables, as well as in words with only R syllables, stress is final.

3.2 I-TSL Functions

Let us now define the I-TSL functions and show how they can handle the Abkhaz stress system. To do so, we extend the notion of *tier projection* used in the TSL languages (Heinz et al., 2011; Baek,

Form	Translation
a̱-ˈt͡sʰa-ga	'(the) hoe'
də-t͡sʰa-la̱-ˈwa-ma	'does (s)he usually go?'
də-t͡sʰa̱-ˈnə	'(s)he having gone'

Table 1: The rightmost consecutive dominant syllable receives primary stress (Spruit, 1986, pp. 50, 53).

Form	Translation
ˈa̱-va-t͡sʼa-ra̱	'to put next to'
də-ˈgəla-gʷuʃa-ma	'did (s)he go and stand, alas?'
a-ˈʁʷakʼʲaməsa	'(the) poniard'

Table 2: Only the leftmost span of Ds contains a primary stress (Spruit, 1986, pp. 44, 47, 73–74).

2018; Mayer and Major, 2018; Graf and Mayer, 2018) to the case of subregular functions. There, tier projections are formalized as functions that delete certain symbols of their inputs.

Definition 4. A *tier-projection function on* Σ is a function $\pi : \Sigma^* \to \Sigma^*$ such that for any $x = x_1 x_2 \ldots x_n \in \Sigma^*$ we have $\pi(x) = y_1 y_2 \ldots y_n$, where for each i, either $y_i = x_i$ or $y_i = \lambda$.

TSL languages make use of tier projection by only enforcing local dependencies based on symbols projected to the tier, thereby bypassing symbols not projected to the tier. To apply the tier projection system to strictly local functions, we only consider symbols on the tier when enforcing strict locality. Whereas i-ISL functions require that their translations by a string x correspond to the last $(i - 1)$-many symbols of x, tier-based i-ISL functions associate translations with the last $(i - 1)$-many symbols *on the tier*, which we identify with $\mathrm{suff}^{i-1}(\pi^{\leftarrow}(x))$.

Definition 5. A function $f : \Sigma^* \to \Gamma^*$ is i-*input tier-based j-input strictly local* (i-I-j-TSL) if there exists an i-ISL tier projection function π on Σ such that for all $x, y \in \Sigma^*$, if $\mathrm{suff}^{j-1}(\pi^{\leftarrow}(x)) = \mathrm{suff}^{j-1}(\pi^{\leftarrow}(y))$, then $f_x^{\to} = f_y^{\to}$. We call π a *tier projection for* f. A function is *input tier-based input strictly local* (I-TSL) if it is i-I-j-TSL for some i and j.

We formalize the Abkhaz stress system as follows. Alphabet symbols represent individual syllables; dominant and recessive syllables are represented as D and R, respectively. Stressed syllables are represented as Ḋ and Ṙ. Following the

137

Form	Translation
a̱-pʰa-'ra̱	'to pleat'
maa-'k'ə	'one handle"

Table 3: Stress is final when all syllables have the same accentual status (Spruit, 1986, pp. 45–46).

discussion from Subsection 3.1, the Abkhaz stress function replaces the leftmost D not followed by another D with D́. If the input does not contain any Ds, then the final R is replaced with Ŕ.

Definition 6. The *Abkhaz stress function* α : $\{D, R\}^* \to \{D, R, \acute{D}, \acute{R}\}^*$ is defined as follows. For $i \geq 0, j > 0$, and $y \in \{\lambda\} \cup R\{D, R\}^*$,

$$\alpha(R^i D^j y) := R^i D^{j-1} \acute{D} y$$
$$\alpha(R^j) := R^{j-1} \acute{R}$$
$$\alpha(\lambda) := \lambda.$$

Proposition 7. *The Abkhaz stress function is 2-I-3-TISL.*

Proof. Let $\pi : \{D, R\}^* \to \{D, R\}^*$ be the tier-projection function defined as follows.

- Any D not preceded by another D is projected.

- Any R preceded by a D is projected.

It is easy to see that π is 2-ISL. Observe that for any x, $\pi(x) \in (DR)^*\{\lambda, D\}$.

We now show that α is 2-I-3-TISL with tier projection π. To that end, we need to show that each translation $\alpha_x^{\rightarrow}$ is determined by $\text{suff}^2(\pi^{\leftarrow}(x))$. Observe that there are four possible values for $\text{suff}^2(\pi^{\leftarrow}(x))$: $\rtimes\ltimes$, $\rtimes D$, DR, or RD. We consider each of these cases one-by-one.

- Suppose $\text{suff}^2(\pi^{\leftarrow}(x)) = \rtimes\ltimes$. This means that $x = R^i$ for some $i \geq 0$. Stress has not yet been assigned, so $\alpha^{\leftarrow}(x) = R^{i-1}$ if $i > 0$ and $\alpha^{\leftarrow}(x) = \lambda$ otherwise. For any $y \in \{D, R\}^*$,

$$\alpha_x^{\rightarrow}(y) = \begin{cases} R\alpha(y), & i > 0 \\ \alpha(y), & i = 0. \end{cases}$$

- Suppose $\text{suff}^2(\pi^{\leftarrow}(x)) = \rtimes D$. This means that $x = R^i D^j$, where $j > 0$ and $i \geq 0$. Stress has not yet been assigned, so $\alpha^{\leftarrow}(x) = R^i D^{j-1}$. For any input of the form $D^m R^n y$, where $m, n \geq 0$ and $y \in \{D, R\}^*$,

$$\alpha_x^{\rightarrow}(D^m R^n y) = \begin{cases} D^m \acute{D} R^n y, & n > 0 \\ D^m y \acute{D}, & R^n y \in D^*. \end{cases}$$

- Suppose $\text{suff}^2(\pi^{\leftarrow}(x)) \in \{DR, RD\}$. Now, stress has already been assigned, so $\alpha^{\leftarrow}(x) = \alpha(x)$ and for all y, $\alpha_x^{\rightarrow}(y) = y$.

In all four cases, we have seen that $\alpha_x^{\rightarrow}$ does not depend on x, though it does depend on $\text{suff}^2(\pi^{\leftarrow}(x))$. Therefore, α is 2-I-3-TISL. $\square$

In the construction described above, the fact that π is allowed to be 2-ISL enables π to only project symbols marking the boundaries between contiguous spans of Ds and Rs. In the original tier-projection mechanism of Heinz et al. (2011), for each symbol $u \in \Sigma$, either all tokens of u must be projected to the tier, or no tokens of u may be projected.

Definition 8. A function is *tier-based j-input strictly local* (j-TISL) if it is 1-I-j-TISL and has a homomorphic tier projection. A function is *tier-based input strictly local* (TISL) if it is j-TISL for some j.

To justify the use of a 2-ISL tier projection, we show that the primitive tier-projection mechanism does not suffice to capture Abkhaz stress.

Proposition 9. *The Abkhaz stress function is not TISL.*

Proof. Let $\pi : \{D, R\}^* \to \{D, R\}^*$ be a homomorphic tier projection. We will show that for every $j > 0$, there exist $x, y, z \in \{D, R\}^*$ such that $\text{suff}^{j-1}(\pi^{\leftarrow}(x)) = \text{suff}^{j-1}(\pi^{\leftarrow}(y))$, but $\alpha_x^{\rightarrow}(z) \neq \alpha_y^{\rightarrow}(z)$.

Fix $j > 0$, and suppose π projects D. Then, $\text{suff}^{j-1}(\pi^{\leftarrow}(D^j)) = \text{suff}^{j-1}(\pi^{\leftarrow}(DRD^j)) = D^{j-1}$, but $\alpha_{D^j}^{\rightarrow}(R) = \acute{D}R$, while $\alpha_{DRD^j}^{\rightarrow}(R) = R$. Next, suppose π projects R. Then, $\text{suff}^{j-1}(\pi^{\leftarrow}(R^j)) = \text{suff}^{j-1}(\pi^{\leftarrow}(DR^j)) = R^{j-1}$, but $\alpha_{R^j}^{\rightarrow}(D) = R\acute{D}$, while $\alpha_{DR^j}^{\rightarrow}(D) = D$. Finally, suppose π projects neither R nor D. Then, $\text{suff}^{j-1}(\pi^{\leftarrow}(R)) = \text{suff}^{j-1}(\pi^{\leftarrow}(DR)) = \rtimes^{j-1}$, but $\alpha_R^{\rightarrow}(D) = R\acute{D}$, while $\alpha_{DR}^{\rightarrow}(D) = D$. Therefore, α is not j-TISL for any j and for any π. $\square$

In addition to exceeding the power of TISL functions, our tier projection is also considerably more sophisticated than the projection used in Baek (2018). There, Baek formalizes LHOL, LHOR, RHOL, and RHOR systems as phonotactic constraints and projects heavy, stressed, word-initial, and word-final syllables to the tier. She achieves this by using the primitive tier-projection mechanism with an augmented alphabet in which

138

syllables are marked as being word-initial, word-final, or word-medial. To avoid feature coding (Rogers, 1997), Baek stipulates that syllables cannot be marked in any other way. Since Dybo's Rule is sensitive to more nuanced structural information, we argue that arbitrary ISL tier projections are required for DO stress systems in general.

4 DS Stress and Weak Determinism

We have now shown that the DO stress system of Abkhaz is I-TISL. This section turns to DS stress systems. Subsection 4.1 introduces the DS stress system of Lhasa Tibetan, and in Subsection 4.2 we show that this stress system is not subsequential. Subsection 4.3 considers two definitions of the weakly deterministic functions, proposed by Heinz and Lai (2013) and McCollum et al. (2018), and argue that the latter definition more naturally describes the Lhasa Tibetan stress system than the former.

4.1 Lhasa Tibetan Stress

We describe here the stress system of Tibetan ([bod], Sino-Tibetan) using data from the Lhasa variety, as described by Dawson (1980). The descriptive generalization about Tibetan stress is as follows: primary stress falls on the leftmost long vowel, and if there are no long vowels, on the leftmost vowel. Stress is indicated with the IPA primary stress diacritic, and long vowels are underlined. Below we illustrate the generalizations about Tibetan stress. All of our data come from Gordon (2007, p. 37), who in turn cites Dawson (1980). The same data can also be found in Odden (1979), who cites personal communication with N. Nornang.

The Lhasa Tibetan stress pattern is illustrated in Tables 4 and 5. When a word contains one or more long vowels, the leftmost long vowel receives the primary stress. When there are no long vowels, the leftmost vowel has primary stress. Thus, this is an example of a DS stress system.

Form	Translation
ám'tô:	'person from Amdo'
kʰá'pá:	'telephone'
'tý:tǔ:	'shirt'

Table 4: The leftmost long vowel receives primary stress.

Form	Translation
'láptá	'school'
'ɲúgú	'pen'
'wòmá	'milk'

Table 5: Default stress is initial.

4.2 Non-Subsequentiality

Intuitively, the behavior of an SFST is to scan its input from left to right, emitting output symbols deterministically as it does so. This paradigm of computation is problematic for DS stress systems such as that of Lhasa Tibetan. In order to determine whether or not the first syllable of its input should be stressed, an SFST implementing Lhasa Tibetan stress must scan the entire input to check for the presence of long vowels. However, once the SFST has determined that an input does not have any long vowels, it no longer has access to the initial syllable, and therefore cannot mark it as stressed. The following discussion makes this intuition rigorous by showing that the Lhasa Tibetan stress system is not subsequential.

We formalize the Lhasa Tibetan stress system as follows. Syllables with long-vowel nuclei are represented as H, while syllables with short-vowel nuclei are represented as L. Stressed syllables are represented as Ḣ and Ĺ, respectively. If an input contains at least one H, then the first H receives stress. Otherwise, the first syllable receives stress.

Definition 10. The *Tibetan stress function* τ : $\{H, L\}^* \to \{H, L, \acute{H}, \acute{L}\}^*$ is defined as follows. For $i \geq 0, j > 0$, and $y \in \{H, L\}^*$,

$$\tau(L^i H y) := L^i \acute{H} y$$
$$\tau(L^j) := \acute{L} L^{j-1}$$
$$\tau(\lambda) := \lambda.$$

Proposition 11. *The Tibetan stress function is not subsequential.*

Proof. We will show that τ has infinitely many translations. Consider a string of the form L^i, where $i > 0$. Observe that $\tau(L^i H) = L^i \acute{H}$ and $\tau(L^i) = \acute{L} L^{i-1}$. Therefore,

$$\text{lcp}(\{\tau(L^i H), \tau(L^i)\}) = \lambda,$$

so $\tau^{\leftarrow}(L^i) = \lambda$, hence $\tau^{\rightarrow}_{L^i}(H) = L^i \acute{H}$. But this means that if $i \neq j$, then

$$L^i \acute{H} = \tau^{\rightarrow}_{L^i}(H) \neq \tau^{\rightarrow}_{L^j}(H) = L^j \acute{H}.$$

Thus, each possible value of i induces a distinct translation $\tau_{\mathrm{L}^i}^{\rightarrow}$, so we conclude that τ is not subsequential. $\qquad\square$

4.3 Weak Determinism

The current subregular approach to non-subsequential processes is represented by the weakly deterministic functions, a class proposed by Heinz and Lai (2013) in order to distinguish the unattested sour grapes harmony process from attested harmony processes.[2] Dominant/recessive and stem-controlled vowel harmony (Heinz and Lai, 2013; McCollum et al., 2018), Tutrugbu ATR harmony (McCollum et al., 2018), and Copperbelt Bemba tone spreading (McCollum et al., 2018; Smith and O'Hara, 2019) have so far been shown to be non-subsequential but weakly deterministic in the sense of Heinz and Lai.

Definition 12 (Heinz and Lai, 2013). A function $f : \Sigma^* \to \Gamma^*$ is *markup-free weakly deterministic* if there exist functions $g : \Sigma^* \to \Sigma^*$ and $h : \Sigma^* \to \Gamma^*$ such that

- $f = h \circ g$;

- either g is left-subsequential and h is right-subsequential or g is right-subsequential and h is left-subsequential; and

- for all $x \in \Sigma^*$, $|g(x)| \leq |x|$.

Elgot and Mezei (1965) show that every finite-state function can be decomposed into a left-subsequential function and a right-subsequential function. In their construction, the first function in the composition encodes state information into its input, which allows the second function to determinize its computation. The above definition attempts to prohibit this kind of encoding by requiring that g cannot introduce new alphabet symbols or increase the length of its input. McCollum et al. (2018) argue that a limited form of state encoding is still possible under Heinz and Lai's criterion, and instead advocate for a more explicit notion of non-interaction between the two functions.

Definition 13 (McCollum et al., 2018). Let $f : \Sigma^* \to \Gamma^*$ be a same-length function.[3] Fix $x \in \Sigma^*$, and write $x = x_1 x_2 \ldots x_n$ and $y = y_1 y_2 \ldots y_n$ so that for each i, $x_i \in \Sigma$ and $y_i \in \Gamma$. The *μ-factors of x with respect to f* are the set

$$\mu(f, x) := \{\langle i, x_i, y_i \rangle | y_i \neq x_i\}.$$

The basic intuition behind McCollum et al.'s criterion is that the two functions in the decomposition cannot feed or bleed one another. They take this to mean that neither function can cause the other to change its behavior for some position of the input.

Definition 14 (McCollum et al., 2018). A function $f : \Sigma^* \to \Gamma^*$ is *interaction-free weakly deterministic* if there exist an alphabet $\Delta \supseteq \Sigma$ and functions $g : \Sigma^* \to \Delta^*$ and $h : \Delta^* \to \Gamma^*$ such that

- $f = h \circ g$;

- either g is left-subsequential and h is right-subsequential or g is right-subsequential and h is left-subsequential; and

- for all $x \in \Sigma^*$, $\mu(f, x) = \mu(g, x) \cup \mu(h, x)$.[4]

This criterion naturally describes the Tibetan stress function. We can decompose this function into a left-subsequential function that assigns stress to the leftmost H and a right-subsequential function that assigns initial stress in the absence of an H. These two functions do not interact, since each only assigns stress if the other does not.

Proposition 15. *The Tibetan stress function is interaction-free weakly deterministic.*

Proof. Let us define $g : \{\mathrm{H, L}\}^* \to \{\mathrm{H, L, \acute{H}}\}^*$ and $h : \{\mathrm{H, L, \acute{H}}\}^* \to \{\mathrm{H, L, \acute{H}, \acute{L}}\}^*$ as follows. For $i \geq 0, y \in \{\mathrm{H, L}\}^*$, and $z \notin \mathrm{L}^+$,

$$g(\mathrm{L}^i \mathrm{H} y) := \mathrm{L}^i \acute{\mathrm{H}} y$$
$$g(\mathrm{L}^i) := \mathrm{L}^i$$
$$h(z) := z$$
$$h(\mathrm{LL}^i) := \acute{\mathrm{L}} \mathrm{L}^i.$$

It is clear that $\tau = h \circ g$, g is left-sequential, and h is right-subsequential. Observe that $h(x) = x$ if $g(x) \neq x$ and $h(x) \neq x$ if $g(x) = x$, so for all x, either $\mu(h, x) = \varnothing$ and $\mu(\tau, x) = \mu(g, x)$ or $\mu(g, x) = \varnothing$ and $\mu(\tau, x) = \mu(h, x)$. Therefore, τ is interaction-free weakly deterministic. $\qquad\square$

---

[2] However, it is currently unknown whether this class of functions is distinct from the class of finite-state functions.

[3] McCollum et al. additionally require that f be sequential. We relax this assumption here.

[4] Note that this criterion implicitly requires that f, g, and h all be same-length.

On the other hand, it is difficult to see how the Tibetan stress function can be made to satisfy Heinz and Lai's definition of weak determinism. The decomposition presented above violates the markup-free criterion because g introduces new alphabet symbols to its input. This is an inherent property of stress assignment, since inputs must be annotated with stress markers. In order to satisfy the markup-free criterion, then, any stress assigned by the first function must be encoded without using a designated stress marker. We conjecture that no such decomposition exists.

5 Discussion

We have now given two separate subregular treatments of DO and DS stress systems. Subsection 5.1 shows how our implementation of the Abkhaz and the Tibetan stress functions mirrors existing phonological analyses of stress systems according to metrical grid theory. Subsection 5.2 discusses the implications of our results for the hierarchy of subregular functions.

5.1 Relation to Metrical Grid Theory

The use of tiers and tier projection functions to investigate phonological complexity is of course not novel. One way of analyzing stress is in terms of so-called *metrical grids* (Liberman, 1975; Hayes, 1995; Kager, 1995; and many others), which are effectively tiers stacked on top of each other. The tiers of metrical grids correspond closely with the tiers used in this paper. In other words, our analysis aligns well with previous analyses of stress. Below we explain metrical grids, and highlight some similarities with the present paper.

The metrical grid below represents the word ˌælə'bæmə 'Alabama' (Kager, 1995, p. 369). Tier 2 identifies the primary stress, tier 1 indicates all stresses, whether primary or secondary, and tier 0 shows the division of the word into syllables.

```
Tier 2            *
Tier 1   *        *
Tier 0   *    *   *    *
         æ    lə  bæ   mə
```

Figure 1: The metrical grid for ˌælə'bæmə 'Alabama.'

Metrical grids can be used to understand the stress systems of Abkhaz and Lhasa Tibetan. The brief overview below follows Kager (1995), which interested readers should consult for a detailed

analysis of both DO and DS systems. For Abkhaz, we begin with a tier 0 where D syllables have two asterisks, and R syllables one. In addition to the final syllable, any ∗∗ on tier 0 not immediately followed by another ∗∗ projects onto tier 1. Finally, the leftmost tier 1 asterisk projects onto tier 2. This gives grids like the one in Figure 2, for the word a-'ʁʷak'ʲaməsa 'the poniard.'

```
Tier 2          *
Tier 1          *           *    *
Tier 0   **    **    *    **    *
         a    ʁʷa   k'ʲa  mə   sa
```

Figure 2: The metrical grid for a-'ʁʷak'ʲaməsa 'the poniard.'

As we saw for English, a tier 2 asterisk identifies the primary stress. It is not clear whether tier 1 asterisks encode secondary stress in Abkhaz, but there are segmental alternations between [ə] and [∅] that are affected by tier 1 (see Spruit, 1986, pp. 73–77).

For words with no dominant syllables, such as maa-'k'ə 'one handle,' we simply project the rightmost syllable from tier 0 onto tier 1. Again, the leftmost (and only) tier 1 asterisk projects onto tier 2.

```
Tier 2                *
Tier 1                *
Tier 0   *    *    *
         ma   a   k'ə
```

Figure 3: The metrical grid for maa-'k'ə 'one handle.'

For Lhasa Tibetan, we have no underlying accentual specifications, but instead place either one or two asterisks on tier 0 depending on whether the vowel is short or long. The leftmost tier 0 ∗∗ is projected onto tier 1.[5] The leftmost ∗ of tier 1 projects onto tier 2, indicating primary stress. For 'týːtûː 'shirt,' this gives the following.

```
Tier 2   *
Tier 1   *    *
Tier 0   **   **
         týː  tûː
```

Figure 4: The metrical grid for 'týːtûː 'shirt.'

---

[5]We are not aware of data on secondary stress.

In words without any long vowels, the same system produces the desired result. The word in Figure 5 is 'wòmá 'milk.' By convention, since tier 1 is empty, we project the leftmost $*$ of tier 0 instead (Kager, 1995, pp. 384–385).

```
Tier 2    *
Tier 1
Tier 0    *    *
          wò   má
```

Figure 5: The metrical grid for 'wòmá 'milk.'

In the analysis of Abkhaz, the projection of tier 1 mirrors the tier projection used in Proposition 7: both the asterisks and the projected Ds and Rs mark the location of Ds not followed by Rs, and both projections are ISL. The projection of tier 2 is ISL if tier 1 is taken to be the input, in the same way that the Abkhaz stress function reflects a strictly local dependency enforced over an ISL tier. In the analysis of Tibetan, the decomposition of τ into g and h is analogous to the convention that tier 2 is projected from tier 0 if tier 1 is empty.

5.2 The Subregular Hierarchy

Our work makes two contributions to the study of the subregular hierarchy. Firstly, our definition of the I-TISL functions naturally incorporates the notion of tier projection developed by Graf and Mayer (2018) into the family of strictly local functions proposed by Chandlee (2014), Chandlee et al. (2015), and Chandlee et al. (In prep). Secondly, we have presented an argument based on stress assignment that McCollum et al.'s (2018) definition of weak determinism is more natural for computational phonology than that of Heinz and Lai (2013).

Intuitively, the difference between DO and DS stress systems is that the former has a consistent directionality, while the latter does not. In our implementation of the Akbhaz stress function, the input is scanned from left to right, and when no appropriate D syllable is found, default final stress is assigned at the end of the computation. Thus, the Abkhaz stress function may be viewed as a "left-to-right" process. The contribution of weak determinism to the Tibetan stress function is that the right-subsequential component allows the process to "change direction" when no H syllable is found. If bidirectionality is the primary contribution of weak determinism to subregular phonology, then

it may be desirable to impose additional structure on the two components of a weakly deterministic function. In Proposition 15, for example, g is 2-TISL, while h is right 1, 1-IOSL.

6 Conclusion

This paper has considered unbounded stress systems in relation to the subregular hierarchy for functions. We have shown that the functions for assigning default-to-opposite (DO) and default-to-same (DS) stress are not part of the same subregular classes. The DO stress function in Abkhaz is subsequential, and belongs to the input tier-based input strictly local (I-TISL) class, which also captures other DO stress systems. The tiers and tier projection functions that we use are linguistically interpretable, sharing many properties with the phonological representations used in metrical analyses of stress. However, we have seen that the DS stress function in Lhasa Tibetan is not subsequential. DS stress can instead be captured using the class of weakly deterministic functions, and therefore we favor McCollum et al.'s (2018) definition of weak determinism over that of Heinz and Lai (2013).

References

Hyunah Baek. 2018. Computational representation of unbounded stress: Tiers with structural features. In *Proceedings of CLS 53 (2017)*, volume 53, pages 13–24, Chicago, IL. Chicago Linguistic Society.

Jane Chandlee. 2014. *Strictly Local Phonological Processes*. PhD Dissertation, University of Delaware, Newark, DE.

Jane Chandlee, Rémi Eyraud, and Jeffrey Heinz. 2015. Output Strictly Local Functions. In *Proceedings of the 14th Meeting on the Mathematics of Language*, pages 112–125, Chicago, IL. Association for Computational Linguistics.

Jane Chandlee, Rémi Eyraud, and Jeffrey Heinz. In prep. Input–output strictly local functions and their efficient learnability.

Willa Dawson. 1980. *Tibetan Phonology*. PhD Dissertation, University of Washington, Seattle, WA.

Vladimir Antonovič Dybo. 1977. Западнокавказкая акцентная система и проблема ее происхождения. In *Конференция «Ностратические языки и ностратическое языкознание»: Тезисы докладов*, pages 41–45, Moscow, Soviet Union. USSR Academy of Sciences.

Calvin C. Elgot and Jorge E. Mezei. 1965. On Relations Defined by Generalized Finite Automata. *IBM Journal of Research and Development*, 9(1):47–68.

Matthew Gordon. 2007. *Syllable Weight: Phonetics, Phonology, Typology*. Routledge, London, United Kingdom.

Thomas Graf and Connor Mayer. 2018. Sanskrit n-Retroflexion is Input-Output Tier-Based Strictly Local. In *Proceedings of the Fifteenth Workshop on Computational Research in Phonetics, Phonology, and Morphology*, pages 151–160, Brussels, Belgium. Association for Computational Linguistics.

Bruce Hayes. 1995. *Metrical Stress Theory: Principles and Case Studies*. University of Chicago Press, Chicago, IL.

Jeffrey Heinz and Regine Lai. 2013. Vowel Harmony and Subsequentiality. In *Proceedings of the 13th Meeting on the Mathematics of Language (MoL 13)*, pages 52–63, Sofia, Bulgaria. Association for Computational Linguistics.

Jeffrey Heinz, Chetan Rawal, and Herbert G. Tanner. 2011. Tier-based Strictly Local Constraints for Phonology. In *Proceedings of the 49th Annual Meeting of the Association for Computational Linguistics: Human Language Technologies*, pages 58–64, Portland, OR. Association for Computational Linguistics.

René Kager. 1995. The Metrical Theory of Word Stress. In John A. Goldsmith, editor, *The Handbook of Phonological Theory*, 1 edition, Blackwell Handbooks in Linguistics, pages 367–402. Wiley-Blackwell, Oxford, United Kingdom.

Mark Yoffe Liberman. 1975. *The Intonational System of English*. PhD Dissertation, Massachusetts Institute of Technology, Cambridge, MA.

Connor Mayer and Travis Major. 2018. A Challenge for Tier-Based Strict Locality from Uyghur Backness Harmony. In *Formal Grammar 2018, 23rd International Conference, FG 2018, Sofia, Bulgaria, August 11-12, 2018, Proceedings*, volume 10950 of *Lecture Notes in Computer Science*, pages 62–83, Berlin, Germany. Springer Berlin Heidelberg.

Adam McCollum, Eric Baković, Anna Mai, and Eric Meinhardt. 2018. The expressivity of segmental phonology and the definition of weak determinism. *LingBuzz*, lingbuzz/004197.

David Odden. 1979. Principles of Stress Assignment: A Crosslinguistic View. *Studies in the Linguistic Sciences*, 9(1):157–176.

José Oncina, Pedro Garcia, and Enrique Vidal. 1993. Learning Subsequential Transducers for Pattern Recognition Interpretation Tasks. *IEEE Transactions on Pattern Analysis and Machine Intelligence*, 15(5):448–458.

George N. Raney. 1958. Sequential Functions. *Journal of the Association for Computing Machinery*, 5(2):177–180.

James Rogers. 1997. Strict LT_2 : Regular :: Local : Recognizable. In *Logical Aspects of Computational Linguistics: First International Conference, LACL '96 Nancy, France, September 23-25, 1996 Selected Papers*, volume 1328 of *Lecture Notes in Computer Science*, pages 366–385, Berlin, Germany. Springer Berlin Heidelberg.

Jacques Sakarovitch. 2009. *Elements of Automata Theory*. Cambridge University Press, Cambridge, United Kingdom.

Caitlin Smith and Charlie O'Hara. 2019. Formal Characterizations of True and False Sour Grapes. In *Proceedings of the Society for Computation in Linguistics*, volume 2, pages 338–341, Amherst, MA. ScholarWorks@UMass Amherst.

Arie Spruit. 1986. *Abkhaz Studies*. PhD Dissertation, Leiden University, Leiden, Netherlands.

Loren Trigo. 1992. Abkhaz Stress Shift. In Brian George Hewitt, editor, *Caucasian Perspectives*, pages 191–235. Lincom Europa, Munich, Germany.

Data mining Mandarin tone contour shapes

Shuo Zhang

CED Applied Research

Bose Corporation

The Mountain Rd, Framingham, MA 01701

shuo_zhang@bose.com

Abstract

In spontaneous speech, Mandarin tones that belong to the same tone category may exhibit many different contour shapes. We explore the use of data mining and NLP techniques for understanding the variability of tones in a large corpus of Mandarin newscast speech. First, we adapt a graph-based approach to characterize the clusters (fuzzy types) of tone contour shapes observed in each tone n-gram category. Second, we show correlations between these realized contour shape types and a bag of automatically extracted linguistic features. We discuss the implications of the current study within the context of phonological and information theory.

1 Introduction

One of the central phenomena of interest in lexical tone production is the deviation of their surface realizations from canonical templates of tone categories(Xu, 1997; Prom-on et al., 2009; Surendran, 2007). In a tone language, different tone categories differing in pitch movements can distinguish different lexical meanings of a syllable (e.g., in Mandarin, the syllable "ma" in a high level pitch contour means "mother", whereas the same syllable spoken in a falling pitch contour means "to scold"). Even though each tone category is defined with a general pitch contour profile (such as level, rising, falling, etc.), they typically exhibit great variability in spontaneous speech. As an example, Figure 1 shows many different realizations of Mandarin tone 1, observed during speech production experiments in the lab.

Previous works in phonology, speech prosody, and tone recognition have investigated this variability by asking questions such as: (1) What factors contribute to the variability in tone production (Xu, 1997)?(2) How can we model the tone contour trajectory in synthesized speech (Prom-on

et al., 2009)? (3) What features can we use to improve the accuracy of automatic tone recognition (Surendran, 2007)? Each of the works was driven by a particular set of theoretical or practical motivations and offered us a slice of understanding into the problem.

In this work, we are interested in looking at the tone variability problem from a data mining perspective: we explore the structure and distribution of tone contour shapes within a large amount of data. By taking a data mining approach, we contrast our work with those works that focus on tone recognition or tone learning (either by machine or by human): we seek to extract tone patterns of empirical significance from a large data set of tones from spontaneous speech.

Working with the MCPST corpus (see Section 3) of Mandarin newscast speech (about 100,000 tones), we ask two questions: (1) For each tone category, what are the (coarse) types/classes of tone contour shapes we observe in this corpus? (2) For a particular tone category, what linguistic factors caused the same tone to be realized as these different types of shapes?

Inspired by works in natural language processing (NLP), we further extend these research questions in two directions. First, we extend our investigation of tone categories into a series of n consecutive tones, or tone n-grams. N-grams is a classic technique in NLP language modeling[1], whereas in the current context, we study tone n-grams due to the importance of context in tone variability (Xu, 1997): a tone category maybe realized differently depending on their neighboring tones. What can we learn from data mining tone contour shapes for tone unigrams, bigrams, and trigrams?

Second, to study prosody interface in MCPST

---

[1]Readers may refer to the classic NLP textbook chapter if needed: https://web.stanford.edu/ jurafsky/slp3/3.pdf.

Proceedings of the 16th Workshop on Computational Research in Phonetics, Phonology, and Morphology, pages 144–153
Florence, Italy. August 2, 2019 ©2019 Association for Computational Linguistics

data, we use automatic methods (NLP and other) to extract linguistic features from the text, including Named Entity Recognition (NER), Coreference resolution, Part-of-speech (POS) tagging, dependency parsing, and other phonological, morphological and contextual features. In order to find out the importance of these linguistic factors in shaping tone variability, we run the following experiment: given a particular tone (or tone n-gram) category, how well can we predict the type of tone contour shape it will take in running speech, using these linguistic features that *exclude* information about the pitch contour $f0$ values?

Previous works showed that many linguistic factors (such as focus, topic, etc.) affect tone production or prosody (see Section 2) . In this work, we extend this to a more comprehensive set of linguistic features, motivated by the information theory account of tone production. We hypothesize that there exists an information content inequality resulting from probability distribution of events in various linguistic domains (phonological, semantic, etc). These inequalities affect speakers' speech production, resulting in gradient variants of tone contour shapes in a given tone category. We investigate the relative importance of these factors in predicting the types of contour shapes any particular tone n-gram will take.

The rest of the paper is organized as follows. Section 2 discusses relevant previous works. Next we describe the data used in this paper in Section 3. In order to characterize the types of contour shapes a tone n-gram will take, we develop a method to derive clusters of tone contour shape types using network analysis (Section 4). In Section 5, we discuss feature engineering and feature extraction from various linguistic domains (syntax, morphology, semantics, information structure, etc.). Section 6 reports machine learning experiments and results on predicting tone contour shape types and the analysis on feature importance. Finally, in Section 7 we discuss the implications of this work in the context of information theory and phonological theory of speech and tone production.

2   Related Work

There has been a long line of research on the variability of tone contour shapes as well as interfacing between other linguistic factors and prosody (Li, 2009; Buring, 2013). In linguistic research

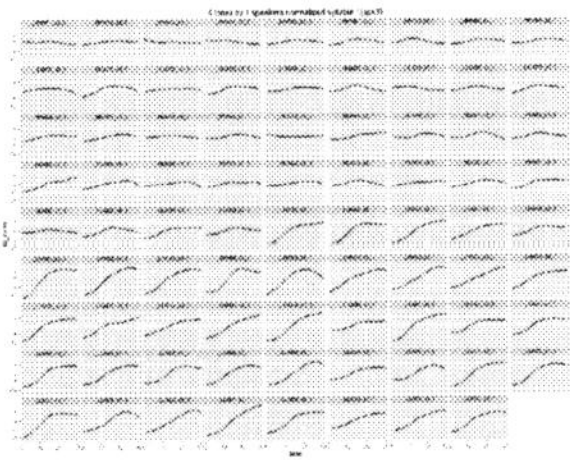

Figure 1: Samples of Mandarin Tone1 by the same speaker in lab speech. Data source: (Xu, 1997). The canonical contours of Mandarin Tone 1,2,3,4 are: high level, low rising, low dipping, high falling, where low and high denote the pitch starting point of the tone.

of Mandarin tones, most works have focused on the effect of local tonal context (e.g., neighboring tones and pitch range, such as (Gauthier et al., 2007; Xu, 1997)) and broader context (e.g., focus, topic, information structure, long term f_0 variations, such as (Xu et al., 2004; Liu et al., 2006; Wang and Xu, 2011)). The data in these works usually consisted of a small number of tone observations obtained in speech production experiments in the lab. They have informed later works on improving the performance of supervised or unsupervised tone recognition ((Levow, 2005; Surendran, 2007) etc.). Other works such as (Surendran, 2007) and (Yu, 2011) have shown the importance of signals in speech outside of f_0 for tone recognition and learning.

In the PENTA (Xu, 1997, 2005) and qTA (quantitative target approximation) models (Prom-on et al., 2009), the surface f_0 contour is viewed as the result of asymptotic approximation to an underlying pitch target, which can be a static target (High or Low) or a dynamic target (Rise or Fall). An important contribution of the qTA is that it provides a mathematical model to account for the process of generating of a particular realization of a tone template, defined by a pitch target (with slope and intercept parameters) and the acceleration rate. As such, the specific shape of the contour then would depend on the starting pitch, ending pitch target, and how fast the pitch moves.

A fundamental theoretical question is how should we view the underlying factors that account for the tone surface variability. Previous research exhibits two opposing theories to this question. The first approach (Cooper et al., 1985; Cooper and Sorenson, 1981) postulates a direct link between communicative functions and surface acoustic forms by finding the acoustic correlates of certain communicative functions, such as focus, stress, newness, questions, etc. Such approaches have met criticisms from phonologists (Ladd, 1996; Liberman and Pierrehumbert, 1984), who argue that prosodic meanings are not directly mapped onto acoustic correlates. Instead, intonational meanings should be first mapped onto phonological structures, which is in turn linked to surface acoustic forms through phonetic implementation rules. In this work, we attempt to show a new middle ground between these two theories.

3 Data

All the data in this work comes from the Mandarin Chinese Phonetic Segmentation and Tone (MCPST) corpus [2], developed by the Linguistic Data Consortium (LDC). It contains 7,849 Mandarin Chinese newscast speech "utterances" and their phonetic segmentation and tone labels. Utterances are defined as the time-stamped between-pause units in the transcribed news recordings. We used the auto-correlation algorithm implemented in Praat [3] for f_0 (pitch) estimation from speech audio signal. We obtained f_0 pitch contour data for 100,161 syllables. After pre-processing the pitch tracks (e.g., speaker-dependent normalization, f_0 outlier detection and removal, pitch interpolation, downsampling), we generate tone unigram, bigram and trigram f_0 data sets, giving rise to a total of 75 unigram (5), bigram (16), and trigram data sets for the prediction task (54) [4]. The total number of tone n-grams in these data sets are on the order of 250k. All tone unigram, bigram, and trigram f_0 vectors are downsampled to length of 30, 100, and 200 samples respectively.

4 Deriving tone n-gram contour shape types through network analysis

4.1 Problem formulation

We define a tone n-gram category as a consecutive sequence of n tones t_i, for $i = 1, ..., n$, where $t_i \in \{0, 1, 2, 3, 4\}$, the five tone categories of Mandarin. In this paper we restrict n to $\{1, 2, 3\}$.

Given the set S (represented as a network) that contains all observations of f_0 vectors that belong to a particular tone n-gram category, an algorithm A, defined in this section, partitions S into k clusters, $c_1, c_2, ..., c_k$, where all tone contours within c_i are highly similar to each other, and members of c_i maximally distinct from c_j for $i \neq j$. For a particular tone n-gram category, we define the centroid f_0 vector of c_i to be its tone contour shape type t_i.

If we denote C to be set of types $\{c_1, c_2, ..., c_k\}$, our goal in this section is to describe the algorithm A that learns a function $g : S \to C$. We adapt an algorithm first proposed by (Gulati et al., 2016), which has been shown to be effective in identifying clusters in time-series data such as pitch contours. It also has several advantages over baseline algorithms such as k-means clustering, including outlier pruning and no need to determine the number of clusters before hand.

On a high level, this method represents all tone contours in a data set as a fully connected network G. It then filters G using heuristics based on the pairwise similarity of tone contour shapes. After the filtering step, only those nodes that have a similarity score beyond a threshold will remain connected. It then leverages network community detection algorithms to optimize the community structure, effectively deriving tone contour shape types $T = \{t_1, t_2, ..., t_k\}$.

4.2 Network construction

To construct the network as described above, we first partition all data in MCPST corpus by their tone n-gram category. For each category, we construct a network where each node stores the f_0 vector of an observation, and the edge between two nodes holds the Euclidean distance between the two f_0 vectors as weights. We derive an undirected, weighted and fully connected network G of tone n-gram patterns for each n-gram category.

4.3 Network filtering

In this step, we take a fully connected network G of a given tone n-gram category and use a principled method to remove edges from the network. Our goal is to find an appropriate threshold so that all edges whose weights (distance between two tone n-gram f_0 vectors) are greater than the threshold will be cut. In the resulting network, only those nodes representing similar enough tone contour shapes will remain connected.

---

[2]https://catalog.ldc.upenn.edu/LDC2015S05

[3]Boersma, Paul and Weenink, David (2019). Praat: doing phonetics by computer [Computer program]. Version 6.0.48, retrieved 17 February 2019 from http://www.praat.org/

[4]Mandarin Chinese has four regular tone categories plus one neutral tone. Since neutral tones occurs infrequently, we did not include them in the analysis of tone bigrams and trigrams due to data sparsity in the conditional distributions. Similarly, we also excluded ngrams categories where the data points are sparse.

Specifically, we decide the threshold value by a six-step process: (1) We search for the appropriate threshold in the set of values $\Phi \in \{1.0, 1.5, 2.0, 2.5, 3.0, 3.5, 4.0, 4.5\}$ for bigrams and trigrams, $\Phi \in \{0.2, 0.4, 0.6, 0.8\}$ for unigrams. These values are empirically chosen; (2) we iterate over this set of values and each time apply a threshold to the network; (3) after we applied the threshold we convert the network to a unweighted network G' where only those nodes that have a distance below the threshold will remain connected; (4) we produce a randomized network G_r by randomly swapping edges from G' k times while keeping the degree of the nodes constant, where k is equal to the number of edges in G'. This can be seen as producing a maximally random network given the degree distribution of the current network; (5) we compute the difference in Clustering Coefficient (CC) of both G' and G_r; (6) after repeating this for all values in T, we pick the threshold that has the largest difference of CCs. [5]

4.4 Community detection

We use the Louvain algorithm (Blondel et al., 2008) to perform community detection, in order to partition the filtered network derived from last step into communities (clusters) $C_1, C_2, ..., C_k$. We pre-tuned the hyperparameters in the network filtering step so that it will result in a small number ($n < 10$) of tightly connected medium-sized communities. Figure 2 shows a histogram of number of shape classes for unigram, bigram, and trigram data sets.

4.5 Outlier community filtering

We propose an extra step of outlier community filtering before deriving our final contour profile classes. In this step, we use a heuristic threshold of $t = 10$ to filter out any communities (clusters) with a size less than t.

4.6 Evaluation of tone contour profile classes

We have leveraged the intrinsic structure of the tone data to derive the tone contour shape types for

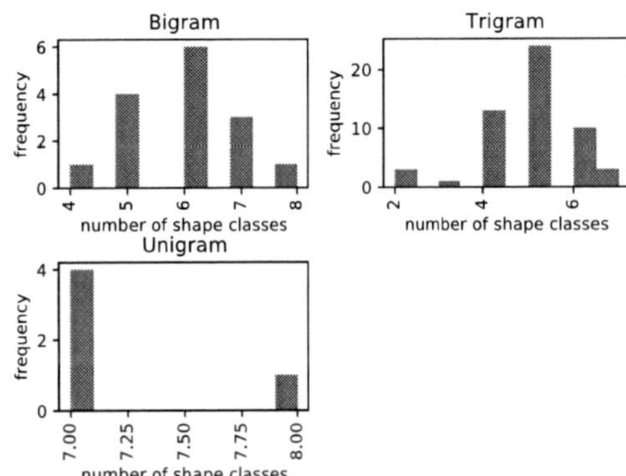

Figure 2: Histogram of number of shape classes in n-gram data sets.

each tone n-gram category. Figure 3 shows examples of learned clusters of tone contour shape types from two n-gram categories of tone unigram, bigram, and trigram, respectively. Without declaring any cognitive or phonological significance of these clusters, these resulting clusters should reflect the similarities of tone contour shapes within any given tone n-gram category: those that are highly similar are grouped into the same cluster. This is an intrinsic property derived from the above method, and is a necessary property sufficient for carrying out the subsequent experiment on predicting the tone contour shape types from linguistic factors.

Nonetheless, we propose two different ways to evaluate the validity of these clusters. First, in the following experiments, we show that we are able to predict these learned tone contour shape types significantly better than randomly assigned clusters (Section 6.2, Figure 4). Second, we train a decision tree classifier to predict the shape type of a given tone n-gram using its f_0 vector and obtained a mean accuracy of 92% (following (Zhang, 2016)). This indicates how well these tone contour shape types can be predicted *with* complete information of its pitch trajectory, which will serve as an upper bound to our next prediction task using linguistic factors *without* information about pitch movements f_0 values.

5 Linguistic features

After we obtained tone contour shape types emerged from each tone n-gram category in the corpus, we now describe the linguistic features used to predict which type of shape the tone n-

---

[5] Clustering coefficient (CC) measures the extent to which the nodes in a network tend to cluster together. Intuitively, it expresses how saturated the network is — how many of the possible connections are actually expressed. The CC for a network of k nodes and n edges is computed as:

$$CC = \frac{2n}{k(k-1)}$$

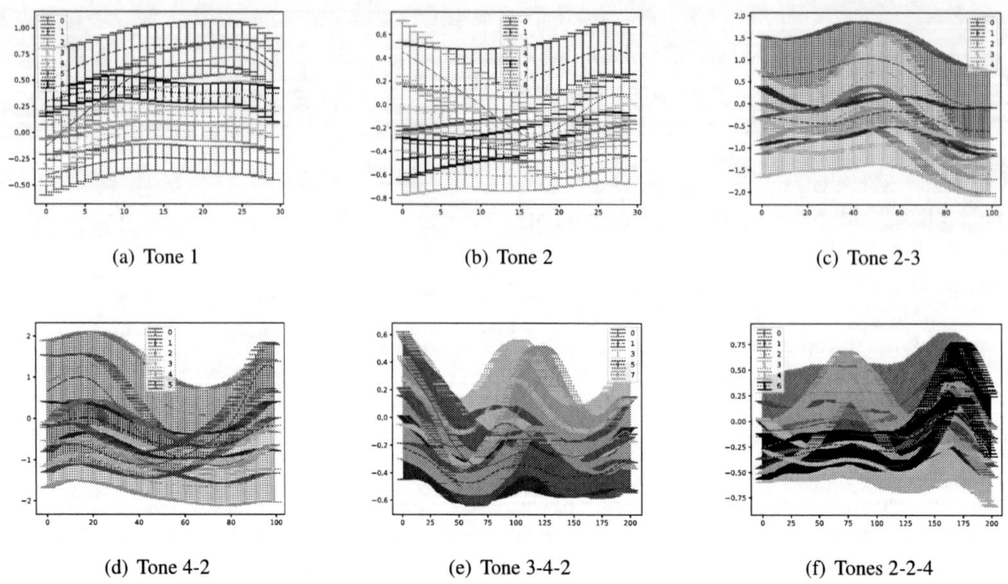

(a) Tone 1   (b) Tone 2   (c) Tone 2-3

(d) Tone 4-2   (e) Tone 3-4-2   (f) Tones 2-2-4

Figure 3: Example contour shape type clusters found in randomly selected tone n-gram categories, with two examples from each of tone unigram, bigram, and trigram. Each cluster is represented by a mean pitch vector with error bars (as shown in the legend). Clusters are indexed by integers shown in legend. X-axis shows number of samples (discrete time index) for the tone contour f_0 vector. Y-axis shows the speaker-normalized pitch values.

gram will take. All syntactic and semantic features are extracted using Stanford CoreNLP for Chinese (Manning et al., 2014).

5.1 Syntactic features

Syntax and prosody has been the subject of investigation in (psycho)linguistic studies (Bard and Aylett, 1999). We extract the part-of-speech (POS) tags for all syllables in a tone n-gram. In addition, we also extract the dependency function (Chen and Manning, 2014) of all syllables in the tone n-gram. Therefore there are $2 * N$ syntactic features where N is the number of syllables included in the tone n-gram data under consideration. The original tag set used in CoreNLP comes from Penn Chinese Treebank[6] and is too fine grained. To avoid data sparseness, we collapsed several categories. For both POS tags and dependency edge function categories, we compute their distributions using the original tag set and we collapse any categories that appear less than 5 times in the data. For POS tags we mapped the original 33 tags onto 5 categories. For dependency functions, we collapsed all tags with a subcategory separated by a colon (e.g., "advmod:loc", "advmod:rcomp", mapped to

______
⁶https://catalog.ldc.upenn.edu/LDC2013T21

"advmod" etc.).

5.2 Semantic features

We extract two semantic features for a tone n-gram data point: (1) whether the tone n-gram includes a named entity; (2) whether the tone n-gram includes a singleton (as opposed to being part of a coreference chain in the discourse). Semantic features such as information structure have been postulated to have an effect on the prosody domain (Buring, 2013). In particular, given information may encode prosodic features different from new information. This could also apply to named entities vs. non-named entities. Named entities points to definite, specific objects in the real world. Whether the token is a singleton (i.e., does not co-refer to an entity with another mention in the text) or part of a coreference chain can be correlated with information structure (Recasens et al., 2013). That is, a singleton may signify new information in discourse, while a non-singleton is part of a coreference chain with potential antecedent or anaphor, pointing to potentially a different information structure. Both can have distinguishing effects on the mental representations and the production of speech prosody (indirectly related to redundancy in (Aylett and Turk, 2004)).

5.3 Morphological features

In Mandarin Chinese, each word usually consists of one to four syllables. Building on the intuition that the first syllable is usually spoken with higher prominence (e.g., neutral tone, which does not carry stress, only occurs on word-final positions), we extract morphological features for each syllable in the given tone n-gram: whether they cross word boundary or not. There are n features in this category in total.

5.4 Phonological features

A basic representation of phonological features is the identity of phonemes in each syllable of the n-gram. However, due to the sparseness of this feature representation, we have designed 7 binary features to encode the phonological properties of the syllables in the tone n-gram: (1) whether the syllable includes a nasal; (2) whether the syllable includes a dipthong; (3) whether the syllable includes a high vowel; (4) whether the syllable includes a low vowel; (5) whether the syllable includes a front vowel; (6) whether the syllable includes a back vowel; (7) whether the syllable includes a round vowel. In addition, we add two contextual tone features: the tone identity of the previous and following syllables of the tone n-gram in question.

5.5 Other features

We add two pitch features to the feature set: the beginning and ending pitch of the tone n-gram. This is based on the notion in generative Mandarin tone modeling (Parallel ENcoding and Target Approximation model, or PENTA) that in speech production, the actual realized tone shape of a given tone category highly depends on the starting point of the pitch contour and its distance to the actual pitch target of the current tone, which affects its course of trajectory when it approximates the target (Prom-on et al., 2009). An additional feature to be included is the position of the current tone n-gram within the context of the current sentence as a percentage. It is a known effect that pitch tends to downdrift in speech production as sentence progresses (Wang and Xu, 2011). Therefore, we also want to account for the effect of sentence position.

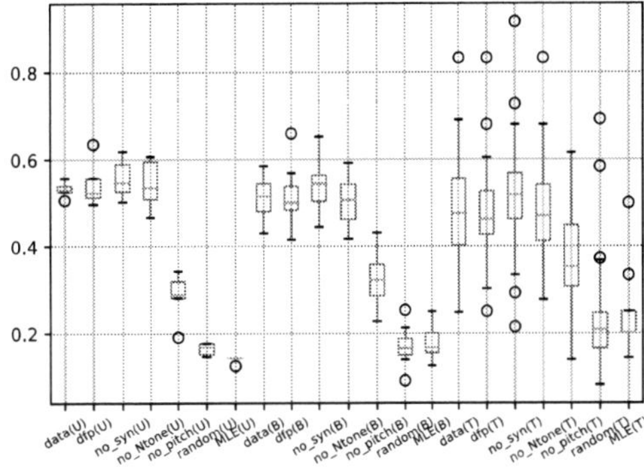

Figure 4: Distribution of classification accuracies for all 75 data sets in unigram(U), bigram(B), trigram(T). For each n-gram the labels on the x-axis are: data:full feature set; dfp:start/end pitch only baseline; no_syn:without syntactic features; no_Ntone:without prev/next tone features; no_pitch:without start/end pitch features; random:baseline with randomly assigned labels; MLE:MLE baseline.

5.6 Bag of features

In this task, we note that the unit of feature extraction is not as straightforward as it would be in classic NLP tasks. That is, instead of a typical syntactic constituent (word, phrase, sentences) as the feature extraction unit, here, our target is tone n-gram, a sequence of n syllables that may or may not be a syntactic constituent. As described above, in many features we have adopted a "Bag of features" approach (similar to the speech coreference resolution work in Roesiger et al. (Röesiger and Riester, 2015)) where each feature describes whether the n-gram contains a certain target value in any position. For some other features, we simply use a set of n features applied to each syllable in the n-gram in question. These are precisely described in Table 1.

6 Predicting tone contour profiles

6.1 Experimental setup

For each of the 5 unigram, 16 bigram, and 54 trigram data sets, the extracted linguistic feature vector $(f_1, f_2, ..., f_m)$ forms the input space X. The contour shape types T forms the output space Y. Our goal is to learn a function $h : X \rightarrow Y$ minimizing expected loss. We use SVM with linear kernel so that we can extract feature importance in subsequent analyses. Each data set is randomly split into 90/10 for train and test. Since the classes

Table 1: Feature set overview. 1...N indicates this feature is computed for all syllables in the N-gram. Total number is N*10+7 features, 37 for trigrams and 27 for bigrams, etc.

Syntactic	Morphological	Semantic	Phonological	Others
$POS\_Tag_{1...N}$	$Tok\_Bound_{1...N}$	is_entity	$is\_nasal_{1...N}$	sent_position
$Dep\_Func_{1...N}$		is_singleton	$is\_dipthong_{1...N}$	start_pitch
			$is\_round_{1...N}$	end_pitch
			$is\_front_{1...N}$	prev_tone
			$is\_back_{1...N}$	next_tone
			$is\_high_{1...N}$	
			$is\_low_{1...N}$	

are balanced in Y, we evaluate the classifier performance directly with accuracy on the test sets.

6.2 Results

To visualize model performances on a large number of tone n-gram data sets (75), we choose the boxplot because of its efficiency to convey statistical information of the distribution of the results across all data sets. Figure 4 gives an overview of our proposed model classification accuracies for all unigram(U), bigram(B), and trigram(T) data sets, as compared to several baselines. In this figure, data, dfp, no_syn, no_Ntone, and no_pitch denote results using different sets of features: full set, start/end pitch only, no syntactic features, no prev/next tone features, and no start/end pitch features, respectively. The random baseline uses the same set of linguistic features as our proposed model but the target tone contour shape type is randomly assigned (while keeping the number of shape types constant). Finally, the Maximum Likelihood Estimation (MLE) baseline reflects chance level performance if linguistic factors are independent from the output tone contour shape types, and is calculated as $1/d$, where d is the number of output classes in a data set.

First, the proposed model significantly outperforms MLE baselines for unigrams, bigrams, and trigrams. Second, the accuracy for predicting learned tone contour shape types is significantly higher than randomly assigned clusters. This serves as a sanity check for the validity of these learned tone contour shape types. Overall, this result supports the hypothesis that a variety of linguistic and contextual features are strongly correlated with the realization of a particular category of tone n-grams. In particular, we observe that using the set of features excluding the syntactic features (POS tags and dependency functions) allows the model to achieve the best median accuracy in

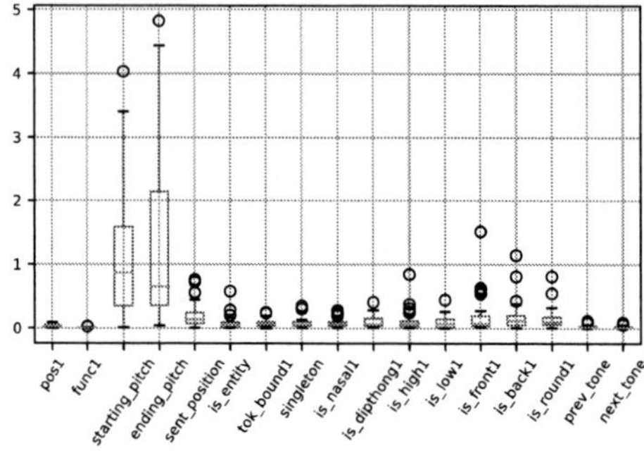

Figure 5: Feature weights for all unigram data sets.

all n-grams (no_syn baseline). In Section 6.3, we provide a more detailed analysis and discussion of feature importance.

A significant trend to note in Figure 4 is that we observe a negative correlation between the model accuracy and the baseline (MLE, random) accuracy as the value of n becomes larger in n-grams. This is striking because it indicates a decrease in predictive power as n grows larger. Moreover, the variance on model accuracy also increases as n becomes larger. From inspecting the tone contour shape types we obtained (such as those showed in Figure 3), we attribute this to three factors from the data perspective: (1) the dimensionality of unigram, bigram, and trigram f_0 vectors in our data set are different (increase); (2) the number of data sets also increases as n grew larger; (3) the complexity of tone contour shapes tend to increase from unigram to bigram to trigram. On a linguistic level, we hypothesize that the longer the window of n-grams, the stronger an effect of unaccounted factors come into play (longer range prosodic factors such as focus and topic, as demonstrated in (Xu et al., 2004)).

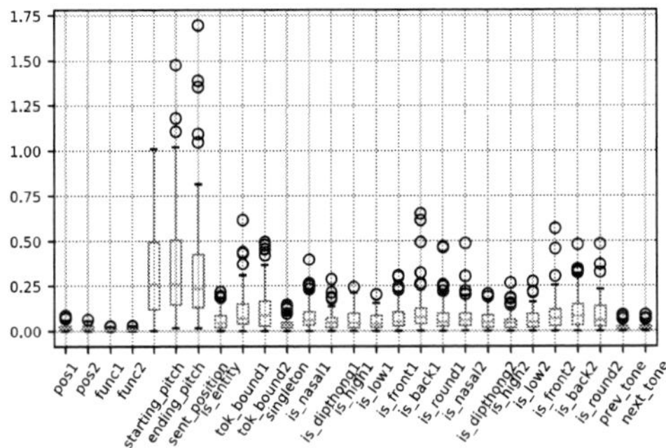

Figure 6: Feature weights for all bigram data sets.

6.3 Feature importance

To analyze feature importance, we extracted weight vectors (coefficients) associated with all features in the linear SVM classifiers (following (Guyon et al., 2002)) for all data sets in each of the n-grams. We take the absolute values of feature weights and normalize them to be comparable across data sets. We then aggregated feature weights for all classes and across all data sets in a given n-gram.

Figure 5, 6, 7 show the distribution of feature weights (importance) for all features for unigram, brigram, and trigram data. Since feature importance values tend to behave similarly according to their linguistic domains, we group them together instead of analyzing the features individually. We observe three levels of feature importance based on the weights, consistent among different n-grams: (1) High: starting pitch, ending pitch, and sentence position (especially when $n > 1$). The importance of starting and ending pitch is consistent with the qTA model of Mandarin tones (Prom-on et al., 2009). The latter (sentence position) is consistent with the effect of downdrift (Wang and Xu, 2011). (2) Medium: Phonological features and morphological token boundary features, as well as coreference (singleton) and entity, which are information structure of the discourse and semantics (givenness, newness of information in speech). (3) Low: Syntactic (pos tag, dependency functions) and contextual features (previous and next tone). This is consistent with (Bard and Aylett, 1999) and (Surendran, 2007)[7].

---

[7]Specifically, (Bard and Aylett, 1999) showed the dissociation of syntax with de-accent in spontaneous speech, and (Surendran, 2007) showed that context did not help tone

To have a more detailed understanding of the feature importance, Figure 4 shows how the model performs with partially ablated feature sets across different n-grams. First, to understand the role of start/end pitch vs. non-pitch linguistic features, we observe that the `dfp` baseline (using only start/end pitch features) has lower results than other models with linguistic features. This is true for all the markers on the boxplots (min, max, first quantile, median, third quantile) when comparing `dfp` to `no_syn`. However, there is also considerable overlap in these accuracy distributions to different degrees as n varies, which indicates cases where the `dfp` baseline outperforms the other models with more linguistic features. To see this possibility, we plotted the difference (delta) in accuracies values for all data sets for the pair of baselines `no_syn` - `dfp` in Figure 8. It shows that for 80% of the data sets, the `no_syn` baseline with linguistic features outperforms the pitch-only baseline in most data sets by a margin of less than 20% in accuracy improvements.

Second, comparing across different n-grams, the `no_pitch` baseline (only linguistic features) performs worse in unigram, and the best in trigrams. This shows that the pitch feature is less important when n becomes larger in n-grams. The same trend is observed in the weights of the pitch features in feature importance. This observation is also consistent with (Prom-on et al., 2009): the target approximation of tones only operates on the syllable units. Therefore the effect of start/end pitch should diminish when $n>1$. Third, even though feature weights are small for previous/next tones, in these results we didn't see an improvement when we exclude these features in the `no_Ntone` baseline. Finally, we confirm the importance of the non-pitch linguistic features since the `no_pitch` baseline significantly outperforms the `random` and the `MLE` baselines.

7 Discussion

In this work, we first described a method to mine tone contour shape types from a large amount of tone data. These shape types, as well as those mined from tone n-grams with larger values of n ($n>3$), can be further analyzed with linguistic knowledge to better understand the behaviors of tones in different tonal contexts in future works. We also showed that using linguistic and contex-

---

recognition as much as expected.

151

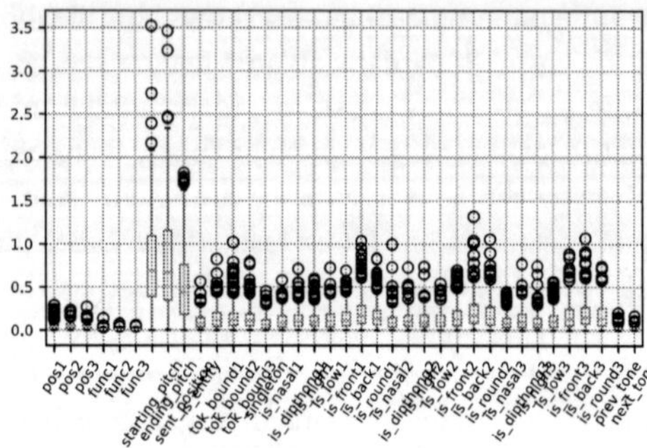

Figure 7: Feature weights for all trigram data sets.

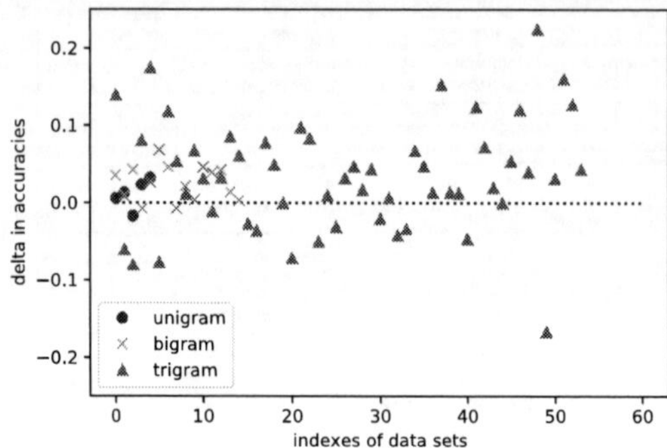

Figure 8: Delta (differences in accuracies): no_syn - dfp baselines. A point above the y=0 line indicates the model with linguistic features outperforms the model with pitch only features.

tual factors, we can predict with reasonable accuracy the contour shape type that a tone n-gram will take in the MCPST data. We analyzed the feature importance to form a relative ranking of the linguistic factors. These results should be interpreted with caution because they are constrained by the particular representations of the linguistic features used in this study, as well as the accuracy of the NLP softwares used to extract them. Nonetheless, we envision that by mining correlates between speech prosody and automatic analysis of linguistic features extracted from the data, this line of work could have potential applications in improving the quality and naturalness of prosody in speech synthesis such as Text-To-Speech (TTS) technologies.

Previous works targeting information theory and information structure in prosody domain have largely looked at acoustic correlates directly, such as accent and duration, all of which may in turn have an impact on the shape of tone contours in speech production. Therefore, looking at tone contour shapes can be thought of as a different level of manifestation of such phenomena, an amalgamation of single dimension acoustic correlates (e.g., duration and intensity). It is also a level that is more difficult to quantify and measure in the traditional linguistic/phonetic investigations on a smaller scale. One possible extension of this work in the future is to look at specific ways tone contour shapes correlate with particular features when they are perturbed in a certain direction. Moreover, it is also of interest to demonstrate this change in a quantified manner using the information theory formulation.

In Section 2 we raised a fundamental theo-

retical question of whether there is a direct link between communicative functions and surface acoustic forms, a question that we found disagreement in literature (as summarized in (Xu, 2005) and in Section 2 of the current paper). In this paper, we showed that by taking a data driven approach, we can predict the contour shape type of a prosodic category (such as a tone n-gram) using linguistic factors, even though we are not predicting its exact shape. In doing so, we give an approximate solution for a middle ground between the two theories.

Acknowledgements

We thank Sankalp Gulati, Xavier Serra, Amir Zeldes, Elizabeth Zsiga, George Wilson, Richard Wright and Gina-Anne Levow for insights and discussions, as well as the anonymous reviewers for valuable comments on the previous versions of this paper.

References

Matthew Aylett and Alice Turk. 2004. The smooth signal redundancy hypothesis: a functional explanation for relationships between redundancy, prosodic prominence, and duration in spontaneous speech. *Language and speech*, 47(Pt 1):31–56.

E. G. Bard and M. P. Aylett. 1999. The dissociation of deaccenting, givenness, and syntactic role in spontaneous speech. In *in ICPhs99*, pages 1753–1756.

Vincent D. Blondel, Jean-Loup Guillaume, Renaud Lambiotte, and Etienne Lefebvre. 2008. Fast unfolding of communities in large networks. *Journal of Statistical Mechanics: Theory and Experiment*, 10008(10):6.

Daniel Buring. 2013. *Syntax, information structure, and prosody*, Cambridge Handbooks in Language and Linguistics, pages 860–896. Cambridge University Press.

Danqi Chen and Christopher D. Manning. 2014. A fast and accurate dependency parser using neural networks. In *Proceedings of the 2014 Conference on Empirical Methods in Natural Language Processing, EMNLP 2014, October 25-29, 2014, Doha, Qatar, A meeting of SIGDAT, a Special Interest Group of the ACL*, pages 740–750.

E Cooper, J Eady, and R Mueller. 1985. Acoustical aspects of contrastive stress in question-answer contexts. *The Journal of the Acoustical Society of America*, 77:2142–2156.

E Cooper and M Sorenson. 1981. Fundamental frequency in sentence production. *New York: Spring-Verlag.*

Bruno Gauthier, Rushen Shi, and Yi Xu. 2007. Learning phonetic categories by tracking movements. *Cognition*, 103(1):80–106.

Sankalp Gulati, Joan Serra, Vignesh Ishwar, and Xavier Serra. 2016. Discovering raga motifs by characterizing communities in networks of melodic patterns. *Proc. of IEEE International Conf. on Acoustics, Speech, and Signal Processing (ICASSP), pp. 286-290, Shanghai, China.*

Isabelle Guyon, Jason Weston, Stephen Barnhill, and Vladimir Vapnik. 2002. Gene selection for cancer classification using support vector machines. *Machine Learning*, 46(1):389–422.

R Ladd. 1996. Intonational phonology. *Cambridge University Press, Cambridge.*

Gina-Anne Levow. 2005. Context in multi-lingual tone and pitch accent recognition. *Interspeech*, pages 1809–1812.

Kening Li. 2009. The information structure of mandarin chinese: Syntax and prosody. *PhD Dissertation, Department of Linguistics, University of Washington.*

M Liberman and J Pierrehumbert. 1984. Intonational invariance under changes in pitch range and length. *M. Aronoff and R. Oehrle (Eds.), Language Sound Structure. M.I.T. Press, Cambridge, Massachusetts*, pages 157–233.

Fang Liu, Dinoj Surendran, and Yi Xu. 2006. Classification of statement and question intonation in mandarin. In *Proceedings of Speech Prosody.*

Christopher D. Manning, Mihai Surdeanu, John Bauer, Jenny Finkel, Steven J. Bethard, and David McClosky. 2014. The Stanford CoreNLP natural language processing toolkit. In *Association for Computational Linguistics (ACL) System Demonstrations*, pages 55–60.

Santitham Prom-on, Yi Xu, and Bundit Thipakorn. 2009. Modeling tone and intonation in Mandarin and English as a process of target approximation. *The Journal of the Acoustical Society of America*, 125(1):405–24.

Marta Recasens, Marie-Catherine de Marneffe, and Christopher Potts. 2013. The life and death of discourse entities: Identifying singleton mentions. In *Proceedings of the 2013 Conference of the North American Chapter of the Association for Computational Linguistics: Human Language Technologies*, pages 627–633, Atlanta, Georgia. Association for Computational Linguistics.

Ina Röesiger and Arndt Riester. 2015. Using prosodic annotations to improve coreference resolution of spoken text. In *Proceedings of the 53rd Annual Meeting of the Association for Computational Linguistics and the 7th International Joint Conference on Natural Language Processing*, volume 2.

Dinoj Surendran. 2007. Analysis and Automatic Recognition of Tones in Mandarin Chinese. *PhD Thesis, Department of Computer Science, University of Chicago.*

Bei Wang and Yi Xu. 2011. Differential prosodic encoding of topic and focus in sentence-initial position in Mandarin Chinese. *Journal of Phonetics*, 39(4):595–611.

Yi Xu. 1997. Contextual tonal variations in Mandarin. *Journal of Phonetics*, 25(1):61–83.

Yi Xu. 2005. Speech melody as articulatorily implemented communicative functions. *Speech Communication*, 46(3-4):220–251.

Yi Xu, Ching X Xu, Xuejing Sun, Haskins Laboratories, and New Haven. 2004. On the Temporal Domain of Focus. *Speech Prosody*, pages 81–84.

Kristine Yu. 2011. The learnability of tones from the speech signal. *PhD Dissertation, Department of Linguistics, UCLA.*

Shuo Zhang. 2016. Mining linguistic tone patterns with symbolic representation. In *Proceedings of the 14th SIGMORPHON Workshop on Computational Research in Phonetics, Phonology, and Morphology*, pages 1–9. Association for Computational Linguistics.

Convolutional neural networks for low-resource morpheme segmentation: baseline or state-of-the-art?

Alexey Sorokin,

Neural Networks and Deep Learning Laboratory, Moscow Institute of Physics and Technology
Faculty of Mathematics and Mechanics, Moscow State University
`alexey at sorokin dot mail dot ru`

Abstract

We apply convolutional neural networks to the task of shallow morpheme segmentation using low-resource datasets for 5 different languages. We show that both in fully supervised and semi-supervised settings our model beats previous state-of-the-art approaches. We argue that convolutional neural networks reflect local nature of morpheme segmentation better than other neural approaches.

Morpheme segmentation consists in dividing a given word to meaningful individual units, morphs, which are surface realizations of underlying abstract morphemes. For example, a word *unexpectedly* could be segmented as *un-expect-ed-ly*, and the morpheme *-ed* may be also realized as *-t* like in *learn-t*. The generated segmentation may be used as input representation for machine translation (Mager et al., 2018) or morphological tagging (Matteson et al., 2018) or for automatic annotation of digital linguistic resources. Briefly, information about internal morpheme structure makes the data less sparse since an out-of-vocabulary word may share its morphemes with other words already present in the training set. This helps to recover semantic and morphological properties of an unknown word, which otherwise will be unaccessible. The task of morpheme segmentation is especially important for agglutinative languages, such as Finnish or Turkish, where a word is formed by attaching a sequence of affixes to its stem. This affixes reflect both derivational and inflectional processes. A common example from Turkish is *evlerinizden 'from your houses'*, which is decomposed as:

ev	ler	iniz	den
house	+PL	*your*+PL	+ABL

The task of morpheme segmentation is even harder for polysynthetic languages: while in agglutinative languages morphemes are usually in one-to-one correspondence with morphological features, for polysynthetic languages this matching is more complex with no clear bound between compound words and sentences. For example, in Chuckchi language the whole phrase '*The house broke*' can be expressed as

ɣa	ra	semat	ɬen
+PF	house	break	+PF+3SG

Consequently, polysynthetic language demonstrate extremely high morpheme-to-word ratio, which leads to high type-token ratio, which makes their automatic processing harder. Even further, this processing is performed in low-resource setting since most polysynthetic languages have only few hundreds or thousands of speakers and consequently tend to lack annotated digital resources. Hence, the algorithms initially designed for less complex languages with more data (mostly for English) may change significantly their properties when applied to low-resource polysynthetic data. That is especially the case for neural methods, which are (often erroneously[1]) believed to be more data-hungry than earlier approaches.

However, in 2019 it is insufficient to just say "neural networks" in case of NLP, since there are various neural networks whose properties may differ significantly. Leaving aside the immense diversity of network architectures, they can be separated in three main categories: the convolutional ones (CNNs), where convolutional windows capture local regularities; the recurrent ones, where GRUs and LSTMs memorize potentially unbounded context; and sequence-to-sequence (seq2seq) models, which perform string transductions using encoder-decoder approach. Among the three, convolutional neural networks are the least

---

[1] see (Zeman et al., 2018) and (Cotterell et al., 2017) that show that both in morphological tagging and automatic word inflection neural networks are clearly superior, though their architecture should be adapted for the lack of data.

Proceedings of the 16th Workshop on Computational Research in Phonetics, Phonology, and Morphology, pages 154–159
Florence, Italy. August 2, 2019 ©2019 Association for Computational Linguistics

explored, however, we argue that they are more effective for surface morpheme segmentation.

In our work we support two claims: 1) convolutional networks improve seq2seq approaches for neural morpheme segmentation 2) language model trained on unlabeled data may be useful to further improve their performance. We apply our models to 4 indigenous languages, spoken in Mexico: Mexicanero, Nahuatl, Wixarika and Yorem Nokki, since the scores for them are available in recent studies Kann et al. (2018). We also test our approach on North Sámi data from Grönroos et al. (2019).

1 Related work.

Automatic morpheme segmentation was extensively studied in pre-neural years of modern NLP. The investigations had two principal directions: several researchers tried to implement the approach of Harris (1970) and Andreev (1965) to find a quantitative counterpart of morpheme boundaries in terms of letter statistics. These methods were mainly unsupervised and include the well-known Morfessor system: Creutz and Lagus (2002) and its successors Creutz and Lagus (2007) and (Virpioja et al., 2013) (the latter uses semi-supervised learning). There was also an extensive work in the field of adaptor grammars.[2](Johnson et al., 2007; Sirts and Goldwater, 2013; Eskander et al., 2018) However, both these approaches are generative by their nature and are based on a probabilistic model of word structure. The most successful pure machine learning method was CRF-based model designed in Ruokolainen et al. (2013, 2014), which still remains state-of-the-art on several morpheme segmentation datasets.

There were several attempts to apply neural networks for morpheme segmentation and closely related problem of word segmentation, which is enevitable for Chinese, Japanese and other languages with similar graphics. The first one was probably Wang et al. (2016), which used window LSTMs, latter works include Kann et al. (2016) and Ruzsics and Samardzic (2017) which applied the sequence-to-sequence approach. Our study is conducted on the material from Kann et al. (2018), where the sequence-to-sequence model with atten-

Figure 1: Morpheme segmentation of word *pre-train-s* expressed with BMES scheme.

tion was applied to the material of 4 indigenous North-American languages, both is supervised and semi-supervised manner. All these studies solve morpheme segmentation as sequence transduction. In contrast, Shao (2017) treated morpheme and word segmentation as sequence labeling task which can be solved with BiRNN-CRF network.

The main inspiration for our work is Sorokin and Kravtsova (2018), who demonstrated, that at least for Russian (a fusional language with lots of data available) convolutional neural networks significantly outperform all other approaches, also being the less data-consuming (see also (Bolshakova and Sapin, 2019) for detailed comparison). The recent study of Grönroos et al. (2019) modified the decoder in seq2seq architecture to make its independent of the previous timesteps, which makes their model essentially an LSTM-based sequence tagger.

2 Model architecture.

Basing on the ideas from Sorokin and Kravtsova (2018), we decide to refrain from seq2seq approaches and reduce the morpheme segmentation task to sequence labeling problem. We solve this problem using convolutional neural networks. Each segmentation in the training set is encoded using BMES-scheme as illustrated on Figure 1. Here, S denotes single-letter morpheme; in case the morph is at least two letters long B stands for morpheme beginning, E for its end and M for all interior letters. Thus, the task of the algorithm is to predict the sequence of labels given the sequence of letters (probably, enriched with special BEGIN and END symbols). Due to the local nature of CNNs, the model cannot see any symbols except those surrounding the current one. However, the width of this local window may be up to 9 letters,[3] which makes the model powerful enough to capture all relevant local context.

2.1 Basic model.

Our basic architecture closely follows the model of Sorokin and Kravtsova (2018). The input of

---

[2]Roughly speaking, an adaptor grammar tries to learn from data a probabilistic context-sensitive grammar for morph sequences.

[3]In case of two layers with convolution width 5.

the algorithm is a sequence of 0/1-encodings, which are transformed to symbol embeddings by an embedding layer. These embeddings are passed through several stacked convolutional layers of different widths, as, for example, in Kim et al. (2016), the final outputs of all layers are concatenated. For better convergence we insert batch normalization and dropout layers between consecutive convoluions. The obtained context encodings are passed through a dense layer with softmax activation which generates a probability distribution over possible tags. Since not every sequence of tags corresponds to a valid morpheme segmentation, we find the most probable segmentation using Viterbi algorithm.

2.2 Multitask training and one-side convolutions.

Kann et al. (2018) demonstrates that pretraining on auxiliary task of autoencoding, which is the restoration of original input sequence, can be beneficial for morpheme segmentation. Autoencoding is an appealing complementary task since it does not require additional labeled data. It is especially suitable for encoder-decoder architecture since the memorization of input sequence is the natural job of the encoder. However, this objective does not fit in our paradigm since we try to avoid global architectures, such as recurrent ones and especially seq2seq, in favor of the local ones. Following modern trends in NLP, we select language modelling as an auxiliary task, predicting not only the morpheme boundary of the current symbol but also the following symbol. However, this approach fails with basic CNN architecture since the convolutional window observes the next symbol and can easily memorize it.

Therefore we slightly modify our model: instead of using a symmetric window around current symbol, we have two groups of convolutions: the left and right ones. The left observes the current symbols and also some symbols preceding it, while the right does not see preceding symbols, but only the current one and the ones following it. We again use windows of different size and concatenate their outputs, thus obtaining for each position t two context embeddings $\overleftarrow{h}_t$ (left) and $\overrightarrow{h}_t$ (right). They are used to obtain the required distribution $\mathbf{p}_t$ over morphological labels as well as two auxiliary distribution $\mathbf{q}_{t-1}$ and $\mathbf{q}_{t+1}$ over preceding and following symbols, respectively:

$$\begin{aligned}
\mathbf{p}_t &= \mathrm{softmax}_{morph}(U[\overrightarrow{h}_t, \overleftarrow{h}_t]), \\
\mathbf{q}_{t-1} &= \mathrm{softmax}_{symb}(V_l\overleftarrow{h}_t), \\
\mathbf{q}_{t+1} &= \mathrm{softmax}_{symb}(V_r\overrightarrow{h}_t).
\end{aligned}$$

Note that this architecture with "unidirectional" convolutions can be used without auxiliary objective as well.

3 Data.

We evaluate our model on two datasets: the dataset of 4 indigenous North American languages from Kann et al. (2018) and the North Sami dataset from Grönroos et al. (2019). In this section we briefly characterize the languages, for more complete description we refer the reader to the cited papers or to linguistic resources such as WALS(Haspelmath et al., 2005).

1. The 4 mexican languages: Mexicanero, Nahuatl, Wixarika and Yorem Nokki all belong to Yuta-Aztecan family. They are mostly agglutinative and have extremely complex verb morphology. Some stems and even affixes in case of Mexicanero are Spanish borrowings.

2. North Sámi is a Finno-Ugric language spoken in the North of Finland, Sweden, Norway and Russia. It is morphologically complex, featuring derivational, inflectional and compounding processes. It also has regular but complicated morphonological variation.

The quantitative characteristics of the datasets used in our study are given in Table 1. For mexican languages we used the same data as in Kann et al. (2018). The number of unlabeled words used for semi-supervised models differ because of different preprocessing.[4]

4 Experiments

4.1 Model parameters.

We use symbol embeddings of size 32. The basic model contains two parallel convolutional groups

---

[4]It is not an obstacle for fair comparison since the main goal of our paper is to compare supervised versions of the model.

[5]As in Kann et al. (2018), the same list of words is used for Mexicanero and Yorem Nokki due to their close relatedness.

[6]Actual word lists are larger but we restrict it to random 100000 words to speed up training.

Language	Train	Dev	Test	Unlabeled
Mexicanero	427	106	355	978[5]
Nahuatl	540	134	449	36149
Wixarika	665	176	553	13092
Yorem Nokki	511	127	425	978[5]
North Sámi	1044	200	796	100000[6]

Table 1: Size of the datasets used for evaluation.

of width 5 and 7, each group having 2 layers and 96 neurons on each of the layers. The unidirectional convolutional model has 64 filters for each window width from 1 to 4 and 2 convolutional layers as well. Dropout rate was 0.2.

Neural networks are implemented using Keras framework with TensorFlow backend. They are trained with Adam optimizer for at most 50 epochs, training is stopped when the accuracy on development set do not improve for 10 epochs. In case of multitask training the language models are trained for 5 epochs jointly with the main model, batches for different tasks are sampled in random order. The size of mini-batch is 32 for all the runs.

4.2 Results.

Our first evaluation scores the basic model on datasets from Kann et al. (2018) and Grönroos et al. (2019). We compare our with their seq2seq model, the CRF model of Ruokolainen et al. (2013) and the semi-supervised neural model (the one of Kann et al. (2018) using autoencoding and the one of Grönroos et al. (2019) trained with Harris features). The supervised CRF model is retrained by ourselves, while other scores except our own are taken from the original papers. We report two metrics, micro-averaged (per morpheme boundary) boundary F1[7] and word accuracy, which is the fraction of correctly segmented words. All our scores are averaged over 5 independent runs with different random initialization, the standard error is also reported.

Analyzing the results in Table 2, we see that our basic model always outperforms sequence-to-sequence model by a substantial margin, also being ahead of conditional random fields on 4 datasets of 5. That answers our first question: convolutional neural networks seem to work bet-

ter than other approaches supervised morpheme segmentation even in extremely low-resource setting. In Table 3 we present the scores for our unidirectional model both in its supervised version and in the semi-supervised one, which is trained using multitask learning. We observe that unidirectional convolutions work better than the traditional ones and the multitask training imporves the scores slightly more further.

We conclude that on the mentioned datasets our model outperforms other tested approaches, setting a new state-of-the-art score for them. We also note that one-side CNNs are better than the basic ones, though they have 4 times more parameters. However, basic CNNs of comparable size do not perform better than the smaller ones due to severe overfitting. Gains from semi-supervised training are the more substantial the more data we have, thus the effect on Mexicanero and Yorem Nokki with less than 1000 unlabeled words is the most modest.

5 Conclusion and future work.

We demonstrate that convolutional neural networks outperform other segmentation models in low-resource setting. We argue that this is due to their ability to capture local dependencies, while morpheme segmentation is essentially local by its nature. A similar observation on sentence-level tasks was made in Yin et al. (2017) which demonstrated that CNNs perform better in tasks like answer selection that do not envolve long-distance relations. However, the claims made on 6 languages (5 of the present article and Russian in Sorokin and Kravtsova (2018) and Bolshakova and Sapin (2019)), 4 of which belong to the same family certainly need further proof on other languages and datasets. However, we note that CNNs are (arguably) more effective not only in terms of performance quality, but also in terms of training complexity.

Nonetheless promising, our results still leave a

---

[7]The work of Kann et al. (2018) reports macro-averaged one, therefore we do not present their boundary F1. We think the micro-averaged version better reflects algorithm properties since the impact of words with larger number of morphemes is higher.

Language	Word accuracy				Boundary F1			
	CNN(our)	seq2seq	CRF	semi-sup	CNN(our)	seq2seq	CRF	semi-sup
Mexicanero	79,4 (0,4)	75,0	78,3	**80,5**	89,7(0,3)	NA	89,2	NA
Nahuatl	59,9 (1,0)	55,9	**64,4**	60,3	77,4(1,0)	NA	80,4	NA
Wixarika	61,4 (0,6)	57,5	58,6	**61,9**	88,2(0,5)	NA	87,8	NA
Yorem Nokki	69,2(0,7)	65,7	65,9	**71,0**	82,6(0,7)	NA	80,3	NA
North Sámi	**71,6**(0,8)	69,1	70,9	71,1	80,8(0,9)	NA	80,0	NA

Table 2: Results of our basic CNN segmentation model in comparison with sequence-to-sequence model (seq2seq), conditional random fields (CRF) and semi-supervised extension of seq2seq (semi-sup). Seq2seq and semi-supervised results for Yuto-Aztecan languages are from Kann et al. (2018), for North Sámi from Grönroos et al. (2019).

Language	Convolutional (our)			Other	
	basic	one-side	one-side+LM	best semi-sup	best
Mexicanero	79,4(0,4)	**80,6**(1,3)	80,1(1,6)	80,5	80,5
Nahuatl	59,9(1,0)	62,8(0,6)	**64,4**(1,1)	60,3	**64,4**
Wixarika	61,4(0,6)	62,9(1,5)	**64,8**(1,1)	61,9	61,0
Yorem Nokki	69,2(0,7)	70,5(0,9)	**71,7**(0,9)	71,0	71,0
North Sámi	71,6(0,8)	72,0(0,5)	**72,5**(0,3)	71,1	71,1

Table 3: Results of our extended CNN models in comparison with the basic one and state-of-the-art. Results for Yuto-Aztecan languages are from Kann et al. (2018), for North Sámi from Grönroos et al. (2019).

huge room for improvement. First of all, the absolute numbers are quite low, only less than two thirds of the words are segmented correctly. The first thing to study is the learning curve of neural segmentation algorithm: it is not so important that a model achieves 60% accuracy on 1000 annotated words, more important is whether it may reach 80% given another thousand of training examples. Another open direction is the incorporation of linguistic features, such as Harris-like distributional measures used in Ruokolainen et al. (2014) or intra-segment interactions regulated by adaptor grammars.

Sometimes morpheme segmentation also requires normalization of morphemes (e.g *studied* $\mapsto$ *study + ed*). This task is not that straightforward to address with CNNs since the problem is no more reduced to sequence labeling. This is exactly the case for Semitic languages, where morpheme segmentation often depends not only from the word itself, but from wider context (Zeldes, 2018). Since neural networks can work with input vectors of any origin, CNN models have the potential for these tasks also and we hope to address some of these questions in future research.

Acknowledgements

The research was conducted under support of National Technological Initiative Foundation and Sberbank of Russia. Project identifier 0000000007417F630002. The author also thanks Manuel Mager for providing the datasets and help with their processing.

References

Nikolai Dmitrievich Andreev, editor. 1965. *Statictical and combinatorial language modelling (Statistiko-kombinatornoe modelirovanie iazykov, in Russian)*. Nauka.

Elena Bolshakova and Alexander Sapin. 2019. Improving neural morphological tagging using language models. In *Computational Linguistics and Intellectual Technologies: Proceedings of the International Conference "Dialogue*, pages 105–113.

Ryan Cotterell, Christo Kirov, John Sylak-Glassman, Géraldine Walther, Ekaterina Vylomova, Patrick Xia, Manaal Faruqui, Sandra Kübler, David Yarowsky, Jason Eisner, et al. 2017. Conll-sigmorphon 2017 shared task: Universal morphological reinflection in 52 languages. *arXiv preprint arXiv:1706.09031*.

Mathias Creutz and Krista Lagus. 2002. Unsupervised discovery of morphemes. In *Proceedings of the*

ACL-02 workshop on Morphological and phonological learning-Volume 6, pages 21–30. Association for Computational Linguistics.

Mathias Creutz and Krista Lagus. 2007. Unsupervised models for morpheme segmentation and morphology learning. *ACM Transactions on Speech and Language Processing (TSLP)*, 4(1):3.

Ramy Eskander, Owen Rambow, and Smaranda Muresan. 2018. Automatically tailoring unsupervised morphological segmentation to the language. In *Proceedings of the Fifteenth Workshop on Computational Research in Phonetics, Phonology, and Morphology*, pages 78–83.

Stig-Arne Grönroos, Sami Virpioja, and Mikko Kurimo. 2019. North sámi morphological segmentation with low-resource semi-supervised sequence labeling. In *Proceedings of the Fifth International Workshop on Computational Linguistics for Uralic Languages*, pages 15–26.

Zellig S Harris. 1970. Morpheme boundaries within words: Report on a computer test. In *Papers in Structural and Transformational Linguistics*, pages 68–77. Springer.

Martin Haspelmath, Matthew S Dryer, David Gil, and Bernard Comrie. 2005. The world atlas of language structures.

Mark Johnson, Thomas L Griffiths, and Sharon Goldwater. 2007. Adaptor grammars: A framework for specifying compositional nonparametric bayesian models. In *Advances in neural information processing systems*, pages 641–648.

Katharina Kann, Ryan Cotterell, and Hinrich Schütze. 2016. Neural morphological analysis: Encoding-decoding canonical segments. In *Proceedings of the 2016 Conference on Empirical Methods in Natural Language Processing*, pages 961–967.

Katharina Kann, Manuel Mager, Ivan Meza-Ruiz, and Hinrich Schütze. 2018. Fortification of neural morphological segmentation models for polysynthetic minimal-resource languages. *arXiv preprint arXiv:1804.06024*.

Yoon Kim, Yacine Jernite, David Sontag, and Alexander M Rush. 2016. Character-aware neural language models. In *Thirtieth AAAI Conference on Artificial Intelligence*.

Manuel Mager, Elisabeth Mager, Alfonso Medina-Urrea, Ivan Meza, and Katharina Kann. 2018. Lost in translation: Analysis of information loss during machine translation between polysynthetic and fusional languages. *arXiv preprint arXiv:1807.00286*.

Andrew Matteson, Chanhee Lee, Young-Bum Kim, and Heuiseok Lim. 2018. Rich character-level information for korean morphological analysis and part-of-speech tagging. *arXiv preprint arXiv:1806.10771*.

Teemu Ruokolainen, Oskar Kohonen, Sami Virpioja, and Mikko Kurimo. 2013. Supervised morphological segmentation in a low-resource learning setting using conditional random fields. In *Proceedings of the Seventeenth Conference on Computational Natural Language Learning*, pages 29–37.

Teemu Ruokolainen, Oskar Kohonen, Sami Virpioja, et al. 2014. Painless semi-supervised morphological segmentation using conditional random fields. In *Proceedings of the 14th Conference of the European Chapter of the Association for Computational Linguistics, volume 2: Short Papers*, pages 84–89.

Tatyana Ruzsics and Tanja Samardzic. 2017. Neural sequence-to-sequence learning of internal word structure. In *Proceedings of the 21st Conference on Computational Natural Language Learning (CoNLL 2017)*, pages 184–194.

Yan Shao. 2017. Cross-lingual word segmentation and morpheme segmentation as sequence labelling. *arXiv preprint arXiv:1709.03756*.

Kairit Sirts and Sharon Goldwater. 2013. Minimally-supervised morphological segmentation using adaptor grammars. *Transactions of the Association for Computational Linguistics*, 1:255–266.

Alexey Sorokin and Anastasia Kravtsova. 2018. Deep convolutional networks for supervised morpheme segmentation of russian language. In *Conference on Artificial Intelligence and Natural Language*, pages 3–10. Springer.

Sami Virpioja, Peter Smit, Stig-Arne Grönroos, Mikko Kurimo, et al. 2013. Morfessor 2.0: Python implementation and extensions for morfessor baseline.

Linlin Wang, Zhu Cao, Yu Xia, and Gerard de Melo. 2016. Morphological segmentation with window lstm neural networks. In *Thirtieth AAAI Conference on Artificial Intelligence*.

Wenpeng Yin, Katharina Kann, Mo Yu, and Hinrich Schütze. 2017. Comparative study of cnn and rnn for natural language processing. *arXiv preprint arXiv:1702.01923*.

Amir Zeldes. 2018. A characterwise windowed approach to hebrew morphological segmentation. *arXiv preprint arXiv:1808.07214*.

Daniel Zeman, Jan Hajič, Martin Popel, Martin Potthast, Milan Straka, Filip Ginter, Joakim Nivre, and Slav Petrov. 2018. Conll 2018 shared task: Multilingual parsing from raw text to universal dependencies. In *Proceedings of the CoNLL 2018 Shared Task: Multilingual Parsing from Raw Text to Universal Dependencies*, pages 1–21.

What do phone embeddings learn about Phonology?

Sudheer Kolachina
sudheer.kpg08@gmail.com

Lilla Magyar
lillamagyar0929@gmail.com

Abstract

Recent work has looked at evaluation of phone embeddings using sound analogies and correlations between distinctive feature space and embedding space. It has not been clear what aspects of natural language phonology are learnt by neural network inspired distributed representational models such as word2vec. To study the kinds of phonological relationships learnt by phone embeddings, we present artificial phonology experiments that show that phone embeddings learn paradigmatic relationships such as phonemic and allophonic distribution quite well. They are also able to capture co-occurrence restrictions among vowels such as those observed in languages with vowel harmony. However, they are unable to learn co-occurrence restrictions among the class of consonants.

1 Introduction

Over the last few years, distributed representation models based on neural networks such as word2vec (Mikolov et al., 2013a) and GloVe (Pennington et al., 2014) have been of much importance in speech and natural language processing (NLP). The word2vec technique is a shallow neural network that takes a text corpus as input and outputs a vector space containing all unique words in the text. The dense vector representations of words induced using word2vec have been shown to capture multiple degrees of similarities between words. Mikolov et al. (2013a,b) show that word embeddings can solve word analogy questions and sentence completion tasks. Mikolov et al. (2013b) show that word embeddings represent words in continuous space, making it possible to perform algebraic operations, such as vector(King) − vector(Man) + vector(Woman) = vector(Queen). Considerable attention has been paid to evaluating these vector rep-

resentations using human judgement datasets (Baroni et al., 2014; Levy et al., 2015). Asr and Jones (2017) use artificial language experiments to study the difference between similarity and relatedness in evaluating distributed semantic models. *Phone embeddings* induced from phonetic corpora have been used in tasks such as word inflection (Silfverberg et al., 2018) and sound sequence alignment (Sofroniev and Çöltekin, 2018). Silfverberg et al. (2018) show that dense vector representations of phones learnt using various techniques are able to solve analogies such as **p** is to **b** as **t** is to **X**, where **X** = **d**. They also show that there is a significant correlation between distinctive feature space and the phone embedding space.

Our goal in this paper is to understand better the evaluation of phone embeddings. We argue that significant correlation between distinctive feature space and phone embedding space cannot be automatically interpreted as the model's ability to capture facts about the phonology of natural language. Since many distinctive features tend to be phonetically based, natural classes denoted by these features capture *phonetic facts* as well as *phonological facts*. For example, the feature [$\pm long$] denotes the distinction between long and short vowels, which is a language-independent phonetic fact. But, whether this distinction is a phonological fact varies from language to language. It is important to make this distinction between phonetic facts and phonological facts when evaluating phone embeddings for their learning of phonology. In this paper, we propose an alternative methodology to evaluate word2vec's ability to learn phonological facts. We define artificial languages with different kinds of phoneme-allophone distinctions and co-occurrence restrictions and study how well phone embeddings capture these relationships. Several interesting insights regarding the relationship between phonetics and phonol-

Proceedings of the 16th Workshop on Computational Research in Phonetics, Phonology, and Morphology, pages 160–169
Florence, Italy. August 2, 2019 ©2019 Association for Computational Linguistics

ogy, the role of distinctive features and the task of distinctive feature/phoneme induction accrue from our experiments.

2 Background and Related work

One major difference between words and phones is that while words are meaningful units in language, phones have no meaning in themselves. However, as with words, there are clear patterns of organization of individual phones in a language. One well-known pattern in phonology is the distinction between **contrastive** and **complementary** distribution. Two phones are said to be in contrastive distribution if they occur in the same context and create a meaning contrast. For example, **b** and **k** occur in word-initial position and create a contrast in meaning, such as in **bæt** versus **kæt**. This is why they are considered distinct phonemes in the language. On the other hand, **pʰ** and **p** never occur in the same context, which is referred to as being in complementary distribution. Since they are phonetically related, they are considered *allophones*, variants of the same underlying phoneme. The notions of contrastive and complementary distribution are purely based on context. They can be considered instances of paradigmatic similarity discussed in the distributed semantic literature. Allophony also involves the notion of phonetic similarity. Another pattern in natural language phonology is that of **co-occurrence restrictions**. A well-known example is homorganic consonant clusters. For example, in nasal plus stop clusters, the nasal must have identical place of articulation to the following stop. Yet another example of co-occurrence restriction in phonology is the phenomenon of vowel harmony. In some languages, a word can only have vowels which agree with respect to certain features, such as backness, rounding or height. Co-occurrence restrictions can be considered to be instances of syntagmatic similarity whereby words that frequently occur together form a syntagm (phrase). Again, most types of co-occurrence restrictions involve phonetic similarity.

The traditional method to describe phones in phonology is in terms of distinctive features (Jakobson et al., 1951). Distinctive features allow phones to be grouped into *natural classes*, which are established on the basis of participation in common phonological processes. They allow for generalizations about phonotactic contexts to be captured in an economical way. In addition to distinctive features in phonology, there are also phonetic features that describe the articulatory and acoustic properties of phones (Ladefoged and Johnson, 2010). However, in practice, there is considerable overlap between phonological distinctive features and phonetic features. This already poses an interesting question about the nature of the relationship between phonetics and phonology, which as we will see, is relevant to the evaluation of phone embeddings.

Next, let us examine the notion of correlation between distinctive feature space and phone embedding space to evaluate phone embeddings as proposed by Silfverberg et al. (2018). Pair-wise featural similarity is estimated using a metric such as Hamming distance or Jaccard index applied to feature representations of phones. Pair-wise contextual similarity is estimated as cosine similarity between phone embeddings induced using a technique like `word2vec`. The correlation between pairwise featural similarity and pairwise contextual similarity is estimated using Pearson's r or Spearman's ρ. The value of this correlation is shown for a number of languages in table 1. Data for Shona and Wargamay are taken from Hayes and Wilson (2008)[1]. Similar datasets were constructed for Telugu and the Vedic variety of Sanskrit[2]. For English, the CMU phonetic dictionary was used with a feature representation based on Parrish (2017) with some minor extensions. The `word2vec` implementation in the Gensim toolkit (Řehůřek and Sojka, 2010) was used to induce phone embeddings using the following parameters- CBOW, dimensionality of 30, window size of 4, negative sampling of 3, minimum count of 5, learning rate of 0.05. We use CBOW which predicts the most likely phone given a context of 4 phones in either direction as this is intuitively similar to the task of a phonologist. It would be interesting to compare CBOW and Skipgram architectures and also, study the effect of different parameters on this correlation between distinctive feature space and phone embedding space. However, this is not the goal of our study. In this paper, we restrict our attention to the linguistic significance of this correlation.

All languages in Table 1 show a significant positive correlation between distinctive feature space

---

[1] https://linguistics.ucla.edu/people/hayes/Phonotactics/index.htm#simulations
[2] Datasets and code available at https://github.com/skolachi/sigmorphoncode

Language	Size	Pearson	Spearman
English	135091	0.589	0.612
Shona	4395	0.431	0.575
Telugu	19627	0.349	0.350
Wargamay	5910	0.411	0.428
Vedic	45334	0.351	0.285
English	4000	0.129	0.161
Shona	4000	0.507	0.533
Telugu	4000	0.202	0.206
Wargamay	4000	0.219	0.387
Vedic	4000	0.146	0.159

Table 1: Correlation between distinctive feature space and embedding space, all values significant ($p < 0.01$)

and embedding space. What is the physical interpretation of this correlation? Firstly, it is important to note the use of this correlation to evaluate phone embeddings presupposes that these hand-crafted distinctive features are the gold standard descriptions of the phonology of these languages. Even if this were the case, the kind of distinctive features used to describe phones plays an important role in the interpretation of this correlation. If feature specifications of phones are based mostly on their phonetic properties, a positive correlation between featural space and embedding space indicates that phonetically similar phones tend to occur in similar contexts. In other words, the natural classes of phonology are tightly constrained by phonetics. To illustrate this point, we take the example of Wargamay natural classes derived from the distinctive features of Hayes and Wilson (2008) shown in Table 2. Examining the pairwise cosine similarities of phones based on embeddings induced by word2vec in the agglomerative clustering (WPGMA) dendrogram heatmap shown in Figure 1, word2vec CBOW embeddings identify the following natural classes- ii1, uu1, aa1 ($[+long, +main, +stress]$), i1, u1, a1 ($[-long, +main, +stress]$), i2, u2, a2 ($[-long, -main, +stress]$), i0, u0, a0 ($[-long, -stress]$) and $[-syllabic]$ which denotes the set of all consonants. Among the set of consonants, the velar consonants N, g ($[+dorsal]$) show up in the same cluster, as do the bilabials b and m. Sonorant consonants like R, l, n, w form one cluster and $[+approximant]$ r, y form another cluster. Notice that all these classes are based on place and manner of articulation. Therefore, it is not clear if the observed clustering is to interpreted as the model's learning of phonology or the fact phonetic features strictly constrain the contexts in which phones occur. Furthermore, as with word

meaning, when embeddings of two phones show high similarity, it is not clear if it is an instance of paradigmatic similarity (phonemic relationship) or syntagmatic similarity (co-occurrence restriction).

Feature	Class
-high	a0,a1,a2,aa1
+high	i0,i1,i2,ii1,u0,u1,u2,uu1,w,y
+long	aa1,ii1,uu1
-long	a0,a1,a2,i0,i1,i2,u0,u1,u2
+back	a0,a1,a2,aa1,u0,u1,u2,uu1,w
-back	i0,i1,i2,ii1,y
-approximant	N,b,d,g,j,m,n,nj
+approximant	R,a0,a1,a2,aa1,i0,i1,i2,ii1,l,r,u0,u1,u2,uu1,w,y
-sonorant	b,d,g,j
+sonorant	N,R,a0,a1,a2,aa1,i0,i1,i2,ii1,l,m,n,nj,r,u0,u1,u2,uu1,w,y
+syllabic	a0,a1,a2,aa1,i0,i1,i2,ii1,u0,u1,u2,uu1
-syllabic	N,R,b,d,g,j,l,m,n,nj,r,w,y
+main	a1,aa1,i1,ii1,u1,uu1
-main	a0,a2,i0,i2,u0,u2
+stress	a1,a2,aa1,i1,i2,ii1,u1,u2,uu1
-stress	a0,i0,u0
-consonantal	a0,a1,a2,aa1,i0,i1,i2,ii1,u0,u1,u2,uu1,w,y
+consonantal	N,R,b,d,g,j,l,m,n,nj,r
+anterior	d,l,n,r
-anterior	R,j,nj,y
+lateral	l
-lateral	R,r
+coronal	R,d,j,l,n,nj,r,y
+dorsal	N,g
+labial	b,m

Table 2: Natural classes derived from distinctive features

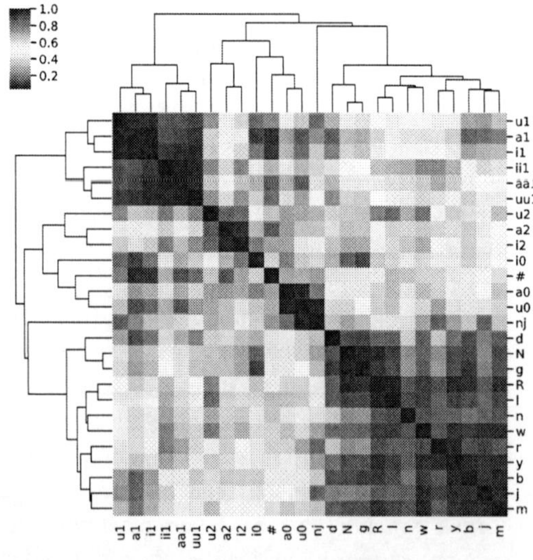

Figure 1: Phone clusters of Wargamay

Asr and Jones (2017) use an artificial language experiment to study the difference in performance of word embeddings between paradigmatic and syntagmatic tasks. In section 3, we propose a similar approach to study word2vec's ability to learn different kinds of phonological patterns. While natural language phonology can be complex with many interleaved phenomena, artificial language phonology makes it possible to test learning of each pattern independently. In addition, previous work on phonological learning such as Hayes and Wilson (2008) assumes that distinctive features exist *a priori*. In our experiments with artificial languages, we explore the possibility of deriving distinctive features from phone embeddings which capture contextual distributions of phones.

3   Learning artificial phonology with `word2vec`

In this section, we present experiments with `word2vec` on learning artificial languages with different kinds of phonological relationships. The languages studied in this experiment are described below. The minimal word is bimoraic CVC. The maximum word length is set at three syllables. Word boundary is indicated using #.

1. **Language 1** contains only open (CV) syllables in polysyllabic words. Monosyllabic words are all CVC. The set of possible consonants is **p t k** and the set of possible vowels is **a e i o u**.

2. **Language 2** is the same as Language 1 with the difference that intervocalic consonants are voiced- **b d g** instead of **p t k**. In other words, there is allophonic variation within the class of consonants.

3. **Language 3** is the same as Language 2 with the following differences: Final syllables in polysyllabic words are optionally closed, that is, codas are allowed. Word-initial consonants are aspirated, **P T K**. Word-final consonants are voiceless **p t k**. Thus, an additional degree of allophony for consonants is introduced.

4. **Language 4** is the same as Language 3 with the addition of nasal codas: **m n N (ŋ)** in all syllables. In the final syllable, the nasal and the voiceless stop form a coda cluster.

5. **Language 5** is the same as Language 4 with the difference that nasal codas are optional. This language is the union of Languages 3 and 4.

6. **Language 6** is the same as Language 5 with a restriction on nasal coda based on the place of articulation of the following voiced consonant. In other words, only **mb nd Ng** combinations are allowed.

7. **Language 7** is the same as Language 6 with the addition that **r** is optionally allowed following a voiced consonant. In other words, onset clusters **br dr gr** are permitted in medial syllables.

8. **Language 8** is the same as Language 7 with the addition that a sibilant **s** is optionally allowed in the coda position of the final syllable. This language allows a variety of contexts in the final syllable- voiceless stops, nasals and nasal+stop clusters, sibilant **s**, sibilant+stop clusters **sp st sk** and also nasal+sibilant+stop clusters.

9. **Language 9** is the same as Language 8 with the restriction that the nasal + sibilant + voiceless stop cluster in coda position must be homorganic- only **nst** is allowed.

10. **Language 10** is the same as Language 9 with the restriction that only high vowels **i u** can occur in initial syllables.

11. **Language 11** is the same as Language 10 with the difference that it has vowel harmony with respect to backness. Thus, words can only have either $[-back]$ (front) vowels **i e** or $[+back]$ vowels **u o**.

12. **Language 12** is the same as Language 11 with the difference that the transparent vowel **a** is permitted in non-initial syllables of polysyllabic words.

Phone embeddings were induced using the same parameters as in the previous section- CBOW, dimensionality 30, context window 4, negative sampling 3, minimum count 5 and learning rate 0.05. The number of words in each language is shown in table 3, alongside the correlations between distinctive feature space and embedding space. A set of distinctive features similar to those of Hayes and Wilson (2008) are used to estimate these correlations. Since the value of cosine similarity is bounded on $[-1, 1]$, we also use Euclidean distance to estimate correlation between contextual similarity based on phone embeddings and featural similarity. We will return to the issue of the significance of these correlations shortly.

Language	size	Pearson's r	
		Cosine	Euclidean
Language 1	3645	0.873	0.882
Language 2	3645	0.632	0.408
Language 3	14445	0.573	0.396
Language 4	372780	0.477	0.362
Language 5	878625	0.470	0.354
Language 6	139635	0.503	0.343
Language 7	549135	0.500	0.305
Language 8	988455	0.394	0.263
Language 9	878625	0.421	0.254
Language 10	351450	0.481	0.286
Language 11	57690	0.476	0.277
Language 12	127962	0.430	0.209

Table 3: Correlation between embedding and distinctive feature space, all values significant at $p < 0.01$

As can be noticed from the descriptions, each language defines different sets of equivalence relations among phones based on the contexts in which they occur. For example, in Language 3, aspirated stops occur word-initially, voiced stops occur inter-vocalically and voiceless stops occur word-finally. The task of phonology is to capture generalizations about these *natural classes*. Notice that although these natural classes are based on phonetic features such as aspiration and voicing, word2vec has no access to these features. The goal of our experiments is to investigate the extent to which these natural classes can be inferred solely based on phone embeddings. The embedding space for each language is visualized using T-distributed Stochastic Neighbor Embedding (t-SNE) plots. Multiple plots were generated for different values of perplexity and learning rate using the implementation in scikit-learn toolkit (Buitinck et al., 2013). The plots shown in Figure 2 correspond to perplexity 3 and learning rate 100. In addition, phone clusters derived using agglomerative clustering of cosine similarities between phone embeddings are also shown. Euclidean distance was used to plot the dendrogram heatmaps[3].

From the plots, we observe that phone embeddings capture the different context classes with varying degrees of success. Languages 1-3 were designed with unique contexts for each class of phones and the embeddings show clear separation between these classes. In Language 4-5,

---

[3]The interpretation of these distance-based heatmaps differs from the cosine similarity-based heatmap of Wargamay presented in the previous section.

where nasal codas are allowed, the t-SNE plot shows less separation between nasal codas and word-initial aspirated voiceless stops. This is due to the fact that in monosyllabic words, aspirated stops and nasals co-occur within the same context (bimoraic) window. This is an unintended co-occurrence restriction learnt by word2vec. However, this pattern in monosyllabic words has no effect on the phone clusters in the dendrogram. Nasals and aspirated stops form separate clusters in the dendrogram. In Language 6, a co-occurrence constraint that nasal obstruent clusters be homorganic was introduced. Interestingly, the t-SNE plot for this language has nasals showing up with vowels. The syntagmatic relationship (co-occurrence restriction) between nasals and homo-organic voiced obstruents introduced in this language is not seen in the t-SNE plot of the embedding space. But, the dendrogram heatmap for this language shows nasals and voiced obstruents forming a high-level cluster. It is plausible that with hyperparameter tuning, co-occurrence restrictions such as nasal-voiced obstruent clusters are captured even in the t-SNE plots of embedding space. Co-occurrence restrictions in phonology are much more rigid than word relatedness since the size of the phone inventory in a language is many degrees smaller than the size of the vocabulary.

A similar pattern is observed with languages 7, 8 and 9, where other kinds of co-occurrence relations between consonants are introduced. The t-SNE plot for Language 7 fails to capture the onset clusters **br dr gr** introduced in this language. The lateral **r** shows up with the word boundary. The dendrogram for this language fails to recover word-initial aspirated stops as a separate class. In Language 8, the introduction of the optional sibilant in the coda position of the final syllable has a same effect on the embedding space as visualized by the t-SNE plot. Nasals, aspirated stops, lateral, sibilant and word boundary are less separated in the t-SNE plot. In the dendrogram plot, the sibilant forms a cluster with the nasals and word boundary. Both the t-SNE and dendrogram plots for Language 9 are almost identical to those Language 8 indicating that the homorganic restriction on nasal sibilant voiceless stop clusters in the final syllable has no effect on the embedding space. In other words, phone embeddings are unable to learn these co-occurrence restrictions. Languages

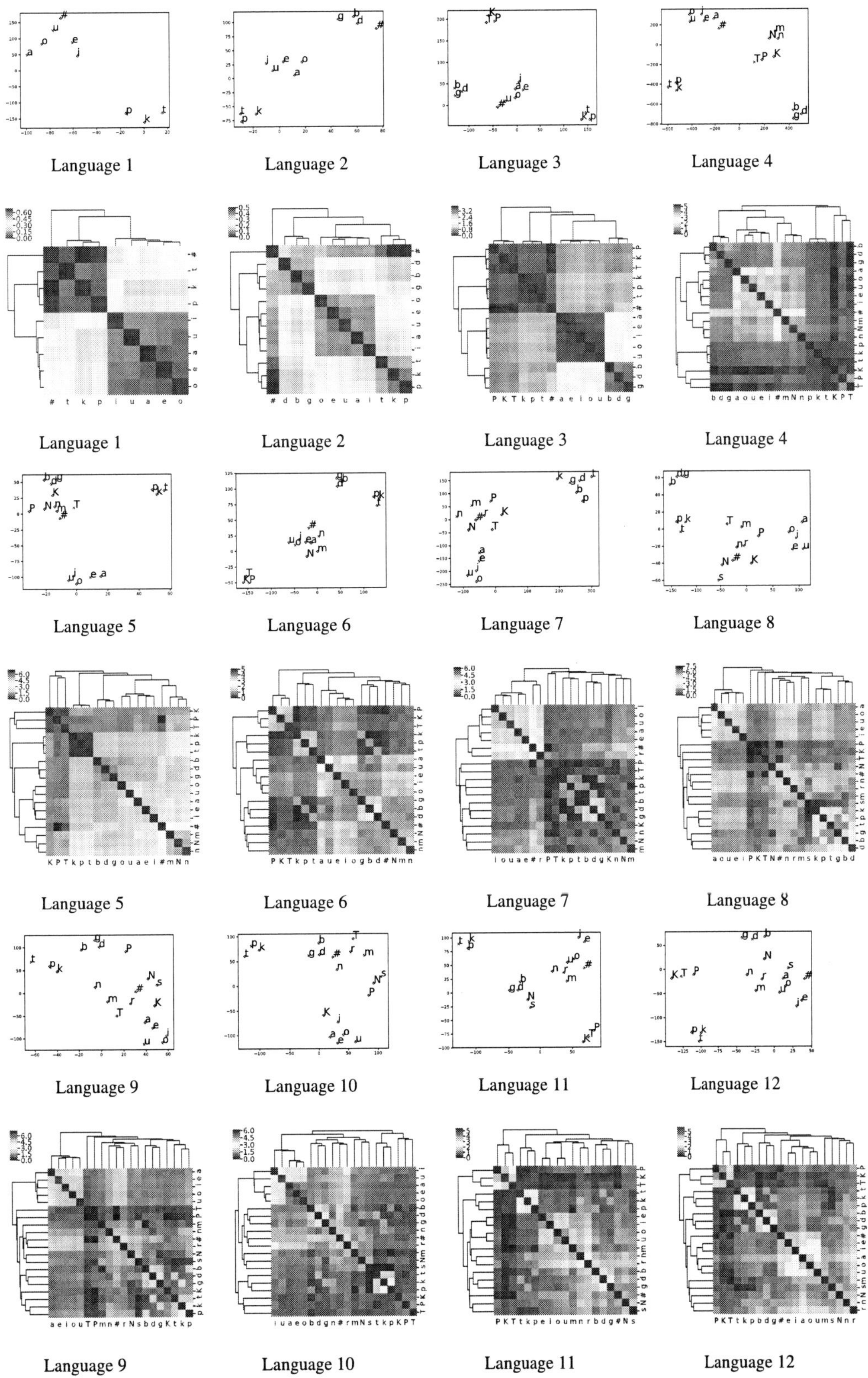

Figure 2: Embedding space of artificial languages

10-12 introduce contextual restrictions on vowels. In Language 10, only high vowels occur in the word-initial position and phone embeddings capture this distinct class of vowels as shown by the dendrogram heatmap. Languages 11 and 12 show a similar pattern with respect to a different feature, backness. Both of them are harmony languages, which still obey the constraint that vowels in initial syllables must be $[+high]$. Interestingly, vowels cluster with respect to $[\pm back]$ rather than $[\pm high]$ as can be seen from the plots. Evidence for agreement between vowels with respect to backness is three times more frequent than the evidence with respect to agreement between vowels in initial syllable with respect to height. Although vowel harmony is also an instance of co-occurrence restriction (syntagmatic relationship), `word2vec` infers these classes accurately. The number of vowels in a language tends to be much lower than the number of consonants. And therefore, it seems that a co-occurrence restriction between vowels is a relatively larger sample of the set of all possible vowel sequences ($5*5*5 = 125$ in this language) compared to a co-occurrence restriction between two or more consonants. The transparent vowel **a** has no effect on the distances between the other vowels in Language 12.

The ability of phone embeddings to learn phonology in our artificial language experiments can be summarized as follows-

1. Phone embeddings are able to capture paradigmatic relationships among phones very well. For example, word-initial aspirated stops, intervocalic voiced stops, word-final voiceless stops and vowels are recovered as separate classes in most languages.

2. Phone embeddings are also able to capture positional restrictions as well as co-occurrence restrictions on vowels as shown by Languages 10-12.

3. Phone embeddings are not able to capture co-occurrence restrictions among consonants such as homorganic nasal-voiced obstruent clusters, voiced obstruent-lateral cluster and homorganic nasal-sibilant-voiceless stop clusters. This observation is similar to one reported in the distributed semantic literature that word embeddings capture similarity better than relatedness (Asr et al., 2018). Based on insights from the word embedding

literature, context embeddings denoted by the hidden to output layer weight matrix, are supposed to be able to capture better syntagmatic relationships like co-occurrence restrictions. In addition, it is plausible that these co-occurrence restrictions among consonants can be learnt using autosegmental tier-based representations. We leave this investigation to future work.

4 Distinctive Features and Phoneme Induction

The main argument of this paper is that phone embeddings should be evaluated in terms of their ability to capture phonological relationships. Applying this bottom-up approach to natural language phonology is not straightforward since the full set of phonological relationships is not known beforehand. Even the method of evaluating phone embeddings using the correlation between distinctive feature space and phone embedding space, as mentioned earlier, presupposes that the gold standard specification of distinctive features for that particular language is known. However, this is seldom the case. Natural languages are highly complex with processes such as borrowing, loanword adaptation and language changes such as drift. This is why experimenting with artificial phonology can be informative.

The artificial languages in our experiment had increasing levels of complexity, since the goal was to tease apart learnability of different phenomena. Recall that a fixed set of distinctive features along the lines of Hayes and Wilson (2008) was used to estimate the correlation between distinctive feature space and phone embedding space. Notice in table 3 that the value of this correlation goes down as we move from Language 1 to Language 12 regardless of the distance metric used to estimate distance between embeddings. Unlike the cross-linguistic comparison in section 2, the distinctive features are the same across languages. We observe that as the size of the phone inventory and the number of distinct context classes increase, the degree of correlation between feature space and embedding space decreases. How can this trend be accounted for? Examining the distances in the clustermaps, we observe that as the number of context classes goes up, intra-phone distances, especially among the class of consonants tend to increase. This can be noticed by comparing the clusters corresponding to voiceless consonants and vowels between Language 1 and Language 12. Given the continuous space nature of phone embeddings and the dimensionality reduction property of `word2vec`, this is expected. When the weights of the neural network corresponding to a particular phone or phone-sequence are adjusted, the changes affect similar items (Mikolov et al., 2013b). This inverse "dispersion" effect is also relevant to the correlation between distinctive feature space and embedding space- the value of featural distance between phones is constant across languages when estimated using a fixed distinctive feature representation. But, as the number of context classes increases, distances between phone embeddings increase and the cumulative effect on the correlation between phonetic space and embedding space is downward. Thus, this correlation value clearly cannot be used as an evaluation metric for cross-linguistic comparison. Even within a language, a higher correlation value does not necessarily indicate better learning of phonology/phonetics. Rather it indicates a low inverse dispersion effect. One way to interpret the results of Silfverberg et al. (2018, pp.140) is that phone classes based on context are much less spread out in embedding space when learnt using supervised RNN compared to `word2vec`. At best, this can be interpreted as a difference in the dimensionality reduction properties of the two techniques.

This also raises an interesting question about the degree of specification of phones. Phonologists assume a language independent feature specification of phones. The results of our experiments suggest the following possibility- could the granularity of feature specification be dependent on how separable the different classes of phones are in embedding space? In other words, do learners infer distinctive features of phones based on the contexts in which they occur? If certain phone classes can be inferred purely based on context, phonetic features that distinguish these classes can be underspecified. For example, in Language 10, the difference between high and non-high vowels in a language could be inferred based on context. For such a language, is it necessary to include height ($[\pm high]$) as a distinctive feature? Intuitively, the task of distinctive feature induction is related to phoneme induction.

A quantitative approach to phoneme induction based on phone embeddings and phonetic features

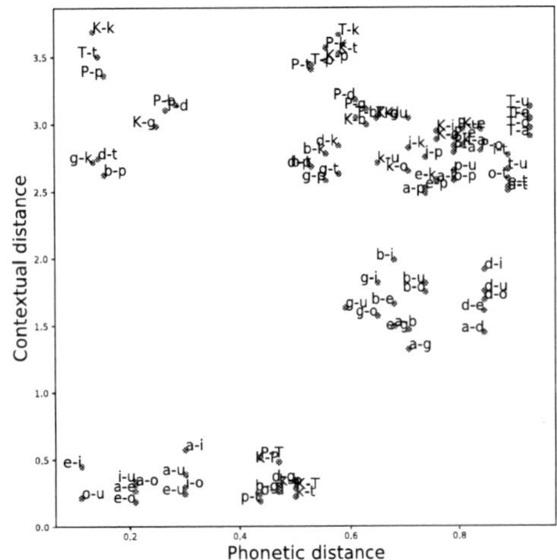

Figure 3: Contextual distance versus Phonetic distance

can be outlined as follows. If embeddings of two phones show low similarity (or high distance), their contexts are very different. If the phones show a high degree of phonetic similarity, then this is very likely to be a case of allophony. If embeddings of two phones show high degree of similarity (or low distance), then their contexts are very similar. If the phones show low degree of phonetic similarity, these are clearly two distinct phonemes in the language. If the phones also show a high degree of phonetic similarity, then this could be either an instance of a phonemic relationship or a co-occurrence restriction. The feature specifications of such phones can be compared to discover distinctive features of phonology. If no such feature is found, it means the default phonetic feature specification is too coarse-grained. If more than one distinctive feature is found, the feature specification is too fine-grained. The exact feature corresponding to the contrast between two phones can be discovered by iterating over the full set of features of the two phones and checking if leaving out a particular feature leads to a drop in the overall correlation between distinctive feature space and embedding space. These ideas are illustrated by the plots in Figures 3 and 4. Figure 3 shows a scatter plot of phone pairs along the phonetic distance-contextual distance axes for Language 3 in the artificial language experiment. Allophonic phone pairs such as **P-p**, **p-b**, **T-t**, **t-d**, **K-k**, **k-g**, etc. show up at the top left corner of the scatter

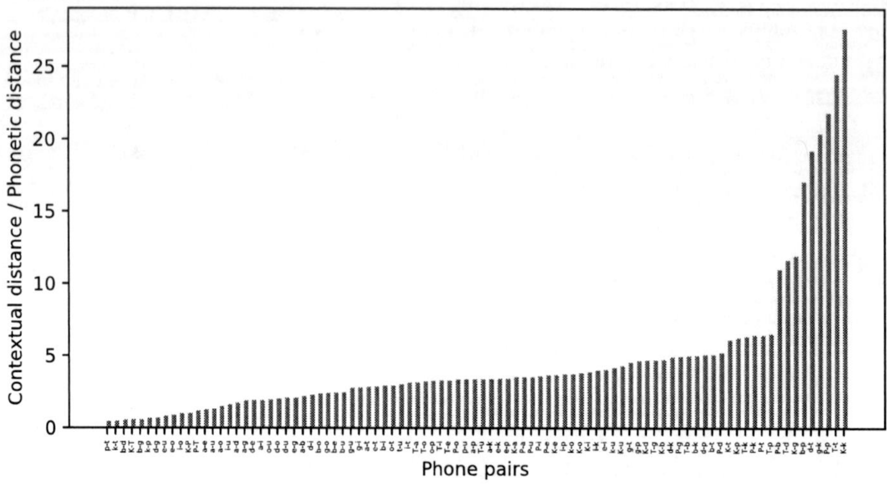

Figure 4: Allophonic index derived from embeddings

plot. The phonetic feature specifications of these pairs can be compared to discover that voicing and aspiration are not phonemic in this language. Similarly, phone pairs that show up at the bottom left corner of this plot such as the 10 pairs of vowels and **P-T**, **P-K**, **K-T**, **p-t**, **t-k**, **p-k**, **b-d**, **d-g** and **g-b** are all phonemic contrasts. The phonetic specifications of these phone pairs can be compared to discover that both height and backness are contrastive for vowels and place of articulation is contrastive for consonants. The remaining phone pairs in the top right corner of the scatter plot are all phonemic contrasts. However, they might not yield any new distinctive features. The bar plot in Figure 4 is another way of visualizing the usefulness of distances between phone embeddings to identify phonemic versus allophonic relationships. We define allophonic index as the ratio of contextual distance estimated using phone embeddings to phonetic distance. The higher the value of this index for a phone pair, the more likely the pair is to be allophonic. The sorted bar plot in Figure 4 corresponding to artificial Language 3 shows allophonic pairs at the right edge and phonemic pairs at the left edge. A precise formulation of a phoneme/distinctive feature induction algorithm based on these metrics is reserved for future work.

5   Conclusions and Future work

This paper presents a discussion of evaluation of phone embeddings. Artificial language experi-ments are used to study `word2vec`'s ability to learn different kinds of phonological relationships. The results show that phone embeddings are able to capture phonemic and allophonic relationships quite well. Phone embeddings are also able to capture co-occurrence restrictions among vowels found in harmony languages. Phone embeddings do not perform well on capturing co-occurrence restrictions among consonants. The experimental results also show an interesting correlation between size and complexity of phone inventory and magnitude of inter-phone distances based on phone embeddings. An analysis of the limitation of correlation between embedding space and distinctive feature space to evaluate phone embeddings for their learning of phonology is also provided. The analytical framework presented here and the proposal for distinctive feature induction will be developed in future work and can be applied to diverse problems ranging from bootstrapping pronunciations of OOV words in ASR to modeling historical phonology. A similar analysis of sound analogies is required to better understand their significance to phonology.

6   Acknowledgements

We thank Giorgio Magri and Mark Steedman for useful comments and discussion. Thanks are also due to the anonymous reviewers for their much useful feedback.

References

Fatemeh Torabi Asr and Michael Jones. 2017. An artificial language evaluation of distributional semantic models. In *Proceedings of the 21st Conference on Computational Natural Language Learning (CoNLL 2017)*, pages 134–142. Association for Computational Linguistics.

Fatemeh Torabi Asr, Robert Zinkov, and Michael Jones. 2018. Querying word embeddings for similarity and relatedness. In *Proceedings of the 2018 Conference of the North American Chapter of the Association for Computational Linguistics: Human Language Technologies, Volume 1 (Long Papers)*, pages 675–684. Association for Computational Linguistics.

Marco Baroni, Georgiana Dinu, and Germán Kruszewski. 2014. Don't count, predict! a systematic comparison of context-counting vs. context-predicting semantic vectors. In *Proceedings of the 52nd Annual Meeting of the Association for Computational Linguistics (Volume 1: Long Papers)*, pages 238–247. Association for Computational Linguistics.

Lars Buitinck, Gilles Louppe, Mathieu Blondel, Fabian Pedregosa, Andreas Mueller, Olivier Grisel, Vlad Niculae, Peter Prettenhofer, Alexandre Gramfort, Jaques Grobler, Robert Layton, Jake VanderPlas, Arnaud Joly, Brian Holt, and Gaël Varoquaux. 2013. API design for machine learning software: experiences from the scikit-learn project. In *ECML PKDD Workshop: Languages for Data Mining and Machine Learning*, pages 108–122.

Bruce Hayes and Colin Wilson. 2008. A maximum entropy model of phonotactics and phonotactic learning. *Linguistic inquiry*, 39(3):379–440.

Roman Jakobson, C Gunnar Fant, and Morris Halle. 1951. *Preliminaries to speech analysis: The distinctive features and their correlates*. MIT press.

Peter Ladefoged and Keith Johnson. 2010. *A course in Phonetics*. Thomson Wadsworth Boston.

Omer Levy, Yoav Goldberg, and Ido Dagan. 2015. Improving distributional similarity with lessons learned from word embeddings. *Transactions of the Association for Computational Linguistics*, 3:211–225.

Tomas Mikolov, Kai Chen, Greg Corrado, and Jeffrey Dean. 2013a. Efficient estimation of word representations in vector space. *arXiv preprint arXiv:1301.3781*.

Tomas Mikolov, Wen-tau Yih, and Geoffrey Zweig. 2013b. Linguistic regularities in continuous space word representations. In *Proceedings of the 2013 Conference of the North American Chapter of the Association for Computational Linguistics: Human Language Technologies*, pages 746–751.

Allison Parrish. 2017. Poetic sound similarity vectors using phonetic features. In *Thirteenth Artificial Intelligence and Interactive Digital Entertainment Conference*.

Jeffrey Pennington, Richard Socher, and Christopher Manning. 2014. Glove: Global vectors for word representation. In *Proceedings of the 2014 Conference on Empirical Methods in Natural Language Processing (EMNLP)*, pages 1532–1543. Association for Computational Linguistics.

Radim Řehůřek and Petr Sojka. 2010. Software Framework for Topic Modelling with Large Corpora. In *Proceedings of the LREC 2010 Workshop on New Challenges for NLP Frameworks*, pages 45–50, Valletta, Malta. ELRA. http://is.muni.cz/publication/884893/en.

Miikka P Silfverberg, Lingshuang Mao, and Mans Hulden. 2018. Sound analogies with phoneme embeddings. *Proceedings of the Society for Computation in Linguistics (SCiL) 2018*, pages 136–144.

Pavel Sofroniev and Çağrı Çöltekin. 2018. Phonetic vector representations for sound sequence alignment. In *Proceedings of the Fifteenth Workshop on Computational Research in Phonetics, Phonology, and Morphology*, pages 111–116.

Inverting and Modeling Morphological Inflection

Yohei Oseki
Faculty of Science & Engineering
Waseda University
oseki@aoni.waseda.jp

Yasutada Sudo
Department of Linguistics
University College London
y.sudo@ucl.ac.uk

Hiromu Sakai
Faculty of Science & Engineering
Waseda University
hsakai@waseda.jp

Alec Marantz
Department of Linguistics & Psychology
New York University
marantz@nyu.edu

Abstract

Previous "wug" tests (Berko, 1958) on
Japanese verbal inflection have demonstrated
that Japanese speakers, both adults and children, cannot inflect novel present tense forms
to "correct" past tense forms predicted by
rules of existent verbs (de Chene, 1982; Vance,
1987, 1991; Klafehn, 2003, 2013), indicating
that Japanese verbs are merely stored in the
mental lexicon. However, the implicit assumption that present tense forms are bases for verbal inflection should not be blindly extended to
morphologically rich languages like Japanese
in which both present and past tense forms are
morphologically complex without inherent direction (Albright, 2002). Interestingly, there
are also independent observations in the acquisition literature to suggest that past tense forms
may be bases for verbal inflection in Japanese
(Klafehn, 2003; Murasugi et al., 2010; Hirose,
2017; Tatsumi et al., 2018). In this paper,
we computationally simulate two directions
of verbal inflection in Japanese, Present $\mapsto$
Past and Past $\mapsto$ Present, with the rule-based
computational model called Minimal Generalization Learner (MGL; Albright and Hayes,
2003) and experimentally evaluate the model
with the bidirectional "wug" test where humans inflect novel verbs in two opposite directions. We conclude that Japanese verbs can be
computed online via some generalizations and
those generalizations do depend on the direction of morphological inflection.

1 Introduction

In her seminal "wug" test, Berko (1958) demonstrated that English speakers, both adults and children, can inflect novel nouns (e.g. *wug*) and novel
verbs (e.g. *rick*) to "correct" plural forms (e.g.
wugs) and "correct" past tense forms (e.g. *ricked*),
respectively. This demonstration strongly suggests that, since the novel words cannot be ex-
perienced before by the experimental participants
and thus accessed from the mental lexicon, the inflected forms must have been produced online via
some productive generalizations, whose nature has
been actively debated in the literature (O'Donnell,
2015; Yang, 2016).

Nevertheless, "wug" tests might be too easy to
"pass" in morphologically sparse languages like
English in which present tense forms are unsuf-
fixed and homonymous (except 3rd person singular) with infinitival forms, and past tense forms
are generated via simple affixation. In fact, previous "wug" tests on Japanese verbal inflection have
demonstrated that Japanese speakers, both adults
and children, cannot inflect novel present tense
forms to "correct" past tense forms predicted by
rules of existent verbs (de Chene, 1982; Vance,
1987, 1991; Klafehn, 2003, 2013). The results of
these previous "wug" tests have been taken to indicate that Japanese verbs are merely stored in the
mental lexicon, not produced online via productive generalizations.

However, the implicit assumption that present
tense forms are bases for verbal inflection should
not be blindly extended to morphologically rich
languages like Japanese. As pointed out by Albright (2002), various factors conspire to determine which cell of the paradigm should be identified as the base and, consequently, in which
direction morphological inflection should be implemented. In particular, unlike English whose
present and past tense forms are asymmetrically
complex, both present and past tense forms are
suffixed in Japanese and thus morphologically
complex without inherent direction, as in Table 1:

Proceedings of the 16th Workshop on Computational Research in Phonetics, Phonology, and Morphology, pages 170–177
Florence, Italy. August 2, 2019 ©2019 Association for Computational Linguistics

Final segment		Meaning	Root	Present	Past
V-final	/e/	'eat'	$\sqrt{\text{tabe}}$	tabe-ru	tabe-ta
	/i/	'wear'	$\sqrt{\text{ki}}$	ki-ru	ki-ta
C-final	/r/	'mow'	$\sqrt{\text{kar}}$	kar-u	kat-ta
	/t/	'win'	$\sqrt{\text{kat}}$	kat-u	kat-ta
	/w/	'buy'	$\sqrt{\text{kaw}}$	ka-u	kat-ta
	/m/	'read'	$\sqrt{\text{yom}}$	yom-u	yon-da
	/b/	'call'	$\sqrt{\text{yob}}$	yob-u	yon-da
	/n/	'die'	$\sqrt{\text{sin}}$	sin-u	sin-da
	/k/	'draw'	$\sqrt{\text{kak}}$	kak-u	ka-ita
	/s/	'lend'	$\sqrt{\text{tas}}$	kas-u	kas-ita
	/g/	'sniff'	$\sqrt{\text{kag}}$	kag-u	ka-ida

Table 1: Japanese verbal inflection (McCawley, 1968)

Interestingly, there are independent observations in the acquisition literature to suggest that past tense forms may be bases for verbal inflection in Japanese. First, Japanese children acquire past tense forms around age 2 before present tense forms (Clancy, 1985; Klafehn, 2003), unlike English children who acquire present tense or infinitival forms first (Brown, 1973). Second, Japanese children exclusively produce past tense forms as Root Infinitive analogues before age 2 (Murasugi et al., 2010), unlike bona fide Root Infinitives in English (Wexler, 1994). Third, Japanese children overregularize present tense forms (e.g. *sim-u* 'die'; Hirose, 2017), but not past tense forms like English (e.g. *go-ed*; Klafehn, 2003). Finally, Japanese children seem to have an inductive bias to prefer past tense forms to present tense forms (Tatsumi et al., 2018). Those observations converge on the hitherto unexplored hypothesis that past tense forms are bases in Japanese.

In this paper, inspired by the acquisition literature (Klafehn, 2003; Murasugi et al., 2010; Hirose, 2017; Tatsumi et al., 2018), we computationally simulate two directions of verbal inflection in Japanese, Present $\mapsto$ Past and Past $\mapsto$ Present, with the rule-based computational model called Minimal Generalization Learner (MGL; Albright and Hayes, 2003) and experimentally evaluate the model with the bidirectional "wug" test where humans inflect novel verbs in two opposite directions. The following questions will be addressed:

1. Which direction is computationally less complex for the model?

2. Which direction is experimentally more accurate for humans?

3. In which direction do the model and humans correlate more strongly?

Model complexity will be measured via three evaluation metrics derived from the confidence scores of rules induced based on the lexicon of existent verb pairs (Albright, 2002). In addition, human accuracy and the correlation between the model and humans are explicitly evaluated against the model, avoiding impressionistic interpretations as in previous "wug" tests, where "the meaning of the word 'pass' is a 60% or better score" (Klafehn, 2013, p.182).

The organization of this paper is as follows. Section 2 describes the methodological details of the Minimal Generalization Learner, the bidirectional "wug" test, and the statistical analyses to compare the two. Section 3 presents the results of model complexity, human accuracy, and the correlation between the model and humans, corresponding to the three questions above. Section 4 summarizes the results and discuss theoretical implications. Section 5 concludes the paper.

2 Methods

2.1 Minimal Generalization Learner

Training: The rule-based computational model called *Minimal Generalization Learner* (MGL; Albright and Hayes, 2002, 2003) was employed from the literature. The MGL was trained on the lexicon of 1269 existent verb pairs (Suski, 1942) in two directions (Present $\mapsto$ Past and Past $\mapsto$ Present), with V-V compounds and light verb constructions removed in order to avoid inflation of the number of particular inflections. Then, rules were induced through minimal generalization for each direction. See Albright and Hayes (2002, 2003) for the rule induction algorithm.

Testing: Novel verbs were then fed into the trained MGL as input and the inflected forms of those verbs were produced as output with the reliability and confidence scores defined below.

Reliability score: The reliability score of a rule, $\hat{p}$, is defined as Equation 1:

$$\hat{p} = \frac{\text{\# forms correctly derived (= hits)}}{\text{\# forms potentially derived (= scope)}} \quad (1)$$

Confidence score: Since weak rules supported by smaller data should be penalized (Mikheev, 1997), the reliability score of a rule is transformed into the confidence score, π, defined as Equation 2:

$$\pi = \hat{p}^* - z(1 - \alpha)/2 \times \sqrt{\frac{\hat{p}^* \times (1 - \hat{p}^*)}{n}} \quad (2)$$

where $\hat{p}^*$ is the smoothed reliability $\hat{p}^* = \frac{hits+0.5}{scope+1}$, $\sqrt{\frac{\hat{p}^* \times (1-\hat{p}^*)}{n}}$ is the estimated variance, and α is the free parameter called confidence value (the higher α, the greater penalty for weak rules) assumed here as $\alpha = .75$.

Mean confidence: Three evaluation metrics can be derived from the confidence score (cf. Albright, 2002). First, the mean confidence score of winning outputs is defined as Equation 3:

$$\bar{\pi} = \frac{1}{n} \sum_{i \in I}^{n} \max_{o \in O_i} \pi_o \tag{3}$$

where I is the the the set of all inputs, O_i is the set of all outputs derived from the input i, and π_o is the confidence score of the output o. The higher mean confidence, the more efficient grammar.

Mean margin: Second, the mean confidence margin of winning outputs is defined as Equation 4:

$$\bar{\Delta} = \frac{1}{n} \sum_{i \in I}^{n} [\max_{o \in O_i} \pi_o - \max_{s \in S_i}(\pi_s, 0)] \tag{4}$$

where S is the subset of all outputs derived from the input i without winning outputs. The higher mean margin, the more efficient grammar.

Mean entropy: Finally, the mean confidence entropy of possible outputs is defined as Equation 5:

$$\bar{H} = \frac{1}{n} \sum_{i \in I}^{n} \sum_{o \in O_i}^{|O_i|} \pi_o \log_2 \pi_o \tag{5}$$

where the confidence scores of all outputs derived from the input, O, are normalized, such that the scores sum up to 1. Unlike the metrics above, the lower mean entropy, the more efficient grammar.

2.2 Bidirectional "Wug" Test

Participants: The bidirectional "wug" test was conducted with the within-participants design. The experimental participants were 45 undergraduate students at Waseda University in Japan. They were given a ¥500 book coupon for their participation. The 6 participants who were non-native speakers of Japanese or misinterpreted the instructions were excluded from statistical analyses, resulting in 39 participants in total.

Stimuli: Bisyllabic novel roots ("wug" roots) were created by randomly combining two open syllables (CV). The open syllables were extracted from the lexicon of 1269 existent verb stems (Suski, 1942), with V-V compounds and light verb constructions removed, and only those with token frequency ≥ 20 were included. The "wug" roots that resemble actual Japanese words or contain repetitions of the same segments were excluded. Since the native Japanese words cannot generally start with voiced obstruents (Tanaka and Yashima, 2013) or /r/ (Labrune, 2014), the "wug" roots starting with those segments were also excluded. Then, 32 past tense forms of the "wug" roots were created as target stimuli in the Past $\mapsto$ Present direction, by attaching (i) the V-final past tense endings /ta/ to 16 "wug" roots (i.e. 8 ending with /e/ and 8 ending with /i/) and (ii) the 4 C-final past tense endings (i.e. /tta/, /nda/, /ita/, and /ida/) to 4 "wug" roots each, hence 16 V-final and 16 C-final past tense forms. In the same vein, 32 present tense forms of the "wug" roots were created as target stimuli in the Present $\mapsto$ Past direction, by attaching (i) the V-final present tense ending /ru/ to 16 "wug" roots (i.e. 8 ending with /e/ and 8 ending with /i/) and (ii) the 8 C-final present tense endings (i.e. /tu/, /u/, /mu/, /bu/, /nu/, /ku/, /su/, and /gu/) to 2 "wug" roots each, hence 16 V-final and 16 C-final present tense forms. Note that the 4 V-final past tense forms whose roots end with /hi/ and 2 C-final present tense forms ending with /nu/ turned out to be not attested in the training data and thus excluded from the statistical analyses.

The 4 frames were also created in which the target stimuli are presented. Each frame consisted of two sentences A and B. In the Present $\mapsto$ Past direction, A sentences include present tense forms, while B sentences contain a blank and elicit past tense forms. In the Past $\mapsto$ Present direction, A sentences include past tense forms, while B sentences contain a blank and elicit present tense forms. In order to make sure that the participants produce target forms in B sentences, temporal adverbs are placed at the sentence initial position to maximally contrast sentences A and B. Specifically, A sentences constitute "Temporal Adverb + Proper Noun + **Verb** + Evidential", whereas B sentences "Temporal Adverb + Proper Noun + _____ + Sentence Final Particle", where the participants are asked to inflect the **Verb**.

Procedure: The task was written production "wug" test in the form of the questionnaire. At the top of the questionnaire were some biographical questions such as (i) birthplaces of participants and their parents, (ii) whether participants were born and grew up in Japan, and (iii) whether parents spoke Japanese to participants at home.

The English translation of the original Japanese instructions is reproduced below:

> "This experiment examines your intuition about Japanese. There are 2 blocks and 48 questions in each block, where both actual and novel verbs in Japanese appear. For each question, please change bold and underlined **verbs** of A sentences to appropriate forms and complete the underlined portion of B sentences. Since there are no correct or incorrect answers, please answer the questions based on your intuition without too much reflection."

The experiment was divided into two blocks, corresponding to Present $\mapsto$ Past and Past $\mapsto$ Present directions, and the order of the two directions was counterbalanced across participants. At the beginning of each block were two example questions with answers in B sentences completed, one example with an actual verb and another with a novel verb. The order of stimulus presentation was randomized across participants by creating 2 random orders for each direction, hence 4 different versions of randomization. The 16 actual verbs, 8 V-final and 8 C-final, were interspersed as fillers in each block, on the condition that no more than 3 target stimuli were presented in sequence.

2.3 Statistical Analyses

Human accuracy: In contrast with the previous "wug" tests, the human accuracies were explicitly evaluated against the MGL. The winning outputs with highest confidence scores were defined as "correct" among possible outputs derived from each input by the MGL. For example, suppose that the MGL produced three possible outputs X, Y, and Z for an input, among which X was the winning output with the highest confidence score. If the output X was produced by 30 participants, the human accuracy would be 30/39 = .769.

Correlation between model and humans: The correlation between model confidence scores and human production probabilities were also analyzed (Albright and Hayes, 2003). The human production probabilities can be simply computed by dividing the frequencies of produced outputs by the number of participants. Given the distribution of human production probabilities being bimodal, nonparametric Kendall's rank correlation analyses were performed in R between model confidence scores and human production probabilities. The outputs not produced by both model and humans were not included in the correlation analyses.

3 Results

3.1 Model Complexity

The result of model complexity is summarized in Table 2, where three model complexity metrics, mean confidence score ($\bar{\pi}$), mean confidence margin ($\bar{\Delta}$), and mean confidence entropy ($\bar{H}$), are shown for each direction of verbal inflection:

	Present $\mapsto$ Past	Past $\mapsto$ Present
Mean confidence ($\bar{\pi}$)	.904	**.959**
Mean margin ($\bar{\Delta}$)	.724	**.849**
Mean entropy ($\bar{H}$)	.387	**.294**

Table 2: Result of model complexity

The three evaluation metrics all converge on the conclusion that the Past $\mapsto$ Present direction is computationally less complex than the Present $\mapsto$ Past direction: the mean confidence and margin were higher, while the mean entropy was lower. On closer inspection, the confidence scores of possible outputs for /ru/-final present tense forms were almost a tie in the Present $\mapsto$ Past direction, which increased the mean entropy.

3.2 Human Accuracy

The result of human accuracy is summarized in Table 3, where the accuracies of the current experiment are shown for each direction of verbal inflection and compared with six previous "wug" tests (de Chene, 1982; Vance, 1987, 1991; Klafehn, 2003, 2013):

Reference	Modality	Task	Accuracy
de Chene (1982)	oral	production	46%
Vance (1987)	written	choice	51%
Vance (1991)	written	choice	63%
Klafehn (2003)	written	choice	53%
Klafehn (2013)	oral	production	32%
Present $\mapsto$ Past	written	production	48%
Past $\mapsto$ Present	written	production	**72%**

Table 3: Result of human accuracy

First, the accuracy of the Present $\mapsto$ Past direction (48%) is generally comparable to the literature, especially the oral production experiment by (46%; de Chene, 1982), despite different participants and stimuli between the experiments. Second, and more importantly, the accuracy of the

Past $\mapsto$ Present direction (72%) was significantly higher than the literature, even the forced choice experiments (Vance, 1987, 1991; Klafehn, 2003), which would be regarded as "pass" on the assumption that "the meaning of the word 'pass' is a 60% or better score" (Klafehn, 2013).

3.3 Correlation Between Model and Humans

The result of correlation between the model and humans is shown in Figure 1, where the x-axis is the model confidence score computed by the MGL ("Model confidence score"), whereas the y-axis is the human production probability of the forms produced by the experimental participants ("Human production probability"). Color represents the Past $\mapsto$ Present (red) and Present $\mapsto$ Past (blue) directions. Shape of the data points represents C-final (circle; •) and V-final (triangle; ▲) roots. The lines are the fitted linear models.

There were 1248 forms in total produced for each direction (39 participants * 32 stimuli = 1248 forms). In the Past $\mapsto$ Present direction, 1225 forms were present tense forms, while 23 forms were errors (i.e. non-present tense forms). Out of the 1225 present tense forms, 956 forms were also produced by the MGL. In the Present $\mapsto$ Past direction, 1225 forms were past tense forms, while 23 forms were errors (i.e. non-past tense forms). Out of the 1225 past tense forms, 821 forms were also produced by the MGL. Kendall's rank correlation analyses revealed that the model confidence scores and human production probabilities were strongly correlated in the Past $\mapsto$ Present direction ($z = 5.0618$, $\tau = 0.534$, $p < 0.001***$), but only weakly in the Present $\mapsto$ Past direction ($z = 2.3058$, $\tau = 0.2448$, $p < 0.05*$).

4 Discussion

In summary, the results demonstrated that (i) the Past $\mapsto$ Present direction was computationally less complex than the Present $\mapsto$ Past direction, (ii) the Past $\mapsto$ Present direction was experimentally more accurate than the Present $\mapsto$ Past direction, and (iii) the model and humans were correlated strongly in the Past $\mapsto$ Present direction, but only weakly in the Present $\mapsto$ Past direction. The present work should be regarded as the computational psycholinguistic approach to the Paradigm Cell Filling Problem (Ackerman et al., 2009) and, importantly, the result of model complexity harmonizes well with the Low Entropy Conjecture (Ackerman and Malouf, 2013), which may in turn provides an insight into SIGMOR-PHON Shared Task on morphological reinflection (Cotterell et al., 2018). In the following, two theoretical implications will be discussed: the past tense debate and language learning.

4.1 The Past Tense Debate

In the context of the past tense debate on rule vs. analogy (Pinker and Ullman, 2002), three logically possible models have been proposed in the literature: the single route rule-based model (Yang, 2002), the single route analogy-based model (Rumelhart and McClelland, 1986), and the dual route model (Pinker and Prince, 1988). The results above at least indicate that Japanese verbs can be computed online via some generalizations and those generalizations do depend on the direction of morphological inflection, contrary to the conclusion of previous "wug" tests that Japanese verbs are merely stored in the mental lexicon (de Chene, 1982; Vance, 1987, 1991; Klafehn, 2003, 2013). However, although the MGL is "rule-based", the nature of those generalizations is still an open question to be addressed via the systematic comparison with contemporary analogy-based models such as Recurrent Neural Networks (RNN: Kirov and Cotterell, 2018) and Naive Discriminative Learning (NDL: Baayen et al., 2011) couched in Word and Paradigm models of morphology (Stump, 2001; Blevins, 2006).

In addition, given the different strength of correlation with the rule-based computational model in two opposite directions, we can hypothesize that the Past $\mapsto$ Present direction is rule-based, while other directions including the Present $\mapsto$ Past direction is analogy-based. Then, following the electroencephalography (EEG) experiment by Kobayashi et al. (2012) who demonstrated that rule and analogy are indexed by event-related potential (ERP) components called LAN and N400, respectively, we predict that the Past $\mapsto$ Present direction is reflected by LAN, whereas the Present $\mapsto$ Past direction by N400. This prediction is summarized in Table 4 and left for future research.

Direction	Wug	Model	Route	ERP
Past $\mapsto$ Present	"pass"	Symbolic	Rule	LAN
Present $\mapsto$ Past	"fail"	Neural	Analogy	N400

Table 4: Prediction of ERP components

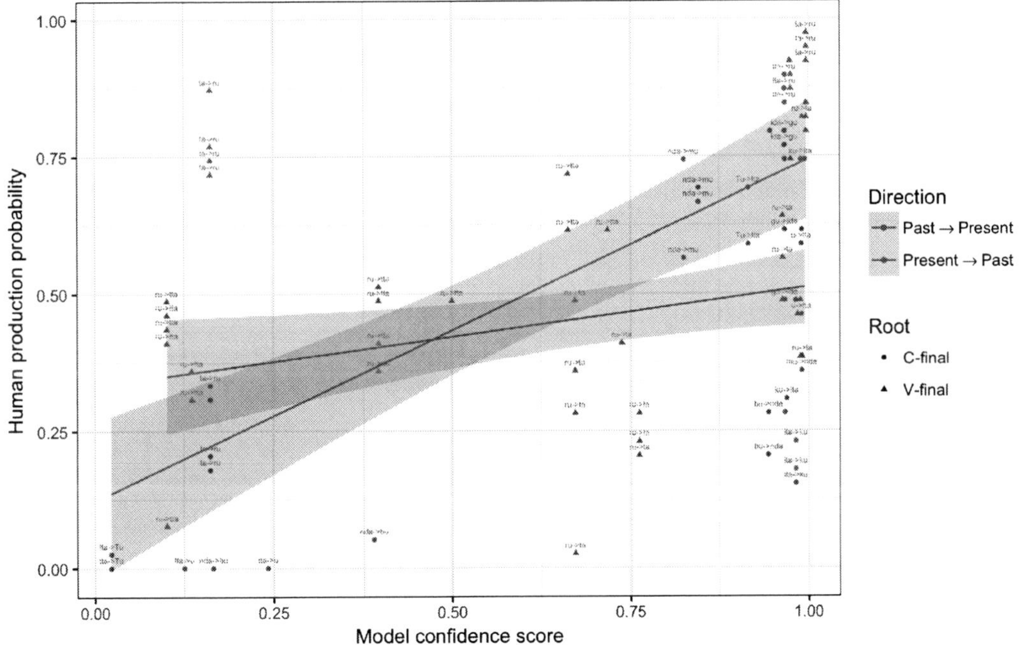

Figure 1: Result of correlation between the model and humans

4.2 Human and Machine Language Learning

The results above further suggest that human language learning can provide insights into machine language learning. Interestingly, the Past ↦ Present direction was motivated by not only the language acquisition literature (Klafehn, 2003; Murasugi et al., 2010; Hirose, 2017; Tatsumi et al., 2018) but also artificial language learning by Yin and White (2018) who show that humans have an inductive bias against neutralization and homophony. In other words, the Past ↦ Present direction is preferred to the Present ↦ Past direction because the present tense forms of /r/, /t/, /w/-final "wug" roots and /m/, /b/, /n/-final "wug" roots are neutralized into the homonymous past tense forms ending with /tta/ and /nda/, respectively.

Nevertheless, there were several limitations with the current experiment. First, the assumption that the training data is fed to the model in pairs organized as paradigms is unrealistic due to Zipf's law (Zipf, 1949), where paradigms are almost always incomplete in human language learning (Yang, 2017; Blevins et al., 2017). In order to simulate realistic language learning, child-directed speech (CDS) should be employed as the training data, especially given that relative frequencies of present and past tense forms seem to be diverse (Tatsumi et al., 2018). Second, the MGL is "rule-based" but learns only product-oriented generalizations (Becker and Gouskova, 2016) in that present and past tense forms are mapped to each other without underlying roots. In order to test source-oriented generalizations over underlying roots, morphological decomposition must be implemented to retrieve the roots from which present and past tense forms are derived (Taft, 1979, 2004). Finally, different "wug" roots were employed in two directions of verbal inflection (though created similarly) so that different results might be attributed to different roots, which remains to be controlled in future.

5 Conclusion

In this paper, inspired by the acquisition literature (Klafehn, 2003; Murasugi et al., 2010; Hirose, 2017; Tatsumi et al., 2018), we computationally simulated two directions of verbal inflection, Present ↦ Past and Past ↦ Present, with the rule-based computational model called Minimal Generalization Learner (MGL; Albright and Hayes, 2003) and experimentally evaluated the model with the bidirectional "wug" test where humans inflected novel verbs in two opposite directions, addressing the following questions:

1. Which direction is computationally less complex for the model?

2. Which direction is experimentally more accurate for humans?

3. In which direction do the model and humans correlate more strongly?

The results revealed that (i) the Past $\mapsto$ Present direction was computationally less complex than the Present $\mapsto$ Past direction, (ii) the Past $\mapsto$ Present direction was experimentally more accurate than the Present $\mapsto$ Past direction, and (iii) the model and humans were correlated strongly in the Past $\mapsto$ Present direction, but only weakly in the Present $\mapsto$ Past direction. We conclude that Japanese verbs can be computed online via some generalizations (pace de Chene, 1982; Vance, 1987, 1991; Klafehn, 2003, 2013) and those generalizations do depend of the direction of morphological inflection.

Acknowledgments

We would like to thank Takane Ito, Ryo Otoguro, Yoko Sugioka, and SIGMORPHON anonymous reviewers for valuable suggestions. This work was supported by JSPS KAKENHI Grant Number JP18H05589.

References

Farrell Ackerman, James Blevins, and Robert Malouf. 2009. Parts and wholes: Implicative patterns in inflectional paradigms. In James Blevins and Juliette Blevins, editors, *Analogy in Grammar: Form and Acquisition*, pages 54–82. Oxford University Press, New York.

Farrell Ackerman and Robert Malouf. 2013. Morphological organization: The low entropy conjecture. *Language*, 89:429–464.

Adam Albright. 2002. *The Identification of Bases in Morphological Paradigms*. Ph.D. thesis, UCLA.

Adam Albright and Bruce Hayes. 2002. Modeling English past tense intuitions with Minimal Generalization. *Proceedings of the Sixth Meeting of the ACL Special Interest Group in Computational Phonology*.

Adam Albright and Bruce Hayes. 2003. Rule vs. analogy in English past tenses: a computational/experimental study. *Cognition*, 90:119–161.

Harald Baayen, Petar Milin, Dusica Filipovic Durdevic, Peter Hendrix, and Marco Marelli. 2011. An Amorphous Model for Morphological Processing in Visual Comprehension Based on Naive Discriminative Learning. *Psychological Review*, 118:438–481.

Michael Becker and Maria Gouskova. 2016. Source-Oriented Generalizations as Grammar Inference in Russian Vowel Deletion. *Linguistic Inquiry*, 47:391–425.

Jean Berko. 1958. The Child's Learning of English Morphology. *Word*, 14:150–177.

James Blevins. 2006. Word-based morphology. *Journal of Linguistics*, 42:531–573.

James Blevins, Petar Milin, and Michael Ramscar. 2017. The Zipfian Paradigm Cell Filling Problem. In Ferenc Kiefer, James Blevins, and Huba Bartos, editors, *Morphological paradigms and functions*, pages 141–158. Brill, Leiden.

Roger Brown. 1973. *A first language*. Harvard University Press, Cambridge, MA.

Brent de Chene. 1982. The segmentation of Japanese verbs: Experimental evidence. *Papers in Japanese Linguistics*, 8:29–61.

Patricia Clancy. 1985. The acquisition of Japanese. In Dan Slobin, editor, *The crosslinguistic study of language acquisition*, pages 373–524. Lawrence Erlbaum Associates, Hillsdale, NJ.

Ryan Cotterell, Christo Kirov, John Sylak-Glassman, Géraldine Walther, Ekaterina Vylomova, Arya D. McCarthy, Katharina Kann, Sebastian Mielke, Garrett Nicolai, Miikka Silfverberg, David Yarowsky, Jason Eisner, and Mans Hulden. 2018. The CoNLL–SIGMORPHON 2018 Shared Task: Universal Morphological Reinflection. *CoNLL*.

Yuki Hirose. 2017. *The Adventure of Little Linguists*. Iwanami Publisher, Tokyo.

Christo Kirov and Ryan Cotterell. 2018. Recurrent Neural Networks in Linguistic Theory: Revisiting Pinker and Prince (1988) and the Past Tense Debate. *Transactions of the Association for Computational Linguistics*, pages 651–665.

Terry Klafehn. 2003. *Emergent properties of Japanese verbal inflection*. Ph.D. thesis, University of Hawaii.

Terry Klafehn. 2013. Myth of the wug test. *BLS*, 37:170–184.

Yuki Kobayashi, Yoko Sugioka, and Takane Ito. 2012. ERP Responses to Violations in Japanese Verb Conjugation Patterns. In *Proceedings of the Annual Meeting of the Cognitive Science Society*, pages 611–616.

Laurence Labrune. 2014. The phonology of Japanese /r/: A panchronic account. *Journal of East Asian Linguistics*, 23:1–25.

James McCawley. 1968. *The Phonological Component of a Grammar of Japanese*. Mouton, The Hague.

Andrei Mikheev. 1997. Automatic rule induction for unknown-word guessing. *Computational Linguistics*, 23:405–423.

Keiko Murasugi, Chisato Fuji, and Tomoko Hashimoto. 2010. What's acquired later in an agglutinative language. *Nanzan Linguistics*, 6:47–78.

Timothy O'Donnell. 2015. *Productivity and Reuse in Language*. MIT Press, Cambridge, MA.

Steven Pinker and Alan Prince. 1988. On language and connectionism. *Cognition*, 28:73–193.

Steven Pinker and Michael Ullman. 2002. The past and future of the past tense. *Trends in Cognitive Sciences*, 6:456–462.

David Rumelhart and James McClelland. 1986. On learning the past tenses of English verbs. In David Rumelhart and James McClelland, editors, *Parallel distributed processing: Explorations in the microstructure of cognition*, pages 216–271. MIT Press, Cambridge, MA.

Gregory Stump. 2001. *Inflectional Morphology: A eory of Paradigm Structure*. Cambridge University Press, Cambridge.

Peter Suski. 1942. *Conjugation of Japanese Verbs in the Modern Spoken Language*. P.D. and Ione Perkins, South Pasadena.

M. Taft. 1979. Recognition of affixed words and the word frequency effect. *Memory and Cognition*, 7:263–272.

M. Taft. 2004. Morphological decomposition and the reverse base frequency effect. *The Quarterly Journal of Experimental Psychology*, 57:745–765.

Yu Tanaka and Jun Yashima. 2013. Deliberate markedness in Japanese hypocoristics. *Proceedings of GLOW in Asia IX*, pages 283–297.

Tomoko Tatsumi, Ben Ambridge, and Julian Pine. 2018. Testing an input-based account of children's errors with inflectional morphology: an elicited production study of Japanese. *Journal of Child Language*, 45:1144–1173.

Timothy Vance. 1987. *An introduction to Japanese phonology*. State University of New York Press, New York.

Timothy Vance. 1991. A new experimental study of Japanese verbal morphology. *Journal of Japanese Linguistics*, 13:145–156.

Ken Wexler. 1994. Optional Infinitives, Head Movement, and Economy of Derivation. In *Verb Movement*, pages 305–350. Cambridge University Press, Cambridge.

Charles Yang. 2002. *Knowlwedge and Learning in Natural Language*. Oxford University Press, Oxford.

Charles Yang. 2016. *The Price of Linguistic Productivity*. MIT Press, Cambridge, MA.

Charles Yang. 2017. Rage against the machine: Evaluation metrics in the 21st century. *Language Acquisition*, 24:100–125.

Sora Heng Yin and James White. 2018. Neutralization and homophony avoidance in phonological learning. *Cognitive Science*, 179:89–101.

George Zipf. 1949. *Human behavior and the principle of least effort: An introduction to human ecology*. Addison-Wesley, Cambridge, MA.

Augmenting a German Morphological Database by Data-Intense Methods

Petra Steiner

Friedrich-Schiller-Universität Jena

Jena, Germany

`petra.steiner@uni-jena.de`

Abstract

This paper deals with the automatic enhancement of a new German morphological database. While there are some databases for flat word segmentation, this is the first available resource which can be directly used for deep parsing of German words. We combine the entries of this morphological database with the morphological tools SMOR and Moremorph and a context-based evaluation method which builds on a large Wikipedia corpus. We describe the state of the art and the essential characteristics of the database and the context method. The approach is tested on an inflight magazine of Lufthansa. We derive over 5,000 new instances of complex words. The coverage for the lemma types reaches up to over 99 percent. The precision of new found complex splits and monomorphemes is between 0.93 and 0.99.

1 Introduction

German is a language with complex processes of word formation, of which the most common are compounding and derivation. Segmentation and analysis of the resulting word forms are challenging as spelling conventions do not permit spaces as indicators for boundaries of constituents as in (1).

(1)   Verkehrsamt 'tourist office'

For long orthographical word forms, many combinatorially possible analyses exist, though usually only one of them has a conventionalized meaning (see Figure 1). For instance, for *Verkehrsamt* 'traffic office, tourist office', word segmentation tools can yield the wrong split containing one with the smaller number of word tokens *Verkehr* 'traffic' and *Samt* 'velvet'.

In this case, there is a linking element within the word form which could be wrongly interpre-

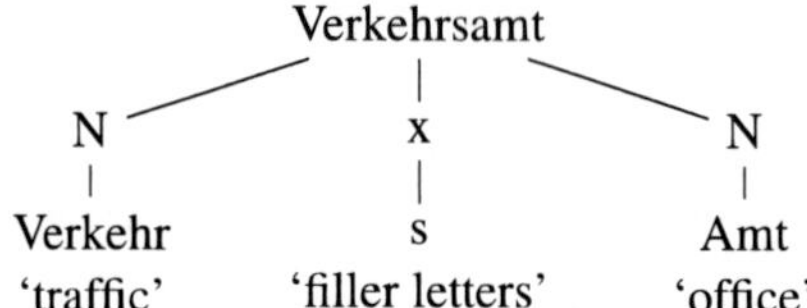
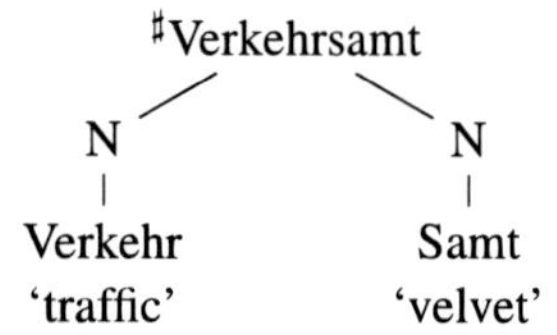

Figure 1: Ambiguous analysis of *Verkehrsamt* 'tourist office'

tated as part of a morph. Such elements function as morphophonological structure markers.[1]

German compounds can consist of derivatives, or compounds can be subject to further derivation. In (1), *Verkehr* is the result of a conversion process from *verkehren* 'to run, to fly', which again consists of a prefix and a verb stem (see Figure 2). On each level of morphological segmentation, the number of possible analyses is 2^n. This number can be reduced by excluding implausible constructions such as suffixes at the beginning of a construct. On the other hand, it has to be multiplied by the number of homonyms for the segmented forms. Therefore, automatic segmentations with more than ten possible analyses for one word are no rare case.

However, finding the correct segmentations and morphological structures is essential for terminologies and translation (memory) tools, information retrieval, and as input for tex-

---

[1] By some approaches, such linking elements are considered as a special kind of morphemes and called *Fugenmorpheme*. We like to avoid such classifications and use the labels *filler letters* or *interfix*.

Proceedings of the 16th Workshop on Computational Research in Phonetics, Phonology, and Morphology, pages 178–188

Florence, Italy. August 2, 2019 ©2019 Association for Computational Linguistics

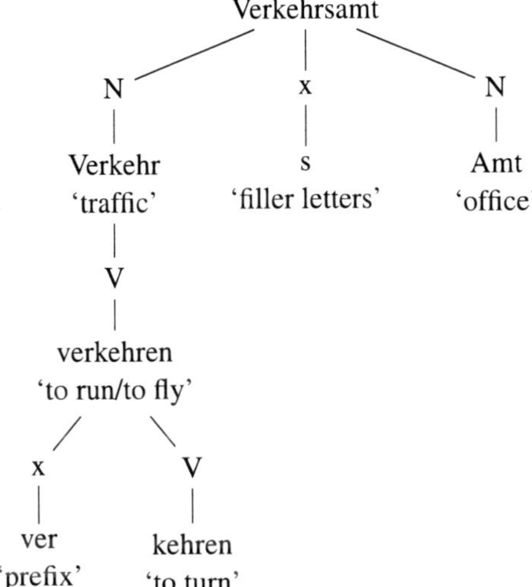

Figure 2: Complex analysis of *Verkehrsamt* 'tourist office'

tual analyses. Deep parsing of complex morphological structures produces disambiguation such as *(Fremde|n|verkehr)|s|amt* 'tourism office' instead of the tautological interpretation ♯*Fremde|n|(Verkehr|s|amt)* 'foreigner tourist office'.[2] Such analyses can help improving the quality of translation and retrieval tasks.

Moreover, counts of morphs, and morphological structures are useful for inducing hypotheses about statistical tendencies and quantitative laws, e.g. Menzerath's law (Cramer, 2005) or the Principle of Early Immediate Constituents (Hoffmann, 1999), which has not yet been corroborated for the word level by statistical tests.

In this paper, we will apply a hybrid approach for finding the correct splits of words and augmenting a morphological database. In Section 2, we provide a concise overview of previous work in word segmentation and word parsing for German. In Section 3, we introduce two linguistic tools we will be using later. *SMOR* is a well-known morphological tool. We describe how we modified its lexicon and exploited and changed its internal results by the add-on module *Moremorph*. Section 4 introduces our morphological database which was built on the basis of the linguistic databases CELEX and GermaNet. Section 5 describes the data-intense procedures for the morphological analyses and supervised database

enhancements. In Section 6, we test our method on a corpus of an inflight journal. Finally, we discuss our results and give an outlook for future developments.

2 Related Work

The first developments in morphological segmentation tools for German date back to the Nineties. Most of them are based on finite state machines. Gertwol (Haapalainen and Majorin, 1995), MORPH (Hanrieder, 1996), Morphy (Lezius, 1996; Lezius et al., 1998) and later SMOR (Schmid et al., 2004) and TAGH (Geyken and Hanneforth, 2006) generate morphological analyses for complex German words, yielding results for derivatives and compounds. All these analyses are flat word splittings and often include dozens of segmentation versions.

There are different ways to tackle such kind of ambiguity, most of which are applied merely to compounds and yield flat segmentations of the immediate constituent level.

Cap (2014) and Koehn and Knight (2003) use ranking scores, such as the geometric mean, for the different morphological analyses and then choose the segmentation with the highest ranking.

Another approach consists in exploitation the sequence of letters, e.g. by pattern matching with tokens (Henrich and Hinrichs, 2011, 422) or lemmas (Weller-Di Marco, 2017). Ziering and van der Plas (2016) use normalization methods which are combined with ranking by the geometric mean. Ma et al. (2016) apply Conditional Random Fields modeling for letter sequences. Daiber et al. (2015) extract candidates of compound splits by string comparisons with corpus data.

Recent approaches exploit semantic information for the ranking of compound splittings. Riedl and Biemann (2016) utilize look-ups of similar terms inside a distributional thesaurus. Their ranking score is a modification of the geometric mean.

Ziering et al. (2016) use the cosine as a measure for semantic similarity between compounds and their hypothetical constituents and combine these similarity values by computing the geometric means and other scores for each produced split. The scores are then used as factors to be multiplied by the scores of former splits.

One of the few approaches tackling deep morphological analyses is Ziering et al. (2016). Their investigation considers left-branching compounds

---

[2]The complete structure of Fremdenverkehrsamt 'tourism traffic office, tourist office' is represented in Figure 4.

consisting of three lexemes. Their distributional semantic modelling often fails to find the correct binary split if the head is too ambiguous to correlate strongly with the first part. But in general, using the semantic context is a sensitive disambiguation method. Ziering and van der Plas (2016) develop a splitter which makes use of normalization methods and can be used recursively by re-analyzing the results of splits. Their evaluation is based on the binary compounds of GermaNet (Hamp and Feldweg, 1997; Henrich and Hinrichs, 2011).

Würzner and Hanneforth (2013) use a probabilistic context free grammar for full morphological parsing, but restrict their approach to derivational adjectives.

Most these approaches build upon corpus data. Only Henrich and Hinrichs (2011) enrich the output of morphological segmentation with information from the annotated compounds of GermaNet to disambiguate such structures. This can in a further step yield hierarchical structures but presupposes that the entries for the components exist inside the database. Steiner and Ruppenhofer (2018) build on this idea to derive more complex morphological structures from lexical resources. In 5, we come back to this and will exploit their resource.

3 SMOR: A Morphological Tool for German and its Add-On Moremorph

3.1 SMOR

SMOR is a widely used morphological segmentation tool (e.g. Cap (2014), Henrich and Hinrichs (2011), Steiner and Ruppenhofer (2015), Ziering et al. (2016)). It is based on two-level morphology (Koskenniemi, 1984) and implemented as a set of finite-state transducers. For German, a large set of lexicons is available. These lexicons contain information about inflection, parts of speech and classes of word formation, e.g. abbreviations and truncations. The tag set used is compatible with the STTS (Stuttgart Tübingen tag set, Schiller et al. (1995)).

SMOR produces different levels of granularity and different representation formats with different transducers and options. Example (2) and (3) show two simplified outputs of fine-grained analyses for *Verkehrsamt* 'traffic office, tourist office' and *Fremdenverkehrsamt* 'foreign-traffic office, tourist office'. For the sake of simplicity, we removed case and number.

(2) Verkehr<NN>Samt<+NN>
     Verkehr<NN>Amt<+NN>
     ver<VPREF>kehren<V>Samt<+NN>

(3) Fremdenverkehr<NN>Samt<+NN>
     Fremdenverkehr<NN>Amt<+NN>
     Fremd<Adj>verkehr<NN>Samt<+NN>
     Fremd<Adj>verkehr<NN>Amt<+NN>
     Fremd<Adj>ver<VPREF>kehren<V>Samt<+NN>

In (2), the word form *Verkehrsamt* 'tourist office' is analyzed in three different ways, of which two show the erroneous interpretation of the string *samt* 'velvet' as a noun. (3) shows the same error in three of its five segmentations. The categories consist of parts of speech (<NN>, <V>) for free morphs and the position of bound morphemes (e.g. <VPREF> for 'verbal prefix').

3.2 Moremorph

While SMOR is a reliable foundation for the analysis of word forms which have not been found before, it comes with some small drawbacks. Moremorph aims at improving and adjusting the output of SMOR.

As can be seen from the second line of (2), the SMOR output does not indicate if there are filler letters (or interfixes) inside a word.

However, the information exists inherently in intermediate SMOR output which can be reanalyzed by Moremorph. Therefore, filler letters (FL) can be marked as in (4):

(4) Verkehr s Amt NN FL NN <NN>

This annotation shows the morphs on the lexical level, their classes with filler letters, and finally the part of speech of the word form in angle brackets. (5) presents the Moremorph representation of (3). In the last three analyses, there is one tag more than the number of splits due to the noun conversion of *fremd* 'foreign' to *Fremde* 'foreigner'.

(5) a. Fremdenverkehrsamt
         Fremdenverkehr Samt
         NN NN <NN>

     b. Fremdenverkehrsamt
         Fremdenverkehr s Amt
         NN FL NN <NN>

c. Fremdenverkehrsamt
fremd en Verkehr Samt
ADJ NNSUFF FL NN NN <NN>

d. Fremdenverkehrsamt
fremd en Verkehr s amt
ADJ NNSUFF FL NN FL NN <NN>

e. Fremdenverkehrsamt
fremd en ver kehr Samt
ADJ NNSUFF FL VPREF V NN
<NN>

Moremorphs uses SMOR lexicons which we adapted to the current task. The original version of the names lexicon comprised 14,998 entries, the final extended version 16,718 entries. During the project, the lexicon was constantly extended and cleaned and its entries were revised. The final version used for the current work comprises 42,205 entries. Many changes of the rule sets were made in cooperation with Helmut Schmid according to our suggestions. For example, we changed the sets of characters or added adverbs as possible tag class for numbers. Other changes include the derivation of adjectives from names of location. Some of the finite-state transducers had to be changed for this.

We also standardized inconsistent analyses for orthographical variants with and without hyphenations and added some more special characters to the inventory of word structuring means.

This leads to consistent analyses for orthographical variants such as in (6). Also word forms with some other special characters not covered by SMOR can be processed now, as in (7).

(6) a. Flughafen Köln-Bonn 'Airport Cologne-Bonn'
b. Flughafen Köln/Bonn 'Airport Cologne/Bonn'.

(7) "Team Lufthansa"-Partner

(8) shows the output for (6-b) with the structuring character tagged as HYPHEN.

(8) Köln/Bonn Köln / Bonn
NPROP HYPHEN NPROP <NPROP>

4 A Lexical Database with Deep-Level Morphological Information

While most morphological analyzers build on the results of word splitters, we decided to take up a hybrid approach which combines the reliable entries of a morphological database with the augmented and further processed analyses of SMOR and Moremorph. Here, also another morphological tool could be chosen.

The German morphological tree database extracts its entries from a. the refurbished CELEX database (Baayen et al., 1995; Steiner, 2016) for German morphology (Burnage, 1995; Gulikers et al., 1995) and b. the compound analyses from the GermaNet database (Hamp and Feldweg, 1997; Henrich and Hinrichs, 2011; Steiner, 2017). For both preprocessed datasets, the derivation of complex structures was performed recursively, by combining the GermaNet analyses with the analyses from CELEX.

The tree building tool provides different parameters for the analysis. We chose to enrich the data with information on diachronic derivation and permitted a depth of six levels for the morphological analyses. (9) shows the morphological structures for (9-a) *Verkehrsamt* 'tourist office', (9-b) *Verkehrsanlage* 'traffic facility', and (9-c) *Verkehrsbehinderung* 'traffic obstruction'. (9-b) comprises diachronic derivational information, showing the noun *Anlage* 'facility/lay out' as derived from the verb *anlegen* 'lay out'.

(9) a. Verkehrsamt
(*Verkehr*
(*verkehren*
ver|
kehren))|
s|
Amt

b. Verkehrsanlage
(*Verkehr*
(*verkehren*
ver|
kehren))|
s|
(*Anlage*
(*anlegen*
an|
legen))

c. Verkehrsbehinderung
    (*Verkehr*
      (*verkehren*
      ver|
      kehren))|
    s|
    (*Behinderung*
      (*behindern*
      be|
      hindern)|
    ung)

The number of entries for this databases of the morphological trees amounts to 101,588. In addition, we extracted 6,339 types of monomorphemes from the refurbished German CELEX database.

5 Combining Morphological Databases with a Segmenter

In the following, we combine the morphological database with a morphological segmenter and a contextual evaluation process. If the database look-up fails, the time-consuming word splitting and evaluation is started. Then the output of Moremorph is analyzed by a contextual method by exploiting a very large corpus. If this fails, frequencies counts of a very large corpus is the back-off strategy. The new analyses are added to a set of new splits.

At the end of each word analysis, all subparts of the word are being searched within the database and the newsplit set. This leads to incrementally more fine-grained entries.

Figure 3 presents an overview. It shows two databases of morphological trees: the German morphological tree database and a incremental database for all newly found morphological analyses. Furthermore, it comprises a set of monomorphemes.

5.1 Basic Look-Up

As shown in Figure 3, a look-up finds the respective tree or the simplex form for the word within the lexicons. Before this is added to the results, all of its subparts are being looked up within the databases and the new splits. These subanalyses are being integrated to its new analysis. Old entries within the lexical databases are being substituted for the new ones.

5.2 Finding Splits

If neither an entry inside the tree lexicons nor in the list of monomorphemes can be found, the Moremorph analyses are taken as the start for the further analysis. For each analysis, e.g. the five different ones of example (5), every possible combination of subtrees has to build. Some of them can be filtered out, because they are linguistically implausible, e.g. when a hypothetical subpart finishes with a prefix.

All plausible combinations of strings and tags undergo a contextual analysis, if occurrences for all subparts can be found within at least one text of the large corpus. Otherwise, a procedure of using the overall document frequencies together with a back-off strategy will be invoked.

5.2.1 Morphological Segmentation based on Contextual Information

For (unknown) compounds, we presuppose that each component can be found within the same close environments. Therefore, the frequencies of components in texts should be much lower for erroneous splits than the frequencies for correct segmentations.

We chose a large set of texts for the retrieval: the freely available and annotated German Wikipedia Korpus of 2015 (Margaretha and Lüngen, 2014).[3] We restricted ourselves to the 1.8 million texts subcorpus of the articles. The corpus was tokenized by a modified version of the tool from Dipper (2016) and lemmatized by the TreeTagger (Schmid, 1999). Text indices were built both for tokenized and lemmatized forms. For each text, all frequencies of lemmas and tokens were stored.

For each morphological split of a word form wf ($\text{sp}_{wf,n}$), the intersection of all texts comprising the word form wf and their hypothetical components $c_{wf,sp,1..n}$ is retrieved from the text indices. For every text t which includes all components for the word form wf ($c_{wf,sp,1}...c_{wf,sp,n}$) of a morphological split, the document frequencies (df) of the components are being retrieved and added to the sum of text frequencies score (Stf). For every hypothetical analysis, the highest value is chosen and the morphological analysis with this score is stored (Equation 1).

---

[3] see http://www1.ids-mannheim.de/kl/projekte/korpora/verfuegbarkeit.html

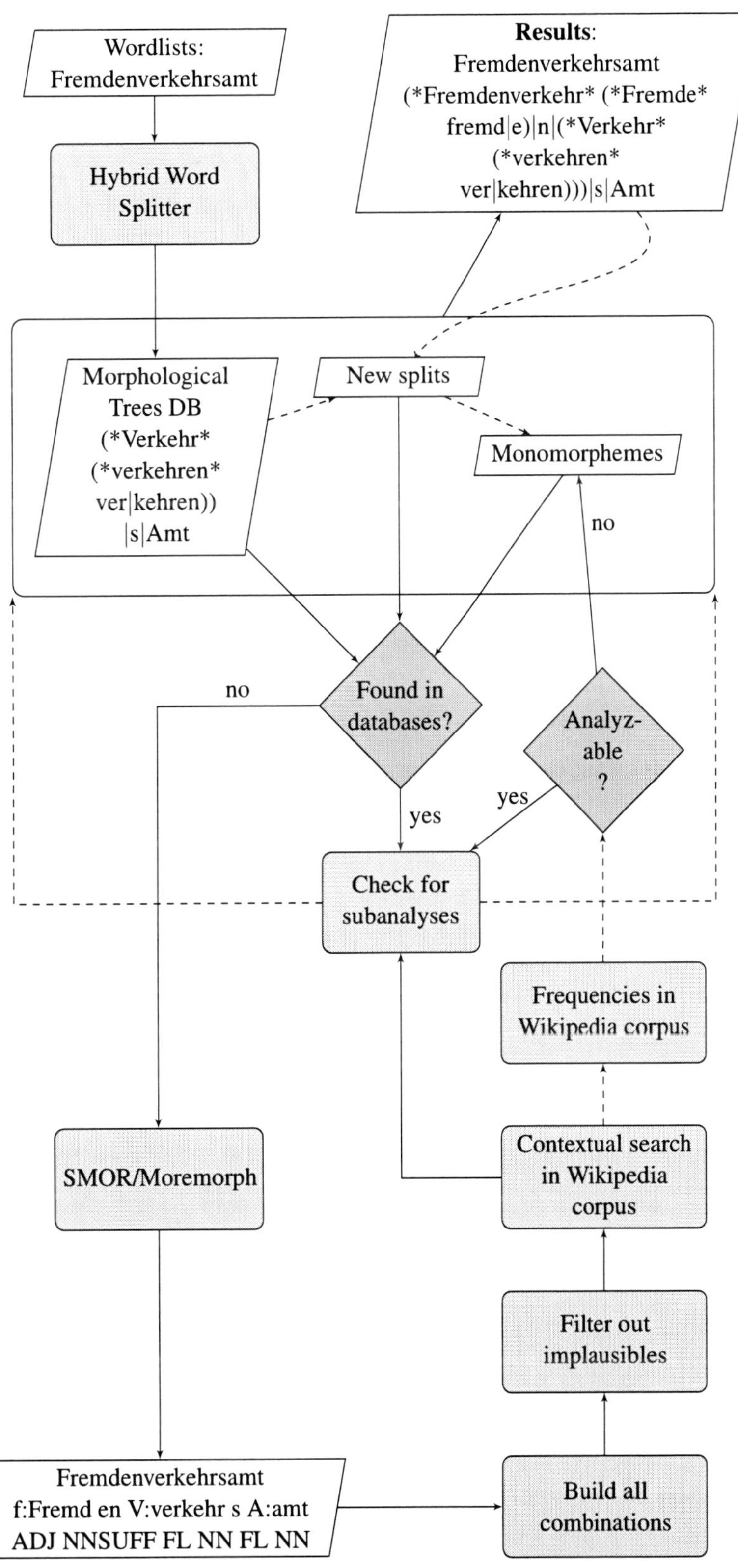

Figure 3: Hybrid word analysis: Morphological trees database, word segmenter, and two different evaluation procedures as alternative methods for word splitting

$$Best - Stf_{wf,sp,t} = \max_{1,t} \sum_{c_{wf,sp,1}}^{c_{wf,sp,n}} df_{1,n} \qquad (1)$$

Finally, for every hypothetical analysis, the highest value is chosen and the morphological analysis with this score is processed and stored.

5.2.2 Morphological Segmentation based on Document Frequencies

In case that no text can be found which includes the word form *wf* and the components of any of the hypothetical analyses, the corpus itself is considered as a textual enviroment in the widest sense. For each split, the sum of frequencies are being calculated. The hypothetical analysis with the highest value is chosen and the morphological analysis with this score is processed for the storage. In all other cases, the analysis will yield the hypothetical analysis of a monomorpheme.

5.3 Substitution of Analyses

Whenever an analysis by the $Best - Stf$ score or another look-up has been found, the analyses for its immediate constituents are being searched in the databases. By this, the lexicons can be incrementally enlarged and enriched. Figure 4 shows an example from our test corpus, which we used for the evaluation in Section 6.

The results are added to a database of new splits and can be added to the previous database after an evaluation.

6 Evaluation

6.1 Data

For testing the performance, we use *Korpus Magazin Lufthansa Bordbuch (MLD)* which is part of the DeReKo-2016-I (Institut für Deutsche Sprache, 2016) corpus[4]. It is an in-flight magazine with articles on traveling, consumption and aviation. For the tokenization, we enlarged and costumized the tokenizer by Dipper (2016) for our purposes. Multi-word units were automatically identified based on the multi-word dataset which we had augmented before. The resulting data comprises 276 texts with 5,202 paragraphs,

---

[4]See Kupietz et al. (2010) and http://www1.ids-mannheim.de/kl/projekte/korpora/archiv/mld.html for further information.

16,046 sentences and 260,114 tokens. The number of word-form types is 38,337. We are analyzing the lemmatized version of this corpus which was produced by the TreeTagger (Schmid, 1999), it comprises 27,902 lemma types.

6.2 Results

6.2.1 Coverage

15,622 lemma types can be found within the database. 12,280 lemma types are not covered by the databases, so they were re-analyzed by SMOR/Moremorph. We manually checked the results for the first 1,000 lemma types which could not be found in the database. Very often, these are derivatives, rare or nounce words, proper names or words containing proper names as in (10).

(10)   a.   ordnend 'ordering, regulatory'
       b.   Paris-Erfahrung 'Paris experience'
       c.   Winterspaß 'winter fun'

The details of the check against the German tree database are included in Table 1, with a coverage of 55.99% for the lemma types. This direct lookup saves a lot of computational effort. According to the quality of the database which is based on GermaNet and CELEX, the recall is extremely close to these numbers.

The remaining 44.01% of all lemma types were evaluated in the following way: We checked every split of the first thousand analyzed words. For ambiguous analyses, we accepted those which included a monomorphemic and a correct derivational analysis, as in (11), with (11-a) showing the segmentation of verb stem and derivational suffix.

(11)   a.   ordnend ordn end V PPres ADJ-SUFF <ADJ>
       b.   ordnend ordnend V <V>

If one or more splits were erroneous, as in (12-a), the analysis was rejected.

(12)   a.   Winterspaß Winter spaß NN NN <NN> 'winter fun'
       b.   #Winterspaß Winter s paß NN FL NN <NN> 'winter|s, filler letter| pass/passport'

We found 26 wrongly segmented words inside the sample of a thousand words from the SMOR/Moremorph output. This shows a good quality of the analysis. However, unknown

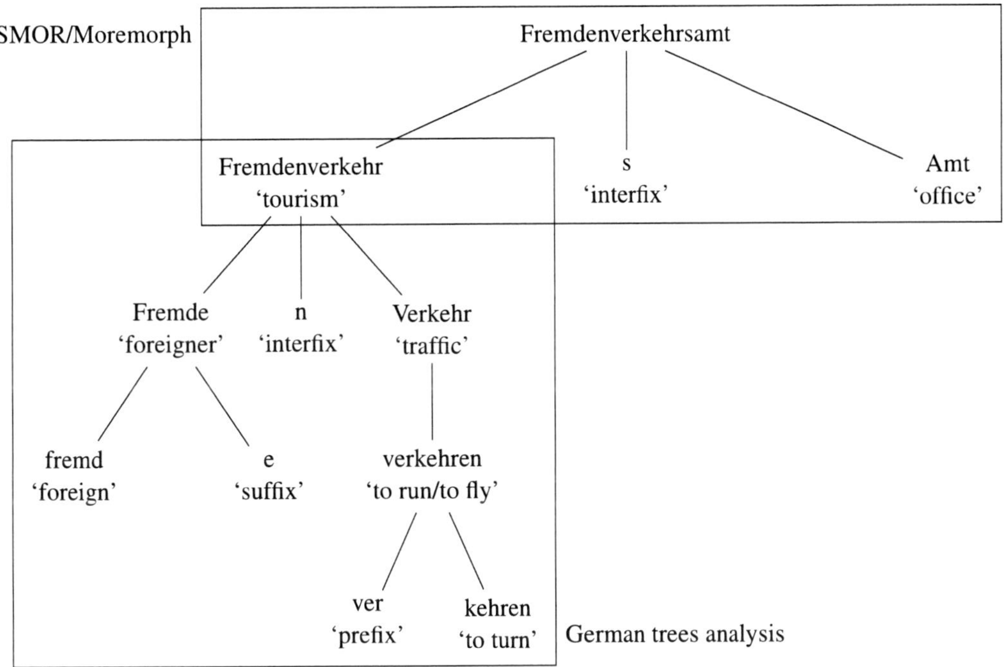

Figure 4: Database look-up and SMOR/Moremorph: Morphological analysis of *Fremdenverkehrsamt* 'tourist office'

types were re-analysed as hypothetical monomorphemes during the further analysis. Often, these were names of airplane types or similar expressions. Therefore, the number of analyzed lemma types (27,902) corresponds to a full coverage. SMOR/Moremorph on its own was able to process 13,461 lemmas, the rest was classified as unknown. This good coverage is a direct result of the adjustment of the lexicons, which we described in 3.2, especially concerning the names lexicons.

	lemma types	corpus size
MLD corpus	27,902	260,114

	lemma types	coverage
Tree DB + monomorphs	15,622	55.99%
+ SMOR & Moremorphs	27,902	100%

Table 1: Coverage of DBs and SMOR analyses

6.2.2 Precision

The complete analyses of the hybrid morphological parsing yield 5,307 entries in the newsplit database and 5,973 new entries inside the monomorphemes. We analyzed the first 1,000 entries of the newly found splits and the first 2,000 entries within the monomorpheme set. Of the first set, we found 65 wrongly or imperfectly analyzed word forms. Most of them are three-part compounds such as (13) whose correct components were not found within a text. The morphemes were identified, but the ambiguity could not be resolved.

(13) (Berg|Regen|Wald) 'mountain rain forest'

Another error are wrong analyses of derivative nouns which starts with a verb particle such as (14-a) , which is a derivative form of *anfahren* 'to approach' (14-b) and not a compound of *an* 'at, to' and *Fahrt* 'ride'. There is a systematic mistake here which is caused by the high frequency of the first part which is usually a homograph of a preposition.

(14) a. ♯An|(*Fahrt* fahren|t) 'approach'
     b. (*anfahren* an|fahren)|t 'approach'

The set of monomorphs comprise many new complex numbers and proper names. All of them were correctly included. Only three assignments are questionable. However, as these are proper names such as *Anneliese* which consists of two proper names *Anna* and *Liese*, and/or the analysis in CELEX was monomorphemous too (as for *Allerheiligen* 'All Saints'), the quality is very high. Therefore, the precision can be considered as high for this test corpus: 0.935 for new splits and 0.998 for newly found monomorphs.

6.3 Discussion

The results for the first hybrid deep-level morphology analyzer are promising. However, the errors concerning verb particles are systematic. They can be explained by the high frequency of verb particles in texts, which are often homographs of a preposition. For future research, we plan an adjustment by a factor which takes into account the relationship between word length in characters and word frequency as observed by Zipf and others (Prün, 2005). Köhler (1986) derives this relationship by a synergetic model. He corroborates the functional connection between the frequency classes of words and their average length. A measure directly derived from this function would penalize word segmentations with small morphemes and assign more weight to longer (and rare) components.

7 Conclusion and Outlook

This paper demonstrates how updating and exploiting linguistic databases for morphological analyses can be performed. By simple look-up, we reached a coverage of 56% of lemma types. As both underlying databases, CELEX and GermaNet, were manually revised, we can speak of very reliable analyses. The remaining unanalyzed words can be mostly covered by a conventional word segmenter after adjusting its lexicons. These analyses have a flat structure and undergo a procedure of constructing all combinations of possible analyses and a context-based search for the hypothetical constituents in a large corpus. The results for the lemma types are very promising: Over 99% of all words were covered by the combined morphological analyses.

New morphological analyses from the tree-building process can be added to the German tree database after a process of careful evaluation and selection.

The direction of the future research is therefore straightforward: it will lead towards creating complex analyses out of existing ones and augmenting the lexical databases.

8 Acknowledgement

Work for this publication was partially supported by the German Research Foundation (DFG) under grant RU 1873/2-1. I would like to thank the reviewers for their valuable feedback and my colleague Josef Ruppenhofer for making this work possible.

References

Harald Baayen, Richard Piepenbrock, and Léon Gulikers. 1995. The CELEX lexical database (CD-ROM).

Gavin Burnage. 1995. CELEX: A Guide for Users. In Harald Baayen, Richard Piepenbrock, and Léon Gulikers, editors, *The CELEX Lexical Database (CD-ROM)*. Linguistic Data Consortium, Philadelphia, PA.

Fabienne Cap. 2014. *Morphological processing of compounds for statistical machine translation*. Ph.D. thesis, Universität Stuttgart.

Irene M. Cramer. 2005. Das Menzerathsche Gesetz (Menzerath's law). In Reinhard Köhler, Gabriel Altmann, and Raĭmond Genrikhovich Piotrovskiĭ, editors, *Quantitative Linguistik / Quantitative Linguistics - Ein internationales Handbuch / An International Handbook*, pages 659–687. M. de Gruyter.

Joachim Daiber, Lautaro Quiroz, Roger Wechsler, and Stella Frank. 2015. Splitting compounds by semantic analogy. In *Proceedings of the 1st Deep Machine Translation Workshop*, pages 20–28. ÚFAL MFF UK.

Stefanie Dipper. 2016. Tokenizer for German.

Alexander Geyken and Thomas Hanneforth. 2006. TAGH: A Complete Morphology for German based on Weighted Finite State Automata. In *Finite State Methods and Natural Language Processing. 5th International Workshop, FSMNLP 2005, Helsinki, Finland, September 1-2, 2005. Revised Papers*, volume 4002, pages 55–66. Springer.

Léon Gulikers, Gilbert Rattink, and Richard Piepenbrock. 1995. German Linguistic Guide. In Harald Baayen, Richard Piepenbrock, and Léon Gulikers, editors, *The CELEX Lexical Database (CD-ROM)*. Linguistic Data Consortium, Philadelphia, PA.

Mariikka Haapalainen and Ari Majorin. 1995. GERTWOL und morphologische Disambiguierung für das

Deutsche. In *Proceedings of the 10th Nordic Conference on Computational Linguistics, Helsinki, Finland.*

Birgit Hamp and Helmut Feldweg. 1997. GermaNet - a Lexical-Semantic Net for German. In *Proceedings of ACL Workshop Automatic Information Extraction and Building of Lexical Semantic Resources for NLP Applications*, pages 9–15.

Gerhard Hanrieder. 1996. MORPH - Ein modulares und robustes Morphologieprogramm für das Deutsche in Common Lisp. In Roland Hauser, editor, *Linguistische Verifikation Dokumentation zur Ersten Morpholymics 1994*, pages 53–66. Niemeyer, Tübingen.

Verena Henrich and Erhard Hinrichs. 2011. Determining Immediate Constituents of Compounds in GermaNet. In *Proceedings of the International Conference Recent Advances in Natural Language Processing 2011*, pages 420–426. Association for Computational Linguistics.

Christiane Hoffmann. 1999. Word order and the Principle of "Early Immediate Constituents" (EIC). *Journal of Quantitative Linguistics*, 6(2):108–116.

Institut für Deutsche Sprache. 2016. Deutsches Referenzkorpus / Archiv der Korpora geschriebener Gegenwartssprache 2016-I (Release from 31.03.2016).

Philipp Koehn and Kevin Knight. 2003. Empirical methods for compound splitting. In *Proceedings of the Tenth Conference of the European Chapter of the Association for Computational Linguistics-Volume 1*, pages 187–193. Association for Computational Linguistics.

R. Köhler. 1986. *Zur linguistischen Synergetik: Struktur und Dynamik der Lexik*, volume 31 of *Quantitative linguistics*. Brockmeyer.

Kimmo Koskenniemi. 1984. A general computational model for word-form recognition and production. In *Proceedings of the 10th International Conference on Computational linguistics*, pages 178–181. Association for Computational Linguistics.

Marc Kupietz, Cyril Belica, Holger Keibel, and Andreas Witt. 2010. The German reference corpus DeReKo: A primordial sample for linguistic research. In *Proceedings of the Seventh International Conference on Language Resources and Evaluation (LREC'10)*, pages 1848–1854, Valletta, Malta. European Language Resources Association (ELRA).

Wolfgang Lezius. 1996. Morphologiesystem Morphy. In *Linguistische Verifikation. Dokumentation zur ersten Morpholympics 1994*, pages 25–35. Niemeyer.

Wolfgang Lezius, Reinhard Rapp, and Manfred Wettler. 1998. A freely available morphological analyzer, disambiguator and context sensitive lemmatizer for German. In *36th Annual Meeting of the Association for Computational Linguistics and 17th International Conference on Computational Linguistics, COLING-ACL '98, August 10-14, 1998, Université de Montréal, Montréal, Quebec, Canada. Proceedings of the Conference.*, pages 743–748.

Jianqiang Ma, Verena Henrich, and Erhard Hinrichs. 2016. Letter Sequence Labeling for Compound Splitting. In *Proceedings of the 14th SIGMORPHON Workshop on Computational Research in Phonetics, Phonology, and Morphology*, pages 76–81, Berlin, Germany. Association for Computational Linguistics.

Eliza Margaretha and Harald Lüngen. 2014. Building linguistic corpora from wikipedia articles and discussions. *JLCL*, 29(2):59–82.

Claudia Prün. 2005. Das Werk von G. K. Zipf (The work of G. K. Zipf). In Reinhard Köhler, Gabriel Altmann, and Rajmund G. Piotrowski, editors, *Quantitative Linguistik / Quantitative Linguistics - Ein internationales Handbuch / An International Handbook*, pages 142–152. DeGruyter.

Martin Riedl and Chris Biemann. 2016. Unsupervised Compound Splitting With Distributional Semantics Rivals Supervised Methods. In *Proceedings of the Conference of the North American Chapter of the Association for Computational Linguistics: Human Language Technologies (NAACL-HLT 2016)*, pages 617–622. Association for Computational Linguistics.

Anne Schiller, Simone Teufel, Christine Stöckert, and Christine Thielen. 1995. Vorläufige Guidelines für das Tagging deutscher Textcorpora mit STTS. Technical report, Universität Stuttgart, Institut für maschinelle Sprachverarbeitung, and Seminar für Sprachwissenschaft, Universität Tübingen.

Helmut Schmid. 1999. Improvements in Part-of-Speech Tagging with an Application to German. In Susan Armstrong, Kenneth Church, Pierre Isabelle, Sandra Manzi, Evelyne Tzoukermann, and David Yarowsky, editors, *Natural Language Processing Using Very Large Corpora*, pages 13–25. Springer Netherlands, Dordrecht.

Helmut Schmid, Arne Fitschen, and Ulrich Heid. 2004. SMOR: A German computational morphology covering derivation, composition and inflection. In *Proceedings of the Fourth International Conference on Language Resources and Evaluation (LREC'04)*. European Language Resources Association (ELRA).

Petra Steiner. 2016. Refurbishing a Morphological Database for German. In *Proceedings of the Tenth International Conference on Language Resources and Evaluation LREC 2016, Portorož, Slovenia, May 23-28, 2016*. European Language Resources Association (ELRA).

Petra Steiner. 2017. Merging the trees. building a morphological treebank for German from two resources. In *Proceedings of the 16th International Workshop on Treebanks and Linguistic Theories, January 23–24, 2018*, TLT'16, pages 146 160, Prague, Czech Republic.

Petra Steiner and Josef Ruppenhofer. 2015. Growing trees from morphs: Towards data-driven morphological parsing. In *Proceedings of the International Conference of the German Society for Computational Linguistics and Language Technology, GSCL 2015, University of Duisburg-Essen, Germany, 30th September - 2nd October 2015*, pages 49–57.

Petra Steiner and Josef Ruppenhofer. 2018. Building a Morphological Treebank for German from a Linguistic Database. In *Proceedings of the Eleventh International Conference on Language Resources and Evaluation (LREC 2018)*, pages 3882 – 3889, Miyazaki, Japan. European Language Resources Association (ELRA).

Marion Weller-Di Marco. 2017. Simple Compound Splitting for German. In *Proceedings of the 13th Workshop on Multiword Expressions (MWE 2017)*, pages 161–166, Valencia, Spain. Association for Computational Linguistics.

Kay-Michael Würzner and Thomas Hanneforth. 2013. Parsing morphologically complex words. In *Proceedings of the 11th International Conference on Finite State Methods and Natural Language Processing, FSMNLP 2013, St. Andrews, Scotland, UK, July 15-17, 2013*, pages 39–43.

Patrick Ziering, Stefan Müller, and Lonneke van der Plas. 2016. Top a splitter: Using distributional semantics for improving compound splitting. In *Proceedings of the 12th Workshop on Multiword Expressions*, pages 50–55, Berlin, Germany. Association for Computational Linguistics.

Patrick Ziering and Lonneke van der Plas. 2016. Towards Unsupervised and Language-independent Compound Splitting using Inflectional Morphological Transformations. In *Human Language Technologies, San Diego California, USA, June 12-17, 2016*, pages 644–653. Association for Computational Linguistics.

Unsupervised Morphological Segmentation for Low-Resource Polysynthetic Languages

Ramy Eskander
Columbia University
Dept. of Computer Science
`rnd2110@columbia.edu`

Judith L. Klavans
University of Maryland
UMIACS
`jklavans@umd.edu`

Smaranda Muresan
Columbia University
Data Science Institute
`smara@columbia.edu`

Abstract

Polysynthetic languages pose a challenge for morphological analysis due to the root-morpheme complexity and to the word class "squish". In addition, many of these polysynthetic languages are low-resource. We propose *unsupervised* approaches for morphological segmentation of low-resource polysynthetic languages based on Adaptor Grammars (AG) (Eskander et al., 2016). We experiment with four languages from the Uto-Aztecan family. Our AG-based approaches outperform other unsupervised approaches and show promise when compared to supervised methods, outperforming them on two of the four languages.

1 Introduction

Computational morphology of polysynthetic languages is an emerging field of research. Polysynthetic languages pose unique challenges for computational approaches, including machine translation and morphological analysis, due to the root-morpheme complexity and to word class gradations (Homola, 2011; Mager et al., 2018d; Klavans, 2018a). Previous approaches include rule-based methods based on finite state transducers (Farley, 2009; Littell, 2018; Kazeminejad et al., 2017), hybrid models (Mager et al., 2018b; Moeller et al., 2018), and supervised machine learning, particularly deep learning approaches (Micher, 2017; Kann et al., 2018). While each rule-based method is developed for a specific language (Inuktitut (Farley, 2009), or Arapaho (Littell, 2018; Moeller et al., 2018)), machine learning, including deep learning approaches, might be more rapidly scalable to many additional languages.

We propose an *unsupervised* approach for morphological segmentation of polysynthetic languages based on Adaptor Grammars (Johnson et al., 2007). We experiment with four Uto-Aztecan languages: Mexicanero (MX), Nahuatl (NH), Wixarika (WX) and Yorem Nokki (YN) (Kann et al., 2018). Adaptor Grammars (AGs) are nonparametric Bayesian models that generalize probabilistic context free grammars (PCFG), and have proven to be successful for unsupervised morphological segmentation, where a PCFG is a morphological grammar that specifies word structure (Johnson, 2008; Sirts and Goldwater, 2013; Eskander et al., 2016, 2018). Our main goal is to examine the success of Adaptor Grammars for unsupervised morphological segmentation when applied to polysynthetic languages, where the morphology is synthetically complex (not simply agglutinative), and where resources are minimal. We use the datasets introduced by Kann et al. (2018) in an unsupervised fashion (unsegmented words). We design several AG learning setups: 1) use the best-on-average AG setup from Eskander et al. (2016); 2) optimize for language using just the small training vocabulary (unsegmented) and dev vocabulary (segmented) from Kann et al. (2018); 3) approximate the effect of having some linguistic knowledge; 4) learn from all languages at once and 5) add additional unsupervised data for NH and WX (Section 3). We show that the AG-based approaches outperform other unsupervised methods — *Morfessor* (Creutz and Lagus, 2007) and *MorphoChain* (Narasimhan et al., 2015)) —, and that for two of the languages (NH and YN), the best AG-based approaches outperform the best supervised methods (Section 4).

2 Languages and Datasets

Typically, polysynthetic languages demonstrate holophrasis, i.e. the ability of an entire sentence to be expressed as what is considered by native speakers to be just one word. To illustrate, consider the following example from Inuktitut (Kla-

Proceedings of the 16th Workshop on Computational Research in Phonetics, Phonology, and Morphology, pages 189–195
Florence, Italy. August 2, 2019 ©2019 Association for Computational Linguistics

vans, 2018b), where the morpheme -tusaa- is the root and all the other morphemes are synthetically combined with it in one unit:

tusaa-tsia-runna-nngit-tu-alu-u-jung
hear-well-be.able-NEG-DOE-very-BE-PT.1S
I can't hear very well.

Another example from WX, one of the languages in the dataset for this paper (from (Mager et al., 2018c)) shows this complexity:

yu-huta-me ne-p+-we-iwa
an-two-ns 1sg:s-asi-2pl:o-brother
I have two brothers.

In linguistic typology, the broader gradient is: isolating/analytic to synthetic to polysynthetic. Agglutinating refers to the clarity of boundaries between morphemes. This more specific gradation is: agglutinating to mildly fusional to fusional. Thus a language might be characterized overall as polysynthetic and agglutinating, i.e. generally a high number of morphemes per word, with clear boundaries between morphemes and thus easily segmentable. Another language might be characterized as polysynthetic and fusional, so again, many morphemes per word, but many phonological and other processes so it is difficult to segment morphemes.

Thus, morphological analysis of polysynthetic languages is challenging due to the root-morpheme complexity and to word class gradations. Linguists recognize a gradience in word classes, known as "squishiness", a term first discussed in Ross (1972) who argued that, instead of a fixed, distinct inventory of syntactic categories, a quasi-continuum from verb, adjective and noun best reflects most lexical distinctions. The root-morpheme complexity and the word class "squish" makes developing segmented training data with reliability across annotators difficult to achieve. Kann et al. (2018) have made a first step by releasing a small set of morphologically segmented datasets although even in these carefully curated datasets, the distinction between affix and clitic is not always indicated. We use these datasets in an unsupervised fashion (i.e., we use the unsegmented words). These datasets were taken from detailed descriptions in the Archive of Indigenous Languages collection for MX (Canger, 2001), NH (de Suárez, 1980), WX (Gómez and López, 1999), and YN (Freeze, 1989). They were constructed so they include both segmentable as well as non-

	Mexicanero	Nahuatl	Wixarika	Yorem N.
train	427	540	665	511
train$_{Bible}$	-	14.7K	16.6K	-
dev	106	134	176	127
test	355	449	553	425

Table 1: Number of words in train, dev, test splits from Kann et al. (2018) + additional Bible data

segmentable words to ensure that methods can correctly decide against splitting up single morphemes. However, as noted above, there is a gradation of polysynthesis, so the delineation of language types is not clear-cut. For these four languages, the more agglutinative is WX; Leza (2004) has observed 20 morphemes per word for this language.

Each training, development and test example consists of one word. Table 1 contains the count of words in the training, development and test. Unlike Kann et al. (2018), for training we do not use the segmented version of the data (our approach is unsupervised). In addition to the datasets, for NH and WX we also have available the Bible (Christodouloupoulos and Steedman, 2015; Mager et al., 2018a), which we consider for one of our experimental setups as additional training data. In the dataset from (Kann et al., 2018), the maximum number of morphemes per word for MX is seven with an average of 2.13; for NH, six with an average of 2.2; for WX, maximum of ten with an average of 3.3; and for YN, the maximum is ten, with an average of 2.13.

3 Using Adaptor Grammars for Polysynthetic Languages

An Adaptor Grammar is typically composed of a PCFG and an adaptor that adapts the probabilities of individual subtrees. For morphological segmentation, a PCFG is a morphological grammar that specifies word structure, where AGs learn latent tree structures given a list of words. In this paper, we experiment with the grammars and the learning setups proposed by Eskander et al. (2016), which we outline briefly below.

Grammars. We use the nine grammars from Eskander et al. (2016, 2018) that were designed based on three dimensions: 1) how the grammar models word structure (e.g., prefix-stem-suffix vs. morphemes), 2) the level of abstraction in nonterminals (e.g., compounds, morphemes and submorphemes) and 3) how the output boundaries are specified (see Table 2 for a sample grammars). For example, the PrStSu+SM grammar models the

Grammar	Main Representation	Compound	Morph	SubMorph	Segmentation Level
Morph+SM	Morph+	No	Yes	Yes	Morph
PrStSu+SM	Prefix+Stem+Suffix	No	Yes	Yes	Prefix-Stem-Suffix
PrStSu+Co+SM	Prefix+Stem+Suffix	Yes	Yes	Yes	Prefix-Stem-Suffix

Table 2: Sample grammar setups used by Eskander et al. (2018, 2016). Compound = Upper level representation of the word as a sequence of compounds; Morph = affix/morpheme representation as a sequence of morphemes. SubMorph (SM) = Lower level representation of characters as a sequence of sub-morphemes. "+" denotes *one or more*.

word as a complex prefix, a stem and a complex suffix, where the complex prefix and suffix are composed of zero or more morphemes, and a morpheme is a sequence of sub-morphemes. The boundaries in the output are based on the prefix, stem and suffix levels.

Learning Settings. The input to the learner is a grammar and a vocabulary of unsegmented words. We consider the three learning settings in (Eskander et al., 2016): Standard, Scholar-seeded Knowledge and Cascaded. The Standard setting is language-independent and fully unsupervised, while in the Scholar-seeded-Knowledge setting, some linguistic knowledge (in the form of affixes taken from grammar books) is seeded into the grammar trees before learning takes place. The Cascaded setting simulates the effect of seeding scholar knowledge in a language-independent manner by first running an AG of high precision to derive a set of affixes, and then seeding those affixes into the grammars.

3.1 AG Setups for Polysynthetic Languages

We experimented with several setups using AGs for unsupervised segmentation.

Language-Independent Morphological Segmenter. LIMS is the best-on-average AG setup obtained by Eskander et al. (2016) when trained on six languages (English, German, Finnish, Estonian, Turkish and Zulu), which is the Cascaded PrStSu+SM configuration. We use this AG setup for each of the four languages. We refer to this system as AG_{LIMS}.

Best AG Configuration per Language. In this experimental setup, we consider all nine grammars from Eskander et al. (2016) using both the Standard and the Cascaded approaches and choosing the one that is best for each polysynthetic language by training on the training set and evaluating on the development set. We denote this system as AG_{BestL}.

Using Seeded Knowledge. To approximate the effect of Scholar-seeded-Knowledge in Eskander et al. (2016), we used the training set to de-

rive affixes and use them as scholar-seeded knowledge added to the grammars (before the learning happens). However, since affixes and stems are not distinguished in the training annotations from Kann et al. (2018), we only consider the first and last morphemes that appear at least five times. We call this setup $AG_{BestL}^{Scholar}$.

Multilingual Training. Since the vocabulary in Kann et al. (2018) for each language is small, and the languages are from the same language family, one data augmentation approach is to train on all languages and test then on each language individually. We call this setup AG_{Multi}.

Data Augmentation. In this setup, we examine the performance of the best AG configuration per language (AG_{BestL}) when more data is available. We merge the training corpus with unique words in the New Testament of the Bible (train$_{Bible}$). We run this only on NH and WX since the Bible text is only available for these two languages. We denote this setup as AG_{Aug}.

4 Evaluation and Discussion

We evaluate the different AG setups on the blind test set from Kann et al. (2018) and compare our AG approaches to state-of-the-art unsupervised systems as well as supervised models including the best supervised deep learning models from Kann et al. (2018). As the metric, we use the segmentation-boundary F1-score, which is standard for this task (Virpioja et al., 2011).

Evaluating different AG setups. Table 3 shows the performance of our AG setups on the four languages. The best AG setup learned for each of the four polysynthetic languages (AG_{BestL}) is the PrStSu+SM grammar using the Cascaded learning setup. This is an interesting finding as the Cascaded PrSTSu+SM setup is in fact AG_{LIMS} — the best-on-average AG setup obtained by Eskander et al. (2016) when trained on six languages (English, German, Finnish, Estonian, Turkish and Zulu). This achieves F1-scores of 0.775, 0.744, 0.768 and 0.820 on MX, NH,

Language	AG_{LIMS}	AG_{BestL}	AG_{Multi}	$AG_{BestL}^{Scholar}$	AG_{Aug}	$Morfessor$	$Morphochain$
Mexicanero	0.775	0.775	0.770	**0.798**	-	0.528	0.283
Nahuatl	0.744	0.744	0.723	0.742	**0.759**	0.505	0.259
Wixarika	0.768	0.768	0.746	**0.787**	0.783	0.709	0.283
Yorem Nokki	**0.820**	**0.820**	0.775	0.804	–	0.549	0.351

Table 3: AG systems compared to unsupervised baselines. Bold indicates best scores

Language	$BestAG$	$S2S$	CRF	$BestMTT$	$BestDA$
Mexicanero	0.798	0.862	0.864	**0.879**	0.868
Nahuatl	**0.759**	0.727	0.749	0.739	0.732
Wixarika	0.787	0.796	0.793	0.802	**0.816**
Yorem Nokki	**0.820**	0.773	0.774	0.808	0.792

Table 4: Best AG results compared to supervised approaches from Kann et al. (2018). Bold indicates best scores.

WX and YN, respectively. Seeding affixes into the grammar trees ($AG_{BestL}^{Scholar}$) improves the performance of the Cascaded $PrStSu + SM$ setup only for MX and WX (additional absolute F1-scores of 0.023 and 0.019, respectively). However, it does not help for NH, while it even decreases the performance on YN. This occurs because AGs are able to recognize the main affixes in the Cascaded setup, while the seeded affixes were either abundant or conflicting with the automatically discovered ones. The multilingual setup (AG_{Multi}) does not improve the performance on any of the languages. This could be because the datasets are too small to generalize common patterns across languages. Finally, augmenting with Bible text in the cases of NH and WX leads to an absolute F1-score increase of 0.015 for both languages when compared to AG_{BestL}. There are two possible explanations for why we only see a slight increase when adding more data: 1) AGs are able to generalize from small data and 2) the added Bible data represents a domain that is different from those of the datasets we are experimenting with as only 4.8% and 9% of the words in the training sets from Kann et al. (2018) appear in the augmented data of NH and WX, respectively. Overall, AG_{BestL} is the best setup for YN, $AG_{BestL}^{Scholar}$ is the best setup for MX and WX, while AG_{Aug} is the best for NH.

Comparison with unsupervised baselines. We consider $Morfessor$ (Creutz and Lagus, 2007), a commonly-used toolkit for unsupervised morphological segmentation, and $MorphoChain$ (Narasimhan et al., 2015), another unsupervised morphological system based on constructing morphological chains. Our AG approaches significantly outperform both $Morfessor$ and $MorphoChain$ on all four languages, as shown in Table 3.

Comparison with supervised baselines. To obtain an upper bound, we compare the best AG setup to the best supervised neural methods presented in Kann et al. (2018) for each language. We consider their best multi-task approach (*BestMTT*) and the best data-augmentation approach (*BestDA*), using F1 scores from their Table 4 for each language. In addition, we report the results on their other supervised baselines: a supervised seq-to-seq model (*S2S*) and a supervised CRF approach. As can be seen in Table 4, our unsupervised AG-based approaches outperform the best supervised approaches for NH and YN with absolute F1-scores of 0.010 and 0.012, respectively. An interesting observation is that for YN we only used the words in the training set of Kann et al. (2018) (unsegmented), without any data augmentation. For MX and WX, the neural models from Kann et al. (2018) (BestMTT and BestDA), outperform our unsupervised AG-based approaches.

Error Analysis. For the purpose of error analysis, we train our unsupervised segmentation on the training sets and perform the analysis of results on the output of the development sets based on our best unsupervised models AG_{BestL}. Since there is no distinction between stems and affixes in the labeled data, we only consider the morphemes that appear at least three times in order to eliminate open-class morphemes in our statistics.

We first define the degree of ambiguity of a morpheme to be the percentage of times its sequence of characters does not form a segmentable morpheme when they appear in the training set. We also define the degree of ambiguity of a language as the average degree of ambiguity of the morphemes in that language. Table 5 shows the number of morphemes, average length of a morpheme (in characters) and the degree of morpheme

	Mexicanero	Nahuatl	Wixarika	Yorem Nokki
Number of Morphemes	343	479	434	424
Average Length of a Morpheme	3.17	3.16	3.19	3.40
Degree of Ambiguity	69.81%	73.97%	74.49%	58.67%

Table 5: Morpheme-based Statistics

Language	word	Gold Segmentation	AG_{BestL} segmentation
Mexicanero	tawanitika	tawani+ti+ka	tawani+tika
	unipodero	u+ni+podero	u+ni+pode+ro
	tikipiyal	ti+ki+piya+l	ti+ki+piya+l
Nahuatl	nannechtlatlaniliake	nan+nech+tla+tlanilia+'ke	nan+nech+tlatla+nilia+'ke
	omokokowaya	o+mo+kokowa+ya	o+mo+kokowa+ya
Wixarika	nep@tiwarutiwawiriwa	ne+p@+ti+wa+r+u+ti+wawi+ri+wa	ne+p@+ti+waru+ti+wawiriwa
	pep@netsiuta	pe+p@+ne+tsi+u+ta	pe+p@+ne+tsi+u+ta
Yorem Nokki	ßohoßareka	ßoho + ßa+ re+ ka	ßoho + ßare+ ka
	haikimsu'e	haiki+m+su+'e	haiki+m+su+'e

Table 6: Examples of correct and incorrect segmentation

ambiguity in each language. Looking at the two languages where our models perform worse than the supervised models, we notice that MX has the least number of morphemes, and our unsupervised methods tend to oversegment; WX has the highest degree of ambiguity with a large number of one-letter morphemes, which makes the task more challenging for unsupervised segmentation as opposed to the case of a supervised setup. Analyzing all the errors that our AG-based models made across all languages, we noticed one, or a combination, of the following factors: a high degree of morpheme ambiguity, short morpheme length and/or low frequency of a morpheme.

Examples. Table 6 shows some examples of correctly and incorrectly segmented words by our models (blue indicates correct morphemes while red are wrong ones). For MX, our models fail to recognize *ka* as a correct affix 100% of the time due to its high degree of ambiguity (71.79%), while we often wrongly detect *ro* as an affix, most likely since *ro* tends to appear at the end of a word; our approaches tend to oversegment in such cases. On the other hand, our method correctly identify *ki* as a correct affix 100% of the time since it appears frequently in the training data. For NH, the morpheme *tla* has a high degree of ambiguity at 79.12%, which lead the model to fail in recognizing it as an affix (see an example in Table 6). On the other hand, NH has a higher percentage of correctly recognized morphemes, due to their less ambiguous nature and higher frequency (such as *ke, tl* or *mo*). For WX, a large portion of errors stem from one-letter morphemes that are highly ambiguous (e.g., *u, a, e, m, n, p* and *r*), in addition to having morphemes in the training set which are not frequent enough to learn from, such as *ki,nua* and *wawi* (see Table 6). Examples of correct segmentation involve morphemes that are more frequent and less ambiguous (*pe, p@* and *ne*). For YN, ambiguity is the main source of segmentation errors (e.g., *wa, wi* and *ßa*).slight

5 Conclusions

Unsupervised approaches based on Adaptor Grammars show promise for morphological segmentation of low-resource polysynthetic languages. We worked with the AG grammars developed by Eskander et al. (2016, 2018) for languages that are not polysynthetic. We showed that even when using these approaches and very little data, we can obtain encouraging results, and that using additional unsupervised data is a promising path.

Acknowledgements

This research is based upon work supported in part by the Office of the Director of National Intelligence (ODNI), Intelligence Advanced Research Projects Activity (IARPA), (contract # FA8650-17-C-9117) and the Army Research Laboratory (ARL). The views and conclusions herein are those of the authors and should not be interpreted as necessarily representing official policies, expressed or implied, of ODNI, IARPA, ARL or the U.S. Government. The U.S. Government is authorized to reproduce and distribute reprints for governmental purposes notwithstanding any copyright annotation therein.

References

Una Canger. 2001. *Mexicanero de la Sierra Madre Occidental*, volume 24 of *Archivo de lenguas indígenas de México*. Centro de Estudios Lingüísticos y Literarios, México.

Christos Christodouloupoulos and Mark Steedman. 2015. A massively parallel corpus: the bible in 100 languages. *Language Resources and Evaluation*, 49(2):375–395.

Mathias Creutz and Krista Lagus. 2007. Unsupervised models for morpheme segmentation and morphology learning. *ACM Trans. Speech Lang. Process.*, 4(1):3:1–3:34.

Ramy Eskander, Owen Rambow, and Smaranda Muresan. 2016. Automatically tailoring unsupervised morphological segmentation to the language. In *Proceedings of the Twenty-Sixth International Conference on Computational Linguistics (LREC)*, Osaka, Japan.

Ramy Eskander, Owen Rambow, and Tianchun Yang. 2018. Extending the use of adaptor grammars for unsupervised morphological segmentation of unseen languages. In *Proceedings of the Fifteenth SIGMORPHON Workshop on Computational Research in Phonetics, Phonology, and Morphology*, Brussels, Belgium.

Benoit Farley. 2009. The uqailaut project. Accessed on 10 Jan 2019.

Ray Freeze. 1989. *May de los Capomos*. Sinaloa.

P. Gómez and P.G. López. 1999. *Huichol de San Andrés Cohamiata, Jalisco*. Archivo de lenguas indígenas de México. Colegio de México.

Petr Homola. 2011. Parsing a polysynthetic language. In *Proceedings of the International Conference Recent Advances in Natural Language Processing 2011*, pages 562–567, Hissar, Bulgaria. RANLP 2011 Organising Committee.

Mark Johnson. 2008. Unsupervised word segmentation for Sesotho using adaptor grammars. In *Proceedings of the Tenth Meeting of ACL Special Interest Group on Computational Morphology and Phonology*, pages 20–27, Columbus, Ohio. Association for Computational Linguistics.

Mark Johnson, Thomas L. Griffiths, and Sharon Goldwater. 2007. Adaptor grammars: a framework for specifying compositional nonparametric bayesian models. In *Advances in Neural Information Processing Systems 19*, pages 641–648, Cambridge, MA. MIT Press.

Katharina Kann, Jesus Manuel Mager Hois, Ivan Vladimir Meza Ruiz, and Hinrich Schütze. 2018. Fortification of neural morphological segmentation models for polysynthetic minimal-resource languages. In *Proceedings of the 2018 Conference of the North American Chapter of the Association for Computational Linguistics: Human Language Technologies, Volume 1 (Long Papers)*, pages 47–57.

Ghazaleh Kazeminejad, Andrew Cowell, and Mans Hulden. 2017. Creating lexical resources for polysynthetic languages—the case of arapaho. In *Proceedings of the 2nd Workshop on the Use of Computational Methods in the Study of Endangered Languages*, pages 10–18. Association for Computational Linguistics.

Judith L. Klavans. 2018a. Computational challenges for polysynthetic languages. In *Proceedings of the Workshop on Computational Modeling of Polysynthetic Languages (COLING 2018)*, pages 1–11. Association for Computational Linguistics.

Judith L. Klavans. 2018b. *On Clitics and Cliticization: The Interaction of Morphology, Phonology, and Syntax*, 2 edition. London, Routledge.

José Luis Leza. 2004. *Lenguas y literaturas indígenas de Jalisco*. Secretaría de Cultura, Gobierno Estatal de Jalisco. Colección: Las culturas populares de Jalisco, Guadalajara, Mexico.

Patrick Littell. 2018. Finite-state morphology for kwak'wala: A phonological approach. In *Proceedings of the Workshop on Computational Modeling of Polysynthetic Languages (COLING 2018)*, pages 21–30. Association for Computational Linguistics.

Manuel Mager, Diónico Carrillo, and Ivan Meza. 2018a. Probabilistic finite-state morphological segmenter for wixarika (huichol) language. *Journal of Intelligent & Fuzzy Systems*, 34(5):3081–3087.

Manuel Mager, Diónico Carrillo, and Iván V. Meza-Ruíz. 2018b. Probabilistic finite-state morphological segmenter for wixarika (huichol) language. *Journal of Intelligent and Fuzzy Systems*, 34(5):3081–3087.

Manuel Mager, Ximena Gutierrez-Vasques, Gerardo Sierra, and Ivan Meza-Ruiz. 2018c. Challenges of language technologies for the indigenous languages of the americas. In *Proceedings of the 27th International Conference on Computational Linguistics*, pages 55–69.

Manuel Mager, Elisabeth Mager, Alfonso Medina-Urrea, Ivan Vladimir Meza Ruiz, and Katharina Kann. 2018d. Lost in translation: Analysis of information loss during machine translation between polysynthetic and fusional languages. In *Proceedings of the Workshop on Computational Modeling of Polysynthetic Languages (COLING 2018)*, pages 73–83.

Jeffrey Micher. 2017. Improving coverage of an inuktitut morphological analyzer using a segmental recurrent neural network. In *Proceedings of the 2nd Workshop on the Use of Computational Methods in the Study of Endangered Languages*, pages 101–106. Association for Computational Linguistics.

Sarah Moeller, Ghazaleh Kazeminejad, Andrew Cowell, and Mans Hulden. 2018. A neural morphological analyzer for arapaho verbs learned from a finite state transducer. In *Proceedings of the Workshop on Computational Modeling of Polysynthetic Languages (COLING 2018)*, pages 12–20. Association for Computational Linguistics.

Karthik Narasimhan, Regina Barzilay, and Tommi Jaakkola. 2015. An unsupervised method for uncovering morphological chains. In *Twelfth AAAI Conference on Artificial Intelligence*.

John R. Ross. 1972. Endstation hauptword: The category squish. *Chicago Linguistic Society*, 8:316–328.

Kairit Sirts and Sharon Goldwater. 2013. Minimally-supervised morphological segmentation using adaptor grammars. *Transactions of the Association for Computational Linguistics*, 1(May):231–242.

Yolanda Lastra de Suárez. 1980. *N´aJhuatl Acaxochitlán, Hidalgo*, volume 10 of *Archivo de lenguas indígenas de México*. Colegio de México, México.

Sami Virpioja, Ville T. Turunen, Sebastian Spiegler, Oskar Kohonen, and Mikko Kurimo. 2011. Empirical comparison of evaluation methods for unsupervised learning of morphology. *Traitement Automatique des Langues*, 52(2):45–90.

Weakly deterministic transformations are subregular

Andrew Lamont
University of Massachusetts Amherst
alamont@linguist.umass.edu

Charlie O'Hara
University of Southern California
charleso@usc.edu

Caitlin Smith
Johns Hopkins University
csmit372@jhu.edu

Abstract

Whether phonological transformations in general are subregular is an open question. This is the case for most transformations, which have been shown to be subsequential, but it is not known whether weakly deterministic mappings form a proper subset of the regular functions. This paper demonstrates that there are regular functions that are not weakly deterministic, and, because all attested processes so far studied are weakly deterministic, supports the subregular hypothesis.

1 Introduction

Phonological transformations, i.e., mappings from underlying representations onto surface representations, are computationally regular (Johnson, 1972; Kaplan and Kay, 1994). Most phonological transformations have further been shown to belong to the *subsequential* classes, which form a proper subset of the regular relations (Oncina et al., 1993; Mohri, 1997). These include *strictly local* transformations (Chandlee, 2014; Chandlee and Heinz, 2018), and long-distance transformations where target segments may depend on information arbitrarily far away in one direction (Chandlee and Heinz, 2012; Chandlee et al., 2012; Gainor et al., 2012; Heinz and Lai, 2013; Payne, 2014, 2017; Luo, 2017).

Two classes of phonological transformations have been shown not to be subsequential. The first, *weakly deterministic* transformations (Heinz and Lai, 2013), comprise mostly long-distance bidirectional processes such as root-controlled vowel harmony. For such transformations, some targets depend on information arbitrarily far to their left, such as suffix vowels assimilating to root vowels, and others depend on information arbitrar-

ily far to their right, such as prefix vowels assimilating to root vowels. These transformations have phonologically intuitive decompositions into a left-subsequential transformation and a related right-subsequential transformation, such as treating regressive and progressive harmony from the root as distinct processes.

Here, we make use of the original definition of weakly deterministic transformations as proposed by Heinz and Lai (2013). Note that this definition differs crucially from the revised definition proposed by McCollum et al. (2018), which properly captures the bidirectional harmony cases discussed above, without capturing any of the second class of mappings.

The second class of non-subsequential transformations are the *unbounded circumambient* transformations (Jardine, 2016a; McCollum et al., 2018), which are characterized by target segments depending on information both arbitrarily far to their left and arbitrarily far to their right. Unlike bidirectional harmonies, these processes do not decompose into phonologically intuitive transformations, and are conjectured not to be weakly deterministic (Heinz and Lai, 2013; Jardine, 2016a). However, every unbounded circumambient process studied so far has been shown to be weakly deterministic either by taking advantage of the alphabet (Graf, 2016) or by using predictable substrings as markup (McCollum et al., 2018; O'Hara and Smith, 2018, 2019; Lamont, 2019; Smith and O'Hara, 2019).

To make this concrete, we illustrate the latter strategy for unbounded tonal plateauing (UTP). In UTP, all tone-bearing units must surface with high tone if there is a high tone somewhere to their left and a high tone somewhere to their right. For example, in Luganda, the input /mu-tém-a-bi-sikí/ maps onto [mùtémábísíkí] 'log-chopper' (Hyman and Katamba, 2010; Jardine, 2016a), with all vow-

196

Proceedings of the 16th Workshop on Computational Research in Phonetics, Phonology, and Morphology, pages 196–205
Florence, Italy. August 2, 2019 ©2019 Association for Computational Linguistics

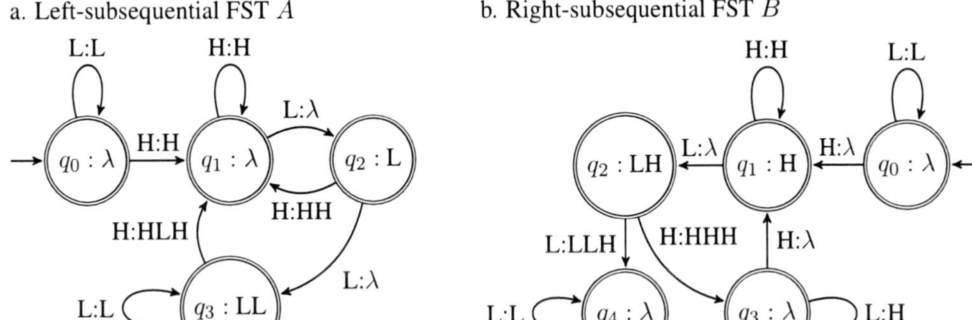

Figure 1: Weakly deterministic UTP: $B(A(i)) = UTP(i)$.

els between the high tones of /-tém-/ 'to chop' and /-sikí-/ 'log' surfacing with high tones.

Because there is no bound on how far the left or right triggering high tones can be from a given target, UTP cannot be modeled by a subsequential finite state transducer (FST) (Karttunen (2003);[1] see Jardine (2016b) for a formal proof). While no subsequential FST can identify which tone-bearing units are *targets*, one can identify which high tones are *triggers*. Marking triggering high tones makes it possible for a second subsequential FST to read the string in the opposite direction and correctly identify the targets.

This markup strategy is implemented by the FSTs in Figure 1. The left-subsequential FST A (1a) marks which high tones are triggers, and the right-subsequential FST B (1b) uses this information to complete the transformation. Because the structural description for UTP is symmetrical, it is arbitrary that the first machine reads left-to-right. A machine reading right-to-left would do equally well to markup inputs. Figure 2 illustrates a derivation mapping an input i /HLHHLLLLH/ onto an output with all high tones; the symbols ⋊ and ⋉ are used to explicitly mark the left and right

---

[1] We are grateful to an anonymous reviewer for drawing our attention to this paper.

---

word boundaries, respectively.

A makes the first pass through i, removing and inserting the substring HLH. It maps HLH onto H̲H̲H̲ (2a), modeling UTP in a local context. Following the first high tone, A prefixes every high tone span with HLH: H…LLH → H…H̲L̲H̲ (2b). Because all HLH substrings that were present in the input have been removed, HLH substrings now only appear in contexts where another high tone is arbitrarily far to their left. This unambiguously encodes the unbounded context for UTP: H…H.

B makes the second pass through i, interpreting the markup left by A: HLH is an instruction to start or continue spreading high tone, and LLH is an instruction to stop. B maps HLH onto H̲H̲H̲, and spreads the high tone leftwards until another high tone: HL^{n}HLH → H̲H̲^{n}H̲H̲H̲ (2c). This repeats until B reaches the left end of the string.

We present this analysis only to demonstrate that UTP is weakly deterministic according to the definition given by Heinz and Lai (2013): UTP is a regular function that can be decomposed into a left-subsequential transformation and a right-subsequential transformation, where the first mapping is both length- and alphabet-preserving. Encoding instructions in intermediate representations is strikingly unphonological and is not intended as a plausible interpretation of the process.

Similar analyses have shown that all unbounded circumambient processes studied so far are in fact weakly deterministic: high tone spreading in Copperbelt Bemba (McCollum et al., 2018; O'Hara and Smith, 2018, 2019; Smith and O'Hara, 2019), vowel harmony in Tutrugbu (McCollum et al., 2018), and Sour Grapes spreading (Lamont, 2019). At present, then, there are no exceptions to

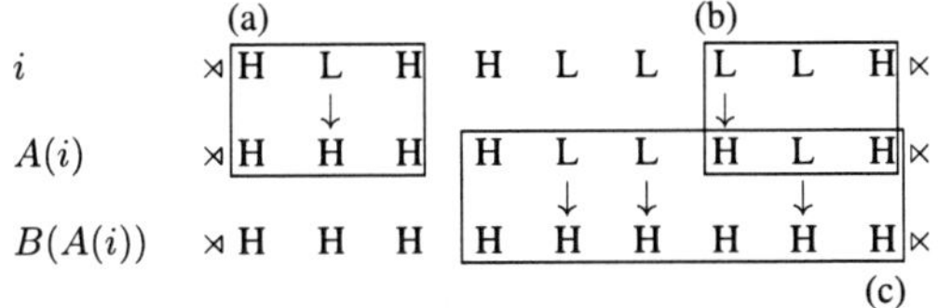

Figure 2: Example of weakly deterministic UTP.

the hypothesis that phonological transformations are weakly deterministic (Heinz and Lai, 2013). However, it is not known whether the weakly deterministic class is a proper subset of the regular functions. If it is, then there are no exceptions to the hypothesis that phonological transformations are *subregular* (Heinz, 2018). If it is not, then some weaker hypothesis, such as phonological transformations being regular, holds.

In this paper, we show that there are regular functions that are not weakly deterministic, supporting the subregular hypothesis. Section 2 presents two such mappings, variations of attested transformations. Section 3 generalizes the class of weakly deterministic unbounded circumambient transformations. Section 4 concludes.

2 Non-weakly deterministic regular functions

This section presents two regular functions that are not weakly deterministic: *first-last UTP* and *double-edged spread*. Both are variations on attested phonological transformations analyzed by Jardine (2016a), and both are defined over a binary alphabet of high tones H and low tones L. If the hypothesis that phonological transformations are weakly deterministic is correct, then neither should exist in natural language phonology.

2.1 First-last UTP

First-last UTP is a variation on UTP where plateauing only occurs if the two high tone triggers are at the word edges.[2] That is, inputs that begin and end with high tones surface with all high tones, e.g., /HLLLH/ → [HHHHH], and inputs that begin or end with low tones surface faithfully, e.g., /HLLHL/ → [HLLHL].

First-last UTP is a regular function, which is modeled by the non-deterministic FST in Figure 3. From the start state q_0, if the first symbol read is a low tone, then the FST transitions to q_1, and writes out the rest of the input faithfully. If the first symbol read is a high tone, then the machine transitions to q_2, where it must decide what to do with following low tones. It can either take the upper path to q_4, where low tones are replaced with high tones, or take the lower path to q_3, where low tones are written faithfully. If the upper path is taken, the input must end with a high tone for the

---

[2]As an anonymous reviewer points out, Schützenberger (1961) discusses a similar mapping.

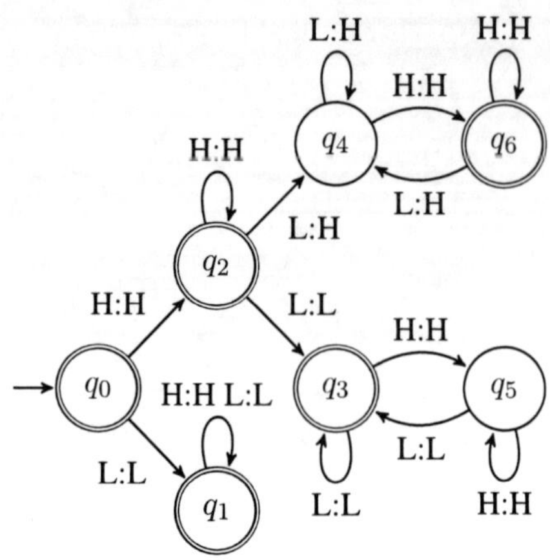

Figure 3: FST for first-last UTP.

FST to accept the mapping, and if the lower path is taken, the input must end with a low tone.

First-last UTP is not subsequential. In strings with initial and final high tones, the triggers circumscribe an unbounded number of targets, which no subsequential FST can identify. We showed in the previous section that a subsequential FST can not only identify the context for spreading in UTP, but one can also unambiguously mark it. This is not the case for first-last UTP: while a subsequential FST can identify the context for spreading, i.e., ⋊H...H⋉, marking it up is impossible.

The markup strategy for UTP exploits the fact that the string HLH never surfaces; it is always mapped onto HHH. Because the first FST removes all instances of HLH that were present in the input, the second FST knows that any remaining HLH strings encode the context for spreading. Furthermore, because the markup string overwrites segments that will be neutralized, there is no harm in changing them to HLH. In first-last UTP, every string surfaces faithfully in some context, such as ⋊L{H, L}*L⋉. There is no string that always neutralizes, and there is no guarantee that changes introduced by the first FST can be undone by the second FST. Thus, some strings that should surface faithfully will instead surface with markup.

This boils down to a pigeonhole argument. Because subsequential FSTs can only model functions that are unbounded on one side, the context for spreading must be identified within k segments from one of the word edges: ⋊H...{H, L}$^{k-1}$H⋉ reading left-to-right, or ⋊H{H, L}$^{k-1}$...H⋉ reading right-to-left. This leaves k segments for markup, and, over the binary alphabet Σ = {H,

L}, a total of 2^k possible strings. There are not enough strings to unambiguously encode inputs that should surface faithfully. Setting aside one string to encode spreading leaves $2^k - 1$ strings for non-spreading contexts. Assuming the first FST is left-subsequential, it has to encode 2^k suffixes from faithful inputs with initial low tones $\ltimes L \ldots \{H, L\}^k \rtimes$ and 2^{k-1} suffixes from those with initial high tones $\ltimes H \ldots \{H, L\}^{k-1} L \rtimes$. Some faithful input that ends with the designated markup string will have to be changed so that the second FST does not overwrite it with all high tones. However, it is impossible for the second FST to know that it was changed. Thus, at least two inputs that should surface unchanged will be incorrectly mapped onto the same output. The markup strategy is impossible, and first-last UTP is not weakly deterministic.

2.2 Double-edged spread

In Copperbelt Bemba, the rightmost high tone spreads unboundedly far to the right edge of the word, and other high tones undergo local spreading (Bickmore and Kula, 2013; Kula and Bickmore, 2015; Jardine, 2016a). For example, the high tone of the subject marker /bá-/ spreads to the end of a word when no high tone follows, as in /bá-ka-mu-londolol-a/ → [bákámúlóóndólólá] 'they will introduce him/her'. When the locative enclitic /=kó/ is added, its high tone blocks unbounded spreading, and other high tones only spread locally, as in /bá-ka-londolol-a−kó/ → [bákálóòndòlòlàkó] 'they will introduce'. Inputs without high tones surface with all low tones, such as /u-ku-tul-a/ → [ùkùtùlà] 'to pierce'.

As mentioned in Section 1, this mapping is weakly deterministic (McCollum et al., 2018; O'Hara and Smith, 2018, 2019; Smith and O'Hara, 2019), and follows along the same lines as UTP. When the context for unbounded spreading is met, the first FST marks up one of the triggers, either the rightmost high tone or the right edge of the input, or, when the triggers are within a bounded window, performs the entire mapping. For example, if a left-subsequential FST makes the first pass, it markups the right edge because it cannot identify the rightmost high tone. In bounded spreading contexts, where only one segment is targeted, the FST completes the mapping: $HL\rtimes \to HH\underline{H}\rtimes$. In unbounded spreading contexts, it leaves the string HL as markup: $H \ldots LL\rtimes \to H \ldots \underline{HL}\rtimes$.

The right-subsequential FST that makes the second pass interprets a final high tone as an instruction to do nothing, and a final low tone as an instruction to replace low tones until it reaches another high tone: $HL^nHL\rtimes \to H\underline{H}^nHH\rtimes$.

As with the string HLH in UTP, HL never surfaces word-finally in Copperbelt Bemba, and is an effective markup string. Similarly, because local spreading guarantees that HL does not surface word-internally, it can be used to markup the triggering high tone when the first FST is right-subsequential, provided it also removes all instances of HL from the input.

Intuitively, the reverse mapping, where the leftmost high tone spreads unboundedly to the left edge of the word and other high tones spread locally, is also weakly deterministic. We are not aware of an attested example in tonal phonology, but Tutrugbu vowel harmony presents a case of unbounded leftward spread (McCollum and Essegbey, 2018; McCollum et al., 2018).

Double-edged spread is a variation on the Copperbelt Bemba mapping where the leftmost high tone spreads unboundedly to the left edge of the word, the rightmost high tone spreads unboundedly to the right edge of the word, and no other tone spreads, e.g., /LLLHLLHLLHLLL/ → [HHHHLLHLLHHHH]. Inputs without high tones surface faithfully, e.g., /LLLL/ → [LLLL].

Double-edged spread is a regular function, which is modeled by the non-deterministic FST in Figure 4. From the start state q_0, if the first symbol read is a low tone, then the FST must decide what to do. It can either transition to state q_1 to anticipate an all low-toned input, or it can transition to q_2 to begin spreading an anticipated

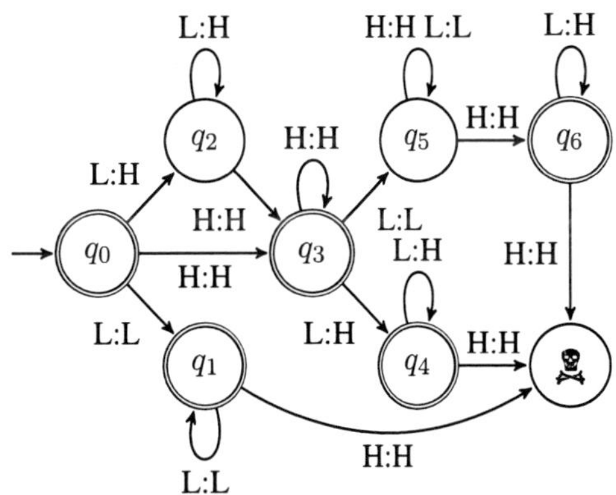

Figure 4: FST for double-edged spread.

high tone. If the FST encounters any high tones in q_1, it transitions into the sink state indicated with the skull and crossbones ☠, and the mapping is not accepted. From q_2, the FST transitions to q_3 once it has identified the leftmost high tone. If the leftmost high tone is word-initial, then the FST transitions directly to q_3 from the start state. Having identified the leftmost high tone, the FST must now identify the rightmost high tone. From q_3, it can either transition to q_4, expecting the string to contain only one high tone span, or transition to q_5 to anticipate a later high tone. From q_5, the FST must eventually transition to q_6 to accept the mapping. Encountering an unexpected high tone in q_4 or q_5 leads to the sink state.

Double-edged spread is not weakly deterministic, but the argument is different than the one for first-last UTP. In double-edged spread, only the leftmost and rightmost high tones spread. Thus, as in first-last UTP, every string surfaces faithfully in some context, such as ⋊LH{H, L}*HL⋉. This means that there is no unambiguous way to markup the high tone triggers; only the word edges can be marked up. Because the high tone triggers may be arbitrarily far away, each word edge must be marked up by a subsequential FST that starts at the opposite end of the string: a right-subsequential FST is required to mark the left edge of the string, and a left-subsequential FST is required to mark the right edge of the string. After an edge is marked as the context for spreading, a subsequential FST reading in the opposite direction can complete the mapping. Thus, to spread the leftmost high tone, a right-subsequential FST must make the first pass, marking up the left edge of the string as an instruction to the left-subsequential FST that makes the second pass. Spreading the rightmost high tone requires a left-subsequential FST to make the first pass, and a right-subsequential FST to make the second pass. For both high tones to spread, the two FSTs are paradoxically ordered, and a weakly deterministic analysis is impossible. Modeling double-edged spread with markup requires a third pass by a subsequential FST.

We conjecture that the weakly deterministic class forms a hierarchy as in Figure 5. We call functions where it does not matter whether the first pass is made a left-subsequential FST or a right-subsequential FST *bi-weakly deterministic*. To our knowledge, all attested phonological transforma-

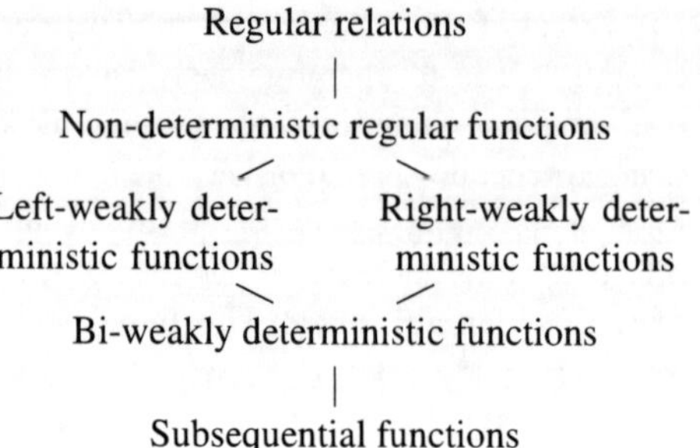

Figure 5: Subregular hierarchy of functions.

tions belong to this class. For other mappings, the order is crucial. For example, to model a hypothetical variant of Copperbelt Bemba without local spreading, markup must be placed at the right edge of the word, and so the first pass must be made by a left-subsequential FST. We call such functions *left-weakly deterministic*. The reverse, where the first pass must be made by a right-subsequential FST, we call *right-weakly deterministic*.

3 Weakly deterministic unbounded circumambient mappings

The previous section demonstrated that there are regular functions that are not weakly deterministic. Like the attested transformations analyzed by Jardine (2016a), first-last UTP and double-edged spread are both unbounded circumambient mappings. Alternative definitions of weak determinism have been proposed which properly exclude all unbounded circumambient mappings (Graf, 2016; McCollum et al., 2018), but it is also important to characterize exactly which unbounded circumambient mappings are weakly deterministic because this makes falsifiable predictions. In this section, we present an initial characterization.

Jardine (2016a, 249) defines unbounded circumambient mappings as in Definition 3.1.

Definition 3.1. An UNBOUNDED CIRCUMAMBIENT MAPPING is a mapping for which:

1. Its application is dependent on information (i.e., the presence of a *trigger* or *blocker*) on *both* sides of the target, and

2. *On both sides,* there is no bound on how far this information may be from the target.

Unbounded circumambient mappings can be represented with rewrite rules such as (1). Some target X is mapped onto Y when circumscribed by triggers L and R. An unbounded number of non-blocking segments N may intervene between the target and the triggers; this set includes targets and transparent segments, and may include other triggers. We assume L and R are not empty strings and are bounded; that is, there exists a k such that k is larger than $|L| + |R|$.

$$X \to Y / L \, N^* \_ N^* \, R \qquad (1)$$

For example, UTP can be represented as in (2). The left and right triggers are both high tones, and the set of non-blocking segments N includes high tones and low tones.

$$L \to H / H\{H, L\}^*\_\{H, L\}^*H$$
$$\Sigma = \{H, L\}, \ N = \{H, L\} \qquad (2)$$

Mappings that involve blocking, such as unbounded spreading in Copperbelt Bemba, can also be represented this way as in (3). The left trigger is a high tone and the right trigger is the right edge of the word. High tones block unbounded spreading, so the set N only contains low tones.

$$L \to H / HL^*\_L^* \ltimes$$
$$\Sigma = \{H, L\}, \ N = \{L\} \qquad (3)$$

Mappings of this type are weakly deterministic if they meet the criteria in Theorem 3.1.

Theorem 3.1. An unbounded circumambient mapping with bounded triggers is weakly deterministic if and only if:

1. There exists at least one bounded substring LXR that is banned from all licit output strings, that is made up of only symbols in the alphabet (no word-boundaries), or

2. There exists at least one bounded substring $\rtimes LXR$ (or $LXR \ltimes$) that is banned from all licit output strings, that contains just one word-boundary, and the triggering substring R (or L) is a blocker, i.e., $R \notin N$ (or $L \notin N$)

The first criterion is exemplified by UTP, where the substring HLH is banned from ever surfacing. The second criterion is exemplified by unbounded spreading in Copperbelt Bemba. The substring HL$\ltimes$ is banned from ever surfacing, and the left

trigger H blocks preceding high tones from undergoing unbounded spreading.

As an aside, we note an intriguing connection between banned substrings and infinite rule schemata proposed by Chomsky and Halle (1968), where rules with unbounded structural descriptions are understood as infinitely many rules with finite contexts. Under that approach, the representation of UTP in (2) would be broken down into the list of rules in (4). The first rule ensures that HLH does not surface, guaranteeing that there is a banned bounded substring.

$$L \to H / H\_H$$
$$L \to H / HL\_H$$
$$L \to H / H\_LH$$
$$L \to H / HLL\_H$$
$$\dots \qquad (4)$$

The rest of this section proves Theorem 3.1. Section 3.1 identifies the contexts where a subsequential FST requires more information than it has access to. Section 3.2 discusses the conditions under which those contexts can be disambiguated by another subsequential FST. Sections 3.2.1 and 3.2.2 demonstrate that when the conditions in Theorem 3.1 are met, it is possible for the first FST to smuggle disambiguating information to the second FST. Section 3.2.3 sketches the inverse, that mappings that do not meet the criteria in Theorem 3.1 are not weakly deterministic.

For simplicity, we assume throughout this section that the first pass is made by a right-subsequential FST, and the mapping is completed by a left-subsequential FST. A similar argument can be made by symmetry for the opposite order.

3.1 Identifying ambiguous contexts

Subsequential FSTs cannot model unbounded circumambient mappings (Karttunen, 2003; Heinz and Lai, 2013; Jardine, 2016a). Following the proofs given by Heinz and Lai (2013) and Jardine (2016b), in a left-subsequential mapping, the realization of any target X in the input is predictable from material that may be unboundedly far to its left or at most k segments to its right. In an unbounded circumambient mapping, contexts as simple as LXN^{k+1}, where X maps to Y if an R follows and maps to X otherwise, cannot be identified by a left-subsequential FST. We refer to these contexts as *ambiguous* because a subsequential FST does not have enough information to correctly determine the output for X.

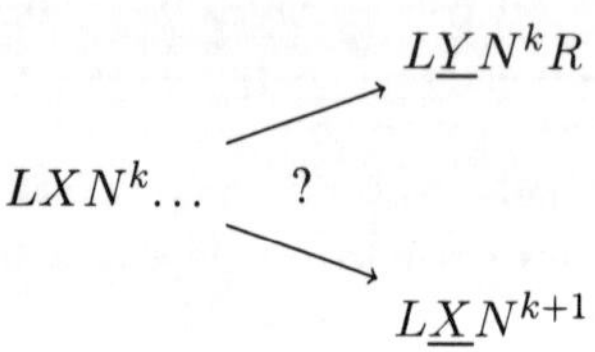

Figure 6: Ambiguous context for the mapping $X \rightarrow Y \mathbin{/} LN^* \_ N^* R$.

There are two types of contexts that may appear in an input, which are defined by the behavior of a target X. We refer to contexts where X is mapped onto itself as *faithful* contexts, and contexts where X is mapped onto some other segment Y as *unfaithful* contexts. In subsequential mappings, every position in the string is unambiguously a faithful or unfaithful context, and changes between contexts depend only on material boundedly far ahead of where the FST is currently printing. For example, in a left-subsequential mapping represented by the rewrite rule $X \rightarrow Y \mathbin{/} LN^* \_$, any X that follows an L is mapped onto Y. Thus, the beginning of the input is a faithful context, and everything following an L is an unfaithful context. The first L in the input unambiguously signals the change from a faithful to an unfaithful context. Blocking segments B unambiguously signal the change back to a faithful context.

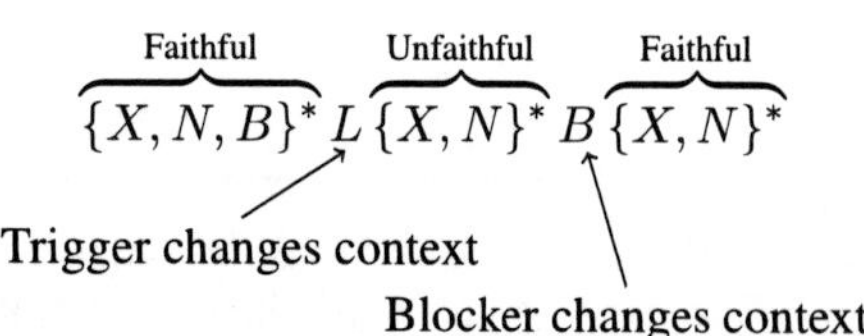

Figure 7: Faithful and unfaithful contexts for the mapping $X \rightarrow Y \mathbin{/} LN^* \_$, where $B \notin N$.

Unbounded circumambient mappings are not subsequential because contexts may not be unambiguously faithful or unfaithful. On its own, a trigger L does not unambiguously signal the change from a faithful context to an unfaithful context; it only does so when there is an R somewhere to its right. For a subsequential FST to process such contexts, they must first be *disambiguated*. Thus, for an unbounded circumambient mapping to be weakly deterministic, all ambiguous contexts must

be marked up by a subsequential FST that makes the first pass through the input.

We define ambiguous contexts in Lemma (3.2).

Lemma 3.2. In an unbounded circumambient mapping, ambiguous contexts occur:

1. After any left trigger (L): $L\ldots\_$, and

2. After any right trigger (R) that follows a left trigger without an intervening blocker (unless R itself is a blocker): $L\ldots R\ldots\_$.

Proof. First, we show that ambiguous contexts appear after Ls. The behavior of X in the context LN^*XN^*, depends on following segments. If an R follows, the context is unfaithful: LN^*XN^*R is precisely the structural description of the rule. Otherwise, the context is faithful: LN^*XN^*. Clearly, if $R = L$, R creates ambiguous contexts in the same way.

Next, we show that if $R \neq L$, R creates ambiguous contexts following L if and only if R is not a blocker. The context following an R that is not preceded by an L is unambiguously faithful. If R is a blocker, the context following an R that is preceded by an L is also unambiguously faithful. Because R is a blocker, it is not in N, and therefore, LN^*R cannot meet the structural description of the rewrite rule in (1) regardless of the following context. If R is not a blocker, it is a part of N. Thus, the string $LN^*RN^*\_$ can be rewritten as the prefix of the structural description $LN^*\_$ and segments unboundedly far to the right determine the context. $\qquad\square$

3.2 Markup strategies

For an unbounded circumambient mapping to be weakly deterministic, the right-subsequential FST that makes the first pass must disambiguate all potentially ambiguous contexts. Reading right-to-left, this FST is able to use information arbitrarily far to the right, and so it can identify the ambiguous contexts.

Regardless of whether an ambiguous context comes from an L or R, the right-subsequential FST knows the context is an unfaithful context if it consists of a string of non-blocking segments followed by an R, i.e., LN^*R. To provide this information to the left-subsequential FST, Ls must be somehow marked up in these contexts (as must Rs if Rs are not blockers). In order for the marked up information to be useful to the left-subsequential

FST it must either be within k segments of the trigger or arbitrarily far to its left.

There are two crucial cases: either L contains a word-boundary and is therefore unique, or L does not contain a word-boundary, and there may be arbitrarily many of them in the input. We show first that if L does not contain a word-boundary, then there is a substring that can act as a markup. If L does contain a word-boundary, we show that there is a markup substring only if R is a blocker.

3.2.1 L does not contain word-boundaries

Lemma 3.3. If there exists an L and an R that do not contain word-boundaries, the unbounded circumambient mapping is weakly deterministic.

Proof. First, we show that such a mapping can contain a potentially unbounded number of ambiguous contexts, requiring an unbounded number of potential markup locations. If L and R do not contain word-boundaries, for any k, and any m, a word exists containing a substring of the form $(LT^k XT^k RB)^m$, where B is some blocker, and where T is the set of "Transparent segments and Targets"—segments that are not left triggers, right triggers, or blockers. The behavior of the Xs in such a word cannot be predicted by a subsequential FST regardless of its direction. The presence of the blocker B means that even if the triggers are non-blockers, the behavior of each X is independently based on the most local L and R.[3] Each ambiguous context requires 1 bit of information indicating whether it is a faithful or unfaithful context. Thus, for the subsequential FST making the first pass to disambiguate ambiguous contexts, at least m bits of markup are required. Because m can grow to become unboundedly large, the amount of markup must also grow as m becomes larger.

As illustrated in Section 1, the right-subsequential FST that makes the first pass must do two things. First, it must map all substrings up to length k of the form LT^*XT^*R to $LT^*\underline{Y}T^*R$ (as well as if L is non-blocking, any substrings up to length k of the form LT^*XT^*L that are followed by R). Given this first action, any substring underlyingly containing LXR will be changed, and, as a result, LXR can be used as markup. In order to transmit the needed m bits of information, markup must be placed after any L

that is in an unfaithful context (that is, followed by a string of non-blockers and then an R), and (if R is a non-blocker) any R unambiguously followed by a faithful context: that is, any R that is not followed by another R. However, if a blocker or other trigger appears within k segments of such a trigger, no markup is needed because the presence of a blocker is sufficient to show that there is a faithful context, and any unfaithful context between two triggers within k segments is handled by the first part of this function.

This leaves L or R followed by an unbounded number of segments that are either targets or transparent segments. We define a k-SUBSTRING OF UNCERTAINTY as any substring in this context, of the shape $(L, R)T^k$. Following an L, the number of possible k-substrings of uncertainty depends on the number of segments in T (specifically, $|T|^k$). A successful markup strategy would replace some of these k segments, but must still contain enough information to reconstruct the string. Any underlying substring of length k that starts with LXR, has been changed already, allowing any substring of that sort to be used as an intermediate markup. LXR is some finite length $j \leq k$. Thus, there are a number of potential markup substrings of the form $LXR\Sigma^{k-j}$, equal to the number of symbols in the alphabet to the $k - j$ power.

For the markup strategy to be successful there need to be at least $|T|^k$ possible markup strings, so that all contrastive k-substrings of uncertainty can be reconstructed, therefore if $|\Sigma|^{k-j} \geq |T|^k$ the process is weakly deterministic. Since the triggers L and R and any blockers B are not in the set T, the non-blocker segments must be less than the full alphabet Σ.[4] If T is a proper subset of Σ, since $|\Sigma| > |T|$,

$$\frac{|\Sigma|}{|T|} > 1 \tag{5}$$

$|\Sigma|^j$ is bounded by definition, and α^x grows unboundedly if $\alpha > 1$, so there exists a k such that:

$$\left(\frac{|\Sigma|}{|T|}\right)^k \geq |\Sigma|^j \tag{6}$$

$$|\Sigma|^{k-j} \geq |T|^k \tag{7}$$

Therefore, for some k, there are more banned substrings of length k that begin with LXR ($|\Sigma|^{k-j}$), than there are contrastive k-substrings of uncertainty that must be reconstructed ($|T|^k$). $\square$

---

[3] If the process in question lacks blocking segments, the amount of markup necessary can only *decrease*, simplifying the proof of weak determinism.

[4] If all triggers and blockers are longer than one segment, the same logic holds using substrings rather than segments.

3.2.2 L contains word-boundaries

If a word-boundary is included in all potential markup substrings, only processes where there is at most one ambiguous context can be weakly deterministic.

Lemma 3.4. If all left (or right) triggers include a word-boundary, but there exists a right (or left) trigger from the other side that does not include a word-boundary, and it blocks application of the process, the process is weakly deterministic.

Proof. If all left triggers L include the left boundary of the word $\rtimes$, the substring LXR cannot be used freely as a markup. However, this can greatly decrease the number of potential k-substrings of uncertainty in the word, as there can only be one L per word. If right triggers block, then there is no k-substring of uncertainty local to any R in the word. Thus the markup strategy must only encode one additional bit of information not present in the original string, so we can make use of the one potential markup location, the k-substring of uncertainty local to the left edge of the word. In this case, LXR substrings could be used to markup the beginning of the word, as long as an R exists that does not include the end of the word $\ltimes$. This is simply a reversed case of the Copperbelt Bemba markup used by McCollum et al. (2018) and demonstrated in Section 2.2, as only the first R in the word would spread all the way to the beginning of the word.

Like the Copperbelt Bemba case, if the reverse is true – that is, if all right triggers R include the right edge of the word – it is impossible for a right-subsequential FST to markup any information in the string, because the only markup location is at the right edge of the word, before the FST is aware of any left triggers in the word; but as above, if there exists an L that does not include a word-boundary, and L are blockers, the process is weakly deterministic using a left-subsequential FST to markup information on the right side of the word first. $\qquad\square$

3.2.3 Summary

In both of the weakly deterministic cases, the number of potential locations for markup strings is at least as many as the number of k-substrings of uncertainty in a word. The cases of non-weakly deterministic unbounded circumambient mappings have a limited number of possible markup locations because all banned substrings include at least one word boundary.

In the first-last UTP case in Section 2.1, there is at most one k-substring of uncertainty possible in a word ($\rtimes\mathrm{H}\,\mathrm{L}^k$), but no banned substring that can be placed as markup in that position because all banned substrings include both word-boundaries.

The other types of non-weakly deterministic unbounded mappings can be seen in the double-edged spreading in Section 2.2, or the true sour grapes mapping described in O'Hara and Smith (2019). In each of these mappings, there are potentially unbounded numbers of k-substrings of uncertainty (for double-edged spreading both $\rtimes\mathrm{L}^k$ and any HL^k), but all banned substrings include a word boundary, restricting the number of possible markup locations to one.

4 Conclusion

This paper demonstrated that the class of weakly deterministic mappings as defined by Heinz and Lai (2013) forms a proper subset of the class of regular functions. This was shown by examining two hypothetical mappings, first-last UTP and double-edged spread, that are regular but not weakly deterministic. The lack of non-weakly deterministic phonological transformations may be demonstrative of an upper bound on the complexity of phonological mappings.

We have also characterized the necessary and sufficient conditions by which an unbounded circumambient mapping is weakly deterministic. This characterization reveals that the set of non-weakly deterministic unbounded circumambient mappings are those that make crucial reference to both edges of the word.

Acknowledgments

This work has greatly benefited from discussions with Eric Baković, Rajesh Bhatt, Jeff Heinz, Adam Jardine, Anna Mai, Adam McCollum, Eric Meinhardt, and audiences at SCAMP 2018, AMP 2018, LSA 2019, and SCiL 2019, as well as comments from three anonymous reviewers for SIGMORPHON. All remaining errors are of course our own.

References

Lee S. Bickmore and Nancy C. Kula. 2013. Ternary spreading and the OCP in Copperbelt Bemba. *Studies in African Linguistics*, 42(2):101–132.

Jane Chandlee. 2014. *Strictly local phonological processes*. Ph.D. thesis, University of Delaware.

Jane Chandlee, Angeliki Athanasopoulou, and Jeffrey Heinz. 2012. Evidence for classifying metathesis patterns as subsequential. In *Proceedings of the 29th West Coast Conference on Formal Linguistics*, pages 303–309.

Jane Chandlee and Jeffrey Heinz. 2012. Bounded copying is subsequential: Implications for metathesis and reduplication. In *Proceedings of SIGMOR-PHON 2012*, pages 42–51.

Jane Chandlee and Jeffrey Heinz. 2018. Strict locality and phonological maps. *Linguistic Inquiry*, 49(1):23–59.

Noam Chomsky and Morris Halle. 1968. *The Sound Pattern of English*. Harper & Row, New York.

Brian Gainor, Regine Lai, and Jeffrey Heinz. 2012. Computational characterizations of vowel harmony patterns and pathologies. In *Proceedings of the 29th West Coast Conference on Formal Linguistics*, pages 63–71.

Thomas Graf. 2016. Weak determinism is not too weak: A reply to Jardine (2016). Unpublished manuscript, Stony Brook University.

Jeffrey Heinz. 2018. The computational nature of phonological generalizations. In Larry M. Hyman and Frans Plank, editors, *Phonological Typology*, pages 126–195. Mouton.

Jeffrey Heinz and Regine Lai. 2013. Vowel harmony and subsequentiality. In *Proceedings of the 13th Meeting on the Mathematics of Language*, pages 52–63.

Larry M. Hyman and Francis X. Katamba. 2010. Tone, syntax and prosodic domains in Luganda. *ZAS Papers in Linguistics*, 53:69–98.

Adam Jardine. 2016a. Computationally, tone is different. *Phonology*, 33(2):247–283.

Adam Jardine. 2016b. Computationally, tone is different. *Phonology*, 33(2). Supplemental materials.

C. Douglas Johnson. 1972. *Formal Aspects of Phonological Description*. Mouton, The Hague.

Ronald Kaplan and Martin Kay. 1994. Regular models of phonological rule systems. *Computational Linguistics*, 20(3):331–378.

Lauri Karttunen. 2003. Finite-state technology. In Ruslan Mitkov, editor, *The Oxford Handbook of Computational Linguistics*, pages 339–357. Oxford University Press, Oxford.

Nancy C. Kula and Lee S. Bickmore. 2015. Phrasal phonology in Copperbelt Bemba. *Phonology*, 32(1):147–176.

Andrew Lamont. 2019. Sour Grapes is phonotactically complex. Paper presented at LSA 2019 Annual Meeting.

Huan Luo. 2017. Long-distance consonant agreement and subsequentiality. *Glossa*, 2(52).

Adam G. McCollum, Eric Baković, Anna Mai, and Eric Meinhardt. 2018. The expressivity of segmental phonology and the definition of weak determinism. Unpublished manuscript, University of California San Diego. Available at `https://ling.auf.net/lingbuzz/004197`.

Adam G. McCollum and James Essegbey. 2018. Unbounded harmony is not always myopic: Evidence from Tutrugbu. In *Proceedings of the 35th West Coast Conference on Formal Linguistics*, pages 251–258.

Mehryar Mohri. 1997. Finite-state transducers in language and speech processing. *Computational Linguistics*, 23(2):269–311.

Charlie O'Hara and Caitlin Smith. 2018. Weakly deterministic characterizations of unbounded tonal and featural spreading. Talk at SCAMP 2018.

Charlie O'Hara and Caitlin Smith. 2019. Computational complexity and sour-grapes-like patterns. In *Supplemental Proceedings of the Annual Meeting on Phonology 2018*.

José Oncina, Pedro García, and Enrique Vidal. 1993. Learning subsequential transducers for pattern recognition tasks. *IEEE Transactions on Pattern Analysis and Machine Intelligence*, 15(5):448–458.

Amanda Payne. 2014. Dissimilation as a subsequential process. In *Proceedings of the 44th Meeting of the North East Linguistic Society*, volume 2, pages 79–90, Amherst, MA. Graduate Linguistics Student Association.

Amanda Payne. 2017. All dissimilation is computationally subsequential. *Language*, 93(4):e353–e371.

Marcel-Paul Schützenberger. 1961. A remark on finite transducers. *Information and Control*, 4:185–196.

Caitlin Smith and Charlie O'Hara. 2019. Formal characterizations of true and false sour grapes. In *Proceedings of the Society for Computation in Linguistics 2019*, volume 2, pages 338–341.

Encoder-decoder models for latent phonological representations of words

Cassandra L. Jacobs
University of California, Davis
clxjacobs@ucdavis.edu

Frédéric Mailhot
Autodesk Inc.
fred.mailhot@autodesk.com

Abstract

We use sequence-to-sequence networks trained on sequential phonetic encoding tasks to construct compositional phonological representations of words. We show that the output of an encoder network can predict the phonetic durations of American English words better than a number of alternative forms. We also show that the model's learned representations map onto existing measures of words' phonological structure (phonological neighborhood density and phonotactic probability).

1 Introduction

The representation of linguistic categories is a fundamental problem in (psycho)linguistics and natural language processing. The formation of complex representations from more basic components is relevant at all levels of linguistic representation, semantic, syntactic, and phonological. Finding good representations for words' phonological[1] structure is critical in psycholinguistics, where we wish to understand the phonological structure of the lexicon, which has been shown to be relevant for language comprehension and production.

The distributional hypothesis defines a word by the context in which it occurs (Harris, 1954; Firth, 1957). This approach has been extended more recently to other types of compositional structures, for example in characterizing the meanings and forms of sentences (Cer et al., 2018; Joulin et al., 2017; Conneau et al., 2017; Devlin et al., 2018). In this paper we explore whether distributional approaches can capture important phonological dependencies.

---

[1]There are disagreements in the literature about the location (Hale and Reiss, 2008) and even existence (Ohala, 1990b) of the boundary/interface between phonetics and phonology, so we remain as theory-agnostic as possible, freely using "phonological"/"phonetic" and "segment"/"phone" interchangeably.

Specifically, we test the extent to which recurrent *encoder-decoder* models (Cho et al., 2014; Sutskever et al., 2014) can learn representations that characterize the phonological structure of the lexicon while also having linguistic and psychological validity (Sibley et al., 2008). We propose that this approach can be used to learn viable lexical-level phonological representations. The output of the encoder component of our model yields promising results in the prediction of phonetic duration, outperforming a number of alternate phonological representations of words.

2 Quantifying a word's phonology

Given a set of discrete phonetic symbols i.e. graphemes with conventionalized pronunciations such as the International Phonetic Alphabet, it is trivial to represent any word's pronunciation as a sequence of such symbols. Conversely, relating sequences of such symbols (*viz.* words) to each other, as well as to the entire lexicon is less obvious. This challenge has led to a proliferation of measurements that characterize a word's phonetic or phonological relationship with all other words in the lexicon. We summarize some salient examples below, and briefly discuss some of their shortcomings.

2.1 Metrics insensitive to serial order

Phonological neighborhood density (PND). This measure is defined as the number of words having a Levenshtein edit distance of one from a given word (in terms of phonetic or phonological symbols) (Luce and Pisoni, 1998; Levenshtein, 1966). Under this definition, a word like "cat" has many neighbors, while a word like "molt" has fewer. This measure is simple to calculate and a wide variety of resources exist for obtaining these measures across many languages (Marian et al., 2012; Baayen et al., 1993; Luce and Pisoni, 1998).

Proceedings of the 16th Workshop on Computational Research in Phonetics, Phonology, and Morphology, pages 206–217
Florence, Italy. August 2, 2019 ©2019 Association for Computational Linguistics

While conceptually simple, PND is insensitive to the position of a segment within a word (e.g. word-initial versus word-final substitutions), and so "sat" and "cab" are treated as equally similar to "cat". Additionally, identifying a word's phonological neighbors using the Levenshtein distance metric requires specifying how many sounds can be added, deleted, or substituted, and potentially the allowable edit distance[2], increasing the number of choice points in determining what a "neighborhood" is.

Frequency-weighted phonological neighborhood density. An augmented version of PND, which weights phonological neighbors in proportion to their lexical frequencies (standardly estimated from large corpora; Marian et al., 2012). So, a more common word like "hat" would contribute more to the neighborhood density of "cat" than a less common word like "cap", even though they are at equal string edit distance. Whether and to what extent density measures should be frequency-weighted is an empirical question, though these measures seem to better reflect psycholinguistic processes than frequency-insensitive measures.

Feature-wise similarity. In the phonological literature it is standard to represent segments as collections of articulatory or acoustic features, e.g. [+voice], [-obstruent] (Chomsky (1968) is the canonical reference). Some linguists (e.g. Frisch (1996), *inter alia*) have posited that words like "cat" and "cap", which differ only in the place of articulation of their final segments (alveolar versus labial), should be considered more similar than e.g. "cat" and "can", which differ in both voicing and manner of articulation. This measure of similarity is potentially controversial, as there are theoretical and empirical questions as to which features to include, or even whether phonetic features exist at all (Stevens and Blumstein, 1981; Marslen-Wilson and Warren, 1994).

2.2 Metrics incorporating serial order

All of the previously described measures effectively characterize words as unordered collections of segments. These characterizations are incomplete because they fail to capture the fact that words unfold over time in usage. Representing the positions of phones within a word is critical for ex-

plaining a number of aspects of language processing. For example, the beginnings of words contribute more strongly than their ends to psycholinguistic effects that are attributed to their phonological representations (Levelt et al., 1999; Sevald and Dell, 1994, *inter alia*), and a word's phonological similarity to the rest of the words in the lexicon has important consequences for speech comprehension (Buz and Jaeger, 2016; Metsala, 1997). Some computational models encode segments as a function of their linear position within a syllable, e.g. in a *onset-vowel-coda* format (e.g. Dell, 1986; Sevald and Dell, 1994). Other approaches include segment n-grams to encode local aspects of serial order (e.g. Seidenberg and McClelland, 1989; Davis, 2010) and the oft-lamented Wickelphone (Houghton and Hartley, 1996). Most closely related to the present approach, some work has demonstrated the viability of sequence encoder models for representing sequences of characters or phonetic segments (Sibley et al., 2008).

2.3 Incorporating variability into representations

Psycholinguistic measures that quantify words' phonological properties in the lexicon generally ignore their variability in pronunciation. In usage, segmental context, or lexical factors such as word frequency, can significantly influence the phonetic realization of a given phone, ranging from assimilatory processes (Ohala, 1990a) to massive reduction and even complete omission (Pitt et al., 2005; Johnson, 2004, *inter alia*). For example, there are over 200 distinct transcriptions of the word "and" in the Buckeye corpus (Pitt et al., 2005), and its normative, dictionary pronunciation (i.e. [ænd]) only accounts for 3% of its realizations.

Measures such as PND rely on single, fixed pronunciations (generally normative/dictionary-based) and corpus-derived lexical frequencies to estimate how many similar-sounding words a given word has, but take no account of variability in realization. As there is evidence that listeners remember and can access/use individual exemplars of perceived speech (Pierrehumbert, 1980; Goldinger, 1998), it seems natural to model distinct realizations within the lexical network. The variability in a word's realizations may especially matter for identifying phonological competitors (Luce and Pisoni, 1998; Marian et al., 2012; Vaden et al., 2009). For example, words like "sand" and

---

[2]See e.g. Suárez et al., 2011 who allow edit distance greater than one, and track the mean distance to a fixed number of neighbors

"and" may rarely compete during lexical access, given that "and" is rarely pronounced similarly to "sand." By incorporating the variability available in naturalistic speech corpora, we hope to provide a better characterization of a word's phonological properties and its relation to the lexicon.

3 Latent phonological representations

Representing arbitrary-length sequences of phones with a single distributed representation has a number of potential practical and conceptual advantages. On the practical side, these representations have a fixed dimensionality, so finding meaningful groupings or clusters is computationally more tractable than directly clustering variable-length sequences. Moreover, projecting these sequences into a latent space offers the potential of discovering hidden relationships or variables that affect phonological or lexical structure.

Our aim in this paper is to test whether and to what extent recent approaches to building sentence representations can also be applied to the phonological domain. Both simpler and more complex latent representations can be constructed to characterize the phonological forms of words. We first discuss potential "naïve" means of accomplishing this, and then move into discussion of our proposed model.

Principal components on bag-of-n-phones

A number of document classification schemes and information retrieval tasks have treated documents as a product of the vector representations of words learned by principal components analysis (PCA; Landauer and Dumais, 1997). We apply this to the phonetic domain as well. By analogy to a bag of words, we refer to bag-of-phones (unigram features) and bag-of-n-phones (higher-order segment co-occurrence categories), which can then be fed into a dimensionality reduction algorithm like principal components analysis (PCA) as an approximate composition function to produce latent phonological representations of words.

doc2vec

Another dimensionality reduction method extends the continuous bag-of-words algorithm used to learn word vectors (Mikolov et al., 2013) to the document domain. Specifically, the model learns to compose (predict) a document (i.e. a word) from its phonological contents. doc2vec (Le and

Mikolov, 2014) has been used in information retrieval and natural language processing applications (Lau and Baldwin, 2016) and so may be a viable way to obtain lexical phonological representations. As with bag-of-phones, this model is insensitive to serial order.

Sequential representations

Encoder-decoder or *sequence-to-sequence* (*seq2seq* henceforth) neural network architectures have shown considerable success in encoding sentences (*viz.* sequences of words) for tasks such as machine translation (Sutskever et al., 2014; Cho et al., 2014). These methods may be appropriate as a means of composing segmental representations, as they are intrinsically sensitive to ordering, easily take usage frequencies into account (directly from training corpora), and have been shown to be effective learners of sequential distributional properties of their training data.

4 Seq2seq model

We trained seq2seq models to either reproduce their input, or to recover (predict) normative (dictionary) pronunciations from the phonetic transcriptions of words in the Buckeye corpus (Pitt et al., 2005), a dataset of monologues provided in response to interviewer questions about the talkers' hometown of Columbus, Ohio. The corpus contains approximately 300,000 words.

Data inclusion criteria. There are some transcription errors in the Buckeye corpus, and so we excluded combinations of phones that did not occur at least ten times. This removes many errors, but a few remain. For example, the segment "h" occurs in some transcriptions but is not part of the character set of the transcription dictionary, and is thus likely an error of omission for actual digraphs from the dictionary; "th", "hh", etc. Despite the presence of these remaining errors, we do not correct the transcriptions of any words. In total, 57 phone/segment categories are represented. Full documentation of the coding scheme used in the corpus can be read in Pitt et al. (2005). For bag-of-n-phones features, we add the additional characters "w_s" and "w_e" as word boundary characters, signaling the starts and ends of words, respectively.

There are no standard train/dev/test splits for the Buckeye corpus, and so we restricted ourselves to randomly selected 80/20 train/test split (Pitt et al., 2005) for training all models.

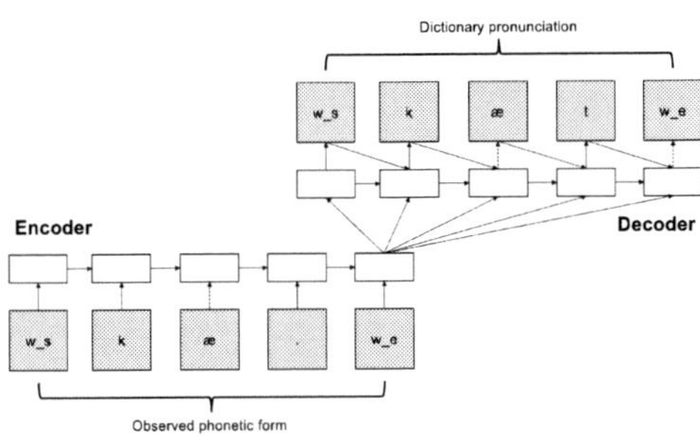

Figure 1: Encoder-decoder LSTM architecture (Normative decoder; for the Observed decoder, the output is the observed phonetic sequence).

Model architecture. Methodologically, we approach the problem with an eye to restricting the computational power of our model, and to restricting the space of hyperparameters to explore. To this end, our models use a basic recurrent encoder-decoder architecture, with an input-side embedding layer, and single-layer, unidirectional[3] LSTMs (Hochreiter and Schmidhuber, 1997) on the encoder and decoder sides. The encoder takes as input a sequence of phone indices (e.g. "cat" → ['k', 'ae', 'tq'] → [11, 1, 20]), embeds them, and encodes the sequence in the space defined by the LSTM. The encoder LSTM's final hidden state is provided as input to the decoder, whose task is to "unroll" this latent representation. The outputs of the decoder LSTM are successively fed through a softmax, sequentially outputting class probabilities for each character class in the phone vocabulary, which are then decoded via simple *argmax* (see Figure 1).

4.1 Training

Hyperparameters. The number of training epochs was empirically determined on the basis of asymptoting training loss, which we determined to be 25 epochs. We used a cross-entropy loss function, using the Adam optimizer (Kingma and Ba, 2015) with a learning rate of 0.001. Other Adam parameters were at default values in the `dynet` python implementation as of this writing (version 2.0.3; Neubig et al., 2017). All hyperparameters were selected on the basis of asymptoting loss on a small subset of the training set. The embedding

layer had 32 dimensions, and the encoder and decoder LSTMs were 64-dimensional.

Tasks. We trained two models to perform slightly different decoding tasks; the *Normative Decoder* model, and the *Observed Decoder* model. In both tasks, the inputs are transcriptions of observed realizations of words in the Buckeye corpus, which include e.g. phonetic changes and omissions. The *Normative Decoder's* task is to output the word's normative pronunciation (e.g. [k, ae, tq] → [k, ae, t]), while the *Observed Decoder* model is trained as a sequential autoencoder (e.g. Chung et al., 2016); the task is to reproduce the input sequence exactly. Both are potentially viable approaches to the creation of lexical phonological representations and show similar performance in the downstream tasks reported on below, which may be useful for researchers who only have access to normative pronunciations.

We evaluated the performance of the model on the 20% held-out portion of the corpus.

4.2 Lexical representations

Once the model is trained, any sequence of phones can be input to the encoder, yielding a latent phonological representation of that sequence. As with character-based NLP models, the comparatively low dimensionality of the input space (57 segments) mitigates sparsity issues, consequently we can obtain latent phonological representations not just of vocabulary words that have been trained but also for rare, out-of-vocabulary (OOV) words and non-words. We plot some aspects of the learned representations in Figures 2 and 3. One pattern that is particularly apparent is that the left-to-right serial nature of the encoder leads to representations that strongly encode the final segment in their representations, for both consonants and vowels.

5 Evaluation

As a preliminary investigation of the information encoded in the learned lexical representations, we assess their ability to model phonetic duration, which is known to be sensitive to phonotactic probability and phonological overlap (Gahl et al., 2012; Watson et al., 2015; Buz and Jaeger, 2016; Yiu and Watson, 2015; Goldrick and Larson, 2008; Vitevitch and Luce, 2005), in addition to other factors like contextual predictability (e.g.

---

[3]While we do not perform these experiments here, we believe that a Bi-LSTM encoder (Schuster and Paliwal, 1997) will enable further advances in constructing psycholinguistically predictive word representations.

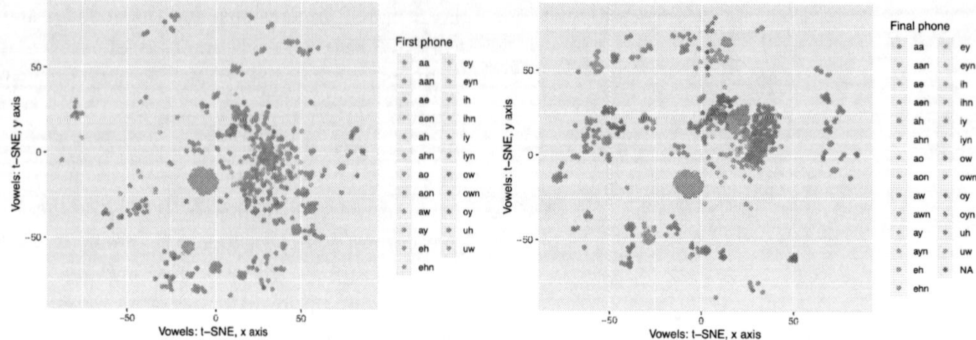

Figure 2: Topology of word vectors from phonological encoder models learned by t-SNE (Maaten and Hinton, 2008). Degree to which word vectors encode vowel information. Clusters largely prioritize word-final information, especially the last segment. Left graph represents the identities of the first segment. Right graph represents the identities of the final segment. The strong encoding of the final segment may be due to the model architecture using uni-directional recurrent layers.

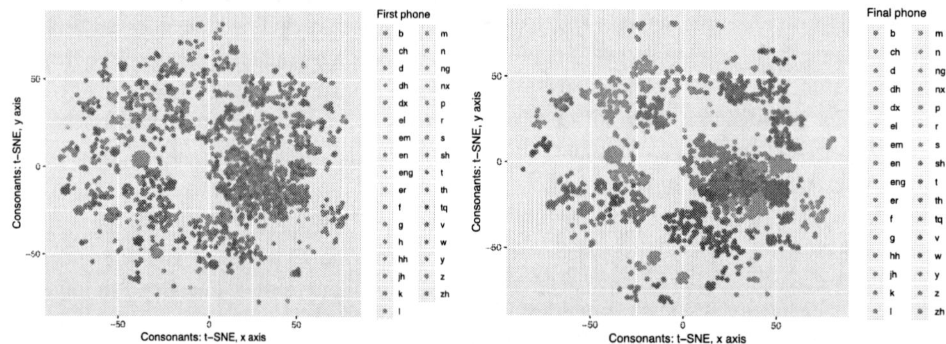

Figure 3: Topology of word vectors, t-SNE projection (Maaten and Hinton, 2008). Degree to which word vectors encode consonant information. Clusters largely prioritize word-final information, especially the last segment. Left graph represents the identities of the first segment. Right graph represents the identities of the final segment.

Cohen Priva and Jaeger, 2018; Seyfarth, 2014). We show that the encoder creates sequence representations that are useful for predicting word duration, and compare the success of the encoder to several other models, described below.

5.1 Predicting word duration

Ultimately we are interested in whether latent phonological representations have predictive validity for phonetic cues, potentially in conjunction with other phonological and lexical representations. Word duration has been shown to be strongly related to phonological structure (Gahl et al., 2012), because duration may reflect the mechanics of the phonological sequencing process in language production (Yiu and Watson, 2015; Watson et al., 2015; Fox et al., 2015) or because speakers lengthen words in dense neighborhoods to promote the listener's understanding (Tily and Kuper-

man, 2012).

We built a series of nested statistical models designed to predict whole-word phonetic duration. The durations were obtained by summing up the durations of each of the annotated phonetic segments for an individual word, which are themselves derived from time stamps extracted from the Buckeye metadata. Whole-word durations were log transformed due to their positive skew; failing to account for this can make statistical inference more difficult (Campbell, 1992). All models were constructed using ridge (L1 norm) regression using the `scikit-learn` package in Python (version 0.2.0; Pedregosa et al., 2011). We report goodness of fit measures in all cases by R^2 values (the coefficient of determination; provided automatically by the *score* function within the ridge regression model object).

All duration models were trained on the same

80-20% split that was used to train the encoder-decoder. Consequently, there were 282,742 observations (words) during training, and 70,686 words at test. The vocabulary for the bag-of-words representations was estimated from the training data. All models are summarized in Table 1.

5.2 Baseline models

Word embeddings. A word's distributional properties, such as its part of speech and meaning; latent part-of-speech; or word-frequency information may reliably predict a word's duration (Seyfarth, 2014; Turnbull et al., 2018; Priva, 2015). Consequently, we incorporate 100-dimensional word embeddings into the regression models. We obtained these word embeddings from gensim's (Řehůřek and Sojka, 2010) skip-gram implementation trained on the Fisher corpus (Cieri et al., 2004), which we selected due to its size, which is critical for generating good word embeddings (Antoniak and Mimno, 2018), and because it belongs to the same domain as the Buckeye corpus (conversational speech).

The skip-gram model used a context window of 5 words and a negative sampling size of 5. We used a zero vector to represent OOV (e.g. Columbus, Ohio-specific place names that would not occur in the Fisher corpus). Word embeddings were, on their own, not a strong predictor of word duration ($R^2 = 0.082$) on the test set, but nevertheless account for some of the variance in word duration.

Bag-of-phones models. Bag-of-words representations are a useful and informative baseline in other NLP tasks, especially text classification (Wang and Manning, 2012). We obtained bag-of-phone representations by learning a vocabulary on the training data and creating sparse count vectors in which the features represent individual phones. A simple bag-of-uniphones model, which ignores order information, has greater predictive power than word embeddings on the test set ($R^2=0.140$). This shows that it is possible to at least partly predict the duration of a given word's realization from relatively unstructured phonological information.

Bag-of-n-phones. Unlike bag-of-words representations, bag-of-ngrams encode localized order information. We constructed n-gram features of phone combinations (bag-of-n-phones) of lengths 2 to 5, using a cutoff frequency of 10 observations. These more complex representations performed similarly to the simpler bag-of-phones model on the test set ($R^2 = 0.140$).

We also tested whether incorporating word boundary information into these models ("w_s" and "w_e" phones) would induce boundary-sensitive phonotactics, but this also did not provide additional gains over simpler models ($R^2 = 0.138$ and $R^2 = 0.140$).

Principal components analysis over bag-of-n-phones. Following from the previous section, we take our bag-of-n-phones representations and feed them into a truncated singular value decomposition model to obtain latent representations of words ("documents"). This representation explained a slightly greater amount of variance in word duration than word embeddings ($R^2 = 0.106$). However, this method performed far worse than the bag-of-phones and bag-of-n-phones models described in the previous section, indicating that some information is lost in this dimensionality reduction method.

doc2vec. Our doc2vec model vectors were trained to predict a word from a phonological representation. The resulting vectors had the same dimensionality as the PCA vectors and the encoder output of the seq2seq models. Surprisingly, doc2vec performed the worst of models that we considered ($R^2 = -0.05$).

seq2seq. The outputs of the encoders for the Observed and Normative decoder models were among the best we considered, both on their own and in conjunction with other measures. Interestingly, the *Observed Decoder* provides a much closer fit to phonetic duration than word embeddings, bag-of-phones, PCA, doc2vec, and the *Normative Decoder* representations. When combined with bag-of-phones and word embedding information, the *Observed Decoder* representations explain the greatest amount of variance in word duration ($R^2 = 0.181$), suggesting that these latent phonological representations encode useful information for characterizing word form.

The disparity between the *Observed* and *Normative* decoder models may be a consequence of the *Normative* model's more difficult learning problem. One potential explanation is that despite training the two models for equal lengths of time (25 epochs), the Normative decoder was not trained to the same criterion as the Observed decoder. Future work should explore whether the worse performance of the Normative decoder model is due to the precision of its representations

Simple	Test R^2	No. features	Combined	Test R^2	No. features
Word embeddings (WE)	0.082	100	**BoP + wb + WE**	0.161	159
Bag-of-phones (BoP)	0.140	57	**+ Observed decoder**	**0.181**	223
+ w_s + w_e (wb)	0.140	59	+ Normative decoder	0.177	223
Bag-of-n-phones (BoNP)	0.140	1700	BoNP + wb + WE	0.159	5018
+ w_s + w_e (wb)	0.138	4918	+ Observed decoder	0.175	5082
PCA bag-of-n-phones	0.106	64	+ Normative decoder	0.173	5082
doc2vec	-0.05	64	Observed + WE	0.149	164
Observed decoder	**0.149**	64	Normative + WE	0.141	164
Normative decoder	0.140	64			

Table 1: Ablation study. Effectiveness of features and combinations of features for predicting (log) phonetic duration.

or due to what is embedded in the representations themselves.

6 Probing phonological structure

While it is clear that seq2seq representations of the phonological forms of words are partially predictive of a phonetic phenomenon (duration), whether the representations encode anything useful about the lexicon requires further investigation. In this section, we explore whether characterizing the similarity space of these phonological word vectors can approximate standard measures of a word's phonological properties. The results show that the vectors produce coherent clusters of words with different phonological properties. We also show that there are correlations between our measures and phonotactic probability.

6.1 Latent phonological neighborhood density

While it is not commonly the case that similarity scores follow a normal distribution, in our case, the similarity scores for words are by visual spot inspection roughly symmetric and normally distributed, so we chose to characterize individual words w_i by the mean and standard deviation of their similarity scores to every other word in the lexicon. Although not *a priori* obvious, one possibility is that these metrics correlate with other lexical metrics, for example, a wide standard deviation could mean that a word has a number of different ways it can be similar to other words, whereas a narrow standard deviation suggests that the word is fairly unique.

6.2 The similarity structure of the lexicon

The distributions of similarity scores show some interesting properties. Unlike the measurements of phonological neighborhood density provided in Vaden et al. (2009), which follow a quasi-Zipfian distribution, a histogram of the mean word-lexicon similarities across the whole vocabulary shows a very different pattern. In particular, there appear to be three distinct clusters of similarity scores, as shown in Figure 4.

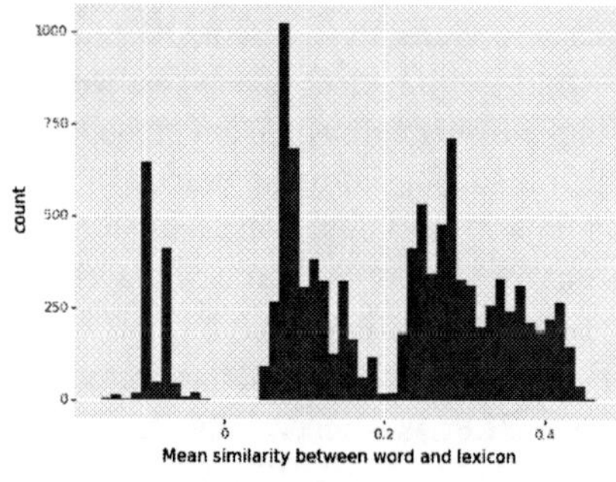

Figure 4: Three clusters of similarity scores from Observed Decoder model.

Words in the first cluster, which show negative average similarity scores, were highly frequent words, typically encompassing function words (e.g. *but*, *about*, *the*). The second cluster appeared to include less high-frequency terms (e.g. *day*, *brain*, *wants*). Finally, the rightmost cluster typically had higher similarity scores, representing low frequency and longer words (e.g. *devices*, *widely*, *element*).[4] Going forward, a meta-model

____

[4]We thank our reviewers for pointing out that all of these properties are correlated with word length in segments (e.g. highly frequent words are on average shorter), which is a useful baseline that we will explore in future work.

will be necessary to determine what factors determine a word's mean lexicon-similarity value.

6.3 Correlation with existing phonological properties

Ideally, a new measure of phonological form should relate to measures already known to affect speech production. For example, a significant correlation with a particular word's mean or standard deviation similarity to all the other words in the lexicon would suggest that our measures characterize the lexicon in a similar way to existing measures. Similarly, because our latent representations encode sequences, we expect them to correlate with phonotactic probability (Vitevitch and Luce, 2004). So, as a final set of analyses, we sought to test whether and to what extent the Observed decoder learns representations that can tell us about a word's relationship to the rest of the lexicon.

There are two measures of interest that have received some attention in the speech production literature. For the present analyses, we reference the phonological neighborhood density metrics as well as the phonotactic probability scores for words in Buckeye that are also in the Irvine Phonotactic Online Dictionary (IPhOD; Vaden et al., 2009). We show that our measures (both mean and standard deviation) strongly correlate with phonotactic probability and IPhoD's additional PND measure. This suggests that the vectors' usefulness extends to researchers who wish to explore the phonological similarity structure of the lexicon for psycholinguistic research.

Phonological neighborhood density. Given the importance of phonological neighborhood density (PND) in speech production (Luce and Pisoni, 1998; Vitevitch and Luce, 2005; Metsala, 1997; Mirman, 2011), we correlated the (log) number of phonological neighbors with our latent density scores and phonetic duration. A phonological neighbor is a word that differs by a single sound (either an addition, a substitution, or a deletion; Levenshtein, 1966). PND ((log) # of neighbors, Figure 5) has a strong negative correlation with mean word-lexicon similarity (greater mean similarity translates to fewer neighbors; $\rho = -.59$) while the standard deviation of word-lexicon similarity shows a non-linear relationship with neighborhood density.

Phonotactic probability. Phonotactic proba-
bility is a measure of the phonological typicality of a word, computed from product of uni-phone and bi-phone probabilities of that word pronunciation, in the same fashion that sentence probabilities are computed in a standard bigram language model (Vitevitch and Luce, 2004, 2005). In our final analysis, we compare the mean and standard deviation of a word's similarity to all other word types, including alternate pronunciations of the same word, to existing measures of phonotactic probability. As with phonological neighborhood density, we see significant positive correlations between our phonological similarity measures (both means and standard deviations; $\rho = 0.41$ and $\rho = 0.13$, respectively) between phonotactic probabilities, which we visualize in Figure 5.

7 Conclusion

The results presented here suggest that encoder-decoder models are a promising framework for composing segment-based representations of words. The models also characterize words' phonological forms relative to the rest of the lexicon. We believe that encoder-decoder models' usefulness extends beyond that of many existing approaches, as they can seamlessly generate gestalt representations for out-of-vocabulary words and even nonce words. Our approach has a number of potential advantages for the cognitive modeling of language processing in both comprehension and production tasks, or indeed in any task that can be modeled with phonological word representations. Importantly, the encoder-decoder modeling framework is flexible, learning both from observed, quasi-phonetic realizations of words as well as from idealized, normative (dictionary-based) pronunciations, and allows for many variations in expressivity and computational power.

The reported correlations between phonological neighborhood density, phonotactic probability, latent phonological similarity, and phonetic duration motivate a need to better understand the embedding representations themselves. We have presented considerable evidence that the models capture some non-trivial dependencies between phonetic segments that can characterize word forms. Going forward, we believe that our latent phonological representations may be useful for designing stimuli, or provide an alternative to standard covariates in psycholinguistic experiments such

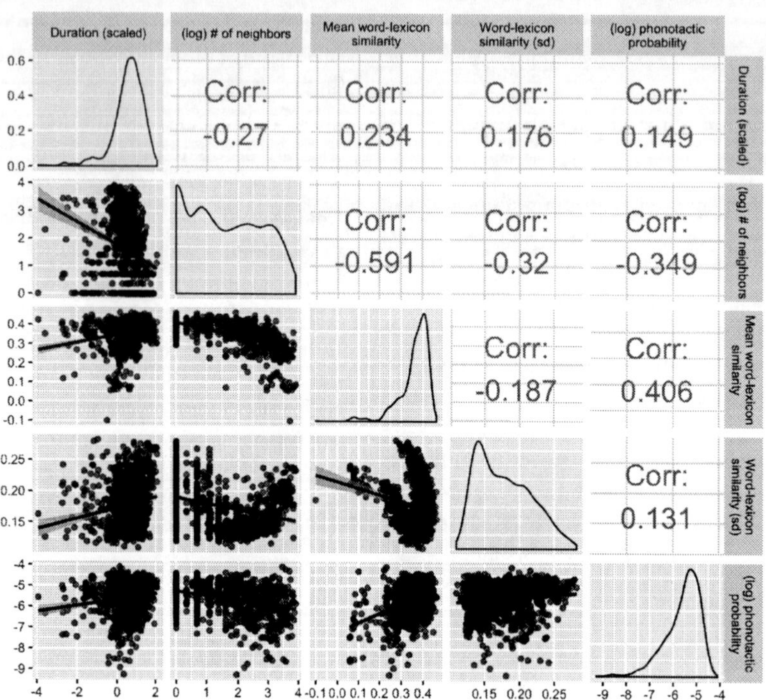

Figure 5: Correlation between a word's phonetic duration in Buckeye, phonological neighborhood density, global word-lexicon similarity (mean and standard deviation), and phonotactic probability.

as phonological neighborhood density and phonotactic probability. Finally, our results on the Normative-Decoder suggest that low-resource languages with only a pronunciation dictionary are also a viable means of learning these representations, assuming that there is a corresponding corpus of conversational data. In sum, we have demonstrated that our approach is useful for modeling of phonological structure.

References

Maria Antoniak and David Mimno. 2018. Evaluating the stability of embedding-based word similarities. *Transactions of the Association of Computational Linguistics*, 6:107–119.

R Harald Baayen, Richard Piepenbrock, and Rijn van H. 1993. The {CELEX} lexical data base on {CD-ROM}. *Linguistic Data Consortium*.

Esteban Buz and T Florian Jaeger. 2016. The (in) dependence of articulation and lexical planning during isolated word production. *Language, Cognition and Neuroscience*, 31:404–424.

W Nick Campbell. 1992. Syllable-based segmental duration. *Talking machines: Theories, models, and designs*, pages 211–224.

Daniel Cer, Yinfei Yang, Sheng-yi Kong, Nan Hua, Nicole Limtiaco, Rhomni St John, Noah Constant, Mario Guajardo-Cespedes, Steve Yuan, Chris Tar, et al. 2018. Universal sentence encoder. *arXiv preprint arXiv:1803.11175*.

Kyunghyun Cho, Bart van Merrienboer, Caglar Gulcehre, Dzmitry Bahdanau, Fethi Bougares, Holger Schwenk, and Yoshua Bengio. 2014. Learning phrase representations using rnn encoder–decoder for statistical machine translation. *Proceedings of the 2014 Conference on Empirical Methods in Natural Language Processing (EMNLP)*, pages 1724–1734.

Noam Chomsky. 1968. *The sound pattern of English*. Studies in language. Harper & Row, New York.

Yu-An Chung, Chao-Chung Wu, Chia-Hao Shen, Hung-Yi Lee, and Lin-Shan Lee. 2016. Audio word2vec: Unsupervised learning of audio segment representations using sequence-to-sequence autoencoder. *Interspeech 2016*, pages 765–769.

Christopher Cieri, David Miller, and Kevin Walker. 2004. The fisher corpus: a resource for the next generations of speech-to-text. In *LREC*, volume 4, pages 69–71.

Uriel Cohen Priva and T Florian Jaeger. 2018. The interdependence of frequency, predictability, and informativity in the segmental domain. *Linguistics Vanguard*, 4.

Alexis Conneau, Douwe Kiela, Holger Schwenk, Loïc Barrault, and Antoine Bordes. 2017. Supervised learning of universal sentence representations from natural language inference data. In *Proceedings of the 2017 Conference on Empirical Methods in Natural Language Processing*, pages 670–680.

Colin J Davis. 2010. The spatial coding model of visual word identification. *Psychological Review*, 117:713–758.

Gary S Dell. 1986. A spreading-activation theory of retrieval in sentence production. *Psychological Review*, 93:283–321.

Jacob Devlin, Ming-Wei Chang, Kenton Lee, and Kristina Toutanova. 2018. Bert: Pre-training of deep bidirectional transformers for language understanding. *arXiv preprint arXiv:1810.04805*.

John R Firth. 1957. A synopsis of linguistic theory, 1930-1955. *Studies in linguistic analysis*.

Neal P Fox, Megan Reilly, and Sheila E Blumstein. 2015. Phonological neighborhood competition affects spoken word production irrespective of sentential context. *Journal of Memory and Language*, 83:97–117.

Stefan Frisch. 1996. *Similarity and frequency in phonology*. Ph.D. thesis, Northwestern University.

Susanne Gahl, Yao Yao, and Keith Johnson. 2012. Why reduce? phonological neighborhood density and phonetic reduction in spontaneous speech. *Journal of Memory and Language*, 66:789–806.

Stephen D Goldinger. 1998. Echoes of echoes? an episodic theory of lexical access. *Psychological Review*, 105:251–279.

Matthew Goldrick and Meredith Larson. 2008. Phonotactic probability influences speech production. *Cognition*, 107:1155–1164.

Mark Hale and Charles Reiss. 2008. *The Phonological Enterprise*. Studies in language. Oxford University Press, New York.

Zellig S Harris. 1954. Distributional structure. *Word*, 10:146–162.

Sepp Hochreiter and Jürgen Schmidhuber. 1997. Long short-term memory. *Neural computation*, 9(8):1735–1780.

George Houghton and Tom Hartley. 1996. Parallel models of serial behaviour: Lashley revisited. *Psyche: An Interdisciplinary Journal of Research on Consciousness*.

Keith Johnson. 2004. Massive reduction in conversational american english. In *Spontaneous speech: Data and analysis. Proceedings of the 1st session of the 10th international symposium*, pages 29–54. Citeseer.

Armand Joulin, Edouard Grave, Piotr Bojanowski, and Tomas Mikolov. 2017. Bag of tricks for efficient text classification. In *Proceedings of the 15th Conference of the European Chapter of the Association for Computational Linguistics: Volume 2, Short Papers*, volume 2, pages 427–431.

Diederik P. Kingma and Jimmy Ba. 2015. Adam: A method for stochastic optimization. In *Proceedings of the 3rd International Conference on Learning Representations (ICLR)*.

Thomas K Landauer and Susan T Dumais. 1997. A solution to plato's problem: The latent semantic analysis theory of acquisition, induction, and representation of knowledge. *Psychological Review*, 104:211–240.

Jey Han Lau and Timothy Baldwin. 2016. An empirical evaluation of doc2vec with practical insights into document embedding generation. In *Proceedings of the 1st Workshop on Representation Learning for NLP*, pages 78–86.

Quoc Le and Tomas Mikolov. 2014. Distributed representations of sentences and documents. In *International conference on machine learning*, pages 1188–1196.

Willem JM Levelt, Ardi Roelofs, and Antje S Meyer. 1999. A theory of lexical access in speech production. *Behavioral and Brain Sciences*, 22:1–38.

Vladimir I Levenshtein. 1966. Binary codes capable of correcting deletions, insertions, and reversals. In *Soviet Physics Doklady*, volume 10, pages 707–710.

Paul A Luce and David B Pisoni. 1998. Recognizing spoken words: The neighborhood activation model. *Ear and Hearing*, 19:1–36.

Laurens van der Maaten and Geoffrey Hinton. 2008. Visualizing data using t-sne. *Journal of Machine Learning Research*, 9:2579–2605.

Viorica Marian, James Bartolotti, Sarah Chabal, and Anthony Shook. 2012. Clearpond: Crosslinguistic easy-access resource for phonological and orthographic neighborhood densities. *PloS one*, 7(8):e43230.

William Marslen-Wilson and Paul Warren. 1994. Levels of perceptual representation and process in lexical access: words, phonemes, and features. *Psychological review*, 101(4):653.

Jamie L Metsala. 1997. An examination of word frequency and neighborhood density in the development of spoken-word recognition. *Memory & Cognition*, 25(1):47–56.

Tomas Mikolov, Ilya Sutskever, Kai Chen, Greg S Corrado, and Jeff Dean. 2013. Distributed representations of words and phrases and their compositionality. In *Advances in Neural Information Processing Systems*, pages 3111–3119.

Daniel Mirman. 2011. Effects of near and distant semantic neighbors on word production. *Cognitive, Affective, & Behavioral Neuroscience*, 11(1):32–43.

Graham Neubig, Chris Dyer, Yoav Goldberg, Austin Matthews, Waleed Ammar, Antonios Anastasopoulos, Miguel Ballesteros, David Chiang, Daniel Clothiaux, Trevor Cohn, Kevin Duh, Manaal Faruqui, Cynthia Gan, Dan Garrette, Yangfeng Ji, Lingpeng Kong, Adhiguna Kuncoro, Gaurav Kumar, Chaitanya Malaviya, Paul Michel, Yusuke Oda, Matthew Richardson, Naomi Saphra, Swabha Swayamdipta, and Pengcheng Yin. 2017. Dynet: The dynamic neural network toolkit. *arXiv preprint arXiv:1701.03980*.

John J Ohala. 1990a. The phonetics and phonology of aspects of assimilation. *Papers in Laboratory Phonology*, 1:258–275.

John J Ohala. 1990b. There is no interface between phonology and phonetics: a personal view. *Journal of Phonetics*, 18:153–171.

F. Pedregosa, G. Varoquaux, A. Gramfort, V. Michel, B. Thirion, O. Grisel, M. Blondel, P. Prettenhofer, R. Weiss, V. Dubourg, J. Vanderplas, A. Passos, D. Cournapeau, M. Brucher, M. Perrot, and E. Duchesnay. 2011. Scikit-learn: Machine learning in Python. *Journal of Machine Learning Research*, 12:2825–2830.

Janet Breckenridge Pierrehumbert. 1980. *The phonology and phonetics of English intonation*. Ph.D. thesis, Massachusetts Institute of Technology.

Mark A Pitt, Keith Johnson, Elizabeth Hume, Scott Kiesling, and William Raymond. 2005. The buckeye corpus of conversational speech: labeling conventions and a test of transcriber reliability. *Speech Communication*, 45:89–95.

Uriel Cohen Priva. 2015. Informativity affects consonant duration and deletion rates. *Laboratory Phonology*, 6(2):243–278.

Radim Řehůřek and Petr Sojka. 2010. Software Framework for Topic Modelling with Large Corpora. In *Proceedings of the LREC 2010 Workshop on New Challenges for NLP Frameworks*, pages 45–50, Valletta, Malta. ELRA. http://is.muni.cz/publication/884893/en.

M. Schuster and K.K. Paliwal. 1997. There is no interface between phonology and phonetics: a personal view. *IEEE Transactions on Signal Processing*, 45:2673–2681.

Mark S Seidenberg and James L McClelland. 1989. A distributed, developmental model of word recognition and naming. *Psychological Review*, 96:523–568.

Christine A Sevald and Gary S Dell. 1994. The sequential cuing effect in speech production. *Cognition*, 53:91–127.

Scott Seyfarth. 2014. Word informativity influences acoustic duration: Effects of contextual predictability on lexical representation. *Cognition*, 133(1):140–155.

Daragh E Sibley, Christopher T Kello, David C Plaut, and Jeffrey L Elman. 2008. Large-scale modeling of wordform learning and representation. *Cognitive Science*, 32(4):741–754.

Kenneth N Stevens and Sheila E Blumstein. 1981. The search for invariant acoustic correlates of phonetic features. *Perspectives on the study of speech*, pages 1–38.

Lidia Suárez, Seok Hui Tan, Melvin J Yap, and Winston D Goh. 2011. Observing neighborhood effects without neighbors. *Psychonomic Bulletin & Review*, 18(3):605–611.

Ilya Sutskever, Oriol Vinyals, and Quoc V Le. 2014. Sequence to sequence learning with neural networks. In *Advances in Neural Information Processing Systems*, pages 3104–3112.

Harry Tily and Victor Kuperman. 2012. Rational phonological lengthening in spoken dutch. *The Journal of the Acoustical Society of America*, 132(6):3935–3940.

Rory Turnbull, Scott Seyfarth, Elizabeth Hume, and T Florian Jaeger. 2018. Nasal place assimilation trades off inferrability of both target and trigger words. *Laboratory Phonology: Journal of the Association for Laboratory Phonology*, 9(1).

Kenneth I Vaden, HR Halpin, and Gregory S Hickok. 2009. Irvine phonotactic online dictionary, version 2.0. [data file]. *Available from http://www.iphod.com*.

Michael S Vitevitch and Paul A Luce. 2004. A web-based interface to calculate phonotactic probability for words and nonwords in english. *Behavior Research Methods, Instruments, & Computers*, 36:481–487.

Michael S Vitevitch and Paul A Luce. 2005. Increases in phonotactic probability facilitate spoken nonword repetition. *Journal of Memory and Language*, 52:193–204.

Sida Wang and Christopher D. Manning. 2012. Baselines and bigrams: simple, good sentiment and topic classification. *Proceedings of the 50th Annual Meeting of the Association for Computational Linguistics: Short Papers*, 2:90–94.

Duane G Watson, Andrés Buxó-Lugo, and Dominique C Simmons. 2015. The effect of phonological encoding on word duration: Selection takes time. In *Explicit and implicit prosody in sentence processing*, pages 85–98. Springer.

Loretta K Yiu and Duane G Watson. 2015. When overlap leads to competition: Effects of phonological encoding on word duration. *Psychonomic Bulletin &
Review*, 22:1701–1708.

Action-Sensitive Phonological Dependencies

Yiding Hao
Yale University
New Haven, CT, USA
`yiding.hao@yale.edu`

Dustin Bowers
University of Arizona
Tucson, AZ, USA
`bowersd@email.arizona.edu`

Abstract

This paper defines a subregular class of functions called the *tier-based synchronized strictly local* (TSSL) functions. These functions are similar to the the tier-based input–output strictly local (TIOSL) functions, except that the locality condition is enforced not on the input and output streams, but on the computation history of the minimal subsequential finite-state transducer. We show that TSSL functions naturally describe rhythmic syncope while TIOSL functions cannot, and we argue that TSSL functions provide a more restricted characterization of rhythmic syncope than existing treatments within Optimality Theory.

1 Introduction

The subregular program in phonology seeks to define subclasses of the regular languages and finite-state functions that describe attested phonotactic constraints and phonological processes. These subclasses provide a natural framework for typological classification of linguistic phenomena while allowing for the development of precise theories of language learning and processing. The traditional view in subregular phonology is that most phonotactic dependencies are described by *tier-based strictly local* languages (TSL, Heinz et al., 2011; McMullin and Hansson, 2016; McMullin, 2016), while most phonological process are described by *strictly local* functions (Chandlee, 2014; Chandlee et al., 2015, In prep). These classes of languages and functions are defined by a principle known as *locality*—that dependencies between symbols must occur over a bounded distance within the string. To account for longer-distance dependencies, Heinz et al. (2011) proposes a *tier projection* mechanism that allows irrelevant intervening symbols to be exempt from the locality condition.

Recent work in subregular phonology has identified a number of exceptions to the traditional view. On the language side, unbounded culminative stress systems (Baek, 2018), Uyghur backness harmony (Mayer and Major, 2018), and Sanskrit n-retroflexion (Graf and Mayer, 2018) have been shown to lie outside the class of TSL languages. These observations have led to an enhancement of Heinz et al.'s (2011) tier projection system. On the function side, a number of processes, including bidirectional harmony systems (Heinz and Lai, 2013) and certain tonal processes (Jardine, 2016), have been shown to be not subsequential, and therefore not strictly local. At least two proposals, both known as the *weakly deterministic* functions, have been made in order to capture these processes (Heinz and Lai, 2013; McCollum et al., 2018).

This paper identifies *rhythmic syncope* as an additional example of a phonological process that is not strictly local. In rhythmic syncope, every second vowel of an underlying form is deleted in the surface form, starting with either the first or the second vowel. While rhythmic syncope cannot be expressed as a local dependency between symbols, it can be viewed as a local dependency between *actions* in the computation history of the minimal subsequential finite-state transducer (SFST). We formalize such dependencies by proposing the *tier-based synchronized strictly local* functions (TSSL). See Bowers and Hao (To appear) for a discussion of TSSL functions oriented towards the phonological literature.

This paper is structured as follows. Section 2 enumerates standard definitions and notation used throughout the paper, while Section 3 reviews existing work on strictly local functions. Section 4 introduces rhythmic syncope and shows that it is not strictly local. Section 5 presents two equivalent definitions of the TSSL functions—an al-

Proceedings of the 16th Workshop on Computational Research in Phonetics, Phonology, and Morphology, pages 218–228
Florence, Italy. August 2, 2019 ©2019 Association for Computational Linguistics

gebraic definition and a definition in terms of a canonical SFST. Section 6 develops some formal properties of the TSSL functions, showing that they are incomparable to the full class strictly local functions. Section 7 compares our proposal to existing OT treatments of rhythmic syncope, and Section 8 concludes.

2   Preliminaries

As usual, $\mathbb{N}$ denotes the set of nonnegative integers. Σ and Γ denote finite alphabets not including the left and right word boundary symbols $\rtimes$ and $\ltimes$, respectively. The length of a string x is denoted by $|x|$, and λ denotes the empty string. Alphabet symbols are identified with strings of length 1, and individual strings are identified with singleton sets of strings. For $k \in \mathbb{N}$, α^k denotes α concatenated with itself k-many times, $\alpha^{<k}$ denotes $\bigcup_{i=0}^{k-1} \alpha^i$, α^* denotes $\bigcup_{i=0}^{\infty} \alpha^i$, and α^+ denotes $\alpha\alpha^*$. The *longest common prefix* of a set of strings A is the longest string $\mathrm{lcp}(A)$ such that every string in A begins with $\mathrm{lcp}(A)$. The *k-suffix* of a string x, denoted $\mathrm{suff}^k(x)$, is the string consisting of the last k-many symbols of $\rtimes^k x$.

A *subsequential finite-state transducer* (SFST) is a 6-tuple $T = \langle Q, \Sigma, \Gamma, q_0, \rightarrow, \sigma \rangle$, where

- Q is the set of *states*, with $q_0 \in Q$ being the *start state*;

- Σ and Γ are the *input* and *output alphabets*, respectively;

- $\rightarrow : Q \times \Sigma \to Q \times \Gamma^*$ is the *transition function*; and

- $\sigma : Q \to \Gamma^*$ is the *final output function*.

For $x \in \Sigma^*$; $y \in \Gamma^*$; and $q, r \in Q$, the notation $q \xrightarrow{x:y} r$ means that T emits y to the output stream and transitions to state r if it reads x in the input stream while it is in state q. Letting $f : \Sigma^* \to \Gamma^*$, we say that T *computes* f if for every $x \in \Sigma^*$, $f(x) = y\sigma(q)$, where $q_0 \xrightarrow{x:y} q$. A function is *subsequential* if it is computed by an SFST.

An SFST $T = \langle Q, \Sigma, \Gamma, q_0, \rightarrow, \sigma \rangle$ is *onward* if for every state q other than q_0,

$$\mathrm{lcp}\left(\left\{ y \,\middle|\, \exists x \exists r.q \xrightarrow{x:y} r \right\} \cup \{\sigma(q)\} \right) = \lambda.$$

Putting T in onward form allows us to impose structure on the timing with which SFSTs produce output symbols.

Definition 1. Let $f : \Sigma^* \to \Gamma^*$. We define the function $f^{\leftarrow} : \Sigma^* \to \Gamma^*$ by

$$f^{\leftarrow}(x) := \mathrm{lcp}\left(\{f(xy) | y \in \Sigma^* \} \right).$$

For any $x, y \in \Sigma^*$, $f_x^{\rightarrow}(y)$ denotes the string such that $f(xy) = f^{\leftarrow}(x)f_x^{\rightarrow}(y)$. We refer to $f_x^{\rightarrow}$ as the *translation of f by x* and to $f^{\leftarrow}$ as f *top*.[1]

Suppose T computes f. The following facts are apparent.

- Fix $w, x \in \Sigma^*$ and write $q_0 \xrightarrow{x:y} q$ and $q_0 \xrightarrow{x:z} r$. If $q = r$, then $f_w^{\rightarrow} = f_y^{\rightarrow}$.

- T is onward if and only if for all $q \in Q \backslash \{q_0\}$, if $q_0 \xrightarrow{x:y} q$, then $y = f^{\leftarrow}(x)$.

These observations allow us to construct the *minimal SFST for f* by identifying each state with a possible translation $f_x^{\rightarrow}$ (Raney, 1958).

Let A and B be alphabets that are possibly infinite. A function $h : A^* \to B^*$ is a *homomorphism* if for every $x, y \in A^*$, $h(xy) = h(x)h(y)$.

3   Background

The *strictly local functions* are classes of subsequential functions proposed by Chandlee (2014), Chandlee et al. (2015), and Chandlee et al. (In prep) as transductive analogues of the strictly local languages (McNaughton and Papert, 1971). Whereas phonotactic dependencies can usually be described using *tier-based strictly local* languages (Heinz et al., 2011; McMullin and Hansson, 2016; McMullin, 2016), Chandlee (2014) has argued that local phonological processes can be modelled as strictly local functions when they are viewed as mappings between underlying representations and surface representations. A survey overview of the related literature can be found in Heinz (2018).

Intuitively, strictly local functions are functions computed by SFSTs in which each state represents the $i - 1$ most recent symbols in the input stream and the $j - 1$ most recent symbols in the output stream along with the current input symbol, for some parameter values i, j fixed. Such functions are "local" in the sense that the action performed on each input symbol depends only on information about symbols in the input and output streams

---

[1] This terminology follows Sakarovitch (2009, pp. 692–693). In the transducer inference literature, Oncina et al. (1993) refer to $f_x^{\rightarrow}$ as the *tails of x in f*, and Chandlee et al. (2015) refer to $f^{\leftarrow}$ as the *prefix function associated to f*.

within a bounded distance. In this paper, we augment strictly local functions with *tier projection*, a mechanism introduced by Heinz et al. (2011) and elaborated by Baek (2018), Mayer and Major (2018), and Graf and Mayer (2018) that allows the locality constraint to bypass irrelevant alphabet symbols, extending the distance over which dependencies may be enforced.

Definition 2. For any alphabet Σ, a *tier on Σ* is a homomorphism $\tau : \Sigma^* \to \Sigma^*$ such that for each $a \in \Sigma$, either $\tau(a) = a$ or $\tau(a) = \lambda$. In the former case, we say that a is *on* τ; in the latter case, we say that a is *off* τ.

Chandlee (2014), Chandlee et al. (2015), and Chandlee et al. (In prep) give two definitions of the strictly local functions. Firstly, they state the locality condition in terms of the algebraic representation of minimal SFSTs.

Definition 3. Fix $i, j > 0$ and let τ be a tier on $\Sigma \cup \Gamma$. A function $f : \Sigma^* \to \Gamma^*$ is *i, j-input–output strictly local on tier τ (i, j-TIOSL)* if for all $w, x \in \Sigma^*$, if

- $\mathrm{suff}^{i-1}(\tau(w)) = \mathrm{suff}^{i-1}(\tau(x))$ and

- $\mathrm{suff}^{j-1}(\tau(f^{\leftarrow}(w))) = \mathrm{suff}^{j-1}(\tau(f^{\leftarrow}(x)))$,

then $f^{\rightarrow}_w = f^{\rightarrow}_x$. A function is *$i$-input strictly local on tier τ (i-TISL)* if it is $i, 1$-TIOSL on tier τ, and it is *j-output strictly local on tier τ (j-TOSL)* if it is $1, j$-TIOSL on tier τ.

Secondly, they define strictly local functions in terms of canonical SFSTs that directly encode $(i-1)$-suffixes of the input stream and $(j-1)$-suffixes of the output stream in their state names.

Definition 4. Fix $i, j > 0$ and let τ be a tier on $\Sigma \cup \Gamma$. An SFST $T = \langle Q, \Sigma, \Gamma, q_0, \to, \sigma \rangle$ is *i, j-input–output strictly local on tier τ (i, j-TIOSL)* if the following conditions hold.

- $Q = (\{\rtimes\} \cup \Sigma)^{i-1} \times (\{\rtimes\} \cup \Gamma)^{j-1}$ and $q_0 = \langle \rtimes^{i-1}, \rtimes^{j-1} \rangle$.

- If $\langle a, b \rangle \xrightarrow{x:y} \langle c, d \rangle$, then $c = \mathrm{suff}^{i-1}(\tau(ax))$ and $d = \mathrm{suff}^{j-1}(\tau(by))$.

An SFST is *i-input strictly local on tier τ (i-TISL)* if it is $i, 1$-TIOSL on tier τ, and it is *j-output strictly local on tier τ (j-TOSL)* if it is $1, j$-TIOSL on tier τ.

These definitions turn out to be equivalent when the canonical SFSTs are required to be onward.

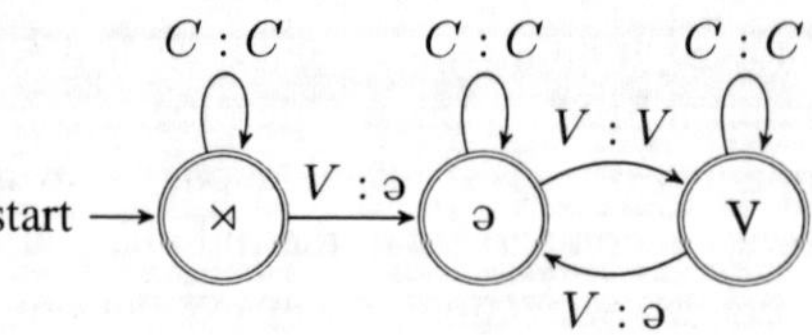

Figure 1: An SFST for rhythmic reduction.

Theorem 5 (Chandlee, 2014; Chandlee et al., 2015, In prep). *A function is i, j-TIOSL on tier τ if and only if it is computed by an onward SFST that is i, j-TIOSL on tier τ.*

Example 6. *Rhythmic reduction* is a phonological process in which alternating vowels in a word undergo reduction. The examples in (7) show rhythmic reduction in the Odawa variety of Ojibwe circa 1912, as documented by Edward Sapir. In our representation of reduction, vowels are reduced to ə, starting from the first vowel. There is no reason to believe that ə appears in underlying forms.

(7) Rhythmic reduction in Ojibwe circa 1912 (Rhodes et al., 2012)

    a. /mʌkɪzɪnʌn/ ⤳ [məkɪzənʌn] 'shoes'

    b. /gʊtɪgʊmɪnʌgɪbɪnaːd/ ⤳ [gətɪgəmɪnəgɪbənaːd] 'if he rolls him'

Figure 1 shows an SFST that implements the rhythmic reduction pattern illustrated in (7). We represent the pattern using an alphabet of three symbols: C, representing consonants; V, representing vowels that have not been reduced; and ə, representing vowels that have been reduced. Observe that this SFST is onward and 2-TOSL, with C off the tier: each state represents the most recent vowel in the ouput stream.[2]

4 Rhythmic Syncope

Rhythmic syncope is a phonological process in which every second vowel in a word is deleted. The examples of (8) show rhythmic syncope in Macushi, in which deletion begins with the first vowel.[3]

(8) Rhythmic syncope in Macushi (Hawkins, 1950)

<hr>

[2]For clarity, we omit the $\langle \lambda, \cdot \rangle$ portions of the state names.

[3]The synchronic status of rhythmic syncope is a matter of current discussion, as its development appears to push a phonological system into dramatic restructuring (Bowers, To appear).

220

a. /piripi/ $\leadsto$ [pripi] 'spindle'

b. /wanamari/ $\leadsto$ [wnamri] 'mirror'

In this section, we show that rhythmic syncope is not TIOSL. To see this, we formalize rhythmic syncope as a function over two alphabet symbols: C, representing consonants, and V, representing vowels. This idealization does not affect the argument that rhythmic syncope is not TIOSL, presented in Proposition 10.

Definition 9. The *rhythmic syncope function* $\rho :$ $\{C, V\}^* \to \{C, V\}^*$ is defined as follows. For $c_0, c_1, \ldots, c_n \in C^*$,

$$\rho(c_0 V c_1 V c_2 \ldots V c_n) = c_0 v_1 c_1 v_2 c_2 \ldots v_n c_n,$$

where for each i, $v_i = V$ if i is even and $v_i = \lambda$ if i is odd.

The intuition underlying the argument presented below is that $(i-1)$-suffixes of the input and $(j-1)$-suffixes of the output do not contain information about whether vowels occupy even or odd positions within the input and output strings. Therefore, while an i, j-TIOSL SFST can record the most recent vowels read from the input stream and emitted to the output stream, this information is not sufficient for determining whether or not the SFST should delete a vowel.

Proposition 10. *The rhythmic syncope function is not i, j-TIOSL on tier τ for any $i, j > 0$ and any* $\tau : \{C, V\}^* \to \{C, V\}^*$.

Proof. Let $k > i$ be even. Consider the strings $w := V^k$ and $x := V^{k+1}$. Observe that $\rho^{\leftarrow}(w) = \rho^{\leftarrow}(x) = V^{k/2}$; thus $\text{suff}^{j-1}(\tau(\rho^{\leftarrow}(w))) = \text{suff}^{j-1}(\tau(\rho^{\leftarrow}(x)))$. Now, if V is on τ, then $\text{suff}^{i-1}(\tau(w)) = V^{i-1} = \text{suff}^{i-1}(\tau(x))$, and if V is off τ, then $\text{suff}^{i-1}(\tau(w)) = \rtimes^{i-1} = \text{suff}^{i-1}(\tau(x))$. Thus, if ρ is i, j-TIOSL on tier τ, then $\rho_w^{\to} = \rho_x^{\to}$. However, letting $y := V^{k/2}$, observe that

$$y = \rho(wV) = \rho^{\leftarrow}(w)\,\rho_w^{\to}(V) = y\,\rho_w^{\to}(V)$$
$$yV = \rho(xV) = \rho^{\leftarrow}(x)\,\rho_x^{\to}(V) = y\,\rho_x^{\to}(V).$$

This means that $\rho_w^{\to}(V) = \lambda$ but $\rho_x^{\to}(V) = V$, so ρ is not i, j-TIOSL on tier τ. $\square$

5 Synchronized Strictly Local Functions

Proposition 10 raises the question of how to characterize the kind of computation that effects rhythmic syncope. To investigate this question, Figure 2

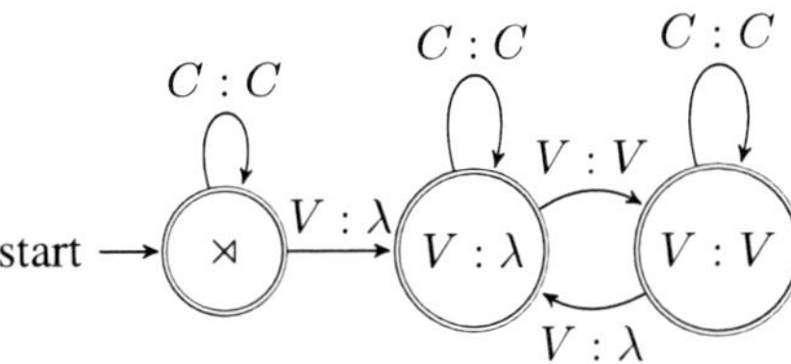

Figure 2: An SFST for rhythmic syncope.

shows a natural SFST implementation of rhythmic syncope. The states in this SFST record the most recent action performed by the SFST. If the most recent action was to delete a vowel ($V : \lambda$), then the next vowel the SFST encounters is not deleted ($V : V$); otherwise, the next vowel is deleted. This SFST is strikingly similar to the rhythmic reduction SFST in Figure 1. There, the special symbol ɔ, which is not part of the input alphabet, indicates the location of a reduced vowel, effectively recording the previous action in the output. Since there is no way to mark the location of a deleted symbol, the SFST in Figure 2 explicitly records its previous action in its state names. Thus, the rhythmic syncope SFST may be seen as a generalization of the rhythmic reduction SFST. The goal of this section is to define a class of functions, known as the *tier-based synchronized strictly local* (TSSL) functions, based on this intuition. Following Section 2, we begin by defining the TSSL functions algebraically in terms of the minimal SFST, and then we define a canonical SFST format for the TSSL functions.

Recall that at each time step, an SFST must read exactly one input symbol while producing an output string of any length. Since the minimal SFST for a function f must produce $f^{\leftarrow}(z)$ after reading the input string z, we can determine the possible actions of f by comparing $f^{\leftarrow}(z)$ with $f^{\leftarrow}(zx)$ for arbitrary $z \in \Sigma^*$ and $x \in \Sigma$.

Definition 11. Let $f : \Sigma^* \to \Gamma^*$. The *actions of f* are the alphabet $\mathcal{A}(f) \subseteq \Sigma \times \Gamma^*$ defined as follows.

$$\mathcal{A}(f) := \{\langle x, y \rangle \mid \exists z \in \Sigma^* . f^{\leftarrow}(zx) = f^{\leftarrow}(z)y\}$$

We denote elements $\langle x, y \rangle$ of $\mathcal{A}(f)$ by $x : y$.

Strings over $\mathcal{A}(f)$ represent computation histories of the minimal SFST for f.

Definition 12. Let $x \in \Sigma^*$ and let $f : \Sigma^* \to \Gamma^*$. The *run of f on input x* is the string $f^{\leftarrow}(x) \in \mathcal{A}(f)^*$ defined as follows.

- If $|x| \leq 1$, then $f^{\Leftarrow}(x) := x : f^{\leftarrow}(x)$.

- If $x = yz$, where $|y| \geq 1$ and $|z| = 1$, then $f^{\Leftarrow}(x) := f^{\Leftarrow}(y)(z : w)$, where w is the unique string such that $f^{\leftarrow}(x) = f^{\leftarrow}(y)w$.

The notation $f^{\Leftarrow}$ allows us to define the TSSL functions in a straightforward manner, highlighting the analogy to the TIOSL functions.

Definition 13. Fix $k > 0$ and let τ be a tier on $\Sigma \times \Gamma^*$. A function $f : \Sigma^* \to \Gamma^*$ is k-*synchronized strictly local on tier* τ (k-TSSL) if for all $x, y \in \Sigma^*$, if $\mathrm{suff}^{k-1}(\tau(f^{\Leftarrow}(x))) = \mathrm{suff}^{k-1}(\tau(f^{\Leftarrow}(y)))$, then $f_x^{\rightarrow} = f_y^{\rightarrow}$.

Now, let us define the canonical SFSTs for TSSL functions. We define the actions of an SFST to be its possible transition labels.

Definition 14. Let $T = \langle Q, \Sigma, \Gamma, q_0, \to, \sigma \rangle$ be an SFST. The *actions of* T are the alphabet

$$\mathcal{A}(T) := \{\langle x, y \rangle | \exists q \exists r . \to (q, x) = \langle r, y \rangle\}.$$

We denote elements $\langle x, y \rangle$ of $\mathcal{A}(T)$ by $x : y$.

Again, the definition of the TSSL SFSTs is directly analogous to that of the TIOSL SFSTs.

Definition 15. Fix $k > 0$ and let τ be a tier on $\Sigma \times \Gamma^*$. An SFST $T = \langle Q, \Sigma, \Gamma, q_0, \to, \sigma \rangle$ is k-*synchronized strictly local on tier* τ (k-TSSL) if the following conditions hold.

- $Q = (\{\rtimes\} \cup \mathcal{A}(T))^{k-1}$ and $q_0 = \rtimes^{k-1}$.

- For every $q \in Q$, if $\to(q, x) = \langle r, y \rangle$, then

$$r = \mathrm{suff}^{k-1}\left(\tau\left(q(x : y)\right)\right).$$

As is the case with TIOSL SFSTs, TSSL SFSTs compute exactly the class of TSSL functions when they are required to be onward.

Theorem 16. *Fix $k > 0$, and let τ be a tier on $\Sigma \times \Gamma^*$. A function is k-TSSL on tier τ if and only if it is computed by an onward SFST that is k-TSSL on tier τ.*

We leave the proof of this fact to Appendix A.

6 Properties of TSSL Functions

Having now defined the TSSL functions, this section investigates some of their formal properties. Subsection 6.1 compares the TSSL functions to the TISL, TOSL, and TIOSL functions. Subsection 6.2 observes that TSSL SFSTs compute a large class of functions when they are not required to be onward.

6.1 Relation to TIOSL Functions

A natural first question regarding the TSSL functions is that of how they relate to previously-proposed classes of subregular functions. We know from the discussion of rhythmic syncope that the TSSL functions are not a subset of the TIOSL functions: we have already seen that the rhythmic syncope function is 2-TSSL but not i, j-TIOSL for any i, j. We will see in this subsection that the TIOSL functions are not a subset of the TSSL functions, though both function classes fully contain the TISL and TOSL functions. Therefore, the two function classes are incomparable, and offer two different ways to generalize the TISL and TOSL functions.

The fact that the TSSL functions contain the TISL and TOSL functions follows from the observation that actions contain information about input and output symbols. Remembering the i most recent actions automatically entails remembering the i most recent input symbols, and the j most recent output symbols can be extracted from the j most recent actions if deletions are ignored.

Proposition 17. *Fix $k > 0$. Every k-TISL function and every k-TOSL function is k-TSSL.*

Proof. Let $f : \Sigma^* \to \Gamma^*$, and let τ be a tier on $\Sigma \cup \Gamma$. First, suppose that f is k-TISL on tier τ. Let υ be a tier on $\Sigma \times \Gamma^*$ defined as follows: an action $x : y$ is on υ if and only if x is on τ. Now, suppose $w, x \in \Sigma^*$ are such that $\mathrm{suff}^{k-1}(\upsilon(f^{\Leftarrow}(w))) = \mathrm{suff}^{k-1}(\upsilon(f^{\Leftarrow}(x)))$. Write

$$\upsilon(f^{\Leftarrow}(w)) = (w_1 : y_1)(w_2 : y_2)\ldots(w_n : y_n)$$
$$\upsilon(f^{\Leftarrow}(x)) = (x_1 : z_1)(x_2 : z_2)\ldots(x_n : z_n).$$

Then, we have $\tau(w) = w_1 w_2 \ldots w_n$ and $\tau(x) = x_1 x_2 \ldots x_n$. For all $i > n - k + 1$, $w_i : y_i = x_i : z_i$, and therefore $w_i = x_i$. But this means that $\mathrm{suff}^{k-1}(\tau(w)) = \mathrm{suff}^{k-1}(\tau(x))$, and since f is k-TISL on tier τ, $f_w^{\leftarrow} = f_x^{\leftarrow}$. We conclude that f is k-TSSL on tier υ.

Next, suppose that f is k-TOSL on tier τ. Let φ be a tier on $\Sigma \times \Gamma^*$ defined as follows: an action $x : y$ is on φ if and only if $\tau(y) \neq \lambda$. Now, suppose $w, x \in \Sigma^*$ are such that $\mathrm{suff}^{k-1}(\varphi(f^{\Leftarrow}(w))) = \mathrm{suff}^{k-1}(\varphi(f^{\Leftarrow}(x)))$. Write

$$\varphi(f^{\Leftarrow}(w)) = (w_1 : y_1)(w_2 : y_2)\ldots(w_n : y_n)$$
$$\varphi(f^{\Leftarrow}(x)) = (x_1 : z_1)(x_2 : z_2)\ldots(x_n : z_n).$$

Now, $\tau(f^{\leftarrow}(w)) = y_1 y_2 \ldots y_n$ and $\tau(f^{\leftarrow}(x)) = z_1 z_2 \ldots z_n$. Again, for all $i > n - k + 1$ we have

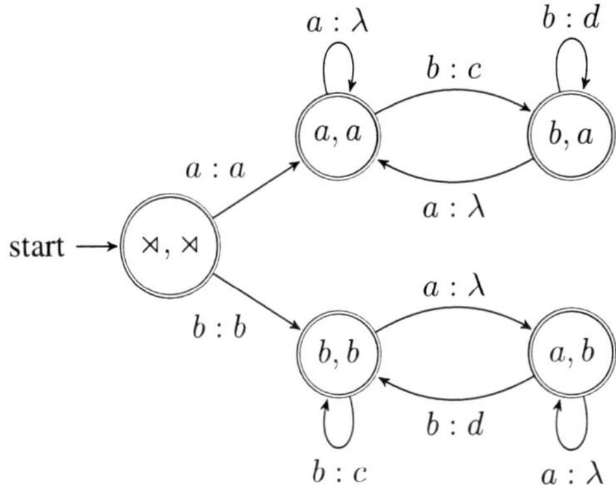

Figure 3: An onward $2,2$-TIOSL SFST computing a function that is not k-TSSL for any k.

$w_i : y_i = x_i : z_i$, so $y_i = z_i$. Observe that

$$\mathrm{suff}^{k-1}(\tau(f^{\Leftarrow}(w))) = \mathrm{suff}^{k-1}(y_j y_{j+1} \ldots y_n)$$

$$= \mathrm{suff}^{k-1}(z_j z_{j+1} \ldots z_n) = \mathrm{suff}^{k-1}(\tau(f^{\Leftarrow}(x))),$$

where $j = n - k + 2$. Since f is k-TOSL on tier τ, $f_w^{\rightarrow} = f_x^{\rightarrow}$, so f is k-TSSL on tier φ. $\square$

This intuition does not carry over to the TIOSL functions. In Proposition 17, the proposed action tiers ignore symbols off the input and output tiers, thus ensuring that the relevant input and output symbols can always be recovered from the computation history. This approach encounters problems when an onward TIOSL SFST deletes symbols on the tier. Such SFSTs perform actions of the form $x : \lambda$, where x is on the tier. These actions do not record any output symbols, but they must be kept on the tier in a TSSL implementation so that the input symbol x can be recovered. If too many $(x : \lambda)$s are performed consecutively, they can overwhelm the memory of a TSSL SFST, causing it to forget the most recent output symbols. The following construction features exactly this kind of behavior.

Proposition 18. *There exists a function that is i, j-TIOSL for some i, j but not k-TSSL for any k.*

Proof. Let T be the SFST shown in Figure 3, and let $f : \{a, b\}^* \rightarrow \{a, b, c, d\}^*$ be the function computed by T.[4] Observe that T is onward and $2, 2$-TIOSL on tier τ, where a and b are on τ but c and d are not, so f is $2, 2$-TIOSL on tier τ. T always copies the first symbol of its input to the

---

[4]The angle brackets are omitted from the state names.

output. Thereafter, T behaves as follows: all as are deleted; a b is changed to a c if the most recent input symbol is the same as the first input symbol; a b is changed to a d otherwise. For example, $f(baabb) = bdc$.

Let $k > 0$, and let v be a tier on $\{a, b\} \times \{a, b, c, d\}^*$. Suppose that either $k = 1$ or $a : \lambda$ is not on v, and consider the strings $w := ba$ and $x := b$. Observe that $f^{\Leftarrow}(w) = (b : b)(a : \lambda)$ and $f^{\Leftarrow}(x) = (b : b)$. Either $\mathrm{suff}^{k-1}(v(f^{\Leftarrow}(x))) = \rtimes^{k-2}(b : b) = \mathrm{suff}^{k-1}(v(f^{\Leftarrow}(x)))$ if $k > 1$ and $b : b$ is on v, or $\mathrm{suff}^{k-1}(v(f^{\Leftarrow}(x))) = \rtimes^{k-1} = \mathrm{suff}^{k-1}(v(f^{\Leftarrow}(x)))$ if $k = 1$ or $b : b$ is not on v. However, $f_w^{\rightarrow}(b) = d$ but $f_x^{\rightarrow}(b) = c$, so f cannot be k-TSSL on tier v.

Next, suppose that $k > 1$ and $a : \lambda$ is on v. Consider the input strings $w := a^{k+1}$ and $x := ba^k$. Observe that $f^{\Leftarrow}(w) = (a : a)(a : \lambda)^k$ and $f^{\Leftarrow}(x) = (b : b)(a : \lambda)^k$, thus

$$\mathrm{suff}^{k-1}(v(f^{\Leftarrow}(w))) = (a : \lambda)^{k-1}$$
$$= \mathrm{suff}^{k-1}(v(f^{\Leftarrow}(x))).$$

However, $f_w^{\rightarrow}(b) = c$ but $f_x^{\rightarrow}(b) = d$, so f is not k-TSSL on tier v. $\square$

6.2 Non-Onward TSSL SFSTs

The equivalence between the two definitions of the TSSL functions presented in Section 5 crucially depends on the criterion that TSSL SFSTs be onward. In this subsection we show that without this criterion, TSSL SFSTs compute a rich class of subsequential functions. To illustrate how this is possible, let us consider an example that witnesses the separation between TSSL functions and TSSL SFSTs.

Proposition 19. *There exists a 2-TSSL SFST that computes a function that is not k-TSSL for any k.*

Proof. Consider the SFST in Figure 4. This SFST is clearly 2-TSSL on a tier containing all actions, and the function it computes is given by $f(xy) = xyx$, where $x \in \{a, b\}$ and $y \in \{a, b\}^*$. Observe that for any $z \in \{a, b\}^*$, $f^{\Leftarrow}(z) = z$. Therefore, writing $z = z_1 z_2 \ldots z_n$ with $|z_i| = 1$ for each i,

$$f^{\Leftarrow}(z) = (z_1 : z_1)(z_2 : z_2) \ldots (z_n : z_n).$$

We need to show that f is not k-TSSL for any $k > 0$ and for any tier τ over $\{a, b\} \times \{a, b\}^*$.

Fix k and τ. Suppose $a : a$ is on τ, and consider the input strings $w = a^{k+1}$ and $x = ba^k$. Observe

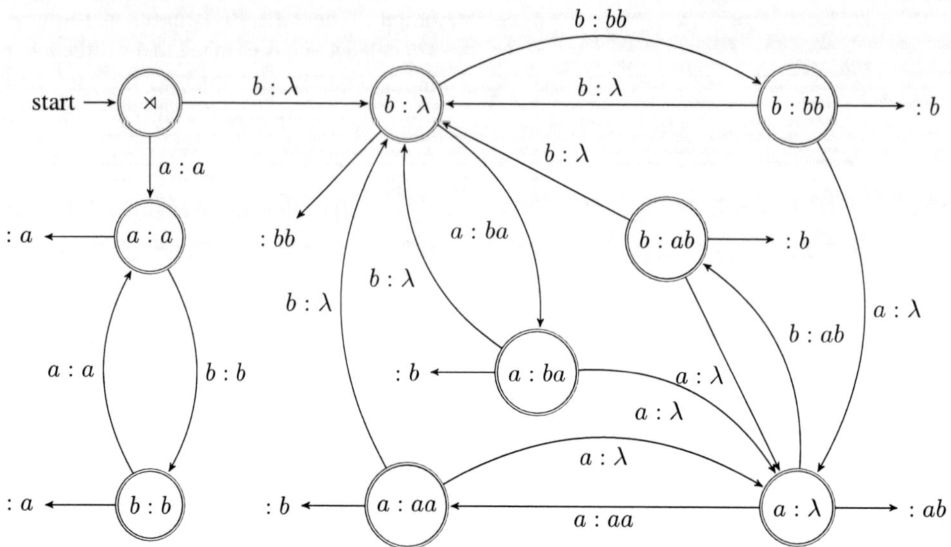

Figure 4: A non-onward 2-TSSL SFST computing a function that is not k-TSSL for any k.

that $f^{\Leftarrow}(w) = (a:a)^{k+1}$ and $f^{\Leftarrow}(x) = (b:b)(a:a)^k$, so

$$\mathrm{suff}^{k-1}(\tau(f^{\Leftarrow}(w))) = (a:a)^{k-1}$$
$$= \mathrm{suff}^{k-1}(\tau(f^{\Leftarrow}(x))).$$

However, $f_w^{\rightarrow}(\lambda) = a$ but $f_x^{\rightarrow}(\lambda) = b$, so f is not k-TSSL on tier τ.

Next, suppose $a : a$ is not on τ, and consider the input strings $w = b$ and $x = ab$. We have $f^{\Leftarrow}(w) = b : b$ and $f^{\Leftarrow}(x) = (a:a)(b:b)$, so

$$\mathrm{suff}^{k-1}(\tau(f^{\Leftarrow}(w))) = \mathrm{suff}^{k-1}(\tau(b:b))$$
$$= \mathrm{suff}^{k-1}(\tau(a:a)\tau(b:b))$$
$$= \mathrm{suff}^{k-1}(\tau((a:a)(b:b)))$$
$$= \mathrm{suff}^{k-1}(\tau(f^{\Leftarrow}(x))).$$

However, $f_w^{\rightarrow}(\lambda) = b$ but $f_x^{\rightarrow}(\lambda) = a$, so f is not k-TSSL on tier τ. $\qquad\square$

Let f be the function described in Proposition 19. As discussed in the proof, an onward SFST computing f must copy the current input symbol to the output stream during each time step. At the end of the computation, the final output function is responsible for adding the first input symbol to the end of the output string. Any onward TSSL SFST that attempts to compute f will eventually forget the identity of the first input symbol, so the final output function cannot determine what to add to the output. The SFST T in Figure 4 avoids this problem by exploiting its non-onwardness. If the

first symbol of its input is an a, then T behaves in an onward manner, copying the current input symbol at each time step. This can be seen in the left column of the state diagram. If the first symbol of T's input is a b, then T alternates between producing no output and producing two symbols of output. Every time T performs a non-deleting action $x : y$, y contains both the symbol that the onward SFST would produce at the current time step and the symbol that the onward SFST would have produced at the previous time step. This way, T encodes the identity of the first symbol of its input using the manner in which it produces output—if T produces output at every time step, then the first symbol is an a, and if it produces output every two time steps, then the first symbol is a b. In general, this kind of encoding trick can be applied to a wide range of SFSTs, including all SFSTs V that do not perform deletions. Informally, we enumerate the states of V by $\{q_0, q_1, \ldots, q_n\}$, and we construct a TSSL SFST S that simulates V by producing output at various frequencies. For each i, S produces output every $i + 1$ time steps if V is in state q_i. If S remembers at least $2(n + 1)$-many actions, then it can always deduce V's state at any point in the computation, allowing it to simulate V.

7 Rhythmic Syncope in Phonology

The view of rhythmic syncope we have presented here differs substantially in approach from existing treatments of rhythmic syncope in phonological theory. McCarthy (2008) identifies two major approaches to rhythmic syncope in Optimality Theory. In the *pseudo-deletion* approach (e.g., Kager, 1997), the locations of symbols deleted by syncope are marked with blank symbols. This essentially makes rhythmic syncope identical to rhythmic reduction, which we have seen is 2-TOSL. McCarthy himself proposes a *Harmonic Serialism* approach in which rhythmic syncope is implemented in multiple steps. Firstly, stress is assigned to every second vowel in the underlying form. Then, the unstressed vowels are deleted, resulting in syncope. This kind of derivation is illustrated in (20).

(20) Rhythmic syncope in Harmonic Serialism (McCarthy, 2008)[5]

/wanamari/	Underlying Form
wanámarí	Stress
[wnámrí]	Syncope

In both approaches, rhythmic syncope is decomposed into a 2-TOSL function and a homomorphism. In the pseudo-deletion approach, the 2-TOSL function is rhythmic reduction, and the homomorphism removes the əs. In (20), the rhythmic stress step is 2-TOSL, while the syncope step is a homomorphism. In general, this kind of approach is extremely powerful.

Proposition 21. *Every subsequential function f can be written in the form $f = h \circ g$, where g is 2-TOSL and h is a homomorphism.*

Proof. Let $T = \langle Q, \Sigma, \Gamma, q_0, \to, \sigma \rangle$ be the minimal SFST for f. Define g as follows. Let $g(\lambda) := \langle \sigma, f(\lambda) \rangle$. For $x_1, x_2, \ldots, x_n \in \Sigma$, write

$$q_0 \xrightarrow{x_1:y_1} q_1 \xrightarrow{x_2:y_2} q_2 \xrightarrow{x_3:y_3} \ldots \xrightarrow{x_{n-1}:y_{n-1}} q_n.$$

Then, $g(x_1 x_2 \ldots x_n) := \langle q_1, y_1 \rangle \langle q_2, y_2 \rangle \ldots \langle q_n, y_n \rangle \langle \sigma, \sigma(q_n) \rangle$. Next, define h so that for any $\langle q, y \rangle$, $h(\langle q, y \rangle) = y$. It is clear that $f(x) = h(g(x))$ for every x. We now show that g is 2-TOSL on a tier containing the full output alphabet.

Fix $w, x \in \Sigma^*$. Observe that for all $z \in \Sigma^*$, $g^{\leftarrow}(z) \in (Q \times \Gamma^*)^*$. Therefore, suppose that $\mathrm{suff}^1(g^{\leftarrow}(w)) = \mathrm{suff}^1(g^{\leftarrow}(x)) = \langle q, y \rangle$. This means that $q_0 \xrightarrow{w:u} q$ and $q_0 \xrightarrow{x:v} q$ for some $u, v \in \Gamma^*$, so $g_u^{\to} = g_v^{\to}$ by definition. $\square$

---

[5]The full derivation proposed by McCarthy (2008) includes syllabification and footing steps, which are omitted here for simplicity.

In both pseudo-deletion and Harmonic Serialism, non-segmental phonological symbols are used to encode state information in the output, making rhythmic syncope 2-TOSL. Proposition 21 shows that this technique can be applied to arbitrary SFSTs, and therefore results in massive overgeneration. By contrast, we have already seen that the TSSL functions are a proper subset of the subsequential functions, making action-sensitivity a more restrictive alternative to current approaches to rhythmic syncope.

8 Conclusion

The classic examples of TIOSL phenomena in phonology are local processes and unidirectional spreading processes (Chandlee, 2014). Rhythmic syncope is qualitatively different from these phenomena in that it leaves no evidence that the process has occurred. As we have seen in Section 4, the fact that rhythmic syncope is not TIOSL is a consequence of this property. In defining the TSSL functions, we have proposed that rhythmic syncope should be viewed as a dependency between incremental steps in a derivation, here formalized as the actions of the minimal SFST.

A potential risk of such an analysis is that the notion of "action" is specific to the computational system used to implement rhythmic syncope, and therefore potentially subject to a broad range of interpretations. In this paper, we have used onwardness and the existence of the minimal SFST to formulate a notion of "action-sensitivity" that is both formalism-independent and implementation-independent. In Subsection 6.2, we have seen that action-sensitivity can be made very powerful if we relax our assumptions about the nature of the computation. This means that if action-sensitivity is to be incorporated into phonological analyses of rhythmic syncope, then care should be taken to avoid loopholes like the one featured in Proposition 19. Based on Proposition 21, a similar warning can be made regarding the composition of phonological processes. When decomposing phonemena into several processes, as McCarthy (2008) does in the Harmonic Serialism analysis, care should be taken to ensure that theoretical proposals do not allow for overgeneration.

Outstanding formal questions regarding the TSSL functions include their closure properties and the complexity of learning TSSL functions. We leave such questions to future work.

References

Hyunah Baek. 2018. Computational representation of unbounded stress: Tiers with structural features. In *Proceedings of CLS 53 (2017)*, volume 53, pages 13–24, Chicago, IL, USA. Chicago Linguistic Society.

Dustin Bowers. To appear. The Nishnaabemwin Restructuring Controversy: New Empirical Evidence. *Phonology*.

Dustin Bowers and Yiding Hao. To appear. Rhythmic Syncope in Subregular Phonology. In *Proceedings of the 42nd Annual Penn Linguistics Conference*, volume 26.1 of *Penn Working Papers in Linguistics*, Philadelphia, PA, USA. Penn Graduate Linguistics Society.

Jane Chandlee. 2014. *Strictly Local Phonological Processes*. PhD Dissertation, University of Delaware, Newark, DE, USA.

Jane Chandlee, Rémi Eyraud, and Jeffrey Heinz. 2015. Output Strictly Local Functions. In *Proceedings of the 14th Meeting on the Mathematics of Language*, pages 112–125, Chicago, IL, USA. Association for Computational Linguistics.

Jane Chandlee, Rémi Eyraud, and Jeffrey Heinz. In prep. Input–output strictly local functions and their efficient learnability.

Thomas Graf and Connor Mayer. 2018. Sanskrit n-Retroflexion is Input–Output Tier-Based Strictly Local. In *Proceedings of the Fifteenth Workshop on Computational Research in Phonetics, Phonology, and Morphology*, pages 151–160, Brussels, Belgium. Association for Computational Linguistics.

W. Neil Hawkins. 1950. Patterns of Vowel Loss in Macushi (Carib). *International Journal of American Linguistics*, 16(2):87–90.

Jeffrey Heinz. 2018. The computational nature of phonological generalizations. In Larry M. Hyman and Frans Plank, editors, *Phonological Typology*, number 23 in Phonology and Phonetics, pages 126–195. De Gruyter Mouton, Berlin, Germany.

Jeffrey Heinz and Regine Lai. 2013. Vowel Harmony and Subsequentiality. In *Proceedings of the 13th Meeting on the Mathematics of Language (MoL 13)*, pages 52–63, Sofia, Bulgaria. Association for Computational Linguistics.

Jeffrey Heinz, Chetan Rawal, and Herbert G. Tanner. 2011. Tier-based Strictly Local Constraints for Phonology. In *Proceedings of the 49th Annual Meeting of the Association for Computational Linguistics: Human Language Technologies*, pages 58–64, Portland, OR, USA. Association for Computational Linguistics.

Adam Jardine. 2016. Computationally, tone is different. *Phonology*, 33(2):247–283.

René Kager. 1997. Rhythmic vowel deletion in Optimality Theory. In Iggy Roca, editor, *Derivations and Constraints in Phonology*, pages 463–499. Clarendon Press, Oxford, United Kingdom.

Connor Mayer and Travis Major. 2018. A Challenge for Tier-Based Strict Locality from Uyghur Backness Harmony. In *Formal Grammar 2018, 23rd International Conference, FG 2018, Sofia, Bulgaria, August 11-12, 2018, Proceedings*, volume 10950 of *Lecture Notes in Computer Science*, pages 62–83, Berlin, Germany. Springer Berlin Heidelberg.

John J. McCarthy. 2008. The serial interaction of stress and syncope. *Natural Language & Linguistic Theory*, 26(3):499–546.

Adam McCollum, Eric Baković, Anna Mai, and Eric Meinhardt. 2018. The expressivity of segmental phonology and the definition of weak determinism. *LingBuzz*, lingbuzz/004197.

Kevin McMullin and Gunnar Ólafur Hansson. 2016. Long-Distance Phonotactics as Tier-Based Strictly 2-Local Languages. In *Proceedings of the 2014 Annual Meeting on Phonology*, Proceedings of the Annual Meetings on Phonology, pages 13–24, Cambridge, MA, USA. Linguistic Society of America.

Kevin James McMullin. 2016. *Tier-Based Locality in Long-Distance Phonotactics: Learnability and Typology*. PhD Dissertation, University of British Columbia, Vancouver, Canada.

Robert McNaughton and Seymour A. Papert. 1971. *Counter-Free Automata*. Number 65 in Research Monograph. MIT Press, Cambridge, MA, USA.

José Oncina, Pedro Garcia, and Enrique Vidal. 1993. Learning Subsequential Transducers for Pattern Recognition Interpretation Tasks. *IEEE Transactions on Pattern Analysis and Machine Intelligence*, 15(5):448–458.

George N. Raney. 1958. Sequential Functions. *Journal of the Association for Computing Machinery*, 5(2):177–180.

Richard A. Rhodes, Karl S. Hele, and J. Randolph Valentine. 2012. Algonquian Trade Languages Revisited. In *Papers of the Fortieth Algonquian Conference/Actes Du Congrès Des Algonquinistes*, Papers of the Algonquian Conference, pages 358–369, Albany, NY, USA. State University of New York Press.

Jacques Sakarovitch. 2009. *Elements of Automata Theory*. Cambridge University Press, Cambridge, United Kingdom.

A   Proof of Theorem 16

This appendix proves the equivalence between TSSL functions and onward TSSL SFSTs. We begin by showing how to construct an onward TSSL SFST computing any given TSSL function.

Definition 22. Let $f : \Sigma^* \to \Gamma^*$ be k-TSSL on tier τ. Define the SFST transducer $\mathcal{T}(f) = \langle Q, \Sigma, \Gamma, q_0, \to, \sigma \rangle$ as follows.

- $Q := (\{\rtimes\} \cup \mathcal{A}(f))^{k-1}$ and $q_0 := \rtimes^{k-1}$.

- For each $x \in \Sigma$, $\to(q_0, x) := \langle r, f^\leftarrow(x) \rangle$, where $r = \mathrm{suff}^{k-1}(\tau(x : f^\leftarrow(x)))$.

- For each $q \in Q \setminus \{q_0\}$, let $x \in \Sigma^*$ be such that $\mathrm{suff}^{k-1}(\tau(f^\Leftarrow(x))) = q$, and let $w : y \in \mathcal{A}(f)$ be such that $f^\leftarrow(xw) = f^\leftarrow(x)y$. We define $\to(q, w) := \langle r, y \rangle$, where $r = \mathrm{suff}^{k-1}(\tau(q(w : y)))$.

- Fix $q \in Q$. If $q = q_0$, then $\sigma(q) := f(\lambda)$. Otherwise, we define $\sigma(q) := f_x^\to(\lambda)$, where $\mathrm{suff}^{k-1}(\tau(f^\Leftarrow(x))) = q$.

Remark 23. $\mathcal{T}(f)$ is k-TSSL on tier τ.

Note that in the third and fourth bullet points of Definition 22, the action $w : y$ and the string $f_x^\to(\lambda)$ only depend on q and not on x, since f is k-TSSL on tier τ. We now need to show that $\mathcal{T}(f)$ computes f and that it is onward.

Lemma 24. Let $f : \Sigma^* \to \Gamma^*$ be k-TSSL on tier τ, and write $\mathcal{T}(f) = \langle Q, \Sigma, \Gamma, q_0, \to, \sigma \rangle$. For every $x \in \Sigma^+$, if $q_0 \xrightarrow{x:y} r$, then $y = f^\leftarrow(x)$.

Proof. Let us induct on $|x|$. For the base case, suppose $|x| = 1$. Then, $y = f^\leftarrow(x)$ by definition.

Now, fix $n > 1$, and suppose that if $0 < |u| < n$ and $q_0 \xrightarrow{u:v} r$, then $v = f^\leftarrow(u)$. Fix $w \in \Sigma^{n-1}$ and $x \in \Sigma$, and suppose that $q_0 \xrightarrow{w:y} s \xrightarrow{x:z} t$. By the induction hypothesis, $y = f^\leftarrow(w)$. The definition of $\mathcal{T}(f)$ states that z is the unique string such that $f^\leftarrow(wx) = f^\leftarrow(w)z$. Thus, $yz = f^\leftarrow(w)z = f^\leftarrow(wx)$, and the proof is complete. $\square$

Lemma 25. Let $f : \Sigma^* \to \Gamma^*$ be k-TSSL on tier τ, and write $\mathcal{T}(f) = \langle Q, \Sigma, \Gamma, q_0, \to, \sigma \rangle$. For all $x \in \Sigma^+$, if $q_0 \xrightarrow{x:y} r$, then $r = \mathrm{suff}^{k-1}(\tau(f^\Leftarrow(x)))$.

Proof. Let us induct on $|x|$. For the base case, suppose $|x| = 1$. Since $f^\Leftarrow(x) = x : f^\leftarrow(x)$, by definition $r = \mathrm{suff}^{k-1}(\tau(f^\Leftarrow(x)))$.

Now, fix $n > 1$, and suppose that if $|w| < n$ and $q_0 \xrightarrow{w:y} r$, then $r = \mathrm{suff}^{k-1}(\tau(f^\Leftarrow(w)))$. We need to show that for all $w \in \Sigma^{n-1}$ and $x \in \Sigma$, if $q_0 \xrightarrow{w:y} r \xrightarrow{x:z} s$, then $s = \mathrm{suff}^{k-1}(\tau(f^\Leftarrow(wx)))$. The induction hypothesis gives us $r = \mathrm{suff}^{k-1}(\tau(f^\Leftarrow(w)))$. Since $\langle s, z \rangle = \to(r, x)$, by the definition of $\mathcal{T}(f)$,

$$s = \mathrm{suff}^{k-1}(\tau(r(x : z)))$$

$$= \mathrm{suff}^{k-1}(\tau(r)\tau(x : z))$$
$$= \mathrm{suff}^{k-1}\left(\tau\left(\mathrm{suff}^{k-1}(\tau(f^\Leftarrow(w)))\right)\tau(x : z)\right)$$
$$= \mathrm{suff}^{k-1}(\tau(\tau(f^\Leftarrow(w)))\tau(x : z))$$
$$= \mathrm{suff}^{k-1}(\tau(f^\Leftarrow(w))\tau(x : z))$$
$$= \mathrm{suff}^{k-1}(\tau(f^\Leftarrow(w)(x : z)))$$
$$= \mathrm{suff}^{k-1}(\tau(f^\Leftarrow(wx))), \tag{26}$$

as desired. $\square$

Proposition 27. If $f : \Sigma^* \to \Gamma^*$ is k-TSSL on tier τ, then $\mathcal{T}(f)$ computes f.

Proof. We need to show that for every $x \in \Sigma^*$, $\mathcal{T}(f)$ outputs $f(x)$ on input x. Write $\mathcal{T}(f) = \langle Q, \Sigma, \Gamma, q_0, \to, \sigma \rangle$ and $q_0 \xrightarrow{x:y} q$. By Lemma 24, $y = f^\leftarrow(x)$, and by Lemma 25, $q = \mathrm{suff}^{k-1}(\tau(f^\Leftarrow(x)))$. Definition 22 then states that $\sigma(q) = f_x^\to(\lambda)$, so $y\sigma(q) = f^\leftarrow(x)f_x^\to(\lambda) = f(x)$, thus $\mathcal{T}(f)$ outputs $f(x)$ on input x. $\square$

Corollary 28. If $f : \Sigma^* \to \Gamma^*$ is k-TSSL on tier τ, then $\mathcal{T}(f)$ is onward.

We then complete the proof by showing that every onward TSSL SFST computes a TSSL function.

Lemma 29. Let $T = \langle Q, \Sigma, \Gamma, q_0, \to, \sigma \rangle$ be onward and k-TSSL on tier τ. Let f be the function computed by T. For all $x \in \Sigma^*$, if $q_0 \xrightarrow{x:y} q$, then $q = \mathrm{suff}^{k-1}(\tau(f^\Leftarrow(x)))$.

Proof. Let us induct on $|x|$. For the base case, suppose $|x| = 1$. Since T is onward, $y = f^\leftarrow(x)$, so

$$q = \mathrm{suff}^{k-1}\left(\tau\left(\rtimes^{k-1}(x : y)\right)\right)$$
$$= \mathrm{suff}^{k-1}\left(\tau\left(\rtimes^{k-1}(x : f^\leftarrow(x))\right)\right)$$
$$= \mathrm{suff}^{k-1}\left(\tau\left(\rtimes^{k-1}f^\Leftarrow(x)\right)\right)$$
$$= \mathrm{suff}^{k-1}\left(\tau\left(\rtimes^{k-1}\right)\tau(f^\Leftarrow(x))\right)$$
$$= \mathrm{suff}^{k-1}(\tau(f^\Leftarrow(x))).$$

Now, fix $n > 1$, and suppose that if $|w| < n$ and $q_0 \xrightarrow{w:y} q$, then $q = \mathrm{suff}^{k-1}(\tau(f^\Leftarrow(w)))$. We need to show that for all $w \in \Sigma^{n-1}$ and $x \in \Sigma$, if $q_0 \xrightarrow{w:y} r \xrightarrow{x:z} s$, then $s = \mathrm{suff}^{k-1}(\tau(f^\Leftarrow(wx)))$. The induction hypothesis gives us $r = \mathrm{suff}^{k-1}(\tau(f^\Leftarrow(w)))$, and Definition 15 states that $s = \mathrm{suff}^{k-1}(\tau(r(x : z)))$. A derivation similar to equation (26) then gives us $s = \mathrm{suff}^{k-1}(\tau(f^\Leftarrow(wx)))$, as desired. $\square$

Proof of Theorem 16. Proposition 27 has already shown the forward direction. Let $T = \langle Q, \Sigma, \Gamma, q_0, \rightarrow, \sigma \rangle$ be an onward SFST computing f that is k-TSSL on tier τ. Suppose $x, y \in \Sigma^*$ are such that $\mathrm{suff}^{k-1}(\tau(f^{\Leftarrow}(w))) = \mathrm{suff}^{k-1}(\tau(f^{\Leftarrow}(x)))$. Write $q_0 \xrightarrow{w:y} r$ and $q_0 \xrightarrow{x:z} s$. By Lemma 29, $r = \mathrm{suff}^{k-1}(\tau(f^{\Leftarrow}(w))) = \mathrm{suff}^{k-1}(\tau(f^{\Leftarrow}(x))) = s$, so $f_w^{\rightarrow} = f_x^{\rightarrow}$, thus f is k-TSSL on tier τ. $\qquad\square$

The SIGMORPHON 2019 Shared Task:
Morphological Analysis in Context and Cross-Lingual Transfer for Inflection

Arya D. McCarthy♣ and **Ekaterina Vylomova**♥ and
Shijie Wu♣ and **Chaitanya Malaviya**♠ and **Lawrence Wolf-Sonkin**♦ and
Garrett Nicolai♣ and **Miikka Silfverberg**♯ and **Sebastian Mielke**♣ and
Jeffrey Heinz♭ and **Ryan Cotterell**♣ and **Mans Hulden**♮

♣Johns Hopkins University   ♥University of Melbourne   ♠Allen Institute for AI
♦Google   ♯University of Helsinki   ♭Stony Brook University   ♮University of Colorado

Abstract

The SIGMORPHON 2019 shared task on cross-lingual transfer and contextual analysis in morphology examined transfer learning of inflection between 100 language pairs, as well as contextual lemmatization and morphosyntactic description in 66 languages. The first task evolves past years' inflection tasks by examining transfer of morphological inflection knowledge from a high-resource language to a low-resource language. This year also presents a new second challenge on lemmatization and morphological feature analysis in context. All submissions featured a neural component and built on either this year's strong baselines or highly ranked systems from previous years' shared tasks. Every participating team improved in accuracy over the baselines for the inflection task (though not Levenshtein distance), and every team in the contextual analysis task improved on both state-of-the-art neural and non-neural baselines.

1 Introduction

While producing a sentence, humans combine various types of knowledge to produce fluent output—various shades of meaning are expressed through word selection and tone, while the language is made to conform to underlying structural rules via syntax and morphology. Native speakers are often quick to identify disfluency, even if the meaning of a sentence is mostly clear.

Automatic systems must also consider these constraints when constructing or processing language. Strong enough language models can often reconstruct common syntactic structures, but are insufficient to properly model morphology. Many languages implement large inflectional paradigms that mark both function and content words with a varying levels of morphosyntactic information. For instance, Romanian verb forms inflect for person, number, tense, mood, and voice; meanwhile,

Archi verbs can take on thousands of forms (Kibrik, 1998). Such complex paradigms produce large inventories of words, all of which must be producible by a realistic system, even though a large percentage of them will never be observed over billions of lines of linguistic input. Compounding the issue, good inflectional systems often require large amounts of supervised training data, which is infeasible in many of the world's languages.

This year's shared task is concentrated on encouraging the construction of strong morphological systems that perform two related but different inflectional tasks. The first task asks participants to create morphological inflectors for a large number of under-resourced languages, encouraging systems that use highly-resourced, related languages as a cross-lingual training signal. The second task welcomes submissions that invert this operation in light of contextual information: Given an unannotated sentence, lemmatize each word, and tag them with a morphosyntactic description. Both of these tasks extend upon previous morphological competitions, and the best submitted systems now represent the state of the art in their respective tasks.

2 Tasks and Evaluation

2.1 Task 1: Cross-lingual transfer for morphological inflection

Annotated resources for the world's languages are not distributed equally—some languages simply have more as they have more native speakers willing and able to annotate more data. We explore how to transfer knowledge from high-resource languages that are genetically related to low-resource languages.

The first task iterates on last year's main task: morphological inflection (Cotterell et al., 2018). Instead of giving some number of training examples in the language of interest, we provided only

Proceedings of the 16th Workshop on Computational Research in Phonetics, Phonology, and Morphology, pages 229–244
Florence, Italy. August 2, 2019 ©2019 Association for Computational Linguistics

a limited number in that language. To accompany it, we provided a larger number of examples in either a related or unrelated language. Each test example asked participants to produce some other inflected form when given a lemma and a bundle of morphosyntactic features as input. The goal, thus, is to perform morphological inflection in the low-resource language, having hopefully exploited some similarity to the high-resource language. Models which perform well here can aid downstream tasks like machine translation in low-resource settings. All datasets were resampled from UniMorph, which makes them distinct from past years.

The mode of the task is inspired by Zoph et al. (2016), who fine-tune a model pre-trained on a high-resource language to perform well on a low-resource language. We do not, though, require that models be trained by fine-tuning. Joint modeling or any number of methods may be explored instead.

Example   The model will have access to type-level data in a low-resource target language, plus a high-resource source language. We give an example here of Asturian as the target language with Spanish as the source language.

Low-resource target training data (Asturian)		
facer	"fechu"	V;V.PTCP;PST
aguar	"aguà"	V;PRS;2;PL;IND
⋮	⋮	⋮
High-resource source language training data (Spanish)		
tocar	"tocando"	V;V.PTCP;PRS
bailar	"bailaba"	V;PST;IPFV;3;SG;IND
mentir	"mintió"	V;PST;PFV;3;SG;IND
⋮	⋮	⋮
Test input (Asturian)		
baxar		V;V.PTCP;PRS
Test output (Asturian)		
	"baxando"	

Table 1: Sample language pair and data format for Task 1

Evaluation   We score the output of each system in terms of its predictions' exact-match accuracy and the average Levenshtein distance between the predictions and their corresponding true forms.

2.2   Task 2: Morphological analysis in context

Although inflection of words in a context-agnostic manner is a useful evaluation of the morphological quality of a system, people do not learn morphology in isolation.

In 2018, the second task of the CoNLL–SIGMORPHON Shared Task (Cotterell et al., 2018) required submitting systems to complete an inflectional cloze task (Taylor, 1953) given only the sentential context and the desired lemma – an example of the problem is given in the following lines: A successful system would predict the plural form "dogs". Likewise, a Spanish word form "ayuda" may be a feminine noun or a third-person verb form, which must be disambiguated by context.

The ______ are barking.
    (dog)

This year's task extends the second task from last year. Rather than inflect a single word in context, the task is to provide a complete morphological tagging of a sentence: for each word, a successful system will need to lemmatize and tag it with a morphsyntactic description (MSD).

The	dogs	are	barking	.
the	dog	be	bark	.
DET	N;PL	V;PRS;3;PL	V;V.PTCP;PRS	PUNCT

Context is critical—depending on the sentence, identical word forms realize a large number of potential inflectional categories, which will in turn influence lemmatization decisions. If the sentence were instead "The barking dogs kept us up all night", "barking" is now an adjective, and its lemma is also "barking".

3   Data

3.1   Data for Task 1

Language pairs   We presented data in 100 language pairs spanning 79 unique languages. Data for all but four languages (Basque, Kurmanji, Murrinhpatha, and Sorani) are extracted from English Wiktionary, a large multi-lingual crowd-sourced dictionary with morphological paradigms for many lemmata.[1] 20 of the 100 language pairs are either

---

[1]The Basque language data was extracted from a manually designed finite-state morphological analyzer (Alegria et al., 2009). Murrinhpatha data was donated by John Mansfield; it

distantly related or unrelated; this allows specula-
tion into the relative importance of data quantity
and linguistic relatedness.

Data format For each language, the basic data
consists of triples of the form (lemma, feature bundle, inflected form), as in Table 1. The first feature in the bundle always specifies the core part of
speech (e.g., verb). For each language pair, separate files contain the high- and low-resource training examples.

All features in the bundle are coded according to
the UniMorph Schema, a cross-linguistically consistent universal morphological feature set (Sylak-
Glassman et al., 2015a,b).

Extraction from Wiktionary For each of the
Wiktionary languages, Wiktionary provides a number of tables, each of which specifies the full inflectional paradigm for a particular lemma. As in
the previous iteration, tables were extracted using a
template annotation procedure described in (Kirov
et al., 2018).

Sampling data splits From each language's collection of paradigms, we sampled the training, development, and test sets as in 2018.[2] Crucially,
while the data were sampled in the same fashion,
the datasets are distinct from those used for the
2018 shared task.

Our first step was to construct probability distributions over the (lemma, feature bundle, inflected
form) triples in our full dataset. For each triple, we
counted how many tokens the inflected form has
in the February 2017 dump of Wikipedia for that
language. To distribute the counts of an observed
form over all the triples that have this token as its
form, we follow the method used in the previous
shared task (Cotterell et al., 2018), training a neural network on unambiguous forms to estimate the
distribution over all, even ambiguous, forms. We
then sampled 12,000 triples without replacement
from this distribution. The first 100 were taken as
training data for low-resource settings. The first
10,000 were used as high-resource training sets. As
these sets are nested, the highest-count triples tend
to appear in the smaller training sets.[3]

The final 2000 triples were randomly shuffled
and then split in half to obtain development and
test sets of 1000 forms each.[4] The final shuffling
was performed to ensure that the development set is
similar to the test set. By contrast, the development
and test sets tend to contain lower-count triples
than the training set.[5]

Other modifications We further adopted some
changes to increase compatibility. Namely, we corrected some annotation errors created while scrap-
ing Wiktionary for the 2018 task, and we standardized Romanian t-cedilla and t-comma to t-comma.
(The same was done with s-cedilla and s-comma.)

3.2 Data for Task 2

Our data for task 2 come from the Universal Dependencies treebanks (UD; Nivre et al., 2018, v2.3),
which provides pre-defined training, development,
and test splits and annotations in a unified annotation schema for morphosyntax and dependency
relationships. Unlike the 2018 cloze task which
used UD data, we require no manual data prepa-
ration and are able to leverage all 107 monolingual treebanks. As is typical, data are presented in
CoNLL-U format,[6] although we modify the morphological feature and lemma fields.

Data conversion The morphological annotations
for the 2019 shared task were converted to the Uni-
Morph schema (Kirov et al., 2018) according to
McCarthy et al. (2018), who provide a deterministic mapping that increases agreement across languages. This also moves the part of speech into
the bundle of morphological features. We do not
attempt to individually correct any errors in the UD
source material. Further, some languages received
additional pre-processing. In the Finnish data, we
removed morpheme boundaries that were present
in the lemmata (e.g., puhe#kieli $\mapsto$ puhekieli
'spoken+language'). Russian lemmata in the GSD
treebank were presented in all uppercase; to match

Swahili. Likewise, the low-resource language Telugu had
fewer than 100 forms.

[4]When sufficient data are unavailable, we instead use 50
or 100 examples.

[5]This mimics a realistic setting, as supervised training is
usually employed to generalize from frequent words that appear in annotated resources to less frequent words that do not.
Unsupervised learning methods also tend to generalize from
more frequent words (which can be analyzed more easily by
combining information from many contexts) to less frequent
ones.

[6]https://universaldependencies.org/format.
html

---

is discussed in Mansfield (2019). Data for Kurmanji Kurdish
and Sorani Kurdish were created as part of the Alexina project
(Walther et al., 2010; Walther and Sagot, 2010).

[2]These datasets can be obtained from https://
sigmorphon.github.io/sharedtasks/2019/

[3]Several high-resource languages had necessarily fewer,
but on a similar order of magnitude. Bengali, Uzbek, Kannada,

the 2018 shared task, we lowercased these. In development and test data, all fields except for form and index within the sentence were struck.

4 Baselines

4.1 Task 1 Baseline

We include four neural sequence-to-sequence models mapping lemma into inflected word forms: soft attention (Luong et al., 2015), non-monotonic hard attention (Wu et al., 2018), monotonic hard attention and a variant with offset-based transition distribution (Wu and Cotterell, 2019). Neural sequence-to-sequence models with soft attention (Luong et al., 2015) have dominated previous SIGMOR-PHON shared tasks (Cotterell et al., 2017). Wu et al. (2018) instead models the alignment between characters in the lemma and the inflected word form explicitly with hard attention and learns this alignment and transduction jointly. Wu and Cotterell (2019) shows that enforcing strict monotonicity with hard attention is beneficial in tasks such as morphological inflection where the transduction is mostly monotonic. The encoder is a biLSTM while the decoder is a left-to-right LSTM. All models use multiplicative attention and have roughly the same number of parameters. In the model, a morphological tag is fed to the decoder along with target character embeddings to guide the decoding. During the training of the hard attention model, dynamic programming is applied to marginalize all latent alignments exactly.

4.2 Task 2 Baselines

Non-neural (Müller et al., 2015): The Lemming model is a log-linear model that performs joint morphological tagging and lemmatization. The model is globally normalized with the use of a second order linear-chain CRF. To efficiently calculate the partition function, the choice of lemmata are pruned with the use of pre-extracted edit trees.

Neural (Malaviya et al., 2019): This is a state-of-the-art neural model that also performs joint morphological tagging and lemmatization, but also accounts for the exposure bias with the application of maximum likelihood (MLE). The model stitches the tagger and lemmatizer together with the use of jackknifing (Agić and Schluter, 2017) to expose the lemmatizer to the errors made by the tagger model during training. The morphological tagger is based on a character-level biLSTM embedder that produces the embedding for a word,

Team	Avg. Accuracy	Avg. Levenshtein
AX-01	18.54	3.62
AX-02	24.99	2.72
CMU-03	**58.79**	1.52
IT-IST-01	49.00	**1.29**
IT-IST-02	50.18	1.32
Tuebingen-01†	34.49	1.88
Tuebingen-02†	20.86	2.36
UAlberta-01*	48.33	1.23
UAlberta-02*†	54.75	1.03
UAlberta-03*†	8.45	4.06
UAlberta-04*†	11.00	3.86
UAlberta-05*	4.10	3.08
UAlberta-06*†	26.85	2.65
Baseline	48.55	1.33

Table 2: Task 1 Team Scores, averaged across all Languages; * indicates submissions were only applied to a subset of languages, making scores incomparable. † indicates that additional resources were used for training.

and a word-level biLSTM tagger that predicts a morphological tag sequence for each word in the sentence. The lemmatizer is a neural sequence-to-sequence model (Wu and Cotterell, 2019) that uses the decoded morphological tag sequence from the tagger as an additional attribute. The model uses hard monotonic attention instead of standard soft attention, along with a dynamic programming based training scheme.

5 Results

The SIGMORPHON 2019 shared task received 30 submissions—14 for task 1 and 16 for task 2— from 23 teams. In addition, the organizers' baseline systems were evaluated.

5.1 Task 1 Results

Five teams participated in the first Task, with a variety of methods aimed at leveraging the cross-lingual data to improve system performance.

The University of Alberta (UAlberta) performed a focused investigation on four language pairs, training cognate-projection systems from external cognate lists. Two methods were considered: one which trained a high-resource neural encoder-decoder, and projected the test data into the HRL, and one that projected the HRL data into the LRL, and trained a combined system. Results demonstrated that certain language pairs may be amenable to such methods.

HRL–LRL	Baseline	Best	Team	HRL–LRL	Baseline	Best	Team
adyghe–kabardian	96.0	97.0	Tuebingen-02	hungarian–livonian	29.0	44.0	it-ist-01
albanian–breton	40.0	81.0	CMU-03	hungarian–votic	19.0	34.0	it-ist-01
arabic–classical-syriac	66.0	92.0	CMU-03	irish–breton	39.0	79.0	CMU-03
arabic–maltese	31.0	41.0	CMU-03	irish–cornish	24.0	34.0	it-ist-01
arabic–turkmen	74.0	84.0	CMU-03	irish–old-irish	2.0	6.0	it-ist-02
armenian–kabardian	83.0	87.0	it-ist-01	irish–scottish-gaelic	64.0	66.0	CMU-03
asturian–occitan	48.0	77.0	CMU-03	italian–friulian	56.0	78.0	CMU-03
bashkir–azeri	39.0	69.0	it-ist-02	italian–ladin	55.0	74.0	CMU-03
bashkir–crimean-tatar	70.0	70.0	CMU-03	italian–maltese	26.0	45.0	CMU-03
bashkir–kazakh	80.0	90.0	it-ist-01	italian–neapolitan	80.0	83.0	CMU-03
bashkir–khakas	86.0	96.0	it-ist-02	kannada–telugu	82.0	94.0	CMU-03
bashkir–tatar	68.0	74.0	it-ist-02	kurmanji–sorani	15.0	69.0	CMU-03
bashkir–turkmen	94.0	88.0	it-ist-01	latin–czech	20.1	71.4	CMU-03
basque–kashubian	40.0	76.0	CMU-03	latvian–lithuanian	17.1	48.4	CMU-03
belarusian–old-irish	2.0	10.0	CMU-03	latvian–scottish-gaelic	48.0	68.0	CMU-03
bengali–greek	17.7	74.6	CMU-03	persian–azeri	46.0	69.0	CMU-03
bulgarian–old-church-slavonic	44.0	56.0	CMU-03	persian–pashto	27.0	48.0	CMU-03
czech–kashubian	52.0	78.0	CMU-03	polish–kashubian	74.0	78.0	CMU-03
czech–latin	8.4	42.0	CMU-03	polish–old-church-slavonic	40.0	58.0	CMU-03
danish–middle-high-german	72.0	82.0	it-ist-02	portuguese–russian	27.5	76.3	CMU-03
danish–middle-low-german	36.0	44.0	it-ist-01	romanian–latin	6.7	41.3	CMU-03
danish–north-frisian	28.0	46.0	CMU-03	russian–old-church-slavonic	34.0	64.0	CMU-03
danish–west-frisian	42.0	43.0	CMU-03	russian–portuguese	50.5	88.4	CMU-03
danish–yiddish	76.0	67.0	it-ist-01	sanskrit–bengali	33.0	65.0	CMU-03
dutch–middle-high-german	76.0	78.0	it-ist-01 / it-ist-02	sanskrit–pashto	34.0	43.0	CMU-03
dutch–middle-low-german	42.0	52.0	it-ist-02	slovak–kashubian	54.0	76.0	CMU-03
dutch–north-frisian	32.0	46.0	CMU-03	slovene–old-saxon	10.6	53.2	CMU-03
dutch–west-frisian	38.0	51.0	it-ist-02	sorani–irish	27.6	66.3	CMU-03
dutch–yiddish	78.0	64.0	it-ist-01	spanish–friulian	53.0	81.0	CMU-03
english–murrinhpatha	22.0	42.0	it-ist-02	spanish–occitan	57.0	78.0	CMU-03
english–north-frisian	31.0	42.0	CMU-03	swahili–quechua	13.9	92.1	CMU-03
english–west-frisian	35.0	43.0	CMU-03	turkish–azeri	80.0	87.0	it-ist-02
estonian–ingrian	30.0	44.0	it-ist-02	turkish–crimean-tatar	83.0	89.0	CMU-03 / it-ist-02
estonian–karelian	74.0	68.0	it-ist-01	turkish–kazakh	76.0	86.0	it-ist-02
estonian–livonian	36.0	40.0	it-ist-02	turkish–khakas	76.0	94.0	it-ist-01
estonian–votic	25.0	35.0	it-ist-01	turkish–tatar	73.0	83.0	it-ist-02
finnish–ingrian	54.0	48.0	it-ist-02	turkish–turkmen	86.0	98.0	it-ist-01
finnish–karelian	70.0	78.0	it-ist-01	urdu–bengali	49.0	67.0	CMU-03
finnish–livonian	22.0	34.0	CMU-03 / it-ist-01	urdu–old-english	20.8	40.3	CMU-03
finnish–votic	42.0	40.0	it-ist-02	uzbek–azeri	57.0	70.0	CMU-03
french–occitan	50.0	80.0	CMU-03	uzbek–crimean-tatar	67.0	67.0	CMU-03
german–middle-high-german	72.0	82.0	CMU-03	uzbek–kazakh	84.0	72.0	CMU-03
german–middle-low-german	42.0	52.0	it-ist-02	uzbek–khakas	86.0	92.0	it-ist-01
german–yiddish	77.0	68.0	it-ist-01	uzbek–tatar	69.0	72.0	CMU-03
greek–bengali	51.0	67.0	CMU-03	uzbek–turkmen	80.0	78.0	CMU-03
hebrew–classical-syriac	89.0	95.0	CMU-03	welsh–breton	45.0	86.0	CMU-03
hebrew–maltese	37.0	47.0	CMU-03	welsh–cornish	22.0	42.0	it-ist-01
hindi–bengali	54.0	68.0	CMU-03	welsh–old-irish	6.0	6.0	CMU-03
hungarian–ingrian	12.0	40.0	it-ist-01	welsh–scottish-gaelic	40.0	64.0	CMU-03
hungarian–karelian	62.0	70.0	it-ist-02	zulu–swahili	44.0	81.0	CMU-03

Table 3: Task 1 Accuracy scores

HRL–LRL	Baseline	Best	Team	HRL–LRL	Baseline	Best	Team
adyghe–kabardian	0.04	0.03	Tuebingen-02	hungarian–livonian	2.56	1.81	it-ist-02
albanian–breton	1.30	0.44	it-ist-02	hungarian–votic	2.47	1.11	it-ist-01
arabic–classical-syriac	0.46	0.10	CMU-03	irish–breton	1.57	0.38	CMU-03
arabic–maltese	1.42	1.37	CMU-03	irish–cornish	2.00	1.56	it-ist-01
arabic–turkmen	0.46	0.32	CMU-03	irish–old-irish	3.30	3.12	it-ist-02
armenian–kabardian	0.21	0.14	CMU-03 / it-ist-01	irish–scottish-gaelic	0.96	1.06	CMU-03
asturian–occitan	1.74	0.80	it-ist-01	italian–friulian	1.03	0.72	it-ist-02
bashkir–azeri	1.64	0.69	it-ist-02	italian–ladin	0.79	0.60	CMU-03
bashkir–crimean-tatar	0.39	0.42	CMU-03	italian–maltese	1.39	1.23	CMU-03
bashkir–kazakh	0.32	0.10	it-ist-01	italian–neapolitan	0.40	0.36	it-ist-02
bashkir–khakas	0.18	0.04	it-ist-02	kannada–telugu	0.60	0.14	CMU-03
bashkir–tatar	0.46	0.33	CMU-03	kurmanji–sorani	2.56	0.65	CMU-03
bashkir–turkmen	0.10	0.12	it-ist-01	latin–czech	2.77	1.14	CMU-03
basque–kashubian	1.16	0.42	CMU-03	latvian–lithuanian	2.21	1.69	CMU-03
belarusian–old-irish	3.90	3.14	CMU-03	latvian–scottish-gaelic	1.16	1.00	CMU-03
bengali–greek	2.86	0.59	CMU-03	persian–azeri	1.35	0.74	CMU-03
bulgarian–old-church-slavonic	1.14	1.06	CMU-03	persian–pashto	1.70	1.54	CMU-03
czech–kashubian	0.84	0.36	CMU-03	polish–kashubian	0.34	0.34	CMU-03
czech–latin	2.95	1.36	CMU-03	polish–old-church-slavonic	1.22	0.96	CMU-03
danish–middle-high-german	0.50	0.38	it-ist-02	portuguese–russian	1.70	1.16	CMU-03
danish–middle-low-german	1.44	1.26	it-ist-01	romanian–latin	3.05	1.35	CMU-03
danish–north-frisian	2.78	2.11	CMU-03	russian–old-church-slavonic	1.33	0.86	CMU-03
danish–west-frisian	1.57	1.27	it-ist-02	russian–portuguese	1.04	0.66	CMU-03
danish–yiddish	0.91	0.72	Tuebingen-01	sanskrit–bengali	1.79	1.13	CMU-03
dutch–middle-high-german	0.44	0.36	it-ist-02	sanskrit–pashto	1.54	1.27	it-ist-02
dutch–middle-low-german	1.34	1.16	it-ist-02	slovak–kashubian	0.60	0.34	CMU-03
dutch–north-frisian	2.67	1.99	CMU-03	slovene–old-saxon	2.23	1.14	CMU-03
dutch–west-frisian	2.18	1.18	it-ist-02	sorani–irish	2.40	0.99	CMU-03
dutch–yiddish	0.53	0.72	Tuebingen-01	spanish–friulian	1.01	0.61	CMU-03
english–murrinhpatha	1.68	1.10	it-ist-02	spanish–occitan	1.14	0.57	it-ist-01
english–north-frisian	2.73	2.22	it-ist-02	swahili–quechua	3.90	0.56	CMU-03
english–west-frisian	1.48	1.26	it-ist-02	turkish–azeri	0.35	0.22	it-ist-01
estonian–ingrian	1.56	1.24	it-ist-02	turkish–crimean-tatar	0.24	0.14	CMU-03
estonian–karelian	0.52	0.62	it-ist-02	turkish–kazakh	0.34	0.16	it-ist-02
estonian–livonian	1.87	1.47	it-ist-02	turkish–khakas	0.80	0.06	it-ist-01
estonian–votic	1.55	1.17	it-ist-02	turkish–tatar	0.37	0.21	it-ist-02
finnish–ingrian	1.08	1.20	it-ist-02	turkish–turkmen	0.24	0.02	it-ist-01
finnish–karelian	0.64	0.42	it-ist-01	urdu–bengali	1.12	0.98	CMU-03
finnish–livonian	2.48	1.71	it-ist-01	urdu–old-english	1.72	1.20	CMU-03
finnish–votic	1.25	1.02	it-ist-02	uzbek–azeri	1.23	0.70	CMU-03
french–occitan	1.22	0.69	it-ist-01	uzbek–crimean-tatar	0.49	0.45	CMU-03
german–middle-high-german	0.44	0.32	it-ist-02	uzbek–kazakh	0.20	0.32	CMU-03
german–middle-low-german	1.24	1.16	it-ist-02	uzbek–khakas	0.24	0.18	it-ist-01
german–yiddish	0.46	0.72	Tuebingen-01	uzbek–tatar	0.48	0.35	CMU-03
greek–bengali	1.21	1.02	CMU-03	uzbek–turkmen	0.32	0.42	CMU-03
hebrew–classical-syriac	0.14	0.06	CMU-03	welsh–breton	0.90	0.31	CMU-03
hebrew–maltese	1.24	1.10	CMU-03	welsh–cornish	2.44	1.50	it-ist-01
hindi–bengali	1.18	0.72	UAlberta-02	welsh–old-irish	3.36	3.08	CMU-03
hungarian–ingrian	2.60	1.46	it-ist-01	welsh–scottish-gaelic	1.22	1.08	CMU-03
hungarian–karelian	0.90	0.50	it-ist-01	zulu–swahili	1.24	0.33	CMU-03

Table 4: Task 1 Levenshtein scores

The Tuebingen University submission (Tuebingen) aligned source and target to learn a set of edit-actions with both linear and neural classifiers that independently learned to predict action sequences for each morphological category. Adding in the cross-lingual data only led to modest gains.

AX-Semantics combined the low- and high-resource data to train an encoder-decoder seq2seq model; optionally also implementing domain adaptation methods to focus later epochs on the target language.

The CMU submission first attends over a decoupled representation of the desired morphological sequence before using the updated decoder state to attend over the character sequence of the lemma. Secondly, in order to reduce the bias of the decoder's language model, they hallucinate two types of data that encourage common affixes and character copying. Simply allowing the model to learn to copy characters for several epochs significantly outperforms the task baseline, while further improvements are obtained through fine-tuning. Making use of an adversarial language discriminator, cross lingual gains are highly-correlated to linguistic similarity, while augmenting the data with hallucinated forms and multiple related target language further improves the model.

The system from IT-IST also attends separately to tags and lemmas, using a gating mechanism to interpolate the importance of the individual attentions. By combining the gated dual-head attention with a SparseMax activation function, they are able to jointly learn stem and affix modifications, improving significantly over the baseline system.

The relative system performance is described in Table 5, which shows the average per-language accuracy of each system. The table reflects the fact that some teams submitted more than one system (e.g. Tuebingen-1 & Tuebingen-2 in the table).

5.2 Task 2 Results

Nine teams submitted system papers for Task 2, with several interesting modifications to either the baseline or other prior work that led to modest improvements.

Charles-Saarland achieved the highest overall tagging accuracy by leveraging multi-lingual BERT embeddings fine-tuned on a concatenation of all available languages, effectively transporting the cross-lingual objective of Task 1 into Task 2. Lemmas and tags are decoded separately (with a joint encoder and separate attention); Lemmas are a sequence of edit-actions, while tags are calculated jointly. (There is no splitting of tags into features; tags are atomic.)

CBNU instead lemmatize using a transformer network, while performing tagging with a multilayer perceptron with biaffine attention. Input words are first lemmatized, and then pipelined to the tagger, which produces atomic tag sequences (i.e., no splitting of features).

The team from Istanbul Technical University (ITU) jointly produces lemmatic edit-actions and morphological tags via a two level encoder (first word embeddings, and then context embeddings) and separate decoders. Their system slightly improves over the baseline lemmatization, but significantly improves tagging accuracy.

The team from the University of Groningen (RUG) also uses separate decoders for lemmatization and tagging, but uses ELMo to initialize the contextual embeddings, leading to large gains in performance. Furthermore, joint training on related languages further improves results.

CMU approaches tagging differently than the multi-task decoding we've seen so far (baseline is used for lemmatization). Making use of a hierarchical CRF that first predicts POS (that is subsequently looped back into the encoder), they then seek to predict each feature separately. In particular, predicting POS separately greatly improves results. An attempt to leverage gold typological information led to little gain in the results; experiments suggest that the system is already learning the pertinent information.

The team from Ohio State University (OHIOSTATE) concentrates on predicting tags; the baseline lemmatizer is used for lemmatization. To that end, they make use of a dual decoder that first predicts features given only the word embedding as input; the predictions are fed to a GRU seq2seq, which then predicts the sequence of tags.

The UNT HiLT+Ling team investigates a low-resource setting of the tagging, by using parallel Bible data to learn a translation matrix between English and the target language, learning morphological tags through analogy with English.

The UFAL-Prague team extends their submission from the UD shared task (multi-layer LSTM), replacing the pretrained embeddings with BERT, to great success (first in lemmatization, 2nd in tag-

Team	Lemma Accuracy	Lemma Levenshtein	Morph Accuracy	Morph F1
CBNU-01†	94.07	0.13	88.09	91.84
CHARLES-MALTA-01	74.95	0.62	50.37	58.81
CHARLES-SAARLAND-02†	95.00	0.11	**93.23**	**96.02**
CMU-02	92.20	0.17	85.06	88.97
CMU-DataAug-01‡	92.51	0.17	86.53	91.18
Edinburgh-01	94.20	0.13	88.93	92.89
ITU-01	94.46	0.11	86.67	90.54
NLPCUBE-01	91.43	2.43	84.92	88.67
OHIOSTATE-01	93.43	0.17	87.42	92.51
RUG-01†	93.91	0.14	90.53	94.54
RUG-02	93.06	0.15	88.80	93.22
UFALPRAGUE-01†	**95.78**	**0.10**	93.19	95.92
UNTHILTLING-02†	83.14	0.55	15.69	51.87
EDINBURGH-02*	97.35	0.06	93.02	95.94
CMU-Monolingual*	88.31	0.27	84.60	91.18
CMU-PolyGlot-01*†	76.81	0.54	60.98	75.42
Baseline	94.17	0.13	73.16	87.92

Table 5: Task 2 Team Scores, averaged across all treebanks; * indicates submissions were only applied to a subset of languages, making scores incomparable. † indicates that additional external resources were used for training, and ‡ indicates that training data were shared across languages or treebanks.

ging). Although they predict complete tags, they use the individual features to regularize the decoder. Small gains are also obtained from joining multilingual corpora and ensembling.

CUNI–Malta performs lemmatization as operations over edit actions with LSTM and ReLU. Tagging is a bidirectional LSTM augmented by the edit actions (i.e., two-stage decoding), predicting features separately.

The Edinburgh system is a character-based LSTM encoder-decoder with attention, implemented in OpenNMT. It can be seen as an extension of the contextual lemmatization system Lematus (Bergmanis and Goldwater, 2018) to include morphological tagging, or alternatively as an adaptation of the morphological re-inflection system MED (Kann and Schütze, 2016) to incorporate context and perform analysis rather than re-inflection. Like these systems it uses a completely generic encoder-decoder architecture with no specific adaptation to the morphological processing task other than the form of the input. In the submitted version of the system, the input is split into short chunks corresponding to the target word plus one word of context on either side, and the system is trained to output the corresponding lemmas and tags for each three-word chunk.

Several teams relied on external resources to improve their lemmatization and feature analysis. Several teams made use of pre-trained embeddings. CHARLES-SAARLAND-2 and UFALPRAGUE-1 used pretrained contextual embeddings (BERT) provided by Google (Devlin et al., 2019). CBNU-1 used a mix of pre-trained embeddings from the CoNLL 2017 shared task and fastText. Further, some teams trained their own embeddings to aid performance.

6 Future Directions

In general, the application of typology to natural language processing (e.g., Gerz et al., 2018; Ponti et al., 2018) provides an interesting avenue for multilinguality. Further, our shared task was designed to only leverage a single helper language, though many may exist with lexical or morphological overlap with the target language. Techniques like those of Neubig and Hu (2018) may aid in designing universal inflection architectures. Neither task this year included unannotated monolingual corpora. Using such data is well-motivated from an L1-learning point of view, and may affect the performance of low-resource data settings.

In the case of inflection an interesting future topic could involve departing from orthographic representation and using more IPA-like representations, i.e. transductions over pronunciations. Differ-

Language (Treebank)	Baseline	Best	Team
UD_Afrikaans-AfriBooms	98.41	99.15	UFALPRAGUE-01
UD_Akkadian-PISANDUB	66.83	67.82	CBNU-01 / EDINBURGH-01
UD_Amharic-ATT	98.68	100.00	Multiple
UD_Ancient_Greek-Perseus	94.44	95.24	EDINBURGH-01
UD_Ancient_Greek-PROIEL	96.68	97.49	EDINBURGH-01
UD_Arabic-PADT	94.49	96.08	UFALPRAGUE-01
UD_Arabic-PUD	85.24	87.13	EDINBURGH-01
UD_Armenian-ArmTDP	95.39	95.96	UFALPRAGUE-01
UD_Bambara-CRB	87.02	92.71	UFALPRAGUE-01
UD_Basque-BDT	96.07	97.19	UFALPRAGUE-01
UD_Belarusian-HSE	89.70	92.51	CHARLES-SAARLAND-02
UD_Breton-KEB	93.53	93.83	OHIOSTATE-01
UD_Bulgarian-BTB	97.37	98.36	UFALPRAGUE-01
UD_Buryat-BDT	88.56	90.19	UFALPRAGUE-01
UD_Cantonese-HK	91.61	100.00	Multiple
UD_Catalan-AnCora	98.07	99.38	CHARLES-SAARLAND-02
UD_Chinese-CFL	93.26	99.76	CBNU-01 / UFALPRAGUE-01
UD_Chinese-GSD	98.44	99.98	CBNU-01 / CMU-02 / UFALPRAGUE-01
UD_Coptic-Scriptorium	95.80	97.31	UFALPRAGUE-01
UD_Croatian-SET	95.32	97.52	UFALPRAGUE-01
UD_Czech-CAC	97.82	99.45	CHARLES-SAARLAND-02
UD_Czech-CLTT	98.21	99.47	UFALPRAGUE-01
UD_Czech-FicTree	97.66	99.01	CHARLES-SAARLAND-02
UD_Czech-PDT	96.06	99.42	CHARLES-SAARLAND-02
UD_Czech-PUD	93.58	98.13	UFALPRAGUE-01
UD_Danish-DDT	96.16	98.33	UFALPRAGUE-01
UD_Dutch-Alpino	97.35	98.62	CHARLES-SAARLAND-02
UD_Dutch-LassySmall	96.63	98.21	UFALPRAGUE-01
UD_English-EWT	97.68	99.19	CHARLES-SAARLAND-02
UD_English-GUM	97.41	98.63	UFALPRAGUE-01
UD_English-LinES	98.00	98.62	CHARLES-SAARLAND-02
UD_English-ParTUT	97.66	98.52	UFALPRAGUE-01
UD_English-PUD	95.29	97.89	CHARLES-SAARLAND-02
UD_Estonian-EDT	94.84	97.09	EDINBURGH-01
UD_Faroese-OFT	88.86	89.53	UFALPRAGUE-01
UD_Finnish-FTB	94.88	96.64	EDINBURGH-02
UD_Finnish-PUD	88.27	89.98	UFALPRAGUE-01
UD_Finnish-TDT	95.53	96.60	UFALPRAGUE-01
UD_French-GSD	97.97	99.01	CHARLES-SAARLAND-02
UD_French-ParTUT	95.69	96.66	CHARLES-SAARLAND-02
UD_French-Sequoia	97.67	99.01	UFALPRAGUE-01
UD_French-Spoken	97.98	99.52	post_deadline_RUG-01
UD_Galician-CTG	98.22	98.96	CHARLES-SAARLAND-02
UD_Galician-TreeGal	96.18	98.65	UFALPRAGUE-01
UD_German-GSD	96.26	97.65	ITU-01
UD_Gothic-PROIEL	96.53	97.03	EDINBURGH-01
UD_Greek-GDT	96.76	97.24	EDINBURGH-01
UD_Hebrew-HTB	96.72	98.17	UFALPRAGUE-01
UD_Hindi-HDTB	98.60	98.87	UFALPRAGUE-01
UD_Hungarian-Szeged	95.17	97.47	UFALPRAGUE-01
UD_Indonesian-GSD	99.37	99.61	UFALPRAGUE-01
UD_Irish-IDT	91.69	92.02	OHIOSTATE-01
UD_Italian-ISDT	97.38	98.88	CHARLES-SAARLAND-02 / UFALPRAGUE-01
UD_Italian-ParTUT	96.84	98.87	CHARLES-SAARLAND-02

Language (Treebank)	Baseline	Best	Team
UD_Italian-PoSTWITA	95.60	97.95	UFALPRAGUE-01
UD_Italian-PUD	95.59	98.06	UFALPRAGUE-01
UD_Japanese-GSD	97.71	99.65	CHARLES-SAARLAND-02
UD_Japanese-Modern	94.20	98.67	CHARLES-SAARLAND-02
UD_Japanese-PUD	95.75	99.36	CHARLES-SAARLAND-02
UD_Komi_Zyrian-IKDP	78.91	89.84	RUG-02
UD_Komi_Zyrian-Lattice	82.97	87.91	UFALPRAGUE-01
UD_Korean-GSD	92.25	94.21	UFALPRAGUE-01
UD_Korean-Kaist	94.61	95.78	EDINBURGH-01
UD_Korean-PUD	96.41	99.57	CHARLES-SAARLAND-02
UD_Kurmanji-MG	92.29	94.80	UFALPRAGUE-01
UD_Latin-ITTB	98.17	99.20	CHARLES-SAARLAND-02
UD_Latin-Perseus	89.54	93.49	UFALPRAGUE-01
UD_Latin-PROIEL	96.41	97.37	UFALPRAGUE-01
UD_Latvian-LVTB	95.59	97.23	UFALPRAGUE-01
UD_Lithuanian-HSE	86.42	87.44	OHIOSTATE-01
UD_Marathi-UFAL	75.61	76.69	CHARLES-SAARLAND-02
UD_Naija-NSC	99.33	100.00	Multiple
UD_North_Sami-Giella	93.04	93.47	OHIOSTATE-01
UD_Norwegian-Bokmaal	98.00	99.19	UFALPRAGUE-01
UD_Norwegian-Nynorsk	97.85	99.00	CHARLES-SAARLAND-02
UD_Norwegian-NynorskLIA	96.66	98.22	UFALPRAGUE-01
UD_Old_Church_Slavonic-PROIEL	96.38	97.23	EDINBURGH-01
UD_Persian-Seraji	96.08	96.89	UFALPRAGUE-01
UD_Polish-LFG	95.82	97.94	CHARLES-SAARLAND-02
UD_Polish-SZ	95.18	97.43	CHARLES-SAARLAND-02
UD_Portuguese-Bosque	97.08	98.69	UFALPRAGUE-01
UD_Portuguese-GSD	93.70	99.11	UFALPRAGUE-01
UD_Romanian-Nonstandard	95.86	96.74	UFALPRAGUE-01
UD_Romanian-RRT	96.94	98.60	UFALPRAGUE-01
UD_Russian-GSD	95.67	97.77	UFALPRAGUE-01
UD_Russian-PUD	91.85	95.76	UFALPRAGUE-01
UD_Russian-SynTagRus	95.92	99.01	CHARLES-SAARLAND-02
UD_Russian-Taiga	89.86	100.00	UNTHILTLING-02
UD_Sanskrit-UFAL	64.32	67.34	CMU-Monolingual-01
UD_Serbian-SET	96.72	98.19	UFALPRAGUE-01
UD_Slovak-SNK	96.14	97.57	CHARLES-SAARLAND-02
UD_Slovenian-SSJ	96.43	98.87	CHARLES-SAARLAND-02
UD_Slovenian-SST	94.06	97.20	CHARLES-SAARLAND-02
UD_Spanish-AnCora	98.54	99.46	UFALPRAGUE-01
UD_Spanish-GSD	98.42	99.30	UFALPRAGUE-01
UD_Swedish-LinES	95.85	98.30	UFALPRAGUE-01
UD_Swedish-PUD	93.12	96.63	UFALPRAGUE-01
UD_Swedish-Talbanken	97.23	98.62	CHARLES-SAARLAND-02
UD_Tagalog-TRG	78.38	91.89	Multiple
UD_Tamil-TTB	93.86	96.43	UFALPRAGUE-01
UD_Turkish-IMST	96.41	96.84	UFALPRAGUE-01
UD_Turkish-PUD	86.02	89.03	UFALPRAGUE-01
UD_Ukrainian-IU	95.53	97.85	UFALPRAGUE-01
UD_Upper_Sorbian-UFAL	91.69	93.74	CHARLES-SAARLAND-02
UD_Urdu-UDTB	96.19	96.98	UFALPRAGUE-01
UD_Vietnamese-VTB	99.79	100.00	CMU-02 / UNTHILTLING-02
UD_Yoruba-YTB	98.84	98.84	Multiple

Table 6: Task 2 Lemma Accuracy scores

Language (Treebank)	Baseline	Best	Team	Language (Treebank)	Baseline	Best	Team
UD_Afrikaans-AfriBooms	0.03	0.02	Multiple	UD_Italian-PoSTWITA	0.11	0.05	UFALPRAGUE-01
UD_Akkadian-PISANDUB	0.87	0.85	OHIOSTATE-01	UD_Italian-PUD	0.08	0.04	CHARLES-SAARLAND-02 / UFALPRAGUE-01
UD_Amharic-ATT	0.02	0.00	Multiple	UD_Japanese-GSD	0.04	0.01	Multiple
UD_Ancient_Greek-Perseus	0.14	0.12	EDINBURGH-01	UD_Japanese-Modern	0.07	0.01	CHARLES-SAARLAND-02
UD_Ancient_Greek-PROIEL	0.08	0.06	EDINBURGH-01 / EDINBURGH-02	UD_Japanese-PUD	0.07	0.01	CHARLES-SAARLAND-02 / UFALPRAGUE-01
UD_Arabic-PADT	0.16	0.11	UFALPRAGUE-01	UD_Komi_Zyrian-IKDP	0.38	0.23	RUG-01 / RUG-02
UD_Arabic-PUD	0.41	0.37	EDINBURGH-01	UD_Komi_Zyrian-Lattice	0.34	0.25	UFALPRAGUE-01
UD_Armenian-ArmTDP	0.08	0.07	UFALPRAGUE-01	UD_Korean-GSD	0.18	0.11	Multiple
UD_Bambara-CRB	0.27	0.10	UFALPRAGUE-01	UD_Korean-Kaist	0.09	0.06	EDINBURGH-01
UD_Basque-BDT	0.09	0.06	UFALPRAGUE-01	UD_Korean-PUD	0.06	0.01	Multiple
UD_Belarusian-HSE	0.17	0.12	CHARLES-SAARLAND-02	UD_Kurmanji-MG	0.39	0.10	UFALPRAGUE-01
UD_Breton-KEB	0.16	0.13	ITU-01	UD_Latin-ITTB	0.04	0.02	CHARLES-SAARLAND-02 / UFALPRAGUE-01
UD_Bulgarian-BTB	0.07	0.05	ITU-01 / UFALPRAGUE-01	UD_Latin-Perseus	0.21	0.13	UFALPRAGUE-01
UD_Buryat-BDT	0.27	0.22	UFALPRAGUE-01	UD_Latin-PROIEL	0.08	0.05	CHARLES-SAARLAND-02
UD_Cantonese-HK	0.28	0.00	Multiple	UD_Latvian-LVTB	0.07	0.05	CHARLES-SAARLAND-02 / UFALPRAGUE-01
UD_Catalan-AnCora	0.04	0.01	CHARLES-SAARLAND-02 / UFALPRAGUE-01	UD_Lithuanian-HSE	0.25	0.24	UFALPRAGUE-01
UD_Chinese-CFL	0.10	0.01	NLPCUBE-01	UD_Marathi-UFAL	0.86	0.57	CMU-Monolingual-01
UD_Chinese-GSD	0.02	0.01	Multiple	UD_Naija-NSC	0.01	0.00	Multiple
UD_Coptic-Scriptorium	0.09	0.06	UFALPRAGUE-01	UD_North_Sami-Giella	0.14	0.13	EDINBURGH-01 / OHIOSTATE-01
UD_Croatian-SET	0.09	0.05	CHARLES-SAARLAND-02 / UFALPRAGUE-01	UD_Norwegian-Bokmaal	0.03	0.01	CHARLES-SAARLAND-02 / UFALPRAGUE-01
UD_Czech-CAC	0.05	0.01	CHARLES-SAARLAND-02 / UFALPRAGUE-01	UD_Norwegian-Nynorsk	0.04	0.01	CHARLES-SAARLAND-02
UD_Czech-CLTT	0.04	0.01	CHARLES-SAARLAND-02 / UFALPRAGUE-01	UD_Norwegian-NynorskLIA	0.08	0.03	UFALPRAGUE-01
UD_Czech-FicTree	0.04	0.02	CHARLES-SAARLAND-02 / UFALPRAGUE-01	UD_Old_Church_Slavonic-PROIEL	0.08	0.06	EDINBURGH-01
UD_Czech-PDT	0.06	0.01	CHARLES-SAARLAND-02 / UFALPRAGUE-01	UD_Persian-Seraji	0.19	0.15	UFALPRAGUE-01
UD_Czech-PUD	0.10	0.03	UFALPRAGUE-01	UD_Polish-LFG	0.08	0.04	CHARLES-SAARLAND-02 / UFALPRAGUE-01
UD_Danish-DDT	0.06	0.03	CHARLES-SAARLAND-02 / UFALPRAGUE-01	UD_Polish-SZ	0.08	0.04	UFALPRAGUE-01
UD_Dutch-Alpino	0.05	0.03	CHARLES-SAARLAND-02 / UFALPRAGUE-01	UD_Portuguese-Bosque	0.05	0.02	CHARLES-SAARLAND-02 / UFALPRAGUE-01
UD_Dutch-LassySmall	0.06	0.03	CHARLES-SAARLAND-02 / UFALPRAGUE-01	UD_Portuguese-GSD	0.18	0.05	CHARLES-SAARLAND-02 / UFALPRAGUE-01
UD_English-EWT	0.12	0.01	CHARLES-SAARLAND-02	UD_Romanian-Nonstandard	0.08	0.06	Multiple
UD_English-GUM	0.05	0.02	CHARLES-SAARLAND-02 / UFALPRAGUE-01	UD_Romanian-RRT	0.05	0.02	CHARLES-SAARLAND-02
UD_English-LinES	0.04	0.02	CHARLES-SAARLAND-02 / UFALPRAGUE-01	UD_Russian-GSD	0.07	0.04	CHARLES-SAARLAND-02 / UFALPRAGUE-01
UD_English-ParTUT	0.04	0.02	CHARLES-SAARLAND-02 / UFALPRAGUE-01	UD_Russian-PUD	0.18	0.08	CHARLES-SAARLAND-02 / UFALPRAGUE-01
UD_English-PUD	0.07	0.03	CHARLES-SAARLAND-02	UD_Russian-SynTagRus	0.08	0.02	CHARLES-SAARLAND-02 / UFALPRAGUE-01
UD_Estonian-EDT	0.11	0.05	EDINBURGH-01	UD_Russian-Taiga	0.21	0.00	UWTHILTLING
UD_Faroese-OFT	0.20	0.18	ITU-01	UD_Sanskrit-UFAL	0.85	0.82	CMU-Monolingual-01
UD_Finnish-FTB	0.11	0.08	Multiple	UD_Serbian-SET	0.06	0.03	CHARLES-SAARLAND-02 / UFALPRAGUE-01
UD_Finnish-PUD	0.24	0.18	UFALPRAGUE-01	UD_Slovak-SNK	0.06	0.04	CHARLES-SAARLAND-02
UD_Finnish-TDT	0.10	0.07	UFALPRAGUE-01	UD_Slovenian-SSJ	0.06	0.02	CHARLES-SAARLAND-02 / UFALPRAGUE-01
UD_French-GSD	0.04	0.02	Multiple	UD_Slovenian-SST	0.12	0.05	CHARLES-SAARLAND-02
UD_French-ParTUT	0.07	0.05	RUG-02 / post_deadline_RUG-01	UD_Spanish-AnCora	0.03	0.01	Multiple
UD_French-Sequoia	0.05	0.02	CHARLES-SAARLAND-02 / UFALPRAGUE-01	UD_Spanish-GSD	0.03	0.01	Multiple
UD_French-Spoken	0.04	0.01	post_deadline_RUG-01	UD_Swedish-LinES	0.08	0.03	UFALPRAGUE-01
UD_Galician-CTG	0.04	0.02	Multiple	UD_Swedish-PUD	0.10	0.05	UFALPRAGUE-01
UD_Galician-TreeGal	0.06	0.03	CHARLES-SAARLAND-02 / UFALPRAGUE-01	UD_Swedish-Talbanken	0.05	0.02	CHARLES-SAARLAND-02 / UFALPRAGUE-01
UD_German-GSD	0.08	0.04	ITU-01	UD_Tagalog-TRG	0.49	0.19	CHARLES-SAARLAND-02 / ITU-01
UD_Gothic-PROIEL	0.07	0.06	OHIOSTATE-01	UD_Tamil-TTB	0.14	0.07	UFALPRAGUE-01
UD_Greek-GDT	0.07	0.06	EDINBURGH-01	UD_Turkish-IMST	0.08	0.06	EDINBURGH-01 / ITU-01 / UFALPRAGUE-01
UD_Hebrew-HTB	0.06	0.03	UFALPRAGUE-01	UD_Turkish-PUD	0.34	0.28	ITU-01
UD_Hindi-HDTB	0.02	0.01	Multiple	UD_Ukrainian-IU	0.10	0.03	CHARLES-SAARLAND-02
UD_Hungarian-Szeged	0.10	0.05	UFALPRAGUE-01	UD_Upper_Sorbian-UFAL	0.12	0.10	CHARLES-SAARLAND-02
UD_Indonesian-GSD	0.01	0.01	Multiple	UD_Urdu-UDTB	0.07	0.06	Multiple
UD_Irish-IDT	0.18	0.16	OHIOSTATE-01	UD_Vietnamese-VTB	0.02	0.00	CMU-02 / UNTHILTLING
UD_Italian-ISDT	0.05	0.02	CHARLES-SAARLAND-02 / UFALPRAGUE-01	UD_Yoruba-YTB	0.01	0.01	Multiple
UD_Italian-ParTUT	0.08	0.02	CHARLES-SAARLAND-02				

Table 7: Task 2 Lemma Levenshtein scores

Language (Treebank)	Baseline	Best	Team	Language (Treebank)	Baseline	Best	Team
UD_Afrikaans-AfriBooms	84.90	99.23	CHARLES-SAARLAND-02 / UFALPRAGUE-01	UD_Italian-PoSTWITA	70.09	96.88	CHARLES-SAARLAND-02
UD_Akkadian-PISANDUB	78.22	89.11	CHARLES-SAARLAND-02	UD_Italian-PUD	80.78	96.37	CHARLES-SAARLAND-02
UD_Amharic-ATT	75.43	89.79	UFALPRAGUE-01	UD_Japanese-GSD	85.47	98.41	CHARLES-SAARLAND-02
UD_Ancient_Greek-Perseus	69.88	91.94	UFALPRAGUE-01	UD_Japanese-Modern	94.94	97.47	CHARLES-SAARLAND-02
UD_Ancient_Greek-PROIEL	84.55	92.94	UFALPRAGUE-01	UD_Japanese-PUD	84.33	98.63	UFALPRAGUE-01
UD_Arabic-PADT	76.78	95.66	CHARLES-SAARLAND-02	UD_Komi_Zyrian-IKDP	35.94	75.78	UFALPRAGUE-01
UD_Arabic-PUD	63.07	85.04	UFALPRAGUE-01	UD_Komi_Zyrian-Lattice	45.05	69.78	UFALPRAGUE-01
UD_Armenian-ArmTDP	64.38	93.34	UFALPRAGUE-01	UD_Korean-GSD	79.73	96.77	CHARLES-SAARLAND-02
UD_Bambara-CRB	76.99	93.93	UFALPRAGUE-01	UD_Korean-Kaist	84.30	97.85	CHARLES-SAARLAND-02
UD_Basque-BDT	67.76	92.52	UFALPRAGUE-01	UD_Korean-PUD	76.78	94.67	CHARLES-SAARLAND-02
UD_Belarusian-HSE	54.22	89.93	CHARLES-SAARLAND-02	UD_Kurmanji-MG	68.10	85.57	UFALPRAGUE-01
UD_Breton-KEB	76.52	91.14	UFALPRAGUE-01	UD_Latin-ITTB	77.68	97.64	CHARLES-SAARLAND-02
UD_Bulgarian-BTB	79.64	98.01	CHARLES-SAARLAND-02	UD_Latin-Perseus	55.06	87.76	UFALPRAGUE-01
UD_Buryat-BDT	64.23	88.56	UFALPRAGUE-01	UD_Latin-PROIEL	82.16	93.68	CHARLES-SAARLAND-02
UD_Cantonese-HK	68.57	94.29	CHARLES-SAARLAND-02	UD_Latvian-LVTB	70.33	95.78	CHARLES-SAARLAND-02
UD_Catalan-AnCora	85.57	98.82	CHARLES-SAARLAND-02	UD_Lithuanian-HSE	41.43	80.14	UFALPRAGUE-01
UD_Chinese-CFL	76.71	94.09	UFALPRAGUE-01	UD_Marathi-UFAL	40.11	67.75	CHARLES-SAARLAND-02
UD_Chinese-GSD	75.97	97.13	CHARLES-SAARLAND-02	UD_Naija-NSC	66.42	96.57	UFALPRAGUE-01
UD_Coptic-Scriptorium	87.73	96.22	UFALPRAGUE-01	UD_North_Sami-Giella	66.87	92.46	CHARLES-SAARLAND-02
UD_Croatian-SET	71.42	94.42	UFALPRAGUE-01	UD_Norwegian-Bokmaal	81.27	98.25	CHARLES-SAARLAND-02
UD_Czech-CAC	77.26	98.48	CHARLES-SAARLAND-02	UD_Norwegian-Nynorsk	81.75	98.11	CHARLES-SAARLAND-02
UD_Czech-CLTT	72.60	95.81	UFALPRAGUE-01	UD_Norwegian-NynorskLIA	74.20	96.80	CHARLES-SAARLAND-02
UD_Czech-FicTree	68.34	97.13	CHARLES-SAARLAND-02	UD_Old_Church_Slavonic-PROIEL	84.13	93.01	UFALPRAGUE-01
UD_Czech-PDT	76.70	98.54	CHARLES-SAARLAND-02	UD_Persian-Seraji	86.84	98.31	CHARLES-SAARLAND-02 / UFALPRAGUE-01
UD_Czech-PUD	60.67	95.03	UFALPRAGUE-01	UD_Polish-LFG	65.72	97.13	CHARLES-SAARLAND-02
UD_Danish-DDT	77.22	97.98	CHARLES-SAARLAND-02	UD_Polish-SZ	63.15	95.11	CHARLES-SAARLAND-02
UD_Dutch-Alpino	82.07	98.12	CHARLES-SAARLAND-02	UD_Portuguese-Bosque	78.05	96.22	CHARLES-SAARLAND-02
UD_Dutch-LassySmall	76.78	98.50	CHARLES-SAARLAND-02	UD_Portuguese-GSD	83.87	99.03	CHARLES-SAARLAND-02
UD_English-EWT	80.17	97.85	CHARLES-SAARLAND-02	UD_Romanian-Nonstandard	74.71	95.01	CHARLES-SAARLAND-02
UD_English-GUM	79.57	97.52	CHARLES-SAARLAND-02	UD_Romanian-RRT	81.62	98.19	CHARLES-SAARLAND-02
UD_English-LinES	80.30	97.77	CHARLES-SAARLAND-02	UD_Russian-GSD	63.37	94.92	CHARLES-SAARLAND-02
UD_English-ParTUT	80.31	96.65	CHARLES-SAARLAND-02	UD_Russian-PUD	60.68	91.15	CHARLES-SAARLAND-02
UD_English-PUD	77.59	96.67	CHARLES-SAARLAND-02	UD_Russian-SynTagRus	73.64	98.38	CHARLES-SAARLAND-02
UD_Estonian-EDT	74.03	97.23	CHARLES-SAARLAND-02	UD_Russian-Taiga	52.06	92.09	UFALPRAGUE-01
UD_Faroese-OFT	65.32	87.70	UFALPRAGUE-01	UD_Sanskrit-UFAL	29.65	50.75	UFALPRAGUE-01
UD_Finnish-FTB	72.89	96.85	CHARLES-SAARLAND-02	UD_Serbian-SET	77.05	97.02	CHARLES-SAARLAND-02
UD_Finnish-PUD	70.07	95.62	CHARLES-SAARLAND-02 / UFALPRAGUE-01	UD_Slovak-SNK	64.04	95.41	CHARLES-SAARLAND-02
UD_Finnish-TDT	74.84	97.15	UFALPRAGUE-01	UD_Slovenian-SSJ	73.82	97.04	UFALPRAGUE-01
UD_French-GSD	84.20	98.31	CHARLES-SAARLAND-02	UD_Slovenian-SST	69.57	92.76	CHARLES-SAARLAND-02
UD_French-ParTUT	81.67	95.78	UFALPRAGUE-01	UD_Spanish-AnCora	84.35	98.79	CHARLES-SAARLAND-02
UD_French-Sequoia	81.50	98.15	UFALPRAGUE-01	UD_Spanish-GSD	81.90	95.88	CHARLES-SAARLAND-02
UD_French-Spoken	94.48	98.60	CHARLES-SAARLAND-02	UD_Swedish-LinES	76.93	94.75	CHARLES-SAARLAND-02
UD_Galician-CTG	86.65	98.44	CHARLES-SAARLAND-02	UD_Swedish-PUD	79.97	95.85	UFALPRAGUE-01
UD_Galician-TreeGal	76.40	96.21	CHARLES-SAARLAND-02	UD_Swedish-Talbanken	81.37	98.09	CHARLES-SAARLAND-02
UD_German-GSD	68.35	90.43	CHARLES-SAARLAND-02	UD_Tagalog-TRG	67.57	91.89	CHARLES-SAARLAND-02 / UFALPRAGUE-01
UD_Gothic-PROIEL	81.00	91.02	CHARLES-SAARLAND-02	UD_Tamil-TTB	73.33	91.63	UFALPRAGUE-01
UD_Greek-GDT	77.44	95.95	UFALPRAGUE-01	UD_Turkish-IMST	62.94	92.27	UFALPRAGUE-01
UD_Hebrew-HTB	81.15	97.67	CHARLES-SAARLAND-02	UD_Turkish-PUD	66.30	87.63	post_deadline_RUG-01
UD_Hindi-HDTB	80.60	93.65	CHARLES-SAARLAND-02	UD_Ukrainian-IU	63.59	95.78	CHARLES-SAARLAND-02
UD_Hungarian-Szeged	65.90	95.03	UFALPRAGUE-01	UD_Upper_Sorbian-UFAL	57.70	87.02	UFALPRAGUE-01
UD_Indonesian-GSD	71.73	92.48	CHARLES-SAARLAND-02	UD_Urdu-UDTB	69.97	80.90	UFALPRAGUE-01
UD_Irish-IDT	67.66	86.37	UFALPRAGUE-01	UD_Vietnamese-VTB	69.42	94.54	CHARLES-SAARLAND-02
UD_Italian-ISDT	83.72	98.49	CHARLES-SAARLAND-02	UD_Yoruba-YTB	73.26	93.80	CMU-DataAug-01
UD_Italian-ParTUT	83.51	98.72	UFALPRAGUE-01				

Table 8: Task 2 Morph Accuracy scores

Language (Treebank)	Baseline	Best	Team	Language (Treebank)	Baseline	Best	Team
UD_Afrikaans-AfriBooms	92.87	99.40	UFALPRAGUE-01	UD_Italian-PoSTWITA	87.98	97.90	CHARLES-SAARLAND-02
UD_Akkadian-PISANDUB	80.41	89.06	CHARLES-SAARLAND-02	UD_Italian-PUD	92.24	98.42	CHARLES-SAARLAND-02
UD_Amharic-ATT	87.57	93.15	UFALPRAGUE-01	UD_Japanese-GSD	90.64	98.21	CHARLES-SAARLAND-02
UD_Ancient_Greek-Perseus	88.97	96.72	UFALPRAGUE-01	UD_Japanese-Modern	95.64	97.50	CHARLES-SAARLAND-02
UD_Ancient_Greek-PROIEL	93.55	97.88	UFALPRAGUE-01	UD_Japanese-PUD	89.64	98.49	UFALPRAGUE-01
UD_Arabic-PADT	91.82	97.65	CHARLES-SAARLAND-02	UD_Komi_Zyrian-IKDP	59.52	82.99	UFALPRAGUE-01
UD_Arabic-PUD	86.35	94.66	RUG-01	UD_Komi_Zyrian-Lattice	74.12	82.99	RUG-01 / RUG-02
UD_Armenian-ArmTDP	86.74	96.66	CHARLES-SAARLAND-02	UD_Korean-GSD	85.90	96.27	CHARLES-SAARLAND-02
UD_Bambara-CRB	88.94	95.55	UFALPRAGUE-01	UD_Korean-Kaist	89.45	97.58	CHARLES-SAARLAND-02
UD_Basque-BDT	87.54	96.30	CHARLES-SAARLAND-02	UD_Korean-PUD	88.15	96.76	CHARLES-SAARLAND-02
UD_Belarusian-HSE	78.80	95.68	CHARLES-SAARLAND-02	UD_Kurmanji-MG	86.54	91.28	UFALPRAGUE-01
UD_Breton-KEB	88.34	93.79	UFALPRAGUE-01	UD_Latin-ITTB	93.12	98.96	CHARLES-SAARLAND-02
UD_Bulgarian-BTB	93.85	99.18	CHARLES-SAARLAND-02	UD_Latin-Perseus	78.91	94.65	UFALPRAGUE-01
UD_Buryat-BDT	80.94	90.50	UFALPRAGUE-01	UD_Latin-PROIEL	91.42	97.87	CHARLES-SAARLAND-02
UD_Cantonese-HK	76.80	92.83	CHARLES-SAARLAND-02	UD_Latvian-LVTB	89.55	98.04	CHARLES-SAARLAND-02
UD_Catalan-AnCora	95.73	99.45	CHARLES-SAARLAND-02	UD_Lithuanian-HSE	67.39	87.97	CHARLES-SAARLAND-02
UD_Chinese-CFL	82.05	93.21	UFALPRAGUE-01	UD_Marathi-UFAL	69.71	80.19	CHARLES-SAARLAND-02
UD_Chinese-GSD	83.79	97.04	CHARLES-SAARLAND-02	UD_Naija-NSC	76.73	95.47	UFALPRAGUE-01
UD_Coptic-Scriptorium	93.56	97.17	UFALPRAGUE-01	UD_North_Sami-Giella	85.45	95.33	CHARLES-SAARLAND-02
UD_Croatian-SET	90.39	97.82	CHARLES-SAARLAND-02	UD_Norwegian-Bokmaal	93.17	99.02	CHARLES-SAARLAND-02
UD_Czech-CAC	93.94	99.48	CHARLES-SAARLAND-02	UD_Norwegian-Nynorsk	92.85	98.97	CHARLES-SAARLAND-02
UD_Czech-CLTT	92.61	98.32	UFALPRAGUE-01	UD_Norwegian-NynorskLIA	89.21	97.39	CHARLES-SAARLAND-02
UD_Czech-FicTree	90.32	98.90	CHARLES-SAARLAND-02	UD_Old_Church_Slavonic-PROIEL	91.17	97.13	UFALPRAGUE-01
UD_Czech-PDT	94.23	99.47	CHARLES-SAARLAND-02	UD_Persian-Seraji	93.76	98.68	UFALPRAGUE-01
UD_Czech-PUD	85.73	98.23	UFALPRAGUE-01	UD_Polish-LFG	88.73	98.86	CHARLES-SAARLAND-02
UD_Danish-DDT	90.19	98.68	CHARLES-SAARLAND-02	UD_Polish-SZ	86.24	98.11	CHARLES-SAARLAND-02
UD_Dutch-Alpino	91.25	98.62	CHARLES-SAARLAND-02	UD_Portuguese-Bosque	92.36	98.26	CHARLES-SAARLAND-02
UD_Dutch-LassySmall	87.97	98.83	CHARLES-SAARLAND-02	UD_Portuguese-GSD	91.73	99.10	CHARLES-SAARLAND-02
UD_English-EWT	90.91	98.52	CHARLES-SAARLAND-02	UD_Romanian-Nonstandard	91.70	97.65	CHARLES-SAARLAND-02
UD_English-GUM	89.81	98.11	CHARLES-SAARLAND-02	UD_Romanian-RRT	93.88	98.89	CHARLES-SAARLAND-02
UD_English-LinES	90.58	98.30	CHARLES-SAARLAND-02	UD_Russian-GSD	87.49	97.95	CHARLES-SAARLAND-02
UD_English-ParTUT	89.46	97.35	CHARLES-SAARLAND-02	UD_Russian-PUD	84.31	96.27	CHARLES-SAARLAND-02
UD_English-PUD	87.70	97.58	CHARLES-SAARLAND-02	UD_Russian-SynTagRus	92.73	99.23	CHARLES-SAARLAND-02
UD_Estonian-EDT	91.52	98.69	CHARLES-SAARLAND-02	UD_Russian-Taiga	76.77	95.56	UFALPRAGUE-01
UD_Faroese-OFT	85.73	93.98	UFALPRAGUE-01	UD_Sanskrit-UFAL	57.80	69.63	RUG-01 / RUG-02
UD_Finnish-FTB	89.08	98.38	CHARLES-SAARLAND-02	UD_Serbian-SET	91.75	98.64	CHARLES-SAARLAND-02
UD_Finnish-PUD	87.77	97.98	CHARLES-SAARLAND-02	UD_Slovak-SNK	88.04	98.24	CHARLES-SAARLAND-02
UD_Finnish-TDT	90.66	98.54	CHARLES-SAARLAND-02	UD_Slovenian-SSJ	90.12	98.80	CHARLES-SAARLAND-02
UD_French-GSD	94.63	99.07	CHARLES-SAARLAND-02	UD_Slovenian-SST	82.28	96.20	CHARLES-SAARLAND-02
UD_French-ParTUT	92.19	97.97	UFALPRAGUE-01	UD_Spanish-AnCora	95.35	99.40	CHARLES-SAARLAND-02
UD_French-Sequoia	93.04	99.11	UFALPRAGUE-01	UD_Spanish-GSD	93.95	98.08	CHARLES-SAARLAND-02
UD_French-Spoken	94.80	98.65	CHARLES-SAARLAND-02	UD_Swedish-LinES	88.99	97.67	CHARLES-SAARLAND-02
UD_Galician-CTG	91.35	98.29	CHARLES-SAARLAND-02	UD_Swedish-PUD	90.49	97.40	UFALPRAGUE-01
UD_Galician-TreeGal	89.33	97.88	CHARLES-SAARLAND-02	UD_Swedish-Talbanken	92.65	99.05	CHARLES-SAARLAND-02
UD_German-GSD	88.91	95.90	CHARLES-SAARLAND-02	UD_Tagalog-TRG	87.07	95.04	CHARLES-SAARLAND-02 / UFALPRAGUE-01
UD_Gothic-PROIEL	90.02	96.64	CHARLES-SAARLAND-02	UD_Tamil-TTB	89.22	96.00	UFALPRAGUE-01
UD_Greek-GDT	93.45	98.37	UFALPRAGUE-01	UD_Turkish-IMST	86.10	96.30	UFALPRAGUE-01
UD_Hebrew-HTB	91.79	98.47	CHARLES-SAARLAND-02	UD_Turkish-PUD	87.62	94.96	post_deadline_RUG-01
UD_Hindi-HDTB	93.92	98.04	CHARLES-SAARLAND-02	UD_Ukrainian-IU	86.81	98.10	CHARLES-SAARLAND-02
UD_Hungarian-Szeged	87.62	98.25	UFALPRAGUE-01	UD_Upper_Sorbian-UFAL	81.04	93.51	UFALPRAGUE-01
UD_Indonesian-GSD	86.12	95.16	CHARLES-SAARLAND-02	UD_Urdu-UDTB	89.46	93.45	CHARLES-SAARLAND-02
UD_Irish-IDT	81.58	91.46	UFALPRAGUE-01	UD_Vietnamese-VTB	78.00	94.02	CHARLES-SAARLAND-02
UD_Italian-ISDT	94.46	99.19	CHARLES-SAARLAND-02	UD_Yoruba-YTB	85.47	94.19	CMU-DataAug-01
UD_Italian-ParTUT	93.88	99.21	UFALPRAGUE-01				

Table 9: Task 2 Morph F1 scores

ent languages, in particular those with idiosyncratic orthographies, may offer new challenges in this respect.[7]

Only one team tried to learn inflection in a multilingual setting—i.e. to use all training data to train one model. Such transfer learning is an interesting avenue of future research, but evaluation could be difficult. Whether any cross-language transfer is actually being learned vs. whether having more data better biases the networks to copy strings is an evaluation step to disentangle.[8]

Creating new data sets that accurately reflect learner exposure (whether L1 or L2) is also an important consideration in the design of future shared tasks. One pertinent facet of this is information about inflectional categories—often the inflectional information is insufficiently prescribed by the lemma, as with the Romanian verbal inflection classes or nominal gender in German.

As we move toward multilingual models for morphology, it becomes important to understand which representations are critical or irrelevant for adapting to new languages; this may be probed in the style of (Thompson et al., 2018), and it can be used as a first step toward designing systems that avoid "catastrophic forgetting" as they learn to inflect new languages (Thompson et al., 2019).

Future directions for Task 2 include exploring cross-lingual analysis—in stride with both Task 1 and Malaviya et al. (2018)—and leveraging these analyses in downstream tasks.

7   Conclusions

The SIGMORPHON 2019 shared task provided a type-level evaluation on 100 language pairs in 79 languages and a token-level evaluation on 107 treebanks in 66 languages, of systems for inflection and analysis. On task 1 (low-resource inflection with cross-lingual transfer), 14 systems were submitted, while on task 2 (lemmatization and morphological feature analysis), 16 systems were submitted. All used neural network models, completing a trend in past years' shared tasks and other recent work on morphology.

In task 1, gains from cross-lingual training were generally modest, with gains positively correlating with the linguistic similarity of the two languages.

In the second task, several methods were implemented by multiple groups, with the most successful systems implementing variations of multiheaded attention, multi-level encoding, multiple decoders, and ELMo and BERT contextual embeddings.

We have released the training, development, and test sets, and expect these datasets to provide a useful benchmark for future research into learning of inflectional morphology and string-to-string transduction.

Acknowledgments

MS has received funding from the European Research Council (ERC) under the European Union's Horizon 2020 research and innovation programme (grant agreement No 771113).

References

Željko Agić and Natalie Schluter. 2017. How (not) to train a dependency parser: The curious case of jackknifing part-of-speech taggers. In *Proceedings of the 55th Annual Meeting of the Association for Computational Linguistics (Volume 2: Short Papers)*, pages 679–684, Vancouver, Canada. Association for Computational Linguistics.

Inaki Alegria, Izaskun Etxeberria, Mans Hulden, and Montserrat Maritxalar. 2009. Porting Basque morphological grammars to *foma*, an open-source tool. In *International Workshop on Finite-State Methods and Natural Language Processing*, pages 105–113. Springer.

Toms Bergmanis and Sharon Goldwater. 2018. Context sensitive neural lemmatization with Lematus. In *Proceedings of the 2018 Conference of the North American Chapter of the Association for Computational Linguistics: Human Language Technologies, Volume 1 (Long Papers)*, pages 1391–1400, New Orleans, Louisiana. Association for Computational Linguistics.

Ryan Cotterell, Christo Kirov, John Sylak-Glassman, Géraldine Walther, Ekaterina Vylomova, Arya D. McCarthy, Katharina Kann, Sebastian Mielke, Garrett Nicolai, Miikka Silfverberg, David Yarowsky, Jason Eisner, and Mans Hulden. 2018. The CoNLL–SIGMORPHON 2018 shared task: Universal morphological reinflection. In *Proceedings of the CoNLL–SIGMORPHON 2018 Shared Task: Universal Morphological Reinflection*, pages 1–27, Brussels. Association for Computational Linguistics.

Ryan Cotterell, Christo Kirov, John Sylak-Glassman, Géraldine Walther, Ekaterina Vylomova, Patrick Xia, Manaal Faruqui, Sandra Kübler, David Yarowsky, Jason Eisner, and Mans Hulden. 2017.

---

[7]Although some work suggests that working with IPA or phonological distinctive features in this context yields very similar results to working with graphemes (Wiemerslage et al., 2018).

[8]This has been addressed by Jin and Kann (2017).

CoNLL-SIGMORPHON 2017 shared task: Universal morphological reinflection in 52 languages. *Proceedings of the CoNLL SIGMORPHON 2017 Shared Task: Universal Morphological Reinflection*, pages 1–30.

Jacob Devlin, Ming-Wei Chang, Kenton Lee, and Kristina Toutanova. 2019. BERT: Pre-training of deep bidirectional transformers for language understanding. In *Proceedings of the 2019 Conference of the North American Chapter of the Association for Computational Linguistics: Human Language Technologies, Volume 1 (Long and Short Papers)*, pages 4171–4186, Minneapolis, Minnesota. Association for Computational Linguistics.

Daniela Gerz, Ivan Vulić, Edoardo Ponti, Jason Naradowsky, Roi Reichart, and Anna Korhonen. 2018. Language modeling for morphologically rich languages: Character-aware modeling for word-level prediction. *Transactions of the Association for Computational Linguistics*, 6:451–465.

Huiming Jin and Katharina Kann. 2017. Exploring cross-lingual transfer of morphological knowledge in sequence-to-sequence models. In *Proceedings of the First Workshop on Subword and Character Level Models in NLP*, pages 70–75, Copenhagen, Denmark. Association for Computational Linguistics.

Katharina Kann and Hinrich Schütze. 2016. MED: The LMU system for the SIGMORPHON 2016 shared task on morphological reinflection. In *Proceedings of the 14th SIGMORPHON Workshop on Computational Research in Phonetics, Phonology, and Morphology*, pages 62–70, Berlin, Germany. Association for Computational Linguistics.

Aleksandr E. Kibrik. 1998. Archi. In Andrew Spencer and Arnold M. Zwicky, editors, *The Handbook of Morphology*, pages 455–476. Oxford: Blackwell Publishers.

Christo Kirov, Ryan Cotterell, John Sylak-Glassman, Géraldine Walther, Ekaterina Vylomova, Patrick Xia, Manaal Faruqui, Sebastian J. Mielke, Arya D. McCarthy, Sandra Kübler, David Yarowsky, Jason Eisner, and Mans Hulden. 2018. UniMorph 2.0: Universal Morphology. In *Proceedings of the 11th Language Resources and Evaluation Conference*, Miyazaki, Japan. European Language Resource Association.

Thang Luong, Hieu Pham, and Christopher D. Manning. 2015. Effective approaches to attention-based neural machine translation. In *Proceedings of the 2015 Conference on Empirical Methods in Natural Language Processing*, pages 1412–1421, Lisbon, Portugal. Association for Computational Linguistics.

Chaitanya Malaviya, Matthew R. Gormley, and Graham Neubig. 2018. Neural factor graph models for cross-lingual morphological tagging. In *Proceedings of the 56th Annual Meeting of the Association for Computational Linguistics (Volume 1: Long Papers)*, pages 2653–2663, Melbourne, Australia. Association for Computational Linguistics.

Chaitanya Malaviya, Shijie Wu, and Ryan Cotterell. 2019. A simple joint model for improved contextual neural lemmatization. In *Proceedings of the 2019 Conference of the North American Chapter of the Association for Computational Linguistics: Human Language Technologies, Volume 1 (Long and Short Papers)*, pages 1517–1528, Minneapolis, Minnesota. Association for Computational Linguistics.

John Mansfield. 2019. *Murrinhpatha morphology and phonology*, volume 653. Walter de Gruyter GmbH & Co KG.

Arya D. McCarthy, Miikka Silfverberg, Ryan Cotterell, Mans Hulden, and David Yarowsky. 2018. Marrying Universal Dependencies and Universal Morphology. In *Proceedings of the Second Workshop on Universal Dependencies (UDW 2018)*, pages 91–101, Brussels, Belgium. Association for Computational Linguistics.

Thomas Müller, Ryan Cotterell, Alexander Fraser, and Hinrich Schütze. 2015. Joint lemmatization and morphological tagging with LEMMING. In *Proceedings of the 2015 Conference on Empirical Methods in Natural Language Processing*, pages 2268–2274, Lisbon, Portugal. Association for Computational Linguistics.

Graham Neubig and Junjie Hu. 2018. Rapid adaptation of neural machine translation to new languages. In *Proceedings of the 2018 Conference on Empirical Methods in Natural Language Processing*, pages 875–880, Brussels, Belgium. Association for Computational Linguistics.

Joakim Nivre, Mitchell Abrams, Željko Agić, Lars Ahrenberg, Lene Antonsen, Katya Aplonova, Maria Jesus Aranzabe, Gashaw Arutie, Masayuki Asahara, Luma Ateyah, Mohammed Attia, Aitziber Atutxa, Liesbeth Augustinus, Elena Badmaeva, Miguel Ballesteros, Esha Banerjee, Sebastian Bank, Verginica Barbu Mititelu, Victoria Basmov, John Bauer, Sandra Bellato, Kepa Bengoetxea, Yevgeni Berzak, Irshad Ahmad Bhat, Riyaz Ahmad Bhat, Erica Biagetti, Eckhard Bick, Rogier Blokland, Victoria Bobicev, Carl Börstell, Cristina Bosco, Gosse Bouma, Sam Bowman, Adriane Boyd, Aljoscha Burchardt, Marie Candito, Bernard Caron, Gauthier Caron, Gülşen Cebiroğlu Eryiğit, Flavio Massimiliano Cecchini, Giuseppe G. A. Celano, Slavomír Čéplö, Savas Cetin, Fabricio Chalub, Jinho Choi, Yongseok Cho, Jayeol Chun, Silvie Cinková, Aurélie Collomb, Çağrı Çöltekin, Miriam Connor, Marine Courtin, Elizabeth Davidson, Marie-Catherine de Marneffe, Valeria de Paiva, Arantza Diaz de Ilarraza, Carly Dickerson, Peter Dirix, Kaja Dobrovoljc, Timothy Dozat, Kira Droganova, Puneet Dwivedi, Marhaba Eli, Ali Elkahky, Binyam Ephrem, Tomaž Erjavec, Aline

Etienne, Richárd Farkas, Hector Fernandez Alcalde, Jennifer Foster, Cláudia Freitas, Katarína Gajdošová, Daniel Galbraith, Marcos Garcia, Moa Gärdenfors, Sebastian Garza, Kim Gerdes, Filip Ginter, Iakes Goenaga, Koldo Gojenola, Memduh Gökırmak, Yoav Goldberg, Xavier Gómez Guinovart, Berta Gonzáles Saavedra, Matias Grioni, Normunds Grūzītis, Bruno Guillaume, Céline Guillot-Barbance, Nizar Habash, Jan Hajič, Jan Hajič jr., Linh Hà Mỹ, Na-Rae Han, Kim Harris, Dag Haug, Barbora Hladká, Jaroslava Hlaváčová, Florinel Hociung, Petter Hohle, Jena Hwang, Radu Ion, Elena Irimia, Ọlájídé Ishola, Tomáš Jelínek, Anders Johannsen, Fredrik Jørgensen, Hüner Kaşıkara, Sylvain Kahane, Hiroshi Kanayama, Jenna Kanerva, Boris Katz, Tolga Kayadelen, Jessica Kenney, Václava Kettnerová, Jesse Kirchner, Kamil Kopacewicz, Natalia Kotsyba, Simon Krek, Sookyoung Kwak, Veronika Laippala, Lorenzo Lambertino, Lucia Lam, Tatiana Lando, Septina Dian Larasati, Alexei Lavrentiev, John Lee, Phuong Lê Hồng, Alessandro Lenci, Saran Lertpradit, Herman Leung, Cheuk Ying Li, Josie Li, Keying Li, KyungTae Lim, Nikola Ljubešić, Olga Loginova, Olga Lyashevskaya, Teresa Lynn, Vivien Macketanz, Aibek Makazhanov, Michael Mandl, Christopher Manning, Ruli Manurung, Cătălina Mărănduc, David Mareček, Katrin Marheinecke, Héctor Martínez Alonso, André Martins, Jan Mašek, Yuji Matsumoto, Ryan McDonald, Gustavo Mendonça, Niko Miekka, Margarita Misirpashayeva, Anna Missilä, Cătălin Mititelu, Yusuke Miyao, Simonetta Montemagni, Amir More, Laura Moreno Romero, Keiko Sophie Mori, Shinsuke Mori, Bjartur Mortensen, Bohdan Moskalevskyi, Kadri Muischnek, Yugo Murawaki, Kaili Müürisep, Pinkey Nainwani, Juan Ignacio Navarro Horñiacek, Anna Nedoluzhko, Gunta Nešpore-Bērzkalne, Luong Nguyễn Thị, Huyền Nguyễn Thị Minh, Vitaly Nikolaev, Rattima Nitisaroj, Hanna Nurmi, Stina Ojala, Adédayọ Olúòkun, Mai Omura, Petya Osenova, Robert Östling, Lilja Øvrelid, Niko Partanen, Elena Pascual, Marco Passarotti, Agnieszka Patejuk, Guilherme Paulino-Passos, Siyao Peng, Cenel-Augusto Perez, Guy Perrier, Slav Petrov, Jussi Piitulainen, Emily Pitler, Barbara Plank, Thierry Poibeau, Martin Popel, Lauma Pretkalniņa, Sophie Prévost, Prokopis Prokopidis, Adam Przepiórkowski, Tiina Puolakainen, Sampo Pyysalo, Andriela Rääbis, Alexandre Rademaker, Loganathan Ramasamy, Taraka Rama, Carlos Ramisch, Vinit Ravishankar, Livy Real, Siva Reddy, Georg Rehm, Michael Rießler, Larissa Rinaldi, Laura Rituma, Luisa Rocha, Mykhailo Romanenko, Rudolf Rosa, Davide Rovati, Valentin Roca, Olga Rudina, Jack Rueter, Shoval Sadde, Benoît Sagot, Shadi Saleh, Tanja Samardžić, Stephanie Samson, Manuela Sanguinetti, Baiba Saulīte, Yanin Sawanakunanon, Nathan Schneider, Sebastian Schuster, Djamé Seddah, Wolfgang Seeker, Mojgan Seraji, Mo Shen, Atsuko Shimada, Muh Shohibussirri, Dmitry Sichinava, Natalia Silveira, Maria Simi, Radu Simionescu, Katalin Simkó, Mária Šimková, Kiril Simov, Aaron Smith, Isabela Soares-Bastos, Carolyn Spadine, Antonio Stella, Milan Straka, Jana Strnadová, Alane Suhr, Umut Sulubacak, Zsolt Szántó, Dima Taji, Yuta Takahashi, Takaaki Tanaka, Isabelle Tellier, Trond Trosterud, Anna Trukhina, Reut Tsarfaty, Francis Tyers, Sumire Uematsu, Zdeňka Urešová, Larraitz Uria, Hans Uszkoreit, Sowmya Vajjala, Daniel van Niekerk, Gertjan van Noord, Viktor Varga, Eric Villemonte de la Clergerie, Veronika Vincze, Lars Wallin, Jing Xian Wang, Jonathan North Washington, Seyi Williams, Mats Wirén, Tsegay Woldemariam, Tak-sum Wong, Chunxiao Yan, Marat M. Yavrumyan, Zhuoran Yu, Zdeněk Žabokrtský, Amir Zeldes, Daniel Zeman, Manying Zhang, and Hanzhi Zhu. 2018. Universal dependencies 2.3. LINDAT/CLARIN digital library at the Institute of Formal and Applied Linguistics (ÚFAL), Faculty of Mathematics and Physics, Charles University.

Edoardo Maria Ponti, Helen O'Horan, Yevgeni Berzak, Ivan Vulic, Roi Reichart, Thierry Poibeau, Ekaterina Shutova, and Anna Korhonen. 2018. Modeling language variation and universals: A survey on typological linguistics for natural language processing. *CoRR*, abs/1807.00914.

John Sylak-Glassman, Christo Kirov, Matt Post, Roger Que, and David Yarowsky. 2015a. A universal feature schema for rich morphological annotation and fine-grained cross-lingual part-of-speech tagging. In Cerstin Mahlow and Michael Piotrowski, editors, *Proceedings of the 4th Workshop on Systems and Frameworks for Computational Morphology (SFCM)*, Communications in Computer and Information Science, pages 72–93. Springer, Berlin.

John Sylak-Glassman, Christo Kirov, David Yarowsky, and Roger Que. 2015b. A language-independent feature schema for inflectional morphology. In *Proceedings of the 53rd Annual Meeting of the Association for Computational Linguistics and the 7th International Joint Conference on Natural Language Processing (Volume 2: Short Papers)*, pages 674–680, Beijing, China. Association for Computational Linguistics.

Wilson L Taylor. 1953. "Cloze procedure": A new tool for measuring readability. *Journalism Bulletin*, 30(4):415–433.

Brian Thompson, Jeremy Gwinnup, Huda Khayrallah, Kevin Duh, and Philipp Koehn. 2019. Overcoming catastrophic forgetting during domain adaptation of neural machine translation. In *Proceedings of the 2019 Conference of the North American Chapter of the Association for Computational Linguistics: Human Language Technologies, Volume 1 (Long and Short Papers)*, pages 2062–2068, Minneapolis, Minnesota. Association for Computational Linguistics.

Brian Thompson, Huda Khayrallah, Antonios Anastasopoulos, Arya D. McCarthy, Kevin Duh, Rebecca Marvin, Paul McNamee, Jeremy Gwinnup, Tim Anderson, and Philipp Koehn. 2018. Freezing subnetworks to analyze domain adaptation in neural machine translation. In *Proceedings of the Third Conference on Machine Translation: Research Papers*, pages 124–132, Belgium, Brussels. Association for Computational Linguistics.

Géraldine Walther and Benoît Sagot. 2010. Developing a large-scale lexicon for a less-resourced language: General methodology and preliminary experiments on Sorani Kurdish. In *Proceedings of the 7th SaLTMiL Workshop on Creation and use of basic lexical resources for less-resourced languages (LREC 2010 Workshop)*, Valetta, Malta.

Géraldine Walther, Benoît Sagot, and Karën Fort. 2010. Fast development of basic NLP tools: Towards a lexicon and a POS tagger for Kurmanji Kurdish. In *International conference on lexis and grammar*.

Adam Wiemerslage, Miikka Silfverberg, and Mans Hulden. 2018. Phonological features for morphological inflection. In *Proceedings of the Fifteenth Workshop on Computational Research in Phonetics, Phonology, and Morphology*, pages 161–166, Brussels, Belgium. Association for Computational Linguistics.

Shijie Wu and Ryan Cotterell. 2019. Exact hard monotonic attention for character-level transduction. *arXiv preprint arXiv:1905.06319v1*.

Shijie Wu, Pamela Shapiro, and Ryan Cotterell. 2018. Hard non-monotonic attention for character-level transduction. In *Proceedings of the 2018 Conference on Empirical Methods in Natural Language Processing*, pages 4425–4438, Brussels, Belgium. Association for Computational Linguistics.

Barret Zoph, Deniz Yuret, Jonathan May, and Kevin Knight. 2016. Transfer learning for low-resource neural machine translation. In *Proceedings of the 2016 Conference on Empirical Methods in Natural Language Processing*, pages 1568–1575, Austin, Texas. Association for Computational Linguistics.

Association for Computational Linguistics
209 N. Eighth Street
Stroudsburg, Pennsylvania 18360